The Princeton Review®

Cracking the

SSAT® & ISEE®

2019 Edition

By the Staff of The Princeton Review

PrincetonReview.com

Penguin
Random
House

The Princeton Review
110 East 42nd St., 7th Floor
New York, NY 10017
Email: editorialsupport@review.com

ISBN: 978-1-5247-5793-9
eBook ISBN: 978-1-5247-5828-8
ISSN: 1090-0144

Editor: Sarah Litt
Production Editor: Kathy Carter and Liz Rutzel
Production Artist: Craig Patches

Printed in the United States of America on partially recycled paper.

10 9 8 7 6 5 4 3 2 1

2019 Edition

Editorial

Rob Franek, Editor-in-Chief
Casey Cornelius, Chief Product Officer
Mary Beth Garrick, Director of Production
Selena Coppock, Managing Editor
Meave Shelton, Senior Editor
Colleen Day, Editor
Sarah Litt, Editor
Aaron Riccio, Editor
Orion McBean, Associate Editor

Penguin Random House Publishing Team

Tom Russell, VP, Publisher
Alison Stoltzfus, Publishing Director
Amanda Yee, Associate Managing Editor
Ellen Reed, Production Manager
Suzanne Lee, Designer

Acknowledgments

The Princeton Review would like to thank Anne Morrow Cullens and Anne Goldberg-Baldwin for their hard work revising and developing test material for this book.

Contents

Get More (Free) Content

1 Go to PrincetonReview.com/cracking.

2 Enter the following ISBN for your book: 9781524757939.

3 Answer a few simple questions to set up an exclusive Princeton Review account. (If you already have one, you can just log in.)

4 Click the "Student Tools" button, also found under "My Account" from the top toolbar. You're all set to access your bonus content!

Need to report a potential **content** issue?

Contact **EditorialSupport@review.com**. Include:

- full title of the book
- ISBN number
- page number

Need to report a **technical** issue?

Contact **TPRStudentTech@review.com** and provide:

- your full name
- email address used to register the book
- full book title and ISBN
- computer OS (Mac/PC) and browser (Firefox, Safari, etc.)

The Princeton Review®

Once you've registered, you can...

- Get complete explanations for the SSAT and ISEE Practice Tests

- Take a full-length Elementary-level SSAT exam

- Find any late-breaking information released about the SSAT or ISEE tests

- Get valuable advice about the college application process, including tips for writing a great essay and where to apply for financial aid

- Check to see if there have been any corrections or updates to this edition

- Get our take on any recent or pending updates to the SSAT or ISEE

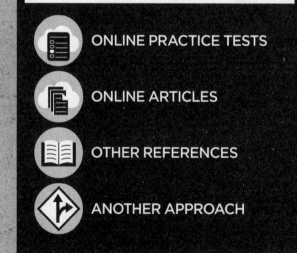

Look for These Icons Throughout the Book

ONLINE PRACTICE TESTS

ONLINE ARTICLES

OTHER REFERENCES

ANOTHER APPROACH

A Parent's
Introduction

HOW CAN I HELP?

Congratulations! Your child is considering attending a private secondary school, and by virtue of the fact that you hold this book in your hands, you have recognized that either the SSAT or the ISEE is an important part of the admissions process. Providing your child with the information contained in this book is an excellent first step toward a strong performance on the SSAT or the ISEE.

As a parent, however, you know well the fine line between support and intrusion. To guide you in your efforts to help your child, we'd like to offer a few suggestions.

Have a Healthy Perspective

Both the SSAT and the ISEE are standardized tests designed to say something about an individual student's chances for success in a private secondary school. Neither is an intelligence test; neither claims to be.

Set realistic expectations for your child. The skills necessary for a strong performance on these tests are very different from those a student uses in school. The additional stress that comes from being expected to do well generally serves only to distract a student from taking a test efficiently.

At the same time, beware of dismissing disappointing results with a simple, "My child doesn't test well." While it is undoubtedly true that some students test better than others, this explanation does little to encourage a student to invest time and effort into overcoming obstacles and improving his or her performance.

Know How to Interpret Performance

Both the SSAT and the ISEE use the same test to measure the performance of students between eighth grade and eleventh grade. It is impossible to interpret scores without considering the grade level of the student. Percentile rankings have much more value than do either raw or scaled scores, and percentiles are the numbers schools use to compare students.

Remember That This Is Not an English or a Math Test

There are both verbal and math questions on the SSAT and on the ISEE. However, these questions are often based on skills and concepts that are different from those used on a day-to-day basis in school. For instance, very few English teachers—at any level—spend a lot of time teaching students how to approach analogy or sentence completion questions.

This may be frustrating for parents, students, and teachers. But in the final judgment, our educational system would take a turn for the worse if it attempted to teach students to do well on the SSAT, the ISEE, or even the SAT. The fact that the valuable skills students learn in school don't directly improve test scores is evidence of a flaw in the testing system, not an indictment of our schools or those who have devoted their professional careers to education.

Realize That All Tests Are Different

Many of the general rules that students are accustomed to applying to tests in school do not apply to either the SSAT or the ISEE. Many students, for instance, actually hurt their scores by trying to work on every question. Although these tests are timed, accuracy is much more important than speed. Once your child learns the format and structure of these tests, he or she will find it easier to apply his or her knowledge to the test and will answer more questions correctly.

Provide All the Resources You Can

This book has been written to provide your child with a very thorough review of all the math, vocabulary, reading, and writing skills that are necessary for success on the SSAT and ISEE. We have also included practice drills for each chapter and practice tests that simulate actual SSAT or ISEE examinations.

The very best practice test questions, however, are naturally the ones written by the organizations who write the real test questions—the Secondary School Admission Test Board (SSATB) for the SSAT and the Educational Resources Bureau (ERB) for the ISEE. We encourage you to contact both these organizations (addresses and phone numbers can be found on page 5) to obtain any resources containing test questions that you can use for additional practice.

One word of caution: Be wary of other sources of SSAT or ISEE practice material. There are a number of test preparation books available (from companies other than The Princeton Review, of course) that are woefully outdated. The ISEE changed quite substantially in 2010, and the SSAT implemented some changes in 2012; many books have not caught up with these changes. In addition, both the SSAT and the ISEE change with time in very subtle ways. Thus, we suggest supplementing the information in this book with ERB's "What to Expect on the ISEE," which you can find at isee.erblearn.org, and "Official Guide to the SSAT" which you can order at ssat.org/prepare/official-guide.

Make sure the materials you choose are, to the greatest extent possible, reflective of the test your child will take and not a test that was given years earlier. Also, try to avoid the inevitable confusion that comes from asking a student to follow two different sets of advice. Presumably, you have decided (or are about to decide) to trust The Princeton Review to prepare your child for this test. In doing so, you have made a wise decision. As we have said, we encourage you to provide any and all sources of additional practice material (as long as it is accurate and reflective of the current test), but providing other test preparation advice tends to muddy the waters and confuse students.

Be Patient and Be Involved

Preparing for the SSAT or the ISEE is like learning how to ride a bicycle. You will watch your child struggle, at first, to develop a level of familiarity and comfort with the test's format and content.

Developing the math, vocabulary, reading, and writing skills that your child will use on the SSAT or the ISEE is a long-term process. In addition to making certain that he or she is committed to spending the time necessary to work through

> The vocabulary list in this book covers all test levels. If you would like a list targeted to younger levels, you can find them online when you register this book!

the chapters of this book, you should also be on the lookout for other opportunities to be supportive. One way to do this is to make vocabulary development into a group activity. In the vocabulary chapter, we provide an extensive list of vocabulary words; learn them as a family, working through flash cards at the breakfast table or during car trips. You may even pick up a new word or two yourself!

Important: If your child is in a lower grade, you may want to offer extra guidance as he or she works through this book and prepares for the test. Because this book covers preparation for the full range of grade levels taking the tests (fourth through eleventh grades), some of the content review will be beyond the areas that your child is expected to know. It is an excellent idea to work through the book along with your younger child, so that he or she doesn't become intimidated by these higher level questions that should be skipped. Go online to see the suggested schedule.

A SHORT WORD ON ADMISSIONS

The most important insight into secondary school admissions that we can offer is that a student's score on the SSAT or the ISEE is only one of many components involved in the admissions decision. While many schools will request SSAT or ISEE scores, all will look seriously at your child's academic record. Think about it—which says more about a student: a single test or years of solid academic performance?

Be an Informed Parent
For the most accurate information about their admissions policies, don't hesitate to call the schools to which your child may apply.

In terms of testing, which is the focus of this book, some schools will specify which test they want applicants to take—the SSAT or ISEE. Others will allow you to use scores from either test. If you are faced with a decision of whether to focus on the SSAT, the ISEE, or both, we encourage you to be an informed consumer. This book contains practice tests for the ISEE and the SSAT, and your child should attempt both. Then, based on the requirements of your desired school and the results of the practice tests, you can decide which test best suits your child. As of August of 2016, students may register to take the ISEE up to three times in a 12-month admission cycle, once in any or all of three testing seasons. The seasons are Fall (August–November), Winter (December–March), and Spring/Summer (April–July). ISEE does not encourage multiple testing, but does offer students and families that option. The SSAT can also be taken multiple times.

There are some differences in subject matter. The SSAT, for example, contains a section on analogies, which many students may not be familiar with; the ISEE includes a section of sentence completions. On the other hand, Middle and Upper Level ISEE test takers will be faced with a number of quantitative comparison questions in the Math section, and these can be tricky at first, especially for younger students.

Resources

SSAT
Secondary School Admission Test Board (SSATB)
609-683-4440
www.ssat.org
info@ssat.org

ISEE
Educational Records Bureau (ERB)
800-989-3721
www.erblearn.org
info@erblearn.org

REGISTERING FOR THE SSAT

Before you go any further in preparing for the SSAT, you must complete one essential step: **sign up for the SSAT**. The test is administered about eight times every year—generally in October, November, December, January, February, March, April, and June. Once you decide which test date you prefer, we encourage you to register as soon as possible. Testing sites can fill up; by registering early, your child will avoid the possibility of having to take the test at an inconvenient or unfamiliar second-choice location. You can register online at www. ssat.org, or call the SSATB at 609-683-4440 to receive a registration form by mail.

The regular registration deadline for the test (at U.S. testing centers) is usually three weeks before the test date. You may return the registration form by mail along with the $132 registration fee ($80 for the Elementary Level test) for test centers in the United States, American Samoa, Puerto Rico, Saipan, USVI, and Canada (or $257 for international test centers), or you may submit your registration form by fax. If you register online, you can pay the fee with a credit card. In some cases, you may be able to obtain an SSAT fee waiver.

> **Plan Ahead**
> Not only will early registration give you one less thing to worry about as the test approaches, but it will also make it easier to get your first-choice test center.

If you forget to register for the test or decide to take the SSAT at the last minute, there is a late registration deadline and, if it is within two weeks of the test date, a rush registration deadline (for U.S. testing centers). If you still have at least two weeks, you can register online late and pay an additional $45 late registration fee. After that point, it's an $85 rush registration fee. If you have already registered and want to change your testing date or location, there's a change fee of $35.

Students who need special testing accommodations must apply for accommodations at least two weeks before the test. Sunday testing is available, but only for those students who are unable to take a Saturday test for religious reasons. Make sure to apply for accommodations early. You won't be able to register until your accommodation has been approved.

REGISTERING FOR THE ISEE

Before you go any further in preparing for the ISEE, you must do one essential thing: **sign up for the ISEE.** Go to the ISEE website, www.iseetest.org, and create an online account to register for the ISEE at an ISEE test site school or Prometric Test Center* in your area.

> Testing fees for the ISEE are:
> • $105 for mail-in or online registration
> • $103 for phone registration
> • $185 for online testing at Prometric Testing Center

Students may register to take the ISEE one time in any or all of three testing seasons. The ISEE testing seasons are defined as Fall (August–November), Winter (December–March), and Spring/Summer (April–July). Families do not have to select schools to receive ISEE scores at the time of registration; they may add them after a test is scored at no extra charge. The regular registration deadline for the ISEE is three weeks before the test date. The registration is $105 and you may use Visa, MasterCard, or American Express.

Late Registration

For one week after the official registration date closes (up to two weeks before the test date), you may register at www.iseetest.org. The fee for late registration is $130.

Walk-in Registration

Walk-in registration is available at a limited number of ISEE test site schools. It is available on a first-come, first-served basis and cannot be assured due to limitations on testing materials and staff. There is an additional $40 fee for this service. If you are a candidate for walk-in registration, you must call the test site school directly to see if you may be accommodated.

* Prometric testing centers offer ISEE tests in over 400 locations throughout the world and the tests are online only.

A Student's Introduction

WHAT DO I DO WITH THIS BOOK?

You've got a hefty amount of paper and information in your hands. How can you work through it thoroughly, without spending eight hours on it the Saturday before the test?

Plan ahead.

Before you start, go online and download the study guide. We've broken down the contents of this book into 12 study sessions and suggested a timeline for you to follow. Some of these sessions will take longer than others, depending on your strengths and weaknesses. If any of them takes more than two hours, take a break and try to finish the session the following day. You may want to do one, two, or three sessions a week, but we suggest you give yourself at least a day or two in between to absorb the information you've just learned. The one thing you should be doing every day is quizzing yourself on vocabulary and making new flash cards.

If You Want to Start Early

If you have more than ten weeks to prepare, start with vocabulary building and essay writing. These skills only improve with time.

We also caution against thinking that you can work through this book during summer vacation, put it aside in September, and be ready to take the test in December. If you want to start that early, work primarily on vocabulary until about 10 weeks before the test. Then you can start on techniques, and they'll be fresh in your mind on the day of the test. If you've finished your preparation too soon and have nothing to practice on in the weeks before the test, you're going to get rusty.

If you know you are significantly weaker in one of the subjects covered by the test, you should begin with that subject so you can practice it throughout your preparation.

At Each Session

Get Your Pencil Moving

You'll get the most out of this book by trying out techniques as you read about them.

At each practice session, make sure you have sharpened pencils, blank index cards, and a dictionary. Each chapter is interactive; to fully understand the techniques we present, you need to be ready to try them out.

As you read each chapter, practice the techniques and do all the exercises. Check your answers in the Answer Key as you do each set of problems, and try to figure out what types of errors you made so you can correct them. Review all of the techniques that give you trouble.

As you begin each session, review the chapter you completed during the previous session before moving on to a new chapter.

The SSATB and the ERB consider their Score Reports proprietary information and we can't reproduce them for our practice tests. You can get an idea of how you did by marking off how many you got right in the answer key after each test. Then go to your (free) Student Tools to get explanations. Keep the learning going!

When You Take a Practice Test

We recommend some specific times to take practice tests in the following session outlines. Here are some guidelines for taking these tests.

- Time yourself strictly. Use a timer, watch, or stopwatch that will ring, and do not allow yourself to go over the allotted time for any section. If you try to do so on the real test, your scores will probably be canceled.

- Take a practice test in one sitting, allowing yourself breaks of no more than two minutes between sections. You need to build up your endurance for the real test, and you also need an accurate picture of how you will do.
- Always take a practice test using an answer sheet with bubbles to fill in, just as you will do for the real test. For the practice tests in this book, use the attached answer sheets. You need to be comfortable transferring answers to the separate sheet because you might end up skipping around a bit.
- Thoroughly fill in each bubble you choose, and make no other marks in the answer area.
- As you fill in the bubble for a question, check to be sure you are on the correct number on the answer sheet. If you fill in the wrong bubble on the answer sheet, it won't matter if you've worked out the problem correctly in your test booklet. All that matters to the machine scoring your test is the No. 2 pencil mark.

The Day of the Exam
- Wake up refreshed from at least eight hours of sleep the night before.
- Eat a good breakfast.
- Arrive at the test center about a half hour early.
- Have with you all the necessary paperwork that shows you have registered for the test, four No. 2 pencils with erasers, and a working black pen. You may also want to take juice or water and a small snack like a granola bar. The test center may not allow you to take food or beverages into the room, but you can leave them in the hall, in case you have a chance to get them during a short break. Do not take a cell phone or any books, papers, or calculators.

  > And bring a sweater! You never know how cold the room might be.

- Remind yourself that you do not have to work out every question on the test to get a good score. Don't let yourself become rushed. Pace yourself.

GENERAL TEST-TAKING TECHNIQUES FOR THE SSAT & ISEE

Pacing
Most people believe that to do well on a test, it is important to answer every question. While this is true of most of the tests you take in school, it is not true of many standardized tests, including the SSAT and ISEE. On this test, it is very possible to score well without attempting all of the questions; in fact, many students can improve their scores by answering fewer questions.

"Wait a second. I can get a better score by attempting *fewer* questions?" Yes. On the SSAT you are penalized only for the questions you answer incorrectly, not for the questions you skip. Because all of the questions are worth the same amount of points, it's just as good to answer a question you understand than waste time with one you don't. So for the most part, you'll give your attention to problems you think you can answer, and decide which questions are too thorny to waste time on. This test-taking approach is just as important to score improvement as your knowledge of vocabulary and math rules!

> On the ISEE, it is best to answer all questions because there is no guessing penalty.

In general, all math and verbal questions on the SSAT and ISEE gradually increase in difficulty from first to last. (The one exception is the Reading section, where question difficulty is mixed.) This means that for most students, the longest and more complicated problems are at the end of each section. For this reason, all students should focus the majority of their attention on the questions they know they can answer. Why rush through these and make careless errors, when you could spend time and get all of them right? Attempt the ones you find more challenging last—if you have time.

Points are not deducted for wrong answers on the SSAT Elementary Level test. Thus, do not leave any answers blank. Even so, pace yourself wisely to increase your accuracy on questions you know or think you know the answers to. This is also true for all levels of the ISEE.

The reason that this approach to pacing can actually *increase* scores is that skipped questions gain you zero points, whereas each incorrect answer reduces your raw score by a quarter-point. Because your raw score will decrease only if you answer a question incorrectly, skipping is the best strategy for a problem that has you completely stumped. Ideally, you will either get a question right or skip it (with some exceptions when you can guess intelligently and aggressively).

Skipping will be a major tool mostly the questions you find most troublesome. Guessing will be part of the whole test, so let's look at how guessing and skipping work together. Again, ISEE students should answer every question.

Guessing

When should you guess? Whenever you can eliminate even one wrong answer with certainty. Yes, really. We'll get to why in a minute. Eliminate the wrong answers and you'll have the right answer by Process of Elimination (we'll explain more about this later). So eliminate the answers that are clearly wrong and guess! Be aggressive.

Over the course of the whole test, this strategy will increase your score. How? Well, let's look again at how SSAT questions are scored, right answers are rewarded, and wrong answers are penalized.

Correct answers: +1 point

Wrong answers: $-\dfrac{1}{4}$ point

Blank answers: 0 points

Suppose we asked you to place a bet on five flips of a coin. There's only one chance in five that it will come up heads, but if it does, you get a dollar. There's a four in five chance of tails; when it's tails, you pay us 25¢. Would you do it? Maybe yes, maybe no. If it came up heads once and tails four times, you'd get a dollar and then pay 25¢ four times, ending up with nothing. You wouldn't lose money, but you wouldn't win any, either. Similarly, there are five choices on every SSAT question, but only one right answer. So if you just guess randomly without eliminating anything first, you will be right about one time and wrong about four times for every five questions you do. That means that the one time you were right, you would get one full raw point (yay!), but you would lose a quarter-point four times (boo!). All of this would bring you right back to where you started.

$$1 - 4(\frac{1}{4}) = 0$$

So random guessing will pretty much keep your score flat. Here is where our guessing strategy comes in. What if, instead of a one-in-five chance of getting heads, the odds were one in four? This time, if four flips usually turned up one head ($1 for you) and three tails (pay out 75¢), you'd make a little money and come out on top. On an SSAT question, if you can eliminate one choice out of the five, you're in the same situation. You now have only four possible answers, and you will be right about once for every *three* times you are wrong. Now the penalty for wrong answers will have less impact. If you narrow it down to three choices, you'll get about one right for every two times you're wrong. Good odds? You bet. That's like making a dollar and losing 50¢. If you can do this throughout the test, you will gradually increase your score. That's why it pays to spend time eliminating the wrong answers and then guessing aggressively.

$$1 - 3(\frac{1}{4}) = \frac{1}{4}$$

Want to use what you've just learned to improve your score? You've come to the right place. Guessing well is one of the most important skills this book can teach you. Strategic guessing and skipping, as simple as they seem, are very powerful score-boosters on standardized tests like the SSAT. Now, let's discuss one more major test-taking approach that should be a part of your game plan.

Process of Elimination

Here's a question you will not see on the SSAT or ISEE, but which will show you how powerful Process of Elimination (POE) can be.

What is the capital of Malawi?

(A) New York
(B) Paris
(C) London
(D) Lilongwe
(E) Washington, D.C.

> **Should I Guess?**
> Random guessing will not improve your Upper or Middle Level SSAT score. Educated guessing, however, is always a good idea.

There are two ways to get this question right. First, you can know that the capital of Malawi is Lilongwe. If you do, good for you! The second is to know that the capital of Malawi is not New York, Paris, London, or Washington, D.C. You don't get more points for knowing the right answer from the start, so one way is just as good as the other. Try to get in the habit of looking at a question and asking, "What are the wrong answers?" instead of "What is the right answer?"

By using POE this way, you will eliminate wrong answers and have fewer answers from which to choose. The result is that you will pick right answers more often. In the example above, you're not even really guessing. You *know* that the other four answers are wrong (or three answers, if you're taking the ISEE), and that's as good as knowing the right answer. In fact, now you *do* know the capital of Malawi. That's the great thing about guessing on a standardized test like the SSAT or ISEE—when you have trouble finding the correct answer, you can often eliminate the wrong ones and come out on top. Now let's look at the same idea in practice in another problem.

> Which of the following cities is the capital of Samoa?
> (A) Vila
> (B) Boston
> (C) Apia
> (D) Chicago
> (E) Los Angeles

You may not know the right answer off the top of your head, but which cities are not the capital of Samoa? You probably know enough about the locations of (B), (D), and (E) to know that Boston, Chicago, and Los Angeles are not the capital of Samoa.

So, what's a good answer to this question? (A) or (C).

What's the right answer? That is not the right question here. The better question is this: should I guess? And the answer is absolutely yes. Yes, yes, yes. You've done a great job of narrowing the answer down to just two choices. On any question where you've done this, you'll have a fifty-fifty chance. In other words, on average you'll get these questions right about half the time (+1 point) and wrong the other half ($-\frac{1}{4}$ point). Even though you'll get some (about half) of these wrong, your score will go up overall, by about 1 point for every 3 questions, and that can make all the difference. Always use POE and guess aggressively. Remember that you should skip the question if you can't eliminate anything at all.

A QUICK SUMMARY

These points about the SSAT and ISEE are important enough that we want to mention them again. Make sure you understand them before you go any farther in this book.

- You do not have to answer every question on the test. Slow down!
- You will not immediately know the correct answer to every question. Instead, look for wrong answers that you can eliminate.
- Random guessing will not improve your score on the SSAT (although it might help with the ISEE). However, educated guessing, which means that you eliminate two or (better) three of the five choices, is a good thing and will improve your score. As a general rule of thumb, if you invest enough time to read and think about the answer to a question, you should be able to eliminate at least one choice and make a good guess!

Part I
The Basics of Both Tests

Chapter 1
Learning
Vocabulary

THE IMPORTANCE OF VOCABULARY

Both the ISEE and the SSAT test synonyms, and you need to know the tested words to get those questions right. While ISEE Sentence Completions and SSAT Analogies allow for a more strategic approach, the fact remains that knowing words is important to scoring points on these questions.

Having a strong vocabulary will also help you throughout your life: on other standardized tests, of course; in college; in your job; and when you read.

Flash Cards
Making *effective* flash cards is important. We'll address how to do so shortly!

BUILDING A VOCABULARY

The best way to build a great vocabulary is to keep a dictionary and flash cards on hand and look up any new words you encounter. For each word you find, make a flash card, and review your flash cards frequently. We'll discuss effective ways of making flash cards shortly.

Reading a lot helps ensure that you will encounter new words. Read newspapers, magazines, and books. If you think you don't like reading, you just haven't found the right material to read. Identify your interests—science, sports, current events, fantasy, you name it—and there will be plenty of material out there that you will look forward to reading.

Not sure what you should read? Ask a parent or favorite teacher. Below are just a few suggestions, but there are so many more.

Title	Area of Interest
Editorial and op-ed pages of *The Washington Post, The New York Times,* and *The Wall Street Journal*	News, politics, and economics
U.S. News and World Report	
The Economist	
The New Yorker	Culture and trends
Scientific American	Science
National Geographic (different editions for different age levels)	Science and environment
The Lord of the Rings by J.R.R. Tolkien	Fantasy and adventure
The Pillars of the Earth by Ken Follett	
The Adventures of Sherlock Holmes by Sir Arthur Conan Doyle	Mystery
Narrative of the Life of Frederick Douglass by Frederick Douglass	Autobiography
Out of Africa by Isak Dinesen	
2001: A Space Odyssey by Arthur C. Clarke	Science Fiction

You can also learn words through vocab-building websites, such as vocabulary.co.il or quizlet.com, which present drills in the form of addictive and rewarding games.

Finally, in the coming pages, you will find lists of words that you may see on the SSAT or ISEE.

The vocabulary list in this chapter is for Upper Level. Lower/Elementary, and Middle Level vocabulary lists can be found online. But it's much more fun to learn words you might not know. Imagine how smart you'll sound!

Making Effective Flash Cards

Most people make flash cards by writing the word on one side and the definition on the other. That's fine as far as it goes, but you can do much better. An effective flash card will provide information that will help you remember the word. Different people learn words in different ways, and you should do what works best for you. Here are some ideas, along with a couple of examples.

Relating Words to Personal Experience

If the definition of a word reminds you of someone or something, write a sentence on the back of your flash card using the word and that person or thing. Suppose, for example, you have a friend named Scott who is very clumsy. Here's a flash card for a word you may not know:

Maladroit

Clumsy

Tripping over his own feet yet again, Scott is quite maladroit.

Relating Words to Roots

Many words are derived from Latin or Greek words. These words often have roots—parts of words—that have specific meanings. If you recognize the roots, you can figure out what the word probably means. Consider the word *benevolent*. It may not surprise you that "bene" means *good*; think *beneficial*. "Vol" comes from a word that means *wish* and also gives us the word *voluntary*. Thus *benevolent* describes someone who is good-hearted (good wish). Your flash card can mention the roots as well as the words *beneficial* and *voluntary* to help you remember how the roots relate to *benevolent*.

Often if you don't know the exact meaning of a word, you can make a good guess as to what the tone of the word is. For example, you may not know what "terse" means, but if a teacher said "My, you're being very terse today," you'd probably assume it meant something bad. Knowing the tone of words can be very helpful even if you can't remember the exact definition. As you go through your flash cards, you can separate them into three piles: positive, negative, and neutral. This will help you more rapidly recognize the tone of advanced vocabulary.

Here are some roots that may show up in words on the SSAT or ISEE.

Root	Meaning	Example
ambi	both	ambidextrous
a/an/anti	not/against	amoral, antibiotics
anim	life	animated
auto	self	autograph
ben	good	beneficial
chron	time	chronology
cis/cise	cut/shorten	scissors, concise
cred	belief	credibility
de/dis	away from/not	deficient, dissent
equ	equal	equality, equate
fort	strength	fortress
gress	movement	progress
il/im/in	not	illegal, imperfect
laud	praise	applaud
loc/loq	speech	eloquent
mag/magna	great	magnify, magnificent
mal	bad	malicious
mis	wrong	mistake
ob	against	obstruct
pac	peace	pact, pacifier
path	feeling	sympathy, apathetic
phil/phile	love	philanthropy, bibliophile
ver	truth	verify
vit/viv	life	vital, revive

Other Methods

There are many other ways to remember words. If you are visually inclined, you might draw pictures to help you remember words. Others use mnemonics (a word that comes from a Greek word for memory), such as sound associations or acronyms (such as PEMDAS: Please Excuse My Dear Aunt Sally). Some people remember words if they speak the words and definitions out loud, in addition to writing flash cards. A great way to remember a word is to start using it in conversation. Ultimately, whatever works for you is the right approach!

Upper Level Vocabulary (SSAT and ISEE)

Includes Lower, Elementary, and Middle Level Vocabulary

Ab through An

Abandon
Abbreviation
Abdicate
Abhor
Abridge
Abrupt
Abundant
Abyss
Acclaimed
Accord
Acknowledge
Acrid
Acumen
Acute
Adamant
Adapt
Adept
Adhere
Adhesive
Admire
Admonish
Adversary
Aesthete
Affiliation
Agenda
Aggrandize
Aggravate
Aggregate
Agile
Ail
Aimless
Akin
Alarmed
Allege
Aloof
Alter
Altruism
Amalgamate
Ambiguous
Ambivalent
Ameliorate
Amiable
Amorphous
Analyze

An through Be

Ancient
Androgynous
Anguish
Animosity
Annex
Antagonistic
Antipathy
Anxious
Apprehension
Approximate
Arbitrary
Arid
Ascertain
Ascetic
Aspect
Aspiration
Assail
Assent
Assert
Assess
Assured
Astonish
Attenuate
Austere
Astute
Audible
Auspicious
Authentic
Authoritative
Avarice
Banal
Barrage
Barren
Barrier
Bashful
Bastion
Bedlam
Bellicose
Belligerent
Bemoan
Benevolent
Benign
Bequest
Betray

Be through Co

Bewilder
Biased
Blatant
Blunt
Bolster
Bombastic
Bourgeois
Brandish
Brash
Brazen
Brittle
Burgeon
Cache
Callow
Candid
Capitulate
Capricious
Cascade
Cater
Cauterize
Cautious
Censor
Chagrin
Chasm
Chronic
Chronicle
Coalesce
Coerce
Commodities
Compassion
Compel
Competent
Composure
Comprehensive
Conceal
Concise
Condemn
Condescending
Condone
Confer
Confine
Conform
Confound
Congenial

Co through De	Di through Ep	Eq through Fo
Conjure	Dignity	Equity
Conniving	Dilute	Equivalent
Connoisseur	Differentiate	Eradicate
Consensus	Disavow	Erratic
Conspicuous	Discreet	Esoteric
Consume	Disgraced	Essential
Contemplation	Dismayed	Esteem
Contented	Dispel	Euphemism
Contradiction	Disparage	Evacuate
Contrite	Disperse	Evade
Controversial	Display	Evict
Conventional	Disputed	Exacerbate
Copious	Dissect	Exalt
Cordial	Distasteful	Exasperate
Corpulent	Distend	Excavate
Corrosion	Distort	Excel
Counsel	Diversity	Exemplify
Counterfeit	Docile	Exhilarating
Cower	Domestic	Exile
Credible	Dominate	Exquisite
Creed	Dormant	Extend
Crucial	Doubtful	Extent
Cunning	Drastic	Extinct
Dawdle	Dread	Extol
Debate	Drenched	Extravagant
Debt	Dubious	Facet
Deceive	Duration	Fallacy
Decline	Eager	Fallow
Decree	Economize	Falter
Defensive	Egotist	Fathom
Defiant	Egress	Fatigue
Deficient	Elegant	Feasible
Deft	Elegy	Feeble
Dejection	Elongate	Feign
Deliberate	Eloquent	Feisty
Delicate	Embodiment	Fickle
Depict	Embryonic	Flaccid
Despair	Emphasize	Flamboyant
Desolate	Endeavor	Flatter
Detest	Enigma	Fleeting
Detrimental	Entrust	Flotsam
Deviate	Envy	Flourish
Devotion	Ephemeral	Fluctuate
Dexterity	Epitome	Foolhardy

Fo through In

Foreseen
Forge
Formulate
Fortunate
Foster
Fragile
Frank
Frugal
Fulcrum
Fundamental
Furious
Furtive
Gap
Genesis
Genial
Generous
Genuine
Germane
Glean
Glint
Glutton
Graceful
Gratified
Grievances
Gullible
Haphazard
Hardship
Hasten
Haughty
Hazard
Hesitate
Hideous
Hinder
Hoard
Homely
Idiosyncrasy
Ignoble
Illuminate
Illustrate
Imbue
Immaculate
Impasse
Imply
Impulsive
Inane
Incident
Incidental
Incision

In through Lu

Incisive
Incite
Incognito
Indifferent
Indignant
Infiltrate
Ingenuity
Ingress
Inhabit
Initial
Innate
Innocuous
Innovate
Inquiry
Insight
Insinuate
Insipid
Insolent
Integrity
Intermission
Integrate
Intricate
Inundate
Invoke
Irate
Jaded
Jargon
Jeer
Jest
Jubilant
Justify
Keen
Kinetic
Knoll
Laudatory
Lavish
Legacy
Lament
Legend
Legitimate
Lenient
Liberate
Limber
Linger
Lofty
Loquacious
Lucrative
Luminous

Lu through Op

Lure
Malicious
Meager
Meander
Meddle
Meek
Menace
Mentor
Merge
Meritorious
Meticulous
Mimic
Mirage
Misery
Model (adjective)
Modify
Molten
Moor
Moral
Morose
Muddled
Mundane
Mystify
Myth
Nag
Narcissism
Navigate
Negate
Neglect
Noncommittal
Nostalgic
Notorious
Novel
Novice
Noxious
Null
Obfuscate
Obscure
Obstacle
Obstinate
Obstruct
Obtuse
Occupy
Ominous
Omit
Onerous
Opaque
Opportune

Op through Pr

Optimistic
Opulent
Ornery
Ostentatious
Overbearing
Overt
Pacify
Pact
Palpable
Paltry
Paradigm
Parody
Parsimonious
Particle
Partisan
Patron
Peak
Pedestrian (adj)
Permeate
Perpetuate
Perplexed
Persevere
Persist
Perturb
Plea
Plight
Pluck (noun)
Plunder
Pompous
Porous
Pragmatic
Precipitate
   (with object)
Precise
Precocious
Predicament
Prediction
Predominate
Prejudiced
Presume
Pretentious
Prevalent
Primary
Pristine
Prominent
Prone
Prophesy
Prototype

Pr through Re

Provoke
Prudent
Pungent
Puny
Puzzled
Qualm
Quiescent
Ratify
Ravenous
Raze
Recalcitrant
Reckless
Refute
Reject
Reluctant
Reminisce
Remote
Rendezvous
Renounce
Renown
Personify
Pervasive
Pessimistic
Petty
Pigment
Pilfer
Pinnacle
Pious
Placate
Plausible
Remonstrate
Remuneration
Reparation
Replete
Replenish
Replica
Reprehensible
Repress
Reprimand
Reproach
Repudiate
Repugnant
Reservations
   (about something)
Residual
Resilience
Restore
Resume

Re through Su

Reticent
Reveal
Revere
Reverent
Robust
Rouse
Routine
Rue
Ruminate
Ruse
Rustic
Ruthless
Salvage
Sate
Satire
Savor
Sedate
Scant
Scarce
Scorn
Seclude
Seldom
Sequence
Shrewd
Simulate
Sincere
Sinister
Solemn
Solitary
Somber
Soothe
Specific
Sporadic
Speck
Spirited
Spontaneous
Stagnate
Stature
Steadfast
Stoic
Stringent
Subside
Succinct
Sullied
Superb
Superfluous
Suppose
Surrogate

Ta through Ul

Tact
Tangible
Taper
Task
Taunt
Tenacious
Terse
Testify to
Thrive
Thwart
Timid
Tiresome
Toil
Torment
Totemic
Tragedy
Trifle
Trite
Tumult
Ultimate

Un through Vi

Uncouth
Undermine
Underscore
Unique
Unruly
Uproot
Utilitarian
Utilize
Vacillate
Vend
Veneration
Vernacular
Versatile
Vetted
Vibrant
Viewpoint
Vigorous
Vigilant
Vindication
Vivacious

Vi through Ze

Vivid
Voracious
Vow
Voyage
Vulnerable
Wane
Wax (verb)
Weary
Wily
Wrath
Writhe
Zany
Zealous (or zeal)

Chapter 2
Fundamental
Math Skills for
the SSAT & ISEE

INTRODUCTION

Whether you are taking the Lower Level ISEE or the Upper Level SSAT, there are some basic math skills that are at the heart of many of the questions on your test. If you are taking the Lower or Elementary Level exams, the content in this section may be something you learned recently or are learning right now. You should go through this chapter very carefully and slowly. If you are having trouble understanding any of the content, you should ask your parents or teachers for help by having them explain it more thoroughly to you. If you are taking the Middle and Upper Level tests, this chapter may serve more as a chance to review some things you may have forgotten or that you need to practice a little. Even the most difficult-seeming questions on the Upper Level exams are built on testing your knowledge of these same skills. Make sure you read the explanations and do all of the drills before going on to either the SSAT or ISEE math chapter. Answers to these drills are provided in Chapter 3.

A Note to Lower, Elementary, and Middle Level Students

This chapter has been designed to give all students a comprehensive review of the math found on the tests. There are four sections: "The Building Blocks," "Algebra," "Geometry," and "Word Problems." At the beginnings and ends of some of these sections, you will notice information about what material you should review and what material is only for Upper Level (UL) students. Be aware that you may not be familiar with all the topics on which you will be working. If you are having difficulty understanding a topic, take this book to your teachers or parents and ask them for additional help.

Lose Your Calculator!

You will *not* be allowed to use a calculator on the SSAT or the ISEE. If you have developed a habit of reaching for your calculator whenever you need to add or multiply a couple of numbers, follow our advice: put your calculator away now and take it out again after the test is behind you. Do your math homework assignments without it, and complete the practice sections of this book without it. Trust us, you'll be glad you did.

Write It Down

Write It Down; Get It Right!
You don't get points for doing the math in your head, so don't do it!

Do not try to do math in your head. You are allowed to write in your test booklet. You *should* write in your test booklet. Even when you are adding just a few numbers together, write them down and do the work on paper. Writing things down not only helps to eliminate careless errors but also gives you something to refer back to if you need to double-check your work.

THE BUILDING BLOCKS

Math Vocabulary

Term	Definition	Examples
Integer	Any number that does not contain either a fraction or a decimal. Can be positive, negative, or zero.	14, 3, 0, –3
Whole number	Positive integers and zero	0, 1, 17
Positive number	Any number greater than zero	$\frac{1}{2}$, 1, 104.7
Negative number	Any number less than zero	$-\frac{1}{2}$, –1, –104.7
Even number	Any number that is evenly divisible by two. **Note:** Zero is an even number!	104, 16, 2, 0, –2, –104
Odd number	Any number that is not evenly divisible by two	115, 11, 1, –1, –11, –115
Prime number	Any number that is divisible by only 1 and itself. **Note:** One is **not** a prime number, but two **is**.	2, 3, 5, 7, 13, 131
Digit	The numbers from 0 through 9	0, 2, 3, 7. The number 237 has digits 2, 7, and 3.
Units (ones) digit	The digit in the ones place	For 281, 1 is in the units place.
Consecutive numbers	Any series of numbers listed in the order they appear on the number line	3, 4, 5 or –1, 0, 1, 2
Distinct numbers	Numbers that are different from one another	2, 7, and 19 are three distinct numbers; 4 and 4 are not distinct because they are the same number.
Divisible by	A number that can be evenly divided by another	12 is divisible by 1, 2, 3, 4, 6, 12.
Sum	The result of addition	The sum of 6 and 2 is 8 because 6 + 2 = 8.
Difference	The result of subtraction	The difference between 6 and 2 is 4 because 6 – 2 = 4.
Product	The result of multiplication	The product of 6 and 2 is 12 because 6 × 2 = 12.
Quotient	The result of division	The quotient when 6 is divided by 2 is 3 because 6 ÷ 2 = 3.
Remainder	The amount left over when dividing	17 ÷ 5 leaves a remainder of 2.
Rational number	A number that can be written as a fraction	$0.\overline{66} = \frac{2}{3}$
Irrational number	A number that cannot be written as a fraction	π or $\sqrt{2}$
Multiple	The result of multiplying a number by an integer (not a fraction)	40 is a multiple of 8 (8 × 5 = 40) and of 5 (5 × 8 = 40).
Factor	Any numbers or symbols that can be multiplied together to form a product	8 and 5 are factors of 40 because 8 × 5 = 40.

The Rules of Zero

Zero has some funny rules. Make sure you understand and remember these rules.

- Zero is neither positive nor negative.
- Zero is even.
- Zero is an integer.
- Zero multiplied by any number is zero.
- Zero divided by any number is zero.
- You cannot divide by zero ($9 \div 0 = $ *undefined*).

The Times Table

Elementary Level
If you haven't learned the Times Table yet, this is a great opportunity to get ahead of your classmates!

Make sure you are comfortable with your multiplication tables up to 12. If you are having trouble with these, break out the flash cards. On one side of the card write down the multiplication problem, and on the other write down the answer. Now quiz yourself. You may also want to copy the table shown below so you can practice. For handy tips on using flash cards effectively, turn to the vocabulary chapter and read the section on flash cards.

	1	2	3	4	5	6	7	8	9	10	11	12
1	1	2	3	4	5	6	7	8	9	10	11	12
2	2	4	6	8	10	12	14	16	18	20	22	24
3	3	6	9	12	15	18	21	24	27	30	33	36
4	4	8	12	16	20	24	28	32	36	40	44	48
5	5	10	15	20	25	30	35	40	45	50	55	60
6	6	12	18	24	30	36	42	48	54	60	66	72
7	7	14	21	28	35	42	49	56	63	70	77	84
8	8	16	24	32	40	48	56	64	72	80	88	96
9	9	18	27	36	45	54	63	72	81	90	99	108
10	10	20	30	40	50	60	70	80	90	100	110	120
11	11	22	33	44	55	66	77	88	99	110	121	132
12	12	24	36	48	60	72	84	96	108	120	132	144

PRACTICE DRILL 1—MATH VOCABULARY

1. How many integers are there between −1 and 6 ? _____

2. List three consecutive odd integers. _____

3. How many odd integers are there between 1 and 9 ? _____

4. What is the tens digit in the number 182.09 ? _____

5. The product of any number and the smallest positive integer is _____

6. What is the product of 5, 6, and 3 ? _____

7. What is the sum of 3, 11, and 16 ? _____

8. What is the difference between your answer to question 6 and your answer to question 7 ? _____

9. List three consecutive negative even integers: _____

10. Is 11 a prime number? _____

11. What is the sum of the digits in the number 5,647 ? _____

12. What is the remainder when 58 is divided by 13 ? _____

13. 55 is divisible by what numbers? _____

14. The sum of the digits in 589 is how much greater than the sum of the digits in 1,207 ? _____

15. Is 21 divisible by the remainder of 19 ÷ 5 ? _____

16. What are the prime factors of 156 ? _____

17. What is the sum of the odd prime factors of 156 ? _____

18. 12 multiplied by 3 is the same as 4 multiplied by what number? _____

19. What are the factors of 72 ? _____

20. How many factors of 72 are even? _____
    How many are odd? _____

> **When You Are Done**
> Check your answers in Chapter 3.

Working with Negative Numbers

It is helpful to think of numbers as having two component parts: the number itself and the sign in front of it (to the left of the number). Numbers that don't have signs immediately to the left of them are positive. So +7 can be, and usually is, written as 7.

Adding

If the signs to the left of the numbers are the same, you add the two numbers and keep the same sign. For example:

$2 + 5 = (+2) + (+5) = +7$ or just plain 7

$(-2) + (-5) = -7$

If the signs to the left of the numbers are different, you subtract the numbers and the answer takes the sign of the larger number. For example:

$5 + (-2) = 5 - 2 = 3$, and because 5 is greater than 2, the answer is +3 or just plain 3.

$(-2) + 5 = 5 - 2 = 3$, and because 5 is greater than 2, the answer is +3 or just plain 3.

$(-5) + 2 = 5 - 2 = 3$, and because 5 is greater than 2, you use its sign and the answer is −3.

Subtracting—Middle and Upper Levels only

All subtraction problems can be converted to addition problems. This is because subtracting is the same as adding the opposite. "Huh?" you say—well, let's test this out on something simple that you already know. We know that $7 - 3 = 4$, so let's turn it into an addition problem and see if we get the same answer.

$$7 - 3 = (+7) - (+3)$$

Okay, so now we reverse only the operation sign and the sign of the number we are subtracting (the second number). The first number stays the same because that's our starting point.

$$(+7) + (-3)$$

Now use the rules for addition to solve this problem. Because the signs to the left are different, we subtract the two numbers $7 - 3 = 4$, and the sign is positive because 7 is greater than 3.

We have just proven that subtraction problems are really just the opposite of addition problems. Now let's see how this works in a variety of examples.

$3 - 7 = (+3) - (+7) = (+3) + (-7) = 7 - 3 = 4$ and, because 7 is greater than 3, the answer is -4.

$-9 - 3 = (-9) - (+3) = (-9) + (-3) = -12$

$13 - (-5) = (+13) - (-5) = (+13) + (+5) = +18$

$(-5) - (-8) = (-5) + (+8) = +3$

This is just one way to look at subtraction problems. If you have a way that works better for you, use that!

PRACTICE DRILL 2—ADDING AND SUBTRACTING NEGATIVE NUMBERS

1. $6 + (–14) =$

2. $13 – 27 =$

3. $(–17) + 13 =$

4. $12 – (–15) =$

5. $16 + 5 =$

6. $34 – (+30) =$

7. $(–7) + (–15) =$

8. $(–42) + 13 =$

9. $–13 – (–7) =$

10. $151 + (–61) =$

11. $(–42) – (–42) =$

12. $5 – (–24) =$

13. $14 + 10 =$

14. $(–5) + (–25) =$

15. $11 – 25 =$

When You Are Done
Check your answers in
Chapter 3.

Multiplying and Dividing

The rules for multiplying and dividing positive and negative integers are so much easier to learn and use than the rules for adding and subtracting them. You simply multiply or divide as normal, and then determine the sign using the rules below.

Positive ($\div$ or $\times$) Positive = Positive

Negative ($\div$ or $\times$) Negative = Positive

Positive ($\div$ or $\times$) Negative = Negative

Negative ($\div$ or $\times$) Positive = Negative

Here are some examples.

$$6 \div 2 = 3 \qquad\qquad 2 \times 6 = 12$$

$$(-6) \div (-2) = 3 \qquad\qquad (-2) \times (-6) = 12$$

$$6 \div (-2) = -3 \qquad\qquad 2 \times (-6) = -12$$

$$(-6) \div 2 = -3 \qquad\qquad (-2) \times 6 = -12$$

If you are multiplying more than two numbers, simply work from left to right and deal with the numbers two at a time.

$$2 \times (-5) \times (-10) = 2 \times (-5) = -10 \text{ and now } (-10) \times (-10) = +100$$

Helpful Rule of Thumb

When multiplying numbers, simply count the number of negative signs. An even number of negative signs (-6×-3) means that the product must be a positive number. An odd number of negative signs (2×-5) means that the product must be negative.

PRACTICE DRILL 3—MULTIPLYING AND DIVIDING NEGATIVE NUMBERS

1. $20 \div (-5) =$

2. $(-12) \times 3 =$

3. $(-13) \times (-5) =$

4. $(-44) \div (-4) =$

5. $7 \times 9 =$

6. $(-65) \div 5 =$

7. $(-7) \times (-12) =$

8. $(-10) \div 2 =$

9. $81 \div 9 =$

10. $32 \div (-4) =$

11. $25 \times (-3) =$

12. $(-24) \times (-3) =$

13. $64 \div (-16) =$

14. $(-17) \times (-2) =$

15. $(-55) \div 5 =$

When You Are Done
Check your answers in
Chapter 3.

ORDER OF OPERATIONS

How would you attack this problem?

$$16 - 45 \div (2 + 1)^2 \times 4 + 5 =$$

To solve a problem like this, you need to know which mathematical operation to do first. The way to remember the order of operations is to use PEMDAS.

Done at the same time from left to right $\left\{\begin{array}{l}\text{\textbf{Parentheses}} \\ \text{\textbf{Exponents}} \\ \text{\textbf{Multiplication}} \\ \text{\textbf{Division}}\end{array}\right.$

$\left.\begin{array}{l}\text{\textbf{Addition}} \\ \text{\textbf{Subtraction}}\end{array}\right\}$ **Done at the same time from left to right**

You can remember the order of operations by using the phrase below:

"Please Excuse My Dear Aunt Sally"

Now, let's give it a try.

$$16 - 45 \div (2 + 1)^2 \times 4 + 5 =$$

1. **Parentheses:**

   $$16 - 45 \div \underline{(2 + 1)}^2 \times 4 + 5 =$$

   $$16 - 45 \div (3)^2 \times 4 + 5 =$$

2. **Exponents:**

   $$16 - 45 \div (3)^2 \times 4 + 5 =$$

   $$16 - 45 \div 9 \times 4 + 5 =$$

3. **Multiplication and division (from left to right):**

$$16 - \underline{45 \div 9} \times 4 + 5 =$$

$$16 - \underline{5 \times 4} + 5 =$$

$$16 - 20 + 5 =$$

4. **Addition and subtraction (from left to right):**

$$\underline{16 - 20} + 5 =$$

$$-4 + 5 = \boxed{1}$$

Just take it one step at a time and you'll be able to do it in no time at all!

PRACTICE DRILL 4—ORDER OF OPERATIONS

1. $10 - 3 + 2 =$

2. $15 + (7 - 3) - 3 =$

3. $3 \times 2 + 3 \div 3 =$

4. $2 \times (4 + 6)^2 \div 4 =$

5. $420 \div (10 + 5 \times 12) =$

6. $20 \times 5 \div 10 + 20 =$

7. $3 + 5 \times 10 \times (7 - 6) \div 2 - 4 =$

8. $10 \times (8 + 1) \times (3 + 1) \div (8 - 2) =$

9. $12 + (5 \times 2)^2 - 33 \div 3 =$

10. $200 - 150 \div 3 \times 2^3 =$

When You Are Done
Check your answers in Chapter 3.

Factors

Factors are all the numbers that divide evenly into your original number. For example, 2 is a factor of 10; it goes in 5 times. However, 3 is not a factor of 10 because 10 divided by 3 does not produce an integer quotient (and therefore does not "go in evenly"). When asked to find the factors of a number, just make a list.

> The factors of 16 are
> > 1 and 16 (always start with 1 and the original number)
> > 2 and 8
> > 4 and 4
> The factors of 18 are
> > 1 and 18
> > 2 and 9
> > 3 and 6

Knowing some of the rules of divisibility can save you some time.

Larger Factors

There's a quick way to figure out if a number is divisible by larger numbers. Simply take the two smaller factors and check both. If a number is divisible by both 2 and 3, then it's divisible by 6. If a number is divisible by both 3 and 4, then it's divisible by 12.

A number is divisible by	If...
2	it ends in 0, 2, 4, 6, or 8
3	the sum of the digits is divisible by 3
4	the number formed by the last two digits is divisible by 4
5	it ends in 0 or 5
8	the number formed by the last three digits is divisible by 8
9	the sum of the digits is divisible by 9
10	it ends in 0

Factor Trees

To find the prime factors of a number, draw a factor tree.

Start by writing down the number and then drawing two branches from the number. Write down any pair of factors of that number. Now if one (or both) of the factors is not prime, draw another set of branches from that factor and write down a pair of factors for that number. Continue until you have only prime numbers at the end of your branches. Each branch end is a prime factor. Remember, 1 is NOT prime!

What are the distinct prime factors of 56? Well, let's start with the factor tree.

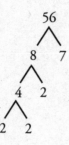

The prime factors of 56 are 2, 2, 2, and 7. Because the question asked for only the distinct prime factors, we have to eliminate the numbers that repeat, so we cross out two of the twos. The distinct prime factors of 56 are 2 and 7.

Multiples

Multiples are the results when you multiply your number by any integer. The number 15 is a multiple of 5 because 5 times 3 equals 15. On the other hand, 18 is a multiple of 3, but not a multiple of 5. Another way to think about multiples is to consider them "counting by a number."

The first seven positive multiples of 7 are:

$$
\begin{array}{rl}
7 & (7 \times 1) \\
14 & (7 \times 2) \\
21 & (7 \times 3) \\
28 & (7 \times 4) \\
35 & (7 \times 5) \\
42 & (7 \times 6) \\
49 & (7 \times 7)
\end{array}
$$

PRACTICE DRILL 5—FACTORS AND MULTIPLES

1. List the first five multiples of:

   2 _____

   4 _____

   5 _____

   11 _____

2. Is 15 divisible by 3 ?

3. Is 81 divisible by 3 ?

4. Is 77 divisible by 3 ?

5. Is 23 prime?

6. Is 123 divisible by 3 ?

7. Is 123 divisible by 9 ?

8. Is 250 divisible by 2 ?

9. Is 250 divisible by 5 ?

10. Is 250 divisible by 10 ?

11. Is 10 a multiple of 2 ?

12. Is 11 a multiple of 3 ?

13. Is 2 a multiple of 8 ?

14. Is 24 a multiple of 4 ?

15. Is 27 a multiple of 6 ?

16. Is 27 a multiple of 9 ?

17. How many numbers between 1 and 50 are multiples of 6 ?

18. How many even multiples of 3 are there between 1 and 50 ?

19. How many numbers between 1 and 100 are multiples of both 3 and 4 ?

20. What is the greatest multiple of 3 less than 50 ?

When You Are Done
Check your answers in
Chapter 3.

Fractions

A fraction really just tells you to divide. For instance, $\frac{5}{8}$ actually means five divided by eight (which equals 0.625 as a decimal).

Another way to think of this is to imagine a pie cut into eight pieces. $\frac{5}{8}$ represents five of those eight pieces of pie.

The parts of a fraction are called the numerator and the denominator. The numerator is the number on top of the fraction. It refers to the portion of the pie, while the denominator is on the bottom of the fraction and tells you how many pieces there are in the entire pie.

$$\frac{\text{numerator}}{\text{denominator}} = \frac{\text{part}}{\text{whole}}$$

Reducing Fractions

Imagine a pie cut into two big pieces. You eat one of the pieces. That means that you have eaten $\frac{1}{2}$ of the pie. Now imagine the same pie cut into four pieces; you eat two. That's $\frac{2}{4}$ this time. But look: The two fractions are equivalent!

> **Remember!**
>
> As the denominator gets smaller, the fraction gets bigger. After all, would you rather have $\frac{1}{4}$ of a cake or $\frac{1}{2}$ of one?

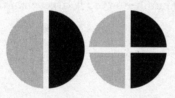

To reduce fractions, simply divide the top number and the bottom number by the same amount. Start out with small numbers like 2, 3, 5, or 10 and reduce again if you need to.

$$\frac{12}{24} \begin{array}{c} \div 2 \\ \div 2 \end{array} = \frac{6}{12} \begin{array}{c} \div 2 \\ \div 2 \end{array} = \frac{3}{6} \begin{array}{c} \div 3 \\ \div 3 \end{array} = \frac{1}{2}$$

In this example, if you happened to see that both 12 and 24 are divisible by 12, then you could have saved two steps. However, don't spend very much time looking for the largest number possible by which to reduce a fraction. Start out with a small number; doing one extra reduction doesn't take very much time and will definitely help prevent careless errors.

PRACTICE DRILL 6—REDUCING FRACTIONS

1. $\dfrac{6}{8} =$

2. $\dfrac{12}{60} =$

3. $\dfrac{20}{30} =$

4. $\dfrac{36}{96} =$

5. $\dfrac{24}{32} =$

6. $\dfrac{16}{56} =$

7. $\dfrac{1,056}{1,056} =$

8. $\dfrac{154}{126} =$

9. What does it mean when the number on top is larger than the one on the bottom?

When You Are Done
Check your answers in Chapter 3.

Improper Fractions and Mixed Numbers

Elementary Level
You may not see this topic.

Changing from Improper Fractions to Mixed Numbers

If you knew the answer to number 9 in the last drill or if you looked it up, you now know that when the number on top is greater than the number on the bottom, the fraction is greater than 1. That makes sense, because we also know that a fraction bar is really just another way of telling us to divide. So, $\frac{10}{2}$ is the same as $10 \div 2$, which equals 5, which is much greater than 1!

A fraction that has a greater numerator than denominator is called an *improper fraction*. You may be asked to change an improper fraction to a mixed number. A *mixed number* is an improper fraction that has been converted into a whole number and a proper fraction. To do this, let's use $\frac{10}{8}$ as the improper fraction that we are going to convert to a mixed number.

Put Away That Calculator!
Remember that a remainder is just the number left over after you do long division; it is not the decimal that a calculator gives you.

First, divide 10 by 8. This gives us our whole number. 8 goes into 10 once.

Now, take the remainder, 2, and put it over the original fraction's denominator: $\frac{2}{8}$.

So the mixed number is $1\frac{2}{8}$, or $1\frac{1}{4}$.

PRACTICE DRILL 7—CHANGING IMPROPER FRACTIONS TO MIXED NUMBERS

1. $\dfrac{45}{9} =$

2. $\dfrac{72}{42} =$

3. $\dfrac{16}{3} =$

4. $\dfrac{5}{2} =$

5. $\dfrac{8}{3} =$

6. $\dfrac{62}{9} =$

7. $\dfrac{15}{10} =$

8. $\dfrac{22}{11} =$

9. $\dfrac{83}{7} =$

10. $\dfrac{63}{6} =$

When You Are Done
Check your answers in
Chapter 3.

Changing Mixed Numbers to Improper Fractions

It's important to know how to change a mixed number into an improper fraction because it may be easier to add, subtract, multiply, or divide a fraction if there is no whole number in the way. To do this, multiply the denominator by the whole number and then add the result to the numerator. Then put this sum on top of the original denominator. For example:

$$1\frac{1}{2}$$

Multiply the denominator by the whole number: $2 \times 1 = 2$

Add this to the numerator: $2 + 1 = 3$

Put this result over the original denominator: $\frac{3}{2}$

$$1\frac{1}{2} = \frac{3}{2}$$

PRACTICE DRILL 8—CHANGING MIXED NUMBERS TO IMPROPER FRACTIONS

1. $6\dfrac{3}{7} =$

2. $2\dfrac{5}{9} =$

3. $23\dfrac{2}{3} =$

4. $6\dfrac{2}{3} =$

5. $7\dfrac{3}{8} =$

6. $7\dfrac{2}{5} =$

7. $10\dfrac{1}{16} =$

8. $5\dfrac{12}{13} =$

9. $4\dfrac{5}{9} =$

10. $33\dfrac{21}{22} =$

When You Are Done
Check your answers in
Chapter 3.

Adding and Subtracting Fractions with a Common Denominator

To add or subtract fractions with a common denominator, just add or subtract the top numbers and leave the bottom numbers alone.

$$\frac{5}{7} + \frac{1}{7} = \frac{6}{7}$$

$$\frac{5}{7} - \frac{1}{7} = \frac{4}{7}$$

Adding and Subtracting Fractions When the Denominators Are Different

In the past, you have probably tried to find common denominators so that you could just add or subtract straight across. There is a different way; it is called the *Bowtie*.

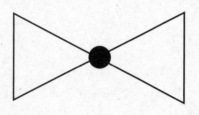

This diagram may make the Bowtie look complicated. It's not. There are three steps to adding and subtracting fractions.

Step 1: Multiply diagonally going up.
First **B × C**. Write the product next to **C**.
Then **D × A**. Write the product next to **A**.

Step 2: Multiply straight across the bottom, **B × D**.
Write the product as the denominator in your answer.

Step 3: To add, add the numbers written next to **A** and **C**.
Write the sum as the numerator in your answer.
To subtract, subtract the numbers written next to A and C. Write the difference as the numerator in your answer.

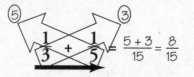

> **No More "Least Common Denominators"**
> Using the Bowtie to add and subtract fractions eliminates the need for the least common denominator, but you may need to reduce the result.

PRACTICE DRILL 9—ADDING AND SUBTRACTING FRACTIONS

1. $\dfrac{3}{8} + \dfrac{2}{3} =$

2. $\dfrac{1}{3} + \dfrac{3}{8} =$

3. $\dfrac{4}{7} + \dfrac{2}{7} =$

4. $\dfrac{3}{4} - \dfrac{2}{3} =$

5. $\dfrac{7}{9} + \dfrac{5}{4} =$

6. $\dfrac{2}{5} - \dfrac{3}{4} =$

7. $\dfrac{10}{12} + \dfrac{7}{2} =$

8. $\dfrac{17}{27} - \dfrac{11}{27} =$

9. $\dfrac{3}{20} + \dfrac{2}{3} =$

(Upper Level)

10. $\dfrac{x}{3} + \dfrac{4x}{6} =$

11. $\dfrac{2x}{10} + \dfrac{x}{5} =$

12. $\dfrac{3y}{6} - \dfrac{y}{12} =$

When You Are Done
Check your answers in
Chapter 3.

Multiplying Fractions—Middle and Upper Levels only

Multiplying can be a pretty simple thing to do with fractions. All you need to do is multiply straight across the tops and bottoms.

$$\frac{3}{7} \times \frac{4}{5} = \frac{3 \times 4}{7 \times 5} = \frac{12}{35}$$

Dividing Fractions—Middle and Upper Levels only

Dividing fractions is almost as simple as multiplying. You just have to flip the second fraction and then multiply.

$$\frac{3}{8} \div \frac{2}{5} = \frac{3}{8} \times \frac{5}{2} = \frac{15}{16}$$

Dividing fractions can be easy as pie; just flip the second fraction and multiply.

PRACTICE DRILL 10—MULTIPLYING AND DIVIDING FRACTIONS

1. $\frac{2}{3} \times \frac{1}{2} =$

2. $\frac{5}{8} \div \frac{1}{2} =$

3. $\frac{4}{5} \times \frac{3}{10} =$

4. $\frac{24}{15} \times \frac{10}{16} =$

5. $\frac{16}{25} \div \frac{4}{5} =$

Remember Reciprocals?

A reciprocal results when you flip a fraction—that is, exchange the numerator and the denominator. So the reciprocal of $\frac{2}{3}$ is what? Yep, that's right: $\frac{3}{2}$.

When You Are Done
Check your answers in Chapter 3.

Decimals

Remember, decimals and fractions are just two different ways of writing the same thing. To change a fraction into a decimal, you just divide the bottom number into the top number.

Be sure you know the names of all the decimal places. Here's a quick reminder.

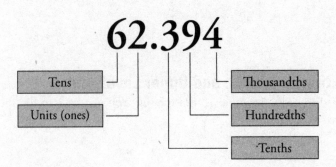

Adding Decimals

To add decimals, just line up the decimal places and add.

$$\begin{array}{r} 48.02 \\ +19.12 \\ \hline 67.14 \end{array}$$

Subtracting Decimals

To subtract, do the same thing. Line up the decimal places and subtract.

$$\begin{array}{r} 67.14 \\ -\ 48.02 \\ \hline 19.12 \end{array}$$

Multiplying Decimals—Middle and Upper Levels only

To multiply decimals, first count the number of digits to the right of the decimal point in the numbers you are multiplying. Then, multiply and, on the product, count that same number of spaces from right to left—this is where you put the decimal point.

$$\begin{array}{r} 0.5 \\ \times\ 4.2 \\ \hline 2.10 \end{array}$$ (two digits to the right of the decimal point)

Dividing Decimals—Middle and Upper Levels only

To divide, move the decimal points in both numbers the same number of spaces to the right until you are working only with integers.

$$12.5 \div 0.25 = 0.25\overline{)12.5}$$

Now move both decimals over two places and solve the problem.

$$25\overline{)1250} = 50$$

And you're done! Remember: you do not put the decimals back into the problem.

PRACTICE DRILL 11—DECIMALS

1. $1.43 + 17.27 =$

2. $2.49 + 1.7 =$

3. $7 - 2.038 =$

4. $4.25 \times 2.5 =$

5. $0.02 \times 0.90 =$

6. $180 \div 0.03 =$

7. $0.10 \div 0.02 =$

When You Are Done
Check your answers in Chapter 3.

Converting Fractions to Decimals and Back Again

From Fractions to Decimals

As we learned when we introduced fractions a little earlier, a fraction bar is really just a division sign.

$$\frac{10}{2} \text{ is the same as } 10 \div 2, \text{ or } 5$$

In the same sense:

$$\frac{1}{2} = 1 \div 2, \text{ or } 0.5$$

In fact, we can convert any fraction to its decimal equivalent by dividing the top number by the bottom number:

$$\frac{11}{2} = 11 \div 2 = 5.5$$

From Decimals to Fractions

To change a decimal to a fraction, look at the digit furthest to the right. Determine what place that digit is in (e.g., tenths, hundredths, and so on) and then put the decimal (without the decimal point) over that number (e.g., 10, 100, and so on). Let's change 0.5 into a fraction.

5 is in the tenths place so we put it over 10.

$$\frac{5}{10} \text{ reduces to } \frac{1}{2}$$

PRACTICE DRILL 12—CONVERTING FRACTIONS TO DECIMALS AND BACK AGAIN

Fill in the table below by converting the fractions to decimals and vice versa. The fractions and decimals in this table are those most often tested on the SSAT and ISEE, so memorize them now and save yourself time later.

Fraction	Decimal
$\frac{1}{2}$	0.5
$\frac{1}{3}$	
$\frac{2}{3}$	
	0.25
	0.75
$\frac{1}{5}$	
	0.4
	0.6
$\frac{4}{5}$	
	0.125

When You Are Done
Check your answers in Chapter 3.

Percents—Middle and Upper Levels only

Percentages are really just an extension of fractions. Let's go back to that pie we were talking about in the section on fractions. Let's say we had a pie that was cut into four equal pieces. If you ate one piece of the pie, then we could say that the *fractional part* of the pie that you have eaten is:

$$\frac{1}{4} \times \frac{\text{(the number of pieces you ate)}}{\text{(the total number of pieces in the pie)}} \times \frac{\text{part}}{\text{whole}}$$

Now let's find out what percentage of the pie you have eaten. Percent literally means "out of 100." When we find a percent, we are really trying to see how many times out of 100 something happens. To determine the percent, you simply take the fractional part and multiply it by 100.

$$\frac{1}{4} \times 100 = \frac{100}{4} = 25\%$$

You've probably seen percents as grades on your tests in school. What does it mean to get 100% on a test? It means you got every question correct. Let's say you got 25 questions right out of a total of 25. So we put the number of questions you got right over the total number of questions and multiply by 100.

$$\frac{25}{25} = 1 \times 100 = 100\%$$

Let's says that your friend didn't do as well on this same test. He answered 20 questions correctly. Let's figure out the percentage of questions he got right.

$$\frac{20}{25} = \frac{4}{5} \times 100 = 80\%$$

What percentage did he get wrong?

$$\frac{5}{25} = \frac{1}{5} = 20\%$$

Notice that the percentage of questions he got right (80%) plus the percentage of questions he got wrong (20%) equals 100%.

PRACTICE DRILL 13—PERCENTS

1. A bag of candies contains 15 butterscotches, 20 caramels, 5 peppermints, and 10 toffees.

   a.) The butterscotches make up what percentage of the candies?_____

   b.) The caramels?_____

   c.) The peppermints?_____

   d.) The toffees?_____

2. A student answered 75% of the questions on a test correctly and left 7% of the questions blank. What percentage of the questions did the student answer incorrectly?_____

3. Stephanie's closet contains 40 pairs of shoes. She has 8 pairs of sneakers, 12 sets of sandals, 16 pairs of boots, and the rest are high heels.

   a.) What percentage of the shoes are sneakers? _____

   b.) Sandals?_____

   c.) Boots?_____

   d.) High heels?_____

   e.) How many high heels does Stephanie own? _____

4. A recipe for fruit punch calls for 4 cups of apple juice, 2 cups of cranberry juice, 3 cups of grape juice, and 1 cup of seltzer. What percentage of the punch is juice?_____

5. Five friends are chipping in for a birthday gift for their teacher. David and Jakob each contribute $13. Stephanie, Kate, and Janice each contribute $8.

   a.) What percentage of the total did the girls contribute?_____

   b.) The boys?_____

When You Are Done
Check your answers in Chapter 3.

More Percents—Middle and Upper Levels Only

Another place you may have encountered percents is at the shopping mall. Stores offer special discounts on their merchandise to entice shoppers to buy more stuff. Most of these stores discount their merchandise by a certain percentage. For example, you may see a $16 shirt that is marked 25% off the regular price. What does that mean?

Percents are not "real" numbers. In the above scenario, the shirt was not $25 less than the regular price (then they'd have to pay you money!), but 25% less. So how do we figure out how much that shirt really costs and how much money we are saving?

To find how much a percent is in "real" numbers, you need to *first take the percent and change it to a fraction.*

Because percent means "out of 100," to change a percent to a fraction, simply put the percent over 100.

$$25\% = \frac{25}{100} = \frac{1}{4}$$

Now let's get back to that shirt. Multiply the regular price of the shirt, $16, by the fraction.

Tip
Changing a decimal to a percent is the same as changing a fraction to a percent. Multiply the decimal by 100 (move the decimal two spaces to the right). So 0.25 as a percent is 0.25 × 100 = 25%.

$$\$16 \times \frac{1}{4} = \$4$$

This means 25% of 16 is $4. You get $4 off the original price of the shirt. If you subtract that from the original price, you find that the new sale price is $12.

Guess what percentage the sale price is of the regular price? If you said 75 percent, you'd be right!

PRACTICE DRILL 14—MORE PERCENTS

Fill in the missing information in the table below.

Fraction	Decimal	Percent
$\frac{1}{2}$	0.5	50%
$\frac{1}{3}$		
	$0.6\overline{6}$	
		25%
	0.75	
$\frac{1}{5}$		
		40%
	0.6	
$\frac{4}{5}$		
		12.5%

1.   25% of 84 =

2. $33\frac{1}{3}$ % of 27 =

3.   20% of 75 =

Tip:
The word *of* in word problems means multiply!

4. 17% of 300 =

5. 16% of 10% of 500 =

6. A dress is marked down 15% from its regular price. If the regular price is $120, what is the sale price of the dress? The sale price is what percentage of the regular price of the dress?

7. Steve goes to school 80% of the 365 days of the year. How many days does Steve go to school?

8. Jennifer answered all 36 questions on her history test. If she got 25% of the questions wrong, how many questions did she get right?

When You Are Done
Check your answers in Chapter 3.

9. During a special one-day sale, the price of a television was marked down 20% from its original price of $100. Later that day, the television was marked down an additional 10%. What was the final sale price?

Exponents—Middle and Upper Levels Only

Exponents are just another way to indicate multiplication. For instance, 3^2 simply means to multiply three by itself two times, so $3^2 = 3 \times 3 = 9$. If you remember that rule, even higher exponents won't seem very complicated. For example:

$$2^5 = 2 \times 2 \times 2 \times 2 \times 2 = 32$$

When in Doubt, Write It Out!
Don't try to compute exponents in your head. Write them out and multiply!

The questions on the SSAT don't generally use exponents higher than four or five, so this is likely to be as complicated as it gets.

The rule for exponents is simple: when in doubt, write it out! Don't try to figure out two times two times two times two times two in your head (just look at how silly it looks written down using words!). Instead, write it as a math problem and just work through it one step at a time.

What would you do if you were asked to solve this problem?

$$Q^3 \times Q^2 =$$

Let's look at this one carefully. Q^3 means $Q \times Q \times Q$ and Q^2 means $Q \times Q$. Put them together and you've got:

$$(Q \times Q \times Q) \times (Q \times Q) =$$

How many Q's is that? Count them. Five! The answer is Q^5. Be careful when multiplying exponents like this so that you don't get confused and multiply the actual exponents, which would give you Q^6. If you are ever unsure, don't spend a second worrying; just write out the exponent and count the number of things you are multiplying.

Square Roots

A square root is just the opposite of squaring a number. $2^2 = 2 \times 2$ or 4, so the square root of 4 is 2.

You will see square roots written this way on a test: $\sqrt{4}$.

PRACTICE DRILL 15—EXPONENTS AND SQUARE ROOTS

1. $2^3 =$

2. $2^4 =$

3. $3^3 =$

4. $4^3 =$

5. $\sqrt{81}$

6. $\sqrt{100}$

7. $\sqrt{49}$

8. $\sqrt{64}$

9. $\sqrt{9}$

When You Are Done
Check your answers in Chapter 3.

More Exponents—Upper Level Only

Multiplying and Dividing Exponents with the Same Base

You can multiply and divide exponents *with the same base* without having to expand out and calculate the value of each exponent. The bottom number, the one you are multiplying, is called the base. (However, note that to multiply $2^3 \times 5^2$ you must calculate the value of each exponent separately and then multiply the results. That's because the bases are different.)

For exponents with the same base, remember MADSPM:
When you *Multiply* with exponents, *Add* them. When you *Divide* with exponents, *Subtract*. When you see *Powers* with exponents, *Multiply*.
The exponent rules do NOT apply when adding or subtracting the bases. Pay attention to the operation that is used in the problem when dealing with exponents!

To multiply, add the exponents.

$$2^3 \times 2^4 = 2^{3+4} = 2^7$$

To divide, subtract the exponents.

$$2^8 \div 2^5 = 2^{8-5} = 2^3$$

To take an exponent to another power, multiply the exponents.

$$(2^3)^3 = 2^{3 \times 3} = 2^9$$

Anything raised to the first power is itself:

$$3^1 = 3 \quad x^1 = x$$

Anything raised to the 0 power is 1:

$$3^0 = 1 \quad x^0 = 1$$

Negative exponents mean reciprocal: flip it over and get rid of the negative sign in the exponent.

$$3^{-2} = \frac{1}{3^2} = \frac{1}{9} \qquad x^{-1} = \frac{1}{x} \qquad 1 \times 10^{-3} = \frac{1}{1,000} \text{ (or 0.001)}$$

PRACTICE DRILL 16—MORE EXPONENTS

1. $3^5 \times 3^3 =$

2. $7^2 \times 7^7 =$

3. $5^3 \times 5^4 =$

4. $15^{23} \div 15^{20} =$

5. $4^{13} \div 4^4 =$

6. $10^{10} \div 10^6 =$

7. $(5^3)^6 =$

8. $(8^{12})^3 =$

9. $(9^5)^5 =$

10. $(2^2)^{14} =$

When You Are Done
Check your answers in
Chapter 3.

REVIEW DRILL 1—THE BUILDING BLOCKS

1. Is 1 a prime number?

2. How many factors does 100 have?

3. $-10 + (-20) =$

4. $100 + 50 \div 5 \times 4 =$

5. $\dfrac{3}{7} - \dfrac{1}{3} =$

6. $\dfrac{4}{5} \div \dfrac{5}{3} =$

7. $1.2 \times 3.4 =$

8. $\dfrac{x}{100} \times 30 = 6$

9. $1^5 =$

10. $\sqrt{16} =$

When You Are Done
Check your answers in
Chapter 3.

11. What are the first 10 perfect squares?

ALGEBRA

An Introduction

If you're a Lower Level, Elementary Level, or Middle Level student, you may not yet have begun learning about algebra in school, but don't let that throw you. If you know how to add, subtract, multiply, and divide, you can solve an algebraic equation. Lower and Elementary Level students only need to understand the section below titled "Solving Simple Equations." Middle Level students should complete all of the "Solving Simple Equations" drills and as much of the Upper Level material as possible. Upper Level students need to go through the entire Algebra section carefully to make sure they can solve each of the question types.

Solving Simple Equations

Algebraic equations involve the same basic operations that we've dealt with throughout this chapter, but instead of using only numbers, these equations use a combination of numbers and letters. These letters are called *variables*. Here are some basic rules about working with variables that you need to understand.

- A variable (usually x, y, or z) replaces an unknown number in an algebraic equation.
- It is usually your job to figure out what that unknown number is.
- If a variable appears more than once in an equation, that variable is always replacing the same number.
- When a variable is directly to the right of a number, with no sign in between them, the operation that is holding them together is multiplication (e.g., $3y = 3 \times y$).
- You can add and subtract like variables (e.g., $2z + 5z = 7z$).
- You cannot add or subtract unlike variables (e.g., $2z$ and $3y$ cannot be combined).

To solve simple algebraic equations, you need to think abstractly about the equation. Let's try one.

$$2 + x = 7$$

What does x equal?

Well, what number plus 2 gives you 7? If you said 5, you were right and $x = 5$.

$$2y = 16$$

In the first equation, we subtracted 2 from both sides. In the second equation, we divided both sides by 2.

What does y equal?

Now you need to ask yourself what multiplied by 2 gives you 16. If you said 8, you were right! $y = 8$.

Tip: You can check to see if you found the right number for the variable by replacing the variable with the number you found in the equation. So in the last problem, if we replace *y* with 8 and rewrite the problem, we get 2 × 8 = 16. And that's true, so we got it right!

PRACTICE DRILL 17—SOLVING SIMPLE EQUATIONS

1. If $35 - x = 23$, then $x =$

2. If $y + 12 = 27$, then $y =$

3. If $z - 7 = 21$, then $z =$

4. If $5x = 25$, then $x =$

5. If $18 \div x = 6$, then $x =$

6. If $3x = 33$, then $x =$

7. If $65 \div y = 13$, then $y =$

8. If $14 = 17 - z$, then $z =$

9. If $\frac{1}{2}y = 24$, then $y =$

10. If $136 + z = 207$, then $z =$

11. If $7x = 84$, then $x =$

12. If $y \div 2 = 6$, then $y =$

13. If $z \div 3 = 15$, then $z =$

14. If $14 + x = 32$, then $x =$

15. If $53 - y = 24$, then $y =$

When You Are Done
Check your answers in
Chapter 3.

Note:
- Lower and Elementary Level students should stop here. The next section you will work on is Geometry.
- All Middle and Upper Level students should continue.

Manipulating an Equation—Middle and Upper Levels Only

To solve an equation, your goal is to isolate the variable, meaning that you want to get the variable on one side of the equation and everything else on the other side.

$$3x + 5 = 17$$

To solve this equation, follow these two steps.

Step 1: Move elements around using addition and subtraction. Get variables on one side and numbers on the other. Simplify.

Step 2: Divide both sides of the equation by the *coefficient*, the number in front of the variable. If that number is a fraction, multiply everything by the denominator.

> **Taking Sides**
> You can do anything you want to one side of the equation, as long as you make sure to do exactly the same thing to the other side.

For example:

$3x + 5 = 17$

$\underline{\quad -5 \quad -5}$ Subtract 5 from both sides to get rid of the numbers on the left side.

$3x \quad = 12$

$\underline{\div 3 \qquad \div 3}$ Divide both sides by 3 to get rid of the 3 on the left side.

$x \quad = 4$

Remember: Whatever you do to one side, you must also do to the other.

PRACTICE DRILL 18—MANIPULATING AN EQUATION

1. If $8 = 11 - x$, then $x =$

2. If $4x = 20$, then $x =$

3. If $5x - 20 = 10$, then $x =$

4. If $4x + 3 = 31$, then $x =$

5. If $m + 5 = 3m - 3$, then $m =$

6. If $2.5x = 20$, then $x =$

7. If $0.2x + 2 = 3.6$, then $x =$

8. If $6 = 8x + 4$, then $x =$

9. If $3(x + y) = 21$, then $x + y =$

10. If $3x + 3y = 21$, then $x + y =$

11. If $100 - 5y = 65$, then $y =$

When You Are Done
Check your answers in
Chapter 3.

Manipulating Inequalities—Middle and Upper Levels Only

Manipulating an inequality is just like manipulating an equation that has an equals sign, except for one rule: if you multiply or divide by a negative number, flip the inequality sign.

Let's try an example.

Helpful Trick
Think of the inequality sign as an alligator, and the alligator always eats the bigger meal.

$$-3x < 6$$

Divide both sides by -3 and then flip the inequality sign.

$$x > -2$$

PRACTICE DRILL 19—MANIPULATING INEQUALITIES

Solve for x.

1. $4x > 16$

2. $13 - x > 15$

3. $15x - 20x < 25$

4. $12 + 2x > 24 - x$

5. $7 < -14 - 3x$

When You Are Done
Check your answers in Chapter 3.

Solving Percent Questions with Algebra—Middle and Upper Levels Only

Learn a Foreign Language

You can memorize "percent language" quickly because there are only four words you need to remember!

Percentages

Solving percent problems can be easy when you know how to translate them from "percent language" into "math language." Once you've done the translation, you guessed it—just manipulate the equation!

Whenever you see words from the following table, just translate them into math terms and go to work on the equation!

Percent Language	Math Language
% or "percent"	out of 100 $\left(\dfrac{x}{100}\right)$
of	times (as in multiplication) (×)
what	your favorite variable (p)
is, are, were, was, did	equals (=)

"What percent" is represented by $\dfrac{x}{100}$.

For example:

24 is 60 percent of what?

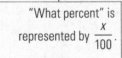

$$24 = \frac{60}{100} \times m$$

PRACTICE DRILL 20—TRANSLATING AND SOLVING PERCENT QUESTIONS

1. 30 is what percent of 250 ?

2. What is 12% of 200 ?

3. What is 25% of 10% of 200 ?

4. 75% of 20% of what number is 12 ?

5. 16% of what number is 25% of 80 ?

6. What percent is equal to $\frac{3}{5}$?

7. 30 is what percent of 75 ?

8. What is 11% of 24 ?

9. What percent of 24 is equal to 48 ?

10. 60% of what percent of 500 is equal to 6 ?

When You Are Done
Check your answers in
Chapter 3.

GEOMETRY

An Introduction

Just as in the previous Algebra section, this Geometry section contains some material that is above the level tested on the Lower/Elementary and Middle Level Exams. These students should not work on sections that are indicated for higher levels.

Perimeter

The perimeter is the distance around the outside of any figure. To find the perimeter of a figure, just add up the lengths of all the sides.

What are the perimeters of these figures?

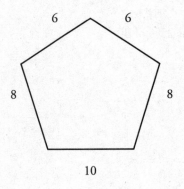

Perimeter = 6 + 6 + 8 + 8 + 10 = 38

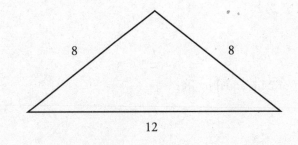

Perimeter = 8 + 8 + 12 = 28

Angles—Middle and Upper Levels Only

Straight Lines

Angles that form a straight line always total 180°.

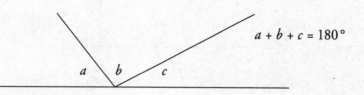

$$a + b + c = 180°$$

Triangles

All of the angles in a triangle add up to 180°.

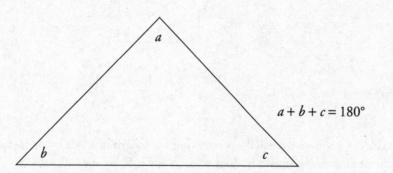

$$a + b + c = 180°$$

The Rule of 180°
There are 180° in a straight line and in a triangle.

Four-Sided Figures

The angles in a square, rectangle, or any other four-sided figure always add up to 360°.

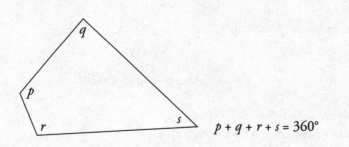

$$p + q + r + s = 360°$$

The Rule of 360°
There are 360° in a four-sided figure and in a circle.

Squares and Rectangles

A *rectangle* is a four-sided figure with four right (90°) angles. Opposite sides are equal in a rectangle. The perimeter is equal to the sum of the sides.

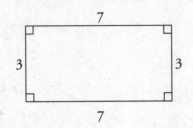

Perimeter = 3 + 3 + 7 + 7 = 20

A *square* is a special type of rectangle in which all the sides are equal.

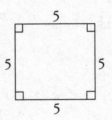

Perimeter = 5 + 5 + 5 + 5 = 20

Because all sides of a square are equal, you can find the length of a side by dividing its perimeter by four. If the perimeter of a square is 20, then each side is 5, because 20 ÷ 4 = 5.

Area

Area is the amount of space taken up by a two-dimensional figure. One way to think about area is as the amount of paper that a figure covers. The larger the area, the more paper the figure takes up.

To determine the area of a square or rectangle, multiply the length (l) by the width (w).

Area of a Rectangle

$A = lw$

Remember the formula:

Area = length × width

What is the area of a rectangle with length 9 and width 4 ?

In this case, the length is 9 and the width is 4, so 9 × 4 = 36. Now look at another example.

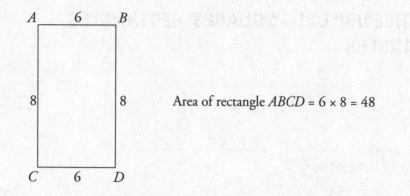

Area of rectangle $ABCD = 6 \times 8 = 48$

The area of squares and rectangles is given in *square feet, square inches,* and so on.

To find the area of a square, you multiply two sides, and because the sides are equal, you're really finding the square of the sides. You can find the length of a side of a square by taking the square root of the area. So if a square has an area of 25, one side of the square is 5.

Area of a Square
$A = s^2$

Volume

Volume is very similar to area, except it takes into account a third dimension. To compute the volume of a figure, you simply find the area and multiply by a third dimension.

For instance, to find the volume of a rectangular object, you would multiply the length by the width (a.k.a. the area) by the height (the third dimension). Since a rectangular solid (like a box) is the only kind of figure you are likely to see in a volume question, simply use the formula below.

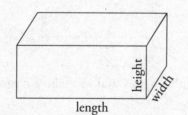

length × width × height = volume

Volume of a Rectangular Solid
$V = lwh$

For example:

    What is the volume of a rectangular fish tank with the
    following specifications?
    length: 6 inches
    height: 6 inches
    width: 10 inches

There isn't much to it. Just plug the numbers into the formula.

    length × width × height = volume
    6 × 10 × 6 = 360

PRACTICE DRILL 21—SQUARES, RECTANGLES, AND ANGLES

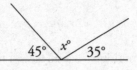

1. What is the value of x ?

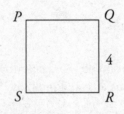

2. What is the value of x ?

3. PQRS is a square. What is its perimeter? Area?

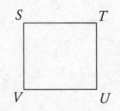

4. ABCD is a rectangle with length 7 and width 3. What is its perimeter? Area?

5. STUV is a square. Its perimeter is 12. What is its area?

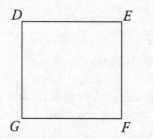

6. *DEFG* is a square. Its area is 81. What is its perimeter?

7. *JKLM* is a rectangle. If its width is 4, and its perimeter is 20, what is its area?

8. *WXYZ* is a rectangle. If its length is 6 and its area is 30, what is its perimeter?

9. What is the volume of a rectangular solid with height 3, width 4, and length 2 ?

When You Are Done
Check your answers in Chapter 3.

Triangles

A triangle is a geometric figure with three sides.

Isosceles Triangles

Any triangle with two equal sides is an isosceles triangle.

If two sides of a triangle are equal, the angles opposite those sides are always equal. Said another way, the sides opposite the equal angles are also equal.

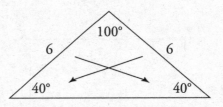

This particular isosceles triangle has two equal sides (of length 6) and therefore two equal angles (40° in this case).

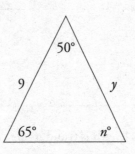

If you already know that the above triangle is isosceles, then you also know that y must equal one of the other sides and n must equal one of the other angles. Since $n = 65$ ($65° + 50° + n° = 180°$), then y must equal 9, because it is opposite the other 65° angle.

Equilateral Triangles

An equilateral triangle is a triangle with three equal sides. If all the sides are equal, then all the angles must be equal. Each angle in an equilateral triangle is 60°.

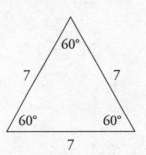

Right Triangles

A right triangle is a triangle with one 90° angle.

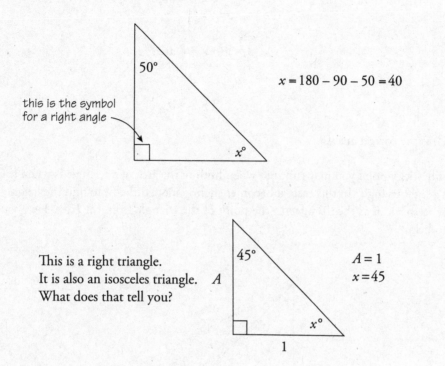

$x = 180 - 90 - 50 = 40$

This is a right triangle.
It is also an isosceles triangle.
What does that tell you?

$A = 1$
$x = 45$

Area

To find the area of a triangle, multiply $\frac{1}{2}$ by the length of the base by the length of the triangle's height, or $\frac{1}{2}b \times h$.

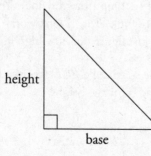

What is the area of a triangle with base 6 and height 3 ?

(A) 3
(B) 6
(C) 9
(D) 12
(E) 18

Elementary and Lower Levels
The test writers may give you the formula for the area of a triangle, but memorizing it will still save you time!

Just put the values you are given into the formula and do the math. That's all there is to it!

Don't Forget!

$A = \dfrac{1}{2}bh$

Remember the base and the height must form a 90° angle.

$$\frac{1}{2}b \times h = \text{area}$$

$$(\frac{1}{2})(6) \times 3 = \text{area}$$

$$3 \times 3 = 9$$

So, (C) is the correct answer.

The only tricky point you may run into when finding the area of a triangle is when the triangle is not a right triangle. In this case, it becomes slightly more difficult to find the height, which is easiest to think of as the distance to the point of the triangle from the base. Here's an illustration to help.

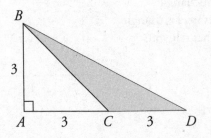

First look at triangle *BAC*, the unshaded right triangle on the left side. Finding its base and height is simple—they are both 3. So using our formula for the area of a triangle, we can figure out that the area of triangle *BAC* is $4\frac{1}{2}$.

Now let's think about triangle *BCD*, the shaded triangle on the right. It isn't a right triangle, so finding the height will involve a little more thought. Remember the question, though: how far up from the base is the point of triangle *BCD*? Think of the shaded triangle sitting on the floor of your room. How far up would its point stick up from the floor? Yes, 3! The height of triangle *BCD* is exactly the same as the height of triangle *BAC*. Don't worry about drawing lines inside the shaded triangle or anything like that, just figure out how high its point is from the ground.

Okay, so just to finish up, to find the base of triangle *BCD* (the shaded one), use the same area formula, and just plug in 3 for the base and 3 for the height.

$$\frac{1}{2}b \times h = \text{area}$$

$$(\frac{1}{2})(3) \times 3 = \text{area}$$

And once you do the math, you'll see that the area of triangle *BCD* is $4\frac{1}{2}$.

Not quite convinced? Let's look at the question a little differently. The base of the entire figure (triangle *DAB*) is 6, and the height is 3. Using your trusty area formula, you can determine that the area of triangle *DAB* is 9. You know the area of the unshaded triangle is $4\frac{1}{2}$, so what's left for the shaded part? You guessed it, $4\frac{1}{2}$.

Similar Triangles—Middle and Upper Levels Only

Similar triangles are triangles that have the same angles but sides of different lengths. The ratio of any two corresponding sides will be the same as the ratio of any other two corresponding sides. For example, a triangle with sides 3, 4, and 5 is similar to a triangle with sides of 6, 8, and 10, because the ratio of each of the corresponding sides (3:6, 4:8, and 5:10) can be reduced to 1:2.

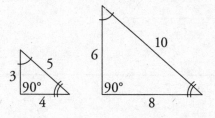

One way to approach similar triangles questions that ask you for a missing side is to set up a ratio or proportion. For example, look at the question below:

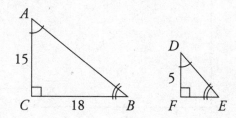

What is the value of *EF*?

A) 4
B) 5
C) 6
D) 7
E) 8

These triangles are similar because they have the same angles. To find side *EF*, you just need to set up a ratio or proportion.

$$\frac{15}{18} = \frac{5}{EF}$$

Cross-multiply to get 15(*EF*) = 18(5).

Divide both sides by 15 to get *EF* = 6.

Therefore, the answer is (C), 6.

The Pythagorean Theorem—Upper Level Only

For all right triangles, $a^2 + b^2 = c^2$, where a, b, and c are the lengths of the triangle's sides.

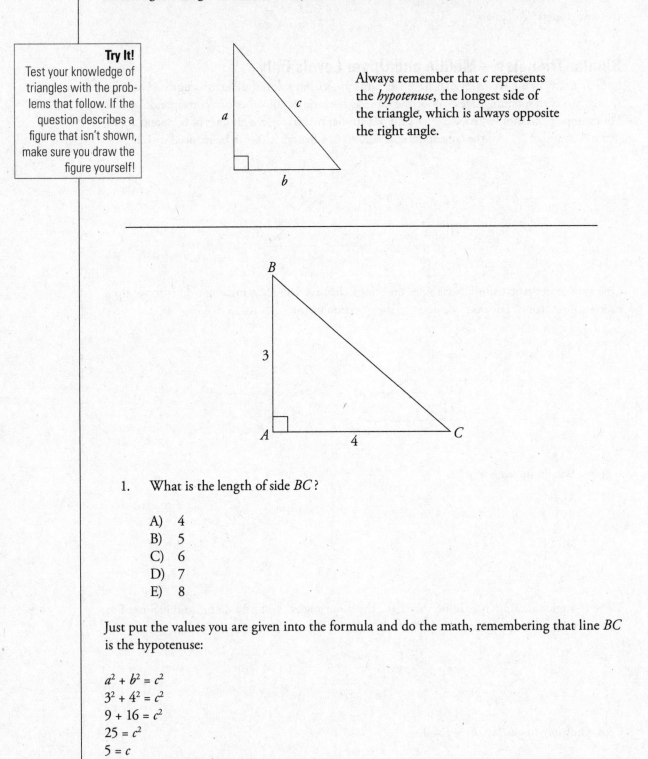

Try It!

Test your knowledge of triangles with the problems that follow. If the question describes a figure that isn't shown, make sure you draw the figure yourself!

Always remember that c represents the *hypotenuse*, the longest side of the triangle, which is always opposite the right angle.

1.   What is the length of side BC?

   A)   4
   B)   5
   C)   6
   D)   7
   E)   8

Just put the values you are given into the formula and do the math, remembering that line BC is the hypotenuse:

$a^2 + b^2 = c^2$
$3^2 + 4^2 = c^2$
$9 + 16 = c^2$
$25 = c^2$
$5 = c$

So, (B) is the correct answer.

PRACTICE DRILL 22—TRIANGLES

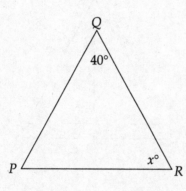

1. What is the value of x?

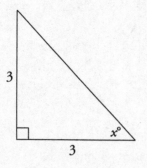

2. Triangle PQR is an isosceles triangle. $PQ = QR$. What is the value of x?

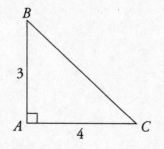

3. What is the area of right triangle ABC?

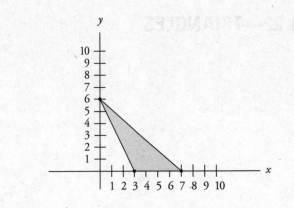

4.   What is the area of the shaded region?

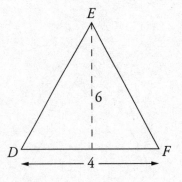

5.   What is the area of triangle *DEF*?

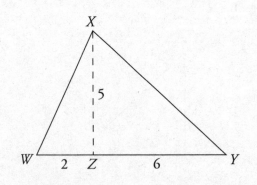

6.   What is the area of triangle *WXZ*? Triangle *ZXY*? Triangle *WXY*?

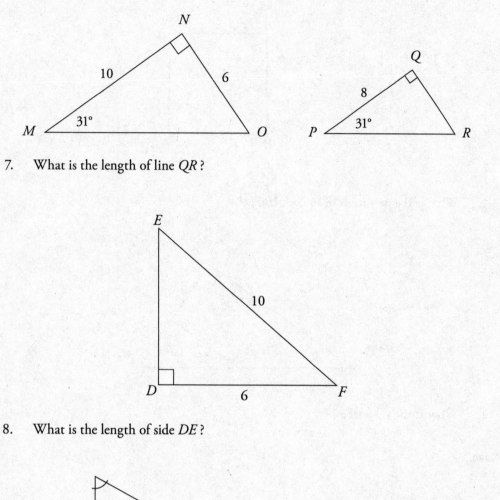

7.   What is the length of line *QR*?

8.   What is the length of side *DE*?

9.   What is the value of *x*?

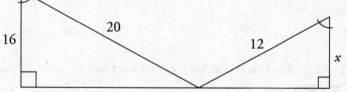

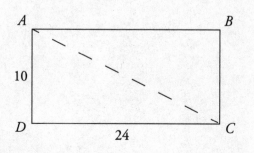

10.   What is the length of the diagonal of rectangle *ABCD*?

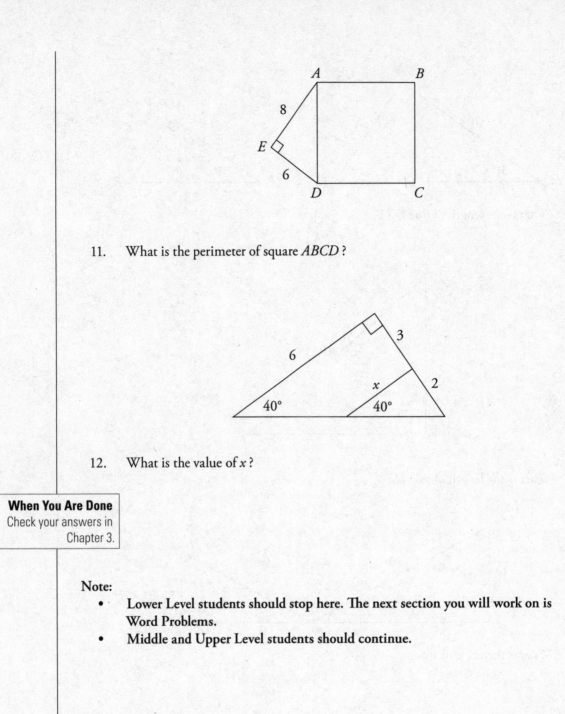

11.   What is the perimeter of square *ABCD* ?

12.   What is the value of *x* ?

When You Are Done
Check your answers in
Chapter 3.

Note:
  • Lower Level students should stop here. The next section you will work on is
    Word Problems.
  • Middle and Upper Level students should continue.

Circles—Middle and Upper Levels Only

You are probably already familiar with the parts of a circle, but let's review them anyway.

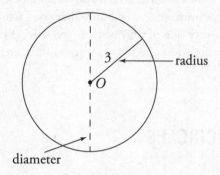

Any line drawn from the origin (the center of the circle) to its edge is called a **radius** (*r*).

Any line that goes from one side of the circle to the other side and passes through the center of the circle is called the **diameter** (*d*). The diameter is two times the length of the radius.

Area and Circumference

Circumference (which is written as *C*) is really just the perimeter of a circle. To find the circumference of a circle, use the formula $2\pi r$ or πd. We can find the circumference of the circle above by taking its radius, 3, and multiplying it by 2π.

$C = 2\pi r$
$C = 2\pi 3$
$C = 6\pi$

The area of a circle is found by using the formula πr^2.

$A = \pi r^2$
$A = \pi 3^2$
$A = 9\pi$

You can find a circle's radius from its circumference by getting rid of π and dividing the number by 2. Or you can find the radius from a circle's area by getting rid of π and taking the square root of the number.

So if a circle has an area of 81π, its radius is 9. If a circle has a circumference of 16π, its radius is 8.

Diameter
$d = 2r$

Circumference
$C = \pi d$

Area
$A = \pi r^2$

What's up with π?

The Greek letter π is spelled "pi" and pronounced "pie." It is a symbol used with circles. Written as a number, π is a nonrepeating, nonending decimal (3.1415927…). We use π to determine the true length of circles. However, on the ISEE and SSAT, we simply leave π as the Greek letter. So when figuring out area or circumference, make sure that you include π in your equation at the beginning and include it in every step of your work as you solve. Remember, π represents a number and it must always be included in either the area or circumference formula.

PRACTICE DRILL 23—CIRCLES

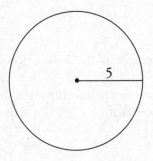

1. What is the circumference of the above circle? What is the area?

2. What is the area of a circle with radius 4 ?

3. What is the area of a circle with diameter 8 ?

4. What is the radius of a circle with area 9π ?

5. What is the diameter of a circle with area 9π ?

6. What is the circumference of a circle with area 25π ?

When You Are Done
Check your answers in
Chapter 3.

3-D Shapes—Upper Level Only

Both the SSAT and ISEE Upper Level tests include 3-D shape geometry questions. While these question types tend to be few and far between, it is important you are prepared for them, just in case they do come up.

Boxes

A three-dimensional box has three important lines: length, width, and height.

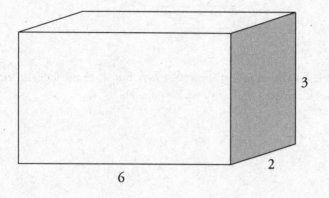

This rectangular box has a length of 6, a width of 2, and a height of 3.

The volume formula of a rectangular box is $V = lwh$.

$V = lwh$
$V = 6(2)(3)$
$V = 36$

Cubes

Cubes are just like rectangular boxes, except that all the sides are equal.

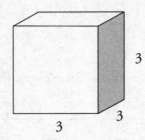

The volume formula for the cube is still just $V = lwh$, but since the length, width and height are all equal it can also be written as $V = s^3$, where s = side.

$V = s^3$
$V = 3^3$
$V = 27$

Cylinders

Cylinders are like circles with height added. For a cylinder with a radius of r and a height of h, the volume formula is $V = \pi r^2 h$.

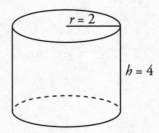

$V = \pi r^2 h$
$V = \pi 2^2 4$
$V = \pi 4(4)$
$V = 16\pi$

PRACTICE DRILL 24—3-D SHAPES

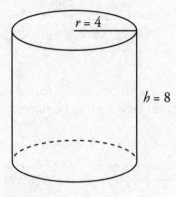

1. What is the volume of this cylinder?

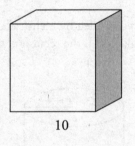

2. What is the volume of this cube?

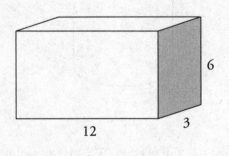

3. What is the volume of this rectangular box?

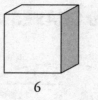

6

4. A cube with a side length of 6 has 54 gallons poured into it. How many more gallons must be poured into the cube for it to be completely filled?

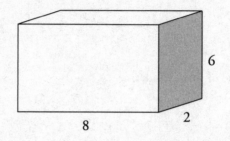

6

8

2

5. The rectangular box pictured is filled by identical cubes with side lengths of 2. How many cubes does it take to fill the rectangular box?

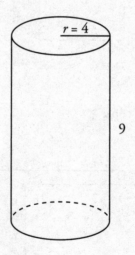

$r = 4$

9

6. The cylinder pictured is $\frac{1}{3}$ full of grain. What is the volume of the grain in the cylinder?

When You Are Done
Check your answers in
Chapter 3.

WORD PROBLEMS

Many arithmetic and algebra problems are written in paragraph form with many words. The hard part is usually not the arithmetic or the algebra; the hard part is translating the words into math. So let's focus on translating.

Key Words and Phrases to Translate

Specific words and phrases show up repeatedly in word problems. You should be familiar with all of those on this page.

What You Read in English	What You Do in Math
and, more than, the sum of, plus	+
less than, the difference between, take away from	−
of, the product of, as much as	×
goes into, divided by, the quotient	÷
is, are, was, were, the result will be, has, have, earns, equals, is the same as	=
what, what number, a certain number	variable (x, y, z)
half of a number	$\frac{1}{2}x$
twice as much as, twice as old as	$2x$
% (percent)	$\overline{}100$
how many times greater	divide the two numbers

Proportions

Proportions show relationships between two sets of information. For example, if you wanted to make cookies and you had a recipe for a dozen cookies but wanted to make two dozen cookies, you would have to double all of the ingredients. That's a proportion. Here's how we'd look at it in equation form.

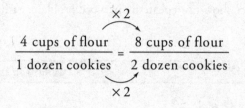

$$\underset{\times 2}{\overset{\times 2}{\frac{4 \text{ cups of flour}}{1 \text{ dozen cookies}} = \frac{8 \text{ cups of flour}}{2 \text{ dozen cookies}}}}$$

Whenever a question gives you one set of data and part of another set, it will ask you for the missing part of the second set of data. To find the missing information, set up the information in fractions like those shown above. Be careful to put the same information in the same place. In our example, we have flour on top and cookies on the bottom. Make sure both fractions have the flour over the cookies. Once we have our fractions set up, we can see what the relationship is between the two elements (in this case, flour and cookies). Whatever that relationship is, it's the same as the relationship between the other two things.

PRACTICE DRILL 25—WORD PROBLEMS

1.   There are 32 ounces in 1 quart. 128 ounces equals how many quarts? How many ounces are there in 7 quarts?

2.   A car travels at a rate of 50 miles per hour. How long will it take to travel 300 miles?

3.   Betty is twice as old as her daughter Fiona. Fiona is twice as old as her dog Rufus. If Rufus is 11, how old is Betty?

4.   A clothing store sold 1,250 pairs of socks this year. Last year, the store sold 250 pairs of socks. This year's sales are how many times greater than last year's sales?

5.   There are 500 students at Eisenhower High School. $\frac{2}{5}$ of the total students are freshmen. $\frac{3}{5}$ of all the freshmen are girls. How many freshman girls are there?

> **When You Are Done**
> Check your answers in Chapter 3.

REVIEW DRILL 2—THE BUILDING BLOCKS

1. If one-third of b is 15, then what is b?

2. If $7x - 7 = 49$, then what is x?

3. If $4(y - 5) = 20$, then what is y?

4. $8x + 1 < 65$. Solve for x.

5. 16 is what percent of 10?

6. What percent of 32 is 24?

7. What is the area of a triangle with base 7 and height 6?

(Middle and Upper Levels)

8. What is the diameter of a circle with an area of 49π?

9. What is the radius of a circle with a circumference of 12π?

10. What is the area of a circle with a diameter of 10?

When You Are Done
Check your answers in
Chapter 3.

Chapter 3
Answer Key to
Fundamental
Math Drills

The Building Blocks

Practice Drill 1—Math Vocabulary

1. 6   0, 1, 2, 3, 4, 5

2. 1, 3, 5   Many sets of integers would answer this question correctly.

3. 3   3, 5, and 7

4. 8   The tens digit is two places to the left of the decimal.

5. That number   The smallest positive integer is 1, and any number times 1 is equal to itself.

6. 90 $5 \times 6 \times 3 = 90$

7. 30 $3 + 11 + 16 = 30$

8. 60 $90 - 30 = 60$

9. −2, −4, −6   2, 4, and 6 are consecutive integers and the question wants negative. Other sets of consecutive integers would also answer the question correctly.

10. Yes   11 is only divisible by 1 and itself.

11. 22 $5 + 6 + 4 + 7 = 22$

12. 6   13 goes into 58, 4 times. $4 \times 13 = 52$ and $58 - 52 = 6$.

13. 1, 5, 11, 55   1, 5, 11, and 55 will all divide into 55 evenly.

14. 12 $5 + 8 + 9 = 22$ and $1 + 2 + 0 + 7 = 10$. $22 - 10 = 12$

15. No   The remainder of $19 \div 5$ is 4. And 21 is not divisible by 4.

16. 2, 2, 3, 13   Draw a factor tree.

```
      156
      / \
     2  78
        / \
       2  39
          / \
         3  13
```

17. 16 $3 + 13 = 16$

18. 9 $12 \times 3 = 36$ and $9 \times 4 = 36$.

19. 1, 2, 3, 4, 6, 8, 9, 12, 18, 24, 36, 72   Remember that factors are the numbers that can be multiplied together to get 72.

20. There are 9 even factors and 3 odd factors.   The even factors are 2, 4, 6, 8, 12, 18, 24, 36, and 72. The odd factors are 1, 3, and 9.

Practice Drill 2—Adding and Subtracting Negative Numbers

1. −8
2. −14
3. −4
4. 27
5. 21
6. 4
7. −22
8. −29
9. −6
10. 90
11. 0
12. 29
13. 24
14. −30
15. −14

Practice Drill 3—Multiplying and Dividing Negative Numbers

1. −4
2. −36
3. 65
4. 11
5. 63
6. −13
7. 84
8. −5
9. 9
10. −8
11. −75
12. 72
13. −4
14. 34
15. −11

Practice Drill 4—Order of Operations

1. 9
2. 16
3. 7
4. 50
5. 6
6. 30
7. 24
8. 60
9. 101
10. −200

Practice Drill 5—Factors and Multiples

1. 2, 4, 6, 8, 10
   4, 8, 12, 16, 20
   5, 10, 15, 20, 25
   11, 22, 33, 44, 55
2. Yes — 3 goes into 15 evenly 5 times.
3. Yes — Use the divisibility rule for 3. The sum of the digits is 9, which is divisible by 3.
4. No — The sum of the digits is 14, which is not divisible by 3.
5. Yes — The only factors of 23 are 1 and 23.
6. Yes — The sum of the digits is 6, which is divisible by 3.
7. No — The sum of the digits is 6, which is not divisible by 9.
8. Yes — 250 ends in a 0, which is an even number and is divisible by 2.
9. Yes — 250 ends in a 0, which is divisible by 5.
10. Yes — 250 ends in a 0, which is divisible by 10.
11. Yes — $2 \times 5 = 10$
12. No — There is no integer that can be multiplied by 3 to equal 11.
13. No — 2 is a factor of 8.
14. Yes — $4 \times 6 = 24$
15. No — There is no integer that can be multiplied by 6 to equal 27.
16. Yes — $3 \times 9 = 27$
17. 8 — 6, 12, 18, 24, 30, 36, 42, 48
18. 8 — Even multiples of 3 are really just multiples of 6.
19. 8 — Multiples of both 3 and 4 are also multiples of 12.
    12, 24, 36, 48, 60, 72, 84, 96
20. 48 — $3 \times 16 = 48$

Practice Drill 6—Reducing Fractions

1. $\dfrac{3}{4}$

2. $\dfrac{1}{5}$

3. $\dfrac{2}{3}$

4. $\dfrac{3}{8}$

5. $\dfrac{3}{4}$

6. $\dfrac{2}{7}$

7. 1

8. $\dfrac{11}{9}$

9. If the number on top is larger than the number on the bottom, the fraction is greater than 1.

Practice Drill 7—Changing Improper Fractions to Mixed Numbers

1. 5

2. $1\dfrac{5}{7}$

3. $5\dfrac{1}{3}$

4. $2\dfrac{1}{2}$

5. $2\dfrac{2}{3}$

6. $6\dfrac{8}{9}$

7. $1\dfrac{1}{2}$

8. 2

9. $11\dfrac{6}{7}$

10. $10\dfrac{1}{2}$

Practice Drill 8—Changing Mixed Numbers to Improper Fractions

1. $\dfrac{45}{7}$ $\dfrac{7 \times 6 + 3}{7} = \dfrac{45}{7}$

2. $\dfrac{23}{9}$ $\dfrac{9 \times 2 + 5}{9} = \dfrac{23}{9}$

3. $\dfrac{71}{3}$ $\dfrac{3 \times 23 + 2}{3} = \dfrac{71}{3}$

4. $\dfrac{20}{3}$ $\dfrac{3 \times 6 + 2}{3} = \dfrac{20}{3}$

5. $\dfrac{59}{8}$ $\dfrac{8 \times 7 + 3}{8} = \dfrac{59}{8}$

6. $\dfrac{37}{5}$ $\dfrac{5 \times 7 + 2}{5} = \dfrac{37}{5}$

7. $\dfrac{161}{16}$ $\dfrac{16 \times 10 + 1}{16} = \dfrac{161}{16}$

8. $\dfrac{77}{13}$ $\dfrac{13 \times 5 + 12}{13} = \dfrac{77}{13}$

9. $\dfrac{41}{9}$ $\dfrac{9 \times 4 + 5}{9} = \dfrac{41}{9}$

10. $\dfrac{747}{22}$ $\dfrac{22 \times 33 + 21}{22} = \dfrac{747}{22}$

Practice Drill 9—Adding and Subtracting Fractions

1. $1\dfrac{1}{24}$ or $\dfrac{25}{24}$ Multiply using Bowtie to get $\dfrac{9}{24} + \dfrac{16}{24} = \dfrac{25}{24} = 1\dfrac{1}{24}$.

2. $\dfrac{17}{24}$ Multiply using Bowtie to get $\dfrac{8}{24} + \dfrac{9}{24} = \dfrac{17}{24}$.

3. $\dfrac{6}{7}$ Did you use the Bowtie? You didn't need to because there was already a common denominator there!

4. $\dfrac{1}{12}$ Multiply using Bowtie to get $\dfrac{9}{12} - \dfrac{8}{12} = \dfrac{1}{12}$.

5. $2\dfrac{1}{36}$ or $\dfrac{73}{36}$ Multiply using Bowtie to get $\dfrac{28}{36} + \dfrac{45}{36} = \dfrac{73}{36} = 2\dfrac{1}{36}$.

6. $-\dfrac{7}{20}$ Multiply using Bowtie to get $\dfrac{8}{20} - \dfrac{15}{20} = -\dfrac{7}{20}$.

7. $4\dfrac{1}{3}$ or $\dfrac{13}{3}$ Multiply using Bowtie to get $\dfrac{20}{24} + \dfrac{84}{24} = \dfrac{104}{24} = \dfrac{13}{3} = 4\dfrac{1}{3}$.

8. $\dfrac{2}{9}$ Did you use the Bowtie? You didn't need to because there was already a common denominator there! Subtract to get $\dfrac{6}{27} = \dfrac{2}{9}$.

9. $\dfrac{49}{60}$ Multiply using Bowtie to get $\dfrac{9}{60} + \dfrac{40}{60} = \dfrac{49}{60}$.

10. x Multiply using Bowtie to get

$$\frac{6x}{18} + \frac{12x}{18} = \frac{18x}{18} = x.$$

11. $\dfrac{2x}{5}$ Multiply using Bowtie to get

$$\frac{10x}{50} + \frac{10x}{50} = \frac{20x}{50} = \frac{2x}{5}.$$

12. $\dfrac{5y}{12}$ Multiply using Bowtie to get

$$\frac{36y}{72} - \frac{6y}{72} = \frac{30y}{72} = \frac{5y}{12}.$$

Practice Drill 10—Multiplying and Dividing Fractions

1. $\dfrac{1}{3}$ $\dfrac{2 \times 1}{3 \times 2} = \dfrac{2}{6} = \dfrac{1}{3}$

2. $1\dfrac{1}{4}$ or $\dfrac{5}{4}$ $\dfrac{5}{8} \times \dfrac{2}{1} = \dfrac{5 \times 2}{8 \times 1} = \dfrac{10}{8} = \dfrac{5}{4}$

3. $\dfrac{6}{25}$ $\dfrac{4 \times 3}{5 \times 10} = \dfrac{12}{50} = \dfrac{6}{25}$

4. 1 $\dfrac{24 \times 10}{15 \times 16} = \dfrac{240}{240} = 1$

5. $\dfrac{4}{5}$ $\dfrac{16}{25} \times \dfrac{5}{4} = \dfrac{16 \times 5}{25 \times 4} = \dfrac{80}{100} = \dfrac{4}{5}$

Practice Drill 11—Decimals

1. 18.7   Don't forget to line up the decimals. Then add.
2. 4.19   After lining up the decimals, remember to add a 0 at the end of 1.7. Then add the two numbers.
3. 4.962   Change 7 to 7.000, line up the decimals, and then subtract.
4. 10.625   Don't forget there are a total of 3 digits to the right of the decimal.
5. 0.018   There are a total of 4 digits to the right of the decimal, but you do not have to write the final 0 in 0.0180.

6. 6,000   Remember to move both decimals right 2 places: $3\overline{)18000}$ with 6000 and don't put the decimals back after dividing!

7. 5   Remember to move both decimals right 2 places: $2\overline{)10}$ with 5 and don't put the decimal back after dividing!

Practice Drill 12—Fractions as Decimals

Fraction	Decimal
$\dfrac{1}{2}$	0.5
$\dfrac{1}{3}$	$0.3\overline{3}$
$\dfrac{2}{3}$	$0.6\overline{6}$
$\dfrac{1}{4}$	0.25
$\dfrac{3}{4}$	0.75
$\dfrac{1}{5}$	0.2
$\dfrac{2}{5}$	0.4
$\dfrac{3}{5}$	0.6
$\dfrac{4}{5}$	0.8
$\dfrac{1}{8}$	0.125

Practice Drill 13—Percents

1. a) 30% $\dfrac{\text{butterscotches}}{\text{total}} = \dfrac{15}{50} = \dfrac{3}{10}$

$\dfrac{3}{10} \times 100 = \dfrac{300}{10} = 30\%$

b) 40% $\dfrac{\text{caramels}}{\text{total}} = \dfrac{20}{50} = \dfrac{2}{5}$

$\dfrac{2}{5} \times 100 = \dfrac{200}{5} = 40\%$

c) 10% $\dfrac{\text{peppermints}}{\text{total}} = \dfrac{5}{50} = \dfrac{1}{10}$

$\dfrac{1}{10} \times 100 = \dfrac{100}{10} = 10\%$

d) 20% $\dfrac{\text{toffees}}{\text{total}} = \dfrac{10}{50} = \dfrac{1}{5}$

$\dfrac{1}{5} \times 100 = \dfrac{100}{5} = 20\%$

2. 18% $100\% = 75\% + 7\% +$ percentage of questions answered incorrectly

3. a) 20% $\dfrac{\text{sneakers}}{\text{total}} = \dfrac{8}{40} = \dfrac{1}{5}$

$\dfrac{1}{5} \times 100 = \dfrac{100}{5} = 20\%$

b) 30% $\dfrac{\text{sandals}}{\text{total}} = \dfrac{12}{40} = \dfrac{3}{10}$

$\dfrac{3}{10} \times 100 = \dfrac{300}{10} = 30\%$

c) 40% $\dfrac{\text{boots}}{\text{total}} = \dfrac{16}{40} = \dfrac{2}{5}$

$\dfrac{2}{5} \times 100 = \dfrac{200}{5} = 40\%$

d) 10% sneakers + sandals + boots + high heels = 100%

20% + 30% + 40% + h = 100%

h = 10%

e) 4   sneakers + sandals + boots + high heels = 40

8 + 12 + 16 + h = 40

h = 4

4. 90% $\dfrac{\text{juice}}{\text{total}} = \dfrac{4+2+3}{4+2+3+1} = \dfrac{9}{10}$

$\dfrac{9}{10} \times 100 = \dfrac{900}{10} = 90\%$

5. a) 48% $\dfrac{\text{girls}}{\text{total}} = \dfrac{3(\$8)}{2(\$13) + 3(\$8)} = \dfrac{24}{50}$

$\dfrac{24}{50} \times 100 = \dfrac{2400}{50} = 48\%$

b) 52% 100% = girls + boys

100 = 48 + b

b = 52

Practice Drill 14—More Percents

Fraction	Decimal	Percent
$\dfrac{1}{2}$	0.5	50%
$\dfrac{1}{3}$	$0.3\overline{3}$	$33\dfrac{1}{3}\%$
$\dfrac{2}{3}$	$0.6\overline{6}$	$66\dfrac{2}{3}\%$
$\dfrac{1}{4}$	0.25	25%
$\dfrac{3}{4}$	0.75	75%
$\dfrac{1}{5}$	0.2	20%
$\dfrac{2}{5}$	0.4	40%
$\dfrac{3}{5}$	0.6	60%
$\dfrac{4}{5}$	0.8	80%
$\dfrac{1}{8}$	0.125	12.5%

1.   21 $25\% = \dfrac{1}{4}$

$$\dfrac{1}{4} \times 84 = \dfrac{84}{4} = 21$$

2.   9 $33\dfrac{1}{3}\% = \dfrac{1}{3}$

$$\dfrac{1}{3} \times 27 = \dfrac{27}{3} = 9$$

3.   15 $20\% = \dfrac{1}{5}$

$$\dfrac{1}{5} \times 75 = \dfrac{75}{5} = 15$$

4.   51 $17\% = \dfrac{17}{100}$

$$\dfrac{17}{100} \times 300 = \dfrac{5100}{100} = 51$$

5.   8 $16\% = \dfrac{16}{100}$

$$10\% = \dfrac{1}{10}$$

$$\dfrac{16}{100} \times \dfrac{1}{10} \times 500 = \dfrac{8000}{1000} = 8$$

6.   The sale price is $102.

15% of $120 = \dfrac{15}{100} \times 120 = \dfrac{180}{100} = 18$.

$120 − $18 = $102. The sale price is 85% of the regular price. 100% − 15% = 85%.

7.   292 $80\% = \dfrac{4}{5}$

$$\dfrac{4}{5} \times 365 = \dfrac{1460}{5} = 292$$

8.   27   If she got 25% wrong, then she got 75% correct.

75% of $36 = \dfrac{3}{4} \times 36 = \dfrac{108}{4} = 27$.

9. $72   If $20\% = \dfrac{1}{5}$, then $\dfrac{1}{5} \times 100 = \dfrac{100}{5} = 20$. The original price ($100) is reduced by $20, so the new price is $80. After an additional 10% mark down $\left(\dfrac{1}{10} \times 80 = \dfrac{80}{10} = 8 \right)$, the discounted price is reduced by $8, so the final sale price is $80 − 8 = 72$.

Practice Drill 15—Exponents and Square Roots

1. 8 $2 \times 2 \times 2 = 8$
2. 16 $2 \times 2 \times 2 \times 2 = 16$
3. 27 $3 \times 3 \times 3 = 27$
4. 64 $4 \times 4 \times 4 = 64$
5. 9 $9^2 = 9 \times 9$ or 81, so $\sqrt{81} = 9$.
6. 10 $10^2 = 10 \times 10$ or 100, so $\sqrt{100} = 10$.
7. 7 $7^2 = 7 \times 7$ or 49, so $\sqrt{49} = 7$.
8. 8 $8^2 = 8 \times 8$ or 64, so $\sqrt{64} = 8$.
9. 3 $3^2 = 3 \times 3$ or 9, so $\sqrt{9} = 3$.

Practice Drill 16—More Exponents

1. 3^8 $3^5 \times 3^3 = 3^{5+3} = 3^8$
2. 7^9 $7^2 \times 7^7 = 7^{2+7} = 7^9$
3. 5^7 $5^3 \times 5^4 = 5^{3+4} = 5^7$
4. 15^3 $15^{23} \div 15^{20} = 15^{23-20} = 15^3$
5. 4^9 $4^{13} \div 4^4 = 4^{13-4} = 4^9$
6. 10^4 $10^{10} \div 10^6 = 10^{10-6} = 10^4$
7. 5^{18} $(5^3)^6 = 5^{3 \times 6} = 5^{18}$
8. 8^{36} $(8^{12})^3 = 8^{12 \times 3} = 8^{36}$
9. 9^{25} $(9^5)^5 = 9^{5 \times 5} = 9^{25}$
10. 2^{28} $(2^2)^{14} = 2^{2 \times 14} = 2^{28}$

Review Drill 1—The Building Blocks

1. No   Remember, 2 is the smallest (and only even) prime number. 1 is NOT prime.

2. 9   1, 2, 4, 5, 10, 20, 25, 50, 100

3. −30

4. 140

5. $\dfrac{2}{21}$ Multiply using Bowtie to get $\dfrac{9}{21} - \dfrac{7}{21} = \dfrac{2}{21}$.

6. $\dfrac{12}{25}$ $\dfrac{4}{5} \times \dfrac{3}{5} = \dfrac{4 \times 3}{5 \times 5} = \dfrac{12}{25}$

7. 4.08   Don't forget there are a total of 2 digits to the right of the decimal.

8. 20   Multiply to get $\dfrac{30x}{100} = 6$. Multiply both sides by 100 to get $30x = 600$, and then divide both sides by 30 to get $x = 20$.

9. 1 $1^5 = 1 \times 1 \times 1 \times 1 \times 1$. Note: 1 to any power will always equal 1.

10. 4 $4^2 = 4 \times 4$ or 16, so $\sqrt{16} = 4$.

11. 1, 4, 9, 16, 25, 36, 49, 64, 81, 100

Algebra

Practice Drill 17—Solving Simple Equations

1. $x = 12$ $35 - 12 = 23$
2. $y = 15$ $15 + 12 = 27$
3. $z = 28$ $28 - 7 = 21$
4. $x = 5$ $5 \times 5 = 25$
5. $x = 3$ $18 \div 3 = 6$
6. $x = 11$ $3 \times 11 = 33$
7. $y = 5$ $65 \div 5 = 13$
8. $z = 3$ $14 = 17 - 3$
9. $y = 48$ $\dfrac{1}{2} \times 48 = 24$
10. $z = 71$ $136 + 71 = 207$
11. $x = 12$ $7 \times 12 = 84$
12. $y = 12$ $12 \div 2 = 6$
13. $z = 45$ $45 \div 3 = 15$
14. $x = 18$ $14 + 18 = 32$
15. $y = 29$ $53 - 29 = 24$

Practice Drill 18—Manipulating an Equation

1. 3   To isolate x, add x to both sides. Then subtract both sides by 8. Check your work by plugging in 3 for x: $8 = 11 - 3$.

2. 5   To isolate x, divide both sides by 4. Check your work by plugging in 5 for x: $4 \times 5 = 20$.

3. 6   To isolate x, add 20 to both sides. Then divide both sides by 5. Check your work by plugging in 6 for x: $5(6) - 20 = 10$.

4. 7   To isolate x, subtract 3 from both sides. Then divide both sides by 4. Check your work by plugging in 7 for x: $4 \times 7 + 3 = 31$.

5. 4   To isolate m, add 3 to both sides. Subtract m from both sides. Then divide both sides by 2. Check your work by plugging in 4 for m: $4 + 5 = 3(4) - 3$.

6. 8   To isolate x, divide both sides by 2.5. Check your work by plugging in 8 for x: $2.5 \times 8 = 20$.

7. 8   To isolate x, subtract 2 from both sides. Then divide both sides by 0.2. Check your work by plugging in 8 for x: $0.2 \times 8 + 2 = 3.6$.

8. $\frac{1}{4}$ To isolate x, subtract 4 from both sides. Then divide both sides by 8. Check your work by plugging in $\frac{1}{4}$ for x: $6 = 8 \times \frac{1}{4} + 4$.

9. 7   To isolate $x + y$, divide both sides by 3. Check your work by plugging in 7 for $x + y$: $3(7) = 21$.

10. 7   To isolate $x + y$, factor out a 3 from both terms on the left side: $3(x + y) = 21$. Then divide both sides by 3. Check your work by plugging in 7 for $x + y$: $3(7) = 21$. Note that this question and the previous question are really the same equation. Did you see it?

11. 7   To isolate y, subtract 100 from both sides. Then divide both sides by -5. Check your work by plugging in 7 for x: $100 - 5 \times 7 = 65$.

Practice Drill 19—Manipulating an Inequality

1. $x > 4$ To isolate x, divide both sides by 4. The sign doesn't change!

2. $x < -2$ To isolate x, subtract 13 from both sides. Then divide both sides by -1. Since you divided by a negative number, flip the sign.

3. $x > -5$ First, combine like terms to get $-5x < 25$. Then divide both sides by -5. Since you divided by a negative number, flip the sign.

4. $x > 4$ To isolate x, add x to both sides. Subtract 12 from both sides. Then divide both sides by 3. The sign doesn't change!

5. $x < -7$ To isolate x, add $3x$ to both sides. Subtract 7 from both sides. Then divide both sides by 3. The sign doesn't change!

Practice Drill 20—Translating and Solving Percent Questions

1. 12   Translation: $30 = \dfrac{x}{100} \times 250$.

    To solve, simplify the right side:

    $\dfrac{x \times 250}{100} = \dfrac{250x}{100}$, which reduces to

    $\dfrac{25x}{10}$. Multiply both sides by 10, and

    then divide both sides by 25. Check

    your work by plugging in 12 for x.

2. 24   Translation: $x = \dfrac{12}{100} \times 200$.

    To solve: $\dfrac{12 \times 200}{100} = \dfrac{2400}{100} = 24$.

3. 5   Translation: $x = \dfrac{25}{100} \times \dfrac{10}{100} \times 200$.

    To solve, reduce the right side:

    $\dfrac{1}{4} \times \dfrac{1}{10} \times 200$. Then simplify:

    $\dfrac{1 \times 1 \times 200}{4 \times 10} = \dfrac{200}{40} = 5$.

4. 80   Translation: $\dfrac{75}{100} \times \dfrac{20}{100} \times n = 12$.

    To solve, reduce the left side:

    $\dfrac{3}{4} \times \dfrac{1}{5} \times n$. Then simplify:

    $\dfrac{3 \times 1 \times n}{4 \times 5} = \dfrac{3n}{20}$. Multiply both

    sides by 20, and divide both sides

    by 3. Check your work by plug-

    ging in 80 in for n.

5. 125   Translation: $\dfrac{16}{100} \times n = \dfrac{25}{100} \times 80$.

    To solve, reduce both sides to

    get $\dfrac{4}{25} \times n = \dfrac{1}{4} \times 80$. Then,

    multiply to get $\dfrac{4n}{25} = \dfrac{80}{4}$. Next,

    cross-multiply to get $16n = 2{,}000$.

    Finally, divide both sides by 16.

    Check your work by plugging in

    125 for n.

6. 60   Translation: $\dfrac{x}{100} = \dfrac{3}{5}$. To solve,

    cross-multiply to get $5x = 300$,

    and then divide both sides by 5.

    Check your work by plugging in

    60 for x.

7. 40   Translation: $30 = \dfrac{x}{100} \times 75$.

    To solve, simplify the right side:

    $\dfrac{x(75)}{100} = \dfrac{75x}{100}$, which reduces to

    $\dfrac{3x}{4}$. Multiply both sides by 4, and

    divide both sides by 3. Check

    your work by plugging in 40 for x.

8. 2.64 or $2\dfrac{16}{25}$ or $\dfrac{66}{25}$

    Translation: $x = \dfrac{11}{100} \times 24$. To solve,

    $\dfrac{11}{100} \times 24 = \dfrac{11 \times 24}{100} = \dfrac{264}{100} = 2.64$.

9. 200 Translation: $\dfrac{x}{100} \times 24 = 48$.

To solve, simplify the left side: $\dfrac{24x}{100}$,

which reduces to $\dfrac{6x}{25}$.

Then multiply both sides by 25,

and divide both sides by 6. Check

your work by plugging in 200 for x.

10. 2 Translation: $\dfrac{60}{100} \times \dfrac{n}{100} \times 500 = 6$.

To solve, reduce the fraction

to $\dfrac{3}{5}$ and simply the left side:

$\dfrac{3 \times n \times 500}{5 \times 100} = \dfrac{1500n}{500} = 3n$.

Then divide both sides by 3.

Check your work by plugging in

2 for n.

Geometry

Practice Drill 21—Squares, Rectangles, and Angles

1. 115° $65° + x° = 180°$

2. 100° $45° + x° + 35° = 180°$

3. The perimeter of *PQRS* is 16.
    $4 + 4 + 4 + 4 = 16$. Its area is also 16. $4^2 = 16$.

4. The perimeter of *ABCD* is 20.
    $7 + 3 + 7 + 3 = 20$. Its area is 21. $7 \times 3 = 21$

5. The area of *STUV* is 9. If the perimeter is 12, then one side of the square is 3 $(12 \div 4 = 3)$. Therefore, the area is $3^2 = 9$.

6. The perimeter of *DEFG* is 36. If the area is 81, then one side of the square is 9 $(\sqrt{81} = 9)$. Therefore, the perimeter is $9 + 9 + 9 + 9 = 36$.

7. The area of *JKLM* is 24. If the perimeter is 20, then $4 + l + 4 + l = 20$. So the length (the other side) of the rectangle is 6. Therefore, the area is $6 \times 4 = 24$.

8. The perimeter of *WXYZ* is 22. If the area is 30, then $6 \times w = 30$. So the width (the other side) of the rectangle is 5. Therefore, the perimeter is $6 + 5 + 6 + 5 = 22$.

9. 24 $V = lwh = 2 \times 4 \times 3 = 24$.

Practice Drill 22—Triangles

1. 45° $180° - 90° = 90°$. Since two sides (legs) of the triangle are both 3, the angles that correspond to those sides are also equal to each other. Therefore, each angle is 45°, so $x = 45°$.

2. 70° $180° - 40° = 140°$. Since sides PQ and QR are equal, then $\angle QPR$ and $x°$ are also equal to each other. Thus, divide 140° by 2 to find that each remaining angle is 70°. So $x = 70°$.

3. 6   Plug the base and height into the area formula for a triangle:
$$A = \frac{1}{2}bh = \frac{1}{2}(4)(3) = 6.$$

4. 12   In this case, count the height and base of the triangle by counting off the ticks on the coordinate plane. The height is 6 and the base is 4, which means that
$$A = \frac{1}{2}bh = \frac{1}{2}(4)(6) = 12.$$

5. 14   Plug the base and height into the area formula for a triangle:
$$A = \frac{1}{2}bh = \frac{1}{2}(4)(7) = 14.$$

6. $WXZ = 5$ $A = \frac{1}{2}bh = \frac{1}{2}(2)(5) = 5$

   $ZXY = 15$ $A = \frac{1}{2}(6)(5) = 15$

   $WXY = 20$ $A = \frac{1}{2}(2+6)(5) = 20$

7. 4.8   These are similar triangles since all the angles are the same. Set up a proportion to solve: $\frac{MN}{NO} = \frac{PQ}{QR}$, so $\frac{10}{6} = \frac{8}{QR}$. Cross-multiply to get $10(QR) = 6(8)$. Divide both sides by 10, and $QR = 4.8$.

8. $DE = 8$ Since this is a right triangle, use the Pythagorean Theorem to find the missing side length: $a^2 + b^2 = c^2$, so $a^2 + 6^2 = 10$. Subtract 36 from both sides and $a^2 = 64$. Take the square root of both sides, and a (or DE) = 8.

9. 9.6   These are similar triangles since all the angles are the same. Set up a proportion to solve: $\frac{16}{20} = \frac{x}{12}$. Cross-multiply to get $16(12) = 20(x)$. Divide both sides by 20, and $x = 9.6$.

10. 26   Remember that all angles in a rectangle are right angles. This diagonal (AC) cuts the rectangle into two right triangles, so use the Pythagorean Theorem to find the missing side length: $a^2 + b^2 = c^2$, so $10^2 + 24^2 = c^2$, and c (or AC) = 26.

11. 40   First, use the right triangle to find AD, which is one side of the square $ABCD$. $8^2 + 6^2 = c^2$, so $c = 10$. Since all sides of a square are equal, the perimeter is $10 + 10 + 10 + 10 = 40$ (or $10(4) = 40$).

12. 2.4   These are similar triangles since all the angles are the same. Set up a proportion to solve: $\frac{6}{3+2} = \frac{x}{2}$. Cross-multiply to get $5x = 6(2)$. Divide both sides by 5, and $x = 2.4$.

Practice Drill 23—Circles

1. Circumference = 10π. Area = 25π. Plug the radius into the circumference formula for a circle: $C = 2\pi r = 2\pi(5) = 10\pi$. Plug the radius into the area formula for a circle: $A = \pi r^2 = \pi(5)^2 = 25\pi$.

2. 16π Plug the radius into the area formula for a circle: $A = \pi r^2 = \pi(4)^2 = 16\pi$.

3. 16π Since $d = 2r$, the radius is $4(8 = 2r)$. Plug the radius into the area formula for a circle: $A = \pi r^2 = \pi(4)^2 = 16\pi$. Note: this is really the same circle as the previous question.

4. 3 Remember, you can find the radius from a circle's area by getting rid of π and taking the square root of 9.

5. 6 Find the radius from a circle's area by getting rid of π and taking the square root of 9. Then multiply the radius by 2 to find the diameter.

6. 10π Find the radius from a circle's area by getting rid of π and taking the square root of 25. Then, plug the radius into the circumference formula for a circle: $C = 2\pi r = 2\pi(5) = 10\pi$.

Practice Drill 24—3-D Shapes

1. 128π Plug the radius and height into the volume formula for a cylinder: $V = \pi r^2 h = \pi(4)^2(8) = 128\pi$.

2. 1,000 Plug the side length into the volume formula for a cube: $V = s^3 = 10^3 = 1,000$.

3. 216 Plug the length, width, and height into the volume formula for a rectangular box: $V = lwh = 12 \times 3 \times 6 = 216$.

4. 162 First, find the volume of the cube: $V = s^3 = 6^3 = 216$. Next, to find the remaining liquid needed to completely fill the cube, subtract the number of gallons already poured into it: $216 - 54 = 162$.

5. 12 One way to solve this problem is to divide the length, width, and height into segments of 2. The length is 8, so 4 cubes could fit along the length of the rectangular box since each cube has a side length of 2. The width of the box is 2, so only 1 cube could fit along the width of the box. That means the bottom layer of the box could hold 4 cubes (4 cubes across by 1 cube deep). The height of the box is 6, so you could stack 3 cubes on top of each other to fill the box. If each layer has 4 boxes and 3 layers of cubes can be stacked, then a total of 12 cubes can fit into the box (4 boxes per layer times 3 layers equals 12 boxes).

6. 48π First, find the volume of the cylinder: $V = \pi r^2 = \pi(4)^2(9) = 144\pi$.

    Since the grain fills only a third of the cylinder, then find $\frac{1}{3}$ of the volume, or $\frac{1}{3}(144\pi) = 48\pi$.

    Just treat the π like a variable in questions like these.

Word Problems

Practice Drill 25—Word Problems

1. 4 quarts

   Set up a proportion:

   $\dfrac{\text{ounces}}{\text{quarts}} = \dfrac{32}{1} = \dfrac{128}{x}$. Then cross-multiply to get $32(x) = 128$. Divide both sides by 32, and $x = 4$.

   224 ounces

   Set up a proportion:

   $\dfrac{\text{ounces}}{\text{quarts}} = \dfrac{32}{1} = \dfrac{x}{7}$. Then cross-multiply to get $32(7) = x$, and $x = 224$.

2. 6 hours

   Set up a proportion:

   $\dfrac{\text{miles}}{\text{hours}} = \dfrac{50}{1} = \dfrac{300}{x}$. Then cross-multiply to get $50x = 300$. Divide both sides by 50, and $x = 6$.

3. 44

   Start with the given age: Rufus's. If Rufus is 11, then find Fiona's age. *Fiona is twice as old as Rufus* translates to: Fiona = 2(Rufus) or $F = 2(11)$, so Fiona is 22. Next find Betty's age. *Betty is twice as old as Fiona* translates to: Betty = 2(Fiona) or $B = 2(22)$. Therefore, Betty is 44.

4. 5

   Translate the parts of the question. *This year's sales* = 1,250, *how many times greater than* means to divide, and *last year's sales* = 250. Thus, $\dfrac{1,250}{250} = 5$.

5. 120

   Translate the first part of the problem: *of* means to multiply and *the total students* = 500.

   So, the number of freshman is $\dfrac{2}{5}(500) = \dfrac{2 \times 500}{5} = \dfrac{1000}{5} = 200$. Now, translate the second part of the problem: *of* means to multiply and *all the freshmen* = 200. Therefore, the number of freshmen girls is $\dfrac{3}{5}(200) = \dfrac{3 \times 200}{5} = \dfrac{600}{5} = 120$.

Review Drill 2—The Building Blocks

1. 45

   Translate the problem: $\dfrac{1}{3}(b) = 15$.

   Multiply both sides by 3, and $b = 45$.

   Check your work by plugging in 45 for b: $\dfrac{1}{3}(45) = 15$.

2. 8

   To isolate x, add 7 to both sides. Then divide both sides by 7. Check your work by plugging in 8 for x: $7(8) - 7 = 49$.

3. 10

   To isolate y, divide both sides by 4. Then add 5 to both sides. Check your work by plugging in 10 for y: $4(10 - 5) = 20$.

4. $x < 8$

   To isolate x, subtract 1 from both sides. Then divide both sides by 8. The sign doesn't change!

5. 160   Translation: $16 = \dfrac{x}{100}(10)$. To

solve, simplify the right side:

$\dfrac{x}{100}(10) = \dfrac{x(10)}{100} = \dfrac{10x}{100}$, which

reduces to $\dfrac{x}{10}$. Then, multiply

both sides by 10. Check your

work by plugging in 160 for x.

6. 75   Translation: $\dfrac{x}{100}(32) = 24$.

To solve, simplify the

left side of the equation:

$\dfrac{x}{100}(32) = \dfrac{x(32)}{100} = \dfrac{32x}{100}$, which

reduces to $\dfrac{8x}{25}$. Then multiply

both sides by 25, and divide both

sides by 8. Check your work by

plugging 75 for x.

7. 21   Plug the base and height into
the area formula for a triangle:

$A = \dfrac{1}{2}bh = \dfrac{1}{2}(7)(6) = 21$.

8. 14   Find the radius from a circle's area by getting rid of π and taking the square root of 49. Then multiply the radius by 2 to find the diameter.

9. 6   Find the radius from a circle's circumference ($C = 2\pi r$) by getting rid of π from both sides (they cancel out), which leaves $12 = 2r$. Divide both sides by 2. Check your work by plugging in 6 for the radius.

10. 25π Be careful not to just fill in a familiar formula with the given numbers. Here, you aren't given r. Instead, you're given the diameter. Since $d = 2r$, the radius is 5 ($10 = 2r$). Plug the radius into the area formula for a circle: $A = \pi r^2 = \pi(5)^2 = 25\pi$.

Chapter 4
Writing the Essay

HOW IS THE ESSAY USED?

Both the ISEE and the SSAT require you to write an essay. While the essay is not graded and does not affect your score, a copy is sent to the schools to which you apply. For this reason, you want to take the essay seriously and use it to show yourself to be thoughtful and likeable.

THE SSAT ESSAY

The Middle and Upper Level tests present two prompts, from which you will select one. The Middle Level test offers two creative writing prompts; the Upper Level test offers one creative writing and one essay style prompt. The instructions tell you that schools would like to get to know you better "through a story," so you should select the prompt that is easier for you to base your story on. The Elementary Level test provides a picture and instructs you to "tell a story" about what happened.

In all cases, you have about one-and-one-half pages on which to write. Elementary Level students have 15 minutes, while Middle and Upper Level students have 25 minutes.

Here are sample prompts.

Elementary Level

Look at the picture and tell a story about what happened. Make sure your story includes a beginning, a middle, and an end.

Middle Level

Ⓐ I picked up the magazine and saw on the cover...

Ⓑ No one else was in the museum.

Upper Level

(A)   Describe a mistake that you would correct if you could go back in time.

(B)   Sometimes, the results are quite different from what you would expect.

THE ISEE ESSAY

All three ISEE tests ask you to "write an essay" on an assigned prompt. You have close to two pages on which to write. You have 30 minutes.

Here are sample prompts.

Lower Level

Who is your favorite teacher? Why have you chosen this person?

Middle Level

If you could solve one problem in the world today, what would you choose and how would you solve the problem?

Upper Level

Name someone you consider to be a success and describe what it is about that person that makes him or her successful.

PLANNING AND WRITING YOUR ESSAY

When you read your ISEE prompt or decide upon your SSAT prompt, do not start writing immediately! It is important that you spend a few minutes thinking about what you want to say and how you will organize your thoughts. A planned essay reads much better than a rambling, free-association essay. Also, the time you spend organizing your thoughts will enable you to write your essay more quickly once you get started. You just need to follow your outline and express the ideas you have already developed.

For the SSAT, you are writing a story, which means you must include a beginning, middle, and end. So your planning time will be used to decide what story you want to tell and how that story progresses. It does not really matter what your story topic is, as long as it responds to the chosen prompt and is delivered in an organized way. Of course, you don't want to be silly; your goal is to make the schools you are applying to like you. On the other hand, you don't have to write a work of creative fiction either. Your story can relate something you have done or seen. If you happen to be a natural storyteller, though, have at it!

> **The Choice is Yours**
> Upper Level SSAT students get to choose between a creative writing or an essay-style prompt. Choose wisely!

For the ISEE, your essay will be a more traditional essay with an introduction, body paragraphs, and a conclusion. Your introduction will summarize the topic and explain your position, and your body paragraphs will include examples or reasons for your position. Thus, you want to spend your planning time deciding how you want to answer the prompt and what examples or reasons you will use to support your point of view. If you are used to using three examples in essays at school, there is no need for that here. You don't have the space or the time. Rather, having one or two well-developed examples or reasons will be fine.

For both tests, be sure to avoid spelling, grammar, and punctuation errors. It is easier to avoid these errors if you have planned your essay in advance. Also, write neatly; again, this is easier if you plan your essay before you write it. Be sure to clearly indent each new paragraph as well. It is a good idea to leave yourself a bit of time at the end to review what you have written, so you can make sure you've written your best possible essay.

> If you need a grammar boost, check out *Grammar Smart, 4th Edition* available everywhere you get books!

You should write one or two practice essays and show them to a parent, teacher, or other adult who can give you feedback. Tell him or her that your goal is to provide an organized, thoughtful, and likeable reply to the prompt, with a minimum of spelling and grammar errors.

On the two pages that follow, write an essay using the prompt (or one of the two prompts for SSAT) on pages 113–114. Be sure to use the prompt for the test level (and test!) you are taking. After you have received feedback from someone, you can write another essay using the second set of prompts.

_____

_____

_____

_____

_____

_____

_____

_____

_____

_____

_____

_____

_____

_____

_____

_____

(Continued on next page)

Are you ready for another prompt?

Middle Level SSAT

Ⓐ   I heard the strange noise and quickly…

Ⓑ   The train pulled out of the station just as I got there.

Upper Level SSAT

Ⓐ   Give three reasons you admire your best friend.

Ⓑ   I couldn't believe she asked me for a favor.

Lower Level ISEE

Describe something you wish you could change about the city or town in which you live.

Middle Level ISEE

If you could spend one week anywhere in the world, where would you go? What would you do there?

Upper Level ISEE

Describe a book or work of art that had an effect on you. What about it affected you?

_____

_____

_____

_____

_____

_____

_____

_____

_____

_____

_____

_____

_____

_____

_____

_____

(Continued on next page)

If you plan to take the SSAT, go on to Chapter 5.
If you plan to take the ISEE, please proceed to
Chapter 13.

Part II
The SSAT

Chapter 5
Everything You Always Wanted to Know About the SSAT

WHAT IS THE SSAT?

The Secondary School Admission Test (SSAT) is a standardized test made up of a writing sample, which is not scored but is sent along with each score report, and a series of multiple-choice questions. There are three different types of sections on the SSAT: Verbal, Reading, and Quantitative (Math). You will receive a score for each of these three section types. In addition, your score report will show an overall score, which is a combination of your verbal, reading, and quantitative scores. You will also receive a percentile score of between 1 percent and 99 percent that compares your test scores with those of other test takers from the previous three years.

What's on the SSAT?

The Verbal section of the SSAT tests your knowledge of vocabulary using two different question types: synonyms and analogies. There are no sentence completions on the SSAT. The Reading section tests your ability to read and understand short passages. These reading passages include both fiction (including poetry and folklore) and nonfiction. The Math sections test your knowledge of general mathematical concepts, including arithmetic, algebra, and geometry. There are no quantitative comparison questions on the Math sections of the SSAT. Remember, there is a guessing penalty on both the Middle and Upper Level SSAT. Each incorrect answer reduces your raw score by a quarter point. However, points are not deducted for wrong answers on the Elementary Level SSAT. Students taking this test should not leave any answers blank.

ML and UL SSAT
The experimental section is not scored and includes verbal, reading, and quantitative questions. SSAT uses this section to test questions that may appear on future tests.

Three Levels

There are three different versions of the SSAT. The Upper Level is taken by students applying to ninth grade or above. The Middle Level test (formerly called the Lower Level test) is taken by students applying to the sixth, seventh, or eighth grades. The Elementary Level test is taken by students applying to the fourth or fifth grade.

Elementary Level

The Elementary Level test is about 2 hours, which includes the four different sections and breaks. There is no experimental section.

Plan Ahead
Not only will early registration give you one less thing to worry about as the test approaches, but it will also get you your first-choice test center.

Quantitative	30 questions	30 minutes
Verbal	30 questions	20 minutes
Reading	28 questions	30 minutes
Writing Sample (ungraded)	1 prompt	15 minutes

Middle Level and Upper Level

For the Middle and Upper Levels, the test lasts about 3 hours, which includes the five different sections, breaks, and a 15-minute experimental section.

Writing Sample (ungraded)	1 essay topic	25 minutes
Quantitative	25 questions	30 minutes
Reading	40 questions	40 minutes
Verbal	60 questions	30 minutes
Quantitative (a second section)	25 questions	30 minutes

This book will focus mainly on the Upper and Middle Level tests, but look out for sidebars containing information about the Elementary Level test. In addition, a practice Elementary Level test is available online when you register this book. You can reference the "Get More (Free) Content" spread at the start of this book, located after the table of contents, for more detailed instructions on how to access that test.

One difference between the Upper and Middle Level tests is their scale. The Upper Level test gives a student **three** scaled scores ranging from 500 on the low end to 800 at the top. Scores on the Middle Level test range from 440 to 710. There are also some small differences in content; for instance, vocabulary on the Middle Level test will more closely reflect what you might have learned up to this point in school, and Upper Level vocab will take it further. Same with Math. In Math, you will see similar general concepts tested (arithmetic, algebra, geometry, charts, and graphs) on both tests, but naturally, the Middle Level test will ask questions based on what you should have learned. However, many of the questions are exactly the same on each level.

> The scale on the Elementary Level test is 300–600.

As you work through the chapters and the drills, you will notice that sets of practice problems do not distinguish between Upper and Middle Level questions. Instead, you will find practice sets that generally increase in difficulty as you move from earlier to later questions. Therefore, if you are taking the Middle Level test, don't worry if you have trouble with questions at the ends of the practice sets. **Students should stop each practice set at the point at which they have reached vocabulary or math concepts with which they are unfamiliar.** This point will be different for every student.

Because the Middle Level SSAT tests fifth, sixth, and seventh graders, and the Upper Level SSAT tests eighth, ninth, tenth, and eleventh graders, there is content on the tests that students testing at the lower end of each of the groups will have difficulty answering. Younger students' scaled scores and percentiles will not be harmed by this fact. Both sets of scores take into consideration a student's age and gender. However, younger students may feel intimidated by this. **If you are at the lower end of your test's age group, there will be questions you are not supposed to be able to answer, and that's perfectly all right.**

Likewise, the material in this book follows the content of the two tests without breaking it down further into age groups or grades. Content that will appear only on the Upper Level test has been labeled as Upper Level only. Students taking the Middle Level test do not need to work on the Upper Level content. Additionally, younger students may not yet have seen some of the material included in the Middle Level review. Parents are advised to help these students with their work and to seek a teacher's advice or instruction if necessary.

Chapter 6
SSAT Math

INTRODUCTION

This section will provide you with a review of all the math that you need to know to do well on the SSAT. When you get started, you may feel that the material is too easy. Don't worry. The SSAT measures your basic math skills, so although you may feel a little frustrated reviewing things you have already learned, basic review is the best way to improve your score.

We recommend that you work through these math sections in order, reading each section and then doing each set of drills. If you have trouble with one section, mark the page so you can come back later to go over it again. Keep in mind that you shouldn't breeze over pages or sections just because they look familiar. Take the time to read over all of the Math sections, so you'll be sure to know all the math you'll need!

Lose Your Calculator!

You will *not* be allowed to use a calculator on the SSAT. If you have developed a habit of reaching for your calculator whenever you need to add or multiply a couple of numbers, follow our advice: put your calculator away now and take it out again after the test is behind you. Do your math homework assignments without it, and complete the practice sections in this book without it. Trust us, you'll be glad you did.

Write It Down

Do not try to do math in your head. You are allowed to write in your test booklet. You *should* write in your test booklet. Even when you are just adding a few numbers together, write them down and do the work on paper. Writing things down will not only help eliminate careless errors but also give you something to refer to if you need to check over your work.

Don't Get Stuck
Make sure you don't spend too much time working on one tough question; there might be easier questions left in the section.

One Pass, Two Pass

Within any Math section you will find three types of questions:

- Those you can answer easily without spending too much time
- Those that, if you had all the time in the world, you could do
- Some questions that you have absolutely no idea how to tackle

When you work on a Math section, start out with the first question. If you think you can do it without too much trouble, go ahead. If not, save it for later. Move on to the second question and decide whether or not to do that one. In general, the questions in each Math section are in a very rough order of difficulty. This means that earlier questions tend to be somewhat easier than later ones. You will likely find yourself answering more questions toward the beginning of the sections and leaving more questions blank toward the end.

Once you've made it all the way through the section, working slowly and carefully to do all the questions that come easily to you, go back and try some of the ones that you think you can do but will take a little longer. You should pace yourself so that time will run out while you're working on the second pass through the section. By working this way, you'll know that you answered all the questions that were easy for you. Using a two-pass system is a smart test-taking strategy.

Guesstimating

Sometimes accuracy is important. Sometimes it isn't.

Which of the following fractions is less than $\frac{1}{4}$?

(A) $\frac{4}{18}$

(B) $\frac{4}{12}$

(C) $\frac{7}{7}$

(D) $\frac{10}{9}$

(E) $\frac{12}{5}$

Before making any kind of calculation, think about this question. It asks you to find a fraction smaller than $\frac{1}{4}$. Even if you're not sure which one is actually smaller, you can certainly eliminate some wrong answers.

Start simple: $\frac{1}{4}$ is less than 1, right? Are there any fractions in the choices that are greater than 1? Get rid of (D) and (E).

Look at (C). $\frac{7}{7}$ equals 1. Can it be less than $\frac{1}{4}$? Eliminate (C). Already, without doing any math, you have a 50 percent chance of guessing the right answer.

> **Some Things Are Easier Than They Seem**
> Guesstimating, or finding approximate answers, can help you eliminate wrong answers and save lots of time.

Here's another good example.

A group of three men buys a one-dollar raffle
ticket that wins $400. If the one dollar that they
paid for the ticket is subtracted and the remainder
of the prize money is divided equally among the
men, how much will each man receive?

(A) $62.50
(B) $75.00
(C) $100.00
(D) $133.00
(E) $200.00

This isn't a terribly difficult question. To solve it mathematically, you would take $400, subtract $1, and then divide the remainder by three. But by using a little bit of logic, you don't have to do any of that.

The raffle ticket won $400. If there were four men, each one would have won about $100 (actually slightly less because the problem tells you to subtract the $1 price of the ticket, but you get the idea). So far so good?

However, there weren't four men; there were only three. This means fewer men among whom to divide the winnings, so each one should get more than $100, right? Look at the choices. Eliminate (A), (B), and (C).

Two choices left. Choice (E) is $200, half of the amount of the winning ticket. If there were three men, could each one get half? Unfortunately not. Eliminate (E). What's left? The right answer!

Guesstimating also works very well with some geometry questions, but just to give you something you can look forward to, we'll save that for the Geometry review.

WORKING WITH CHOICES

In Chapter 2, Fundamental Math Skills for the SSAT & ISEE, we reviewed the concepts that will be tested on the SSAT tests. However, the questions in those practice drills were slightly different from the ones that you will see on your exam. Questions on test day are going to give you five answers to choose from. And as you'll soon see, there are many benefits to working with multiple-choice questions.

A Tip About Choices
Notice that the choices are often in numerical order.

For one, if you really mess up calculating the question, chances are your choice will not be among the ones given. Now you have a chance to go back and try that problem again more carefully. Another benefit is that you may be able to use the information in the choices to help you solve the problems (don't worry; we'll tell you how soon).

We are now going to introduce to you the type of multiple-choice questions you will see on the SSAT. Each one of the following questions will test some skill that we covered in the Fundamental Math Skills chapter. If you don't see how to solve the question, take a look back at Chapter 2 for help.

Math Vocabulary

1. Which of the following is the greatest even integer less than 25 ?

   (A) 26
   (B) 24.5
   (C) 22
   (D) 21
   (E) 0

The first and most important thing you need to do on this—and every—problem is to read and understand the question. What important vocabulary words did you see in the question? There is "even" and "integer." You should always underline the important words in the questions. This way you will make sure to pay attention to them and avoid careless errors.

Now that we understand that the question is looking for an even integer, we can eliminate any answers that are not even or an integer. Cross out (B) and (D). We can also eliminate (A) because 26 is greater than 25 and we want a number less than 25. Now all we have to do is ask which is greater—0 or 22. (C) is the right answer.

Try it again.

Set A = {All multiples of 7}

Set B = {All odd numbers}

2. All of the following are members of both set A and set B above EXCEPT

   (A)   7
   (B) 21
   (C) 49
   (D) 59
   (E) 77

Did you underline the words *multiples of 7* and *odd*? Because all the choices are odd, you can't eliminate any that would not be in Set B, but only (D) is not a multiple of 7. So (D) is the right answer.

The Rules of Zero

Remember the Rules of Zero
Zero is even. It's neither positive nor negative, and anything multiplied by 0 = 0.

3. x, y, and z stand for three distinct numbers, where $xy = 0$ and $yz = 15$. Which of the following must be true?

    (A) $y = 0$
    (B) $x = 0$
    (C) $z = 0$
    (D) $xyz = 15$
    (E) It cannot be determined from the information above.

Because x times y is equal to zero, and x, y, and z are different numbers, we know that either x or y is equal to zero. If y was equal to zero, then y times z should also be equal to zero. Because it is not, we know that it must be x that equals zero. Choice (B) is correct.

The Multiplication Table

4. Which of the following is equal to $6 \times 5 \times 2$?

    (A) $60 \div 3$
    (B) 14×7
    (C) $2 \times 2 \times 15$
    (D) 12×10
    (E) $3 \times 3 \times 3 \times 9$

$6 \times 5 \times 2 = 60$ and so does $2 \times 2 \times 15$. Choice (C) is correct.

Working with Negative Numbers

Don't Do More Work Than You Have To
When looking at answer choices, start with what's easiest for you; work through the harder ones only when you have eliminated all the others.

5. $7 - 9$ is the same as

    (A) $7 - (-9)$
    (B) $9 - 7$
    (C) $7 + (-9)$
    (D) $-7 - 9$
    (E) $-9 - 7$

Remember that subtracting a number is the same as adding its opposite. Choice (C) is correct.

Order of Operations

6. $9 + 6 \div 2 \times 3 =$

   (A) 7
   (B) 9
   (C) 10
   (D) 13
   (E) 18

Remember your PEMDAS rules? Left to right; Since this problem has no parentheses (P) or exponents (E), you can proceed to MD (multiplication and division). Finally, perform the addition. The correct answer is (E).

Factors and Multiples

7. What is the sum of the prime factors of 42 ?

   (A) 18
   (B) 13
   (C) 12
   (D) 10
   (E) 7

> **Factors Are Small; Multiples Are Large**
> The factors of a number are always equal to or less than that number. The multiples of a number are always equal to or greater than that number. Be sure not to confuse the two!

How do we find the prime factors? The best way is to draw a factor tree. Then we will see that the prime factors of 42 are 2, 3, and 7. Add them up and we get 12, (C).

Fractions

8. Which of the following is less than $\frac{4}{6}$?

   (A) $\frac{3}{5}$

   (B) $\frac{4}{6}$

   (C) $\frac{5}{7}$

   (D) $\frac{7}{8}$

   (E) $\frac{9}{7}$

When comparing fractions, you have three choices. You can find a common denominator and then compare the fractions (such as when you add or subtract fractions). You can also change the fractions to decimals. If you have memorized the fraction-to-decimal chart in Fundamentals (Chapter 2), you probably found the right answer without too much difficulty. It's (A). Or, if you remember the Bowtie method, you can compare answers that way too!

Percents

9. Thom's CD collection contains 15 jazz CDs, 45 rap albums, 30 funk CDs, and 60 pop albums. What percent of Thom's CD collection is funk?

(A) 10%
(B) 20%
(C) 25%
(D) 30%
(E) 40%

First we need to find the fractional part that represents Thom's funk CDs. He has 30 out of a total of 150. We can reduce $\frac{30}{150}$ to $\frac{1}{5}$. As a percent, $\frac{1}{5}$ is 20%, (B).

Exponents

Elementary Level
You shouldn't expect to see exponents or roots on your tests.

10. $2^6 =$

(A) 2^3
(B) 3^2
(C) 4^2
(D) 4^4
(E) 8^2

Expand 2^6 out and multiply to find that it equals 64. Choice (E) is correct.

Square Roots

11. The square root of 75 falls between what two integers?

(A) 5 and 6
(B) 6 and 7
(C) 7 and 8
(D) 8 and 9
(E) 9 and 10

If you have trouble with this one, try using the choices and work backward. As we discussed in Fundamentals (Chapter 2), a square root is just the opposite of squaring a number. So let's square the choices. Then we find that 75 falls between 8^2 (64) and 9^2 (81). Choice (D) is correct.

Simple Algebraic Equations

12. $11x = 121$. What does $x = ?$

    (A)   2

    (B)   8

    (C) 10

    (D) 11

    (E) 12

Remember, if you get stuck, use the choices and work backward. Each one provides you with a possible value for x. Start with the middle choice and replace x with it. $11 \times 10 = 110$. That's too small. Now we know that not only is (C) incorrect, but also that (A) and (B) are incorrect because they are smaller than (C). The correct choice is (D).

Solve for *X*

13. If $3y + 17 = 25 - y$, then $y =$

    (A) 1

    (B) 2

    (C) 3

    (D) 4

    (E) 5

> **The Case of the Mysteriously Missing Sign**
> If there is no operation sign between a number and a variable (letter), the operation is multiplication.

Just as above, if you get stuck, use the choices. The correct answer is (B).

Percent Algebra

14. 25% of 30% of what is equal to 18 ?

    (A)   1

    (B)   36

    (C) 120

    (D) 240

    (E) 540

> **Percent**
> *Percent* means "out of 100," and the word *of* in a word problem tells you to multiply.

If you don't remember the math conversion table, look it up in Fundamentals (Chapter 2). You can also use the choices and work backward. Start with (C) and find out what 25% of 30% of 120 is (9). The correct answer is (D).

Geometry

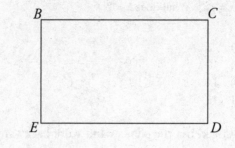

15. *BCDE* is a rectangle with a perimeter of 44. If the length of *BC* is 15, what is the area of *BCDE* ?

(A) 105
(B) 15
(C) 17
(D) 14
(E) It cannot be determined.

From the perimeter, we can find that the sides of the rectangle are 7 and 15. So the area is 105, (A).

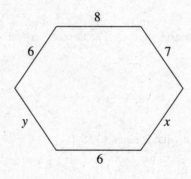

16. If the perimeter of this polygon is 37, what is the value of *x* + *y* ?

(A)   5
(B)   9
(C) 10
(D) 16
(E) 20

The sum of *x* and *y* is equal to the perimeter of the polygon minus the lengths of the sides we know. So (C) is correct.

Word Problems

17. Emily is walking to school at a rate of 3 blocks every 14 minutes. When Jeff walks at the same rate as Emily and takes the most direct route to school, he arrives in 56 minutes. How many blocks away from school does Jeff live?

    (A) 3
    (B) 5
    (C) 6
    (D) 9
    (E) 12

This is a proportion question because we have two sets of data that we are comparing. Set up your fractions.

$$\frac{3 \text{ blocks}}{14 \text{ minutes}} = \frac{\text{Number of blocks Jeff walks}}{56 \text{ minutes}}$$

We know that we must do the same thing to the top and bottom of the first fraction to get the second fraction. Notice that the denominator of the second fraction (56) is 4 times the denominator of the first fraction (14). Therefore, the numerator of the second fraction must be 4 times the numerator of the first fraction (3).

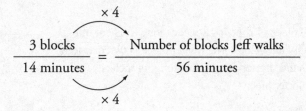

So Jeff walks 12 blocks in 56 minutes. This makes (E) the correct answer.

18. Half of the 30 students in Mrs. Whipple's first-grade class got sick on the bus on the way back from the zoo. Of these students, $\frac{2}{3}$ of them were sick because they ate too much cotton candy. The rest were sick because they sat next to the students who ate too much cotton candy. How many students were sick because they sat next to the wrong student?

    (A)   5
    (B)   10
    (C)   15
    (D)   20
    (E)   25

This is a really gooey fraction problem. Because we've seen the word *of*, we know we have to multiply. First we need to multiply $\frac{1}{2}$ by 30, the number of students in the class. This gives us 15, the number of students who got sick. Now we have another *of*, so we must multiply the fraction of students who ate too much cotton candy, $\frac{2}{3}$, by the number of students who got sick, 15. This gives us 10. So then the remainder, those who were unlucky in the seating plan, is 15 − 10 or 5, (A).

19. A piece of rope is 18 inches long. It is cut into 2 unequal pieces. The longer piece is twice as long as the shorter piece. How long, in inches, is the shorter piece?

    (A)   2
    (B)   6
    (C)   9
    (D)   12
    (E)   18

Again, if you are stuck for a place to start, go to the choices. Because we are looking for the length of the shorter rope, we can eliminate any choice that gives us a piece equal to or longer than half the rope. That gets rid of (C), (D), and (E). Now if we take one of the pieces, we can subtract it from the total length of the rope to get the length of the longer piece. For (B), if 6 is the length of the shorter piece, we can subtract that from 18 and know that the length of the longer piece must be 12. 12 is double 6, so we have the right answer.

PRACTICE DRILL 1—MULTIPLE CHOICE

When you are done, check your answers in Chapter 9. Don't forget to time yourself!

Remember to time yourself during this drill!

1. The sum of five consecutive positive integers is 30. What is the square of the largest of the five positive integers?

    (A) 25
    (B) 36
    (C) 49
    (D) 64
    (E) 81

2. How many factors does the number 24 have?

    (A) 2
    (B) 4
    (C) 6
    (D) 8
    (E) 10

3. If 12 is a factor of a certain number, what must also be factors of that number?

    (A) 2 and 6 only
    (B) 3 and 4 only
    (C) 12 only
    (D) 1, 2, 3, 4, and 6
    (E) 1, 2, 3, 4, 6, and 24

4. What is the smallest number that can be added to the number 1,024 to produce a result divisible by 9 ?

    (A) 1
    (B) 2
    (C) 3
    (D) 4
    (E) 6

5. Which of the following is a multiple of 3 ?

    (A) 2
    (B) 6
    (C) 10
    (D) 14
    (E) 16

6. Which of the following is NOT a multiple of 6 ?

(A) 12
(B) 18
(C) 23
(D) 24
(E) 42

7. Which of the following is a multiple of both 3 and 5 ?

(A) 10
(B) 20
(C) 25
(D) 45
(E) 50

8. A company's profit was $75,000 in 1972. In 1992, its profit was $450,000. The profit in 1992 was how many times as great as the profit in 1972 ?

(A) 2
(B) 4
(C) 6
(D) 10
(E) 60

9. Joanna owns one-third of the pieces of furniture in the apartment she shares with her friends. If there are 12 pieces of furniture in the apartment, how many pieces does Joanna own?

(A) 2
(B) 4
(C) 6
(D) 8
(E) 12

10. A tank of oil is one-third full. When full, the tank holds 90 gallons. How many gallons of oil are in the tank now?

(A) 10
(B) 20
(C) 30
(D) 40
(E) 50

11. Tigger the Cat sleeps three-fourths of every day. In a four-day period, he sleeps the equivalent of how many full days?

(A) $\frac{1}{4}$

(B) $\frac{3}{4}$

(C) 1

(D) 3

(E) 4

12. Which of the following has the greatest value?

(A) $\frac{1}{4} + \frac{2}{3}$

(B) $\frac{3}{4} - \frac{1}{3}$

(C) $\frac{1}{12} \div \frac{1}{3}$

(D) $\frac{3}{4} \times \frac{1}{3}$

(E) $\frac{1}{12} \times 2$

13. $\frac{1}{2} + \frac{2}{3} + \frac{3}{4} + \frac{1}{2} + \frac{1}{3} + \frac{1}{4} =$

(A) $\frac{3}{4}$

(B) 1

(C) 6

(D) 3

(E) 12

14. The product of 0.34 and 1,000 is approximately

    (A)   3.50
    (B) 35
    (C) 65
    (D) 350
    (E) 650

15. $2.398 =$

    (A) $2 \times \dfrac{9}{100} \times \dfrac{3}{10} \times \dfrac{8}{1000}$

    (B) $2 + \dfrac{3}{10} + \dfrac{9}{1000} + \dfrac{8}{100}$

    (C) $2 + \dfrac{9}{100} + \dfrac{8}{1000} + \dfrac{3}{10}$

    (D) $\dfrac{3}{10} + \dfrac{9}{100} + \dfrac{8}{1000}$

    (E) None of the above

Stop. Check your time for this drill: _____

Don't forget to check your answers in Chapter 9.

HOW DID YOU DO?

That was a good sample of some of the kinds of questions you'll see on the SSAT. Now there are a few things to check other than your answers. Remember that taking the test involves much more than just getting answers right. It's also about guessing wisely, using your time well, and figuring out where you're likely to make mistakes. Once you've checked to see what you've gotten right and wrong, you should then consider the points that follow to improve your score.

Time and Pacing

How long did it take you to do the 15 questions? 15 minutes? It's okay if you went a minute or two over. However, if you finished very quickly (in fewer than 10 minutes) or slowly (more than 20 minutes), look at any problems that may have affected your speed. Which questions seriously slowed you down? Did you answer some quickly but not correctly? Your answers to these questions will help you plan which and how many questions to answer on the SSAT.

Question Recognition and Selection

Did you use your time wisely? Did you do the questions in an order that worked well for you? Which kinds of questions were the hardest for you? Remember that every question on the SSAT, whether you know the answer right away or find the question confusing, is worth one point, and that you don't have to answer all the questions to get a good score. In fact, because of the guessing penalty, skipping questions can actually raise your score. So depending on your personal speed, you should concentrate most on getting as many questions you find easy or sort-of easy right as possible, and worry about harder problems later. Keep in mind that in Math sections, the questions generally go from easiest to hardest throughout. Getting the questions you know you know the answers to right takes time, but you know you can solve them—so give yourself that time!

POE and Guessing

Did you actively look for wrong answers to eliminate, instead of just looking for the right answer? (You should.) Did you physically cross off wrong answers to keep track of your POE? Was there a pattern to when guessing worked (more often when you could eliminate one wrong answer, and less often when you picked simpler-looking over harder-looking answers)?

Be Careful

Did you work problems out on a separate piece of paper? Did you move too quickly or skip steps on problems you found easier? Did you always double-check what the question was asking? Often students miss questions that they know how to do! Why? It's simple—they work out problems in their heads or don't read carefully. Work out every SSAT math problem on the page. Consider it a double-check because your handwritten notes confirm what you've worked out in your head.

PRACTICE DRILL 2—MULTIPLE CHOICE—UPPER LEVEL ONLY

While doing the next drill, keep in mind the general test-taking techniques we've talked about: guessing, POE, order of difficulty, pacing, and working on the page and not in your head. At the end of the section, check your answers. But don't stop there: Investigate the drill thoroughly to see how and why you got your answers wrong. And check your time. You should be spending about one minute per question on this drill. When you are done, check your answers in Chapter 9. Don't forget to time yourself!

Remember to time yourself during this drill!

1. How many numbers between 1 and 100 are multiples of both 2 and 7 ?

    (A)   6
    (B)   7
    (C)   8
    (D)   9
    (E)   10

2. What is the smallest multiple of 7 that is greater than 50 ?

    (A)   7
    (B)   49
    (C)   51
    (D)   56
    (E)   63

3. $2^3 \times 2^3 \times 2^2 =$

    (A)   64
    (B) 2^8
    (C) 2^{10}
    (D) 2^{16}
    (E) 2^{18}

4. For what integer value of m does $2m + 4 = m^3$?

    (A)   1
    (B)   2
    (C)   3
    (D)   4
    (E)   5

5. One-fifth of the students in a class chose recycling as the topic for their science projects. If four students chose recycling, how many students are in the class?

    (A)   4
    (B)   10
    (C)   16
    (D)   20
    (E)   24

6. If $6x - 4 = 38$, then $x + 10 =$

   (A) 7
   (B) 10
   (C) 16
   (D) 17
   (E) 19

7. If $3x - 6 = 21$, then what is $x \div 9$?

   (A) 0
   (B) 1
   (C) 3
   (D) 6
   (E) 9

8. Only one-fifth of the chairs in a classroom are in working order. If three additional working chairs are brought in, there are 19 working seats available. How many chairs were originally in the room?

   (A) 16
   (B) 19
   (C) 22
   (D) 80
   (E) 95

9. If a harvest yielded 60 bushels of corn, 20 bushels of wheat, and 40 bushels of soybeans, what percent of the total harvest was corn?

   (A) 50%
   (B) 40%
   (C) 33%
   (D) 30%
   (E) 25%

10. At a local store, an item that usually sells for $45 is currently on sale for $30. By what percent is that item discounted?

   (A) 10%
   (B) 25%
   (C) 33%
   (D) 50%
   (E) 66%

11. Which of the following is most nearly 35% of $19.95 ?

   (A) $3.50
   (B) $5.75
   (C) $7.00
   (D) $9.95
   (E) $13.50

12. Of the 50 hotels in the Hilltop Hotels chain, 5 have indoor swimming pools and 15 have outdoor swimming pools. What percent of all Hilltop Hotels have either an indoor or an outdoor swimming pool?

   (A) 40%
   (B) 30%
   (C) 20%
   (D) 15%
   (E) 5%

13. For what price item does 40% off equal a $20 discount?

   (A) $50.00
   (B) $100.00
   (C) $400.00
   (D) $800.00
   (E) None of the above

14. A pair of shoes is offered on a special blowout sale. The original price of the shoes is reduced from $50 to $20. What is the percent change in the price of the shoes?

   (A) 60%
   (B) 50%
   (C) 40%
   (D) 25%
   (E) 20%

15. Lisa buys a silk dress regularly priced at $60, a cotton sweater regularly priced at $40, and four pairs of socks regularly priced at $5 each. If the dress and the socks are on sale for 20% off the regular price and the sweater is on sale for 10% off the regular price, what is the total amount of her purchase?

   (A) $90.00
   (B) $96.00
   (C) $100.00
   (D) $102.00
   (E) $108.00

16. Thirty percent of $17.95 is closest to

   (A) $2.00
   (B) $3.00
   (C) $6.00
   (D) $9.00
   (E) $12.00

17. Fifty percent of the 20 students in Mrs. Schweizer's third-grade class are boys. If 90 percent of these boys ride the bus to school, which of the following is the number of boys in Mrs. Schweizer's class who ride the bus to school?

(A)   9
(B)   10
(C)   12
(D)   16
(E)   18

18. On a test with 25 questions, Marc scored an 88 percent. How many questions did Marc answer correctly?

(A)   22
(B)   16
(C)   12
(D)   4
(E)   3

19. Four friends each pay $5 for a pizza every Friday night. If they were to start inviting a fifth friend to come with them and still bought the same pizza, how much would each person then have to pay?

(A) $1
(B) $4
(C) $5
(D) $20
(E) $25

20. A stop sign has 8 equal sides of length 4. What is its perimeter?

(A)   4
(B)   8
(C)   12
(D)   32
(E)   It cannot be determined from the information given.

21. If the perimeter of a square is 56, what is the length of each side?

(A)   4
(B)   7
(C)   14
(D)   28
(E)   112

22. The perimeter of a square with a side of length 4 is how much less than the perimeter of a rectangle with sides of length 4 and width 6 ?

(A) 0
(B) 2
(C) 4
(D) 6
(E) 8

23. What is the perimeter of an equilateral triangle, one side of which measures 4 inches?

(A) 12 inches
(B) 8 inches
(C) 6 inches
(D) 4 inches
(E) It cannot be determined from the information given.

24. $x =$

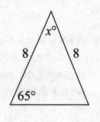

(A) 8
(B) 30
(C) 50
(D) 65
(E) 180

25. If $b = 45$, then $v^2 =$

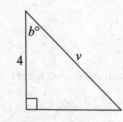

(A) 32
(B) 25
(C) 16
(D) 5
(E) It cannot be determined from the information given.

26. One-half of the difference between the number of degrees in a square and the number of degrees in a triangle is

(A) 45
(B) 90
(C) 180
(D) 240
(E) 360

27. If the area of a square is equal to its perimeter, what is the length of one side?

(A) 1
(B) 2
(C) 4
(D) 8
(E) 10

28. The area of a rectangle with width 4 and length 3 is equal to the area of a triangle with a base of 6 and a height of

(A) 1
(B) 2
(C) 3
(D) 4
(E) 12

29. Two cardboard boxes have equal volume. The dimensions of one box are $3 \times 4 \times 10$. If the length of the other box is 6 and the width is 4, what is the height of the second box?

(A) 2
(B) 5
(C) 10
(D) 12
(E) 24

30. If the area of a square is $64p^2$, what is the length of one side of the square?

(A) $64p^2$
(B) $64p$
(C) $8p^2$
(D) $8p$
(E) 8

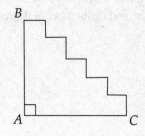

31. If $AB = 10$ and $AC = 15$, what is the perimeter of
     the figure above?

     (A) 25
     (B) 35
     (C) 40
     (D) 50
     (E) It cannot be determined from the information given.

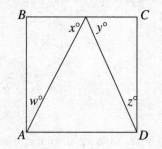

32. If $ABCD$, shown above, is a rectangle, what is the
     value of $w + x + y + z$?

     (A)   90°
     (B) 150°
     (C) 180°
     (D) 190°
     (E) 210°

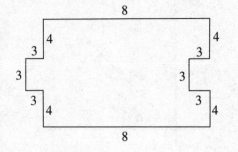

33. What is the area of the figure above if all the angles shown are right angles?

    (A) 38
    (B) 42
    (C) 50
    (D) 88
    (E) 96

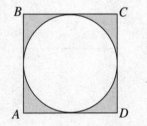

34. In the figure above, the length of side *AB* of square *ABCD* is equal to 4 and the circle has a radius of 2. What is the area of the shaded region?

    (A) $4 - \pi$
    (B) $16 - 4\pi$
    (C) $8 + 4\pi$
    (D) 4π
    (E) 8π

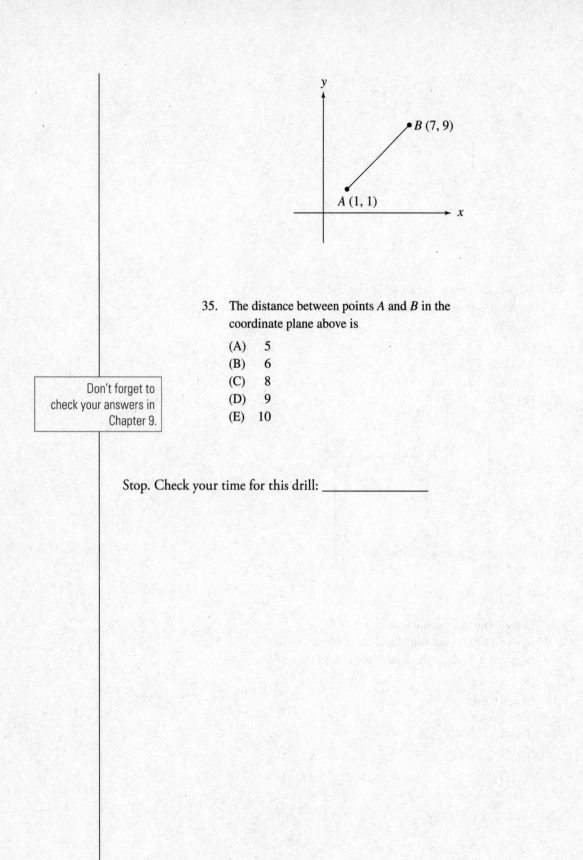

35. The distance between points *A* and *B* in the
     coordinate plane above is

(A)   5
(B)   6
(C)   8
(D)   9
(E)   10

Don't forget to
check your answers in
Chapter 9.

Stop. Check your time for this drill: _____

Ratios

A ratio is like a recipe. It tells you how much of each ingredient goes into a mixture.

For example:

To make punch, mix two parts grape juice with three parts orange juice.

This ratio tells you that for every two units of grape juice, you will need to add three units of orange juice. It doesn't matter what the units are; if you were working with ounces, you would mix two ounces of grape juice with three ounces of orange juice to get five ounces of punch. If you were working with gallons, you would mix two gallons of grape juice with three gallons of orange juice. How much punch would you have? Five gallons.

To work through a ratio question, first you need to organize the information you are given. Do this using the Ratio Box.

In a club with 35 members, the ratio of boys to girls is 3:2. To complete your Ratio Box, fill in the ratio at the top and the "real value" at the bottom.

	Boys	**Girls**	**Total**
Ratio	3 +	2 =	5
Multiplier			
Real Value			35

Then look for a "magic number" that you can multiply by the ratio total to get the real value total. In this case, the magic number is 7. That's all there is to it!

	Boys	**Girls**	**Total**
Ratio	3 +	2 =	5
Multiplier	× 7	× 7	× 7
Real Value	21	14	35

PRACTICE DRILL 3—RATIOS

Remember to time your-
self during this drill!

1. In a jar of lollipops, the ratio of red lollipops to
   blue lollipops is 3:5. If only red lollipops and blue
   lollipops are in the jar and if the total number of
   lollipops in the jar is 56, how many blue lollipops
   are in the jar?

   (A) 35
   (B) 28
   (C) 21
   (D)   8
   (E)   5

2. At Jed's Country Hotel, there are three types of
   rooms: singles, doubles, and triples. If the ratio of
   singles to doubles to triples is 3:4:5, and the total
   number of rooms is 36, how many doubles are
   there?

   (A)   4
   (B)   9
   (C) 12
   (D) 24
   (E) 36

3. Matt's Oak Superstore has exactly three times as
   many large oak desks as small oak desks in its
   inventory. If the store sells only these two types of
   desks, which could be the total number of desks in
   stock?

   (A) 10
   (B) 13
   (C) 16
   (D) 18
   (E) 25

4. In Janice's tennis club, 8 of the 12 players are
   right-handed. What is the ratio of right-handed to
   left-handed players in Janice's club?

   (A) 1:2
   (B) 1:6
   (C) 2:1
   (D) 2:3
   (E) 3:4

5. One-half of the 400 students at Booth Junior High School are girls. Of the girls at the school, the ratio of those who ride a school bus to those who walk is 7:3. What is the total number of girls who walk to school?

    (A) 10
    (B) 30
    (C) 60
    (D) 120
    (E) 140

6. A pet goat eats 2 pounds of goat food and 1 pound of grass each day. When the goat has eaten a total of 15 pounds, how many pounds of grass will it have eaten?

    (A) 3
    (B) 4
    (C) 5
    (D) 15
    (E) 30

Don't forget to check your answers in Chapter 9.

Stop. Check your time for this drill: _____

Averages

There are three parts to every average problem: total, number, and average. Most SSAT problems will give you two of the three pieces and ask you to find the third. To help organize the information you are given, use the Average Pie.

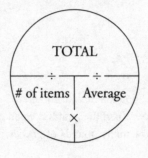

The Average Pie organizes all of your information visually. It makes it easier to see all of the relationships between the pieces of the pie.

- TOTAL = (*# of items*) × (*Average*)

- # of items = $\dfrac{Total}{Average}$

- Average = $\dfrac{Total}{\text{# of items}}$

For example, if your friend went bowling and bowled three games, scoring 71, 90, and 100, here's how you would compute her average score using the Average Pie.

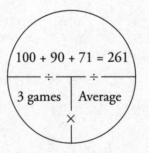

To find the average, you would simply write a fraction that represents $\dfrac{Total}{\text{# of items}}$, in this case $\dfrac{261}{3}$.

The math becomes simple. 261 ÷ 3 = 87. Your friend bowled an average of 87.

Practice working with the Average Pie by using it to solve the following problems.

PRACTICE DRILL 4—AVERAGES

1. The average of 3 numbers is 18. What is 2 times the sum of the 3 numbers?

   (A) 108
   (B) 54
   (C) 36
   (D) 18
   (E)   6

Average
When you see the word *average*, draw an Average Pie.

2. If Set M contains 4 positive integers whose average is 7, then what is the largest number that Set M could contain?

   (A)   6
   (B)   7
   (C) 18
   (D) 25
   (E) 28

Remember to time your-self during this drill!

3. An art club of 4 boys and 5 girls makes craft projects. If the boys average 2 projects each and the girls average 3 projects each, what is the total number of projects produced by the club?

   (A) 14
   (B) 23
   (C) 26
   (D) 54
   (E) 100

4. If a class of 6 students has an average grade of 72 before a seventh student joins the class, then what must the seventh student's grade be to raise the class average to 76 ?

   (A) 100
   (B) 92
   (C) 88
   (D) 80
   (E) 76

5. Catherine scores an 84, 85, and 88 on her first three exams. What must she score on her fourth exam to raise her average to an 89 ?

   (A) 99
   (B) 97
   (C) 93
   (D) 91
   (E) 89

Don't forget to check your answers in Chapter 9.

Percent Change—Upper Level Only

There is one special kind of percent question that shows up on the SSAT: percent change. This type of question asks you to find what percent something has increased or decreased. Instead of taking the part and dividing it by the whole, you will take the difference between the two numbers and divide it by the original number. Then, to turn the fraction to a percent, divide the numerator by the denominator and multiply by 100.

For example:

> The number of people who watched *Empire* last year was 3,600,000. This year, only 3,000,000 are watching the show. By approximately what percent has the audience decreased?

$$\frac{\text{The difference}}{\text{The original}} = \frac{600,000}{3,600,000} \quad \text{(The difference is } 3,600,000 - 3,000,000.\text{)}$$

The fraction reduces to $\dfrac{1}{6}$, and $\dfrac{1}{6}$ as a percent is 17%.

PRACTICE DRILL 5—PERCENT CHANGE

1. During a severe winter in Ontario, the temperature dropped suddenly to 10 degrees below zero. If the temperature in Ontario before this cold spell occurred was 10 degrees above zero, by what percent did the temperature drop?

    (A) 25%
    (B) 50%
    (C) 100%
    (D) 150%
    (E) 200%

2. Fatty's Burger wants to attract more customers by increasing the size of its patties. From now on Fatty's patties are going to be 4 ounces larger than before. If the size of its new patty is 16 ounces, by approximately what percent has the patty increased?

    (A) 25%
    (B) 27%
    (C) 33%
    (D) 75%
    (E) 80%

Stop. Check your time for this drill: _____

$$\%\,change = \frac{difference}{original} \times 100$$

Remember to time yourself during this drill!

Don't forget to check your answers in Chapter 9.

Plugging In

The SSAT will often ask you questions about real-life situations in which the numbers have been replaced with variables. One of the easiest ways to tackle these questions is with a powerful technique called *Plugging In*.

> Mark is two inches taller than John, who is four inches shorter than Terry. If t represents Terry's height in inches, then in terms of t, an expression for Mark's height is
>
> (A) $t + 6$
> (B) $t + 4$
> (C) $t + 2$
> (D) t
> (E) $t - 2$

Take the Algebra Away, and Arithmetic Is All That's Left
When you Plug In for variables, you won't need to write equations and won't have to solve algebra problems. Doing simple arithmetic is always easier than doing algebra.

The problem with this question is that we're not used to thinking of people's heights in terms of variables. Have you ever met someone who was t inches tall?

Whenever you see variables used in the question and in the choices, just Plug In a number to replace the variable.

1. Choose a number for t.
2. Using that number, figure out Mark's and John's heights.
3. Put a box around Mark's height because that's what the question asked you for.
4. Plug your number for t into the choices and choose the one that gives you the number you found for Mark's height.

Here's How It Works

> Mark is two inches taller than John, who is four inches shorter than Terry. If t represents Terry's height in inches, then ~~in terms of t,~~ an expression for Mark's height is
>
> (A) $t + 6$
> (B) $t + 4$
> (C) $t + 2$
> (D) t
> (E) $t - 2$

Cross this out! Because you are Plugging In, you don't need to pay any attention to "in terms of" any variable.

For Terry's height, let's pick 60 inches. This means that $t = 60$.

Remember, there is no right or wrong number to pick. 50 would work just as well.

But given that Terry is 60 inches tall, now we can figure out that, because John is four inches shorter than Terry, John's height must be $(60 - 4)$, or 56 inches.

The other piece of information we learn from the problem is that Mark is two inches taller than John. If John's height is 56 inches, that means Mark must be 58 inches tall.

Here's what we've got:

Terry	60 inches = t
John	56 inches
Mark	58 inches

Now, the question asks for Mark's height, which is 58 inches. The last step is to go through the choices substituting 60 for t and choose the one that equals 58.

(A)	$t + 6$	$60 + 6 = 66$	ELIMINATE
(B)	$t + 4$	$60 + 4 = 64$	ELIMINATE
(C)	$t + 2$	$60 + 2 = 62$	ELIMINATE
(D)	t	60	ELIMINATE
(E)	$t - 2$	$60 - 2 = 58$	PICK THIS ONE!

After reading this explanation, you may be tempted to say that Plugging In takes too long. Don't be fooled. The method itself is often faster and (more importantly) more accurate than regular algebra. Try it out. Practice. As you become more comfortable with Plugging In, you'll get even quicker and better results. You still need to know how to do algebra, but if you do only algebra, you may have difficulty improving your SSAT score. Plugging In gives you a way to break through whenever you are stuck. You'll find that having more than one way to solve SSAT math problems puts you at a real advantage.

PRACTICE DRILL 6—PLUGGING IN

1. At a charity fund-raiser, 200 people each donated x dollars. In terms of x, what was the total number of dollars donated?

    (A) $\dfrac{x}{200}$

    (B) 200

    (C) $\dfrac{200}{x}$

    (D) $200 + x$

    (E) $200x$

2. If 10 magazines cost d dollars, then in terms of d, how many magazines can be purchased for 3 dollars?

    (A) $\dfrac{3d}{10}$

    (B) $30d$

    (C) $\dfrac{d}{30}$

    (D) $\dfrac{30}{d}$

    (E) $\dfrac{10d}{3}$

3. The zoo has four times as many monkeys as lions. There are four more lions than there are zebras at the zoo. If z represents the number of zebras in the zoo, then in terms of z, how many monkeys are there in the zoo?

    (A) $z + 4$
    (B) $z + 8$
    (C) $4z$
    (D) $4z + 16$
    (E) $4z + 4$

Occasionally, you may run into a Plugging In question that doesn't contain variables. These questions usually ask about a percentage or a fraction of some unknown number or price. This is the one time that you should Plug In even when you don't see variables in the answer!

Also, be sure you Plug In good numbers. Good doesn't mean right because there's no such thing as a right or wrong number to Plug In. A good number is one that makes the problem easier to work with. If a question asks about minutes and hours, try Plugging In 30 or 60, not 128. Also, whenever you see the word percent, Plug In 100!

4. The price of a suit is reduced by half, and then the resulting price is reduced by 10%. The final price is what percent of the original price?

(A) 5%
(B) 10%
(C) 25%
(D) 40%
(E) 45%

5. On Wednesday, Miguel ate one-fourth of a pumpkin pie. On Thursday, he ate one-half of what was left of the pie. What fraction of the entire pie did Miguel eat on Wednesday and Thursday?

(A) $\dfrac{3}{8}$

(B) $\dfrac{1}{2}$

(C) $\dfrac{5}{8}$

(D) $\dfrac{3}{4}$

(E) $\dfrac{7}{8}$

6. If p pieces of candy costs c cents, then in terms of p and c, 10 pieces of candy will cost

(A) $\dfrac{pc}{10}$ cents.

(B) $\dfrac{10c}{p}$ cents.

(C) $10pc$ cents.

(D) $\dfrac{10p}{c}$ cents.

(E) $10 + p + c$ cents.

7. If J is an odd integer, which of the following must be true?

(A) $(J \div 3) > 1$
(B) $(J - 2)$ is a positive integer.
(C) $2 \times J$ is an even integer.
(D) $J^2 > J$
(E) $J > 0$

8. If m is an even integer, n is an odd integer, and p is the product of m and n, which of the following is always true?

(A) p is a fraction.
(B) p is an odd integer.
(C) p is divisible by 2.
(D) p is between m and n.
(E) p is greater than zero.

Don't forget to check your answers in Chapter 9.

Stop. Check your time for this drill: _____

Plugging In The Answers (PITA)

Plugging In The Answers is similar to Plugging In. When you have *variables* in the choices, you Plug In. When you have *numbers* in the choices, you should generally Plug In the Answers. The only time this may get tricky is when you have a question that asks for a percent or fraction of some unknown number.

Plugging In the Answers works because on a multiple-choice test, the right answer is always one of the choices. On this type of question, you can't Plug In any number you want because only one number will work. Instead, you can Plug In numbers from the choices, one of which must be correct. Here's an example.

> Nicole baked a batch of cookies. She gave half to her friend Lisa and six to her mother. If she now has eight cookies left, how many did Nicole bake originally?
>
> (A)   8
> (B)   12
> (C)   20
> (D)   28
> (E)   32

See what we mean? It would be hard to just start making up numbers of cookies and hope that eventually you guessed correctly. However, the number of cookies that Nicole baked originally must be either 8, 12, 20, 28, or 32 (the five choices). So pick one—always start with (C)—and then work backward to determine whether you have the right choice.

Let's start with (C): Nicole baked 20 cookies. Now work through the events listed in the question.

She had 20 cookies—from (C)—and she gave half to Lisa. That leaves Nicole with 10 cookies.

What next? She gives 6 to her mom. Now she's got 4 left.

Keep going. The problem says that Nicole now has 8 cookies left. But if she started with 20—(C)—she would only have 4 left. So is (C) the right answer? No.

No problem. Choose another choice and try again. Be smart about which choice you pick. When we used the number in (C), Nicole ended up with fewer cookies than we wanted her to have, didn't she? So the right answer must be a number larger than 20, the number we took from (C).

The good news is that the choices in most Plugging In The Answers questions go in order, so you can choose the next larger or smaller number—you just pick either (B) or (D), depending on which direction you've decided to go.

Back to Nicole and her cookies. We need a number larger than 20. So let's go to (D)—28.

Nicole started out with 28 cookies. The first thing she did was give half, or 14, to Lisa. That left Nicole with 14 cookies.

Then she gave 6 cookies to her mother. 14 – 6 = 8. Nicole has 8 cookies left over. Keep going with the question. It says, "If she now has eight cookies left…" She has eight cookies left and, *voilà*—she's supposed to have 8 cookies left.

What does this mean? It means you've got the right answer! Pick (D) and move on.

If (D) had not worked, and you were still certain that you needed a number larger than (C), you also would be finished. Since you started with the middle, (C), which didn't work, and then you tried the next larger choice, (D), which didn't work either, you could pick the only choice bigger than (C) that was left—in this case (E)—and be done.

This diagram helps illustrate the way you should move through the choices.

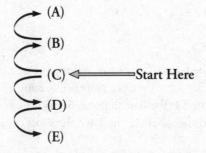

To wrap up, Plugging In The Answers should always go the following way:

1. **Start with (C).** This number is now what you are working with.
2. **Work the problem.** Go through the problem with that number, using information to help you determine if it is the correct answer.
3. **If (C) doesn't work, try another answer.** Remember to think logically about which choice you should check next.
4. **Once you find the correct answer, STOP.**

PRACTICE DRILL 7—PLUGGING IN THE ANSWERS

1. Ted can read 60 pages per hour. Naomi can read 45 pages per hour. If both Ted and Naomi read at the same time, how many minutes will it take them to read a total of 210 pages?

   (A)   36
   (B)   72
   (C)   120
   (D)   145
   (E)   180

Remember to time yourself during this drill!

2. If the sum of *y* and *y* + 1 is greater than 18, which of the following is one possible value for *y* ?

   (A)   −10
   (B)   −8
   (C)   2
   (D)   8
   (E)   10

3. Kenny is 5 years older than Greg. In 5 years, Kenny will be twice as old as Greg is now. How old is Kenny now?

   (A)   5
   (B)   10
   (C)   15
   (D)   25
   (E)   35

4. Three people—Paul, Sara, and John—want to put their money together to buy a $90 radio. If Sara agrees to pay twice as much as John, and Paul agrees to pay three times as much as Sara, how much must Sara pay?

   (A) $10
   (B) $20
   (C) $30
   (D) $45
   (E) $65

5. Four less than a certain number is two-thirds of that number. What is the number?

   (A)   1
   (B)   6
   (C)   8
   (D)   12
   (E)   16

Don't forget to check your answers in Chapter 9.

Stop. Check your time for this drill: _____

GEOMETRY

Guesstimating: A Second Look

Guesstimating worked well back in the introduction when we were just using it to estimate or "ballpark" the size of a number, but geometry problems are undoubtedly the best place to guesstimate whenever you can.

Let's try the next problem. Remember, unless a particular question tells you otherwise, you can safely assume that figures *are* drawn to scale.

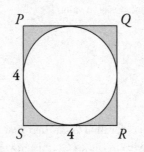

Elementary Level
This question is harder than what you will encounter, but it's a good idea to learn how guesstimating can help you!

A circle is inscribed in square *PQRS*. What is the area of the shaded region?

(A) $16 - 6\pi$
(B) $16 - 4\pi$
(C) $16 - 3\pi$
(D) $16 - 2\pi$
(E) 16π

Wow, a circle inscribed in a square—that sounds tough!

It isn't. Look at the picture. What fraction of the square looks like it is shaded? Half? Three-quarters? Less than half? In fact, about one-quarter of the area of the square is shaded. You've just done most of the work necessary to solve this problem.

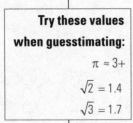

Try these values when guesstimating:

$\pi \approx 3+$

$\sqrt{2} = 1.4$

$\sqrt{3} = 1.7$

Now, let's just do a little math. The length of one side of the square is 4, so the area of the square is 4×4 or 16.

So the area of the square is 16, and we said that the shaded region was about one-fourth of the square. One-fourth of 16 is 4, right? So we're looking for a choice that equals about 4. Let's look at the choices.

(A) $16 - 6\pi$
(B) $16 - 4\pi$
(C) $16 - 3\pi$
(D) $16 - 2\pi$
(E) 16π

This becomes a little complicated because the answers include π. For the purposes of guesstimating, and in fact for almost any purpose on the SSAT, you should just remember that π is a little more than 3.

Let's look back at those answers.

(A)	$16 - 6\pi$	is roughly equal to	$16 - (6 \times 3) = -2$
(B)	$16 - 4\pi$	is roughly equal to	$16 - (4 \times 3) = 4$
(C)	$16 - 3\pi$	is roughly equal to	$16 - (3 \times 3) = 7$
(D)	$16 - 2\pi$	is roughly equal to	$16 - (2 \times 3) = 10$
(E)	16π	is roughly equal to	$(16 \times 3) = 48$

Now let's think about what these answers mean.

Choice (A) is geometrically impossible. A figure *cannot* have a negative area. Eliminate it.

Choice (B) means that the shaded region has an area of about 4. Sounds pretty good.

Choice (C) means that the shaded region has an area of about 7. The area of the entire square was 16, so that would mean that the shaded region was almost half the square. Possible, but doubtful.

Choice (D) means that the shaded region has an area of about 10. That's more than half the square and in fact, almost three-quarters of the entire square. No way; cross it out.

Finally, (E) means that the shaded region has an area of about 48. What? The whole square had an area of 16. Is the shaded region three times as big as the square itself? Not a chance. Eliminate (E).

At this point you are left with only (B), which we feel pretty good about, and (C), which seems a little large. What should you do?

Pick (B) and pat yourself on the back because you chose the right answer without doing a lot of unnecessary work. Also, remember how useful it was to guesstimate and make sure you do it whenever you see a geometry problem, unless the problem tells you that the figure is not drawn to scale!

Weird Shapes

Whenever the test presents you with a geometric figure that is not a square, rectangle, circle, or triangle, draw a line or lines to divide that figure into the shapes that you do know. Then you can easily work with shapes you know all about.

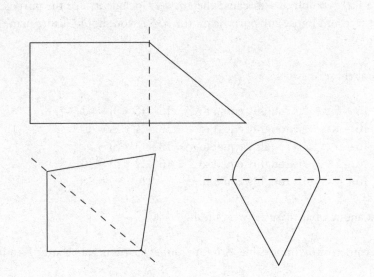

Shaded Regions—Middle and Upper Levels Only

Sometimes geometry questions show you one figure inscribed in another and then ask you to find the area of a shaded region inside the larger figure and outside the smaller figure (like the problem at the beginning of this section). To find the areas of these shaded regions, find the area of the outside figure and then subtract from that the area of the figure inside. The difference is what you need.

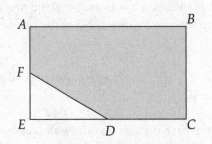

ABCE is a rectangle with a length of 10 and width of 6. Points *F* and *D* are the midpoints of *AE* and *EC*, respectively. What is the area of the shaded region?

(A) 25.5
(B) 30
(C) 45
(D) 52.5
(E) It cannot be determined from the information given.

The first step is to find the area of the rectangle. If you multiply the length by the width, you'll find the area is 60. Now we find the area of the triangle that we are removing from the rectangle. Because the height and base of the triangle are parts of the sides of the rectangle, and points *D* and *F* are half the length and width of the rectangle, we know that the height of the triangle is half the rectangle's width, or 3, and the base of the triangle is half the rectangle's length, or 5.

Using the formula for area of a triangle, we find the area of the triangle is 7.5. Now we subtract the area of the triangle from the area of the rectangle. $60 - 7.5 = 52.5$. The correct choice is (D). Be careful not to choose (E) just because the problem looks tricky!

Functions—Middle and Upper Levels Only

In a function problem, an arithmetic operation is defined and then you are asked to perform it on a number. A function is just a set of instructions written in a strange way.

$$\# x = 3x(x + 1)$$

On the left there is usually a variable with a strange symbol next to or around it.
In the middle is an equals sign.
On the right are the instructions. These tell you what to do with the variable.

$\# x = 3x(x + 1)$ *What does # 5 equal?*

$\# 5 = (3 \times 5)(5 + 1)$ *Just replace each x with a 5!*

Here, the function (indicated by the # sign) simply tells you to substitute a 5 wherever there was an x in the original set of instructions. Functions look confusing because of the strange symbols, but once you know what to do with them, they are just like manipulating an equation.

Sometimes more than one question will refer to the same function. The following drill, for example, contains two questions about one function. In cases such as this, the first question tends to be easier than the second.

PRACTICE DRILL 8—FUNCTIONS

Questions 1 and 2 refer to the following definition.

Remember to time your-
self during this drill!

For all real numbers n, $\$n = 10n - 10$.

1. $\$7 =$

    (A) 70

    (B) 60

    (C) 17

    (D)   7

    (E)   0

2. If $\$n = 120$, then $n =$

    (A) 11

    (B) 12

    (C) 13

    (D) 120

    (E) 130

Questions 3–5 refer to the following definition.

For all real numbers d and y, $d \mathbin{\text{¿}} y = (d \times y) - (d + y)$.

[Example: $3 \mathbin{\text{¿}} 2 = (3 \times 2) - (3 + 2) = 6 - 5 = 1$]

3. $10 \mathbin{\text{¿}} 2 =$

    (A) 20

    (B) 16

    (C) 12

    (D)   8

    (E)   4

4. If $K (4 \mathbin{\text{¿}} 3) = 30$, then $K =$

    (A) 3

    (B) 4

    (C) 5

    (D) 6

    (E) 7

5. $(2 \mathbin{\text{¿}} 4) \times (3 \mathbin{\text{¿}} 6) =$

    (A) $(9 \mathbin{\text{¿}} 3) + 3$

    (B) $(6 \mathbin{\text{¿}} 4) + 1$

    (C) $(5 \mathbin{\text{¿}} 3) + 4$

    (D) $(8 \mathbin{\text{¿}} 4) + 2$

    (E) $(9 \mathbin{\text{¿}} 4) + 3$

Don't forget to
check your answers in
Chapter 9.

Stop. Check your time for this drill: _____

Charts and Graphs

Charts

Chart questions are simple, but you must be careful. Follow these three steps and you'll be well on the way to mastering any chart question.

Don't Be in Too Big of a Hurry
When working with charts and graphs, make sure you take a moment to look at the chart or graph, figure out what it tells you, and then go to the questions.

1. Read any text that accompanies the chart. It is important to know what the chart is showing and what scale the numbers are on.
2. Read the question.
3. Refer to the chart and find the specific information you need.

If there is more than one question about a single chart, the later questions will tend to be more difficult than the earlier ones. Be careful!

Here is a sample chart.

Club Membership by State, 2010 and 2011		
State	**2010**	**2011**
California	300	500
Florida	225	250
Illinois	200	180
Massachusetts	150	300
Michigan	150	200
New Jersey	200	250
New York	400	600
Texas	50	100

There are many different questions that you can answer based on the information in this chart. For instance:

> What is the difference between the number of members who came from New York in 2010 and the number of members who came from Illinois in 2011 ?

This question asks you to look up two simple pieces of information and then do a tiny bit of math.

First, the number of members who came from New York in 2010 was 400.

Second, the number of members who came from Illinois in 2011 was 180.

Finally, look back at the question. It asks you to find the difference between these numbers. 400 − 180 = 220. Done.

> The increase in the number of members from New Jersey from 2010 to 2011 was what percent of the total number of members in New Jersey in 2010 ?

You should definitely know how to do this one! Do you remember how to translate percentage questions? If not, go back to Fundamental Math Skills (Chapter 2).

In 2010, there were 200 club members from New Jersey. In 2011, there were 250 members from New Jersey. That represents an increase of 50 members. To determine what percent that is of the total amount in 2010, you will need to ask yourself, "50 (the increase) is what percent of 200 (the number of members in 2010)?"

Translated, this becomes:

$$50 = \frac{g}{100} \times 200$$

With a little bit of simple manipulation, this equation becomes:

$$50 = 2g$$

and

$$25 = g$$

So from 2010 to 2011, there was a 25% increase in the number of members from New Jersey. Good work!

> Which state had as many club members in 2011 as a combination of Illinois, Massachusetts, and Michigan had in 2010 ?

First, take a second to look up the number of members who came from Illinois, Massachusetts, and Michigan in 2010 and add them together.

$$200 + 150 + 150 = 500$$

Which state had 500 members in 2011? California. That's all there is to it!

Graphs

Some questions will ask you to interpret a graph. You should be familiar with both pie and bar graphs. These graphs are generally drawn to scale (meaning that the graphs give an accurate visual impression of the information) so you can always guess based on the figure if you need to.

The way to approach a graph question is exactly the same as the way to approach a chart question. Follow the same three steps.

1. Read any text that accompanies the graph. It is important to know what the graph is showing and what scale the numbers are on.
2. Read the question.
3. Refer back to the graph and find the specific information you need.

This is how it works.

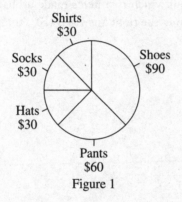

Figure 1

The graph in Figure 1 shows Emily's clothing expenditures for the month of October. On which type of clothing did she spend the most money?

(A) Shoes
(B) Shirts
(C) Socks
(D) Hats
(E) Pants

This one should be simple. You can look at the pieces of the pie and identify the largest, or you can look at the amounts shown in the graph and choose the largest one. Either way, the answer is (A) because Emily spent more money on shoes than on any other clothing items in October.

Emily spent half of her clothing money on which two items?

(A) Shoes and pants
(B) Shoes and shirts
(C) Hats and socks
(D) Socks and shirts
(E) Shirts and pants

Again, you can find the answer to this question two different ways. You can look for which two items together make up half the chart, or you can add up the total amount of money Emily spent ($240) and then figure out which two items made up half (or $120) of that amount. Either way is just fine, and either way the right answer is (B), shoes and shirts.

PRACTICE DRILL 9—CHARTS AND GRAPHS

<u>Questions 1-3</u> refer to the following summary of energy costs by district.

District	1990	1991
A	400	600
B	500	700
C	200	350
D	100	150
E	600	800

(All numbers are in thousands of dollars.)

Remember to time yourself during this drill!

1. In 1991, which district spent twice as much on energy as District A spent in 1990 ?

    (A) A
    (B) B
    (C) C
    (D) D
    (E) E

2. Which district spent the most on energy in 1990 and 1991 combined?

    (A) A
    (B) B
    (C) D
    (D) E
    (E) It cannot be determined from the information given.

3. The total increase in energy expenditure in these districts, from 1990 to 1991, is how many dollars?

    (A) $800
    (B) $1,800
    (C) $2,400
    (D) $2,600
    (E) $800,000

Questions 4 and 5 refer to Figure 2, which shows the number of compact discs owned by five students.

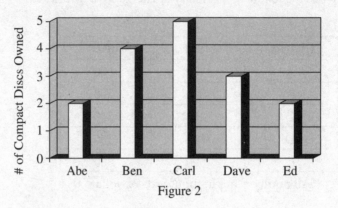

Figure 2

4. Carl owns as many CDs as which two other students combined?

    (A) Abe and Ben
    (B) Ben and Dave
    (C) Abe and Ed
    (D) Abe and Dave
    (E) Ben and Ed

5. Which one student owns one-fourth of the CDs accounted for in Figure 2 ?

    (A) Abe
    (B) Ben
    (C) Carl
    (D) Dave
    (E) Ed

Questions 6-8 refer to Matt's weekly time card, shown below.

Day	In	Out	Hours Worked
Monday	2:00 P.M.	5:30 P.M.	3.5
Tuesday			
Wednesday	2:00 P.M.	6:00 P.M.	4
Thursday	2:00 P.M.	5:30 P.M.	3.5
Friday	2:00 P.M.	5:00 P.M.	3
Saturday			
Sunday			

6. If Matt's hourly salary is $6, what were his earnings for the week?

    (A) $6
    (B) $14
    (C) $21
    (D) $54
    (E) $84

7. What is the average number of hours Matt worked on the days he worked during this particular week?

    (A)   3
    (B)   3.5
    (C)   4
    (D)   7
    (E)   14

8. The hours that Matt worked on Monday accounted for what percent of the total number of hours he worked during this week?

    (A)   3.5
    (B)   20
    (C)   25
    (D)   35
    (E)   50

Don't forget to check your answers in Chapter 9.

Stop. Check your time for this drill: _____

PRACTICE DRILL 10—MIDDLE AND UPPER LEVELS ONLY

When you are done, check your answers in Chapter 9. Don't forget to time yourself!

1. If p is an odd integer, which of the following must be an odd integer?

   (A) $p^2 + 3$
   (B) $2p + 1$
   (C) $p \div 3$
   (D) $p - 3$
   (E) $2(p^2)$

2. If m is the sum of two positive even integers, which of the following CANNOT be true?

   (A) $m < 5$
   (B) $3m$ is odd
   (C) m is even
   (D) m^3 is even
   (E) $m \div 2$ is even

3. The product of $\frac{1}{2}b$ and a^2 can be written as

   (A) $(ab)^2$

   (B) $\dfrac{a^2}{b}$

   (C) $2a \times \dfrac{1}{2}b$

   (D) $\dfrac{a^2 b}{2}$

   (E) $\dfrac{a^2 b^2}{2}$

4. Damon has twice as many records as Graham, who has one-fourth as many records as Alex. If Damon has d records, then in terms of d, how many records do Alex and Graham have together?

   (A) $\dfrac{3d}{2}$

   (B) $\dfrac{3d}{4}$

   (C) $\dfrac{9d}{2}$

   (D) $\dfrac{5d}{2}$

   (E) $2d$

5. $x^a = (x^3)^3$

$y^b = \dfrac{y^{10}}{y^2}$

What is the value of $a \times b$?

(A) 17
(B) 30
(C) 48
(D) 45
(E) 72

6. One six-foot Italian hero serves either 12 children or 8 adults. Approximately how many sandwiches do you need to feed a party of 250, 75 of whom are children?

(A) 21
(B) 24
(C) 29
(D) 30
(E) 32

7. Liam and Noel are traveling from New York City to Dallas. If they traveled $\dfrac{1}{5}$ of the distance on Monday and $\dfrac{1}{2}$ of the distance that remained on Tuesday, what percentage of the trip do they have left to travel?

(A) 25%
(B) 30%
(C) 40%
(D) 50%
(E) 80%

8. $\dfrac{1}{4}$ of a bag of potato chips contains 10 grams of fat. Approximately how many grams of fat are in $\dfrac{1}{6}$ of that same bag of chips?

(A) 5.5
(B) 6.5
(C) 7.5
(D) 8.5
(E) 9.5

9. Students in Mr. Greenwood's history class are collecting donations for a school charity drive. If the total number of students in the class, x, donated an average of y dollars each, in terms of x and y, how much money was collected for the drive?

(A) $\dfrac{x}{y}$

(B) xy

(C) $\dfrac{xy}{x}$

(D) $\dfrac{y}{x}$

(E) $2xy$

10. If $e + f$ is divisible by 17, which of the following must also be divisible by 17 ?

(A) $(e \times f) - 17$
(B) $e + (f \times 17)$
(C) $(e \times 17) + f$
(D) $(e + f) / 17$
(E) $(e \times 3) + (f \times 3)$

11. Joe wants to find the mean number of pages in the books he has read this month. The books were 200, 220, and 260 pages long. He read the 200 page book twice, so it will be counted twice in the mean. If he reads one more book, what is the fewest number of pages it can have to make the mean no less than 230 ?

(A) 268
(B) 269
(C) 270
(D) 271
(E) 272

12. Sayeeda is a point guard for her basketball team. In the last 3 games, she scored 8 points once and 12 points in each of the other two games. What must she score in tonight's game to raise her average to 15 points?

(A) 28
(B) 27
(C) 26
(D) 25
(E) 15

13. What is the greatest common factor of $(3xy)^3$ and $3x^2y^5$?

    (A) xy
    (B) $3x^2y^5$
    (C) $3x^2y^3$
    (D) $27x^3y^3$
    (E) $27x^5y^8$

14. The town of Mechanicville lies due east of Stillwater and due south of Half Moon Crescent. If the distance from Mechanicville to Stillwater is 30 miles, and from Mechanicville to Half Moon Crescent is 40 miles, what is the shortest distance from Stillwater to Half Moon Crescent?

    (A) 10
    (B) 50
    (C) 70
    (D) 100
    (E) It cannot be determined from the information given.

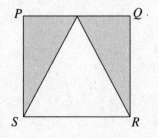

15. *PQRS* is a square with an area of 144. What is the area of the shaded region?

    (A) 50
    (B) 72
    (C) 100
    (D) 120
    (E) It cannot be determined from the information given.

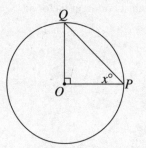

16. *PO* and *QO* are radii of the circle with center *O*.
    What is the value of *x* ?

    (A) 30
    (B) 45
    (C) 60
    (D) 90
    (E) It cannot be determined from the information given.

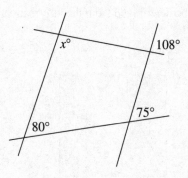

17. What is the value of *x* ?

    (A) 360
    (B) 100
    (C)   97
    (D)   67
    (E) It cannot be determined from the information given.

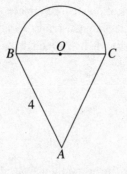

18. *ABC* is an equilateral triangle. What is the perimeter of this figure?

    (A) $4 + 2\pi$
    (B) $4 + 4\pi$
    (C) $8 + 2\pi$
    (D) $8 + 4\pi$
    (E) $12 + 2\pi$

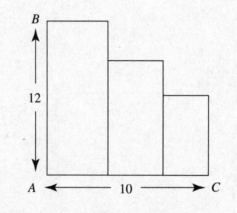

19. What is the perimeter of this figure?

    (A) 120
    (B) 44
    (C) 40
    (D) 36
    (E) It cannot be determined from the information given.

20. How many meters of police tape are needed to wrap around a rectangular crime scene that measures 6 meters wide by 28 meters long?

   (A)   34 meters
   (B)   68 meters
   (C)   90 meters
   (D)   136 meters
   (E)   168 meters

21. Billy Bob's Beans are currently packaged in cylindrical cans that contain 9 servings. The cans have a height of 20 cm and a diameter of 18 cm. Billy Bob wants to introduce a new single-serving can. If he keeps the height of the can the same, what should the diameter of the single-serving can be?

   (A)   3
   (B) $3\sqrt{2}$
   (C)   4.5
   (D)   6
   (E) $6\sqrt{2}$

Stop. Check your time for this drill: _____

Don't forget to check your answers in Chapter 9.

MATH REVIEW

Make sure you can confidently answer all of the following questions before you take your test.

1. Is zero an integer? _____

2. Is zero positive or negative? _____

3. What operation do you perform to find a sum? _____

4. What operation do you perform to find a product?

   _____

5. What is the result called when you divide? _____

6. Is 312 divisible by 3 ? _____

   Is 312 divisible by 9 ? _____

   (Actually, dividing isn't fair—use your divisibility rules!)

7. What does the "E" in PEMDAS stand for? _____

8. Is 3 a factor of 12 ? _____

   Is 12 a factor of 3 ? _____

9. Is 3 a multiple of 12 ? _____

   Is 12 a multiple of 3 ? _____

10. What is the tens digit in the number 304.275 ? _____

11. What is the tenths digit in the number 304.275 ?

    _____

12. $2^3 =$ _____

13. In "math language," the word *percent* means _____.

14. In "math language," the word *of* means _____.

15. In a Ratio Box, the last column on the right is always the

    _____.

16. Whenever you see a problem involving averages, draw the

    _____.

17. When a problem contains variables in the question and in the

    answers, I will _____.

18. To find the perimeter of a square, I _____ the

    length(s) of _____ side(s).

19. To find the area of a square, I _____ the length(s)

    of _____ sides(s).

20. There are _____ degrees in a straight line.

21. A triangle has _____ angles, which total

    _____ degrees.

22. A four-sided figure contains _____ degrees.

23. An isosceles triangle has _____ equal sides; a(n)

    _____ triangle has three equal sides.

24. The longest side of a right triangle is called the _____

    and is located opposite the _____.

25. To find the area of a triangle, I use the formula _____.

Don't forget to
check your answers in
Chapter 9.

Chapter 7
SSAT Verbal

INTRODUCTION

The Verbal section on the SSAT consists of:

Elementary Level
You will have 15 synonyms and 15 analogies.

- 30 synonym questions (questions 1 to 30)
- 30 analogy questions (questions 31 to 60)

That's 60 questions—but you have only 30 minutes! Should you try to spend 30 seconds on each question to get them all done? NO!

You Mean I Don't Have to Answer All the Questions?

Nope. You'll actually improve your score by answering fewer questions, as long as you're still using all of the allotted time.

"Allotted Time"?
If you can't define *allotted*, make a flash card for it! Look in Chapter 1 for ideas on how to use flash cards to learn new words.

Remember, this test is designed for students in three or four different grade levels. There will be vocabulary in some of these questions that is aimed at students older than you, and almost no one in your grade will get those questions right. On the SSAT score report, you will be compared only with students in your own grade. The younger you are in your test level, the fewer questions you are expected to complete. Fifth graders are expected to do the least number of questions on the Middle Level test. Eighth graders are expected to do the least number of questions on the Upper Level test.

Why rush through the questions you can get right to get to the really tough ones that almost nobody gets? That approach only ensures that you will make hasty, careless errors. Work slowly on the questions that have vocabulary that you know to make sure you get them right. Then try the ones that have some advanced words in them.

Which Questions Should I Answer?

The questions are arranged in a rough order of difficulty—the more complex synonyms tend to come toward the end of the synonym section, and the advanced analogies tend to come at the end of the analogy section. However, everyone is different, and some questions are harder for certain people than they are for others. You know some words that your friends don't, and vice versa.

Bubble Practice
Whenever you do a practice test, use the sample answer sheet so you get used to skipping around when you're filling in bubbles.

You get as many points for a question you find easy as you do for one you find more complicated. So here's the plan: do all the questions that you find easy first. Easy questions will be those for which you know the definitions of all the words involved. Then go back through and do the questions with words that sound familiar, even if you are not sure of their dictionary definitions—these are words you sort of know. As you work through these questions, you'll probably be concentrating mostly on the beginning and middle of each section, but don't be afraid to glance ahead—there may be some words you know toward the end. Remember to skip a number on the answer sheet when you skip a question.

Knowing your own vocabulary is the key to quickly deciding if you can answer a question easily.

Know Yourself

Categorize the words you see in SSAT questions into:

- Words you know
- Words you sort of know
- Words you really don't know

Be honest with yourself when it comes to deciding whether you know a word or not so you can tell which of the techniques you learn in this book works best for each question you tackle. Keep your idea of the word's meaning flexible because the test writers sometimes use the words in ways that you and I do not! (They claim to use dictionary definitions.)

The easiest way to get a verbal question right is by making sure all the words in it fall into the first category—words you know. The best way to do this is by learning new vocabulary *every day*. Check out the Vocabulary chapter (Chapter 1) for the best ways to do this.

You can raise your verbal score moderately just by using the techniques we teach in this chapter. But if you want to see a substantial rise, you need to build up your vocabulary, too.

Eliminate Choices

With math questions, there's always a correct answer; the other answers are simply wrong. With verbal questions, however, things are not that simple. Words are much more slippery than numbers. So verbal questions have *best* answers, not *correct* ones. The other answers aren't necessarily wrong, but the people who score the SSAT think they're not as good as the *best* ones. This means that your goal is to eliminate *worse* choices in the Verbal and Reading sections.

Get used to looking for *worse* answers. There are many more of them than there are *best* answers, so *worse* answers are easier to find! When you find them, cross them out in the question booklet to make sure you don't spend any more time looking at them. No matter which other techniques you use to answer a question, eliminate wrong answers first instead of trying to magically pick out the best answer right away.

One thing to remember for the Verbal section: you should not eliminate choices that contain words you don't know. If you don't know what a word means, it could be the right answer.

> **Cross Out the Bad Ones**
> Even when none of the answers look particularly right, you can usually eliminate at least one.

What If I Can't Narrow It Down to One Answer?

Should you guess? Yes. If you can eliminate even one choice, you should guess from the remaining choices.

Where Do I Start?

In the Verbal section, do analogies first—they're easier to get right when you don't know all the words in the question.

Take two passes over each section, in the following order:

- analogies with words you know
- analogies with words you sort of know
- analogies with words you really don't know
- synonyms with words you know
- synonyms with words you sort of know

There is no need to ever try to attempt synonyms with words that you really don't know. You will rarely be able to eliminate choices in a synonym question for which you do not know the stem word.

REVIEW—THE VERBAL PLAN

Pacing and Verbal Strategy

When I start the Verbal section, with which question number do I start? _____

What's the order in which I answer questions in the Verbal section?

1. _____

2. _____

3. _____

4. _____

5. _____

How many choices must I have eliminated to guess productively? _____

Can I eliminate choices that contain words I don't know? _____

If you have trouble answering any of the questions above, reread this chapter!

Knowing My Vocabulary

Look at each of the following words and decide if it's a word that you know, sort of know, or really don't know. If you know it, write down its definition.

insecticide (noun)   _____

trifle (verb)   _____

repugnant (adjective)   _____

mollify (verb)   _____

camouflage (verb)   _____

historic (adjective)   _____

Use a dictionary to check the ones you thought you knew or sort of knew. Make flash cards for the ones you didn't know, the ones you sort of knew, and any that you thought you knew but for which you actually had the wrong definition.

ANALOGIES

What Is an Analogy?

An analogy, on the SSAT, asks you to:

1. Decide how two words are related.
2. Choose another set of words that has the same relationship.

It looks like this:

> A is to B as
>
> (A) C is to D
> (B) C is to D
> (C) C is to D
> (D) C is to D
> (E) C is to D

Or like this:

> A is to B as C is to
>
> (A) D
> (B) D
> (C) D
> (D) D
> (E) D

A, B, C, and D stand for words. We will call any words that are in the question part of the analogy the *stem words*. To figure out the relationship, ignore the "A is to B as C is to D" sentence that they've given you. It doesn't tell you what you need to know. Cross out "is to" and "as."

Next use the techniques that we describe on the next few pages depending on the words in the question. Get your pencil ready because you need to try these strategies out as we go along.

When You Know the Words

Make a Sentence
Here's an analogy for which you'll know all the words.

> Kitten is to cat as
>
> (A) bull is to cow
> (B) snake is to frog
> (C) squirrel is to raccoon
> (D) puppy is to dog
> (E) spider is to fly

You want to be sure you get a question like this one right because it's worth just as much as an advanced one. Here's how to be sure you don't make a careless mistake.

Picture what the first two words ("A" and "B") stand for and how those two words are related.

> Kitten is to cat as   (Cross out "is to" and "as."
>   Just picture a kitten and a cat.)

Shop Around
Try every choice in a verbal question to be sure you're picking the *best* answer there.

Make a sentence to describe what you see. (We sometimes call this a "definitional" sentence.) A good sentence will do two things:

- Define one of the words using the other one.

- Stay short and simple.

> A kitten _____ cat.
> (Make a sentence.)

Now look at the choices and eliminate any that cannot have the same relationship as the one you've got in your sentence.

> (A) bull is to cow
> (B) snake is to frog
> (C) squirrel is to raccoon
> (D) puppy is to dog
> (E) spider is to fly

If your sentence was something like "A kitten is a young cat," you can eliminate all but (D). After all, a bull is not a young cow; a snake is not a young frog; a squirrel is not a young raccoon; and a spider is not a young fly. If you had a sentence that did not work, think about how you would define a kitten. Stay away from sentences that use the word *you*, as in "You see kittens with female cats." Also avoid sentences like "A kitten is a cat." These sentences don't give you a definition or description of one of the words. Get specific. Yes, a kitten is a cat, but what *else* do you know about it?

As you go through the choices, cross out the choices as you eliminate them. In the kitten analogy, you probably knew that (D) was a good fit for your sentence, but don't stop there! Always check all the answers. On the SSAT, often a so-so answer will appear before the *best* answer in the choices, and you don't want to get sidetracked by it. Try *all* the answers so you can be sure to get all the analogies you find easy right.

In making your sentence, you can start with either of the first two words. Try to start your sentence by defining the first word, but if that doesn't work, start by defining the second word.

House is to tent as (Cross out "is to" and "as." Picture a house and a tent.)

A house _____ tent.

(Can you make a definitional sentence? Not really.)

A tent _____ house.

(Make a sentence. Now eliminate choices.)

House is to tent as bed is to

(A) table
(B) stool
(C) floor
(D) blanket
(E) hammock

Draw an arrow to remind yourself that you started with the second word instead of the first, as we have here. If you reverse the words in your sentence, you need to reverse them when you're trying out the choices, too. If you have a sentence like, "A tent is a temporary house," then you can eliminate all but (E).

Write your sentence above the question, between the two words. It's a good idea to do this as you start practicing analogies, and most students find it helpful to write out their sentences all the time. If you have a tendency to change your sentence as you go through the answers, you should always write it down.

Notice that in the house analogy, they've *given* you the first word of the answer pair. Some of the analogies will be like this, but they're really no different from the others. You'll still be using the same techniques for them, and you may find them a little easier.

Make Another Sentence

Why would you ever need to change your sentence? Let's see.

If at First You Don't Succeed...

Then try the other word! You can start your sentence with the first word (A) or the second word (B).

Motor is to car as
(Cross out. Picture them. Write a sentence. Eliminate.)

(A) knob is to door
(B) shovel is to earth
(C) bulb is to lamp
(D) sail is to boat
(E) pond is to ocean

Did you get it down to one? If not, make your sentence more specific. You may have said "A car has a motor," in which case you can only eliminate (B) and (E). The best words to use are active verbs and descriptive adjectives. What does a motor *do* for a car? Make a more specific sentence. (Remember to draw an arrow if you start with the word *car*.)

A motor makes a car move. You could also say that a car is powered by a motor. Either sentence will help you eliminate all but (D). When your sentence eliminates some, but not all, of the choices, make it more specific.

If you have trouble picturing the relationship or making a more specific sentence, ask yourself questions that will help you get at how the two words are related.

Below are some questions to ask yourself that will help you make sentences. ("A" and "B" are the first two words in the analogy. Remember, you can start with either one.) Refer back to these questions if you get stuck when trying to make a sentence.

Help!
These questions will help you come up with a sentence that defines one of the words in an analogy. Refer to them as much as you need to, until you are asking yourself these questions automatically.

- What does A/B do?
- What does A/B mean?
- How does A/B work?
- What does A/B look like?
- How is A/B used?
- Where is A/B found?
- How do A and B compare?
- How are A and B associated?

PRACTICE DRILL 1—MAKING SENTENCES

Try making a sentence for each of these analogies for which you know both words. Use the questions above to guide you if you have trouble. Avoid using "A is B" or "A is the opposite of B." Instead, try using "has" or "lacks," or you can use "with" or "without." Use active verbs. Check your sentences in Chapter 9 before you move on to the next practice set. Don't forget to time yourself!

1. Chapter is to book as _____ is a section of a _____

2. Scale is to weight as _____

3. Striped is to lines as _____

4. Anger is to rage as _____

5. Rehearsal is to performance as _____

6. Mechanic is to car as _____

7. Traitor is to country as _____

8. Aggravate is to problem as _____

9. Trout is to fish as _____

10. General is to army as _____

11. Law is to crime as _____

12. Buckle is to belt as _____

13. Truculent is to fight as _____

14. Cure is to illness as _____

15. Toxic is to poison as _____

16. Mountain is to pinnacle as _____

17. Perilous is to safety as _____

18. Humanitarian is to philanthropy as _____

19. Notorious is to reputation as _____

20. Miser is to generosity as _____

> **When You Are Done**
> Make flash cards for the words you sort of know or don't know at all.

PRACTICE DRILL 2—BASIC ANALOGY TECHNIQUES

For each analogy that has words you know:

- Make a sentence.
- Try out your sentence on the choices.
- Eliminate the choices that don't fit.
- If you need to, make your sentence more specific and eliminate again.
- If there are words you don't know or just sort of know in a question, skip it.
- If there are words you don't know or just sort of know in a choice, do not eliminate it. Just narrow your choices down as far as you can.
- As always, look up the words you can't define and write them down on flash cards.

When you are done, check your answers in Chapter 9.

1. Chapter is to book as

   (A) glass is to water
   (B) lamp is to light
   (C) scene is to play
   (D) stew is to meat
   (E) elevator is to building

2. Refrigerator is to cool as furnace is to

   (A) radiator
   (B) house
   (C) oil
   (D) heat
   (E) furniture

3. Fish is to fin as

   (A) fruit is to stem
   (B) bird is to wing
   (C) insect is to shell
   (D) cod is to school
   (E) dog is to tail

4. Driver is to car as

   (A) pilot is to airplane
   (B) police officer is to highway
   (C) secretary is to letter
   (D) baker is to cake
   (E) carpenter is to house

5. Clock is to time as thermometer is to

   (A) air
   (B) pressure
   (C) wind
   (D) ice
   (E) temperature

6. Envelope is to letter as

   (A) suitcase is to clothes
   (B) pen is to paper
   (C) box is to cardboard
   (D) table is to wood
   (E) frame is to picture

7. Librarian is to library as curator is to

   (A) museum
   (B) studio
   (C) mall
   (D) workshop
   (E) garden

8. Pen is to write as

   (A) pencil is to point
   (B) actor is to perform
   (C) knife is to cut
   (D) desk is to sit
   (E) ink is to stain

9. Hurricane is to breeze as

   (A) storm is to tempest
   (B) fire is to flame
   (C) tidal wave is to ripple
   (D) cloud is to sunlight
   (E) temperature is to weather

10. Circle is to ball as

    (A) square is to cube
    (B) pyramid is to triangle
    (C) point is to line
    (D) side is to rectangle
    (E) hexagon is to polygon

11. Egg is to shell as banana is to

    (A) fruit
    (B) tree
    (C) bunch
    (D) peel
    (E) seed

12. Cup is to quart as

    (A)   week is to time
    (B)   minute is to hour
    (C)   liter is to metric
    (D)   coin is to dollar
    (E)   spoon is to measure

13. Coach is to team as

    (A)   captain is to platoon
    (B)   singer is to chorus
    (C)   batter is to baseball
    (D)   teacher is to homework
    (E)   king is to queen

14. Bat is to mammal as

    (A)   boar is to hog
    (B)   porpoise is to shark
    (C)   butterfly is to insect
    (D)   whale is to fish
    (E)   reptile is to lizard

15. Famished is to hungry as

    (A)   clean is to dirty
    (B)   destitute is to poor
    (C)   worried is to lonely
    (D)   misdirected is to lost
    (E)   worried is to scared

16. Sterilize is to germ as

    (A)   cut is to surgeon
    (B)   sneeze is to dust
    (C)   scour is to grime
    (D)   inject is to virus
    (E)   rinse is to mouth

17. Director is to actors as conductor is to

    (A)   writers
    (B)   dancers
    (C)   painters
    (D)   musicians
    (E)   playwrights

18. Applicant is to hire as

    (A) judge is to jury
    (B) candidate is to elect
    (C) cashier is to work
    (D) student is to study
    (E) writer is to research

19. Stale is to bread as

    (A) American is to cheese
    (B) rancid is to meat
    (C) thick is to milk
    (D) dry is to rice
    (E) pulpy is to juice

20. Prejudice is to unbiased as worry is to

    (A) adamant
    (B) active
    (C) blithe
    (D) concerned
    (E) occupied

When You Know Only One of the Words

Working Backward

If you know only one of the words, go straight to the choices. Make a sentence with each choice. Keep your sentence as definitional as possible. If your sentence uses *can* or *might* or *could*, or if you find yourself really reaching to try to make up a sentence, then the relationship is not a strong definitional one and that answer is probably not right. Eliminate it. Each time you can create a good sentence with an choice, you should then try the sentence with the stem words. If you don't know a word in a choice, do not eliminate it.

Cygnet is to swan as

(A)	chicken is to egg	a chicken lays eggs—a cygnet lays swans?
(B)	frog is to snake	a snake can eat a frog—not strong
(C)	turtle is to raccoon	no sentence—not strong
(D)	puppy is to dog	a puppy is a young dog—a cygnet is a young swan?
(E)	spider is to fly	some spiders eat flies—not strong

Pick the *best* or most likely relationship for *cygnet* and *swan*. Which relationship is most like a definition?

Cross out (C), because we couldn't make a sentence at all. Choices (B) and (E) are not great because snakes and spiders eat other things, too, and their definitions are not based on what they eat. Eliminate them. Now look at (A) and (D). Try their sentences on the stem words. Could something lay a swan? Probably not! Could something be a young swan? Sure, there could be a word that means *baby swan*. Sure enough, *cygnet* is exactly that.

Try Working Backward with these analogies.

Kinesiology is to motion as

(A)   numerology is to progress   _____

(B)   navigation is to ocean   _____

(C)   astronomy is to weather   _____

(D)   criminology is to perversion   _____

(E)   psychology is to mind   _____

Only (B) and (E) allow you to make strong sentences. Navigation is how you get around on the ocean. Psychology is the study of the mind. So try those sentences: Could kinesiology be how you get around on the motion? No. Could kinesiology be the study of human motion? Yep. We got it down to (E).

Apiary is to bees as

(A)   stable is to horses   _____

(B)   jar is to honey   _____

(C)   florist is to flowers   _____

(D)   dirt is to ants   _____

(E)   leash is to dog   _____

Eliminate (B), (D), and (E) because the word relationships are not strong. A stable is a place where horses are kept. A florist is someone who works with flowers. Now, do you think that an apiary is a place where bees are kept? Possibly. Do you think an apiary is someone who works with bees? Also possible. Take a guess between (A) and (C). Look up *apiary* and make a flash card for it.

PRACTICE DRILL 3—WORKING BACKWARD

We've hidden one of the words in the stem pair, so you can't know it. But you'll still be able to take a good guess at the answer. Work backward.

- Make sentences with the choices.
- Eliminate the sentences that don't show a strong, definitional relationship.
- Try out each definitional sentence on the stem words.
- If it helps, say "something" when you have to insert the unknown word.
- Does it seem possible that the unknown word has that definition? If not, eliminate it.
- Don't eliminate any choices that contain words you don't know.
- Get as far as you can, and then guess.

When you are done, check your answers in Chapter 9.

1.   Island is to ??????? as

    (A)   castle is to moat
    (B)   star is to galaxy
    (C)   river is to delta
    (D)   bay is to peninsula
    (E)   earth is to hemisphere

2.   ??????? is to king as

    (A)   legality is to lawyer
    (B)   monarchy is to sovereign
    (C)   hierarchy is to heir
    (D)   feudalism is to farmer
    (E)   duplicity is to thief

3.   ??????? is to enthusiasm as submissive is to

    (A)   solitude
    (B)   defiance
    (C)   conviction
    (D)   admiration
    (E)   withdrawn

4.   ??????? is to jury as

    (A)   eradicate is to problem
    (B)   quarantine is to patient
    (C)   elect is to politician
    (D)   liquidate is to opponent
    (E)   evacuate is to city

5.   ??????? is to shape as

    (A)   amorous is to trust
    (B)   temporal is to patience
    (C)   enticing is to guile
    (D)   bland is to zest
    (E)   classical is to harmony

When You Sort of Know the Words

Use "Side of the Fence"

If you can't make a definitional sentence because you're not sure what the words mean, but you've got some idea from having seen the words before, determine whether the words are on the same side of the fence or different sides. That is, are they similar enough to be grouped together, or are they different enough that you'd say they're on different sides of a fence? If they are similar in meaning, write "S" next to the pair. If their meanings are more like opposites, write "D." So cat and kitten would get an "S," while black and white would get a "D."

Because the answer pair has to have the same relationship as that of the stem words, you can eliminate any answers that don't match. If your words are similar, you can eliminate any answers that are different. If your words are different, you can eliminate any answers that are similar.

PRACTICE DRILL 4—JUDGING "SIDE OF THE FENCE"

Mark the following pairs of words as "S" (similar) or "D" (different).

1. healthy is to ailing _____
2. limitless is to end _____
3. rapture is to happiness _____
4. humane is to brutality _____
5. obscure is to sight _____
6. incendiary is to flame _____
7. apathetic is to passion _____
8. boast is to vain _____
9. tactful is to diplomacy _____
10. innocent is to guile _____
11. miser is to greedy _____
12. frivolous is to serious _____

Now we can try a whole analogy.

Lurid is to horror as

(A) comical is to amusement
(B) illegal is to law
(C) cowardly is to fear
(D) ghastly is to serenity
(E) humane is to treatment

Don't try to make a sentence—just decide if *lurid* and *horror* are similar or different. Then make the same decision for all the choices. You should wind up with a question that looks as follows:

Lurid is to horror as   S

(A) comical is to amusement   S
(B̶) illegal is to law   D
(C) cowardly is to fear   S
(D̶) ghastly is to serenity   D
(E̶) humane is to treatment   nice phrase, but it's
                                                          not a relationship

Now you can guess from just two answers—you've increased your odds considerably! Remember to mark up your test booklet as you eliminate, and guess even if you've eliminated only one choice. If you're not sure of the definition of *lurid*, or any other word on this page, make a flash card for it!

PRACTICE DRILL 5—USING "SIDE OF THE FENCE"

In these analogies, we've taken out the stem words but told you whether they're similar or different. Eliminate the answers that you know are definitely wrong because you've written a letter next to them that doesn't match the letter next to the stem words. Remember, you can't eliminate answers that contain words you don't know!

1. (SIMILAR WORDS)

   (A) miserly is to greed
   (B) gentle is to harm
   (C) famous is to privacy
   (D) objective is to opinion
   (E) fanciful is to theory

2. (SIMILAR WORDS)

   (A) athletic is to shapely
   (B) darkened is to light
   (C) free is to liberated
   (D) brave is to cowardly
   (E) normal is to unusual

3. (DIFFERENT WORDS)

   (A) refurbish is to worn
   (B) repaint is to beautiful
   (C) shining is to new
   (D) revive is to tired
   (E) cultivate is to fertile

4. (SIMILAR WORDS)

   (A) humid is to moisture
   (B) displeased is to anger
   (C) silent is to discourse
   (D) pointless is to relevance
   (E) guilty is to neutral

5. (DIFFERENT WORDS)

   (A) flourish is to revive
   (B) wilt is to deaden
   (C) protect is to harm
   (D) heal is to injure
   (E) discuss is to debate

6. (DIFFERENT WORDS)

   (A) modify is to vary
   (B) mutter is to speak
   (C) vacillate is to stand
   (D) rectify is to fix
   (E) verify is to discover

7. (DIFFERENT WORDS)

   (A) charitable is to selfish
   (B) favorable is to despised
   (C) productive is to arid
   (D) predictable is to ordinary
   (E) verbose is to tacit

8. (SIMILAR WORDS)

   (A) anticipate is to hope
   (B) alleviate is to lessen
   (C) innovate is to predict
   (D) disseminate is to gather
   (E) elucidate is to muddle

9. (SIMILAR WORDS)

   (A) slander is to libel
   (B) avenge is to forgive
   (C) provoke is to calm
   (D) quibble is to argue
   (E) satiate is to fill

10. (SIMILAR WORDS)

   (A) supreme is to zenith
   (B) infallible is to certain
   (C) prevalent is to vacant
   (D) listless is to energetic
   (E) pessimistic is to negative

Don't forget to
check your answers in
Chapter 9.

Work Backward

You can use this technique for words you just sort of know, in addition to using it on analogies where you just know one of the words. Try it on this one. *Patent* is a word we all sort of know.

Patent is to inventor as

(A)   advertisement is to merchant   _____

(B)   money is to consumer   _____

(C)   monopoly is to customer   _____

(D)   copyright is to author   _____

(E)   novelty is to journalist   _____

Choices (C) and (E) should be crossed out for sure—the words are not strongly related. You've made sentences with the other choices. Which sentence works best with *patent* and *inventor*? Choice (D).

When You Really Don't Know Either of the Words

If you have never seen the stem words before, you're better off putting a circle around the question number in the test booklet and skipping the question. If you have time to go back to the ones you've circled and skipped, then try this.

Work Backward as Much as You Can

Go straight to the choices, and make sentences with them. Now, you can't try the sentences with the stem words because you don't know the stem words, right? So just look at the sentences you have. Which ones are not likely to be correct? The ones that are not like definitions. Eliminate those choices—the ones in which the words are not related in such a way that you need one to define the other.

Look at these possible choices and decide if they're definitional or if you should eliminate them on a question for which you do not know the stem words. Write a sentence for the answers you'd keep.

PRACTICE DRILL 6—WORKING BACKWARD AS MUCH AS YOU CAN

1. tooth is to chewing _____

2. hammer is to wood _____

3. archipelago is to islands _____

4. engine is to smoke _____

5. angry is to violence _____

6. jest is to humorous _____

7. wind is to season _____

Remember that you're not trying to answer all the questions. There are bound to be words on the test that you do not know. Don't sweat it. Check your Pacing Chart to see how many analogies you need to complete. To reach their target scores, most students don't need to attempt analogies with words they don't know at all.

Review—The Analogies Plan

If I Know the Words

If I know the words, then I

_____

_____

_____

A sentence is good if it's _____ and _____ .

If my sentence eliminates some, but not all, choices, I can

_____

_____

A specific, definitional sentence uses words that are _____

Some questions that can help me make a sentence are

_____   _____

_____   _____

_____   _____

If I know the words but can't make a sentence, then I ask myself

_____

_____

_____

_____

_____

_____

And finally, if none of these questions works with A and B (the first two words in the analogy), then I ask myself

_____

If I Know One of the Words

If I know one of the words, then I _____

which means that I _____

and then I _____

If I Sort of Know the Words

If I sort of know the words, then I _____

I can also _____

If I Don't Know the Words

If I don't know the words, I _____

If I have time left, then I go back and _____

If you have trouble with any of the questions above, go back and reread the appropriate part of this chapter.

PRACTICE DRILL 7—ALL ANALOGIES TECHNIQUES

Elementary Level
Stop after question 13.

The following questions ask you to find relationships between words. For each question, select the answer choice that best completes the meaning of the sentence.

1. Chocolate is to candy as
   (A) fish is to mammal
   (B) meat is to animal
   (C) cat is to animal
   (D) brick is to house
   (E) fire is to forest

2. Pound is to weight as
   (A) decibel is to sound
   (B) inch is to foot
   (C) quart is to liter
   (D) fathom is to height
   (E) length is to distance

3. Class is to student as
   (A) cast is to actor
   (B) teacher is to staff
   (C) conductor is to band
   (D) director is to play
   (E) musician is to band

4. Composer is to symphony as
   (A) mechanic is to auto
   (B) major is to troops
   (C) architect is to building
   (D) tycoon is to wealth
   (E) writer is to paragraph

5. Link is to chain as
   (A) obstacle is to course
   (B) group is to member
   (C) sidewalk is to path
   (D) mural is to museum
   (E) word is to sentence

6. Tadpole is to frog as caterpillar is to
   (A) worm
   (B) cocoon
   (C) crawl
   (D) larvae
   (E) butterfly

7. Cuff is to wrist as
   (A) string is to hood
   (B) buckle is to waist
   (C) cap is to hat
   (D) vest is to body
   (E) collar is to neck

8. Congregation is to worshippers as
   (A) galaxy is to stars
   (B) party is to politics
   (C) mine is to gems
   (D) job is to employers
   (E) pottery is to shards

9. Tactile is to touch as
   (A) delectable is to drink
   (B) audible is to sound
   (C) potable is to food
   (D) servile is to obey
   (E) nutritious is to meal

10. Conviction is to opinion as
   (A) report is to story
   (B) reverence is to admiration
   (C) debate is to argument
   (D) appeal is to affectation
   (E) ascend is to precipice

11. Caricature is to drawing as
   (A) joke is to punch line
   (B) watercolor is to painting
   (C) hyperbole is to statement
   (D) star is to feature
   (E) dynamite is to blast

12. Deceleration is to speed as
   (A) adulation is to praise
   (B) descent is to altitude
   (C) tyranny is to leader
   (D) hydration is to water
   (E) fear is to hatred

13. Dull is to insipid as diverting is to
   (A) expecting
   (B) feeling
   (C) astounding
   (D) entertaining
   (E) surprising

14. Voracious is to food as
   (A) greedy is to money
   (B) gluttonous is to obesity
   (C) clarity is to water
   (D) generosity is to object
   (E) veracity is to truth

15. Adroit is to motion as
    (A) bridled is to emotion
    (B) unfettered is to restraint
    (C) superior is to skill
    (D) ubiquitous is to presence
    (E) articulate is to speech

16. Anesthetic is to pain as
    (A) lamp is to light
    (B) mnemonic is to memory
    (C) exercise is to diet
    (D) understanding is to comprehension
    (E) muffler is to noise

17. Impeccable is to adequate as
    (A) impressionable is to eager
    (B) inexhaustible is to sufficient
    (C) impossible is to prepared
    (D) intangible is to popular
    (E) impractical is to sensible

18. Symmetrical is to amorphous as
    (A) metric is to moronic
    (B) shapely is to muscled
    (C) balanced is to unshaped
    (D) flowing is to lined
    (E) external is to internal

19. Incessant is to intermittent
    (A) amazed is to underwhelming
    (B) horizontal is to inclined
    (C) celebrated is to opulent
    (D) timid is to brazen
    (E) eternal is to perpetual

20. Penicillin is to antibiotic
    (A) healthcare is to pharmacist
    (B) medicine is to prescription
    (C) coughing is to symptom
    (D) mold is to bacteria
    (E) antibacterial is to sanitization

21. Cobbler is to shoe
    (A) tanner is to horse
    (B) blacksmith is to sword
    (C) porter is to doorbell
    (D) dentist is to floss
    (E) nurse is to symptoms

22. Fortify is to protect
    (A) blitz is to attack
    (B) evoke is to elicit
    (C) pacify is to incense
    (D) recommend is to advocate
    (E) invite is to accompany

23. Delinquent is to reprimand
    (A) thief is to steal
    (B) virtuoso is to recognize
    (C) prophet is to trust
    (D) jury is to deliberate
    (E) tutor is to guide

24. Disinfect is to pristine
    (A) insult is to grateful
    (B) swim is to upstream
    (C) shape is to bend
    (D) adore is to envious
    (E) learn is to uncomplicated

25. Inconspicuous is to overlook as unfounded is to
    (A) scorn
    (B) investigate
    (C) reject
    (D) convolute
    (E) offend

26. Student is to graduate
    (A) guru is to savant
    (B) connoisseur is to amateur
    (C) famine is to feast
    (D) dilettante is to dabbler
    (E) novice is to master

27. Appreciative is to gratitude
    (A) ashamed is to compunction
    (B) amicable is to aloofness
    (C) ravenous is to starvation
    (D) pity is to destitute
    (E) meticulous is to adoration

28. Egg is to dozen
    (A) player is to crowd
    (B) day is to week
    (C) puppies is to litter
    (D) goose is to gaggle
    (E) day is to month

29. Illogical is to reason
    (A) rude is to impertinence
    (B) classified is to catalogue
    (C) hasty is to prudence
    (D) brazen is to plethora
    (E) improvised is to spontaneity

30. Payment is to debt
    (A) relief is to hurricane
    (B) cover-up is to crime
    (C) injury is to repair
    (D) recall is to defect
    (E) blanket is to snow

Don't forget to
check your answers in
Chapter 9.

SYNONYMS

What Is a Synonym?

On the SSAT, a synonym question asks you to choose the choice that comes closest in meaning to the stem word (the word in capitals). Often the best answer won't mean the exact same thing as the stem word, but it will be closer than any of the other choices.

Just like analogies, you need to decide which vocabulary category the synonym stem word falls into for you, so you know which technique to use. First, try all the synonyms for which you know the stem word, and then go back and try the ones with stem words you sort of know.

When You Know the Stem Word

Write Down Your Own Definition

Come up with a simple definition—a word or a phrase. Write it next to the stem word. Then look at the answers, eliminate the ones that are farthest from your definition, and choose the closest one.

It's very simple. Don't let the test writers put words into your mouth. Make sure you're armed with your own definition before you look at their choices. They often like to put in a word that is a close second to the best answer, and if you've got your own synonym ready, you'll be able to make the distinction.

If you need to, cover the answers with your hand, so you can think of your definition before looking. Eventually you may not have to write down your definitions, but you should start out that way.

As you compare the choices with your definition, cross out the ones that are definitely not right. Crossing out choices is something you should *always* do—it saves you time because you don't go back to choices you've already decided were not the best.

As always, don't eliminate the words you don't know.

Try this one. Write your definition of WITHER before you look at the choices.

WITHER: _____ (definition)

(A) play
(B) spoil
(C) greatly improve
(D) wilt
(E) give freely

The stem word means *shrivel* or *dry up*. Which answer is closest? (D). You may have been considering (B), but (D) is closer.

PRACTICE DRILL 8—WRITE YOUR OWN DEFINITION

Write your definition—just a word or two—for each of these stem words.

1. BIZARRE: _____

2. PREFACE: _____

3. GENEROUS: _____

4. MORAL (n): _____

5. ALTER: _____

6. REVOLVE: _____

7. HOPEFUL: _____

8. LINGER: _____

9. ASSIST: _____

10. CONSTRUCT: _____

11. STOOP: _____

12. CANDID: _____

13. TAUNT: _____

14. COARSE: _____

15. VAIN: _____

16. SERENE: _____

17. UTILIZE: _____

18. VIGOROUS: _____

19. PROLONG: _____

20. BENEFIT: _____

Write Another Definition

Why would you ever need to change your definition? Let's see.

> MANEUVER:
>
> (A) avoidance
> (B) deviation
> (C) find
> (D) contrivance
> (E) invent

Your definition may be something like *move* or *control* if you know the word from hearing it applied to cars. But that definition isn't in the choices. The problem is that you're thinking about *maneuver* as a verb. However, *maneuver* can also be a noun. It means *a plan, scheme,* or *trick*. Now go back and eliminate. The answer is (D).

The SSAT sometimes uses secondary definitions, which can be the same part of speech or a different part of speech from the primary definition. Just stay flexible in your definitions, and you'll be fine.

PRACTICE DRILL 9—WRITE ANOTHER DEFINITION

Write down as many definitions as you can think of for the following words. Your definitions may be the same part of speech or different. If you have a hard time thinking of different meanings, look the word up.

1. POINT: _____

2. INDUSTRY: _____

3. FLAG: _____

4. FLUID: _____

5. CHAMPION: _____

6. TABLE: _____

7. SERVICE: _____

PRACTICE DRILL 10—BASIC SYNONYM TECHNIQUES

Try these synonyms.

- Use the definition for the stem word that you wrote down before.
- Look at the choices and eliminate the ones that are farthest from your definition.

1. BIZARRE:
   - (A) lonely
   - (B) unable
   - (C) odd
   - (D) found
   - (E) able

2. PREFACE:
   - (A) introduce
   - (B) state
   - (C) propose
   - (D) jumble
   - (E) make able

3. GENEROUS:
   - (A) skimpy
   - (B) faulty
   - (C) ample
   - (D) unusual
   - (E) cold

4. MORAL:
   - (A) imitation
   - (B) full
   - (C) real
   - (D) upright
   - (E) sure

5. ALTER:
   - (A) sew
   - (B) make up
   - (C) react
   - (D) total
   - (E) change

6. REVOLVE:
   - (A) push against
   - (B) go forward
   - (C) leave behind
   - (D) turn around
   - (E) move past

7. HOPEFUL:

   (A) discouraging
   (B) promising
   (C) fulfilling
   (D) deceiving
   (E) frustrating

8. LINGER:

   (A) hurry
   (B) abate
   (C) dawdle
   (D) attempt
   (E) enter

9. ASSIST:

   (A) work
   (B) discourage
   (C) appeal
   (D) hinder
   (E) help

10. CONSTRUCT:

    (A) build
    (B) type
    (C) live in
    (D) engage
    (E) enable

11. STOOP:

    (A) raise
    (B) elevate
    (C) condescend
    (D) realize
    (E) imagine

12. CANDID:

    (A) picture
    (B) honest
    (C) prepared
    (D) unfocused
    (E) rehearsed

13. TAUNT:

    (A) delay
    (B) stand
    (C) show
    (D) horrify
    (E) tease

14. COARSE:

    (A) smooth
    (B) crude
    (C) polite
    (D) furious
    (E) emotional

15. VAIN:

    (A) conceited
    (B) beautiful
    (C) talented
    (D) unattractive
    (E) helpless

16. SERENE:

    (A) helpful
    (B) normal
    (C) calm
    (D) disastrous
    (E) floating

17. UTILIZE:

    (A) pass on
    (B) break down
    (C) resort to
    (D) rely on
    (E) make use of

18. VIGOROUS:

    (A) slothful
    (B) aimless
    (C) energetic
    (D) glorious
    (E) victorious

19. PROLONG:

    (A) affirmative
    (B) lengthen
    (C) exceed
    (D) assert
    (E) resolve

20. BENEFIT:

    (A) cooperate
    (B) struggle
    (C) assist
    (D) deny
    (E) appeal

Don't forget to check your answers in Chapter 9.

When You Sort of Know the Stem Word

Why Should You Attempt Synonyms Last? Why Are They More Complicated than Analogies?

Synonyms can be harder to beat than analogies because the SSAT gives you no context with which to figure out words that you sort of know. But that doesn't mean you should try to answer only the synonyms you find easy. You can get the medium ones, too. You just need to create your own context to figure out words you don't know very well.

Keep in mind that your goal is to eliminate the worst answers, to make an educated guess. You'll be able to do this for every synonym that you sort of know, and even if you just eliminate one choice, *guess*. You'll gain points overall.

Make Your Own Context

You can create your own context for the word by figuring out how you've heard it used before. Think of the other words you've heard used with the stem word. Is there a certain phrase that comes to mind? What does that phrase mean?

If you still can't come up with a definition for the stem word, just use the context in which you've heard the word to eliminate answers that wouldn't fit at all in that same context.

How about this stem word:

ABOMINABLE

Where have you heard *abominable*? The Abominable Snowman, of course. Think about it—you know it's a monster-like creature. Which choices can you eliminate?

ABOMINABLE:

(A)	enormous	*the enormous snowman? maybe*
(B)	terrible	*the terrible snowman? sure*
~~(C)~~	rude	*the rude snowman? probably not*
~~(D)~~	showy	*the showy snowman? nope*
~~(E)~~	talkative	*the talkative snowman? only Frosty!*

You can throw out everything but (A) and (B). Now you can guess, with a much better shot at getting the answer right than guessing from five choices. Or you can think about where else you've heard the stem word. Have you ever heard something called an *abomination*? Was it something terrible or was it something enormous? Choice (B) is the answer.

Try this one. Where have you heard this stem word? Try the answers in that context.

SURROGATE:

(A) friendly
(B) requested
(C) paranoid
(D) numerous
(E) substitute

Have you heard the stem word in *surrogate mother*? If you have, you can definitely eliminate (B), (C), and (D), and (A) isn't great either. A surrogate mother is a substitute mother.

Try one more.

ENDANGER:

(A) rescue
(B) frighten
(C) confuse
(D) threaten
(E) isolate

Everyone's associations are different, but you've probably heard of *endangered species* or *endangered lives*. Use either of those phrases to eliminate choices that can't fit into it. Rescued species? Frightened species? Confused species? Threatened species? Isolated species? Choice (D) works best.

PRACTICE DRILL 11—MAKING YOUR OWN CONTEXT

Write down the phrase in which you've heard each word.

1. COMMON:_____

2. COMPETENT: _____

3. ABRIDGE : _____

4. UNTIMELY: _____

5. HOMOGENIZE: _____

6. DELINQUENT: _____

7. INALIENABLE: _____

8. PALTRY: _____

9. AUSPICIOUS: _____

10. PRODIGAL: _____

PRACTICE DRILL 12—USING YOUR OWN CONTEXT

1. COMMON:

   (A) beautiful
   (B) novel
   (C) typical
   (D) constant
   (E) similar

2. COMPETENT:

   (A) angry
   (B) peaceful
   (C) well-written
   (D) capable
   (E) possible

3. ABRIDGE:

   (A) complete
   (B) span
   (C) reach
   (D) shorten
   (E) retain

4. UNTIMELY:

   (A) late
   (B) punctual
   (C) dependent
   (D) inappropriate
   (E) continuous

5. HOMOGENIZE:

   (A) make the same
   (B) send away
   (C) isolate
   (D) enfold
   (E) purify quickly

6. DELINQUENT:

   (A) underage
   (B) negligent
   (C) superior
   (D) advanced
   (E) independent

7. INALIENABLE:

   (A) misplaced
   (B) universal
   (C) assured
   (D) democratic
   (E) changeable

8. PALTRY:

   (A) meager
   (B) colored
   (C) thick
   (D) abundant
   (E) indistinguishable

9. AUSPICIOUS:

   (A) supple
   (B) minor
   (C) doubtful
   (D) favorable
   (E) ominous

10. PRODIGAL:

   (A) wasteful
   (B) amusing
   (C) disadvantaged
   (D) lazy
   (E) virtuous

> Don't forget to
> check your answers in
> Chapter 9.

Use Word Parts to Piece Together a Definition

Prefixes, roots, and suffixes can help you figure out what a word means. You should use this technique in addition to (not instead of) word association, because not all word parts retain their original meanings.

You may have never seen this stem word before, but if you've been working on your Vocabulary chapter, you know that the root *pac* or *peac* means peace. You can see the same root in *Pacific,* *pacifier,* and the word *peace* itself. So what's the answer to this synonym?

PACIFIST:

   (A) innocent person
   (B) person opposed to war
   (C) warmonger
   (D) wanderer of lands
   (E) journeyman

The answer is (B).

In the following stem word, we see *cred*, a word part that means "belief" or "faith." You can see this word part in *incredible*, *credit*, and *credibility*. The answer is now simple.

CREDIBLE:

(A) obsolete
(B) believable
(C) fabulous
(D) mundane
(E) superficial

Choice (B) again. What are the word parts in the following stem word?

MONOTONOUS:

(A) lively
(B) educational
(C) nutritious
(D) repetitious
(E) helpful

Mono means "one." *Tone* has to do with sound. If something keeps striking one sound, how would you describe it? (D) is the answer.

The only way you'll be able to use root words is if you know them. Get cracking on the Vocabulary chapter!

Words You Really Don't Know
Don't waste time on words you've never seen if you don't know any of their word parts.

PRACTICE DRILL 13—ALL SYNONYMS TECHNIQUES

Directions: Each of the following questions consists of one word followed by five words or phrases. You are to select the one word or phrase whose meaning is closest to the word in capital letters.

Elementary Level
Stop after question 10.

1. ATROCITY:
   (A) hardship
   (B) abomination
   (C) punishment
   (D) utopia
   (E) fortress

2. INDULGENT:
   (A) spoiled
   (B) dugout
   (C) doting
   (D) insolent
   (E) overwhelming

3. REPROACH:
   (A) reinvent
   (B) replenish
   (C) refinish
   (D) reinstate
   (E) rebuke

4. SCANT:
   (A) spare
   (B) ample
   (C) inconsistent
   (D) insufficient
   (E) noticeable

5. ANNIHILATE:
   (A) obliterate
   (B) repair
   (C) heal
   (D) annotate
   (E) undermine

6. AMENDMENT:
   (A) law
   (B) sanction
   (C) endorsement
   (D) correction
   (E) meeting

7. EMULATE:
   (A) simulate
   (B) evaluate
   (C) copy
   (D) instigate
   (E) forge

8. EPITOME:
   (A) epicenter
   (B) paradox
   (C) apex
   (D) embodiment
   (E) paradigm

9. COUNTENANCE:
   (A) self-importance
   (B) appearance
   (C) creativity
   (D) empathy
   (E) disdain

10. COMMANDEER:
    (A) sanction
    (B) authorize
    (C) seize
    (D) instruction
    (E) entertain

11. RESILIENT:
    (A) rebounding
    (B) affluent
    (C) silent
    (D) extravagant
    (E) resounding

12. VAGRANT:
    (A) roaming
    (B) fibrous
    (C) irritable
    (D) varied
    (E) allowed

13. EVICT:
    (A) strain
    (B) prosper
    (C) incite
    (D) eject
    (E) remain

14. PROLIFERATE:
    (A) perforate
    (B) stem
    (C) generate
    (D) contract
    (E) destroy

15. ADHERE
    (A) fracture
    (B) hold off
    (C) lose
    (D) surround
    (E) obey

16. DISCREPANCY
    (A) qualm
    (B) unique
    (C) scrupulous
    (D) disparity
    (E) conspicuous

17. INCREDULOUS
    (A) complicated
    (B) believable
    (C) voluminous
    (D) skeptical
    (E) envious

18. INVOKE
    (A) rebuke
    (B) invest
    (C) summon
    (D) innovate
    (E) take away

19. OPULENT
    (A) indolent
    (B) vocal
    (C) haughty
    (D) luxurious
    (E) ovular

20. ARSENAL
    (A) fire pit
    (B) supply
    (C) pavement
    (D) barracks
    (E) commander

21. VIRTUOSO
    (A) realistic
    (B) righteous
    (C) moral
    (D) master
    (E) pious

22. SAGE
    (A) foolish
    (B) herbal
    (C) sumptuous
    (D) ancient
    (E) insightful

23. VISTA
    (A) wisdom
    (B) industrial
    (C) rural
    (D) view
    (E) port

24. SURREPTITIOUS
    (A) secret
    (B) understanding
    (C) successful
    (D) shocking
    (E) unexpected

25. PERTURBATION
    (A) commotion
    (B) excitement
    (C) consternation
    (D) understanding
    (E) jurisdiction

26. MERCURIAL
    (A) stern
    (B) melancholy
    (C) effusive
    (D) erratic
    (E) cunning

27. ACQUIESCE
    (A) control
    (B) acquire
    (C) quiet
    (D) gratify
    (E) consent

28. INSUBORDINATE
    (A) subdued
    (B) obedient
    (C) defiant
    (D) grateful
    (E) suppressed

29. QUERULOUS
    (A) winsome
    (B) whining
    (C) spiteful
    (D) arguing
    (E) crafty

30. ENERVATE
    (A) drain
    (B) unnerve
    (C) irritate
    (D) energize
    (E) provoke

Don't forget to check your answers in Chapter 9.

Chapter 8
SSAT Reading

AN OPEN BOOK TEST

Keep in mind when you approach the Reading Section of the test that *it is an open book test*. But you can't read the passages in advance of the test to prepare, and you have a limited amount of time to get through the passages and questions. So, what does this all mean? You will be much better served to take a *strategic* approach.

Read with a Purpose

When you read for school, you have to read everything—carefully. Not only is there no time for such an approach on the SSAT, but reading carefully at the outset does not even make sense. Each passage has only a few questions, and all you need to read and process is the information that will provide answers to those questions. As only questions can generate points, your goal is to get to the questions as quickly as possible.

Even so, it does help to have a high-level overview of the passage before you attack the questions. There are two ways to accomplish this goal.

- If you are a fairly fast reader, get through the passage quickly, ignoring the nitty-gritty and focusing on the overall point of each paragraph.
- If you don't read quickly enough to read the entire passage in a way that will provide you with the overall point of the paragraphs, read the first sentence of each paragraph. For a very short passage, you should read through it quickly, however.

Once you have identified the point of each paragraph, those points will flow into the overall purpose of the passage and also provide a map of where to find detailed information. Once you have established the purpose and map, you should go right to the questions.

Answering Questions

Some questions are about particular parts of a passage, while others are about the passage as a whole. Depending on how well you understood the purpose of the passage, you may be able to answer big picture questions quite easily. Detail questions, on the other hand, will require some work; after all, you didn't get lost in the details when you got through the passage quickly!

For a particular detail question, you will need to go back to the passage with the question in mind and *find the answer in the passage*. Let's repeat that last part: you should *find the answer in the passage*. If you know what the answer should look like, it is much easier to evaluate the answers. True, some questions cannot be answered in advance, such as "Which one of the following questions is answered in the passage?" But the general rule is *find the answer* before you go to the choices.

> By reading more quickly up front, you have more time to spend on finding the answer to a particular question.

In all cases, you should use effective Process of Elimination. Correct answers are fully supported by the text of the passage. There is no reading between the lines, connecting the dots, or getting inside the author's head. If you are down to two answers, determine which one is not supported by the text of the passage. It takes only one word to doom an otherwise good answer.

In short, follow this process for detail questions:

- Read and understand the question.
- Go to the passage and *find the answer* (unless the question is too open-ended).
- Use Process of Elimination, getting rid of any answer that is not consistent with the answer you found and/or is not fully supported by the text of the passage.

We will look at some specific question types shortly, but if you follow the general approach outlined here, you will be able to answer more questions accurately.

Pacing

Let's amend that last statement: you will be able to answer more questions accurately if you have a sound pacing plan. While reading up front more quickly will generate more time for the questions, getting through all the passages and all the questions in the time allotted is difficult for almost all students.

The number of reading passages varies on the test, some short and some quite long. Some might be fairly quick reads and some might seem more dense. They cover a broad array of topics, from history to science to fiction and even poetry. You may relate to some passages but not to others. On top of that, if you are rushing through the section to make sure you answer every single question, you are likely making a lot of mistakes. Slow down to increase your accuracy.

> Doing fewer passages accurately can generate more points than rushing through more passages.

How many passages should you do? That depends on you. You should attack as many passages as you can while still maintaining a high degree of accuracy. If, for example, eliminating one passage allows you to answer all but one or two questions correctly, while rushing through all the passages creates a lot of silly mistakes, skip one passage.

Also, pick your passages wisely. You don't get extra credit for answering questions on a complicated passage correctly. If you begin a passage and are thinking "Uh, what?" move on to another passage. You might end up coming back to the passage, or you may never look at it again. What is most important is that you nail the easier passages before you hit the harder-seeming ones.

STEP ONE: READING THE PASSAGE

Let's put the new reading approach into practice.

Label the Paragraphs

After you read each paragraph, ask yourself what you just read. Put it in your own words—just a couple of words—and label the side of the paragraph with your summary. This way you'll have something to guide you back to the relevant part of the passage when you answer a question. The key to labeling the paragraphs is to practice—you need to do it quickly, coming up with one or two words that accurately remind you of what's in the paragraph.

If the passage has only one paragraph, come up with a single label. Poems do not need to be labeled.

State the Main Idea

After you have read the entire passage, ask yourself the following two questions:

- **"What?"** What is the passage about?
- **"So what?"** What's the author's point about this topic?

The answers to these questions will show you the main idea of the passage. Scribble down this main idea in just a few words. The answer to "What?" is the thing that was being talked about—"bees" or "weather forecasting." The answer to "So what?" gives you the rest of the sentence—"Bees do little dances that tell other bees where to go for pollen," or "Weather forecasting is complicated by many problems."

Don't assume you will find the main idea in the first sentence. While often the main idea is in the beginning of the passage, it is not *always* in the first sentence or even the first paragraph. The beginning may just be a lead-in to the main point.

PRACTICE DRILL 1—GETTING THROUGH THE PASSAGE

As you quickly read each paragraph, label it. When you finish the passage, answer "What?" and "So what?" to get the main idea.

> Contrary to popular belief, the first European known to lay eyes on America was not Christopher Columbus or Amerigo Vespucci but a little-known Viking by the name of Bjarni Herjolfsson. In the summer of 986, Bjarni sailed from Norway to Iceland, heading for the Viking settlement where his father Heriulf resided.
>
> 5   When he arrived in Iceland, Bjarni discovered that his father had already sold his land and estates and set out for the latest Viking settlement on the subarctic island called Greenland. Discovered by a notorious murderer and criminal named Erik the Red, Greenland lay at the limit of the known world. Dismayed, Bjarni set out for this new colony.
>
> 10   Because the Vikings traveled without chart or compass, it was not uncommon for them to lose their way in the unpredictable northern seas. Beset by fog, the crew lost their bearings. When the fog finally cleared, they found themselves before a land that was level and covered with woods.
>
> They traveled farther up the coast, finding more flat, wooded country. Farther
> 15   north, the landscape revealed glaciers and rocky mountains. Though Bjarni realized this was an unknown land, he was no intrepid explorer. Rather, he was a practical man who had simply set out to find his father. Refusing his crew's request to go ashore, he promptly turned his bow back out to sea. After four days' sailing, Bjarni landed at Herjolfsnes on the southwestern tip of Greenland, the
> 20   exact place he had been seeking all along.

"What" is this passage about? _____

"So what?" What's the author's point? _____

What type of passage is this? _____

Check your answers in Chapter 9 to be sure you're on the right track. For detailed explanations, check your Student Tools.

STEP TWO: ANSWERING THE QUESTIONS

Now, we're getting to the important part of the Reading section. This is where you need to spend time in order to avoid careless errors. After reading a passage, you'll have a group of questions that are in no particular order. The first thing you need to decide is whether the question you're answering is general or specific.

General Questions

General questions are about the passage as a whole. They come in a variety of forms but ideally all can be answered based on your initial read.

Main idea
- Which of the following best expresses the main point?
- The passage is primarily about
- The main idea of the passage is
- The best title for this passage would be

Purpose
- The purpose of the passage is
- The author wrote this passage to

Tone/attitude
- The author's tone is
- The attitude of the author is one of

Odd ball
- Where would you be likely to find this passage?
- Which is likely to happen next?
- The author will most likely discuss next

Notice that these questions all require you to know the main idea, but the ones at the beginning of the list don't require anything else, and the ones toward the end require you to use a bit of common sense.

Answering a General Question

Keep your answers to "What?" and "So what?" in mind. The answer to a general question will concern the main idea. If it helps, you can go back to your paragraph labels. The labels will allow you to look at the passage again without getting bogged down in the details.

- For a straight **main idea** question, just ask yourself, "What was the 'What? So what?' for this passage?"
- For a **general purpose** question, ask yourself, "Why did the author write this?"

- For a **tone/attitude** question, ask yourself, "How did the author feel about the subject?" Think about tone as you would a text message. Would you say the author feels ☺ or ☹? These signs can help you with Process of Elimination.
- For an **oddball** question, use common sense and sound Process of Elimination.

Answer the question in your own words before looking at the choices. Eliminate answers that are not consistent with your predicted answer, as well as those that are too broad or too narrow. They should be "just right."

PRACTICE DRILL 2—ANSWERING A GENERAL QUESTION

Use the passage about Vikings that you just read and labeled. Reread your main idea and answer the following questions. Use the questions on the previous page to help you paraphrase your own answer before looking at the choices. When you're done, check your answers in Chapter 9. For detailed explanations, go to your Student Tools.

1. This passage is primarily about

    (A) the Vikings and their civilization
    (B) the waves of Viking immigration
    (C) sailing techniques of Bjarni Herjolfsson
    (D) one Viking's glimpse of the New World
    (E) the hazards of Viking travel

> What was the answer to "What?" and "So what?" for this passage?

2. What was the author's purpose in writing this passage?

    (A) To turn the reader against Italian adventurers
    (B) To show his disdain for Erik the Red
    (C) To demonstrate the Vikings' nautical skills
    (D) To correct a common misconception about the European discovery of America
    (E) To prove the Vikings were far more advanced than previously thought

> Why did the author write this passage? Think about the main idea.

Specific Questions

Specific questions are about a detail or section of the passage. While the questions can be presented in a number of different ways, they boil down to questions about WHAT the author said, WHY the author said something, and Vocab-in-Context.

What?
- According to the passage/author
- The author states that
- Which of these questions is answered by the passage?
- The author implies in line X
- It can be inferred from paragraph X
- The most likely interpretation of X is

Why?
- The author uses X to
- Why does the author say X?

Vocab-in-Context
- What does the passage mean by X?
- X probably represents/means
- Which word best replaces the word X without changing the meaning?
- As it is used in X, _____ most nearly means

Specific interpretation
- The author would be most likely to agree with which one of the following?
- Which one of the following questions is answered in the passage?

Once you have read and understood the question, go to the passage to find the answer. You should be able to find the answer quickly:

- Use your **paragraph labels** to go straight to the information you need.
- Use the **line or paragraph reference**, if there is one, but be careful. With a line reference ("In line 10…"), be sure to read the whole surrounding paragraph, not just the line. If the question says, "In line 10…," then you need to read lines 5 through 15 to actually find the answer.
- Use words that stand out in the question and passage. Names, places, and long words will be easy to find back in the passage. We call these **lead words** because they lead you back to the right place in the passage.

Once you're in the right area, answer the question in your own words. Then look at the choices and eliminate any that aren't like your answer or are not supported by the text of the passage.

For Vocab-in-Context questions, be sure to come up with your own word, based on the surrounding sentences. It does not matter if you do not know the word being tested, as long as you can figure it out from context. Also, even if you do know the word, it may be used in an unusual way. So, always ignore the word and come up with your own before Process of Elimination.

Questions with Special Formats

I, II, III questions The questions that have three Roman numerals are confusing and time-consuming. They look like this:

According to the passage, which of the following is true?

    I.   The sky is blue.

    II.   Nothing rhymes with "orange."

    III.   Smoking cigarettes increases lung capacity.

    (A)   I only
    (B)   II only
    (C)   III only
    (D)   I and II only
    (E)   I, II, and III

On the SSAT, you will need to look up each of the three statements in the passage. This will always be time-consuming, but you can make them less confusing by making sure you look up just one statement at a time.

For instance, in the question above, say you look back at the passage and see that the passage says statement I is true. Write a big "T" next to it. What can you eliminate now? Choices (B) and (C). Now you check out II and you find that sure enough, the passage says that, too. So II gets a big "T" and you cross off (A). Next, looking in the paragraph you labeled "Smoking is bad," you find that the passage actually says that smoking decreases lung capacity. What can you eliminate? Choice (E).

You may want to skip a I, II, III question because it will be time-consuming, especially if you're on your last passage and there are other questions you can do instead. If you have time, you can always come back to this question.

EXCEPT/LEAST/NOT questions This is another confusing type of question. The test writers are reversing what you need to look for, asking you which answer is false.

> All of the following can be inferred from the passage
> EXCEPT

Before you go any further, cross out the "EXCEPT." Now, you have a much more positive question to answer. Of course, as always, you will go through *all* the choices, but for this type of question you will put a little "T" or "F" next to the answers as you check them out. Let's say we've checked out these answers:

(A)	Americans are patriotic.	**T**
(B)	Americans have great ingenuity.	**T**
(C)	Americans love war.	**F**
(D)	Americans do what they can to help one another.	**T**
(E)	Americans are brave in times of war.	**T**

Which one stands out? The one with the "F." That's your answer. You made a confusing question much simpler than the test writers wanted it to be. If you don't go through all the choices and mark them, you run the risk of accidentally picking one of the choices that you know is true because that's what you usually look for on reading questions.

You should skip an EXCEPT/LEAST/NOT question if you're on your last passage and there are other questions you can do instead. If you have time, you can always come back to this question.

PRACTICE DRILL 3—ANSWERING A SPECIFIC QUESTION

Use the passage about Vikings that you just read and labeled. Use your paragraph labels and the lead words in each question to get to the part of the passage you need, and then put the answer in your own words before going back to the choices. When you're done, check your answers in Chapter 9. For detailed explanations, go to your Student Tools.

1. According to the passage, Bjarni Herjolfsson left Norway to

   (A) found a new colony
   (B) open trading lanes
   (C) visit a relative
   (D) map the North Sea
   (E) settle in Greenland

   > What's the lead word here? *Norway.* Norway should also be in one of your labels.

2. Bjarni's reaction upon landing in Iceland can best be described as

   (A) disappointed
   (B) satisfied
   (C) amused
   (D) indifferent
   (E) fascinated

   > What's the lead word here? *Iceland.* Again, this should be in one of your labels.

3. "The crew lost their bearings," in the third paragraph, probably means that

   (A) the ship was damaged beyond repair
   (B) the crew became disoriented
   (C) the crew decided to mutiny
   (D) the crew went insane
   (E) the ship's compass broke

   > For a paragraph reference, just go back and read that paragraph. Replace the words they've quoted with your own.

4. It can be inferred from the passage that prior to Bjarni Herjolfsson's voyage, Greenland

   (A) was covered in grass and shrubs
   (B) was overrun with Vikings
   (C) was rich in fish and game
   (D) was populated by criminals
   (E) was as far west as the Vikings had traveled

   > What's the lead word here? *Greenland.* Is it in one of your labels? What does that part of the passage say about Greenland? Paraphrase before looking at the answers!

Which answer is closest to what the author said overall?

When You Are Done
Check your answers in Chapter 9.

5. With which of the following statements about Viking explorers would the author most probably agree?

(A) Greenland and Iceland were the Vikings' final discoveries.

(B) Viking explorers were cruel and savage.

(C) The Vikings' most startling discovery was an accidental one.

(D) Bjarni Herjolfsson was the first settler of America

(E) All Viking explorers were fearless.

STEP THREE: PROCESS OF ELIMINATION

Before you ever look at a choice, you've come up with your own answer, in your own words. What do you do next?

Well, you're looking for the closest answer to yours, but it's a lot easier to eliminate answers than to try to magically zone in on the best one. Work through the answers using Process of Elimination. As soon as you eliminate an answer, cross off the letter in your test booklet so that you no longer think of that choice as a possibility.

How Do I Eliminate Choices?

On a General Question

Eliminate an answer that is:

- Too small. The passage may mention it, but it's only a detail—not a main idea.
- Not mentioned in the passage.
- In contradiction to the passage—it says the opposite of what you read.
- Too big. The answer tries to say that more was discussed than really was.
- Too extreme. An extreme answer is too negative or too positive, or it uses absolute words like *all, every, never,* or *always.* Eliminating extreme answers can make tone/attitude questions especially quick.
- Against common sense. The passage is not likely to back up answers that just don't make sense at all.

On a Specific Question

Eliminate an answer that is:

- too extreme
- in contradiction to passage details
- not mentioned in the passage
- against common sense

If you look back at the questions you did for the Viking passage, you'll see that many of the wrong choices fit into the categories above.

On a Tone Question

Eliminate an answer that is:

- too extreme
- opposite meaning
- against common sense. These are answers that make the author seem confused or uninterested, which an SSAT author will never be.

What Kinds of Answers Do I Keep?

Best answers are likely to be:

- paraphrases of the words in the passage
- traditional and conservative in their outlook
- moderate, using words like *may, can,* and *often*

When You've Got It Down to Two

If you've eliminated all but two answers, don't get stuck and waste time. Keep the main idea in the back of your mind and step back.

- Reread the question.
- Look at what makes the two answers different.
- Go back to the passage.
- Which answer is worse? Eliminate it.

REVIEW—THE READING PLAN

The Passages

After I read each paragraph, I _____ it.

After I read an entire passage, I ask myself: _____ ? _____ ?

I am better at doing the following types of passages:

_____

_____

_____

The Questions

The five main types of general questions, and the questions I can ask myself to answer them, are:

_____ _____

_____ _____

_____ _____

_____ _____

_____ _____

To find the answer to a specific question, I can use the following three clues:

_____

_____

If the question says, "In line 22," where do I begin reading for the answer?

_____

The Answers

On a general question, I eliminate answers that are

_____

_____

_____

_____

_____

_____

On a specific question, I eliminate answers that are

_____

_____

_____

_____

When I've got it down to two possible answers, I

_____

_____

_____

If you have trouble with any of these questions, be sure to reread this chapter before moving on.

When you're done, check your answers in Chapter 9. For detailed explanations, go to your Student Tools.

PRACTICE DRILL 4—ALL READING TECHNIQUES—ALL LEVELS

In 2011, the National Aeronautics and Space Administration (NASA) ended the Space Shuttle program, which was the United States' manned space flight program after the Apollo programs took astronauts to the moon. NASA's Space Shuttle program used five shuttles in its thirty-year program—*Columbia*, *Challenger*, *Discovery*, *Endeavor*, and *Atlantis* all carried astronauts and
5 cargo into space. Shuttles were used to build the International Space Station (known as the ISS) and deploy the Hubble Telescope. The ISS orbits the Earth and is crewed by astronauts from all over the world. Currently, astronauts reach the station on Russian Soyuz spacecraft.

Today, NASA is working to design and build spacecraft for exploration further into space so humans can return to the moon, explore Mars, or even visit an asteroid. NASA has sent
10 robotic labs to Mars, the moon, and beyond. NASA is also working in partnership with private companies to develop a commercial space industry to supply the ISS and carry out experiments in low earth orbit. Companies such as Space X, Blue Origin, Boeing, and Lockheed Martin are working to develop rockets that can take satellites, cargo, and eventually humans into outer space.

Space X has already successfully launched missions to the ISS and launched satellites
15 and experiments into orbit on a rocket called the *Falcon 9*. In the same way the Space Shuttle Program made space travel easier and less expensive by reusing the shuttles many times, Space X is able to launch frequently by reusing its rockets and boosters.

The commercial space flight industry has many exciting possibilities for scientific discovery both in creating faster travel on earth and traveling beyond our planet to explore the solar system.

1. Which of the following best summarizes the author's main point?

(A) Space X is a more successful company than NASA.
(B) The United States' space program is reliant on Russia for space travel.
(C) In order to explore the solar system, the commercial space flight industry will create faster travel.
(D) NASA's purpose is to supply the ISS and conduct experiments in space.
(E) It is still possible for the United States to make scientific advancements without NASA's Space Shuttle program.

2. According to the passage, which of the following is NOT true of NASA?

(A) NASA collaborates with private companies such as ISS.
(B) NASA's Space Shuttle program terminated after thirty years.
(C) NASA has plans for man to return to outer space.
(D) *Columbia*, *Challenger*, *Discovery*, *Endeavor*, and *Atlantis* comprised NASA's shuttle fleet.
(E) Prior to 2011, NASA sent manned missions into space.

3. The author's attitude when discussing space exploration is best described as

(A) critical
(B) dubious
(C) jubilant
(D) sanguine
(E) tenacious

4. It can most likely be inferred from the passage that when NASA ended the Space Shuttle program,

(A) the United States lost momentum in future space discoveries.
(B) numerous men and women lost their jobs and their dreams of space travel.
(C) NASA also retired their five shuttles from manned space flight.
(D) the United States had more money and resources to allocate toward privately operated space missions.
(E) NASA turned to rockets and boosters for future manned space missions.

5. The word "reach" in line 7 could be replaced by which of the following without changing the author's meaning?

(A) Attain
(B) Extend
(C) Influence
(D) Arrive at
(E) Get in touch with

PRACTICE DRILL 5—ALL READING TECHNIQUES—ALL LEVELS

Martial arts traditions are practiced all over the world. Some of the most well-known martial arts are the Japanese art of Karate and the Korean art of Taekwondo. One reason for the popularity of these arts in the United States is that many American service members were introduced to them: Karate after World War II in Japan and Taekwondo during the Korean Conflict in the 1950s. During this time, many
5   service members learned these fighting styles and brought them back to the United States when they finished their service in the armed forces.

In Japan, Karate is usually called *karate do*. The word "do" is translated to mean "way." Traditionally, when the name of a martial art style ends in "do" (e.g., *taekwondo, judo, karate do, aikido*), it denotes a "way" or philosophically based martial art. In other words, practitioners are learning their particular
10   style as a path to develop this art and to improve their mental focus, physical fitness, self-defense skills, and perhaps spirituality. This is in contrast to martial arts that are practiced for military use or law enforcement. These martial art styles end in "jutsu" (e.g., *ninjutsu*, Japanese *jujutsu*).

Today, many people practice martial arts as a sport because of the physical benefits and practical applications of the skills they learn. Some styles focus on traditional techniques such as strikes, blocks,
15   and kicks. Others incorporate traditional weapons training such as bo staffs, nunchucks, and swords. While it is tempting to evaluate which style is "best," each style of martial arts has advantages and disadvantages in terms of effectiveness in combat. However, the benefits to all practitioners of following the "way" of martial arts are increased focused, fitness, and, hopefully, fun.

1. The passage was most likely taken from

   (A) a newspaper article
   (B) an encyclopedia
   (C) an advertisement for Karate lessons
   (D) a fitness magazine
   (E) a speaking engagement

2. The author suggests which of the following about martial arts?

   (A) There are some benefits of martial arts that all practitioners experience.
   (B) Karate and Taekwondo are the most well-known martial arts.
   (C) Practicing martial arts is now considered a sport and no longer a style of art.
   (D) Japanese revere Karate more than other martial arts.
   (E) Karate and Taekwondo are the only martial arts American service members have encountered while serving their country.

3. The word "This" mentioned in line 11 most likely refers to

   (A) karate
   (B) practitioners of martial arts
   (C) self-defense skills
   (D) philosophy and the arts
   (E) martial arts styles ending in *do*

4. According to the author, a martial arts practice of *aikido*

   (A) is a form of *karate do*
   (B) incorporates traditional weapons training
   (C) was created by American service members during World War II
   (D) offers physical and mental benefits
   (E) is more focused on developing mental focus than on self defense skills

5. The passage provides information that helps answer which of the following questions?

   I. How many different types of martial art styles end in the word *do*?
   II. What is the best style of martial arts?
   III. What role did American service members play in the popularity of martial arts in the United States?

   (A) I only
   (B) II only
   (C) III only
   (D) I and II only
   (E) I and III only

6. The tone of the passage is primarily

   (A) conceited
   (B) heretical
   (C) admiring
   (D) informative
   (E) philosophical

PRACTICE DRILL 6—ALL READING TECHNIQUES— MIDDLE AND UPPER LEVELS

The following speech was given by Samuel Clemens on April 14, 1907, following a children's performance of *The Prince and the Pauper*. Nearly one thousand children were in the audience during this speech.

> I have not enjoyed a play so much, so heartily, and so thoroughly since I played Miles Hendon twenty-two years ago. I used to play in this piece (*The Prince and the Pauper*) with my children, who, twenty-two years ago, were little youngsters. One of my daughters was the Prince, and a neighbor's daughter was the Pauper, and the children of other neighbors
> 5 played other parts. But we never gave such a performance as we have seen here to-day. It would have been beyond us.
> My late wife was the dramatist and stage-manager. Our coachman was the stage-manager, second in command. We used to play it in this simple way, and the one who used to bring in the crown on a cushion—he was a little fellow then—is now a clergyman way up high—six
> 10 or seven feet high—and growing higher all the time. We played it well, but not as well as you see it here, for you see it done by practically trained professionals.
> I was especially interested in the scene which we have just had, for Miles Hendon was my part. I did it as well as a person could who never remembered his part. The children all knew their parts. They did not mind if I did not know mine. I could thread a needle nearly as well
> 15 as the player did whom you saw to-day. The words of my part I could supply on the spot. The words of the song that Miles Hendon sang here I did not catch. But I was great in that song....
> This theatre is a part of the work, and furnishes pure and clean plays. This theatre is an influence. Everything in the world is accomplished by influences which train and educate. When you get to be seventy-one and a half, as I am, you may think that your education is
> 20 over, but it isn't.
> If we had forty theatres of this kind in this city of four millions, how they would educate and elevate! We should have a body of educated theatre-goers.
> It would make better citizens, honest citizens. One of the best gifts a millionaire could make would be a theatre here and a theatre there. It would make of you a real Republic, and
> 25 bring about an educational level.

1. The speaker's primary purpose is to

   (A) caution listeners against subpar theater practices
   (B) compare previous performances of the play
   (C) congratulate the performance of a children's play
   (D) advocate for better arts education
   (E) reminisce over his previous theatrical endeavors

2. The passage could be from the viewpoint of which of the following?

   (A) a perceptive critic
   (B) a devoted patron of the arts
   (C) an exuberant stage manager
   (D) an enthusiastic producer
   (E) an aloof commentator

3. The word "furnishes" in line 17 could be replaced by which of the following without changing the speaker's meaning?

   (A) provides
   (B) stocks
   (C) equips
   (D) reclines
   (E) adorns

4. The speaker uses the phrase "If we had forty theatres of this kind in this city of four millions" in the fifth paragraph to show

    I.   the valuable role theater serves in society
    II. building new theaters would guarantee residents of the city would attend productions
    III. theater can enrich the education and morals of its attendees
    IV. all wealthy patrons should invest in theater construction

    (A) I only
    (B) I and II only
    (C) I and III only
    (D) I, III, and IV only
    (E) II, III, and IV only

5. The tone of the first three paragraphs is primarily

    (A) informative
    (B) indifferent
    (C) whimsical
    (D) nostalgic
    (E) indignant

PRACTICE DRILL 7—ALL READING TECHNIQUES—MIDDLE AND UPPER LEVELS

There is no practice which has been more extensively eulogized in all ages than early rising; and this universal impression is an indication that it is founded on true philosophy....

Now the mass of any nation must always consist of persons who labor at occupations which demand the light of day. But in aristocratic countries, especially in England, labor is regarded
5 as the mark of the lower classes, and indolence is considered as one mark of a gentleman. This impression has gradually and imperceptibly, to a great extent, regulated their customs, so that, even in their hours of meals and repose, the higher orders aim at being different and distinct from those who, by laborious pursuits, are placed below them. From this circumstance, while the lower orders labor by day and sleep at night, the rich, the noble, and the honored sleep by
10 day, and follow their pursuits and pleasures by night.

It will be found that the aristocracy of London breakfast near midday, dine after dark, visit and go to Parliament between ten and twelve at night, and retire to sleep toward morning. In consequence of this, the subordinate classes who aim at gentility gradually fall into the same practice. The influence of this custom extends across the ocean, and here, in this democratic
15 land, we find many who measure their grade of gentility by the late hour at which they arrive at a party. And this aristocratic folly is growing upon us, so that, throughout the nation, the hours for visiting and retiring are constantly becoming later, while the hours for rising correspond in lateness.

1. The passage was most likely taken from a/an

   (A) diary entry
   (B) history book
   (C) article in an academic journal
   (D) observation from sleep specialists
   (E) fictional novel

2. The author uses the phrase "There is no practice which has been more extensively eulogized in all ages" to show that early rising is

   (A) necessary for all ages
   (B) no longer useful in modern society
   (C) recommended more than any other practice
   (D) a highly revered practice
   (E) a practice for the working class

3. The word "labor" mentioned in the second paragraph most likely refers to

   (A) farming tasks
   (B) leisure
   (C) distress
   (D) computer jobs
   (E) physical work

4. What does the author mean when she says "this democratic land" in the third paragraph?

   (A) London
   (B) France
   (C) Europe
   (D) England
   (E) The United States

5. Which of the following titles best fits the content of the passage?

   (A) "The Importance of Early Rising"
   (B) "A Caution Against Aristocratic Folly"
   (C) "Pursuits and Pleasures by Night: the Story of a Socialite"
   (D) "Labor by Day, Sleep at Night: Life of a Laborer"
   (E) "Evening Customs of Aristocrats"

6. The author admires people who

   (A) conduct their business at night
   (B) toil at physical labor
   (C) aim at gentility
   (D) are early risers
   (E) are wealthy and noble

PRACTICE DRILL 8—ALL READING TECHNIQUES— MIDDLE AND UPPER LEVELS

The Children's Hour

Between the dark and the daylight,
  When the night is beginning to lower,
Comes a pause in the day's occupations,
  That is known as the Children's Hour.

5 I hear in the chamber above me
  The patter of little feet,
The sound of a door that is opened,
  And voices soft and sweet.

From my study I see in the lamplight,
10 Descending the broad hall stair,
Grave Alice, and laughing Allegra,
  And Edith with golden hair.
A whisper, and then a silence:
  Yet I know by their merry eyes
15 They are plotting and planning together
  To take me by surprise.

A sudden rush from the stairway,
  A sudden raid from the hall!
By three doors left unguarded
20 They enter my castle wall!

They climb up into my turret
  O'er the arms and back of my chair;
If I try to escape, they surround me;
  They seem to be everywhere.

25 They almost devour me with kisses,
  Their arms about me entwine,
Till I think of the Bishop of Bingen
  In his Mouse-Tower on the Rhine!

Do you think, o blue-eyed banditti,
30 Because you have scaled the wall,
Such an old mustache as I am
  Is not a match for you all!
I have you fast in my fortress,
  And will not let you depart,
35 But put you down into the dungeon
  In the round-tower of my heart.

And there will I keep you forever,
  Yes, forever and a day,
Till the walls shall crumble to ruin,
40 And moulder in dust away!

---

1. Which of the following best describes actions of the children?

   (A) soft and sweet
   (B) grave and laughing
   (C) Plotting and planning
   (D) climbing and surrounding
   (E) devouring and entwining

2. In the last two stanzas of the poem, the speaker indicates that

   (A) he will lock the children in a dungeon for their shenanigans
   (B) his love for the children is everlasting
   (C) he will keep the children captive in his fortress
   (D) the children will have to tear down the walls if they ever wish to escape
   (E) his love is no match for dungeon walls

3. The sensory image most important to this passage is

   (A) the sound of the sudden raid from the hall
   (B) the sight of the girls descending down the stairs
   (C) the sound of pattering little feet
   (D) the sensation of kisses and hugs
   (E) the sight of blue eyes and moustaches

4. Which of the following words could be substituted for "banditti" (line 29) without changing the meaning of the verse?

   (A) bandits
   (B) musicians
   (C) vines
   (D) children
   (E) mice

5. Which of the following best describes the main idea of the poem?

   (A) The speaker is distracted by the children's mischievous activities.
   (B) The speaker cherishes the time of day when he can break from his work and play with his children.
   (C) A poet depicts the games of children who inhabit an imaginary fortress.
   (D) The children are scheming of ways to attack their captor and escape the castle.
   (E) The children are listening to a story before for their bedtime

PRACTICE DRILL 9—ALL READING TECHNIQUES— MIDDLE AND UPPER LEVELS

It was just then that Miss Minchin entered the room. She was very like her house, Sara felt: tall and dull, and respectable and ugly. She had large, cold, fishy eyes, and a large, cold, fishy smile. It spread itself into a very large smile when she saw Sara and Captain Crewe. She had heard a great many desirable things of the young soldier from the lady who had recommended
5   her school to him. Among other things, she had heard that he was a rich father who was willing to spend a great deal of money on his little daughter.

"It will be a great privilege to have charge of such a beautiful and promising child, Captain Crewe," she said, taking Sara's hand and stroking it. "Lady Meredith has told me of her unusual cleverness. A clever child is a great treasure in an establishment like mine."
10   Sara stood quietly, with her eyes fixed upon Miss Minchin's face. She was thinking something odd, as usual.

"Why does she say I am a beautiful child?" she was thinking. "I am not beautiful at all. Colonel Grange's little girl, Isobel, is beautiful. She has dimples and rose-colored cheeks, and long hair the color of gold. I have short black hair and green eyes; besides which, I am a thin
15   child and not fair in the least. I am one of the ugliest children I ever saw. She is beginning by telling a story."

She was mistaken, however, in thinking she was an ugly child. She was not in the least like Isobel Grange, who had been the beauty of the regiment, but she had an odd charm of her own. She was a slim, supple creature, rather tall for her age, and had an intense, attractive little face.
20   Her hair was heavy and quite black and only curled at the tips; her eyes were greenish gray, it is true, but they were big, wonderful eyes with long, black lashes, and though she herself did not like the color of them, many other people did. Still she was very firm in her belief that she was an ugly little girl, and she was not at all elated by Miss Minchin's flattery.

"I should be telling a story if I said she was beautiful," she thought; "and I should know I
25   was telling a story. I believe I am as ugly as she is—in my way. What did she say that for?"

After she had known Miss Minchin longer she learned why she had said it. She discovered that she said the same thing to each papa and mamma who brought a child to her school.

1. By saying that "She was mistaken, however, in thinking she was an ugly child" in line 17, the author means that

(A) beauty is in the eye of the beholder
(B) Sara has a distorted view of herself
(C) to some people, Sara's beauty surpasses Isobel's
(D) Miss Minchin mistook Sara for Isobel
(E) Miss Minchin's standards of beauty are flawed

2. Which of the following is probably true of Miss Minchin?

(A) She is dishonest to the parents who bring their children to her school.
(B) Her obsequious nature is appreciated by Sara.
(C) She never fails to see the beauty in all of her children.
(D) Her commentary is predictable when welcoming newcomers.
(E) She favors the children of rich fathers when admitting new students.

3. In line 15, "fair" could be replaced by which of the following without changing the author's meaning?

    (A) attractive
    (B) corpulent
    (C) just
    (D) light-colored
    (E) pleasant

4. The narrator's tone in the passage is primarily

    (A) critical
    (B) disparaging
    (C) emotional
    (D) objective
    (E) partisan

5. In line 1, the phrase "She was very like her house" is an example of a(n)

    (A) allegory
    (B) metaphor
    (C) personification
    (D) pun
    (E) simile

6. Sara most likely mentions Isobel Grange in order to

    (A) clarify a position
    (B) set a standard of comparison
    (C) pose a new topic of conversation
    (D) challenge a belief
    (E) reminisce about a dear friend

7. Throughout the passage, "a story" could be replaced by which of the following without changing the author's meaning?

    (A) an account
    (B) an anecdote
    (C) a fable
    (D) a fib
    (E) a rumor

Chapter 9
Answers and
Explanations for
SSAT Practice Drills

SSAT MATH

Practice Drill 1—Multiple Choice

1. **D** Use PITA to solve this question. Since the question asks for *the square of the largest of the five consecutive integers*, label the choices as such. Then, start with (C) to get rid of choices more effectively. If 49 were the square of the largest integer, the integer would be 7, and other consecutive integers would be 6, 5, 4, and 3. The sum of these numbers 3 + 4 + 5 + 6 + 7 = 25, which is less than 30. Therefore, eliminate (A), (B), and (C), since these are too small. Try (D): the square root of 64 is 8, and the other integers would therefore be 7, 6, 5, and 4. 4 + 5 + 6 + 7 + 8 = 30, so the correct answer is (D).

2. **D** List the factors of 24: 1 and 24, 2 and 12, 3 and 8, and 4 and 6. This totals 8 different factors of 24. The correct answer is (D).

3. **D** Since 12 is a factor of a certain number, Plug In for that certain number. For instance, Plug In 36, since 12 is a factor, and use POE. 2 and 6 are factors of 36, but they are not the only factors of 36 listed in the choices. Eliminate (A). Similarly, 3 and 4 are not the only factors of 36 listed, so eliminate (B). 12 is a factor, but it is not the only factor listed, so eliminate (C). 24 is not a factor of 36, so eliminate (E). Choice (D) contains all the other factors listed in previous choices. The correct answer is (D).

4. **B** Use long division to find the remainder of 1,024 divided by 9. The remainder is 7, so add 2 to the total to make the number be divisible by 9. The correct answer is (B). Alternatively, you can use the divisibility rule for 9—the sum of the digits is divisible by 9. 1 + 0 + 2 + 4 = 7, so if 2 is added to that, the sum is 9, which is divisible by 9. Remember, the question asks for the *smallest* number that can be added to 1,024.

5. **B** A multiple of 3 will be 3 times a number. 2 is not a multiple of 3, so eliminate (A). 3 × 2 = 6, so (B) is a multiple of 3. 10, 14, and 16 are not divisible by 3, and therefore cannot be multiples of 3. The correct answer is (B).

6. **C** The question asks which number is NOT a multiple of 6. 6 × 2 = 12 and 6 × 3 = 18, so (A) and (B) are multiples. 6 does not divide evenly into 23, so keep (C). 6 × 4 = 24 and 6 × 7 = 42, so (D) and (E) are also multiples. The correct answer is (C).

7. **D** The question is essentially asking for a number that is divisible by both 3 and 5. 10, 20, and 25, and 50 are all divisible by 5, but not by 3. Eliminate (A), (B), (C), and (E). 45 ÷ 3 = 15 and 45 ÷ 5 = 9, so 45 is divisible by both 3 and 5. The correct answer is (D). Remember, you can also use the divisibility rules for 3 and 5 to help with this question! All the numbers end in either 5 or 0, so they are all divisible by 5. However, only (D) has digits that add up to a number divisible by 3.

8. **C** Since the question is asking for a specific amount and has real numbers in the choices, one way to solve this problem is to use PITA to test the answers, starting with (C). 75,000 × 6 = 450,000, which works. The correct answer is (C). Alternatively, you can translate the words. *How many times as great as* means divide the two numbers, so $\frac{\text{profit in 1992}}{\text{profit in 1972}} = \frac{450,000}{75,000} = 6$.

9. **B** Use PITA since the question is asking for a specific value and there are real numbers in the choices. The question asks for Joanna's portion of the furniture, which is one-third of the total. Therefore, 3 times however many pieces she owns will equal the total (12 pieces). Start with (C): $6 \times 3 = 18$, which is too large. Eliminate (C), (D), and (E). Try (B): $4 \times 3 = 12$, which works. The correct answer is (B).

10. **C** Since the question asks for a specific value, use PITA to answer the question, starting with (C). The choices represent the amount of oil in the tank now, which is one-third of the total amount. Choice (C) is 30. Is 30 one-third of the total amount (90 gallons) the tank holds? $30 = \frac{1}{3}(90)$ is true, so the correct answer is (C).

11. **D** Tigger sleeps $\frac{3}{4}$ of each day. To find how many days he sleeps over the course of four days, multiply: $\frac{3}{4} \times 4$. Simplify to solve: $\frac{3 \times 4}{4} = \frac{12}{4} = 3$. The correct answer is (D).

12. **A** To find the greatest value, use the choices and ballpark wherever possible to help. Choice (A) is close to 1, so use this as a comparison point. Choice (B) is smaller, since it is less than $\frac{1}{2}$. Pay attention to the division sign in (C): $\frac{1}{12} \div \frac{1}{3} = \frac{1}{12} \times \frac{3}{1} = \frac{3}{12}$, which is also less than $\frac{1}{2}$. In (D), multiply the fractions: $\frac{3}{4} \times \frac{1}{3} = \frac{3 \times 1}{4 \times 3} = \frac{3}{12}$, which is equal to (C) and therefore less than $\frac{1}{2}$. Do the same with (E): $\frac{1}{12} \times 2 = \frac{1 \times 2}{12} = \frac{2}{12}$. This is even smaller than (C) and (D), so eliminate (E). The greatest value is (A).

13. **D** Rearrange these values by grouping together fractions with like denominators: $\frac{1}{2} + \frac{1}{2} = 1$, $\frac{2}{3} + \frac{1}{3} = \frac{3}{3} = 1$, and $\frac{3}{4} + \frac{1}{4} = \frac{4}{4} = 1$. Then add the whole numbers: $1 + 1 + 1 = 3$. The correct answer is (D).

14. **D** When multiplying by a factor of 10, simply move the decimal point to the right for each zero. In this case, you are multiplying by 1,000, so move the decimal point to the right three places for the three zeros in 1,000. The decimal 0.34 becomes 340, which is closest to 350. The correct answer is (D).

15. **C** The question is testing knowledge of decimal places. The answer should not have multiplication in it, so eliminate (A). Eliminate (D) as well since it does not have 2 included. In the number 2.398, 0.3 is equivalent to $\frac{3}{10}$, 0.09 to $\frac{9}{100}$, and 0.008 to $\frac{8}{1,000}$. This correlates to (C), which is the correct answer.

Practice Drill 2—Multiple Choice—Upper Level Only

1. **B** First, since there are fewer multiples of 7, list the multiples of 7 from 1 to 99. The multiples are 7, 14, 21, 28, 35, 42, 49, 56, 63, 70, 77, 84, 91, and 98. The multiples that would also be multiples of 2 would be the even numbers: 14, 28, 42, 56, 70, 84, and 98. This is a total of 7 numbers. The correct answer is (B).

2. **D** Let the choices help here. Since the number must be greater than 50, eliminate (A) and (B). 51 is not a multiple of 7, so eliminate (C). 56 is a multiple of 7, and it is the smallest of the remaining choices. Therefore, the correct answer is (D). Note, 63 is a multiple of 7, but it is not the *smallest* multiple *greater than 50*.

3. **B** Remember, with exponents, you can write it out! $2^3 = 2 \times 2 \times 2$ and $2^2 = 2 \times 2$, so you have $(2 \times 2 \times 2) \times (2 \times 2 \times 2) \times (2 \times 2)$. Count up the number of 2s that you have, which is 8, and make that number the new exponent: 2^8. The correct choice is (B). Alternatively, you can use MADSPM: when multiplying the same base, add the exponents. Simply add $3 + 3 + 2 = 8$. The answer will be 2^8.

4. **B** Use PITA to Plug In the choices for m, starting with (C). Plug 3 in for m: $2(3) + 4 = 10$ and $3^3 = 27$, which are not equal. Since 3 is too large, eliminate (C), (D), and (E). Next try (B): $2(2) + 4 = 8$ and $2^3 = 8$. Since this works, stop here. The correct answer is (B).

5. **D** For word problem questions, translate the words to their math equivalents. If 4 (the students who chose recycling) is equal to one-fifth of the students in the class, then $4 = \frac{1}{5} \times n$, where n is the number of students in the class. To solve, multiply both sides by 5, and $n = 20$. There are 20 students in the class. The correct choice is (D).

6. **D** First, solve for x and then find what the question is asking: $x + 10$. Start with $6x - 4 = 38$. Add 4 to each side, and $6x = 42$. Divide by 6 on each side to find that $x = 7$. Now plug 7 into $x + 10$ to find that $7 + 10 = 17$. The correct answer is (D).

7. **B** Note that the question asks for $\frac{x}{9}$, not just for x. Start with $3x - 6 = 21$. Add 6 to both sides, and $3x = 27$. Divide by 3 on each side, and $x = 9$. Plug this into the equation: $\frac{x}{9} = \frac{9}{9} = 1$. The correct answer is (B).

8. **D** Since the question asks for a specific value, use PITA to answer the question, starting with (C). The choices represent the original number of chairs. Notice that with (C), there is a problem. If there were 22 chairs originally and only one-fifth worked, that would leave a remainder—22 does not divide by 5 evenly. Eliminate (C). Next try (D) since 80 is a multiple of 5. If there were 80 chairs originally, there would be 16 chairs in working order since $\frac{1}{5} \times 80 = \frac{80}{5} = 16$. The problem states that 3 more chairs were added: $16 + 3 = 19$, which is the number of available working seats. Since this works, stop here. The correct answer is (D).

9. **A** To find a percentage, find the portion the question asks for out of the total. First, find the total of all the grains: 60 bushels of corn + 20 bushels of wheat + 40 bushels of soybeans = 120 total bushels. The question asks for the percent of corn, so $\frac{\text{corn}}{\text{total}} = \frac{60}{120} = \frac{1}{2}$, which is equal to $\frac{50}{100}$ or 50%. The correct answer is (A).

10. **C** To find percent change, use the formula % change $= \frac{\text{difference}}{\text{original}} \times 100$. The difference here is $45 − $30 = $15, and the item was originally $45, so $\frac{15}{45} \times 100$. This reduces to $\frac{1}{3} \times 100$. To solve, $\frac{1 \times 100}{3} = \frac{100}{3} = 33\frac{1}{3}\%$. The correct answer is (C).

11. **C** Use Ballparking! 19.95 is roughly 20 and 35% is close to $\frac{1}{3}$, so $\frac{1}{3}$ of 20 is between 6 and 7. Eliminate (D) and (E) since both are too big. Choices (A) and (B) are too small, so that leaves (C) as the closest. The correct answer is (C).

12. **A** The question asks for the percentage of hotels that have swimming pools, indoor or outdoor. There are 5 indoor pools and 15 outdoor pools, making a total of 20 pools. There are 50 total hotels, so $\frac{\text{pools}}{\text{total hotels}} = \frac{20}{50} = \frac{2}{5} = 0.4$, or 40%. The correct answer is (A).

13. **A** Use the choices to see which original value will yield $20. Just by Ballparking, you can eliminate (B), (C), and (D) since these are too large. 40% of any of these numbers will be greater than $20. Try (A): 40% of 50 translates into $\frac{40}{100}(50) = \frac{2}{5}(50) = \frac{2 \times 50}{5} = \frac{100}{5} = 20$. This matches the information in the question, so the correct answer is (A).

14. **A** To find percent change, use the formula % change $= \frac{\text{difference}}{\text{original}} \times 100$. The original value is $50 and the final value is $20, so the difference is $30. $\frac{30}{50} \times 100$ reduces to $\frac{3}{5} \times 100 = \frac{3 \times 100}{5} = \frac{300}{5} = 60$. The correct answer is (A).

15. **C** Take this question in bite-sized pieces. The dress is originally priced at $60 and is 20% off. 20% of 60 is the same as saying $\frac{1}{5}(60) = \frac{60}{5} = 12$. Therefore, the discounted dress price is $60 − $12 = $48. Do the same to the other items. The cotton sweater is regularly $40 and is on sale for 10% off. $\frac{1}{10}(40) = \frac{40}{10} = 4$, so the discounted sweater price is $40 − $4 = $36. There are four pairs of socks for $5 each, and these are also 20% off. $\frac{1}{5}(5) = \frac{5}{5} = 1$, so the discounted price of each pair of socks is $5 − $1 = $4. There are four pairs, so multiply 4 by 4 to find the total for the socks on sale, which is $16. The question asks for the total, so find the sum: $48 + $36 + $16 = $100. The correct answer is (C).

16. C Use Ballparking to answer this question. $17.95 is close to $18. 30% is close to $\frac{1}{3}$, so $\frac{1}{3}(18) = \frac{18}{3} = 6$. The correct answer is (C).

17. A Take this question in bite-sized pieces. 50% of the 20 students are boys. This means that half of the students are boys, so $\frac{1}{2}(20) = \frac{20}{2} = 10$. Since there are 10 boys, 90% of the 10 boys take the bus to school, which is equal to $\frac{90}{100}(10) = \frac{900}{100} = 9$. The correct answer is (A).

18. A To find how many questions Marc answered correctly, ballpark! 88% is a large percentage, so eliminate anything too small. Eliminate (C), (D), and (E) since they are all less than half (or 50%) of 25. 88% is close to 80%, which is $\frac{4}{5}$. What's $\frac{4}{5}$ of 25? $\frac{4}{5}(25) = \frac{4 \times 25}{5} = \frac{100}{5} = 20$. So the closest answer will be a little bigger than 20. That leaves (A), which is the correct answer.

19. B Take this question in bite-sized pieces. If four friends each pay $5 for a pizza, the pizza costs $4 \times 5 =$ $20. Therefore, if a fifth friend joins, then $5 \times p = 20$. Divide both sides by 5, and each friend pays $4. The correct answer is (B).

20. D To find the perimeter, add all of the sides. Since there are 8 lengths of 4, $4 + 4 + 4 + 4 + 4 + 4 + 4 + 4 = 32$, or $8 \times 4 = 32$. The correct answer is (D).

21. C The perimeter is all the sides added together. The sides of a square are all equal, so divide 56 by 4 to find that each side has a length of 14. The correct answer is (C).

22. C Take this question in bite-sized pieces. First, find the perimeter of a square with a side length of 4 by adding up all the sides: $4 + 4 + 4 + 4 = 16$. Next, the perimeter of the rectangle with length 4 and width 6 is $4 + 4 + 6 + 6 = 20$. The question asks for the difference between the two, so $20 - 16 = 4$. The correct answer is (C).

23. A An equilateral triangle has equal sides. Therefore, if one side has a length of 4, all three sides have a length of 4. Add all the sides to find the perimeter: $4 + 4 + 4 = 12$. The correct answer is (A).

24. C All triangles have a total of 180°. This triangle is isosceles since two sides are equal. This means that the two angles opposite the sides are equal as well. Therefore, there are two angles that equal 65°. 65° + 65° = 130°. The remaining side is 50° since $180 - 130 = 50$. The correct answer is (C).

25. A If $b° = 45°$, the other angle must also be 45° since $180 - 90 - 45 = 45$, which makes this an isosceles right triangle. Therefore, the other leg of the triangle is also 4. From here, use the Pythagorean Theorem to find v^2: $4^2 + 4^2 = v^2$. Simplify the left side of the equation to get $16 + 16 = 32$. The correct answer is (A).

26. B Translate this question into math: *One-half of something* means to multiply by $\frac{1}{2}$, *difference between* means to subtract, *degrees in a square* is 360°, and *degrees in a triangle* is 180°. Thus, the equation will be $\frac{1}{2}(360 - 180)$. Simplify to get $\frac{1}{2}(180) = 90$. The correct answer is (B).

27. C Since the question asks for a specific value, use PITA to answer this question, starting with (C). If the side length of a square is 4, its perimeter is 16 because $4 + 4 + 4 + 4 = 16$ and its area is also 16 because $4^2 = 16$. Since those are equal, stop here. The correct answer is (C).

28. **D** First find the area of the rectangle with a width of 4 and length of 3: $A = l \times w = 3 \times 4 = 12$. The area of the triangle is also equal to 12, so $A = \frac{1}{2}bh = 12$. Plug in the given value for the base: $\frac{1}{2}(6)h = 12$. Simplify to find that $3h = 12$, and then divide both sides by 3. The height must be 4, so the correct answer is (D).

29. **B** First, find the volume of the box that has all dimensions known. $V = lwh$, so $V = 3 \times 4 \times 10 = 120$. Since the other box has the same volume, $120 = 6 \times 4 \times h$. $120 = 24h$, so $h = 5$. The correct answer is (B).

30. **D** Use the formula for the area of a square: $A = s^2$. If $A = 64p^2$, then to find the side length of the square, take the square root: $\sqrt{64} = 8$. Eliminate (A) and (B) since both choices have 64. For the square root of p^2, you can plug in for p. Pick an easy number like 2. If $p = 2$, then $p^2 = 4$. So $\sqrt{p^2} = \sqrt{4} = 2$, which means your answer should equal 2 when you plug in for p. Choice (C) has p^2, which would be 4, so eliminate (C). Choice (D) has p, which is 2. Keep it! Choice (E) is missing p, so it can't be correct. The correct answer is (D).

31. **D** The length of AB is the same as all the different heights added together on the right-hand side of the figure. Therefore, the perimeter will contain two lengths of 10. Similarly, the length of AC is the same as all the different lengths added together that are across the figure (in this case, above) AC, so there will be two lengths of 15. To find the perimeter, add all the sides: $P = 10 + 10 + 15 + 15 = 50$. The correct answer is (D).

32. **C** Notice the three triangles that have been created within the rectangle. Look at the two right triangles that surround the larger (possibly) equilateral triangle in the middle. Since each triangle has a right angle, the other two angles must equal 90° since 180° − 90° = 90°. Thus, in the triangle on the left side that includes side AB, $w + x = 90°$, and in the triangle on the right side that includes side CD, $y + z = 90°$. Add all these together to find that 90° + 90° = 180°. The correct answer is (C).

33. **D** Notice that the part that juts out on the left side of the shape would fit into the indented part on the right side of the shape. Filling in the hole would make a rectangle with a length of 8 and a width of 4 + 3 + 4 = 11. To find the area of a rectangle, use the formula $A = l \times w$. Therefore, $A = 8 \times 11 = 88$. The correct answer is (D).

34. **B** Take this question in bite-sized pieces. The question asks for the shaded region, so you want the part inside the square but outside the circle. In other words, if you find the area of the square and the area of the circle, you can find the shaded region by removing what you do not need (the area of the circle). First, find the area of the square. The side of the square is equal to 4, so $A = s^2 = 4^2 = 16$. Eliminate (A), (C), (D), and (E), since these do not contain 16. For added security, find the area of the circle. The radius is 2, so $A = \pi r^2 = \pi(2)^2 = 4\pi$. Remember to subtract that from the area of the square, so the full answer is $16 - 4\pi$. The correct answer is (B).

35. **E** To find the distance between two points, draw a right triangle and use the Pythagorean Theorem. Draw a line straight down from point B and directly right from point A. That point will be (7, 1), which you can label C. The distance from A to C is 6, and the distance from C to B is 8. Use the Pythagorean Theorem to find the missing side: $6^2 + 8^2 = c^2$. Simplify the left side to get 36 + 64 = 100. Take the square root of both sides to get $c = 10$. The correct answer is (E).

Practice Drill 3—Ratios

1. **A**   When the question asks about ratios, make a Ratio Box. The ratio of red to blue lollipops is 3:5, so place this information in the ratio row. Add across to find that 3 + 5 = 8, and put 8 in the total column for this row. The question states that the total number of lollipops is 56. Put this number in the total column in the actual number row. Now, ask yourself what times 8 equals 56. Well, 7 × 8 = 56, so the multiplier is 7. To find the number of blue lollipops, multiply 5 × 7 = 35. The correct answer is (A).

	RED	**BLUE**	**TOTAL**
Ratio	3	5	8
Multiplier	× 7	× 7	× 7
Actual Number	21	35	56

2. **C**   The ratio of single rooms to doubles to triples is 3:4:5, so label the boxes and place this ratio in the top row. Add 3 + 4 + 5 to find the total for the room types is 12. Put 12 in the total column for the ratio row. The question states that there are 36 total rooms in the hotel, so this number goes in the total column for the actual number row. 12 times what equals 36? Since 12 × 3 = 36, the multiplier is 3. Find the number of doubles by multiplying: 4 × 3 = 12. The correct answer is (C).

	SINGLES	**DOUBLES**	**TRIPLES**	**TOTAL**
Ratio	3	4	5	12
Multiplier	× 3	× 3	× 3	× 3
Actual Number	9	12	15	36

3. **C**   The question states that the superstore *has exactly three times as many large oak desks as small oak desks*, so the ratio of large desks to small desks is 3:1. Write this information into the ratio row, and add the two numbers together to get the total for the ratio row: 3 + 1 = 4. So 4 goes into the total column for the ratio row. The actual total is not given; however, that number will have to be a multiple of 4 since 4 times the multiplier will equal the total actual number. Since the question asks for the total number of desks, look at the choices. You can eliminate (A), (B), (D), and (E) because these numbers are not multiples of 4. Only 16 is a possible actual total because the multipliers must be integers. You can check to see that 16 works by plugging it into the ratio box. Remember, the desks must be integers since the store isn't selling partial desks!

	LARGE DESKS	**SMALL DESKS**	**TOTAL**
Ratio	3	1	4
Multiplier	× 4	× 4	× 4
Actual Number	12	4	16

4. **C**   This question gives information about the total number of players first, so place this information in the bottom row and add 8 and 4 to find the total for the actual number row. Be careful to order the ratio in the way the question asks. There are more right-handed players, so the first number should be the bigger of the two numbers. Eliminate (A) and (B)! Next, divide out the largest possible common denominator, in this case 4, to find the most reduced form of the ratio. That means the ratio of right-handed players to left-handed players is 2:1. The correct answer is (C). Note: If you chose (A), you set up the Ratio Box backwards, showing left-handed players to right-handed players. Read carefully!

	RIGHT-HANDED	LEFT-HANDED	TOTAL
Ratio	2	1	3
Multiplier	× 4	× 4	× 4
Actual Number	8	4	12

5. **C**   Take the question one step at a time: Half of the 400 students are girls, so there are 200 girls. This number will go in the total column for the actual number row. The ratio of the girls who ride the bus to those who walk is 7:3, which will go in the ratio row of the box. Add 7 and 3 to find the total number: 10. 10 times what equals 200? If 10 × 20 = 200, then the multiplier is 20. The question asks how many girls walk to school, so multiply 3 × 20 = 60 to get the total girls walking to school. The correct answer is (C).

	BUS	WALK	TOTAL
Ratio	7	3	10
Multiplier	× 20	× 20	× 20
Actual Number	140	60	200

6. **C**   The ratio of goat food to grass is 2:1, so place this in the ratio row of the box. The question also states that the goat eats 15 total pounds per day, so place this number in the total column of the actual number row. To find the multiplier, find the total of the ratio, 2 + 1 = 3, and find what times 3 equals 15. Since 3 × 5 = 15, the multiplier is 5. The question asks for the total amount of grass the goat eats, so 1 × 5 = 5. The correct answer is (C).

	GOAT FOOD	GRASS	TOTAL
Ratio	2	1	3
Multiplier	× 5	× 5	× 5
Actual Number	10	5	15

Practice Drill 4—Averages

1. **A** Use an Average Pie to solve this question: . Place 3 in the *# of items* portion and 18 in the *average* place. Multiply these numbers to find the total, which is 54. The question asks for twice the sum, which is the same as twice the total, so 2 × 54 = 108. The correct answer is (A).

2. **D** Whenever a question mentions average, use an Average Pie to solve . Place 4 in the *# of items* portion, and 7 in the *average* place. Find the total by multiplying the two together: 4 × 7 = 28. Eliminate (E) right away because that is the total. The question asks for the largest number the set could contain, so start with the largest remaining number in the choices: 25. If 25 were the largest number in the set, the other numbers would be 1, 1, and 1. This is a possibility, since the problem does not say the numbers have to be distinct. Since this works, the correct answer is (D).

3. **B** Use two Average Pie to organize the information in this question—every time you see the word *aver-age* draw an Average Pie . The first pie represents the information about the boys: 4 boys average 2 projects each, so place 4 in the *# of items* place and 2 in the *average* place. To find the total number of projects the boys complete, multiply 4 and 2 to find a total of 8 projects. Repeat this same process with the girls in the second pie. The 5 girls average 3 projects each, so place these numbers in their respective places in the average pie, and multiply to find a total of 15 projects. The question asks for the total number of projects in the class, so 8 + 15 = 23. The correct answer is (B).

4. **A** Use two Average Pie to organize the information in this question—every time you see the word *average* draw an Average Pie . There are 6 students with an average test score of 72. Place 6 in the *# of items* place and 72 in the *average* place. Find the total number of points by multiplying 6 × 72 = 432. Make a separate Average Pie for the next portion of the question. If a seventh student joins the class, the *# of items* place now contains 7, and the desired *average* is 76. Multiply these together to find that 7 × 76 = 532. The difference between 532 and 432 is 100, so the seventh student must score 100 to change the average to 76. The correct answer is (A).

5.   A   First, add the three scores to find Catherine's current point total. 84 + 85 + 88 = 257. Next, make an

Average Pie with 4 in the *# of items* place since there will be a fourth test, and 89 as the desired *average*. Multiply 4 × 89 to find a total of 356. Subtract the totals to find that 356 − 257 = 99. This means that she must score a 99 on the fourth test to raise her average to an 89. The correct answer is (A).

Practice Drill 5—Percent Change

1.   E   The question is testing percent change since it asks *by what percent did the temperature drop?* To find

percent change, use the formula % change = $\dfrac{\text{difference}}{\text{original}}$ × 100. The change in temperature was 20

degrees: 10° − (−10°) = 20°. Since the question asks for the percent the temperature *dropped*, the *larger*

number will be the original number. Thus, the equation should read $\dfrac{20}{10}$ × 100, which reduces to 2 ×

100 = 200. The correct answer is (E).

2.   C   The question is testing percent change since it asks *by what percent did the patty increase?* To find per-

cent change, use the formula % change = $\dfrac{\text{difference}}{\text{original}}$ × 100. The change in patty size is 4, which is

given in the question. The new patty size is 16 oz, so the original patty size must have been 12 oz since

16 − 4 = 12. The equation will read $\dfrac{4}{12}$ × 100, which reduces to $\dfrac{1}{3}$ × 100 = $\dfrac{100}{3}$ = 33$\dfrac{1}{3}$. The correct

answer is (C).

Practice Drill 6—Plugging In

1.   E   This is a Plugging In question because there are variables in the choices and the question stem

contains the phrase *in terms of*. Plug In a value, work through the problem to find a target answer,

and then check each of the choices to see which yields the target answer. For instance, Plug In *x* =

$3. The question asks for the total amount of money donated, so 3 × 200 = 600. The target answer

is $600. Now, plug 3 into the choices for *x* to see which choice matches your target answer (600).

Eliminate (A) because $\dfrac{3}{200}$ is way too small. Eliminate (B) as well because 200 ≠ 600. Eliminate

(C) because $\dfrac{200}{3}$ is still too small. Eliminate (D) because 200 + 3 or 203 ≠ 600. Choice (E) works

because 200(3) = 600. The correct answer is (E).

2. **D** This is a Plugging In question because there are variables in the choices and the question stem contains the phrase *in terms of.* Plug In a value, work through the problem to find a target answer, and then check each of the choices to see which yields the target answer. For instance, Plug In 6 for *d* dollars. If 10 magazines cost $6, then $3 would buy 5 magazines—you spend half as much money, so you can get only half as many magazines. So 5 is the target answer. Now, plug 6 into the choices to see which answer yields 5, the target answer. Eliminate (A) because $\frac{3 \times 6}{10} = \frac{18}{10} = 1.8$ does not equal 5. Eliminate (B) because 30(6) is way too large. Choice (C) is a fraction, $\frac{6}{30} = \frac{1}{5}$, so it will not equal 5. Choice (D) works, as $\frac{30}{6} = 5$, so keep this choice. Remember to try all five choices when Plugging In, so check (E) as well: $\frac{10 \times 6}{3} = \frac{60}{3} = 20$. Eliminate (E) since 20 ≠ 5. The correct answer is (D).

3. **D** This is a Plugging In question because there are variables in the choices and the question stem contains the phrase *in terms of.* Plug In a value, work through the problem to find a target answer, and then check each of the choices to see which yields the target answer. *The zoo has four times as many monkeys as lions*, so, for instance, Plug In 40 for the monkeys, which translates to 4 × lions, = 40, so there are 10 lions. *There are four more lions than zebras*, which means that 10 − 4 = 6 zebras, so z = 6. The question asks *how many monkeys are there in the zoo*, so the target answer is 40. Now, plug 6 into the choices for *z* to see which choice matches your target answer (40). Eliminate (A) because 6 + 4 = 10 is too small. Eliminate (B) because 6 + 8 = 14 is still too small. In (C), 4 × 6 = 24 is still not equal to 40, so eliminate (C). Since 4(6) + 16 = 40, keep (D). Remember to try all five choices when Plugging In, so check (E) as well. 4(6) + 4 = 28, which is too small, so eliminate (E). The correct answer is (D).

4. **E** When there are percents or fractions without a starting or ending value in the question stem, feel free to Plug In. For instance, Plug In $100 for the starting price of the suit. It is *reduced by half,* so one-half of $100 is $50, and the new price of the suit is $50. The suit is then *reduced by 10%,* so 10% of $50 is $\frac{10}{100}(50) = \frac{1}{10}(50) = \frac{50}{10} = 5$. Subtract this from $50 to find the new price of the suit: 50 − 5 = 45. The final price is $45. The *final price is what percent of the original* translates to $45 = \frac{x}{100}(100)$, which makes the math easy! 45 = *x*, so the correct answer is (E).

5. **C** When there are percents or fractions without a starting or ending value in the question stem, feel free to Plug In. What number would make the math easy? 8 is a common denominator for $\frac{1}{4}$ and $\frac{1}{2}$, so draw a circle and divide it into 8 equal parts. Shade in the number of pieces he has eaten. On Wednesday, he ate $\frac{1}{4}$ of the pie, so $\frac{1}{4}$ of 8 is 2 slices, leaving 6 slices for later. The next day, he ate $\frac{1}{2}$

of what was left. Half of 6 slices is 3, so he ate 3 slices. There are now 3 out of 8 slices left. Beware of choosing (A), however! The question asks how much he ate, so add up the slices he consumed. There should be 5 slices shaded (2 + 3 = 5), so the correct answer is (C).

6. **B** This is a Plugging In question because there are variables in the choices and the question stem contains the phrase *in terms of*. Plug In a value, work through the problem to find a target answer, and then check each of the choices to see which yields the target answer. For instance, say that p pieces of candy is equal to 5 pieces, and c cents is 10 cents. Therefore, 10 pieces of candy will cost 20 cents—you have twice as many pieces, so it will cost twice as much money. So, the target answer is 20. Now, Plug In your values for p and c into the choices to find the choice that equals your target answer (20). Eliminate (A) because $\frac{5 \times 10}{10} = \frac{50}{10} = 5$, which is too small. $\frac{10 \times 10}{5} = \frac{100}{5} = 20$, so keep (B). Remember to check the remaining choices when Plugging In. Cross off (C) because 10(5)(10) = 500, which is way too large. $\frac{10 \times 5}{10} = \frac{50}{10} = 5$, so eliminate (D) as well. Finally, eliminate (E) because 10 + 5 + 10 or 25 ≠ 20. The correct answer is (B).

7. **C** In this question, J is an odd integer, so Plug In an odd integer for J. Since this is a *must be* question, see if there is a number that would make the answer untrue. Plug In 1 for J to make (A) untrue, since $\frac{1}{3}$ is not greater than 1. This number for J will also eliminate (B) since 1 – 2 = –1, which is not a positive integer. Choice (C) is true since 2 × 1 = 2, which is an even integer. Eliminate (D) since $1^2 = 1$ is not greater than 1. Finally, eliminate (E) since J could be negative. For example, if $J = –3$, –3 is not greater than 0. Check that value for (C) to be sure it always works. Again, if $J = –3$, then 2 × –3 = –6, which is still an even integer. Since it always works, the correct answer is (C).

8. **C** Try Plugging In values that satisfy the question stem, and eliminate choices. It may be necessary to Plug In twice on *must be true* or *always true* questions. If m is an even number, let $m = 2$, and let $n = 3$ since it must be an odd integer. If p is the product of m and n, then $p = (2)(3) = 6$. Now check the choices. Eliminate (A) because p is not a fraction. Eliminate (B) as well since p is not an odd integer. Keep (C) because 6 is divisible by 2. 6 is not between 2 and 3, so eliminate (D). Finally, keep (E) because 6 is greater than zero. Plug In again to compare the remaining choices. Perhaps keep one number the same, so $n = 3$, but make $m = –2$ instead of 2. Now $p = (–2)(3) = –6$. Choice (C) still works since –6 is divisible by 2, but (E) no longer works since p is less than zero. Since it is always true, the correct answer is (C).

Practice Drill 7—Plugging In The Answers

1. **C** The question is asking for a specific value and there are real numbers in the choices, so use PITA to solve. Ted can read 60 pages per hour, which is 60 pages in 60 minutes, and Naomi can read 45 pages in 60 minutes. Combined, they can read 105 pages (60 + 45) in 60 minutes. Now, start with (C) to see which answer will yield a total of 210 pages. If they read for 120 minutes, they will read double the amount they did in 60 minutes: 105 × 2 = 210. This satisfies the question, so (C) is correct.

2. **E** The question is asking for a specific value and there are real numbers in the choices, so use PITA to solve, starting with (C). If $y = 2$, then $y + (y + 1) = 2 + (2 + 1) = 2 + 3 = 5$, which is too small. Therefore, eliminate (C) as well as (A) and (B) since those values for y are also too small. Now try (D): if $y = 8$, then $y + (y + 1) = 8 + (8 + 1) = 8 + 9 = 17$, which is still too small, so eliminate (D). The correct answer must be (E). If you're pressed for time, pick (E) and move on. If you have time later to come back and check, great! It's okay to be aggressive and go with (E) if you know the other choices don't work. There has to be a correct answer!

3. **C** The question is asking for a specific value and there are real numbers in the choices, so use PITA to solve, starting with (C). The choices represent Kenny's age now. If Kenny is 15 years old and he is 5 years older than Greg, then Greg must be 10. In 5 years, Kenny will be 20. *Twice as old as Greg is now* would be 2(10) = 20. Since the two numbers match, stop here. The correct answer is (C).

4. **B** The question is asking for a specific value and there are real numbers in the choices, so use PITA to solve, starting with (C). The choices represent how much Sara pays. If Sara pays $30 and she pays twice as much as John, then John would have paid $15 since $\frac{1}{2} \times 30 = 15$. Paul paid three times as much as Sara, so he would have paid $3 \times 30 = 90$. This added together is more than $90, so eliminate (C), (D), and (E), as all of these will amount to a total that is too much. Try (B): if Sara paid $20, John would have paid $10 since $\frac{1}{2} \times 20 = 10$. Paul paid $3 \times 20 = 60$. Add these amounts together to find that $20 + $10 + $60 = $90, which satisfies the question. The correct answer is (B).

5. **D** First, translate the English into math and then use PITA to test the choices. *Four less than a certain number* translates to $n - 4$, and two-thirds of a number translates to $\frac{2}{3} \times n$. So the equation is $n - 4 = \frac{2}{3} \times n$. Now, Plug In the Answers to find the one that satisfies the equation, starting with (C). If $n = 8$, then the equation will read $8 - 4 = \frac{2}{3}(8)$. Since $4 \neq \frac{16}{3}$, eliminate (C) and try another choice. Try (D). If $n = 12$, then $12 - 4 = \frac{2}{3}(12)$, which is $8 = \frac{24}{3}$ or 8 = 8. Since 12 works, stop here. The correct answer is (D).

Practice Drill 8—Functions

1. **B**   Don't be scared off by these types of questions! Simply follow the directions and plug numbers into the equation where specified. In this case, replace n with the given number (7). Thus, the equation should read $7 = 10(7) – 10$. Simplify the equation to $7 = 70 – 10 = 60$. The correct answer is (B).

2. **C**   The question asks which of the choices will yield a result of 120. Therefore, use PITA to solve, starting with (C). If $n = 13$, then replace 13 for n in the given equation: $13 = 10(13) – 10$. Simplify to find that $13 = 130 – 10 = 120$. This works, so the correct answer is (C).

3. **D**   In this function, simply plug in the number to the left of the weird symbol for d and the number to the right of the weird symbol for y exactly as the example directs. The function should read $d \, ¿ \, y = 10 \, ¿ \, 2 = (10 \times 2) – (10 + 2)$, which simplifies to $(20) – (12) = 8$. The correct answer is (D).

4. **D**   This question asks to first find the result of the function, and then to find the unknown K. Take this question in bite-sized pieces. Start with the parentheses first. Solve for $4 \, ¿ \, 3$: $(4 \times 3) – (4 + 3) = (12) – (7) = 5$. Next, plug 5 into the equation to find K: $K(5) = 30$. Divide by 5 on both sides to find that K equals 6. The correct answer is (D).

5. **A**   You will need to set the equation up based on the function defined, and then use PEMDAS to simplify and solve for the end result. Take this question in bite-sized pieces. Start with the first set of parentheses: $(2 \, ¿ \, 4) = (2 \times 4) – (2 + 4) = (8) – (6) = 2$. Next, work with the second set of parentheses: $(3 \, ¿ \, 6) = (3 \times 6) – (3 + 6) = (18) – (9) = 9$. Put these values back into the original equation: $(2 \, ¿ \, 4) \times (3 \, ¿ \, 6) = (2) \times (9) = 18$. Now, test the choices to see which expression yields 18 as well. Try (A): $(9 \times 3) – (9 + 3) + 3 = (27) – (12) + 3 = 18$. Since this matches, stop here. The correct answer is (A). Remember, if you find a question too time consuming, skip it and move on! You can come back to it later if you have time.

Practice Drill 9—Charts and Graphs

1. **E**   First, find what District A spent in 1990: $400,000 (pay attention to the note below the table: the numbers are in thousands of dollars). Look for double this amount. $800,000 is listed in the table for the value in 1991 for District E. The correct answer is (E).

2. **D**   Add across to find which district spent the most, keeping in mind that these are all in the thousands (though this doesn't really matter to find the largest sum). District E has the largest sum: $600,000 + $800,000 = $1,400,000. The correct answer is (D).

3. **E**   Remember that these numbers are in the thousands. Add down to find the sum of the values in 1990: $1,800,000. Do the same with the values in 1991 to find a sum of $2,600,000. Find the difference of these values: $2,600,000 – $1,800,000 = $800,000. The correct answer is (E).

4. **D**   Check the graph. Carl owns 5 CDs, so the other two people together must own a total of 5 CDs. Eliminate (A) because Abe has 2 and Ben has 4, totaling 6. Eliminate (B) as well because Ben has 4 and Dave has 3, which is 7. Choice (C) is incorrect since both Abe and Ed have 2, so this only amounts to 4. Choice (D) works because Abe has 2 and Dave has 3, amounting to 5. There can be only one correct answer, so the correct answer is (D).

5. **B**   To find which student owns one-fourth of all the CDs, first add all the CDs to find a total. Your work from the previous question will help! Abe = 2, Ben = 4, Carl = 5, Dave = 3, and Ed = 2, which yields a total of 16 CDs. $\frac{1}{4}$ of 16 is $\frac{1}{4} \times 16 = \frac{16}{4} = 4$, so Ben is the student who has 4 CDs. The correct answer is (B).

6. **E** To find Matt's earnings for the week, first add up all his hours and then multiply by his hourly salary ($6/hour). He works 3.5 + 4 + 3.5 + 3 = 14 hours over the week, so 14 × 6 = 84. The correct answer is (E).

7. **B** Remember, if you see the word average, you can use an Average Pie . The previous question helped you find the total number of hours Matt worked: 14. Put that number in the *total* place. He worked 4 days—note the question says *on the days he worked* not the number of days in a week. Put 4 in the *# of items* place. Divide these two numbers to find the average: $\frac{14}{4}$ = 3.5. If you're pressed for time, instead of doing the long division, let the choices help! Since 14 is not divisible by 4, eliminate all the integers. The correct answer is (B).

8. **C** One way to solve this problem is to translate the words into math: *the hours he worked on Monday* is 3.5, a*ccounted for* is equals, *what percent* is $\frac{x}{100}$, and the *total hours he worked* is 14. The equation is 3.5 = $\frac{x}{100}$ × 14. Simplify the right side: $\frac{x}{100}$ × 14 = $\frac{x(14)}{100}$ = $\frac{14x}{100}$. Multiply both sides by 100 to get 350 = 14x. Divide both sides by 14, and x = 25. The correct answer is (C). You can also find a percent by dividing the desired amount by the total amount: Matt worked 3.5 hours on Monday and a total of 14 hours, so $\frac{3.5}{14}$ = $\frac{35}{140}$ = $\frac{1}{4}$, or 25%.

Practice Drill 10—Middle and Upper Levels Only

1. **B** Since there are variables in the choices, Plug In a value for *p*, paying attention to the restrictions in the question. If *p* is an odd integer, make sure to Plug In an odd integer, for instance *p* = 3. Now, test the choices to see which ones can be eliminated. Cross off (A) because $(3)^2$ + 3 = 9 + 3 = 12, which is not odd. Choice (B) works since 2(3) + 1 = 6 + 1 = 7, which is odd. Choice (C) works since $\frac{3}{3}$ = 1 . Choice (D) does not work since 3 − 3 = 0. Remember 0 is even, not odd. Eliminate (E) because $2(3^2)$ = 2(9) = 18, which is not odd. Plug In a second time for the remaining choices. Try *p* = 5. Choice (B) still works because 2(5) + 1 = 10 + 1 = 11, but eliminate (C) because $\frac{5}{3}$ is no longer an integer. The correct answer is (B).

2. **B** The wording on this problem is tricky. It asks for which CANNOT be true, so try to find examples that COULD be true to eliminate choices. Pay attention to the restrictions in the problem,

and Plug In two positive even integers: say 4 and 6. Thus, $4 + 6 = 10 = m$. Next, eliminate choices that WORK. Choice (A) does not work since 10 is greater than 5. Keep it. Choice (B) does not work because $3(10) = 30$, which is even, not odd. Keep it. Eliminate (C) because $m = 10$, which is even, so it works. Eliminate (D) as well because 10^3 ends in a zero, which is also even, so this statement works. Choice (E) doesn't work because $\frac{10}{2} = 5$, which is odd. Keep it. Now, Plug In a second time for the remaining choices. Try new numbers, and remember that the numbers do not have to be distinct from one another. Try Plugging In 2 for both positive even integers. Thus, $2 + 2 = 4 = m$. Check the remaining answers and eliminate the choices that WORK. For (A), 4 is less than 5. That works, so eliminate (A). For (B), $3(4) = 12$, which does not work since it's even, so keep it. Finally for (E), $\frac{4}{2} = 2$ is even, which works, so eliminate (E). The only choice left is (B), which is the correct answer.

3. **D**   This is a Plugging In question because there are variables in the choices. Plug In a value, work through the problem to find a target answer, and then check each of the choices to see which yields the target answer. Let $b = 4$ and $a = 3$. Finding the *product* means multiply, so $\frac{1}{2}(4) \times 3^2 = 2 \times 9 = 18$. The target answer is 18. Now, Plug In your values for b and a into the choices to find the choice that equals your target answer (18). Eliminate (A) since $(3 \times 4)^2 = (12)^2 = 144$, which is too big. Eliminate (B) since $\frac{3^2}{4} = \frac{9}{4}$ and is not equal to 18. Also eliminate (C) since $2(3) \times \frac{1}{2}(4) = 6 \times 2 = 12$, which does not equal 18. Choice (D) works: $\frac{3^2 \times 4}{2} = \frac{9 \times 4}{2} = \frac{36}{2} = 18$. Keep it. Remember to try all five choices when Plugging In, so check (E) as well. $\frac{3^2 \times 4^2}{2} = \frac{9 \times 16}{2} = \frac{144}{2} = 72$, which is too big, so eliminate (E). The correct answer is (D).

4. **D**   There are variables in the choices, so Plug In here. For instance, say that Damon has 10 records, so $d = 10$. That means Graham has half as many records, so he has 5 records. Graham has $\frac{1}{4}$ as many records as Alex, so Alex has 4 times as many as Graham: $5 \times 4 = 20$, or 20 records. Together, Graham and Alex have $5 + 20 = 25$ records. So, 25 is the target answer. Now, Plug In 10 for d and find which choice yields 25, your target answer. Eliminate (A) because $\frac{3 \times 10}{2} = \frac{30}{2} = 15$, which is not 25. Eliminate (B) since $\frac{3 \times 10}{4} = \frac{30}{4}$ is even smaller than (A). Choice (C) is too large

since $\dfrac{9 \times 10}{2} = \dfrac{90}{2} = 45$. Choice (D) works because $\dfrac{5 \times 10}{2} = \dfrac{50}{2} = 25$. Remember to try all five choices when Plugging In, so still check (E). 2(10) = 20, which does not work, so eliminate (E). The correct answer is (D).

5. **E**   Use MADSPM to simplify the exponents in the equations first. When raising a power to a power, multiply the exponents together. For the first equation, $\left(x^3\right)^3 = x^{3 \times 3} = x^9$, so a = 9. When dividing by the same base, subtract the exponents. For the second equation, $\dfrac{y^{10}}{y^2} = y^{10-2} = y^8$, so b = 8. The question asks to find $a \times b$, so 9 × 8 = 72. The correct answer is (E).

6. **C**   Take this question one step at a time. If there are 250 people and 75 are children, then there are 175 adults. If one hero sandwich could feed 12 children and there are 75 children at the party, find how many sandwiches are needed for the 75 children: 12 goes into 75 six times evenly since 6 × 12 = 72, which leaves a remainder of 3 children. Part of another sandwich will be needed to feed those children. Therefore, the 75 children will need 6+ sandwiches. Now, do the same for the adults. There are 175 adults at the party. Each hero sandwich can feed 8 adults. 8 only goes into 175 twenty-one times evenly since 8 × 21 = 168. That will leave a remainder of 7 adults (175 – 168 = 7). Remember, 1 sandwich feeds 8 adults, so if there are 7 adults left, you need almost an entire sandwich more. That makes about 22 sandwiches to feed all the adults. 22 + 6 = 28. Remember that a little more than 6 sandwiches were needed to feed all the children (no half-sandwich orders allowed!). Round up, so 29 sandwiches will be needed to feed the entire group. The correct answer is (C). Ballparking is okay here! Note that the next closest answer is 30, which is too many (3 extra sandwiches are not needed), so both (D) and (E) are too large. Choices (A) and (B) are too small even before taking the remainders into account, which makes (C) is the best answer!

7. **C**   When there are percentages in the choices with no starting or ending value, go ahead and Plug In a number. Even though it's not realistic, try Plugging In 100 miles for the distance between New York and Dallas. Yes, it's further, but make the math easy when Plugging In your own number! Liam and Noel drive $\dfrac{1}{5}$ of the distance on Monday, so $\dfrac{1}{5}$ of 100 is $\dfrac{1}{5}(100) = \dfrac{100}{5} = 20$. Subtract this from the total they must drive: 100 – 20 = 80 miles left. On Tuesday, they drive half the remaining distance; half of 80 is 40, so subtract this from 80: 80 – 40 = 40, so there are 40 miles remaining. To find the percentage they still need to drive, divide the remaining mileage from the total to find $\dfrac{\text{part}}{\text{whole}} = \dfrac{40}{100}$. Multiply by 100 to convert to a percent: $\dfrac{40}{100} \times 100 = 40\%$. The correct answer is (C).

8. **B**   Work step by step here. If $\dfrac{1}{4}$ of the bag contains 10 grams of fat, then the entire bag must contain 40 grams of fat since 10 × 4 = 40. To find $\dfrac{1}{6}$ of the bag, divide 40 by 6. This will not be a whole number, but it will be between 6 and 7 using Ballparking (6 × 6 = 36 and 6 × 7 = 42). Thus, the correct answer is (B).

9. **B** There are variables in the choices, so Plug In here. Say there are 20 students in the class, so $x = 20$. If each donates an average of \$3, $y = 3$. Next, find the total amount of money donated: $20 \times 3 = 60$. This is the target answer. Now, Plug In your values for x and y to see which choice yields the target (60). Eliminate (A) because $\dfrac{20}{3}$ is not an integer and is much too small. Choice (B) works because $(20)(3) = 60$. Eliminate (C) because $\dfrac{20 \times 3}{20} = \dfrac{60}{20} = 3$, which is too small. Cross off (D) since it equals $\dfrac{3}{20}$, and (E) is way too large: $(2)(20)(3) = 120$. The correct answer is (B).

10. **E** There are variables in the answers, so Plug In here. If $e + f = 17$, then 17 is divisible by 17, so choose two numbers that add together to equal 17. For instance, $13 + 4 = 17$, so let $e = 13$ and $f = 4$. Now, Plug In to the choices and see which one works. Eliminate (A) because $(13 \times 4) - 17 = 52 - 17 = 35$, which is not divisible by 17. Similarly, eliminate (B) because $13 + (4 \times 17) = 13 + (68) = 81$, which is not divisible by 17 either. Choice (C) does not work because $(13 \times 17) + 4 = (221) + 4 = 225$, which is not divisible by 17. Eliminate (D) because $\dfrac{13 + 4}{17} = \dfrac{17}{17} = 1$, which is not divisible by 17. Keep (E) because $(13 \times 3) + (4 \times 3) = 39 + 12 = 51$, which is divisible by 17. The correct answer is (E).

11. **C** Since the question mentions the mean, create an Average Pie. Joe wants to have an average of 230 or more, so place 230 in the *average* spot of the pie. In the *# of items* place, write in 5 because he has already read 4 books that were 200, 200, 220, and 260 pages long, and he is going to read one more. Multiply to find the total number of pages he must read: $5 \times 230 = 1,150$. He has already read $200 + 200 + 220 + 260 = 880$ pages, so find the difference between these two totals to see how many pages long the fifth book must at least be: $1,150 - 880 = 270$. The correct answer is (C).

12. **A** Since the question mentions average, create an Average Pie. Sayeeda wants to raise her average to 15 on the fourth game, so write 15 in the *average* spot and 4 in for the *# of items*. Multiply these two numbers together to find the total points: $4 \times 15 = 60$. In the first three games, she scored $8 + 12 + 12 = 32$ points. The difference that she must score in the fourth game is $60 - 32 = 28$ points. The correct answer is (A).

13. **C** First, simplify the first expression: $(3xy)^3 = 3^3x^3y^3 = 27x^3y^3$. While comparing it to the other expression, $3x^2y^5$, you can work in bite-sized pieces. Start with the coefficients. The greatest common factor of 3 and 27 is 3. Eliminate (A), (D), and (E) since those don't contain 3. Both of the remaining answers contain x^2, so compare y in the two expressions. One has $y^3 = y \times y \times y$ and the other has $y^5 = y \times y \times y \times y \times y$. The greatest common factor is y^3 since both expressions have at least 3 y's. Eliminate (B). The correct answer is (C).

14.   **B**   To start, draw a picture for this question. Mechanicville must be due east of Stillwater, so draw Mechanicville directly to the right of Stillwater. Mechanicville is also due south of Half Moon Crescent, so draw Half Moon Crescent directly above Mechanicville. Connect each of these cities to form a right triangle. Label the lengths of the sides, 30 miles and 40 miles according to the problem. The length of the hypotenuse will equal the shortest distance from Stillwater to Half Moon Crescent. Use the Pythagorean Theorem to find the hypotenuse ($30^2 + 40^2 = c^2$), or recognize that this is a 3-4-5 right triangle. Therefore, the sides are 30, 40, and 50. The correct answer is (B).

15.   **B**   Ballparking is one way to work through this problem. The shaded region looks to be about half the square, and half of 144 is 72, (B). To be more precise, the side of the square must be 12 since $A = s^2$ and $12^2 = 144$, so the height of each shaded triangle is 12. The base for one triangle ends at P and the base for the other triangle ends at Q, and $PQ = 12$ since it's a side of the square. So make the base for each triangle 6 since the two bases must add up to 12. Plug those values into the formula: $A = \frac{1}{2}bh = \frac{1}{2}(6)(12) = 36$. Since both areas equal 36, the total area of the shaded region is 36 + 36 = 72. The correct answer is (B).

16.   **B**   Even though the length of the radius is unknown, it is still possible to find the angle measurements. There is a 90° angle in the center of the circle, and OQ and OP are both radii of the circle, which means they are the same length. Therefore, this is an isosceles right triangle, meaning the two smaller angles are equal. All triangles have 180º, so 180° – 90° = 90°. The two smaller angles add up to 90°, so $\frac{90°}{2} = 45°$. The correct answer is (B).

17.   **D**   Notice that the four intersecting lines form a quadrilateral. All quadrilaterals contain 360°, so keep a tally of the vertices and find the missing angle. 80° is already provided, so 360° – 80° = 280°. All straight lines add up to 180°, so use the exterior angles to find the interior angles. If one of the exterior angles is 75°, the supplementary angle must be 105°. Subtract this from 280° to find that 280° – 105° = 175°. The other exterior angle, 108°, is opposite the interior vertex. Since opposite angles are equal, the interior vertex must also be 108°. Subtract this from the current total to find that 175° – 108° = 67°. The missing angle is 67°. The correct answer is (D).

18.   **C**   The question states that triangle ABC is equilateral, so all three sides are equal to 4. Label AC as 4 and BC as 4. The question asks for perimeter, not area. So, there are two sides of the triangle that are part of the perimeter, so add them together: $AB + AC = 4 + 4 = 8$. Eliminate (A), (B), and (E) since the choice must have an 8 in it. Now, find the rounded portion. The rounded portion is half of the circumference (i.e., a semicircle). Since you labeled BC as 4, you should see that the diameter of the circle must also be 4. If $C = \pi d$, then half of the circumference is $\frac{1}{2}\pi d$. Plug in the value for

the diameter and simplify: $\frac{1}{2}\pi(4) = 2\pi$. The full expression for the perimeter will then read $8 + 2\pi$.
The correct answer is (C).

19. **B** To find the perimeter, it doesn't matter how the right-hand vertical segments are broken up. Since everything meets at right angles, those segments will all add up to the same height as AB, which is 12. Similarly, it does not matter how the top horizontal lines are divided. They will still add up to the same length as AC, which is 10. Therefore, simply add $10 + 10 + 12 + 12$ to find the perimeter of 44. The correct answer is (B).

20. **B** The length of police tape wrapping around a rectangle is the same as the perimeter. Draw a rectangle and label the length as 28 and the width as 6. Remember, in a rectangle, opposite sides are equal to each other. Calculate the perimeter by adding all the sides: $6 + 6 + 28 + 28 = 68$. The correct answer is (B).

21. **D** Beware! The question asks for the diameter, not the radius. First, find the volume of the cylinder as it is now. The equation for the volume of a cylinder is $V = \pi r^2 h$. Plug in the values for r and h from the question. The question states that the diameter is 18 cm, so the radius is 9 cm, and the height is 20 cm. The equation will read $V = \pi(9^2)(20)$. Simplify to get $V = \pi(81)(20)$. Do not bother doing all this multiplication yet! Since the question asks for the diameter of a single serving which has the same height, take this volume (the volume of 9 servings) and divide by 9 to find the volume of a single serving can: $V = \dfrac{\pi(81)(20)}{9}$, which simplifies to $V = \pi(9)(20)$. To find the diameter, isolate the radius: $r^2 = 9$, which means $r = 3$. Multiply by 2 to find the diameter, so $d = 6$ cm. The correct answer is (D). Remember, for any question that may seem difficult or time consuming, skip it and come back to it later if you have time!

Math Review

1. Yes

2. It is neither positive nor negative.

3. Addition

4. Multiplication

5. The quotient

6. Yes   3 + 1 + 2 = 6, which is divisible by 3;

   No   3 + 1 + 2 = 6, which is not divisible by 9.

7. Exponents

8. Yes   3 goes into 12 evenly 4 times;

   No   12 cannot go into 3.

9. No   No integer times 12 is equal to 3;

   Yes   3 × 4 = 12

10. 0   The tens digit is two places to the left of the decimal.

11. 2   The tenths digit is one place to the right of the decimal.

12. 8   Write it out! 2 × 2 × 2 = 8

13. Over 100, or $\dfrac{x}{100}$

14. Multiplication

15. Total column

16. Average Pie

17. Plug In a number

18. Add; all four

19. Multiply; two (or square one side, since the sides of a square are the same)

20. 180

21. 3; 180

22. 360

23. 2; equilateral

24. Hypotenuse; right angle

25. $A = \dfrac{1}{2}(base)(height)$

SSAT VERBAL

Review—The Verbal Plan

Pacing and Verbal Strategy

Your answers should be similar to the following:

I will start on question number 31, so that I begin with analogies.

I will do the verbal questions in the following order:

1. Analogies with words I know
2. Analogies with words I sort of know
3. Synonyms with words I know
4. Synonyms with words I sort of know
5. Analogies with words I don't know

I need only to eliminate one answer to guess.

No, I cannot eliminate choices that contain words I do not know.

Analogies

Practice Drill 1—Making Sentences

You can abbreviate your sentences as we have done below, using one letter to stand for each stem word. Your sentences should be similar to these.

1. A chapter is a section of a book.

2. A scale is used to measure weight.

3. Striped means having lines.

4. Rage is a very strong anger.

5. Rehearsal is practice for a performance.

6. A mechanic fixes a car.

7. A traitor betrays a country.

8. Aggravate means to make a problem worse.

9. A trout is a type of fish.

10. A general leads an army.

11. Crime occurs when someone breaks the law.

12. A buckle fastens a belt.

13. Truculent means prone to a fight.

14. A cure gets rid of illness.

15. A poison is something toxic.

16. A pinnacle is the top of a mountain.

17. Perilous means lacking safety.

18. A humanitarian practices philanthropy.

19. Notorious means having a bad reputation.

20. A miser is a person without generosity.

Practice Drill 2—Basic Analogy Techniques

1. **C** A chapter is a section of a book.

2. **D** A refrigerator is used to cool.

3. **B** A fish uses a fin to move itself. (Get specific!)

4. **A** A driver operates/steers a car. (Picture it. Get specific!)

5. **E** A clock is used to measure time.

6. **A** An envelope contains/transports a letter. (Watch out for (E); it's close but not the best.)

7. **A** A librarian is the person in charge of a library.

8. **C** A pen is used to write.

9. **C** A hurricane is a very, very strong breeze.

10. **A** A ball is a three-dimensional circle. (Choice (B) is wrong because the words are reversed.)

11. **D** A shell is on the outside of an egg.

12. **B** A cup is a smaller unit of measure than a quart.

13. **A** A coach leads a team.

14. **C** A bat is a type of flying mammal. (Get specific!)

15. **B** Famished means very hungry.

16. **C** To sterilize means to get rid of germs.

17. **D** A director directs/leads actors.

18. **B** An applicant wants to be hired. An applicant wants someone to hire him or her. (Think about who's doing what!)

19. **B** Stale is what bread becomes when it gets old.

20. **C** Unbiased means without prejudice.

Practice Drill 3—Working Backward

1. Choices (A) or (B) because a castle is surrounded by a moat and a galaxy is a group of stars

2. Choice (B) because a monarchy is ruled by a sovereign (Choice (E) is okay, but do thieves always practice duplicity? Not really—just thievery.)

3. Choice (B) because submissive means lacking defiance

4. Choices (B) or (C) because quarantine means to isolate a patient and elect means to choose a politician

5. Choice (D) because bland means lacking zest

Practice Drill 4—Judging "Side of the Fence"

1. D
2. D
3. S
4. D
5. D
6. S
7. D
8. S
9. S
10. D
11. S
12. D

Practice Drill 5—Using "Side of the Fence"

1. A
2. A or C
3. A or D
4. A or B
5. C or D
6. B, C, or E
7. A, B, C, or E
8. A or B
9. A, D, or E
10. A, B, or E

Practice Drill 6—Working Backward as Much as You Can

1. A tooth is used for chewing.

2. Eliminate

3. An archipelago is a group of islands.

4. Eliminate

5. Eliminate

6. To jest means to try to be humorous.

7. Eliminate

Review—The Analogies Plan

Your answers should be similar to the following:

If I know the words, then I make a sentence.

A sentence is good if it's specific and definitional.

If my sentence eliminates some but not all choices, I can make another, more specific, sentence.

A specific, definitional sentence uses words that are descriptive.

Some questions that can help me make a sentence are as follows:

- What does A/B do?
- What does A/B mean?
- How does A/B work?
- What does A/B look like?
- How is A/B used?
- Where is A/B found?
- How do A and B compare?
- How are A and B associated?

(A and B are the first two words in the analogy.)

If I know the words but can't make a sentence, then I ask myself the following:

- Are A and B synonyms?
- Do A and B have something in common?
- Are A and B members of the same group?
- What kind of sequence or pattern are A and B in?
- Do A and B rhyme?
- Do A and B have rearranged letters?

And finally, if none of these questions works with A and B (the first two words in the analogy), then I ask myself the following:

- Can I make a definitional sentence with A and C? (C is the third word in the analogy.)

If I know one of the words, then I work backward, which means that I make a sentence with each choice, and then I try using that sentence with the stem words (the first two words in the analogy).

If I sort of know the words, then I use "Side of the Fence."

I can also work backward.

If I don't know the words, I circle the question in the test booklet and skip it.

If I have time left, then I go back and work backward as much as I can.

Practice Drill 7—All Analogies Techniques

1. **C** Chocolate is a type of candy just as cat is a type of animal.

2. **A** A pound is a unit that measures weight just as decibel is a unit that measure sound.

3. **A** A student is part of a class just as an actor is part of a cast.

4. **C** A composer creates a symphony just as an architect creates (or designs) a building. Note: choice (E) is not as good because while a writer creates a paragraph, a paragraph is not a large, complete work.

5. **E** Many links make up a chain just as many words make up a sentence.

6. **E** A tadpole is a young form of a frog just as a caterpillar is a young form of a butterfly.

7. **E** A cuff is the part of a garment that is at the wrist just as a collar is the part of a garment that is at the neck. Note: buckle in choice (B) is not part of a garment and body in choice (D) is too general.

8. **A** A congregation consists of worshippers just as a galaxy consists of stars. Note: in choice (C) mines don't always contain gems.

9. **B** Tactile means sensed by touch just as audible means sensed by sound.

10. **B** A conviction is a strong opinion just as reverence is strong admiration.

11. **C** A caricature is an exaggerated drawing just as hyperbole is an exaggerated statement.

12. **B** Deceleration is a decrease in speed just as descent is a decrease in altitude.

13. **D** Something insipid is very dull just as something entertaining is very diverting.

14. **A** Voracious means wanting a lot of food just as greedy means wanting a lot of money.

15. **E** Adroit means skilled in motion just as articulate is skilled in speech. Note: skill in choice (C) is too general.

16. **E** An anesthetic dulls pain just as a muffler dulls noise.

17. **B** Impeccable is far beyond adequate just as inexhaustible is far beyond sufficient.

18. **C** Symmetrical means balanced, and amorphous means unshaped. Note: this is a vertical relationship.

19. **D**   Incessant and intermittent are opposites just as timid and brazen are opposites.

20. **C**   Penicillin is a type or kind of antibiotic just as coughing is a kind of symptom.

21. **B**   A cobbler makes a shoe just as a blacksmith makes a sword.

22. **A**   Fortify is a stronger version of protect just as blitz is a stronger version of attack.

23. **B**   Someone reprimands a delinquent just as someone recognizes (i.e. acknowledges) a virtuoso.

24. **E**   Someone disinfects a surface to make it become pristine just as someone learns something to make it become uncomplicated.

25. **C**   Something inconspicuous is easy to overlook just as something unfounded is easy to reject.

26. **E**   A student completes his studies to become a graduate just as a novice completes his studies to become a master.

27. **A**   A person who is appreciative shows gratitude just as a person who is ashamed shows compunction.

28. **B**   An egg is a discrete part of a dozen. A day is a discrete part of a week, which never changes length. Note: choice (E) is wrong because months vary in length.

29. **C**   Someone who makes an illogical choice is acting without reason just as someone who makes a hasty choice is acting without prudence.

30. **D**   Payment takes care of debt just as a recall takes care of a defect. Note: a cover-up doesn't take care of a crime for the better; a cover-up hides a crime.

SYNONYMS

Practice Drill 8—Write Your Own Definition

Possible definitions:

1.   Weird

2.   Introduction

3.   Giving

4.   Doing the right thing

5.   Change

6.   Circle around

7.   Optimistic

8.   Stick around

9.   Help

10. Build

11. Bend down

12. Honest

13. Tease

14. Rough

15. Self-centered

16. Calm

17. Use

18. Full of life

19. Stretch out

20. Help

Practice Drill 9—Write Another Definition

Look up these seven words in a dictionary to see how many different meanings they can have.

Practice Drill 10—Basic Synonym Techniques

1.	C	11.	C
2.	A	12.	B
3.	C	13.	E
4.	D	14.	B
5.	E	15.	A
6.	D	16.	C
7.	B	17.	E
8.	C	18.	C
9.	E	19.	B
10.	A	20.	C

Practice Drill 11—Making Your Own Context

Answers will vary. Possible contexts:

1. Common cold; common man

2. Competent to stand trial

3. Abridged dictionary

4. Untimely demise; untimely remark

5. Homogenized milk

6. Juvenile delinquent; delinquent payments

7. Inalienable rights

8. Paltry sum

9. Auspicious beginning; auspicious occasion

10. Prodigal son

Practice Drill 12—Using Your Own Context

1.	C	6.	B	
2.	D	7.	C	
3.	D	8.	A	
4.	D	9.	D	
5.	A	10.	A	

Practice Drill 13—All Synonyms Techniques

1. B An atrocity is something terrible that has occurred.

2. C To be indulgent is to spoil or fuss over someone. Be careful! To be indulgent does not mean to be spoiled.

3. E To reproach means to scold someone or something.

4. D If a supply is scant, then there is not enough of it to go around.

5. A To annihilate is to destroy.

6. D An amendment is a change or addition to something in order to improve it.

7. C To emulate is to copy the original as closely as possible. To simulate is to create an artificial copy of the original.

8. D The epitome of something is its perfect example or representation.

9. B A countenance is a face or facial expression.

10. C To commandeer means to take control of something.

11. A To be resilient is to have the ability to rebound or be durable.

12. A A vagrant is a homeless or wandering person.

13. D To evict is to uproot or eject.

14. C To proliferate is to create plentifully.

15. E To adhere means to literally stick to something or figuratively to obey rules or orders.

16. A A discrepancy is a difference or inequality between two or more things.

17. D To be incredulous means to be unbelieving.

18. C To invoke is to call upon something, usually a higher power.

19. D Something that is opulent is luxurious or lavish.

20. B An arsenal is a store or supply of commodities or ideas.

21. D A virtuoso, usually a performer, is a master at his or her craft.

22. E Sage advice is wise advice. A very wise person or guru may also be referred to as a sage (noun).

23. **D**   A vista is a view, usually a beautiful one.

24. **A**   Surreptitious means clandestine, secret, or hidden.

25. **C**   Perturbation is a state of being stressed, anxious, or in distress.

26. **D**   Mercurial is often used to describe personality, though it is anything that fluctuates and changes quickly.

27. **E**   Acquiesce is to oblige or agree to something.

28. **C**   Insubordinate is to be defiant or rebellious.

29. **B**   Querulous means to be whining and irritable.

30. **A**   Enervate is to lose energy or exhaust.

READING
Detailed explanations can be found online in your Student Tools.

Practice Drill 1—Getting Through the Passage
You should have brief labels like the following:

Label for 1st paragraph: Norway → Iceland
Label for 2nd paragraph: Iceland → Greenland
Label for 3rd paragraph: lost
Label for 4th paragraph: saw America; landed Greenland
What? A Viking
So what? Found America early
Passage type? History of an event

Practice Drill 2—Answering a General Question
1. D
2. D

Practice Drill 3—Answering a Specific Question
1. C
2. A   Lead word: Iceland
3. B
4. E   Lead word: Greenland
5. C

Review—The Reading Plan

Your answers should be similar to the following:

> After I read each paragraph, I label it.
> After I read an entire passage, I ask myself What? So what?
> I am better at doing these types of passages.

(Answers will vary. You may be better at answering questions related to history passages, science passages, opinion passages, stories, or poems. You may also be better at shorter passages or passages covering topics that you like. Take note of this when you take a practice test.)

The five main types of general questions, and the questions I can ask myself to answer them, are the following:

- Main idea: What was the "What? So what?" for this passage?
- Tone/attitude: How did the author feel about the subject?
- General interpretation: Which answer stays closest to what the author said and how he said it?
- General purpose: Why did the author write this?
- Prediction: How was the passage arranged? What will come next?

To find the answer to a specific question, I can use three clues:

- Paragraph labels
- Line or paragraph reference
- Lead words

If the question says, "In line 22," then I begin reading at approximately line 17.

On a general question, I eliminate answers that are:

- Too small
- Not mentioned in the passage
- In contradiction to the passage
- Too big
- Too extreme
- Against common sense

On a specific question, I eliminate answers that are:

- Too extreme
- In contradiction to passage details
- Not mentioned in the passage
- Against common sense

When I've got it down to two possible answers, I:

- Reread the question
- Look at what makes the two answers different
- Go back to the passage
- Eliminate the answer that is worse

Practice Drill 4—All Reading Techniques—All Levels

1. **E**   In the second and third paragraphs, the author details continued space exploration since the end of the Space Shuttle program. The final paragraph indicates that there are still more discoveries possible.

2. **A**   All of the choices are true, except (A). ISS (the International Space Station) is not a private company that NASA collaborates with.

3. **D**   Be sure to look up any vocabulary words you didn't know and make flash cards for them. The author's tone is positive. Sanguine means optimistic. Jubilant is too strong, and tenacious is a better description of those involved in space exploration.

4. **C**   Remember that for some questions it can be easier to focus on finding four wrong answers rather than to search for the one right answer. The passage never states that the United States lost momentum, nor does the passage contain information about lost jobs or dreams. There is no mention of how much (or little) money the United States has to spend on any space missions. The passage doesn't say what NASA will use for manned space flights in the future—it only says it is designing and building spacecraft, but not that they are specifically using rockets and boosters. Other companies are using rockets. Note that the five shuttles were a part of the former Space Shuttle program. Since that program has now ended, the fleet of shuttles is no longer being using to take humans into space.

5. **D**   Read the sentence and substitute your own word into the sentence. For example, astronauts "get to" the station on Russian Soyuz spacecraft. Choice (D), *arrive at*, is closest in meaning to "get to."

Practice Drill 5—All Reading Techniques—All Levels

1. **B**   With its focus on Martial Arts history and the meaning of words, this passage would most likely appear as an entry in an encyclopedia.

2. **A**   In the last sentence of the passage, the author states that benefits to all practitioners include increased focused, fitness, and (for some) fun.

3. **E**   The sentence states "This is in contrast to Martial Arts that are practiced for military use or law enforcement," which are styles that usually end in *jutsu*. The word "This" is referring to another type of Martial Arts, ones that are practiced for a different purpose (i.e., the styles that end in *do*).

4. **D**   The author mentions *aikido* as a style of Martial Arts that ends in *do*, which the author goes on to explain is a style of Martial Arts that allows practitioners to improve, among other things, their mental focus and physical fitness.

5. **C**   The author doesn't give a complete list of the types of Martial Art styles ending in *do*, only examples. The author never claims that one style is the superior style—each style has advantages and disadvantages. The author does say that armed service members were the ones who brought back these fighting styles to the States after they learned them while deployed.

6. **D**   The author is sharing information about a topic in a neutral way.

Practice Drill 6—All Reading Techniques—Middle and Upper Levels

1. **D**   Remember to answer the question (*why* is the speaker sharing this information?) and not choose an answer about what the speaker is saying. The final three paragraphs explain the purpose of the author's speech—theatre has an influence on society and can educate its citizens, ultimately for the better. If there were more theatres, more lives could be reached, educated, and improved as a result.

2. **B**   The speaker is not a stage manager or a producer. The speaker is also not being aloof or offering a critique of the play. Rather, the speaker is a strong supporter of the arts and feels strongly about what theatre can offer to citizens and their community.

3. **A**   Read the sentence and substitute your own word into the sentence. For example, this theatre "shares" or "offers" pure and clean plays. Choice (A), *provides*, is closest in meaning to "shares" or "offers."

4. **C**   The speaker uses the phrase in the fifth paragraph to show the reach that more theatres could have on a community—"how they would educate and elevate!" He isn't trying to dictate what individuals should do with their money or guarantee attendance numbers at productions. He is indicating the valuable impact the theatre can have on the city because, as a means of education, theatre can better the lives as well as the actions and beliefs of those who attend shows.

5. **D**   In the first three paragraphs, the speaker speaks fondly about his experience as an actor in this same play many years ago and how touched he is by the production he just witnessed.

Practice Drill 7—All Reading Techniques—Middle and Upper Levels

1. **C**   Based on the style, tone, and topic of this passage, it would most likely be found in a scholarly work such as an academic journal.

2. **D**   Eulogize means to praise highly. The author is expressing there is no practice like early rising that has been more highly and universally praised. Thus, early rising is a greatly respected practice.

3. **E**   Those who labor "at occupations which demand the light of day" are those who have occupations that require physical labor. Farming is a type of physical work but not the only kind that would require daylight.

4. **E**   When the author states that "the influence of this custom extends across the ocean, and here, in this democratic land...," she references a specific place. Throughout the passage, the author references England or London, so "Across the ocean" refers to across the Atlantic Ocean. The only option listed as a country that could be across this ocean and is also democratic is (E), *the United States*.

5. **A**   Remember to use other questions to help on trickier questions. Both questions 2 and 6 can help with this question. The correct answer should mention early rising and its importance.

6. **D**   The author speaks highly of early rising and regards staying up late (and thus rising later in the day) as lacking good sense. Thus, she would admire those who get up early.

Practice Drill 8—All Reading Techniques—Middle and Upper Levels

1. **C** The children are planning to ambush the speaker (their father) who is working. The speaker hears them whispering their plans, knows they are attempting a surprise attack, and waits for them to carry it out. Plotting and planning are the main actions of the children since the trick they are playing on their father is the main action in the poem.

2. **B** The walls, fortress, and dungeon are all figurative, as the action of the poem takes place in the speaker's study or office space. The speaker uses those images to explain the eternal love he has for his children.

3. **D** The poem is about the love the speaker has for the children. Kisses and hugs best depict the image of love.

4. **A** The speaker is referring to the children when he calls them *banditti*. Since they are planning a raid and are trying to surround him by climbing into his chair, this word most likely means invaders, which makes *bandits* the closest match.

5. **B** The Children's Hour is the time of night when there "comes a pause in the day's occupations." During this time, the children come to play with their father—a time they all enjoy. The poem is not about a story he tells them or a description of an imaginary game the children play.

Practice Drill 9—All Reading Techniques—Middle and Upper Levels

1. **B** The "she" in this sentence is referring to Sara, so (D) and (E) should be eliminated. While Sara "was very firm in her belief that she was an ugly little girl," the author lists specific features Sara possesses that give her "an odd charm of her own" distinct from Isobel, whom Sara does not look like at all. Since the omniscient narrator gives the reader this information about Sara's looks and compares it to Sara's own thoughts, the narrator allows the reader to see that Sara's perception of herself is not entirely accurate.

2. **D** The last sentence of the passage states that Sara later discovers that Miss Minchin says "the same thing to each papa and mamma who brought a child to her school." Thus, Miss Minchin's actions towards newcomers is known.

3. **A** Read the sentence and substitute your own word. For example, Sara says she is not "pretty" in the least. Choice (A), *attractive*, is closest in meaning to "pretty."

4. **D** Read the question carefully. It asks for the narrator's tone, not a character's tone. The narrator is simply sharing information and details that relate to the story.

5. **E** A simile is a literary device that compares two unlike things and uses the word like or as to set up the comparison.

6. **B** Sara states in the 4th paragraph that she is not beautiful at all and that, in her opinion, Isobel is beautiful. She gives reasons for why she considers Isobel beautiful and why she herself is not. Thus, Sara uses Isobel as a standard for beauty in order to show how she does not meet the Isobel-standard of beauty.

7.   **D**   Read the sentences that use the word "story" and substitute your own word. For example, when Sara says in the last sentence of the 4th paragraph, "she is beginning by telling a story," she means that Miss Minchin is saying something untrue. Each time "story" is used in the passage, it is used to indicate someone is telling a lie.

Part III
SSAT Practice Tests

If you are taking the Elementary Level SSAT, see "Register Your Book Online!" after the Table of Contents for instructions on how to download your full-length practice test from PrincetonReview.com.

HOW TO TAKE A PRACTICE TEST

Here are some reminders for taking your practice test.

- Find a quiet place to take the test where you won't be interrupted or distracted, and make sure you have enough time to take the entire test.

- Time yourself strictly. Use a timer, watch, or stopwatch that will ring, and do not allow yourself to go over time for any section.

- Take a practice test in one sitting, allowing yourself breaks of no more than two minutes between sections.

- Use the attached answer sheets to bubble in your choices.

- Each bubble you choose should be filled in thoroughly, and no other marks should be made in the answer area.

- Make sure to double-check that your bubbles are filled in correctly!

Chapter 10
Upper Level
SSAT Practice Test

Upper Level Practice Test

Be sure each mark *completely* fills the answer space.
Start with number 1 for each new section of the test. You may find more answer spaces than you need.
If so, please leave them blank.

SECTION 1

1 Ⓐ Ⓑ Ⓒ Ⓓ Ⓔ	6 Ⓐ Ⓑ Ⓒ Ⓓ Ⓔ	11 Ⓐ Ⓑ Ⓒ Ⓓ Ⓔ	16 Ⓐ Ⓑ Ⓒ Ⓓ Ⓔ	21 Ⓐ Ⓑ Ⓒ Ⓓ Ⓔ
2 Ⓐ Ⓑ Ⓒ Ⓓ Ⓔ	7 Ⓐ Ⓑ Ⓒ Ⓓ Ⓔ	12 Ⓐ Ⓑ Ⓒ Ⓓ Ⓔ	17 Ⓐ Ⓑ Ⓒ Ⓓ Ⓔ	22 Ⓐ Ⓑ Ⓒ Ⓓ Ⓔ
3 Ⓐ Ⓑ Ⓒ Ⓓ Ⓔ	8 Ⓐ Ⓑ Ⓒ Ⓓ Ⓔ	13 Ⓐ Ⓑ Ⓒ Ⓓ Ⓔ	18 Ⓐ Ⓑ Ⓒ Ⓓ Ⓔ	23 Ⓐ Ⓑ Ⓒ Ⓓ Ⓔ
4 Ⓐ Ⓑ Ⓒ Ⓓ Ⓔ	9 Ⓐ Ⓑ Ⓒ Ⓓ Ⓔ	14 Ⓐ Ⓑ Ⓒ Ⓓ Ⓔ	19 Ⓐ Ⓑ Ⓒ Ⓓ Ⓔ	24 Ⓐ Ⓑ Ⓒ Ⓓ Ⓔ
5 Ⓐ Ⓑ Ⓒ Ⓓ Ⓔ	10 Ⓐ Ⓑ Ⓒ Ⓓ Ⓔ	15 Ⓐ Ⓑ Ⓒ Ⓓ Ⓔ	20 Ⓐ Ⓑ Ⓒ Ⓓ Ⓔ	25 Ⓐ Ⓑ Ⓒ Ⓓ Ⓔ

SECTION 2

1 Ⓐ Ⓑ Ⓒ Ⓓ Ⓔ	9 Ⓐ Ⓑ Ⓒ Ⓓ Ⓔ	17 Ⓐ Ⓑ Ⓒ Ⓓ Ⓔ	25 Ⓐ Ⓑ Ⓒ Ⓓ Ⓔ	33 Ⓐ Ⓑ Ⓒ Ⓓ Ⓔ
2 Ⓐ Ⓑ Ⓒ Ⓓ Ⓔ	10 Ⓐ Ⓑ Ⓒ Ⓓ Ⓔ	18 Ⓐ Ⓑ Ⓒ Ⓓ Ⓔ	26 Ⓐ Ⓑ Ⓒ Ⓓ Ⓔ	34 Ⓐ Ⓑ Ⓒ Ⓓ Ⓔ
3 Ⓐ Ⓑ Ⓒ Ⓓ Ⓔ	11 Ⓐ Ⓑ Ⓒ Ⓓ Ⓔ	19 Ⓐ Ⓑ Ⓒ Ⓓ Ⓔ	27 Ⓐ Ⓑ Ⓒ Ⓓ Ⓔ	35 Ⓐ Ⓑ Ⓒ Ⓓ Ⓔ
4 Ⓐ Ⓑ Ⓒ Ⓓ Ⓔ	12 Ⓐ Ⓑ Ⓒ Ⓓ Ⓔ	20 Ⓐ Ⓑ Ⓒ Ⓓ Ⓔ	28 Ⓐ Ⓑ Ⓒ Ⓓ Ⓔ	36 Ⓐ Ⓑ Ⓒ Ⓓ Ⓔ
5 Ⓐ Ⓑ Ⓒ Ⓓ Ⓔ	13 Ⓐ Ⓑ Ⓒ Ⓓ Ⓔ	21 Ⓐ Ⓑ Ⓒ Ⓓ Ⓔ	29 Ⓐ Ⓑ Ⓒ Ⓓ Ⓔ	37 Ⓐ Ⓑ Ⓒ Ⓓ Ⓔ
6 Ⓐ Ⓑ Ⓒ Ⓓ Ⓔ	14 Ⓐ Ⓑ Ⓒ Ⓓ Ⓔ	22 Ⓐ Ⓑ Ⓒ Ⓓ Ⓔ	30 Ⓐ Ⓑ Ⓒ Ⓓ Ⓔ	38 Ⓐ Ⓑ Ⓒ Ⓓ Ⓔ
7 Ⓐ Ⓑ Ⓒ Ⓓ Ⓔ	15 Ⓐ Ⓑ Ⓒ Ⓓ Ⓔ	23 Ⓐ Ⓑ Ⓒ Ⓓ Ⓔ	31 Ⓐ Ⓑ Ⓒ Ⓓ Ⓔ	39 Ⓐ Ⓑ Ⓒ Ⓓ Ⓔ
8 Ⓐ Ⓑ Ⓒ Ⓓ Ⓔ	16 Ⓐ Ⓑ Ⓒ Ⓓ Ⓔ	24 Ⓐ Ⓑ Ⓒ Ⓓ Ⓔ	32 Ⓐ Ⓑ Ⓒ Ⓓ Ⓔ	40 Ⓐ Ⓑ Ⓒ Ⓓ Ⓔ

SECTION 3

1 Ⓐ Ⓑ Ⓒ Ⓓ Ⓔ	13 Ⓐ Ⓑ Ⓒ Ⓓ Ⓔ	25 Ⓐ Ⓑ Ⓒ Ⓓ Ⓔ	37 Ⓐ Ⓑ Ⓒ Ⓓ Ⓔ	49 Ⓐ Ⓑ Ⓒ Ⓓ Ⓔ
2 Ⓐ Ⓑ Ⓒ Ⓓ Ⓔ	14 Ⓐ Ⓑ Ⓒ Ⓓ Ⓔ	26 Ⓐ Ⓑ Ⓒ Ⓓ Ⓔ	38 Ⓐ Ⓑ Ⓒ Ⓓ Ⓔ	50 Ⓐ Ⓑ Ⓒ Ⓓ Ⓔ
3 Ⓐ Ⓑ Ⓒ Ⓓ Ⓔ	15 Ⓐ Ⓑ Ⓒ Ⓓ Ⓔ	27 Ⓐ Ⓑ Ⓒ Ⓓ Ⓔ	39 Ⓐ Ⓑ Ⓒ Ⓓ Ⓔ	51 Ⓐ Ⓑ Ⓒ Ⓓ Ⓔ
4 Ⓐ Ⓑ Ⓒ Ⓓ Ⓔ	16 Ⓐ Ⓑ Ⓒ Ⓓ Ⓔ	28 Ⓐ Ⓑ Ⓒ Ⓓ Ⓔ	40 Ⓐ Ⓑ Ⓒ Ⓓ Ⓔ	52 Ⓐ Ⓑ Ⓒ Ⓓ Ⓔ
5 Ⓐ Ⓑ Ⓒ Ⓓ Ⓔ	17 Ⓐ Ⓑ Ⓒ Ⓓ Ⓔ	29 Ⓐ Ⓑ Ⓒ Ⓓ Ⓔ	41 Ⓐ Ⓑ Ⓒ Ⓓ Ⓔ	53 Ⓐ Ⓑ Ⓒ Ⓓ Ⓔ
6 Ⓐ Ⓑ Ⓒ Ⓓ Ⓔ	18 Ⓐ Ⓑ Ⓒ Ⓓ Ⓔ	30 Ⓐ Ⓑ Ⓒ Ⓓ Ⓔ	42 Ⓐ Ⓑ Ⓒ Ⓓ Ⓔ	54 Ⓐ Ⓑ Ⓒ Ⓓ Ⓔ
7 Ⓐ Ⓑ Ⓒ Ⓓ Ⓔ	19 Ⓐ Ⓑ Ⓒ Ⓓ Ⓔ	31 Ⓐ Ⓑ Ⓒ Ⓓ Ⓔ	43 Ⓐ Ⓑ Ⓒ Ⓓ Ⓔ	55 Ⓐ Ⓑ Ⓒ Ⓓ Ⓔ
8 Ⓐ Ⓑ Ⓒ Ⓓ Ⓔ	20 Ⓐ Ⓑ Ⓒ Ⓓ Ⓔ	32 Ⓐ Ⓑ Ⓒ Ⓓ Ⓔ	44 Ⓐ Ⓑ Ⓒ Ⓓ Ⓔ	56 Ⓐ Ⓑ Ⓒ Ⓓ Ⓔ
9 Ⓐ Ⓑ Ⓒ Ⓓ Ⓔ	21 Ⓐ Ⓑ Ⓒ Ⓓ Ⓔ	33 Ⓐ Ⓑ Ⓒ Ⓓ Ⓔ	45 Ⓐ Ⓑ Ⓒ Ⓓ Ⓔ	57 Ⓐ Ⓑ Ⓒ Ⓓ Ⓔ
10 Ⓐ Ⓑ Ⓒ Ⓓ Ⓔ	22 Ⓐ Ⓑ Ⓒ Ⓓ Ⓔ	34 Ⓐ Ⓑ Ⓒ Ⓓ Ⓔ	46 Ⓐ Ⓑ Ⓒ Ⓓ Ⓔ	58 Ⓐ Ⓑ Ⓒ Ⓓ Ⓔ
11 Ⓐ Ⓑ Ⓒ Ⓓ Ⓔ	23 Ⓐ Ⓑ Ⓒ Ⓓ Ⓔ	35 Ⓐ Ⓑ Ⓒ Ⓓ Ⓔ	47 Ⓐ Ⓑ Ⓒ Ⓓ Ⓔ	59 Ⓐ Ⓑ Ⓒ Ⓓ Ⓔ
12 Ⓐ Ⓑ Ⓒ Ⓓ Ⓔ	24 Ⓐ Ⓑ Ⓒ Ⓓ Ⓔ	36 Ⓐ Ⓑ Ⓒ Ⓓ Ⓔ	48 Ⓐ Ⓑ Ⓒ Ⓓ Ⓔ	60 Ⓐ Ⓑ Ⓒ Ⓓ Ⓔ

SECTION 4

1 Ⓐ Ⓑ Ⓒ Ⓓ Ⓔ	6 Ⓐ Ⓑ Ⓒ Ⓓ Ⓔ	11 Ⓐ Ⓑ Ⓒ Ⓓ Ⓔ	16 Ⓐ Ⓑ Ⓒ Ⓓ Ⓔ	21 Ⓐ Ⓑ Ⓒ Ⓓ Ⓔ
2 Ⓐ Ⓑ Ⓒ Ⓓ Ⓔ	7 Ⓐ Ⓑ Ⓒ Ⓓ Ⓔ	12 Ⓐ Ⓑ Ⓒ Ⓓ Ⓔ	17 Ⓐ Ⓑ Ⓒ Ⓓ Ⓔ	22 Ⓐ Ⓑ Ⓒ Ⓓ Ⓔ
3 Ⓐ Ⓑ Ⓒ Ⓓ Ⓔ	8 Ⓐ Ⓑ Ⓒ Ⓓ Ⓔ	13 Ⓐ Ⓑ Ⓒ Ⓓ Ⓔ	18 Ⓐ Ⓑ Ⓒ Ⓓ Ⓔ	23 Ⓐ Ⓑ Ⓒ Ⓓ Ⓔ
4 Ⓐ Ⓑ Ⓒ Ⓓ Ⓔ	9 Ⓐ Ⓑ Ⓒ Ⓓ Ⓔ	14 Ⓐ Ⓑ Ⓒ Ⓓ Ⓔ	19 Ⓐ Ⓑ Ⓒ Ⓓ Ⓔ	24 Ⓐ Ⓑ Ⓒ Ⓓ Ⓔ
5 Ⓐ Ⓑ Ⓒ Ⓓ Ⓔ	10 Ⓐ Ⓑ Ⓒ Ⓓ Ⓔ	15 Ⓐ Ⓑ Ⓒ Ⓓ Ⓔ	20 Ⓐ Ⓑ Ⓒ Ⓓ Ⓔ	25 Ⓐ Ⓑ Ⓒ Ⓓ Ⓔ

Upper Level SSAT
Writing Sample
Time - 25 Minutes
1 Topic

<u>Writing Sample</u>

Schools would like to get to know you better through a story you will tell using one of the ideas below. Please choose the idea you find more interesting and write a story using the idea in your first sentence. Please fill in the circle next to the one you choose.

> Ⓐ What did a parent tell you to do that you now wish you had done?

> Ⓑ It was a pleasant surprise.

_____

_____

_____

_____

_____

_____

_____

_____

GO ON TO THE NEXT PAGE.

Upper Level SSAT
Section 1
Time - 30 Minutes
25 Questions

Following each problem in this section, there are five suggested answers. Work each problem in your head or in the blank space provided at the right of the page. Then look at the five suggested answers and decide which one is best.

<u>Note:</u> Figures that accompany problems in this section are drawn as accurately as possible EXCEPT when it is stated in a specific problem that its figure is not drawn to scale.

Sample Problem:

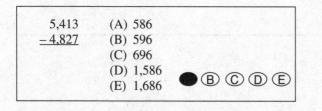

USE THIS SPACE FOR FIGURING.

1. If $h = 2$, and h, i, and j are consecutive even integers and $h < i < j$, what is $h + i + j$?

   (A)   3
   (B)   5
   (C)   9
   (D)   10
   (E)   12

---

2. If $x = \dfrac{1}{2} + \dfrac{1}{3} + \dfrac{1}{4}$ and $y = \dfrac{1}{2} + \dfrac{2}{3} + \dfrac{3}{4}$, then $x + y =$

   (A) 3

   (B) 1

   (C) $\dfrac{2}{3}$

   (D) $\dfrac{1}{24}$

   (E) $\dfrac{1}{3}$

GO ON TO THE NEXT PAGE.

3. If the product of 412.7 and 100 is rounded to the nearest hundred, the answer will be

USE THIS SPACE FOR FIGURING.

1

(A)   400
(B)   4,100
(C)   4,127
(D)   41,270
(E)   41,300

4. If $\frac{4}{5}$ of a number is 28, then $\frac{1}{5}$ of that number is

(A)   4
(B)   7
(C)   21
(D)   35
(E)   112

5. $14 + 3 \times 7 + (12 \div 2) =$

(A)   140

(B)   125

(C) $65\frac{1}{2}$

(D)   41

(E)   20

6. Maggie wants to mail postcards to 25 of her friends and needs one stamp for each postcard. If she buys 3 stamps at a time, how many sets of stamps must she buy in order to mail all of her postcards?

(A)   3
(B)   8
(C)   9
(D)   10
(E)   25

GO ON TO THE NEXT PAGE.

Questions 7 and 8 refer to the following chart.

USE THIS SPACE FOR FIGURING.

1

Money Raised from Candy Sale

Cost of Candy	$1.00	$5.00	$10.00	$15.00
# Sold	100	25	20	5

Figure 1

7. How much more money was raised by the $10.00 candy than by the $5.00 candy?

(A) $32
(B) $50
(C) $75
(D) $125
(E) $200

8. The money raised by the $15.00 candy is approximately what percent of the total money raised from the candy sale?

(A) 15%
(B) 20%
(C) 30%
(D) 45%
(E) 50%

9. An art gallery has three collections: modern art, sculpture, and photography. If the 24 items that make up the modern art collection represent 25% of the total number of items in the gallery, then the average number of items in each of the other two collections is

(A) 8
(B) 24
(C) 36
(D) 96
(E) 288

GO ON TO THE NEXT PAGE.

10. At Calvin U. Smith Elementary School, the ratio of students to teachers is 9:1. What fractional part of the entire population at the school is teachers?

(A) $\dfrac{1}{10}$

(B) $\dfrac{1}{9}$

(C) $\dfrac{1}{8}$

(D) $\dfrac{8}{1}$

(E) $\dfrac{9}{1}$

USE THIS SPACE FOR FIGURING.

11. The Ace Delivery Company employs two drivers to make deliveries on a certain Saturday. If Driver A makes d deliveries and Driver B makes $d + 2$ deliveries, then in terms of d, the average number of deliveries made by each driver is

(A) d

(B) $d + 1$

(C) $d + 2$

(D) $\dfrac{1}{2}d + 2$

(E) $\dfrac{3}{2}d$

12. Which of the following is equal to w ?

(A) $180 - v$
(B) $180 + v$
(C) 105
(D) 115
(E) $2v$

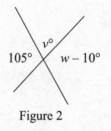

Figure 2

GO ON TO THE NEXT PAGE.

13. Tracy goes to the store and buys only candy bars and cans of soda. She buys 3 times as many candy bars as cans of soda. If she buys a total of 24 items, how many of those items are candy bars?

(A) 3
(B) 12
(C) 18
(D) 21
(E) 24

USE THIS SPACE FOR FIGURING.

1

14. $-\left(\dfrac{4}{3}\right)^3 =$

(A) $\dfrac{64}{27}$

(B) $\dfrac{12}{9}$

(C) $-\dfrac{12}{27}$

(D) $-\dfrac{12}{9}$

(E) $-\dfrac{64}{27}$

15. Of the following choices, which value for x would satisfy the equation $\dfrac{1}{5} + x > 1$?

(A) $\dfrac{3}{4}$

(B) $\dfrac{4}{5}$

(C) $\dfrac{6}{7}$

(D) $\dfrac{6}{8}$

(E) $\dfrac{7}{9}$

GO ON TO THE NEXT PAGE.

16. Given the equations $2x + y = 8$ and $z + y = 8$, find the value of x?

USE THIS SPACE FOR FIGURING.

1

(A) –8
(B) –4
(C) 4
(D) 16
(E) It cannot be determined from the information given.

17. A, B, and C are squares. The length of one side of square A is 3. The length of one side of square B is twice the length of a side of square A, and the length of one side of square C is twice the length of a side of square B. What is the average area of the three squares?

(A) 21
(B) 36
(C) 63
(D) 84
(E) 144

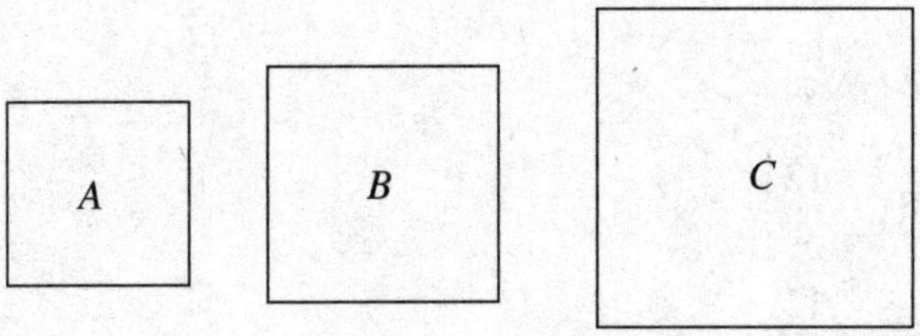

Figure 3

18. There are 12 homes on a certain street. If 4 homes are painted blue, 3 are painted red, and the remaining homes are green, what fractional part of the homes on the street are green?

(A) 7

(B) 5

(C) $\frac{7}{12}$

(D) $\frac{5}{12}$

(E) $\frac{1}{12}$

GO ON TO THE NEXT PAGE.

19. Melissa lives 30 miles from work and Katy lives 40 miles from work. If Melissa and Katy work at the same office, how many miles apart do the girls live from each other?

(A) 10
(B) 35
(C) 50
(D) 70
(E) It cannot be determined from the information given.

USE THIS SPACE FOR FIGURING.

20. If, at a fundraising dinner, x guests each donate $200 and y guests each donate $300, in terms of x and y, what is the total number of dollars raised?

(A) $250(x + y)$

(B) $200x + 300y$

(C) $250xy$

(D) $\dfrac{xy}{250}$

(E) $500xy$

21. A rectangular fish tank with dimensions 2 feet × 3 feet × 4 feet is being filled by a hose that produces 6 cubic feet of water per minute. At this rate, how many minutes will it take to fill the tank?

(A) 24
(B) 6
(C) 4
(D) 3
(E) 2

GO ON TO THE NEXT PAGE.

22. With 4 days left in the Mountain Lake Critter Collection Contest, Mary has caught 15 fewer critters than Natalie. If Mary is to win the contest by collecting more critters than Natalie, at least how many critters per day must Mary catch?

    (A) 4
    (B) 5
    (C) 16
    (D) 30
    (E) 46

USE THIS SPACE FOR FIGURING.

23. If $3x - y = 23$ and x is an integer greater than 0, which of the following is NOT a possible value for y ?

    (A) 9
    (B) 7
    (C) 4
    (D) 1
    (E) −2

24. Anna, A, and Bob, B, are avid readers. If Anna and Bob together read an average of 200 pages in a day and Bob reads fewer pages than Anna, which equation must be true?

    (A) $A - 200 = 200 - B$
    (B) $A = 200$ and $B = 200$
    (C) $A - B = 100$
    (D) $A = 200 + B$
    (E) $A + B = 200$

25. $30.00 is taken off the price of a dress. If the new price is now 60% of the original price, what was the original price of the dress?

    (A) $75.00
    (B) $60.00
    (C) $50.00
    (D) $45.00
    (E) $30.00

STOP
IF YOU FINISH BEFORE TIME IS CALLED,
YOU MAY CHECK YOUR WORK ON THIS SECTION ONLY.
DO NOT TURN TO ANY OTHER SECTION IN THE TEST.

GO ON TO THE NEXT PAGE.

Upper Level SSAT
Section 2
Time - 40 Minutes
40 Questions

Read each passage carefully and then answer the questions about it. For each question, decide on the basis of the passage which one of the choices best answers the question.

The reading passages in this test are brief excerpts or adaptations of excerpts from published material. To make the text suitable for testing purposes, we may have, in some cases, altered the style, contents, or point of view of the original.

Florence Nightingale was a woman ahead of her time. Before the nineteenth century, the profession of nursing was largely untrained. Midwives were the only practitioners who had any training at all. For the most part, sick people were looked after by the women of the house in their own homes.

Florence Nightingale began a school in London, England to set the standards for nursing. She was able to
5 do this because she had already established a reputation for her work with soldiers during the Crimean War. She carried a lamp above her head as she walked among the wounded men, thereby earning the nickname "the lady with the lamp." It was this great lady who lit the way for nursing to become the respected profession it is today.

---

1. The passage is mainly about

(A) the impact of nursing on the soldiers of the Crimean War
(B) Florence Nightingale and her influence on the profession of nursing
(C) the difference between nurses and midwives
(D) how Florence Nightingale earned the nickname "the lady with the lamp"
(E) why only females entered the profession of nursing

2. Which of the following was a method most people used to receive care before Florence Nightingale's time?

(A) They would be cared for only by doctors.
(B) They would be cared for by their children.
(C) They were largely left uncared for.
(D) They were cared for by midwives.
(E) They were cared for by female relatives.

3. The style of the passage is most like that found in a(n)

(A) personal letter to a trusted friend
(B) anthology of short biographies of famous women
(C) history of nineteenth-century England
(D) textbook on medicine
(E) editorial written for a daily paper

4. According to the author, the primary reason that Florence Nightingale was able to open a school for nursing was that

(A) she was already famous for her work in the war
(B) her family was willing to finance her work
(C) she had gained notoriety as a difficult woman to challenge
(D) she had cared for many wealthy sick people herself
(E) she worked endless hours every night

5. According to the passage, all of the following could be said of nurses EXCEPT

(A) prior to Florence Nightingale, only midwives were trained
(B) Florence Nightingale raised the standards of their profession
(C) they are well-respected professionals today
(D) they are exceedingly well paid for their work
(E) prior to Florence Nightingale, their work was done often by female relatives

GO ON TO THE NEXT PAGE.

2

In England during the mid-1600s, a group of poor English farmers led by Gerrard Winstanley united to form an organization known as the True Levelers. Their stated
5 goal was to change the laws regarding real estate and ownable property so that all willing citizens would be able to support themselves through farming. At the time in England, there was great social unrest and food prices were
10 very high. Most of the land throughout the country was strictly divided and controlled by a small number of the elite ruling class. The True Levelers believed that they could "level" the different classes of society by
15 creating communities in which the farmable private land was owned by all and available for agrarian purposes. To fight the unequal system that only benefited the wealthy landowners, the True Levelers defiantly occupied private and
20 public land and began farming.

Because much of farming involves plowing and planting, these groups of communal farmers became better known by the name Diggers. Their hope was that their act of
25 rebellion would stir the sympathies of the other poor people throughout the country. The Digger philosophy was to unite all the poor and working classes behind the idea that the land should be shared. If thousands of common
30 English folk began to claim reasonable access to the land, the powerful landowners would be unable to stop them. In practice for a brief time, Digger communities flourished as they welcomed anyone who wished to merely grow
35 their own food and live freely.

Sadly, the landowners believed the Diggers were a threat and began to take steps to preserve their control over the farmable land. Many members of the Digger communities were
40 harassed, threatened, and jailed. Planting vegetables was viewed as a rebellious act and dealt with as if it were a crime. The majority of land reverted back into the hands of the landowners. Ultimately, most of the Digger
45 communities that had briefly thrived were disbanded. In their place, other political groups arose and continued to protest the various injustices of the time. The Digger name continues to the present day in some English
50 folk songs as a reminder of their ideals.

6. The word "agrarian" is most similar to which of the following?

    (A) Testing
    (B) Private
    (C) Unequal
    (D) Farming
    (E) Aggressive

7. Which of the following can be inferred about the Diggers as described in the passage?

    (A) They had a different political philosophy than the True Levelers.
    (B) They allowed others to join them in their farming activities.
    (C) They were skilled political speakers.
    (C) They defeated the powerful landowners through military force.
    (E) They were exceptional folk singers.

8. Which of the following was the most significant point of conflict between landowners and Diggers?

    (A) The Diggers had the willingness but not the space on which to grow enough food to support themselves.
    (B) Wealthy landowners in England at the time were usually violent.
    (C) There was no agreement between Diggers and True Levelers.
    (D) The quality of vegetables grown by the Diggers was inferior to that produced on wealthy estates.
    (E) The local government did not have any authority in the dispute.

GO ON TO THE NEXT PAGE.

9. The passage is primarily about

 (A) working hard even in challenging times
 (B) social problems in England in the seventeenth century
 (C) the inhumanity of wealthy English landowners
 (D) Gerrard Winstanley's ideas
 (E) the brief history of an English community organization

10. According to the passage, what is the most significant difference between True Levelers and the Diggers?

2

 (A) The True Levelers believed in farming private land, while the Diggers believed in farming public land.
 (B) The True Levelers followed Gerrard Winstanley, while the Diggers had other leaders.
 (C) There is no difference between the two groups, as the names refer to the same people.
 (D) The True Levelers were accepted by landowners, while the Diggers were jailed.
 (E) The True Levelers are not remembered in folk songs, while the Diggers are.

GO ON TO THE NEXT PAGE.

2

Flax has been raised for many thousands of years, for many different reasons. Probably the two most important reasons are for the fabric made from it and the oil produced from it. The woody stem of the flax plant contains the long, strong fibers that are used to make linen. The seeds are rich in an oil important for its industrial uses.

5   The people of ancient Egypt, Assyria, and Mesopotamia raised flax for cloth; Egyptian mummies were wrapped in linen. Since the discovery of its drying ability, the oil from flaxseed, called linseed oil, has been used as a drying agent in paints and varnishes.

The best fiber and the best seed cannot be obtained from the same kinds of plant.
10   Fiber flax grows tall and has few branches. It needs a short, cool growing season with plenty of rainfall evenly distributed. Otherwise, the plants become woody and the fiber is rough and dry. On the other hand, seed flax grows well in places that are too dry for fiber flax. The plants are lower to the ground and have more branches.

11. Which of the following would be the best title for the passage?

   (A) "How Mummies Were Preserved"
   (B) "The Many Uses of the Flax Plant"
   (C) "The Difference Between Seeds and Fibers"
   (D) "The Types of Plant Life Around the World"
   (E) "Ancient Sources of Oil and Linen"

12. The author suggests that ancient people raised flax primarily for

   (A) its oil, used to preserve wood
   (B) its oil, used as a rich source of nutrient
   (C) its fabric, used for their clothes
   (D) its fabric, used to wrap their dead
   (E) its fabric and oil, for industrial uses

13. This passage sounds as if it were an excerpt from

   (A) a letter to the Egyptians
   (B) a book on plant life
   (C) a scientific treatise
   (D) a persuasive essay from an ecologist
   (E) a friendly reminder to a politician

14. Which of the following questions is answered by the passage?

   (A) Can the same plant be grown for the best fabric and the best oil?
   (B) How did the Egyptians wrap their mummies?
   (C) What temperature is optimal for growing flax?
   (D) How is flax harvested?
   (E) Is it possible to produce a new type of flax for fabric and oil production?

15. Which of the following is the author most likely to discuss next?

   (A) How flax is used around the world today
   (B) Other types of useful plants
   (C) Other sources of oil
   (D) The usefulness of synthetic fabrics
   (E) The advantages of pesticides and crop rotation

GO ON TO THE NEXT PAGE.

William, Duke of Normandy, conquered England in 1066. One of the first tasks he undertook as king was the building of a fortress in the city of London. Begun in 1066 and completed several years later by William's son, William Rufus, this structure was called the White Tower.

The Tower of London is not just one building, but an 18-acre complex of buildings. In
5 addition to the White Tower, there are 19 other towers. The Thames River flows by one side of the complex and a large moat, or shallow ditch, surrounds it. Once filled with water, the moat was drained in 1843 and is now covered with grass.

The Tower of London is the city's most popular tourist attraction. A great deal of fascinating history has taken place within its walls. The tower has served as a fortress, royal residence, prison,
10 royal mint, public records office, observatory, military barracks, place of execution, and city zoo.

As recently as 1941, the tower was used as a prison for Adolf Hitler's associate Rudolf Hess. Although it is no longer used as a prison, the tower still houses the crown jewels and a great deal of English history.

16. The primary purpose of this passage is to

  (A) discuss the future of the Tower of London
  (B) discuss the ramifications of using the Tower as a prison
  (C) argue that the Tower is an improper place for crown jewels
  (D) describe and discuss the history of the Tower of London
  (E) debate the relative merits of the uses of the Tower in the past to the present

17. All of the following were uses for the Tower of London EXCEPT

  (A) a place where money was made
  (B) a palace for the royals
  (C) a place where executions were held
  (D) a place of religious pilgrimage
  (E) a place where records were stored

18. Which of the following questions is answered by the passage?

  (A) What controversy has surrounded the Tower of London?
  (B) How much revenue does the Tower generate for England?
  (C) In what year did construction on the Tower of London begin?
  (D) What is the type of stone used in the Tower of London?
  (E) Who was the most famous prisoner in the Tower?

19. When discussing the Tower of London, the author's tone could best be described as

  (A) bewildered
  (B) objective
  (C) overly emotional
  (D) envious
  (E) disdainful

20. Which of the following does the author imply about Rudolf Hess?

  (A) He was executed at the Tower of London.
  (B) He was one of the last prisoners in the Tower of London.
  (C) He died an untimely death.
  (D) He was a tourist attraction.
  (E) He was respectful of the great Tower of London.

21. The author would most probably agree that

  (A) the Tower of London is useful only as a tourist attraction
  (B) the Tower of London could never be built today
  (C) the Tower of London cannot generate enough revenue to justify its expenses
  (D) the Tower of London has a complex history
  (E) the prisoners at the Tower were relatively well treated

GO ON TO THE NEXT PAGE.

2

Most art enthusiasts agree that *Mona Lisa* by Leonardo da Vinci is the most famous painting in the world. It is the portrait of a woman, the wife of Francesco del Giocondo, a wealthy Florentine business man. The name roughly translates from Italian to mean "Madam Lisa" and is a respectful term. Anyone who has ever viewed the painting, seasoned art critic or inexperienced museum visitor, remembers well its greatest feature—Mona Lisa's smile. It is this smile that has captured the imagination of the millions of visitors who have seen the painting over the years.

There is something powerful and alluring contained in Mona Lisa's smile that intrigues all who see it. The reason for her smile has long been the subject of discussion in the art world. But perhaps it is the fact that no one knows why she smiles that makes *Mona Lisa* the most famous of all paintings. There is something so appealing and recognizably human about an unexplained smile to which everyone can relate. Furthermore, if we ever tire of analyzing why

Mona Lisa smiles, we can consider how da Vinci managed to capture the smile. What could he have been thinking while painting? A genuine smile is hard to capture even in a photograph with a modern camera, yet Leonardo da Vinci managed to capture this subtle expression in a painting. It is amazing that da Vinci was able to create for eternity a frozen picture of a smile that in reality lasts less than an instant.

The painting now hangs in the Musée du Louvre in Paris, France. Several different owners have possessed it at various times throughout history, including Louis XIV and Napoleon. It was even temporarily in the possession of a former museum employee who stole it in 1911. He was caught in 1913. It is likely that all who held the painting at one time or another wondered about the Mona Lisa smile, just as today's museum visitors do. Now the painting officially belongs to the French government. In some ways, though, it is really a painting (and a mystery) that belongs to the world.

22. Which of the following best expresses the author's attitude toward the painting?

(A) It should be well protected so that it is not stolen again.
(B) It is difficult to preserve such old masterpieces.
(C) Its greatest appeal is the mystery surrounding it.
(D) There will never be a painter as great as Leonardo da Vinci again.
(E) Everyone should have a chance to own great art.

23. Which of the following is a fact from the passage?

(A) A good smile lasts only a few seconds.
(B) There is tremendous mystery surrounding which painter created *Mona Lisa*.
(C) Napoleon donated *Mona Lisa* to the Musée du Louvre.
(D) There has been some focus on Mona Lisa's smile in artistic communities.
(E) All art historians agree that *Mona Lisa* is the greatest work of art in the world.

24. The author implies which of the following?

(A) A painting can be owned, but the powerful effect of a work of art is available to everyone who sees it.
(B) Leonardo da Vinci was hiding a secret that he wished to reveal through his painting.
(C) *Mona Lisa* has caused much turmoil in the art world due to its peculiar details.
(D) The Musée du Louvre does not have proper equipment in place for capturing modern criminals.
(E) The only detail viewers of *Mona Lisa* can later recall is her smile.

25. The author's tone can best be described as

(A) appreciative
(B) investigative
(C) artistic
(D) confused
(E) indifferent

GO ON TO THE NEXT PAGE.

2

The first old "horseless carriages" of the 1880s may have been worthy of a snicker or two, but not the cars of today. The progress that has been made over the last one hundred thirty years has been phenomenal. In fact, much progress was made even in the first twenty years—in 1903, cars could travel at 70 miles per hour. The major change from
5 the old cars to today is the expense. Whereas cars were once a luxury that only the very wealthy could afford, today, people of all income levels own cars.

In fact, there are so many cars that if they were to line up end to end, they would touch the moon. Cars are used for everyday transportation for millions of people, for recreation, and for work. Many people's jobs depend on cars—police officers, health
10 care workers, and taxi drivers all rely on automobiles.

One thing that hasn't changed is how cars are powered. The first cars ran on gas and diesel fuel just as the most modern ones do. You could argue that today's "most modern" cars are electric or hybrid. The newer cars, however, are much more fuel efficient and much research is devoted to saving fuel and finding new sources of energy for cars.

26. The "progress" mentioned in line 2 most likely refers to

(A) the ability of a car to move forward
(B) technological advancement
(C) research
(D) the new types of fuels available
(E) the cost of the car

27. Which of the following is answered by the passage?

(A) What are some ways people use cars?
(B) Why did people laugh at the "horseless carriage"?
(C) Where will the fuels of the future come from?
(D) When will cars become even more efficient?
(E) How much money is spent on cars today?

28. The passage is primarily concerned with

(A) the problem of fuel consumption
(B) the difficulty of driving
(C) the invention of the car
(D) the development of the car from the past to now
(E) the future of automobiles

29. According to the passage, scientists devote much of their research today to

(A) making cars faster
(B) making more cars
(C) making cars more affordable
(D) making cars more fuel efficient
(E) making cars that hold more people

30. When discussing the technological advances of the early car, the author's tone could best be described as

(A) proud
(B) hesitant
(C) informative
(D) pedantic
(E) sarcastic

31. The author would most likely agree that

(A) cars are incredibly useful to many different sorts of people
(B) the problems we face in the future are very important
(C) cars are more trouble than they are worth
(D) early car owners were all snobs
(E) we will never make the same technological advances as we did in the past

GO ON TO THE NEXT PAGE.

2

> By the rude bridge that arched the flood,
> Their flag to April's breeze unfurled,
> Here once the embattled farmers stood
> And fired the shot heard round the world.
> 5   The foe long since in silence slept;
> Alike the conqueror silent sleeps;
> And Time the ruined bridge has swept
> Down the dark stream which seaward creeps.
> On this green bank, by this soft stream,
> 10   We set to-day a votive stone;
> That memory may their deed redeem,
> When, like our sires, our sons are gone.
> Spirit, that made those heroes dare
> To die, and leave their children free,
> 15   Bid Time and Nature gently spare
>   The shaft we raise to them and thee.

—"Concord Hymn" by Ralph Waldo Emerson

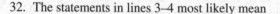

32. The statements in lines 3–4 most likely mean

(A) the narrator is a farmer
(B) the place described is a battle site
(C) a crime took place at that site
(D) the farmers described were all killed
(E) it is a cold day

33. In the poem, the speaker claims which of the reasons for writing this poem?

  I.   To warn future generations about the horrors of war
  II. To keep the memory of the great deeds of soldiers alive
  III. To gain courage to fight himself

(A) I only
(B) II only
(C) II and III only
(D) I and III only
(E) I, II, and III

34. The "votive stone" referred to in line 10 probably refers to

(A) a candle
(B) a weapon
(C) an old stone fence
(D) a war memorial
(E) a natural landmark

35. With which statement would the author most strongly agree?

(A) All war is in vain.
(B) Farming is a difficult life.
(C) It is important to remember the brave soldiers.
(D) How a man fights is as important as how he lives his life.
(E) A memorial is an insignificant way to remember the past.

GO ON TO THE NEXT PAGE.

2

José Ferrer was known as one of the most successful American film actors of his generation, but he actually began his career in theater. He was born January 8, 1909 in
5 Puerto Rico and moved to the United States when he was six years old. His acting skills were first showcased while he attended Princeton University and performed with the Triangle Club, a student acting group
10 whose alumni also include Jimmy Stewart and F. Scott Fitzgerald.

After graduating, Ferrer continued to perform in theater until he made his Broadway debut in 1935 in the play
15 *Charley's Aunt.* He had many successful roles on Broadway, including a role in 1943 when he played the villain Iago in Shakespeare's play *Othello.* The title role of *Othello* in that production was played by the
20 acclaimed actor Paul Robeson. With these two powerful performers, *Othello* became the longest running play in Broadway history (at the time). Ferrer's greatest role, though, was still to come.
25 In 1946, Ferrer was cast in the title role of *Cyrano de Bergerac.* He won the prestigious Tony award as Cyrano, the tragic hero who fights men with supreme courage but cowardly hides his love for the
30 beautiful Roxanne. His success in this role led directly to his repeated performances as Cyrano in a film version (for which he won an Oscar) and a television version (for which he won an Emmy). He is the only
35 actor to win all three of those special awards for playing the same role. This feat is all the more remarkable because Cyrano de Bergerac was known as a desirable role, one that had been played very well previously
40 by other talented actors.

Through these roles, Ferrer earned a reputation on Broadway as an extremely flexible actor, talented enough to play many diverse roles. Eight years after his debut
45 in professional theater, he finally started performing in movies. Once he began appearing in films, that skill translated into many great performances and memorable roles. His film career included both acting
50 and directing opportunities and lasted nearly forty years.

36. Which of the following is the primary purpose of the passage?

(A) To discuss the success of Puerto Rican actors on Broadway
(B) To suggest that José Ferrer was the best actor ever to play Cyrano de Bergerac
(C) To provide a synopsis of the career of a well-regarded American actor
(D) To contrast the history of theater with the history of television
(E) To compare two great Broadway actors, Paul Robeson and José Ferrer

37. The author would most likely agree with which of the following?

(A) Ferrer's career was long because he was able to play many different roles.
(B) Ferrer regretted waiting years before he became a screen actor.
(C) Princeton University's Triangle Club allowed Ferrer to learn from Jimmy Stewart and F. Scott Fitzgerald.
(D) Cyrano de Bergerac is the greatest role ever written for the Broadway stage.
(E) Cyrano de Bergerac was Ferrer's favorite role to perform.

GO ON TO THE NEXT PAGE.

38. Which of the following can be inferred from the passage?

   (A) Most members of the Triangle Club have successful acting careers.
   (B) Ferrer was more honored by his Tony award than by his Emmy or Oscar.
   (C) The record-setting run of *Othello* may have been in part due to Paul Robeson.
   (D) Ferrer did not perform again on Broadway after he began performing in movies.
   (E) Ferrer's performance as Cyrano set a record that still stands today.

39. The author would most likely agree with all of the following EXCEPT

   (A) Paul Robeson was seen by some as a very talented actor
   (B) Ferrer is somewhat responsible for the success of the longest-running Broadway play in history
   (C) some actors consider Cyrano de Bergerac a role they would like to perform
   (D) it is difficult to win prestigious acting awards
   (E) Ferrer's successful performance in Othello was his first Broadway performance

40. Which of the following best describes the author's attitude toward José Ferrer?

   (A) Indifference
   (B) Envy
   (C) Friendship
   (D) Isolation
   (E) Admiration

STOP

IF YOU FINISH BEFORE TIME IS CALLED,
YOU MAY CHECK YOUR WORK ON THIS SECTION ONLY.
DO NOT TURN TO ANY OTHER SECTION IN THE TEST.

Upper Level SSAT
Section 3
Time - 30 Minutes
60 Questions

This section consists of two different types of questions. There are directions and a sample question for each type.

Each of the following questions consists of one word followed by five words or phrases. You are to select the one word or phrase whose meaning is closest to the word in capital letters.

Sample Question:

CHILLY:
(A) lazy
(B) nice
(C) dry
(D) cold
(E) sunny   Ⓐ Ⓑ Ⓒ ● Ⓔ

1. CONTORT:
   (A) bend
   (B) deform
   (C) color
   (D) amuse
   (E) occupy

2. GRIM:
   (A) clean
   (B) relaxing
   (C) frown
   (D) harsh
   (E) irresponsible

3. PROHIBIT:
   (A) attempt
   (B) recount
   (C) diminish
   (D) conserve
   (E) forbid

4. VACANT:
   (A) stark
   (B) varied
   (C) dreary
   (D) rented
   (E) huge

5. AUSTERE:
   (A) plentiful
   (B) ornate
   (C) miserly
   (D) severe
   (E) empty

6. QUELL:
   (A) stifle
   (B) dissemble
   (C) articulate
   (D) rock gently
   (E) praise highly

7. FORTIFY:
   (A) emphasize
   (B) strengthen
   (C) revere
   (D) diffuse
   (E) surround

8. PROCLIVITY:
   (A) efficiency
   (B) accuracy
   (C) authenticity
   (D) propensity
   (E) proprietary

GO ON TO THE NEXT PAGE.

9. FORMIDABLE:
    (A) malleable
    (B) powerful
    (C) talented
    (D) fearful
    (E) trainable

10. STYMIE:
    (A) construct
    (B) swindle
    (C) depress
    (D) frustrate
    (E) reason

11. ERRATIC:
    (A) constant
    (B) amiable
    (C) innate
    (D) inconsistent
    (E) caustic

12. CONCILIATE:
    (A) pacify
    (B) replace
    (C) inform
    (D) expose
    (E) surpass

13. REFRACTORY:
    (A) stubborn
    (B) excessive
    (C) ironic
    (D) inhumane
    (E) improper

14. TRUNCATE:
    (A) packed
    (B) shorten
    (C) grow
    (D) remind
    (E) reproach

15. MEAGER:
    (A) gullible
    (B) novel
    (C) sparse
    (D) vulnerable
    (E) providential

16. CREDIBLE:
    (A) obsolete
    (B) plausible
    (C) fabulous
    (D) mundane
    (E) superficial

17. CULPABLE:
    (A) elusive
    (B) unheralded
    (C) esoteric
    (D) worthy of blame
    (E) sanctioned

18. DEPLORE:
    (A) rejoice
    (B) mitigate
    (C) lament
    (D) imply
    (E) prevent

19. ACCLAIM:
    (A) compliment
    (B) feast
    (C) assert
    (D) blame
    (E) compose

20. GUILE:
    (A) vengeance
    (B) fear
    (C) trust
    (D) loathing
    (E) cunning

GO ON TO THE NEXT PAGE.

21. FALLOW:
    (A) prompt
    (B) unused
    (C) deep
    (D) secondary
    (E) recessive

22. CHAMPION:
    (A) deter
    (B) force
    (C) fight
    (D) side with
    (E) change

23. IMBUE:
    (A) renew
    (B) suffuse
    (C) dawdle
    (D) compete
    (E) impress

24. POSTHUMOUS:
    (A) in the future
    (B) post war
    (C) after death
    (D) during the age of
    (E) promptly

25. INAUSPICIOUS:
    (A) colorless
    (B) prudent
    (C) misplaced
    (D) unfortunate
    (E) raising intelligent questions

26. RENAISSANCE:
    (A) carnival
    (B) fortune
    (C) burial
    (D) revival
    (E) earlier time

27. DECOMPOSITION:
    (A) combustion
    (B) infiltration
    (C) perturbation
    (D) equalization
    (E) disintegration

28. AGGRANDIZEMENT:
    (A) assessment
    (B) leniency
    (C) restitution
    (D) annulment
    (E) glorification

29. GULLIBLE:
    (A) stranded
    (B) easily deceived
    (C) distant
    (D) assailable
    (E) scheduled

30. REFUTATION:
    (A) attraction
    (B) rebuttal
    (C) legal activity
    (D) confirmation
    (E) enthusiastic response

GO ON TO THE NEXT PAGE.

The following questions ask you to find relationships between words. For each question, select the answer choice that best completes the meaning of the sentence.

Sample Question:

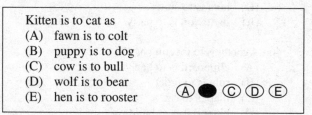

Kitten is to cat as
(A) fawn is to colt
(B) puppy is to dog
(C) cow is to bull
(D) wolf is to bear
(E) hen is to rooster

Choice (B) is the best answer because a kitten is a young cat, just as a puppy is a young dog. Of all the answer choices, (B) states a relationship that is most like the relationship between <u>kitten</u> and <u>cat</u>.

31. Composer is to score as
    (A) conductor is to orchestra
    (B) operator is to telephone
    (C) teacher is to classroom
    (D) attorney is to trial
    (E) author is to book

32. Stanza is to poem as
    (A) sonnet is to play
    (B) drama is to theater
    (C) paragraph is to essay
    (D) teacher is to class
    (E) preface is to book

33. Sovereign is to monarchy as principal is to
    (A) school
    (B) administrators
    (C) workers
    (D) crew
    (E) town

34. Cylinder is to can as
    (A) circle is to square
    (B) perimeter is to area
    (C) cube is to dice
    (D) line is to angle
    (E) arc is to sphere

35. Laughter is to joke as
    (A) read is to story
    (B) question is to answer
    (C) wince is to pain
    (D) talk is to conversation
    (E) cramp is to swim

36. Massive is to weight as
    (A) gargantuan is to size
    (B) acute is to hearing
    (C) tender is to feeling
    (D) simple is to thought
    (E) foolish is to idea

37. Pint is to quart as
    (A) cup is to teaspoon
    (B) mile is to road
    (C) measure is to recipe
    (D) week is to year
    (E) temperature is to thermometer

38. Scrawl is to writing as
    (A) decipher is to code
    (B) babble is to speaking
    (C) carve is to stone
    (D) tango is to dancing
    (E) direct is to acting

3

GO ON TO THE NEXT PAGE.

39. Stoic is to emotion as
    (A) serious is to concern
    (B) soothe is to injury
    (C) amorphous is to shape
    (D) choke is to morsel
    (E) breathe is to life

40. Frugal is to spending as unruly is to
    (A) fractious
    (B) impossible
    (C) obedient
    (D) warmth
    (E) pride

41. Integrity is to honesty as
    (A) comprehension is to instruction
    (B) fame is to happiness
    (C) resolution is to determination
    (D) severity is to compassion
    (E) quotation is to report

42. Lily is to flower as pine is to
    (A) oak
    (B) needle
    (C) forest
    (D) winter
    (E) wood

43. Kitchen is to galley as
    (A) wheel is to car
    (B) fireplace is to heat
    (C) lobby is to apartment
    (D) house is to ship
    (E) exhibit is to museum

44. Blooming is to rose as
    (A) withered is to vine
    (B) prolific is to weed
    (C) fertile is to field
    (D) edible is to corn
    (E) ripe is to tomato

45. Mask is to face as
    (A) coat is to fabric
    (B) shoe is to foot
    (C) belt is to leather
    (D) hem is to skirt
    (E) invitation is to party

46. Agenda is to meeting as
    (A) clipboard is to paper
    (B) rule is to order
    (C) map is to car
    (D) blueprint is to building
    (E) gavel is to podium

47. Pathology is to disease as psychology is to
    (A) mind
    (B) science
    (C) doctor
    (D) anguish
    (E) hospital

48. Autobiography is to author as
    (A) autograph is to signature
    (B) self-sufficiency is to provision
    (C) automation is to worker
    (D) self-portrait is to artist
    (E) autopsy is to doctor

49. Bird is to migration as
    (A) parrot is to imitation
    (B) ranger is to conservation
    (C) bear is to hibernation
    (D) lawyer is to accusation
    (E) traveler is to location

50. Border is to country as
    (A) perimeter is to area
    (B) land is to owner
    (C) road is to street
    (D) area is to volume
    (E) capital is to state

GO ON TO THE NEXT PAGE.

51. Patter is to rain as
    (A) rainbow is to storm
    (B) call is to telephone
    (C) clank is to chain
    (D) volume is to radio
    (E) eruption is to volcano

52. Brazen is to tact as
    (A) lethargic is to energy
    (B) agile is to strength
    (C) humongous is to size
    (D) ancient is to time
    (E) fallen is to grace

53. Taciturn is to words as
    (A) thrifty is to money
    (B) petty is to concern
    (C) silly is to extras
    (D) startled is to surprise
    (E) trusting is to care

54. Scalpel is to razor as surgeon is to
    (A) barber
    (B) gardener
    (C) chef
    (D) patient
    (E) engineer

55. Storyteller is to listener as
    (A) accompanist is to composer
    (B) critique is to commentator
    (C) banter is to humorist
    (D) anthologist is to editor
    (E) pantomime is to viewer

56. Gully is to erosion as
    (A) drought is to precipitation
    (B) mine is to excavation
    (C) clot is to dispersion
    (D) forest is to cultivation
    (E) water is to inundation

57. Drip is to deluge as
    (A) shine is to polish
    (B) warm is to heat
    (C) yearn is to wish
    (D) smolder is to blaze
    (E) bend is to straight

58. Lax is to resolution as
    (A) hapless is to circumstance
    (B) detrimental is to destruction
    (C) deceitful is to sincerity
    (D) vulnerable is to wound
    (E) accessible is to rewarded

59. Hammer is to pound as
    (A) vase is to flowers
    (B) briefcase is to papers
    (C) nail is to wood
    (D) screwdriver is to tool
    (E) jack is to raise

60. Lexicon is to words as anthology is to
    (A) reading
    (B) library
    (C) books
    (D) works
    (E) pages

STOP

IF YOU FINISH BEFORE TIME IS CALLED,
YOU MAY CHECK YOUR WORK ON THIS SECTION ONLY.
DO NOT TURN TO ANY OTHER SECTION IN THE TEST.

Upper Level SSAT
Section 4
Time - 30 Minutes
25 Questions

Following each problem in this section, there are five suggested answers. Work each problem in your head or in the blank space provided at the right of the page. Then look at the five suggested answers and decide which one is best.

<u>Note:</u> Figures that accompany problems in this section are drawn as accurately as possible EXCEPT when it is stated in a specific problem that its figure is not drawn to scale.

Sample Problem:

5,413 − 4,827	(A) 586 (B) 596 (C) 696 (D) 1,586 (E) 1,686 ● Ⓑ Ⓒ Ⓓ Ⓔ

---

1. $2^4 =$

    (A) 24
    (B) 16
    (C) 8
    (D) 6
    (E) 4

USE THIS SPACE FOR FIGURING.

---

2. $x =$

    (A) 30
    (B) 60
    (C) 90
    (D) 120
    (E) 300

    $x°$ $60°$

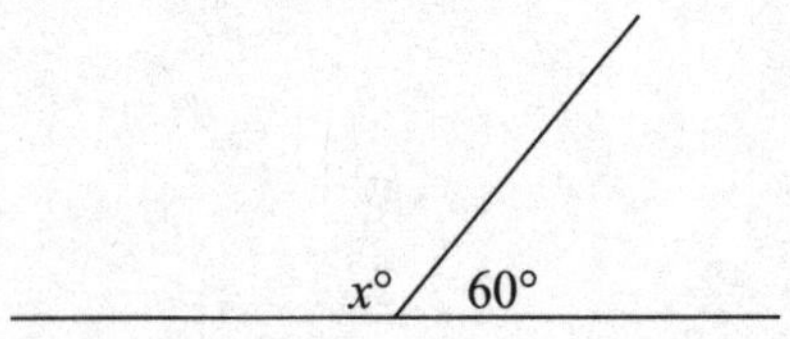

    Figure 1

---

3. If $-4 < x < 2$, how many possible integer values for x are there?

    (A) 6
    (B) 5
    (C) 4
    (D) 3
    (E) 2

GO ON TO THE NEXT PAGE.

Questions 4-6 refer to the following graph.

USE THIS SPACE FOR FIGURING.

4

Ken's Savings Account Balance, 2011–2014

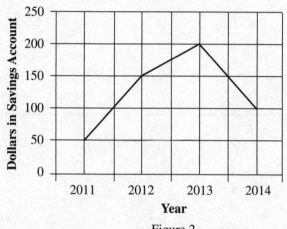

Figure 2

4. By how many dollars did Ken's savings account balance grow from 2011 to 2012 ?

    (A) $25.00
    (B) $50.00
    (C) $75.00
    (D) $100.00
    (E) $150.00

5. The decrease in Ken's account balance from 2013 to 2014 equals what percent of Ken's account balance at the start of 2012 ?

    (A) 100%

    (B) 75%

    (C) $66\frac{2}{3}$ %

    (D) 50%

    (E) 25%

6. If during 2014, Ken withdrew from his account one-half the amount he withdrew in 2013, how many dollars would be left in his account at the end of 2014 ?

    (A) $50
    (B) $75
    (C) $100
    (D) $150
    (E) $200

GO ON TO THE NEXT PAGE.

7. A large square box is made up of smaller square boxes. Each of these smaller boxes has a side length of 3 inches. How many of these smaller boxes are used to create the larger box if the larger box's base has a perimeter of 36 inches?

(A) 9
(B) 27
(C) 36
(D) 64
(E) 108

USE THIS SPACE FOR FIGURING.

8. Calculate $10x - y^2$ when $x = 4$ and $y = 5$.

(A) 4
(B) 7
(C) 15
(D) 25
(E) 30

9. Which of the following fractions is greatest?

(A) $\dfrac{3}{4}$

(B) $\dfrac{5}{8}$

(C) $\dfrac{1}{2}$

(D) $\dfrac{3}{7}$

(E) $\dfrac{5}{9}$

10. If $x + y = z$, then $z =$

(A) 180
(B) 90
(C) 60
(D) 45
(E) 30

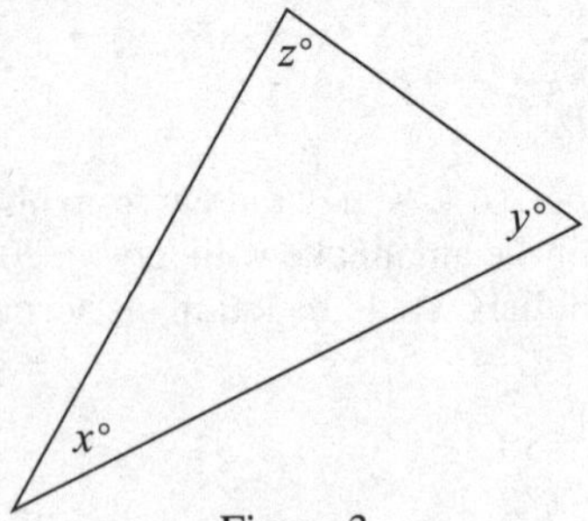

Figure 3

GO ON TO THE NEXT PAGE.

11. Anita bowled a 100, a 120, and an 88 on her first three games. What must her score be on the fourth game to raise her average for the day to a 130 ?

(A) 80

(B) 95

(C) $102\frac{2}{3}$

(D) 145

(E) 212

USE THIS SPACE FOR FIGURING.

4

12. There are 35 girls and 24 boys in a club. One quarter of the boys are wearing red shirts. Forty percent of the girls are wearing yellow shirts. How many more club members are wearing yellow shirts than red shirts?

(A) 1
(B) 3
(C) 8
(D) 9
(E) 12

13. 36 is 16 percent of

(A) 25
(B) 52
(C) 112
(D) 125
(E) 225

14. Mr. Patterson pays $1,200 each month for a storage warehouse that measures 75 feet by 200 feet. What is the monthly cost per square foot?

(A) $0.08
(B) $0.75
(C) $0.80
(D) $8.00
(E) $450.00

GO ON TO THE NEXT PAGE.

15. The ratio of rhubarb plants to tomato plants in Jim's garden is 4 to 5. If there is a total of 45 rhubarb and tomato plants all together, how many of these plants are rhubarb plants?

   (A)   4
   (B)   5
   (C)   9
   (D) 20
   (E) 25

16. If m is a positive integer, and if $3 + 16 \div m$ is an integer less than 19, which of the following must be true of m ?

   (A) $m = 19$
   (B) m is even
   (C) $m = 16$
   (D) m is a prime number
   (E) m is a multiple of four

17. If an item that is discounted by 20% still costs more than $28.00, the original price of the item must be

   (A) less than $3.50
   (B) less than $7.00
   (C) less than $35.00
   (D) equal to $35.00
   (E) more than $35.00

18. What is the perimeter of triangle *MNO* ?

   (A)   3
   (B)   9
   (C) 18
   (D) 27
   (E) It cannot be determined from the information given.

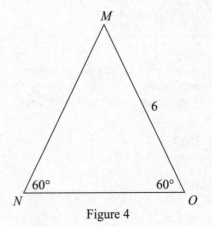

Figure 4

GO ON TO THE NEXT PAGE.

19. It takes Alice between 2 and $2\frac{1}{2}$ hours to drive home from college. If the trip is 100 miles, her average speed, in miles per hour, must always be between

    (A) 10 and 20
    (B) 25 and 30
    (C) 30 and 35
    (D) 40 and 50
    (E) 50 and 60

USE THIS SPACE FOR FIGURING.

20. What is the value of the underlined digit?

    470.1<u>8</u>

    (A) 8 hundredths
    (B) 8 tenths
    (C) 8 ones
    (D) 8 tens
    (E) 8 hundreds

GO ON TO THE NEXT PAGE.

Questions 21 and 22 refer to the following chart.

Number of Patients Seen by Four Doctors During a Certain Week

	Monday	Tuesday	Wednesday	Thursday	Friday	Total
Dr. Adams	6	12	10	0	0	28
Dr. Chou	8	8	0	8	8	32
Dr. Davis	4	0	5	3	4	16
Dr. Rosenthal	0	8	10	6	0	24
Total	18	28	25	17	12	100

Figure 5

21. The number of patients that Dr. Davis saw on Friday represents what percent of the total number of patients she saw during the entire week?

    (A) $33\frac{1}{3}$ %

    (B) 25%

    (C) 10%

    (D) 4%

    (E) It cannot be determined from the information given.

USE THIS SPACE FOR FIGURING.

22. Over the entire week, Dr. Adams and Dr. Davis together saw what percent of the total number of patients seen by all four doctors?

    (A) 16%
    (B) 28%
    (C) 44%
    (D) 50%
    (E) 88%

GO ON TO THE NEXT PAGE.

23. A store sells mints for 50¢ each or $4.80 for a case of 12 mints. The cost per mint is what percent greater when the mints are purchased separately than when purchased in a case?

    (A) 10%
    (B) 20%
    (C) 22%
    (D) 25%
    (E) 30%

USE THIS SPACE FOR FIGURING.

24. Michael sells chocolate covered bananas. On average, he sells 130 chocolate covered bananas each day. Michael is looking to expand business and runs a special on bananas purchased after 4 P.M. Customers will pay only $3.00 rather than $4.00 for a chocolate covered banana. In order to maintain his current revenue, what is the minimum number of customers needed to buy $3.00 bananas if Michael has 40 customers buying $4.00 bananas each day?

    (A)   90
    (B) 120
    (C) 130
    (D) 170
    (E) 360

25. If the length of one of the legs of a right triangle is decreased by 10%, and the length of the other leg is increased by 20%, then what is the approximate percent change in the area of the triangle?

    (A) 2%
    (B) 8%
    (C) 10%
    (D) 15%
    (E) 18%

STOP

IF YOU FINISH BEFORE TIME IS CALLED,
YOU MAY CHECK YOUR WORK ON THIS SECTION ONLY.
DO NOT TURN TO ANY OTHER SECTION IN THE TEST.

Chapter 11
Middle Level
SSAT Practice Test

Middle Level Practice Test

Be sure each mark *completely* fills the answer space.
Start with number 1 for each new section of the test. You may find more answer spaces than you need.
If so, please leave them blank.

SECTION 1

1 Ⓐ Ⓑ Ⓒ Ⓓ Ⓔ	6 Ⓐ Ⓑ Ⓒ Ⓓ Ⓔ	11 Ⓐ Ⓑ Ⓒ Ⓓ Ⓔ	16 Ⓐ Ⓑ Ⓒ Ⓓ Ⓔ	21 Ⓐ Ⓑ Ⓒ Ⓓ Ⓔ
2 Ⓐ Ⓑ Ⓒ Ⓓ Ⓔ	7 Ⓐ Ⓑ Ⓒ Ⓓ Ⓔ	12 Ⓐ Ⓑ Ⓒ Ⓓ Ⓔ	17 Ⓐ Ⓑ Ⓒ Ⓓ Ⓔ	22 Ⓐ Ⓑ Ⓒ Ⓓ Ⓔ
3 Ⓐ Ⓑ Ⓒ Ⓓ Ⓔ	8 Ⓐ Ⓑ Ⓒ Ⓓ Ⓔ	13 Ⓐ Ⓑ Ⓒ Ⓓ Ⓔ	18 Ⓐ Ⓑ Ⓒ Ⓓ Ⓔ	23 Ⓐ Ⓑ Ⓒ Ⓓ Ⓔ
4 Ⓐ Ⓑ Ⓒ Ⓓ Ⓔ	9 Ⓐ Ⓑ Ⓒ Ⓓ Ⓔ	14 Ⓐ Ⓑ Ⓒ Ⓓ Ⓔ	19 Ⓐ Ⓑ Ⓒ Ⓓ Ⓔ	24 Ⓐ Ⓑ Ⓒ Ⓓ Ⓔ
5 Ⓐ Ⓑ Ⓒ Ⓓ Ⓔ	10 Ⓐ Ⓑ Ⓒ Ⓓ Ⓔ	15 Ⓐ Ⓑ Ⓒ Ⓓ Ⓔ	20 Ⓐ Ⓑ Ⓒ Ⓓ Ⓔ	25 Ⓐ Ⓑ Ⓒ Ⓓ Ⓔ

SECTION 2

1 Ⓐ Ⓑ Ⓒ Ⓓ Ⓔ	9 Ⓐ Ⓑ Ⓒ Ⓓ Ⓔ	17 Ⓐ Ⓑ Ⓒ Ⓓ Ⓔ	25 Ⓐ Ⓑ Ⓒ Ⓓ Ⓔ	33 Ⓐ Ⓑ Ⓒ Ⓓ Ⓔ
2 Ⓐ Ⓑ Ⓒ Ⓓ Ⓔ	10 Ⓐ Ⓑ Ⓒ Ⓓ Ⓔ	18 Ⓐ Ⓑ Ⓒ Ⓓ Ⓔ	26 Ⓐ Ⓑ Ⓒ Ⓓ Ⓔ	34 Ⓐ Ⓑ Ⓒ Ⓓ Ⓔ
3 Ⓐ Ⓑ Ⓒ Ⓓ Ⓔ	11 Ⓐ Ⓑ Ⓒ Ⓓ Ⓔ	19 Ⓐ Ⓑ Ⓒ Ⓓ Ⓔ	27 Ⓐ Ⓑ Ⓒ Ⓓ Ⓔ	35 Ⓐ Ⓑ Ⓒ Ⓓ Ⓔ
4 Ⓐ Ⓑ Ⓒ Ⓓ Ⓔ	12 Ⓐ Ⓑ Ⓒ Ⓓ Ⓔ	20 Ⓐ Ⓑ Ⓒ Ⓓ Ⓔ	28 Ⓐ Ⓑ Ⓒ Ⓓ Ⓔ	36 Ⓐ Ⓑ Ⓒ Ⓓ Ⓔ
5 Ⓐ Ⓑ Ⓒ Ⓓ Ⓔ	13 Ⓐ Ⓑ Ⓒ Ⓓ Ⓔ	21 Ⓐ Ⓑ Ⓒ Ⓓ Ⓔ	29 Ⓐ Ⓑ Ⓒ Ⓓ Ⓔ	37 Ⓐ Ⓑ Ⓒ Ⓓ Ⓔ
6 Ⓐ Ⓑ Ⓒ Ⓓ Ⓔ	14 Ⓐ Ⓑ Ⓒ Ⓓ Ⓔ	22 Ⓐ Ⓑ Ⓒ Ⓓ Ⓔ	30 Ⓐ Ⓑ Ⓒ Ⓓ Ⓔ	38 Ⓐ Ⓑ Ⓒ Ⓓ Ⓔ
7 Ⓐ Ⓑ Ⓒ Ⓓ Ⓔ	15 Ⓐ Ⓑ Ⓒ Ⓓ Ⓔ	23 Ⓐ Ⓑ Ⓒ Ⓓ Ⓔ	31 Ⓐ Ⓑ Ⓒ Ⓓ Ⓔ	39 Ⓐ Ⓑ Ⓒ Ⓓ Ⓔ
8 Ⓐ Ⓑ Ⓒ Ⓓ Ⓔ	16 Ⓐ Ⓑ Ⓒ Ⓓ Ⓔ	24 Ⓐ Ⓑ Ⓒ Ⓓ Ⓔ	32 Ⓐ Ⓑ Ⓒ Ⓓ Ⓔ	40 Ⓐ Ⓑ Ⓒ Ⓓ Ⓔ

SECTION 3

1 Ⓐ Ⓑ Ⓒ Ⓓ Ⓔ	13 Ⓐ Ⓑ Ⓒ Ⓓ Ⓔ	25 Ⓐ Ⓑ Ⓒ Ⓓ Ⓔ	37 Ⓐ Ⓑ Ⓒ Ⓓ Ⓔ	49 Ⓐ Ⓑ Ⓒ Ⓓ Ⓔ
2 Ⓐ Ⓑ Ⓒ Ⓓ Ⓔ	14 Ⓐ Ⓑ Ⓒ Ⓓ Ⓔ	26 Ⓐ Ⓑ Ⓒ Ⓓ Ⓔ	38 Ⓐ Ⓑ Ⓒ Ⓓ Ⓔ	50 Ⓐ Ⓑ Ⓒ Ⓓ Ⓔ
3 Ⓐ Ⓑ Ⓒ Ⓓ Ⓔ	15 Ⓐ Ⓑ Ⓒ Ⓓ Ⓔ	27 Ⓐ Ⓑ Ⓒ Ⓓ Ⓔ	39 Ⓐ Ⓑ Ⓒ Ⓓ Ⓔ	51 Ⓐ Ⓑ Ⓒ Ⓓ Ⓔ
4 Ⓐ Ⓑ Ⓒ Ⓓ Ⓔ	16 Ⓐ Ⓑ Ⓒ Ⓓ Ⓔ	28 Ⓐ Ⓑ Ⓒ Ⓓ Ⓔ	40 Ⓐ Ⓑ Ⓒ Ⓓ Ⓔ	52 Ⓐ Ⓑ Ⓒ Ⓓ Ⓔ
5 Ⓐ Ⓑ Ⓒ Ⓓ Ⓔ	17 Ⓐ Ⓑ Ⓒ Ⓓ Ⓔ	29 Ⓐ Ⓑ Ⓒ Ⓓ Ⓔ	41 Ⓐ Ⓑ Ⓒ Ⓓ Ⓔ	53 Ⓐ Ⓑ Ⓒ Ⓓ Ⓔ
6 Ⓐ Ⓑ Ⓒ Ⓓ Ⓔ	18 Ⓐ Ⓑ Ⓒ Ⓓ Ⓔ	30 Ⓐ Ⓑ Ⓒ Ⓓ Ⓔ	42 Ⓐ Ⓑ Ⓒ Ⓓ Ⓔ	54 Ⓐ Ⓑ Ⓒ Ⓓ Ⓔ
7 Ⓐ Ⓑ Ⓒ Ⓓ Ⓔ	19 Ⓐ Ⓑ Ⓒ Ⓓ Ⓔ	31 Ⓐ Ⓑ Ⓒ Ⓓ Ⓔ	43 Ⓐ Ⓑ Ⓒ Ⓓ Ⓔ	55 Ⓐ Ⓑ Ⓒ Ⓓ Ⓔ
8 Ⓐ Ⓑ Ⓒ Ⓓ Ⓔ	20 Ⓐ Ⓑ Ⓒ Ⓓ Ⓔ	32 Ⓐ Ⓑ Ⓒ Ⓓ Ⓔ	44 Ⓐ Ⓑ Ⓒ Ⓓ Ⓔ	56 Ⓐ Ⓑ Ⓒ Ⓓ Ⓔ
9 Ⓐ Ⓑ Ⓒ Ⓓ Ⓔ	21 Ⓐ Ⓑ Ⓒ Ⓓ Ⓔ	33 Ⓐ Ⓑ Ⓒ Ⓓ Ⓔ	45 Ⓐ Ⓑ Ⓒ Ⓓ Ⓔ	57 Ⓐ Ⓑ Ⓒ Ⓓ Ⓔ
10 Ⓐ Ⓑ Ⓒ Ⓓ Ⓔ	22 Ⓐ Ⓑ Ⓒ Ⓓ Ⓔ	34 Ⓐ Ⓑ Ⓒ Ⓓ Ⓔ	46 Ⓐ Ⓑ Ⓒ Ⓓ Ⓔ	58 Ⓐ Ⓑ Ⓒ Ⓓ Ⓔ
11 Ⓐ Ⓑ Ⓒ Ⓓ Ⓔ	23 Ⓐ Ⓑ Ⓒ Ⓓ Ⓔ	35 Ⓐ Ⓑ Ⓒ Ⓓ Ⓔ	47 Ⓐ Ⓑ Ⓒ Ⓓ Ⓔ	59 Ⓐ Ⓑ Ⓒ Ⓓ Ⓔ
12 Ⓐ Ⓑ Ⓒ Ⓓ Ⓔ	24 Ⓐ Ⓑ Ⓒ Ⓓ Ⓔ	36 Ⓐ Ⓑ Ⓒ Ⓓ Ⓔ	48 Ⓐ Ⓑ Ⓒ Ⓓ Ⓔ	60 Ⓐ Ⓑ Ⓒ Ⓓ Ⓔ

SECTION 4

1 Ⓐ Ⓑ Ⓒ Ⓓ Ⓔ	6 Ⓐ Ⓑ Ⓒ Ⓓ Ⓔ	11 Ⓐ Ⓑ Ⓒ Ⓓ Ⓔ	16 Ⓐ Ⓑ Ⓒ Ⓓ Ⓔ	21 Ⓐ Ⓑ Ⓒ Ⓓ Ⓔ
2 Ⓐ Ⓑ Ⓒ Ⓓ Ⓔ	7 Ⓐ Ⓑ Ⓒ Ⓓ Ⓔ	12 Ⓐ Ⓑ Ⓒ Ⓓ Ⓔ	17 Ⓐ Ⓑ Ⓒ Ⓓ Ⓔ	22 Ⓐ Ⓑ Ⓒ Ⓓ Ⓔ
3 Ⓐ Ⓑ Ⓒ Ⓓ Ⓔ	8 Ⓐ Ⓑ Ⓒ Ⓓ Ⓔ	13 Ⓐ Ⓑ Ⓒ Ⓓ Ⓔ	18 Ⓐ Ⓑ Ⓒ Ⓓ Ⓔ	23 Ⓐ Ⓑ Ⓒ Ⓓ Ⓔ
4 Ⓐ Ⓑ Ⓒ Ⓓ Ⓔ	9 Ⓐ Ⓑ Ⓒ Ⓓ Ⓔ	14 Ⓐ Ⓑ Ⓒ Ⓓ Ⓔ	19 Ⓐ Ⓑ Ⓒ Ⓓ Ⓔ	24 Ⓐ Ⓑ Ⓒ Ⓓ Ⓔ
5 Ⓐ Ⓑ Ⓒ Ⓓ Ⓔ	10 Ⓐ Ⓑ Ⓒ Ⓓ Ⓔ	15 Ⓐ Ⓑ Ⓒ Ⓓ Ⓔ	20 Ⓐ Ⓑ Ⓒ Ⓓ Ⓔ	25 Ⓐ Ⓑ Ⓒ Ⓓ Ⓔ

Middle Level SSAT
Writing Sample

Time - 25 Minutes
1 Topic

Writing Sample

Schools would like to get to know you better through a story you tell using one of the ideas below. Please choose the idea you find more interesting and write a story using the idea in your first sentence. Please fill in the circle next to the one you choose.

Ⓐ   What I noticed across the street caused me to...

Ⓑ   The room was surprisingly cold.

_____

_____

_____

_____

_____

_____

_____

_____

_____

GO ON TO THE NEXT PAGE.

Middle Level SSAT
Section 1
Time - 30 Minutes
25 Questions

Following each problem in this section, there are five suggested answers. Work each problem in your head or in the blank space provided at the right of the page. Then look at the five suggested answers and decide which one is best.

Note: Figures that accompany problems in this section are drawn as accurately as possible EXCEPT when it is stated in a specific problem that its figure is not drawn to scale.

Sample Problem:

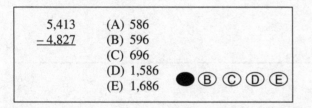

$$\begin{array}{r} 5,413 \\ -\,4,827 \end{array}$$

(A) 586
(B) 596
(C) 696
(D) 1,586
(E) 1,686

● Ⓑ Ⓒ Ⓓ Ⓔ

---

1. Which fraction equals $\frac{2}{3}$?

    (A) $\frac{3}{2}$

    (B) $\frac{3}{6}$

    (C) $\frac{9}{12}$

    (D) $\frac{8}{12}$

    (E) $\frac{5}{6}$

USE THIS SPACE FOR FIGURING.

---

2. Which of the following is an even positive integer that lies between 22 and 27 ?

    (A) 25
    (B) 24
    (C) 22
    (D) 21
    (E) 20

GO ON TO THE NEXT PAGE.

3. In the number 281, the sum of the digits is how much less than the product of the digits?

   (A) 16
   (B) 11
   (C) 10
   (D) 5
   (E) 4

USE THIS SPACE FOR FIGURING.

1

4. $(109 - 102) \times 3 - 4^2 =$

   (A)   5
   (B)   0
   (C)   −5
   (D)   −7
   (E) −336

5. A concert is held at a stadium that has 25,000 seats. If exactly $\frac{3}{4}$ of the seats were filled, to the nearest thousand, how many people attended the concert?

   (A) 10,000
   (B) 14,000
   (C) 15,000
   (D) 19,000
   (E) 21,000

6. The perimeter of a square with an area of 81 is

   (A) 81
   (B) 54
   (C) 36
   (D) 18
   (E) 9

7. If the sum of three consecutive positive integers is 9, what is the middle integer?

   (A) 1
   (B) 2
   (C) 3
   (D) 4
   (E) 5

GO ON TO THE NEXT PAGE.

8. A number greater than 2 that is a factor of both 20 and 16 is also a factor of which number?
   (A) 10
   (B) 14
   (C) 18
   (D) 24
   (E) 30

USE THIS SPACE FOR FIGURING.

1

9. $(2^3)^2 =$

   (A) 2
   (B) 2^5
   (C) 2^6
   (D) 4^5
   (E) 4^6

10. If $\dfrac{1}{2}$ is greater than $\dfrac{M}{16}$, then M could be

    (A) 7
    (B) 8
    (C) 9
    (D) 10
    (E) 32

11. The sum of the lengths of two sides of an equilateral triangle is 4. What is the perimeter of the triangle?

    (A) 2
    (B) 4
    (C) 6
    (D) 8
    (E) 12

GO ON TO THE NEXT PAGE.

Questions 12–14 refer to the following chart.

Stacey's Weekly Mileage

Day	Miles Driven
MONDAY	35
TUESDAY	70
WEDNESDAY	50
THURSDAY	105
FRIDAY	35
SATURDAY	35
SUNDAY	20
Total	**350**

Figure 1

USE THIS SPACE FOR FIGURING.

12. What percentage of her total weekly mileage did Stacey drive on Monday?

    (A) 10%
    (B) 20%
    (C) 35%
    (D) 60%
    (E) 90%

13. The number of miles Stacey drove on Thursday is equal to the sum of the miles she drove on which days?

    (A) Monday and Wednesday
    (B) Saturday and Sunday
    (C) Tuesday, Wednesday, and Friday
    (D) Friday, Saturday, and Sunday
    (E) Monday, Friday, and Saturday

14. The number of miles Stacey drove on Sunday is equal to what percent of the number of miles she drove on Wednesday?

    (A) 10%
    (B) 20%
    (C) 40%
    (D) 50%
    (E) 80%

GO ON TO THE NEXT PAGE.

15. If $x = 5$, which of the following is equal to $\frac{1}{x}$?

    (A) 10
    (B) 20
    (C) 40
    (D) 2
    (E) 3

USE THIS SPACE FOR FIGURING.

16. What is 20% of 25% of 80 ?

    (A)   4%
    (B)   5%
    (C) 10%
    (D) 16%
    (E) 20%

17. During one week, Roy worked 3 hours on Monday, 5 hours on Tuesday, and 8 hours each day on Saturday and Sunday. The following week Roy worked a total of 40 hours. What was the average number of hours Roy worked each week?

    (A) 32
    (B) 28
    (C) 24
    (D) 12
    (E)   6

18. A box with dimensions $4 \times 8 \times 10$ is equal in volume to a box with dimensions $16 \times g \times 2$. What does g equal?

    (A)   2
    (B)   4
    (C)   8
    (D) 10
    (E) 16

GO ON TO THE NEXT PAGE.

19. Otto wants to buy two CDs that regularly sell for *b* dollars each. The store is having a sale in which the second CD costs half price. If he buys the CDs at this store, what is the overall percent he will save on the price of the two CDs?

    (A) 10%

    (B) 25%

    (C) $33\frac{1}{3}$%

    (D) 50%

    (E) 75%

20. In a certain month Ben eats 8 dinners at Italian restaurants, 4 dinners at Chinese restaurants, and 6 dinners at steakhouses. If these dinners account for all Ben's restaurant visits during the month, what percent of Ben's restaurant meals were at steakhouses?

    (A) 75%

    (B) $66\frac{1}{2}$%

    (C) 50%

    (D) $33\frac{1}{3}$%

    (E) 10%

21. What is the area of the shaded region?

    (A) 48
    (B) 36
    (C) 24
    (D) 12
    (E) It cannot be determined from the information given.

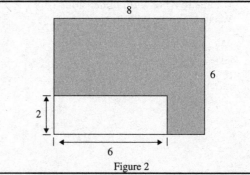

Figure 2

22. In the equation $(2 + \_ + 3)(2) = 16$, what does the _ stand for?

    (A) 3
    (B) 8
    (C) 9
    (D) 10
    (E) 12

GO ON TO THE NEXT PAGE.

23. At Skytop Farm, the ratio of cows to pigs is 16 to 1. Which of the following could be the total number of cows and pigs at the farm?

USE THIS SPACE FOR FIGURING.

(A) 15
(B) 16
(C) 32
(D) 68
(E) 74

24. Sibyl has seen four more films than Linda has seen. Linda has seen twice as many films as Joel has seen. If Sibyl has seen s films, then in terms of s, which of the following is an expression for the number of films Joel has seen?

(A) $\dfrac{s}{2} - 2$

(B) $\dfrac{s}{2} - 4$

(C) $s - 2$

(D) $s - 4$

(E) $\dfrac{8}{s - 2}$

Question 25 refers to the following definition.

For all integers x, @ $x = 2x$

25. @3 – @2 =

(A) @4
(B) @2
(C) @1
(D) @–2
(E) @–3

STOP

IF YOU FINISH BEFORE TIME IS CALLED,
YOU MAY CHECK YOUR WORK ON THIS SECTION ONLY.
DO NOT TURN TO ANY OTHER SECTION IN THE TEST.

Middle Level SSAT
Section 2
Time - 40 Minutes
40 Questions

Read each passage carefully and then answer the questions about it. For each question, decide on the basis of the passage which one of the choices best answers the questions.

The native inhabitants of the Americas arrived from Asia more than 20,000 years ago. They belonged to numerous tribes and many were skilled hunters, farmers, and fishers. Some of the most famous of the tribes of Native Americans are the Sioux, the Cheyenne, the Iroquois, and the Apache.

These tribes settled and developed organized societies. The settlers to North America from Europe fought the Native Americans for land. Geronimo was the last great Native American chief to organize rebellions against the settlers. He led raids across the southwest and into Mexico. Although he eventually was captured, he later became a celebrity.

After a long battle, the United States government moved the Native Americans onto reservations—special sections of land set aside for them—where many still reside today.

---

1. The main purpose of this passage is to

   (A) report on the current status of Native Americans
   (B) offer a solution to the problems of Native Americans
   (C) give a brief history of Native Americans
   (D) discuss ways Native Americans are able to work on reservations
   (E) give a history of different Native American tribes

2. According to the passage, the fate of Geronimo was

   (A) to live out his life in disgrace
   (B) to become a great war hero with no defeats
   (C) to become famous throughout the country
   (D) to die penniless and alone
   (E) to commit suicide

3. The author's tone in regard to the fate of Native Americans is

   (A) passionate
   (B) objective
   (C) disappointed
   (D) ambivalent
   (E) envious

4. Which of the following is the author most likely to discuss next?

   (A) Possible causes of Native American resentment
   (B) The life of the Native American in modern society
   (C) The battle that defeated Geronimo
   (D) The differences among tribes
   (E) A detailed history of the Sioux

5. The passage names all the following as skills possessed by Native Americans EXCEPT

   (A) farming
   (B) hunting
   (C) fishing
   (D) gathering
   (E) fighting

GO ON TO THE NEXT PAGE.

2

Twenty percent of all the land on Earth consists of deserts. When most people think of deserts, they think of searing heat, big sand dunes, and camels. But not all deserts are huge sand piles—many are strewn with rocks and some, like those at high altitudes, may actually be quite cold.

Desert life is interesting and varied as well. Though the desert is a punishing place—it is difficult to find food and water in the desert—many animals live there. Because there is so little water, desert animals have adapted. Camels can survive for days without drinking. Other animals get their water from the insects and plants they eat.

The extreme temperatures of the desert can make life difficult as well. Many of the mammals there have thick fur to keep out the heat and the cold. Some desert animals are nocturnal, sleeping by day and hunting by night when the air is cooler. It may seem that all deserts are the same, but they are as different as the animals that inhabit them.

6. The passage is primarily about

   (A) deserts and desert wildlife
   (B) nocturnal animals
   (C) plant life of the desert
   (D) sources of water in the desert
   (E) average desert temperatures

7. Which of the following can be inferred as an example of an adaptation to desert life?

   (A) The large claws of the lizard
   (B) The heavy outer shell of the beetle
   (C) The long ears of the hedgehog that give off heat to cool the animal
   (D) The large hood of the cobra that scares off predators
   (E) The quick speed of the mongoose so that it may catch its prey

8. The style of the passage is most like that found in a(n)

   (A) scientific thesis
   (B) general book on desert life
   (C) advanced text on animal adaptations
   (D) diary of a naturalist
   (E) biography of a desert researcher

9. According to the passage, camels are well adapted to desert life because

   (A) they have long legs
   (B) they have thick fur that keeps them cool
   (C) they have large hooded eyes
   (D) they are capable of hunting at night
   (E) they can store water for many days

10. According to the passage, some deserts

    (A) are filled with lush vegetation
    (B) are home to large bodies of water
    (C) actually get a good deal of rainfall
    (D) can be in a cold climate
    (E) are home to large, thriving cities

11. The word "punishing" in line 5 most closely means

    (A) beating
    (B) harsh
    (C) unhappy
    (D) deadly
    (E) fantastic

GO ON TO THE NEXT PAGE.

The original Olympic Games started in Greece more than 2,000 years ago. These games were a religious festival, and, at their height, lasted for five days. Only men could compete, and the sports included running, wrestling, and chariot racing.

Today's Olympic Games are quite a bit different. First, there are two varieties: Winter Olympics and Summer Olympics. They each boast many men and women competing in a multitude of sports, from skiing to gymnastics. They are each held every four years, but not during the same year. They alternate so that there are Olympic Games every two years. The Olympics are no longer held only in one country. They are hosted by different cities around the world. The opening ceremony is a spectacular display, usually incorporating the traditional dances and culture of the host city.

The highlight of the opening ceremony is the lighting of the Olympic flame. Teams of runners carry the torch from Olympia, the site of the ancient Greek games. Although the games have changed greatly throughout the centuries, the spirit of competition is still alive. The flame represents that spirit.

12. The passage is primarily concerned with

(A) justifying the existence of the Olympic Games
(B) explaining all about the games in Ancient Greece
(C) discussing the differences between Winter Olympics and Summer Olympics
(D) comparing the modern Olympic Games to those in Ancient Greece
(E) explaining the process for choosing a host country

13. The author mentions "traditional dances and culture of the host city" in order to

(A) give an example of how the opening ceremony is so spectacular
(B) explain the differences among the different host cities
(C) show that Ancient Greek games were quite boring by contrast
(D) make an analogy to the life of the Ancient Greeks
(E) illustrate the complexity of the modern games

14. The author's tone in the passage can best be described as

(A) disinterested
(B) upbeat
(C) gloating
(D) depressing
(E) fatalistic

15. The lighting of the torch is meant to symbolize

(A) the destruction caused in Ancient Greece
(B) the spirit of Ancient Greek competition
(C) the rousing nature of the games
(D) the heat generated in competition
(E) an eternal flame so that the games will continue forever

16. Which of the following can be inferred from the passage?

(A) Women in ancient Greece did not want to compete in the Olympics.
(B) The Olympics were held every year.
(C) The Olympics used to be held in just one country.
(D) Ice skating is a winter event.
(E) Opening ceremonies today are more spectacular than ones in ancient Greece.

GO ON TO THE NEXT PAGE.

Like snakes, lizards, and crocodiles, turtles are reptiles. The earliest fossils recognized as turtles are about 200 million years old and date from the time when dinosaurs roamed Earth. Unbelievably, turtles have changed little in appearance since that time.

There are many different types of turtles in many different climates around the world. In contrast to other reptiles, whose populations are confined largely to the tropics, turtles are most abundant in southeastern North America and southeastern Asia. They live in lakes, ponds, salt marshes, rivers, forests, and even deserts. The sizes of turtles vary. Bog or mud turtles grow no larger than about 4 inches (10 centimeters) long. At the other end of the spectrum is the sea-roving leatherback turtle, which may be more than 6.5 feet (2 meters) in length and weigh more than 1,100 pounds (500 kilograms).

Turtles live longer than most other animals, but reports of turtles living more than a century are questionable. Several kinds, however, have lived more than 50 years in captivity. Even in natural environments, box turtles and slider turtles can reach ages of 20 to 30 years. The ages of some turtles can be estimated by counting the growth rings that form each year on the external bony plates of the shell.

17. The author mentions dinosaurs in the first paragraph to

    (A) illustrate the age of the turtle fossils
    (B) uncover the mystery of turtle origins
    (C) show that turtles may become extinct
    (D) give an example of the type of predator that turtles once faced
    (E) bring the life of the turtle into focus

18. Turtles are different from other reptiles because they

    (A) date back to dinosaur times
    (B) have not adapted to their environment
    (C) live in different climates
    (D) are desert dwellers
    (E) are good pets

19. When the author discusses the theory that turtles may live to be more than 100, the tone can best be described as

    (A) respectful
    (B) ridiculing
    (C) horrified
    (D) interested
    (E) skeptical

20. One of the ways to verify the age of a turtle is to

    (A) measure the turtle
    (B) count the rings on its shell
    (C) examine the physical deterioration of its shell
    (D) weigh the turtle
    (E) subtract its weight from its length

21. The author would most probably agree that

    (A) turtles are more interesting than other reptiles
    (B) there is a lot to be learned about turtles
    (C) turtles live longer than any other animal
    (D) turtles can be very dangerous
    (E) there are no bad turtles

GO ON TO THE NEXT PAGE.

The summer holidays! Those magic words! The mere mention of them used to send shivers of joy rippling over my skin. All my summer holidays, from when I was four years old to when I was seventeen (1920 to 1932), were idyllic. This, I am certain, was because we always went to the same idyllic place, and that place was Norway.

Except for my ancient half-sister and my not-quite-so-ancient half-brother, the rest of us were all pure Norwegian by blood. We all spoke Norwegian and all our relations lived over there. So in a way, going to Norway every summer was like going home.

Even the journey was an event. Do not forget that there were no commercial aeroplanes in those times, so it took us four whole days to complete the trip out and another four days to get home again.

22. The author's goal in writing was to express

(A) his affection for Norway
(B) his dislike of his half-sister and half-brother
(C) dismay at the drudgery of the journey
(D) how different life was back then
(E) his realization that the trip was so long

23. The author uses the word "idyllic" in the first paragraph to mean

(A) scary
(B) pleasant
(C) religious
(D) cold
(E) boring

24. The author uses the analogy that "going to Norway every summer was like going home" to illustrate

(A) how much he dreaded the journey
(B) how frequently they went to Norway
(C) why his half-sister and half-brother were going along
(D) how long they stayed in Norway
(E) how happy and comfortable he was there

25. The author mentions the length of the trip in order to

(A) make the reader sympathetic to his plight
(B) make the reader understand why the trip was an adventure
(C) help the reader visualize the boredom that he faced
(D) give the reader some sympathy for the half-sister and half-brother
(E) help the reader visualize Norway

GO ON TO THE NEXT PAGE.

You may love to walk along the seashore and collect beautiful shells, but do you ever think about whose home that shell was before you found it? That's right, seashells are the home of a whole group of creatures known as shellfish. Some of the most common types of shellfish are the mussel, the clam, and the scallop.

It may surprise you to learn that the shellfish themselves make the shells. They manage to draw calcium carbonate, a mineral, from the water. They use that mineral to build the shell up layer by layer. The shell can grow larger and larger as the shellfish grows in size.

There are two main types of shells. There are those that are a single unit, like a conch's shell, and those that are in two pieces, like a clam's shell. The two-piece shell is called a bivalve, and the two pieces are hinged together, like a door, so that the shell can open and close for feeding.

26. The "home" mentioned in line 2 most likely refers to

(A) the sea
(B) the planet
(C) the places shellfish can be found
(D) the shell
(E) a shelter for fish

27. Which of the following questions is answered by the passage?

(A) How do shellfish reproduce?
(B) How much does the average shellfish weigh?
(C) What is the average life span of a shellfish?
(D) What do shellfish feed on?
(E) How do shellfish make their shells?

28. This passage is primarily concerned with

(A) how shellfish differ from other fish
(B) the life span of shellfish
(C) shellfish and their habitats
(D) a general discussion of shells
(E) the origin of shells

29. The author uses the comparison of the bivalves' hinge to a door in order to

(A) illustrate how the shell opens and closes
(B) explain why the shell is so fragile
(C) give a reason for the shells that are found open
(D) explain the mechanism for how the shells are made
(E) illustrate that shellfish are not so different from other fish

30. What is the best title of the selection?

(A) "A Conch by Any Other Name Would Shell as Sweet"
(B) "Going to the Beach"
(C) "I Can Grow My Own Home!"
(D) "The Prettiest Aquatic Life"
(E) "How to Find Shells"

31. According to the passage, the primary difference between the conch's shell and the clam's shell is that

(A) the conch shell is more valuable than the clam's shell
(B) the conch shell protects better than the clam's shell
(C) the conch shell is more beautiful than the clam's shell
(D) the clam's shell is more difficult for the clam to manufacture than the conch shell is for the conch to manufacture
(E) the conch shell has fewer pieces than the clam shell

GO ON TO THE NEXT PAGE.

> By day the bat is cousin to the mouse;
>
> He likes the attic of an aging house.
>
> His fingers make a hat about his head.
>
> His pulse-beat is so slow we think him dead.
>
> He loops in crazy figures half the night
>
> Among the trees that face the corner light.
>
> But when he brushes up against a screen,
>
> We are afraid of what our eyes have seen:
>
> For something is amiss or out of place
>
> When mice with wings can wear a human face.
>
> —Theodore Roethke

32. The "hat" referred to in line 3 is meant to refer to

    (A) the attic of the house
    (B) the bat's head
    (C) the bat's wings
    (D) the death of the bat
    (E) the mouse

33. The passage uses which of the following to describe the bat?

    I. The image of a winged mouse
    II. The image of a vampire
    III. The way he flies

    (A) I only
    (B) I and II only
    (C) II and III only
    (D) I and III only
    (E) I, II, and III

34. The author mentions the "crazy figures" in line 5 to refer to

    (A) the comic notion of a mouse with wings
    (B) the pattern of the bat's flight
    (C) the shape of the house
    (D) the reason the bat appears dead
    (E) the trees in the yard

35. The author would most probably agree with which of the following statements?

    (A) Bats are useful animals.
    (B) Bats are related to mice.
    (C) Bats are feared by many.
    (D) Most people have bats in their attic.
    (E) Bats are an uninteresting phenomenon.

GO ON TO THE NEXT PAGE.

Did you ever watch a sport and admire the players' uniforms? Perhaps you play a sport and know the thrill of putting on your team's uniform. Uniforms are important for many different reasons, whether you are playing a sport or watching one.

If you are playing a sport, you have many reasons to appreciate your uniform. You may notice how different uniforms are for different sports. That's because they are designed to make participation both safe and easy. If you participate in track and field, your uniform is designed to help you run faster and move more easily. If you participate in a sport like boxing or football, your uniform will protect you as well. You may wear special shoes, like sneakers or cleats, to help you run faster or keep you from slipping.

If you watch sports, you can appreciate uniforms as well. Imagine how difficult it would be to tell the players on a field apart without their uniforms. And of course, as sports fans all over the world do, you can show support for the team you favor by wearing the colors of the team's uniform.

36. The primary purpose of the passage is to

(A) discuss the importance of team spirit
(B) explain why uniforms are important for safety
(C) give a general history of uniforms
(D) help shed light on the controversy surrounding uniforms
(E) give some reasons why uniforms are useful

37. The "support" mentioned in line 12 most probably means

(A) nourishment
(B) salary
(C) endorsement
(D) brace
(E) relief

38. Which of the following best describes the author's attitude toward uniforms?

(A) Most of them are basically the same.
(B) They have many different purposes.
(C) They're most useful as protection against injury.
(D) They are fun to wear.
(E) They don't serve any real purpose.

39. According to the passage, people need special uniforms for track and field sports to

(A) help spectators cheer on the team
(B) distinguish them from other athletes
(C) protect against injury
(D) give them freedom of movement
(E) prevent them from losing

40. According to the passage, the primary reason that spectators like uniforms is that

(A) they help them to distinguish teams
(B) they have such vibrant colors
(C) they make great souvenirs
(D) they are collectible
(E) they are not too expensive

STOP
IF YOU FINISH BEFORE TIME IS CALLED,
YOU MAY CHECK YOUR WORK ON THIS SECTION ONLY.
DO NOT TURN TO ANY OTHER SECTION IN THE TEST.

Middle Level SSAT
Section 3
Time - 30 Minutes
60 Questions

This section consists of two different types of questions. There are directions and a sample question for each type.

Each of the following questions consists of one word followed by five words or phrases. You are to select the one word or phrase whose meaning is closest to the word in capital letters.

Sample Question:

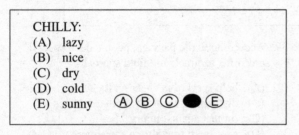

CHILLY:
(A) lazy
(B) nice
(C) dry
(D) cold
(E) sunny   Ⓐ Ⓑ Ⓒ ● Ⓔ

---

1. OBEDIENT:
    (A) amenable
    (B) excessive
    (C) ironic
    (D) inhumane
    (E) improper

2. CONTAMINATE:
    (A) deodorize
    (B) decongest
    (C) deter
    (D) taint
    (E) defoliate

3. WOEFUL:
    (A) wretched
    (B) bloated
    (C) dim
    (D) animated
    (E) reasonable

4. PRACTICAL:
    (A) difficult to learn
    (B) inferior in quality
    (C) providing great support
    (D) having great usefulness
    (E) feeling great regret

5. SCRUTINIZE:
    (A) examine carefully
    (B) announce publicly
    (C) infer correctly
    (D) decide promptly
    (E) warn swiftly

6. CONFIDE:
    (A) judge
    (B) entrust
    (C) secret
    (D) profess
    (E) confuse

7. INITIATE:
    (A) bring to an end
    (B) sign
    (C) commence
    (D) hinder
    (E) guide

8. FORTUNATE:
    (A) lucky
    (B) wealthy
    (C) intelligent
    (D) poor
    (E) downtrodden

GO ON TO THE NEXT PAGE.

9. CRUMBLE:
   (A) eat
   (B) stumble
   (C) dry out
   (D) small
   (E) deteriorate

10. DESPERATE:
    (A) hungry
    (B) frantic
    (C) delicate
    (D) adaptable
    (E) contaminated

11. FRET:
    (A) listen
    (B) provide
    (C) worry
    (D) require
    (E) stash

12. DISGUISE:
    (A) mystery
    (B) convict
    (C) present
    (D) false front
    (E) pressure

13. ASSIST:
    (A) support
    (B) bring
    (C) distrust
    (D) yearn
    (E) destroy

14. REPRIMAND:
    (A) praise
    (B) insure
    (C) liberate
    (D) chide
    (E) forgive

15. EVADE:
    (A) take from
    (B) blind
    (C) help
    (D) sidestep
    (E) successful

16. FATIGUE:
    (A) grow weary
    (B) become fluid
    (C) increase in height
    (D) recede from view
    (E) improve

17. ANTIDOTE:
    (A) foundation
    (B) vacation
    (C) poison
    (D) learning experience
    (E) antitoxin

18. PROPOSE:
    (A) speak up
    (B) marriage
    (C) fall away
    (D) suggest
    (E) lease

19. INCREDIBLE:
    (A) mundane
    (B) uncivilized
    (C) sophisticated
    (D) believable
    (E) extraordinary

20. VIGILANT:
    (A) observant
    (B) sleepy
    (C) overly anxious
    (D) brutal
    (E) moving

GO ON TO THE NEXT PAGE.

21. TATTERED:
    (A) unkempt
    (B) neat
    (C) exuberant
    (D) unruly
    (E) pressed

22. PRECEDE:
    (A) stand alongside
    (B) move toward
    (C) come before
    (D) hurl
    (E) beg

23. LAMENT:
    (A) relish
    (B) drench
    (C) moan
    (D) invent
    (E) incline

24. ENGAGE:
    (A) date
    (B) employ
    (C) train
    (D) dismiss
    (E) fear

25. COMPETENT:
    (A) disastrous
    (B) fast
    (C) cautious
    (D) able
    (E) inanimate

26. SINCERE:
    (A) new
    (B) passionate
    (C) expensive
    (D) genuine
    (E) untold

27. RICKETY:
    (A) strong
    (B) wooden
    (C) antique
    (D) beautiful
    (E) feeble

28. CONSPICUOUS:
    (A) plain as day
    (B) identity
    (C) camouflaged
    (D) shiny
    (E) cramped

29. VERSATILE:
    (A) peaceful
    (B) disruptive
    (C) adaptable
    (D) truthful
    (E) charming

30. CORROBORATION:
    (A) attraction
    (B) confirmation
    (C) legal activity
    (D) unfulfilled expectation
    (E) enthusiastic response

GO ON TO THE NEXT PAGE.

The following questions ask you to find relationships between words. For each question, select the answer choice that best completes the meaning of the sentence.

Sample Question:

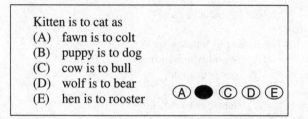

Kitten is to cat as
(A)   fawn is to colt
(B)   puppy is to dog
(C)   cow is to bull
(D)   wolf is to bear
(E)   hen is to rooster

Choice (B) is the best answer because a kitten is a young cat, just as a puppy is a young dog.
Of all the answer choices, (B) states a relationship that is most like the relationship between <u>kitten</u> and <u>cat</u>.

31. Fish is to water as
   (A)   bird is to egg
   (B)   roe is to pouch
   (C)   lion is to land
   (D)   flower is to pollen
   (E)   bee is to honey

32. Sick is to healthy as jailed is to
   (A)   convicted
   (B)   free
   (C)   guilty
   (D)   trapped
   (E)   hurt

33. Dancer is to feet as
   (A)   surgeon is to heart
   (B)   juggler is to hands
   (C)   drummer is to drums
   (D)   conductor is to voice
   (E)   musician is to eyes

34. Bystander is to event as
   (A)   juror is to verdict
   (B)   culprit is to crime
   (C)   tourist is to journey
   (D)   spectator is to game
   (E)   model is to portrait

35. Baker is to bread as
   (A)   shop is to goods
   (B)   butcher is to livestock
   (C)   politician is to votes
   (D)   sculptor is to statue
   (E)   family is to confidence

36. Igneous is to rock as
   (A)   stratum is to dig
   (B)   fossil is to dinosaur
   (C)   computer is to calculator
   (D)   watercolor is to painting
   (E)   calendar is to date

37. Delicious is to taste as melodious is to
   (A)   sound
   (B)   movie
   (C)   ears
   (D)   eyes
   (E)   sight

38. Clog is to shoe as
   (A)   sneaker is to run
   (B)   lace is to tie
   (C)   beret is to hat
   (D)   shirt is to torso
   (E)   sock is to foot

GO ON TO THE NEXT PAGE.

39. Cube is to square as
    (A) box is to cardboard
    (B) circle is to street
    (C) cylinder is to pen
    (D) line is to angle
    (E) sphere is to circle

40. Jam is to fruit as
    (A) bread is to toast
    (B) butter is to milk
    (C) crayon is to color
    (D) height is to stone
    (E) write is to pencil

41. Mile is to quart as
    (A) sky is to height
    (B) coffee is to drink
    (C) pot is to stew
    (D) floor is to ground
    (E) length is to volume

42. Biologist is to scientist as surgeon is to
    (A) doctor
    (B) scar
    (C) cut
    (D) heart
    (E) scalpel

43. Clay is to potter as
    (A) sea is to captain
    (B) magazine is to reader
    (C) marble is to sculptor
    (D) word is to teacher
    (E) bubble is to child

44. Clip is to movie as
    (A) buckle is to shoe
    (B) excerpt is to novel
    (C) jar is to liquid
    (D) room is to house
    (E) filling is to pie

45. Ruthless is to mercy as naive is to
    (A) thoughtfulness
    (B) illness
    (C) worldliness
    (D) contempt
    (E) purity

46. Glacier is to ice as
    (A) rain is to snow
    (B) bay is to sea
    (C) cloud is to storm
    (D) ocean is to water
    (E) pond is to fish

47. Glass is to window as
    (A) wood is to building
    (B) car is to motor
    (C) job is to skills
    (D) fabric is to clothing
    (E) loan is to interest

48. Buttress is to support as scissor is to
    (A) press
    (B) store
    (C) create
    (D) cool
    (E) cut

49. Sneer is to disdain as cringe is to
    (A) loneliness
    (B) bravery
    (C) intelligence
    (D) distrust
    (E) fear

50. Library is to book as
    (A) bank is to money
    (B) museum is to patron
    (C) opera is to audience
    (D) restaurant is to waiter
    (E) concert is to music

51. Famine is to food as
    (A) drought is to water
    (B) paper is to print
    (C) legend is to fantasy
    (D) debate is to issue
    (E) clause is to contract

52. Teacher is to student as
    (A) coach is to player
    (B) assistant is to executive
    (C) nurse is to doctor
    (D) patient is to dentist
    (E) theory is to technician

GO ON TO THE NEXT PAGE.

53. Muffle is to noise as
    (A) engine is to bicycle
    (B) wind is to vane
    (C) dam is to flood
    (D) aroma is to fetid
    (E) nibble is to eat

54. Rest is to exhaustion as
    (A) pack is to vacation
    (B) water is to thirst
    (C) audit is to forms
    (D) jury is to trial
    (E) tide is to ocean

55. Playwright is to script as
    (A) choreographer is to dance
    (B) mathematician is to science
    (C) philosopher is to insight
    (D) enemy is to strategy
    (E) athlete is to prowess

56. Gluttony is to food as
    (A) sheer is to wall
    (B) avarice is to money
    (C) enterprise is to earning
    (D) curiosity is to danger
    (E) mystery is to solution

57. Facile is to effort as
    (A) deception is to trick
    (B) helpful is to friend
    (C) inconsiderate is to thought
    (D) pious is to religion
    (E) incompetent is to task

58. Single-handed is to assistance as anonymous is to
    (A) praise
    (B) authorship
    (C) recognition
    (D) sincerity
    (E) ideas

59. Stable is to horse as kennel is to
    (A) farm
    (B) storage
    (C) dog
    (D) groomer
    (E) boarding

60. Tree is to knee as
    (A) pot is to cot
    (B) bam is to lamb
    (C) forest is to body
    (D) bob is to cob
    (E) seek is to leek

STOP

IF YOU FINISH BEFORE TIME IS CALLED,
YOU MAY CHECK YOUR WORK ON THIS SECTION ONLY.
DO NOT TURN TO ANY OTHER SECTION IN THE TEST.

Middle Level SSAT
Section 4
Time - 30 Minutes
25 Questions

Following each problem in this section, there are five suggested answers. Work each problem in your head or in the blank space provided at the right of the page. Then look at the five suggested answers and decide which one is best.

<u>Note:</u> Figures that accompany problems in this section are drawn as accurately as possible EXCEPT when it is stated in a specific problem that its figure is not drawn to scale.

Sample Problem:

5,413 − 4,827	(A) 586 (B) 596 (C) 696 (D) 1,586 (E) 1,686 ● Ⓑ Ⓒ Ⓓ Ⓔ

1. Which of the following fractions is greatest?

    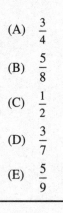

    (A) $\dfrac{3}{4}$

    (B) $\dfrac{5}{8}$

    (C) $\dfrac{1}{2}$

    (D) $\dfrac{3}{7}$

    (E) $\dfrac{5}{9}$

USE THIS SPACE FOR FIGURING.

2. The sum of the factors of 12 is

    (A) 28
    (B) 21
    (C) 20
    (D) 16
    (E) 15

GO ON TO THE NEXT PAGE.

3. $16 + 2 \times 3 + 2 =$

(A) 90
(B) 56
(C) 24
(D) 23
(E) 18

USE THIS SPACE FOR FIGURING.

4

4. $D + E + F + G =$

(A) 45
(B) 90
(C) 180
(D) 270
(E) 360

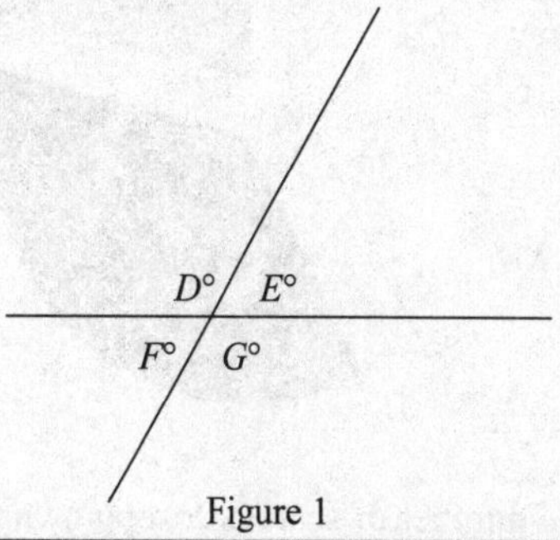

Figure 1

5. What are two different prime factors of 48 ?

(A) 2 and 3
(B) 3 and 4
(C) 4 and 6
(D) 4 and 12
(E) 6 and 8

6. The difference between 12 and the product of 4 and 6 is

(A) 12
(B) 10
(C) 2
(D) 1
(E) 0

7. The sum of the number of degrees in a straight line and the number of degrees in a triangle equals

(A) 720
(B) 540
(C) 360
(D) 180
(E) 90

GO ON TO THE NEXT PAGE.

Questions 8-10 refer to the following graph.

USE THIS SPACE FOR FIGURING.

Joseph's Winter Clothing

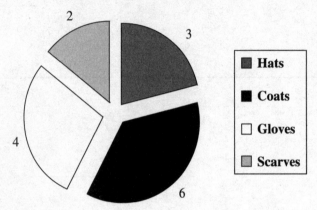

8. The number of scarves Joseph owns plus the number of coats he owns equals

   (A)   5
   (B)   7
   (C)   8
   (D)   9
   (E)   10

9. Hats represent what percentage of the total number of garments accounted for in the graph?

   (A)   10%
   (B)   20%
   (C)   30%
   (D)   50%
   (E)   80%

10. Which types of garments represent one-third of the total number of garments accounted for in the graph?

   (A)   Hats and coats
   (B)   Gloves and scarves
   (C)   Hats and scarves
   (D)   Gloves and coats
   (E)   Hats, gloves, and scarves

GO ON TO THE NEXT PAGE.

11. George bought five slices of pizza for $10. At this price, how many slices of pizza could he buy with $32 ?

   (A) 16
   (B) 15
   (C) 14
   (D) 12
   (E) 10

USE THIS SPACE FOR FIGURING.

12. On a certain English test, the 10 students in Mrs. Bennett's class score an average of 85. On the same test, 15 students in Mrs. Grover's class score an average of 70. What is the combined average score for all the students in Mrs. Bennett's and Mrs. Grover's classes?

   (A) 80
   (B) 77.5
   (C) 76
   (D) 75
   (E) 72

13. If Mary bought p pencils, Jane bought 5 times as many pencils as Mary, and Peggy bought 2 pencils fewer than Mary, then in terms of p, how many pencils did the three girls buy all together?

   (A) $5p - 2$
   (B) 7
   (C) $7p - 2$
   (D) $8p$
   (E) $8p - 2$

14. $\dfrac{4}{1,000} + \dfrac{3}{10} + 3 =$

   (A) 4,033
   (B) 433
   (C) 334
   (D) 3.34
   (E) 3.304

GO ON TO THE NEXT PAGE.

Questions 15 and 16 refer to the following definition.

USE THIS SPACE FOR FIGURING.

4

For all real numbers f, $\boxed{f} = -2f$.

15. $\boxed{0} =$

    (A)   4
    (B)   2
    (C)   0
    (D) −2
    (E) −4

16. $\boxed{2} \times \boxed{3} =$

    (A) $\boxed{24}$
    (B) $\boxed{2}$
    (C) $\boxed{3}$
    (D) $\boxed{-3}$
    (E) $\boxed{-12}$

17. $2\frac{1}{4}\% =$

    (A) 0.0025
    (B) 0.0225
    (C) 0.225
    (D) 2.025
    (E) 2.25

18. The area of triangle UVW is

    (A) $2h^2$
    (B) h^2
    (C) h
    (D) 3
    (E) 2

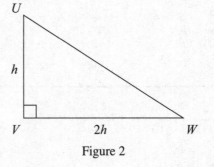

Figure 2

GO ON TO THE NEXT PAGE.

19. 9^4 is equal to which of the following?

    (A) $(3) \times (3) \times (3) \times (3)$
    (B) $(9) \times (3) \times (9) \times (3)$
    (C) $(9) \times (4)$
    (D) $(3) \times (3) \times (3) \times (3) \times (3) \times (3) \times (3) \times (3)$
    (E) $(9) \times (9) + (9) \times (9)$

USE THIS SPACE FOR FIGURING.

20. It costs h cents to make 12 handkerchiefs. At the same rate, how many cents will it cost to make 30 handkerchiefs?

    (A) $30h$

    (B) $\dfrac{5h}{2}$

    (C) $\dfrac{2h}{5}$

    (D) $\dfrac{2}{5h}$

    (E) $5h$

21. A girl collects rocks. If her collection consists of 12 pieces of halite, 16 pieces of sandstone, 8 pieces of mica, and 8 pieces of galaxite, then the average number of pieces of each type of rock in her collection is

    (A) 8
    (B) 11
    (C) 12
    (D) 16
    (E) 44

22. A recipe calls for 24 ounces of water for every two ounces of sugar. If 12 ounces of sugar are used, how many ounces of water should be added?

    (A) 6
    (B) 12
    (C) 24
    (D) 36
    (E) 144

GO ON TO THE NEXT PAGE.

USE THIS SPACE FOR FIGURING.

4

23. The number of people now employed by a certain company is 240, which is 60% of the number employed five years ago. How many more employees did the company have five years ago than it has now?

(A) 160
(B) 360
(C) 400
(D) 720
(E) 960

$$\begin{array}{r} 1B5 \\ \times\ 15 \\ \hline 2{,}025 \end{array}$$

24. In the multiplication problem above, B represents which digit?

(A) 1
(B) 2
(C) 3
(D) 5
(E) 7

25. If the area of each of the smaller squares that make up rectangle *ABCD* is 4, what is the perimeter of rectangle *ABCD* ?

(A) 220
(B) 64
(C) 55
(D) 32
(E) 4

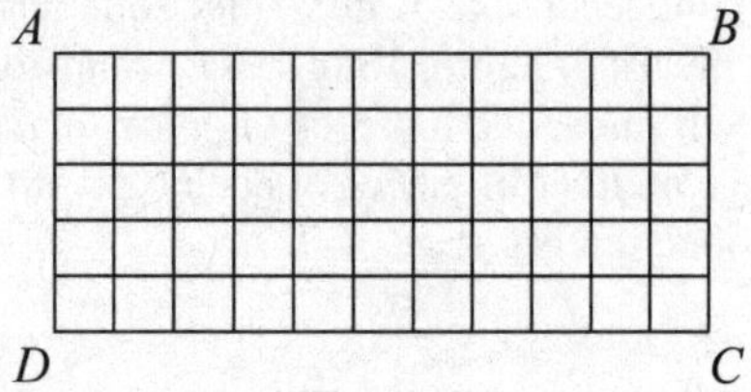

Figure 3

STOP

IF YOU FINISH BEFORE TIME IS CALLED,
YOU MAY CHECK YOUR WORK ON THIS SECTION ONLY.
DO NOT TURN TO ANY OTHER SECTION IN THE TEST.

Chapter 12
Answer Key to SSAT
Practice Tests

ANSWER KEY

Detailed explanations can be found online in your Student Tools.

SSAT UL Math 1

1. E	4. B	7. C	10. A	13. C	16. E	19. E	22. A	25. A
2. A	5. D	8. A	11. B	14. E	17. C	20. B	23. A
3. E	6. C	9. C	12. D	15. C	18. D	21. C	24. A

SSAT UL Reading 2

1. B	5. D	9. E	13. B	17. D	21. D	25. A	29. D	33. B	37. A
2. E	6. D	10. C	14. A	18. C	22. C	26. B	30. C	34. D	38. C
3. B	7. B	11. B	15. A	19. B	23. D	27. A	31. A	35. C	39. E
4. A	8. A	12. D	16. D	20. B	24. A	28. D	32. B	36. C	40. E

SSAT UL Verbal 3

1. A	7. B	13. A	19. A	25. D	31. E	37. D	43. D	49. C	55. E
2. D	8. D	14. B	20. E	26. D	32. C	38. B	44. E	50. A	56. B
3. E	9. B	15. C	21. B	27. E	33. A	39. C	45. B	51. C	57. D
4. A	10. D	16. B	22. D	28. E	34. C	40. C	46. D	52. A	58. C
5. D	11. D	17. D	23. B	29. B	35. C	41. C	47. A	53. A	59. E
6. A	12. A	18. C	24. C	30. B	36. A	42. E	48. D	54. A	60. D

SSAT UL Math 4

1. B	4. D	7. B	10. B	13. E	16. B	19. D	22. C	25. B
2. D	5. C	8. C	11. E	14. A	17. E	20. A	23. D
3. B	6. A	9. A	12. C	15. D	18. C	21. B	24. B

ANSWER KEY

Detailed explanations can be found online in your Student Tools.

SSAT ML Math 1

1. D	4. A	7. C	10. A	13. E	16. A	19. B	22. A	25. C
2. B	5. D	8. D	11. C	14. C	17. A	20. D	23. D	
3. D	6. C	9. C	12. A	15. B	18. D	21. B	24. A	

SSAT ML Reading 2

1. C	6. A	11. B	16. C	21. B	26. D	31. E	36. E
2. C	7. C	12. D	17. A	22. A	27. E	32. C	37. C
3. B	8. B	13. A	18. C	23. B	28. D	33. D	38. B
4. B	9. E	14. B	19. E	24. E	29. A	34. B	39. D
5. D	10. D	15. B	20. B	25. B	30. C	35. C	40. A

SSAT ML Verbal 3

1. A	7. C	13. A	19. E	25. D	31. C	37. A	43. C	49. E	55. A
2. D	8. A	14. D	20. A	26. D	32. B	38. C	44. B	50. A	56. B
3. A	9. E	15. D	21. A	27. E	33. B	39. E	45. C	51. A	57. C
4. D	10. B	16. A	22. C	28. A	34. D	40. B	46. D	52. A	58. C
5. A	11. C	17. E	23. C	29. C	35. D	41. E	47. D	53. C	59. C
6. B	12. D	18. D	24. B	30. D	36. D	42. A	48. E	54. B	60. C

SSAT ML Math 4

1. A	4. E	7. C	10. C	13. C	16. E	19. D	22. E	25. B
2. A	5. A	8. C	11. A	14. E	17. B	20. B	23. A	
3. C	6. A	9. B	12. C	15. C	18. B	21. B	24. C	

Part IV
The ISEE

Chapter 13
Everything You Always Wanted to Know About the ISEE

WHAT IS THE ISEE?

The Independent School Entrance Examination (ISEE) is a standardized test made up of a series of multiple-choice questions and a writing sample. All three levels of the ISEE may be taken online or in the traditional pencil/paper format. The entire test lasts a little less than three hours, during which you will work on five different sections. The writing sample is not scored. The other four sections of the test are scored and your score report will show those scaled scores. You will also receive a percentile score for each section (between 1 percent and 99 percent) that compares your test scores with those of other test takers from the previous three years. In addition, percentiles are then converted into stanines on a scale from 1–9.

Plan Ahead
Early registration will not only give you one less thing to worry about as the test approaches, but will also get you your first-choice test center.

Lower Level

Verbal Reasoning	34 questions	20 minutes
Quantitative Reasoning	38 questions	35 minutes
Reading Comprehension	25 questions	25 minutes
Mathematics Achievement	30 questions	30 minutes
Essay (ungraded)	1 essay topic	30 minutes

Middle Level

Verbal Reasoning	40 questions	20 minutes
Quantitative Reasoning	37 questions	35 minutes
Reading Comprehension	36 questions	35 minutes
Mathematics Achievement	47 questions	40 minutes
Essay (ungraded)	1 essay topic	30 minutes

Prepare Wisely
Print or order "What to Expect on the ISEE" from the ERB at www.erblearn.org.

Upper Level

Verbal Reasoning	40 questions	20 minutes
Quantitative Reasoning	37 questions	35 minutes
Reading Comprehension	36 questions	35 minutes
Mathematics Achievement	47 questions	40 minutes
Essay (ungraded)	1 essay topic	30 minutes

What's on the ISEE?

The Verbal section of the ISEE tests your knowledge of vocabulary using two different question types: synonyms and sentence completions. There are no analogies on the ISEE. The Reading Comprehension section tests your ability to read and understand short passages. These reading passages include both fiction and nonfiction. The Math sections test your knowledge of general mathematical concepts through two different question types: problem-solving questions and quantitative comparison questions. The quantitative comparison questions ask you to compare two columns of data. There are no quantitative comparison questions on the Lower Level ISEE. Remember, there is no guessing penalty on the ISEE. You should select an answer for every question.

Upper Versus Middle Versus Lower Levels

There are, in effect, three different versions of the ISEE. The Lower Level test is taken by students who are, at the time of testing, in the fourth and fifth grades. Students who are in the sixth and seventh grades take the Middle Level test. Students who are in the eighth, ninth, tenth, and eleventh grades take the Upper Level test. All three levels use the same scale. Students receive four scaled scores ranging from 760 on the low end to 940 at the top.

There are few major differences between the Lower, Middle, and Upper Level tests. There are some differences in content, however; for instance, vocabulary on the Middle Level test is less challenging than it is on the Upper Level test. The Middle and Upper Level tests cover the same general math concepts (arithmetic, algebra, geometry, charts, and graphs), but naturally, the Middle Level test will ask slightly easier questions than the Upper Level test. There are no quantitative comparison questions on the Lower Level test. The Lower Level test is 20 minutes shorter than the others.

Because the Lower Level ISEE tests both fourth and fifth graders, the Middle Level tests both sixth and seventh graders, and the Upper Level tests eighth, ninth, tenth, and eleventh graders, there are questions on the tests that students testing at the lower end of each of those groups might have difficulty answering. Younger students' scaled scores and percentiles will not be harmed by this fact. Both sets of scores take into consideration a student's age. However, younger students may feel intimidated by this. If you are at the lower end of your test's age group, there will be questions you are not supposed to be able to answer and that's perfectly all right.

Likewise, the material in this book follows the content of the two tests without breaking it down further into age groups or grades. Content that will appear only on the Upper Level test has been labeled as "Upper Level only." Students taking the Lower and Middle Level tests do not need to work on the Upper Level content. Nevertheless, younger students may not have yet seen some of the material included in the Lower and Middle Level review. Parents are advised to help younger students with their work in this book and seek teachers' advice or instruction if necessary.

Chapter 14
ISEE Math

Taking the Lower Level ISEE? You can skip the section on quantitative comparison (pages 422–434).

INTRODUCTION

This section will provide you with a review of all the math that you need to do well on the ISEE. When you get started, you may feel that the material is too easy. Don't worry. This test measures your basic math skills, so although you may feel a little frustrated reviewing things you have already learned, this type of basic review is undoubtedly the best way to improve your score.

Lose Your Calculator!

You will not be allowed to use a calculator on the ISEE. If you have developed a habit of reaching for your calculator whenever you need to add or multiply a couple of numbers, follow our advice: put your calculator away now, and don't take it out again until the test is behind you. Do your homework assignments without it, and complete the practice sections of this book without it. Trust us, you'll be glad you did.

Write It Down

Do not try to do math in your head. You are allowed to write in your test booklet. You should write in your test booklet. Even when you are just adding a few numbers together, write them down and do the work on paper. Writing things down will not only help eliminate careless errors but will also give you something to refer back to if you need to check over your work.

One Pass, Two Pass

Within any math section, you will find three types of questions:

- those you can answer easily in a short period of time
- those that you can do given enough time
- some questions that you have absolutely no idea how to tackle

When you work on a math section, start out with the first question. If it is one of the first type and you think you can do it without too much trouble, go ahead. If not, mark it and save it for later. Move on to the second question and decide whether or not to do that one.

Once you've made it all the way through the section, working slowly and carefully to answer all the questions that come easily to you, go back and try some of those that you think you can answer but will take you a little longer. You should pace yourself so that time will run out while you're working on the second pass through the section. Make sure you save the last minute to bubble in an answer for any question you didn't get to. Working this way, you'll know that you answered all the questions that were easy for you. Using a two-pass system is good, smart test-taking.

Guesstimating

Sometimes accuracy is important. Sometimes it isn't.

Which of the following fractions is less than $\frac{1}{4}$?

(A) $\dfrac{4}{18}$

(B) $\dfrac{4}{12}$

(C) $\dfrac{7}{7}$

(D) $\dfrac{12}{5}$

Some Things Are Easier Than They Seem
Guesstimating, or finding approximate answers, can help you eliminate wrong answers and save lots of time.

Without doing a bit of calculation, think about this question. It asks you to find a fraction smaller than $\frac{1}{4}$. Even if you're not sure which one is actually smaller, you can certainly eliminate some wrong answers.

Start simple: $\frac{1}{4}$ is less than 1, right? Are there any fractions in the choices that are greater than 1? Get rid of (D).

Look at (C). $\frac{7}{7}$ equals 1. Can it be less than $\frac{1}{4}$? Eliminate (C). Already, without doing any math, you have a 50 percent chance of guessing the right answer.

Here's another good example.

A group of three men buys a one-dollar raffle ticket that wins $400. If the one dollar that they paid for the ticket is subtracted and the remainder of the prize money is divided equally among the men, how much will each man receive?

(A) $62.50
(B) $75.00
(C) $100.00
(D) $133.00

This isn't a terribly difficult question. To solve it mathematically, you would take $400, subtract $1, and then divide the remainder by three. But by using a little logic, you don't have to do any of that.

The raffle ticket won $400. If there were four men, each one would have won about $100 (actually slightly less because the problem tells you to subtract the $1 price of the ticket, but you get the idea). So far so good? However, there weren't four men; there were only three. This means fewer men among whom to divide the winnings, so each one should get more than $100, right?

Look at the choices. Eliminate (A), (B), and (C). What's left? The right answer!

Guesstimating Geometry

Now that you've seen a couple examples that used guesstimating in arithmetic and word problems, you will see how we can also guesstimate geometry problems.

Let's try the problem below. Remember that unless a particular question tells you that a figure is not drawn to scale, you can safely assume that the figure is drawn to scale.

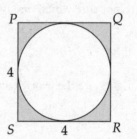

A circle is inscribed in square *PQRS*. What is the area of the shaded region?

(A) $16 - 6\pi$
(B) $16 - 4\pi$
(C) $16 - 3\pi$
(D) 16π

Wow, a circle inscribed in a square—that sounds tough!

It isn't. Look at the picture. What fraction of the square looks like it is shaded? Half? Three-quarters? Less than half? In fact, about one-quarter of the area of the square is shaded. You've nearly guesstimated the answer!

Now, let's do a tiny bit of math. The length of one side of the square is 4, so the area of the square is 4×4 or 16.

So the area of the square is 16 and we said that the shaded region was about one-fourth of the square. One-fourth of 16 is 4, right? So we're looking for a choice that equals about 4. Let's look at the choices.

(A) $16 - 6\pi$

(B) $16 - 4\pi$

(C) $16 - 3\pi$

(D) 16π

This could get a little complicated since the answers include π. However, since you're guesstimating, you should just remember that π is just a little more than 3.

Let's look back at those answers.

(A) $16 - 6\pi$ is roughly equal to $16 - (6 \times 3) = -2$

(B) $16 - 4\pi$ is roughly equal to $16 - (4 \times 3) = 4$

(C) $16 - 3\pi$ is roughly equal to $16 - (3 \times 3) = 7$

(D) 16π is roughly equal to $(16 \times 3) = 48$

Now, let's think about what these answers mean.

Since we guesstimated that the shaded region's area is roughly 4, (B) must be correct...and it is! Pat yourself on the back because you chose the right answer without doing a lot of unnecessary work. Unless the problem tells you that the figure is not drawn to scale, remember how useful guesstimating on geometry problems can be!

Working with Choices

In Chapter 2, Fundamental Math Skills for the SSAT & ISEE, we reviewed the concepts that the ISEE will be testing on the Lower, Middle, and Upper Level tests. However, the questions in the practice drills were slightly different from those that you will see on your exam. The ones on the exam are going to give you four answers from which to choose, not five.

There are many benefits to working with multiple-choice questions. For one, if you really mess up calculating the question, chances are your answer will not be among those given. Now you have a chance to go back and try that problem again more carefully. Another benefit, which this chapter will explore in more depth, is that you may be able to use the information in the choices to help you solve the problems.

We are now going to introduce you to the type of multiple-choice questions you will see on the ISEE. Each one of the questions on the pages that follow will test some skill that we covered in the Fundamental Math Skills chapter. If you don't see how to solve the question, take a look back at Chapter 2 for help.

Math Vocabulary

Notice that the choices are often in either ascending or descending numerical order.

1. Which of the following is the greatest even integer less than 25 ?

    (A) 26
    (B) 24.5
    (C) 22
    (D) 21

The first and most important thing you need to do on this and every problem is to read and understand the question. What important vocabulary words did you see in the question? There is "even" and "integer." You should always underline the important words in the questions. This way, you will make sure to pay attention to them and avoid careless errors.

Now that we understand that the question is looking for an even integer, we can eliminate any answers that are not even or an integer. Cross out (B) and (D). We can also eliminate (A) because 26 is greater than 25 and we want a number less than 25. So (C) is the right answer.

Try it again.

Set A = {All multiples of 7}

Set B = {All odd numbers}

2. Which of the following is NOT a member of both Set A and Set B above?

    (A)   7
    (B) 21
    (C) 49
    (D) 59

Did you underline the words multiples of 7 and odd? Because all the choices are odd, you can't eliminate any that would not be in Set B, but only (D) is not a multiple of 7. So (D) is the right answer.

The Rules of Zero

Remember the Rules of Zero

Zero is even. It's neither + nor –, and anything multiplied by 0 = 0.

3. x, y, and z stand for three distinct numbers, where $xy = 0$ and $yz = 15$. Which of the following must be true?

    (A) $y = 0$
    (B) $x = 0$
    (C) $z = 0$
    (D) $xyz = 15$

The Case of the Mysteriously Missing Sign

If there is no operation sign between a number and a variable (letter), the operation is multiplication.

Because x times y is equal to zero, and x, y, and z are different numbers, we know that either x or y is equal to zero. If y was equal to zero, then y times z should also be equal to zero. Because it is not, we know that it must be x that equals zero. Choice (B) is correct.

The Multiplication Table

4. Which of the following is equal to $6 \times 5 \times 2$?

    (A) $60 \div 3$
    (B) 14×7
    (C) $2 \times 2 \times 15$
    (D) 12×10

Don't Do More Work Than You Have To
When looking at answer choices, start with what's easy for you; work through the harder ones only when you have eliminated all of the others.

$6 \times 5 \times 2 = 60$ and so does $2 \times 2 \times 15$. Choice (C) is correct.

Working with Negative Numbers

5. $7 - 9$ is the same as

    (A) $7 - (-9)$
    (B) $9 - 7$
    (C) $7 + (-9)$
    (D) $-7 - 9$

Remember that subtracting a number is the same as adding its opposite. Choice (C) is correct.

Order of Operations

6. $9 + 6 \times 2 \div 3 =$

    (A) 7
    (B) 9
    (C) 10
    (D) 13

Remember your PEMDAS rules? The multiplication comes first. The correct answer is (D).

Factors and Multiples

7. What is the sum of the prime factors of 42 ?

    (A) 18
    (B) 13
    (C) 12
    (D) 10

Remember!
1 is NOT a prime number.

How do we find the prime factors? The best way is to draw a factor tree. Then we see that the prime factors of 42 are 2, 3, and 7. Add them up and we get 12, (C).

Fractions

8. Which of the following is less than $\frac{4}{6}$?

    (A) $\frac{3}{5}$

    (B) $\frac{2}{3}$

    (C) $\frac{5}{7}$

    (D) $\frac{7}{8}$

When comparing fractions, you have two choices. You can find a common denominator and then compare the fractions (such as when you add or subtract them). You can also change the fractions to decimals. If you have completed and memorized the fraction-to-decimal charts in the Fundamentals chapter (pages 53 and 57), you probably found the right answer without too much difficulty. It's (A).

Percents

9. Thom's CD collection contains 15 jazz CDs, 45 rap albums, 30 funk CDs, and 60 pop albums. What percent of Thom's CD collection is funk?

    (A)   10%
    (B)   20%
    (C)   25%
    (D)   30%

First, we need to find the fractional part that represents Thom's funk CDs. He has 30 out of a total of 150. We can reduce $\frac{30}{150}$ to $\frac{1}{5}$; $\frac{1}{5}$ as a percent is 20%, (B).

Exponents

10. $2^6 =$

    (A) 2^3
    (B) 4^2
    (C) 3^2
    (D) 8^2

Expand 2^6 out and we can multiply to find that it equals 64. Choice (D) is correct.

Square Roots

11. The square root of 75 falls between what two integers?

    (A) 5 and 6
    (B) 6 and 7
    (C) 7 and 8
    (D) 8 and 9

If you have trouble with this one, use the choices and work backward. As we discussed in the Fundamentals chapter, a square root is just the opposite of squaring a number. So let's square the choices. Then we find that 75 falls between 8^2 (64) and 9^2 (81). Choice (D) is correct.

Basic Algebraic Equations

12. $11x = 121$. What does $x = $?

    (A) 2
    (B) 8
    (C) 10
    (D) 11

Remember, if you get stuck, use the choices and work backward. Each one provides you with a possible value for x. Start with a middle choice and replace x with it. $11 \times 10 = 110$. That's too small. Now we know not only that (C) is the incorrect answer, but also that (A) and (B) are incorrect because they are smaller than (C). The correct answer is (D).

Solve for *X*—Upper Level Only

13. $3y + 17 = 25 - y$. What does $y = $?

    (A) 1
    (B) 2
    (C) 3
    (D) 4

Just as on the previous question, if you get stuck, use the choices. The correct answer is (B).

Percent Algebra—Upper Level Only

14. 25% of 30% of what is equal to 18 ?

 (A)   1
 (B) 36
 (C) 120
 (D) 240

If you don't remember the math conversion table, look it up in Fundamentals (Chapter 2). You can also use the choices and work backward. Start with (C), and find out what 25% of 30% of 120 is (9). The correct answer is (D).

Geometry

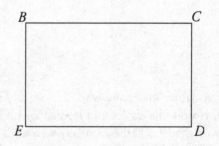

15. *BCDE* is a rectangle with a perimeter of 44. If the length of *BC* is 15, what is the area of *BCDE* ?

 (A) 105
 (B) 17
 (C) 15
 (D) 14

From the perimeter, we can find that the sides of the rectangle are 7 and 15. So the area is 105, (A).

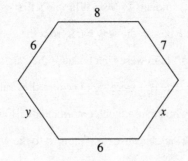

16. If the perimeter of this polygon is 37, what is the value of $x + y$?

    (A) 5
    (B) 9
    (C) 10
    (D) 16

$x + y$ is equal to the perimeter of the polygon minus the lengths of the sides we know. Choice (C) is correct.

Word Problems

17. Emily is walking to school at a rate of 3 blocks every 14 minutes. When Jeff walks at the same rate as Emily, and takes the most direct route to school, he arrives in 42 minutes. How many blocks away from school does Jeff live?

    (A) 3
    (B) 5
    (C) 6
    (D) 9

This is a proportion question because we have two sets of data we are comparing. Set up your fractions.

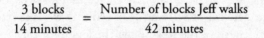

Because we know that we must do the same thing to the top and the bottom of the first fraction to get the second fraction, and because $14 \times 3 = 42$, we must multiply 3×3 to get 9.

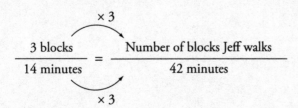

So Jeff walks 9 blocks in 42 minutes. Choice (D) is correct.

18. Half of the 30 students in Mrs. Whipple's first-grade class

    got sick on the bus on the way back from the zoo. Of these

    students, $\frac{2}{3}$ of them were sick because they ate too much

    cotton candy. The rest were sick because they sat next to

    the students who ate too much cotton candy. How many

    students were sick because they sat next to the wrong

    student?

    (A)   5
    (B)   10
    (C)   15
    (D)   20

This is a really gooey fraction problem. Because we've seen the word *of*, we know we have to multiply. First, we need to multiply $\frac{1}{2}$ by 30, the number of students in the class. This gives us 15, the number of students who got sick. Now we have another *of*, so we must multiply the fraction of students who ate too much cotton candy, $\frac{2}{3}$, by the number of students who got sick, 15. This gives us 10. So then the remainder—those who were unlucky in the seating plan—is 15 – 10, or 5, (A).

19. A piece of rope is 18 inches long. It is cut into 2 unequal
    pieces. The longer piece is twice as long as the shorter
    piece. How long is the shorter piece?

    (A)   2
    (B)   6
    (C)   9
    (D)   12

Again, if you are stuck for a place to start, go to the choices. Because we are looking for the length of the shorter rope, we can eliminate any choice that gives us a piece equal to or longer than half the rope. That gets rid of (C) and (D). Now, if we take one of the pieces, we can subtract it from the total length of the rope to get the length of the longer piece. In (B), if 6 is the length of the shorter piece, we can subtract it from 18 and now we know the length of the longer piece is 12. And 12 is twice the length of 6, so we have the right answer.

PRACTICE DRILL 1—LOWER LEVEL

Time yourself on this drill. When you are done, check your answers in Chapter 17.

1. How many factors does the number 24 have?

   (A) 2
   (B) 4
   (C) 6
   (D) 8

2. If 12 is a factor of a certain number, what must also be factors of that number?

   (A) 2 and 6 only
   (B) 3 and 4 only
   (C) 12 only
   (D) 1, 2, 3, 4, and 6

3. Which of the following is a multiple of 3 ?

   (A)   2
   (B)   6
   (C) 10
   (D) 14

4. Which of the following is NOT a multiple of 6 ?

   (A) 12
   (B) 18
   (C) 23
   (D) 24

5. Which of the following is a multiple of both 3 and 5 ?

   (A) 10
   (B) 20
   (C) 25
   (D) 45

6. What is the smallest number that can be added to the number 1,024 to produce a result divisible by 9 ?

   (A) 1
   (B) 2
   (C) 3
   (D) 4

Remember to time yourself during this drill!

7. The sum of five consecutive positive integers is 30. What is the square of the largest of the five positive integers?

(A) 25
(B) 36
(C) 49
(D) 64

8. A company's profit was $75,000 in 1972. In 1992, its profit was $450,000. The profit in 1992 was how many times as great as the profit in 1972 ?

(A) 2
(B) 4
(C) 6
(D) 10

9. Joanne owns one-third of the pieces of furniture in the apartment she shares with her friends. If there are 12 pieces of furniture in the apartment, how many pieces does Joanne own?

(A) 2
(B) 4
(C) 6
(D) 8

10. A tank of oil is one-third full. When full, the tank holds 90 gallons. How many gallons of oil are in the tank now?

(A) 10
(B) 20
(C) 30
(D) 40

11. Ginger the dog sleeps three-fourths of every day. In a four-day period, she sleeps the equivalent of how many full days?

(A) $\dfrac{1}{4}$

(B) $\dfrac{3}{4}$

(C) 1

(D) 3

12. Which of the following has the greatest value?

(A) $\dfrac{1}{4} + \dfrac{2}{3}$

(B) $\dfrac{3}{4} - \dfrac{1}{3}$

(C) $\dfrac{1}{12} \div \dfrac{1}{3}$

(D) $\dfrac{3}{4} \times \dfrac{1}{3}$

13. $\dfrac{1}{2} + \dfrac{2}{3} + \dfrac{3}{4} + \dfrac{1}{2} + \dfrac{1}{3} + \dfrac{1}{4} =$

(A) $\dfrac{3}{4}$

(B) 1

(C) 3

(D) 6

14. The product of 0.34 and 1,000 is approximately

(A)   3.50
(B)   35
(C)   65
(D)   350

15. 2.398 =

(A) $2 \times \dfrac{9}{100} \times \dfrac{3}{10} \times \dfrac{8}{1000}$

(B) $2 + \dfrac{3}{10} + \dfrac{9}{1000} + \dfrac{8}{100}$

(C) $2 + \dfrac{9}{100} + \dfrac{8}{1000} + \dfrac{3}{10}$

(D) $\dfrac{3}{10} + \dfrac{9}{100} + \dfrac{8}{1000}$

Stop. Check your time for this drill: _____

How Did You Do?

That was a good sample of the kinds of questions you'll see on the ISEE. There are a few things to check other than your answers. Remember that taking the test involves much more than just getting answers right. It's also about guessing wisely, using your time well, and figuring out where you're likely to make mistakes. Once you've checked to see what you've gotten right and wrong, you should then consider the following to improve your score.

Time and Pacing

How long did it take you to do the 15 questions? 15 minutes? It's okay if you went a minute or two over. However, if you finished very quickly (in fewer than 10 minutes) or slowly (more than 20 minutes), your pacing is off. Take a look at any problems that may have affected your speed. Were there any questions that seriously slowed you down? Did you answer some quickly but not correctly? In general, don't just look to see what you got right, but rather how you got it right.

Question Recognition and Selection

Did you use your time wisely? Did you do the questions in an order that worked well for you? Did you get stuck on one problem and spend too much time on it? Which kinds of questions were hardest for you? Remember that on the ISEE you must answer every question, but you don't have to work on every problem. Every question on the ISEE, whether you find it easy or hard, is worth one point, and there is no penalty for wrong answers. You should concentrate most on getting all the questions you find easy or sort-of easy right, and worry about doing problems you find harder later. Keep in mind that questions generally go from easiest to hardest throughout the section. Getting the early questions right takes time, but you know you can do it, so give yourself that time! If you don't have time for a question or can't guess wisely, pick a "letter of the day" (the same letter for every problem you can't do), fill it in, and move on. Because there is no penalty for wrong answers, guessing can only help your score.

POE and Guessing

Did you actively look for wrong answers to eliminate, rather than looking for the right answer? (You should.) Did you physically cross off wrong answers to keep track of your POE? Was there a pattern to when guessing worked (more often when you could eliminate one wrong answer and less often when you picked simpler-looking over harder-looking numbers)?

Write It Down

Did you work out the practice questions? Did you move too quickly or skip steps on problems you found easier? Did you always double-check what the question was asking? Students frequently miss questions that they know how to do! Why? It's simple—they work out problems in their heads or don't read carefully. Work out every ISEE math problem on a piece of paper. Consider it a double-check because your handwritten notes confirm what you've worked out in your head.

PRACTICE DRILL 2—MULTIPLE CHOICE—MIDDLE AND UPPER LEVELS ONLY

While doing the next drill, keep in mind the general test-taking techniques we've talked about: guessing, POE, order of difficulty, pacing, choosing a letter-of-the-day for problems that stump you, and working on the page and not in your head. When you are done, check your answers in Chapter 17. But don't stop there: investigate the drill thoroughly to see how and why you got your answers wrong, and check your time. You should be spending about one minute per question on this drill.

1. How many numbers between 1 and 100, inclusive, are both prime and a multiple of 4 ?

   (A)   0
   (B)   12
   (C)   20
   (D)   25

Remember to time yourself during this drill!

2. How many factors do the integers 24 and 81 have in common?

   (A)   1
   (B)   2
   (C)   3
   (D)   4

3. If the final total of a dinner bill—after including a 25% tip—is $50, what was the cost of the dinner before including the tip?

   (A) $12.50
   (B) $25.00
   (C) $37.50
   (D) $40.00

4. How many numbers between 1 and 100 are multiples of both 2 and 7 ?

   (A)   6
   (B)   7
   (C)   8
   (D)   9

5. $2^3 \times 2^3 \times 2^3 =$

   (A) 2^6
   (B) 2^9
   (C) 2^{27}
   (D) 8^9

6. For what integer value of m does $2m + 4 = m^3$?

    (A) 1
    (B) 2
    (C) 3
    (D) 4

7. If $6x - 4 = 38$, then $x + 10 =$

    (A) 7
    (B) 10
    (C) 16
    (D) 17

8. What is the smallest multiple of 7 that is greater than 50 ?

    (A) 7
    (B) 49
    (C) 51
    (D) 56

9. One-fifth of the students in a class chose recycling as the topic for their science projects. If four students chose recycling, how many students are in the class?

    (A) 4
    (B) 10
    (C) 16
    (D) 20

10. If a harvest yielded 60 bushels of corn, 20 bushels of wheat, and 40 bushels of soybeans, what percent of the total harvest was corn?

    (A) 50%
    (B) 40%
    (C) 33%
    (D) 30%

11. At a local store, an item that usually sells for $45 is currently on sale for $30. By what percent is that item discounted?

    (A) 10%
    (B) 25%
    (C) 33%
    (D) 50%

12. Which of the following is most nearly 35% of $19.95 ?

    (A) $3.50
    (B) $5.75
    (C) $7.00
    (D) $9.95

13. A pair of shoes is offered on a special blowout sale. The original price of the shoes is reduced from $50 to $20. What is the percent change in the price of the shoes?

    (A) 60%
    (B) 50%
    (C) 40%
    (D) 25%

14. Four friends each pay $5 for a pizza every Friday night. If they were to start inviting a fifth friend to come with them and still bought the same pizza, how much would each person then have to pay?

    (A) $1
    (B) $4
    (C) $5
    (D) $25

15. If the perimeter of a square is 56, what is the length of each side?

    (A) 4
    (B) 7
    (C) 14
    (D) 28

16. What is the perimeter of an equilateral triangle, one side of which measures 4 inches?

    (A) 12 inches
    (B) 8 inches
    (C) 6 inches
    (D) 4 inches

Lower and Middle levels can stop here. Don't forget to check your answers!

Upper Level Only

17. If $b = 45$, then $v^2 =$

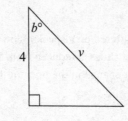

(A) 32
(B) 25
(C) 16
(D) 5

18. One-half of the difference between the number of degrees in a square and the number of degrees in a triangle is

(A) 45
(B) 90
(C) 180
(D) 240

19. If the area of a square is equal to its perimeter, what is the length of one side?

(A) 1
(B) 2
(C) 4
(D) 8

20. The area of a rectangle with width 4 and length 3 is equal to the area of a triangle with a base of 6 and a height of

(A) 1
(B) 2
(C) 3
(D) 4

21. Two cardboard boxes have equal volume. The dimensions of one box are $3 \times 4 \times 10$. If the length of the other box is 6 and the width is 4, what is the height of the second box?

(A) 2
(B) 5
(C) 10
(D) 12

22. If the area of a square is $64p^2$, what is the length of one side of the square?

   (A) $64p^2$
   (B) $8p^2$
   (C) $64p$
   (D) $8p$

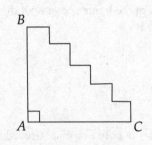

23. If $AB = 10$ and $AC = 15$, what is the perimeter of the figure above?

   (A) 25
   (B) 35
   (C) 40
   (D) 50

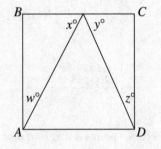

24. If $ABCD$ is a rectangle, what is the value of $w + x + y + z$?

   (A)   90
   (B) 150
   (C) 180
   (D) 190

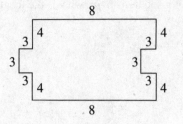

25. What is the area of the figure above if all the angles shown are right angles?

(A) 38
(B) 42
(C) 50
(D) 88

26. How many meters of police tape are needed to wrap around a rectangular crime scene that measures 6 meters wide by 28 meters long?

(A) 34 meters
(B) 68 meters
(C) 90 meters
(D) 168 meters

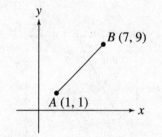

27. The distance between points A and B in the coordinate plane above is

(A) 5
(B) 6
(C) 8
(D) 10

28. *PO* and *QO* are radii of the circle with center *O*. What is the value of *x* ?

    (A) 30
    (B) 45
    (C) 60
    (D) 90

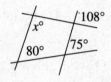

29. What is the value of *x* ?

    (A) 360
    (B) 100
    (C)   97
    (D)   67

30. *ABC* is an equilateral triangle. What is the perimeter of this figure?

    (A) $4 + 2\pi$
    (B) $4 + 4\pi$
    (C) $8 + 2\pi$
    (D) $8 + 4\pi$

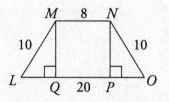

31. In trapezoid *LMNO*, line *LO* has a length of 20. What is the area of the trapezoid?

    (A)   48
    (B)   64
    (C)   88
    (D) 112

When you're finished, check your answers in Chapter 17.

Ratios

A ratio is like a recipe. It tells you how much of each ingredient goes into a mixture.

For example:

To make punch, mix two parts grape juice with three parts orange juice.

This ratio tells you that for every two units of grape juice, you will need to add three units of orange juice. It doesn't matter what the units are; if you were working with ounces, you would mix two ounces of grape juice with three ounces of orange juice to get five ounces of punch. If you were working with gallons, you would mix two gallons of grape juice with three gallons of orange juice. How much punch would you have? Five gallons.

To work through a ratio question, first you need to organize the information you are given. Do this using the Ratio Box.

In a club with 35 members, the ratio of boys to girls is 3:2. To complete your Ratio Box, fill in the ratio at the top and the "real value" at the bottom.

	BOYS	GIRLS	TOTAL
Ratio	3	2	5
Multiplier			
Real Value			35

Then look for a "magic number" that you can multiply by the ratio total to get to the real value total. In this case, the magic number is 7. That's all there is to it!

	BOYS	GIRLS	TOTAL
Ratio	3 +	2 =	5
Multiplier	7	7	7
Real Value	21	14	35

PRACTICE DRILL 3—RATIOS

1. At Jed's Country Hotel, there are three types of rooms: singles, doubles, and triples. If the ratio of singles to doubles to triples is 3:4:5, and the total number of rooms is 36, how many doubles are there?

    (A) 4
    (B) 9
    (C) 12
    (D) 24

2. In Janice's tennis club, 8 of the 12 players are right-handed. What is the ratio of right-handed to left-handed players in Janice's club?

    (A) 1:2
    (B) 1:6
    (C) 2:1
    (D) 2:3

3. A pet goat eats 2 pounds of goat food and 1 pound of grass each day. When the goat has eaten a total of 15 pounds, how many pounds of grass will it have eaten?

    (A) 3
    (B) 4
    (C) 5
    (D) 15

Remember to time yourself during this drill!

Check your answers in Chapter 17.

Stop. Check your time for this drill: _____

Averages

There are three parts to every average problem: total, number, and average. Most ISEE problems will give you two of the three pieces and ask you to find the third. To help organize the information you are given, use the Average Pie.

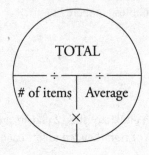

The Average Pie organizes all of your information visually. It makes it easier to see all of the relationships between pieces of the pie.

- TOTAL = (# of items) × (Average)

- # of items = $\dfrac{Total}{Average}$

- Average = $\dfrac{Total}{\# \ of \ items}$

For example, if your friend went bowling and bowled three games, scoring 71, 90, and 100, here's how you would compute her average score using the Average Pie.

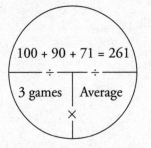

To find the average, you would simply write a fraction that represents $\dfrac{Total}{\# \ of \ items}$, in this case $\dfrac{261}{3}$.

The math becomes simple. 261 ÷ 3 = 87. Your friend bowled an average of 87.

Get used to working with the Average Pie by using it to solve the following problems.

PRACTICE DRILL 4—AVERAGES

1. The average of 3 numbers is 18. What is two times the sum of the 3 numbers?

   (A) 108
   (B) 54
   (C) 36
   (D) 18

Remember to time yourself during this drill!

2. An art club of 4 boys and 5 girls makes craft projects. If the boys average 2 projects each and the girls average 3 projects each, what is the total number of projects produced by the club?

   (A) 14
   (B) 23
   (C) 26
   (D) 54

3. Catherine scores 84, 85, and 88 on her first three exams. What must she score on her fourth exam to raise her average to an 89 ?

   (A) 99
   (B) 97
   (C) 93
   (D) 91

4. If a class of 6 students has an average grade of 72 before a seventh student joins the class, what must the seventh student's grade be to raise the class average to 76 ?

   (A) 100
   (B) 92
   (C) 88
   (D) 80

Check your answers in Chapter 17.

More Practice: Lower Level

5. Anna ate 2 doughnuts on Monday, Wednesday, and Friday and ate 4 doughnuts on Tuesday and Thursday. She did not eat any doughnuts on Saturday or Sunday. What is the average number of doughnuts that Anna ate each day of the week?

(A) 2.0
(B) 2.5
(C) 2.8
(D) 3.0

6. Merry drove 350 miles from New Orleans to Houston in 7 hours. She then drove 240 miles from Houston to Dallas in 4 hours. What was her approximate average rate of speed, in miles per hour (mph), for the entire trip?

(A) 50.0 mph
(B) 53.6 mph
(C) 55.0 mph
(D) 60.0 mph

7. The ticket price to a school's spring musical production is $6. The auditorium has a seating capacity of 300. After having spent $550 on stage production and $250 on advertising, how much profit did the school make, assuming the show was sold out?

(A) $700
(B) $800
(C) $900
(D) $1,000

Check your answers in Chapter 17.

More Practice: Middle and Upper Levels

8. Michael scored an average of 24 points over his first 5 basketball games. How many points must he score in his 6th game to average 25 points over all 6 games?

   (A) 24
   (B) 25
   (C) 30
   (D) 36

9. Dwan measured a total of 245 inches of rainfall in his hometown over one week. During the same week the previous year, his hometown had a total of 196 inches. How many more inches was the daily amount of rainfall for the week this year than the week last year?

   (A) 6
   (B) 7
   (C) 8
   (D) 9

10. Joe wants to find the mean number of pages in the books he has read this month. The books were 200, 220, and 260 pages long. He read the 200 page book twice, so it will be counted twice in the mean. If he reads one more book, what is the fewest number of pages it can have to make the mean no less than 230 ?

   (A) 268
   (B) 269
   (C) 270
   (D) 271

When you're finished, don't forget to check your answers in Chapter 17!

Percent Change—Upper Level Only

There is one special kind of percent question that shows up on the ISEE: percent change. This type of question asks you to find by what percent something has increased or decreased. Instead of taking the part and dividing it by the whole, you will take the difference between the two numbers and divide it by the original number. Then, to turn the fraction to a percent, divide the numerator by the denominator and multiply by 100.

For example:

> The number of people who watched *The Voice* last year was 3,600,000. This year, only 3,000,000 are watching the show. By approximately what percent has the audience decreased?

$$\frac{\text{The difference}}{\text{The original}} = \frac{600,000}{3,600,000} \quad \text{(The difference is } 3,600,000 - 3,000,000.\text{)}$$

The fraction reduces to $\frac{1}{6}$, and $\frac{1}{6}$ as a percent is 17%.

PRACTICE DRILL 5—PERCENT CHANGE

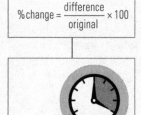

$$\%\,\text{change} = \frac{\text{difference}}{\text{original}} \times 100$$

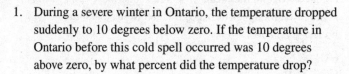

Remember to time yourself during this drill!

Check your answers in Chapter 17.

1. During a severe winter in Ontario, the temperature dropped suddenly to 10 degrees below zero. If the temperature in Ontario before this cold spell occurred was 10 degrees above zero, by what percent did the temperature drop?

    (A) 50%
    (B) 100%
    (C) 150%
    (D) 200%

2. Fatty's Burger wants to attract more customers by increasing the size of its patties. From now on Fatty's patties are going to be 4 ounces larger than before. If the size of its new patty is 16 ounces, by approximately what percent has the patty increased?

    (A) 25%
    (B) 27%
    (C) 33%
    (D) 75%

Plugging In

The ISEE will often ask you questions about real-life situations for which the numbers have been replaced with variables. One of the easiest ways to tackle these questions is with a powerful technique called Plugging In.

> Mark is two inches taller than John, who is four inches
> shorter than Bernal. If b represents Bernal's height in inches,
> then in terms of b, an expression for Mark's height is
>
> (A) $b + 6$
> (B) $b + 4$
> (C) $b + 2$
> (D) $b - 2$

The problem with this question is that we're not used to thinking of people's heights in terms of variables. Have you ever met someone who was b inches tall?

Whenever you see variables used in the question and in the choices, just plug in a number to replace the variable.

1. Choose a number for b.
2. Using that number, figure out Mark's and John's heights.
3. Put a box around Mark's height, because that's what the question asked you for.
4. Plug your number for b into the choices and choose the one that gives you the number you found for Mark's height.

Here's How It Works

> Mark is two inches taller than John, who
> is four inches shorter than Bernal. If b
> represents Bernal's height in inches, then
> ~~in terms of b,~~ an expression for Mark's
> height is
>
> (A) $b + 6$
> (B) $b + 4$
> (C) $b + 2$
> (D) $b - 2$

Cross this out! Because you are Plugging In, you don't need to pay any attention to "in terms of" any variable.

For Bernal's height, let's pick 60 inches. This means that $b = 60$. Remember, there is no right or wrong number to pick. 50 would work just as well.

But given that Bernal is 60 inches tall, now we can figure out that, because John is four inches shorter than Bernal, John's height must be $(60 - 4)$, or 56 inches.

The other piece of information we learn from the problem is that Mark is two inches taller than John. If John's height is 56 inches, that means Mark must be 58 inches tall.

So here's what we've got.

Bernal   60 inches = b
John   56 inches
Mark $\boxed{58}$ inches

Now, the question asks for Mark's height, which is 58 inches. The last step is to go through the choices substituting 60 for b, and choose the one that equals 58.

(A)	$b + 6$	$60 + 6 = 66$	ELIMINATE
(B)	$b + 4$	$60 + 4 = 64$	ELIMINATE
(C)	$b + 2$	$60 + 2 = 62$	ELIMINATE
(D)	$b - 2$	$60 - 2 = 58$	PICK THIS ONE!

After reading this explanation, you may be tempted to say that Plugging In takes too long. Don't be fooled. The method itself is often faster and more accurate than regular algebra. Try it out. Practice. As you become more comfortable with Plugging In, you'll get even quicker and better results. You still need to know how to do algebra, but if you do only algebra, you may have difficulty improving your ISEE score. Plugging In gives you a way to break through whenever you are stuck. You'll find that having more than one way to solve ISEE math problems puts you at a real advantage.

PRACTICE DRILL 6—PLUGGING IN

1. At a charity fund-raiser, 200 people each donated x dollars. In terms of x, what was the total number of dollars that was donated?

    (A) $\dfrac{x}{200}$

    (B) $200x$

    (C) $\dfrac{200}{x}$

    (D) $200 + x$

2. If 10 magazines cost d dollars, how many magazines can be purchased for 3 dollars?

    (A) $\dfrac{3d}{10}$

    (B) $30d$

    (C) $\dfrac{d}{30}$

    (D) $\dfrac{30}{d}$

3. The zoo has four times as many monkeys as lions. There are four more lions than there are zebras at the zoo. If z represents the number of zebras in the zoo, then in terms of z, how many monkeys are there in the zoo?

    (A) $4z$
    (B) $z + 4$
    (C) $4z + 16$
    (D) $4z + 4$

Take the Algebra Away, and Arithmetic Is All That's Left
When you Plug In for variables, you won't need to write equations and won't have to solve algebra problems. Doing simple arithmetic is always easier than doing algebra.

Don't worry about timing yourself on this drill. Focus on the strategy. Plug In for each question so you learn how to use the technique.

Occasionally, you may run into a Plugging In question that doesn't contain variables. These questions usually ask about a percentage or a fraction of some unknown number or price. This is the one time that you should Plug In even when you don't see variables in the answer.

Also, be sure you plug in good numbers. Good doesn't mean right because there's no such thing as a right or wrong number to Plug In. A good number is one that makes the problem easier to work with. If a question asks about minutes and hours, try 30 or 60, not 128. Also, whenever you see the word *percent*, Plug In 100!

More Practice: Lower Level

4. There were 6 pairs of earrings sold at a price of *y* dollars each. In terms of *y*, what is the total amount of money for which these earrings were sold?

   (A) $6 + y$
   (B) $6y$
   (C) 6^y
   (D) $6 + 6y$

5. If *p* pieces of candy costs *c* cents, 10 pieces of candy will cost

   (A) $\dfrac{pc}{10}$ cents

   (B) $\dfrac{10c}{p}$ cents

   (C) $\dfrac{10p}{c}$ cents

   (D) $10pc$ cents

Lower level students can stop here and check answers in Chapter 17. Middle and Upper level students should keep on drilling!

More Practice: Middle Level

6. If *J* is an odd integer, which of the following must be true?
   (A) $(J + 3) > 1$
   (B) $(J - 2)$ is a positive integer.
   (C) $2 \times J$ is an even integer.
   (D) $J > 0$

7. On Monday, Sharon ate one-half of a fruit tart. On Tuesday, Sharon then ate one-fourth of what was left of the tart. What fraction of the tart did Sharon eat on Monday and Tuesday?

   (A) $\dfrac{3}{8}$

   (B) $\dfrac{1}{2}$

   (C) $\dfrac{5}{8}$

   (D) $\dfrac{3}{4}$

More Practice: Middle and Upper Levels

8. The price of a suit is reduced by 20%, and then the resulting price is reduced by another 10%. The final price is what percent off of the original price?

   (A) 20%
   (B) 25%
   (C) 28%
   (D) 30%

9. If m is an even integer, n is an odd integer, and p is the product of m and n, which of the following is always true?

   (A) p is a fraction.
   (B) p is an odd integer.
   (C) p is divisible by 2.
   (D) p is greater than zero.

> Middle level students can stop here and check their answers in Chapter 17. Upper level students have more math fun ahead!

More Practice: Upper Level

10. If p is an odd integer, which of the following must be an odd integer?

    (A) $p^2 + 3$
    (B) $2p + 1$
    (C) $p \div 3$
    (D) $p - 3$

11. If m is the sum of two positive even integers, which of the following CANNOT be true?

    (A) $m < 5$
    (B) $3m$ is odd.
    (C) m is even.
    (D) m^3 is even.

12. Anthony has twice as many baseball cards as Keith, who has one-third as many baseball cards as Ian. If Keith has k baseball cards, how many baseball cards do Anthony and Ian have together?

    (A) $\dfrac{3k}{2}$

    (B) $\dfrac{6k}{2}$

    (C) $\dfrac{8k}{2}$

    (D) $\dfrac{10k}{2}$

13. The product of $\frac{1}{2}b$ and a^2 can be written as

   (A) $(ab)^2$

   (B) $\dfrac{a^2}{b}$

   (C) $2a \times \dfrac{1}{2}b$

   (D) $\dfrac{a^2 b}{2}$

14. $x^a = (x^3)^3$

    $y^b = \dfrac{y^{10}}{y^2}$

    What is the value of $a \times b$?

    (A) 17
    (B) 30
    (C) 48
    (D) 72

15. Hidden Glen Elementary school is collecting donations for a school charity drive. The total number of students in Mr. Greenwood's history class donate an average of y dollars each. The same number of students in Ms. Norris's science class donate an average of z dollars each. In terms of y and z, what is the average amount of donations for each student from both classes?

    (A) $\dfrac{z}{y}$

    (B) $\dfrac{(y + z)}{2}$

    (C) $(y + z)$

    (D) $2(y + z)$

16. What is the greatest common factor of $(3xy)^3$ and $3x^2y^5$?

    (A) xy
    (B) $3x^2y^5$
    (C) $3x^2y^3$
    (D) $27x^3y^3$

Upper level students, it's time to check your answers in Chapter 17.

Plugging In The Answers (PITA)

Plugging In the Answers is similar to Plugging In. When *variables* are in the choices, plug in. When *numbers* are in the choices, Plug In the Answers.

Plugging In the Answers works because on a multiple-choice test, the right answer is always one of the choices. On this type of question, you can't Plug In any number you want because only one number will work. Instead, you can Plug In numbers from the choices, one of which must be correct. Here's an example.

> Nicole baked a batch of cookies. She gave half to her friend
> Lisa and six to her mother. If she now has eight cookies
> left, how many did Nicole bake originally?
>
> (A)   8
> (B)   12
> (C)   20
> (D)   28

See what we mean? It would be hard to just start making up numbers of cookies and hope that eventually you guessed correctly. However, the number of cookies that Nicole baked originally must be either 8, 12, 20, or 28 (the four choices). So pick one—start with either (B) or (C)— and then work backward to determine whether you have the right choice.

Let's start with (C): Nicole baked 20 cookies. Now work through the events listed in the question. She had 20 cookies and she gave half to Lisa. That leaves Nicole with 10 cookies. Then, she gave 6 to her mom. Now she's got 4 left.

Keep going. The problem says that Nicole now has 8 cookies left. But if she started with 20— (C)—she would only have 4 left. So is (C) right? No.

No problem. Pick another choice and try again. Be smart about which choice you pick. When we used the number in (C), Nicole ended up with fewer cookies than we wanted her to have, didn't she? So the right answer must be a number larger than 20, the number we took from (C).

The good news is that the choices in most Plugging In The Answers questions go in consecutive order, so it makes it easier to pick the next larger or smaller number, depending on which direction you've decided to go. We need a number larger than 20. So let's go to (D)—28.

Nicole started out with 28 cookies. The first thing she did was give half, or 14, to Lisa. That left Nicole with 14 cookies. Then she gave 6 cookies to her mother. 14 − 6 = 8. Nicole has eight cookies left over. Keep going with the question. It says, "If she now has eight cookies left…." She has 8 cookies left and, *voilà*—she's supposed to have 8 cookies left.

What does this mean? It means you've got the right answer!

PRACTICE DRILL 7—PLUGGING IN THE ANSWERS

Remember to time your-self during this drill!

1. Ted can read 60 pages per hour. Naomi can read 45 pages per hour. If both Ted and Naomi read at the same time, how many minutes will it take them to read a total of 210 pages?

   (A) 72
   (B) 120
   (C) 145
   (D) 180

2. Three people—Paul, Sara, and John—want to put their money together to buy a $90 radio. If Sara agrees to pay twice as much as John, and Paul agrees to pay three times as much as Sara, how much must Sara pay?

   (A) $10
   (B) $20
   (C) $30
   (D) $45

3. Four less than a certain number is two-thirds of that number. What is the number?

   (A) 1
   (B) 6
   (C) 8
   (D) 12

More Practice: Lower Level

4. There are 12 more girls than boys in a classroom. If there are 30 total students in the classroom, how many girls are there in the classroom?

   (A) 9
   (B) 12
   (C) 20
   (D) 21

5. Victor, Jonathan, and Russell buy a home theater system. Victor pays twice as much as Jonathan, and Victor pays half as much Russell. If the home theater system costs $560, how much does Jonathan pay?

   (A) $60
   (B) $80
   (C) $100
   (D) $120

Lower level students can stop here and check answers in Chapter 17. The rest of you, keep going!

More Practice: Middle and Upper Levels

6. Adam is half as old as Bob and three times as old as Cindy. If the sum of their ages is 40, what is Bob's age?

   (A) 6
   (B) 12
   (C) 18
   (D) 24

7. If $70x + 33y = 4,233$, and x and y are positive integers, x could be which of the following values?

   (A) 42
   (B) 47
   (C) 55
   (D) 60

8. The sum of three positive integers is 9 and their product is 24. If the smallest of the integers is 2, what is the largest?

   (A) 4
   (B) 6
   (C) 8
   (D) 9

9. Lori is 15 years older than Carol. In 10 years, Lori will be twice as old as Carol. How old is Lori now?

   (A) 5
   (B) 12
   (C) 20
   (D) 25

10. A group of people are sharing equally the $30 cost of renting a car. If an additional person joined the group, each person would owe $1 less. How many people are in the group currently?

   (A) 5
   (B) 6
   (C) 10
   (D) 12

Check your answers in Chapter 17.

GEOMETRY

Weird Shapes

Whenever the test presents you with a geometric figure that is not a square, rectangle, circle, or triangle, draw a line or lines to divide that figure into the shapes that you do know. Then you can easily work with shapes you know all about.

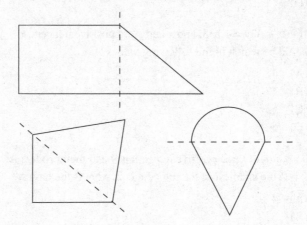

Shaded Regions—Middle and Upper Levels Only

Sometimes geometry questions show you one figure inscribed in another and ask you to find the area of a shaded region inside the larger figure and outside the smaller figure (like the problem at the beginning of this section). To find the areas of these shaded regions, find the area of the outside figure and then subtract the area of the figure inside. The difference is what you need.

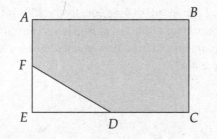

ABCE is a rectangle with a length of 10 and a width of 6. Points F and D are the midpoints of AE and EC, respectively. What is the area of the shaded region?

(A) 25.5
(B) 30
(C) 45
(D) 52.5

The first step is to find the area of the rectangle. Multiply the length by the width and find that the area of the rectangle is 60. Now we find the area of the triangle that we are removing from the rectangle. Because the height and base of the triangle are parts of the sides of the rectangle, and points D and F are half the length and width of the rectangle, we know that the height of the triangle is half the rectangle's width, or 3, and the base of the triangle is half the rectangle's length, or 5. Using the formula for the area of a triangle, we find the area of the triangle is 7.5. Now we subtract the area of the triangle from the area of the rectangle. $60 - 7.5 = 52.5$. The correct answer is (D).

Extra Practice

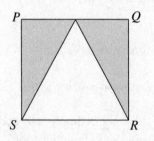

1. *PQRS* is a square with an area of 144. What is the area of the shaded region?

    (A)   50
    (B)   72
    (C)   100
    (D)   120

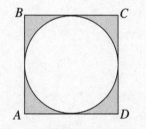

2. In the figure above, the length of side *AB* of square *ABCD* is equal to 4 and the circle has a radius of 2. What is the area of the shaded region?

    (A) $4 - \pi$
    (B) $16 - 4\pi$
    (C) $8 + 4\pi$
    (D) 4π

Functions

In a function problem, an arithmetic operation is defined, and then you are asked to perform it on a number. A function is just a set of instructions written in a strange way.

$$\# \, x = 3x(x + 1)$$

On the left there is usually a variable with a strange symbol next to or around it.

In the middle is an equals sign.

On the right are the instructions. These tell you what to do with the variable.

$\# \, x = 3x(x + 1)$ *What does # 5 equal?*

$\# \, 5 = (3 \times 5)(5 + 1)$ *Just replace each x with a 5!*

Here, the function (indicated by the # sign) simply tells you to substitute a 5 wherever there was an x in the original set of instructions. Functions look confusing because of the strange symbols, but once you know what to do with them, they are just like manipulating an equation.

Sometimes, more than one question will refer to the same function. The following drill, for example, contains two questions about one function. In cases such as this, the first question tends to be easier than the second.

PRACTICE DRILL 8—FUNCTIONS

Questions 1 and 2 refer to the following definition.

For all real numbers n, $\$n = 10n - 10$.

1. $\$7 =$
   (A) 70
   (B) 60
   (C) 17
   (D) 7

2. If $\$n = 120$, then $n =$
   (A) 11
   (B) 12
   (C) 13
   (D) 120

Questions 3-5 refer to the following definition.

For all real numbers d and y, $d \text{ ¿ } y = (d \times y) - (d + y)$.

[Example: $3 \text{ ¿ } 2 = (3 \times 2) - (3 + 2) = 6 - 5 = 1$]

3. $10 \text{ ¿ } 2 =$
   (A) 20
   (B) 16
   (C) 12
   (D) 8

4. If $K (4 \text{ ¿ } 3) = 30$, then $K =$
   (A) 3
   (B) 4
   (C) 5
   (D) 6

5. $(2 \text{ ¿ } 4) \times (3 \text{ ¿ } 6) =$
   (A) $(9 \text{ ¿ } 3) + 3$
   (B) $(6 \text{ ¿ } 4) + 1$
   (C) $(5 \text{ ¿ } 3) + 4$
   (D) $(8 \text{ ¿ } 4) + 2$

Remember to time your-self during this drill!

When you're finished, check your answers in Chapter 17.

Charts and Graphs

Charts

Chart questions usually do not involve much computation, but you must be careful. Follow these three steps and you'll be well on the way to mastering any chart question.

Don't Be in Too Big a Hurry
When working with charts and graphs, make sure you take a moment to look at the chart or graph, figure out what it tells you, and then go to the questions.

1. Read any text that accompanies the chart. It is important to know what the chart is showing and what scale the numbers are on.
2. Read the question.
3. Refer to the chart and find the specific information you need.

If there is more than one question about a single chart, the later questions will tend to be more difficult than the earlier ones. Be careful!

Here is a sample chart.

Club Membership by State, 2012 and 2013

State	2012	2013
California	300	500
Florida	225	250
Illinois	200	180
Massachusetts	150	300
Michigan	150	200
New Jersey	200	250
New York	400	600
Texas	50	100

There are many different questions that you can answer based on the information in this chart. For instance:

> What is the difference between the number of members who came from New York in 2012 and the number of members who came from Illinois in 2013 ?

This question asks you to look up two simple pieces of information and then do a tiny bit of math.

First, the number of members who came from New York in 2012 was 400.

Second, the number of members who came from Illinois in 2013 was 180.

Finally, look back at the question. It asks you to find the difference between these numbers. 400 − 180 = 220. Done.

> The increase in the number of members from New Jersey from 2012 to 2013 was what percent of the total number of members in New Jersey in 2012 ?

You should definitely know how to do this one! Do you remember how to translate percentage questions? If not, go back to Chapter 2.

In 2012, there were 200 club members from New Jersey. In 2013, there were 250 members from New Jersey. That represents an increase of 50 members. To determine what percent that is of the total amount in 2012, you need to ask yourself, "50 (the increase) is what percent of 200 (the number of members in 2012)?"

Translated, this becomes:

$$50 = \frac{g}{100} \times 200$$

With a little bit of simple manipulation, this equation becomes:

$$50 = 2g$$

and

$$25 = g$$

So from 2012 to 2013, there was a 25% increase in the number of members from New Jersey. Good work!

> Which state had as many club members in 2013 as a combination of Illinois, Massachusetts, and Michigan had in 2012 ?

First, take a second to look up the number of members who came from Illinois, Massachusetts, and Michigan in 2012 and add them together.

$$200 + 150 + 150 = 500$$

Which state had 500 members in 2013? California. That's all there is to it!

Graphs

Some questions will ask you to interpret a graph. You should be familiar with both pie and bar graphs. These graphs are generally drawn to scale (meaning that the graphs give an accurate visual impression of the information) so you can always guess based on the figure if you need to.

The way to approach a graph question is exactly the same as the way to approach a chart question. Follow the same three steps.

1. Read any text that accompanies the graph. It is important to know what the graph is showing and what scale the numbers are on.
2. Read the question.
3. Refer back to the graph and find the specific information you need.

This is how it works.

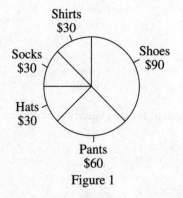

Figure 1

The graph in Figure 1 shows Emily's clothing expenditures for the month of October. On which type of clothing did she spend the most money?

(A) Shoes
(B) Shirts
(C) Socks
(D) Hats

This one is easy. You can look at the pieces of the pie and identify the largest, or you can look at the amounts shown in the graph and choose the largest one. Either way, the answer is (A) because Emily spent more money on shoes than on any other clothing items in October.

Emily spent half of her clothing money on which two items?

(A) Shoes and pants
(B) Shoes and shirts
(C) Hats and socks
(D) Socks and shirts

Again, you can find the answer to this question two different ways. You can look for which two items together make up half the chart, or you can add up the total amount of money Emily spent ($240) and then figure out which two items made up half (or $120) of that amount. Either way is just fine, and either way, the right answer is (B), shoes and shirts.

PRACTICE DRILL 9—CHARTS AND GRAPHS

Questions 1–3 refer to the following summary of energy costs by district.

District	2013	2014
A	400	600
B	500	700
C	200	350
D	100	150
E	600	800

(All numbers are in thousands of dollars.)

Remember to time yourself during this drill!

1. In 2014, which district spent twice as much on energy as District A spent in 2013 ?

   (A) A
   (B) B
   (C) C
   (D) E

2. Which district spent the most on electricity in 2013 and 2014 combined?

   (A) A
   (B) B
   (C) D
   (D) E

3. The total increase in energy expenditure in these districts, from 2013 to 2014, is how many dollars?

   (A) $800
   (B) $1,800
   (C) $2,600
   (D) $800,000

Questions 4 and 5 refer to Figure 2, which shows the number of compact discs owned by five students.

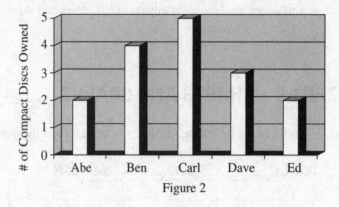

Figure 2

4. Carl owns as many CDs as which two other students combined?

(A) Abe and Ben
(B) Ben and Dave
(C) Abe and Ed
(D) Abe and Dave

5. Which one student owns one-fourth of the CDs accounted for in Figure 2 ?

(A) Abe
(B) Ben
(C) Carl
(D) Dave

Questions 6–8 refer to Matt's weekly time card, shown below.

Day	In	Out	Hours Worked
Monday	2:00 P.M.	5:30 P.M.	3.5
Tuesday			
Wednesday	2:00 P.M.	6:00 P.M.	4
Thursday	2:00 P.M.	5:30 P.M.	3.5
Friday	2:00 P.M.	5:00 P.M.	3
Saturday			
Sunday			

6. If Matt's hourly salary is $6, what were his earnings for the week?

   (A) $14
   (B) $21
   (C) $54
   (D) $84

7. What is the average number of hours Matt worked on the days he worked during this particular week?

   (A) 3
   (B) 3.5
   (C) 4
   (D) 7

8. The hours that Matt worked on Monday accounted for what percent of the total number of hours he worked during this week?

   (A) 3.5
   (B) 20
   (C) 25
   (D) 35

Check your answers in Chapter 17. You can make a chart to see how you've been doing!

QUANTITATIVE COMPARISON—MIDDLE AND UPPER LEVELS ONLY

Lower Level Test Takers

The ISEE's Lower Level test does not include quantitative comparison questions, so you can skip this section.

Quant Comp: Same Book, Different Cover

Quantitative comparison is a type of question—one slightly different from the traditional multiple-choice questions you've seen so far—that tests exactly the same math concepts you have learned so far in this book. There is no new math for you to learn here, just a different approach for this type of question.

You will see a total of 17 quant comp questions in one of your ISEE Math sections.

The Rules of the Game

In answering a quant comp question, your goal is very simple: Determine which column is larger and choose the appropriate answer. There are four possible answers.

(A)   means that Column A is always greater.
(B)   means that Column B is always greater.
(C)   means that Column A is always equal to Column B.
(D)   means that A, B, or C are not always true.

So that you can use POE in quant comp, where there are no choices written out for you, we suggest that you write "A B C D" next to each question. Then when you eliminate an answer, you can cross it off.

Don't Do Too Much Work

Quant comp is a strange, new question type for most students. Don't let it intimidate you, however. Always keep your goal in mind: to figure out which column is larger. Do you care how much larger one column is? We hope not.

They Look Different, but the Math Is the Same

This section will introduce you to quantitative comparison, a different type of question from the "regular" multiple-choice questions you've seen so far. Don't worry—these questions test your knowledge of exactly the same math skills you have already learned in this chapter.

Here's a good example.

Column A	Column B
$2 \times 4 \times 6 \times 8$	$3 \times 5 \times 7 \times 9$

Test takers who don't appreciate the beauty of quant comp look at this one and immediately start multiplying. Look carefully, however, and compare the numbers in both columns.

Of the first numbers in each column, which is larger, 2 or 3 ?

Next, look at the second number in each column. Which is larger, 4 or 5 ?

Now, look at the third numbers. Which is larger, 6 or 7 ?

Finally, look at the fourth numbers. Which is larger, 8 or 9 ?

In each case, column B contains larger numbers. Now, when you multiply larger numbers together, what happens? You guessed it—even larger numbers!

Which column is larger? Without doing a single bit of multiplication you know that (B) is the right answer. Good work!

(D) Means Different

Choice (D) is useful when the relationship between the columns can change. You may have to choose (D) when you have variables in a quant comp problem. For example:

Column A	Column B
$g + 12$	$h - 7$

Which column is larger here depends entirely on what g and h equal, and the problem doesn't give you that information. This is a perfect time to choose (D).

But be careful and don't be too quick to choose (D) when you see a variable.

Column A	Column B
$g + 12$	$g - 7$

With one small change, the answer is no longer (D). Because the variables are the same here, you can determine that no matter what number is represented by g, column A will always be larger. So in this case the answer is (A).

One valuable thing to remember is that when a quant comp question contains no variables and no unknown quantities, the answer cannot be (D).

Column A	Column B
$6 \times 3 \times 4$	$4 \times 6 \times 3$

Even if you somehow forget how to multiply (don't worry, you won't forget), someone somewhere knows how to multiply, so you can get rid of (D).

By the way, look quickly at the last example. First, you eliminate (D) because there are no variables. Do you need to multiply? Nope! The columns contain exactly the same numbers, just written in a different order. What's the answer? You got it: (C)!

PRACTICE DRILL 10—QUANT COMP—MIDDLE AND UPPER LEVELS ONLY

Remember to time your-self during this drill!

(A) means that Column A is always greater
(B) means that Column B is always greater
(C) means that Column A is always equal to Column B
(D) means that A, B, or C are not always true

	Column A	Column B
1.	17×3	$17 \times 2 + 17$
2.	$\dfrac{1}{2}$	$\dfrac{3}{8}$
3.	$b + 80$	$b + 82$

Rob is two inches shorter than Matt.

Joel is four inches taller than Matt.

4.	Rob's height	Joel's height
5.	16^3	4^6

Kimberly lives two miles from school.

Jennifer lives four miles from school.

6.	The distance from Kimberly's house to school	The distance from Kimberly's house to Jennifer's house

Check your answers in Chapter 17.

Quant Comp Plugging In

Think back to the Algebra section. Plugging In helped you deal with variables, right? The same technique works on quant comp questions. There are some special rules you'll need to follow to make sure you can reap all the benefits that Plugging In has to offer you in the Quantitative Comparison section.

Column A	Column B
x	x^2

Follow these three simple steps, and you won't go wrong.

Step 1: Write "A B C D" next to the problem.

Step 2: Plug In an "easy" number for x. By easy number, we mean a nice simple integer, like 3. When you Plug In 3 for x in the above example, column A is 3 and column B is 9, right? Think about the choices and what they mean. Column B is larger, so can the correct answer be (A)? No, eliminate it. Can the correct answer be (C)? No, you can get rid of that one, too!

Step 3: Plug In a "weird" number for x. A weird number might be a little harder to define, but it is something that most test takers won't think of—for instance, zero, one, a fraction, or a negative number. In this case, try plugging in 1. Column A is 1 and column B is also 1. So the columns *can* be equal. Now look at the choices you have left. Choice (B) means that column B is always greater. Is it? No. Cross off (B) and pick (D).

> **Weird Numbers**
> For your second Plug In, try something weird:
> Zero
> One
> Negative
> Extreme
> Fraction

Remember, if you get one result from Plugging In a number and you get a different result by Plugging In another number, you have to pick (D). But don't think too much about these questions, or you'll end up spending a lifetime looking for the perfect "weird" number. Just remember that you always have to Plug In **twice** on quant comp questions.

PRACTICE DRILL 11—QUANT COMP

Remember to time your-
self during this drill!

(A) means that Column
A is always greater
(B) means that Column
B is always greater
(C) means that Column
A is always equal
to Column B
(D) means that A, B, or
C are not always
true

Column A	Column B

$$x > 1$$

1. x x^2

b is an integer and $-1 < b < 1$.

2. $\dfrac{b}{2}$ $\dfrac{b}{8}$

3. p gallons m quarts

x is a positive integer.

4. $\dfrac{x}{4}$ $\dfrac{x}{5}$

w is an integer less than 4.

p is an integer greater than 10.

5. pw w

When you're finished,
check your answers in
Chapter 17.

6. $4c + 6$ $3c + 12$

PRACTICE DRILL 12—QUANT COMP—MIDDLE AND UPPER LEVELS ONLY

Do this drill in three parts. Questions 1–11, 12–28, and 29–45. When you're done with each set, check your progress in Chapter 17. Don't forget to time yourself!

Remember to time yourself during this drill!

(A) means that Column A is always greater
(B) means that Column B is always greater
(C) means that Column A is always equal to Column B
(D) means that A, B, or C are not always true

	Column A	Column B
1.	The total cost of 3 plants that cost $4 each	The total cost of 4 plants that cost $3 each

2.	$30(1 - 2n)$	$30 - 2n$

The product of 3 integers is 48.

3.	The smallest of the 3 integers	1

4.	$(x + y)(x - y)$	$x^2 - y^2$

5.	$(7 - 4) \times 3 - 3$	0

Line m is the graph of $y = x + 4$.

6.	Slope of line m	Slope of line l that is perpendicular to line m

The price of a pair of shoes is $100. The price is increased by 20%. Nobody buys it, so the price is then reduced by 20%.

Column A   Column B

7.   The final price of the pair of shoes after reductions $100

8. $\left(-\dfrac{5}{6}\right)^3$ $\left(-\dfrac{5}{6}\right)^5$

9. $\left(\dfrac{5}{6}\right)^4$ $\left(\dfrac{5}{6}\right)^6$

10. $\left(-\dfrac{5}{6}\right)^2$ $\left(-\dfrac{5}{6}\right)^4$

11. $\left(\dfrac{5}{6}\right)^3$ $\left(\dfrac{5}{6}\right)^5$

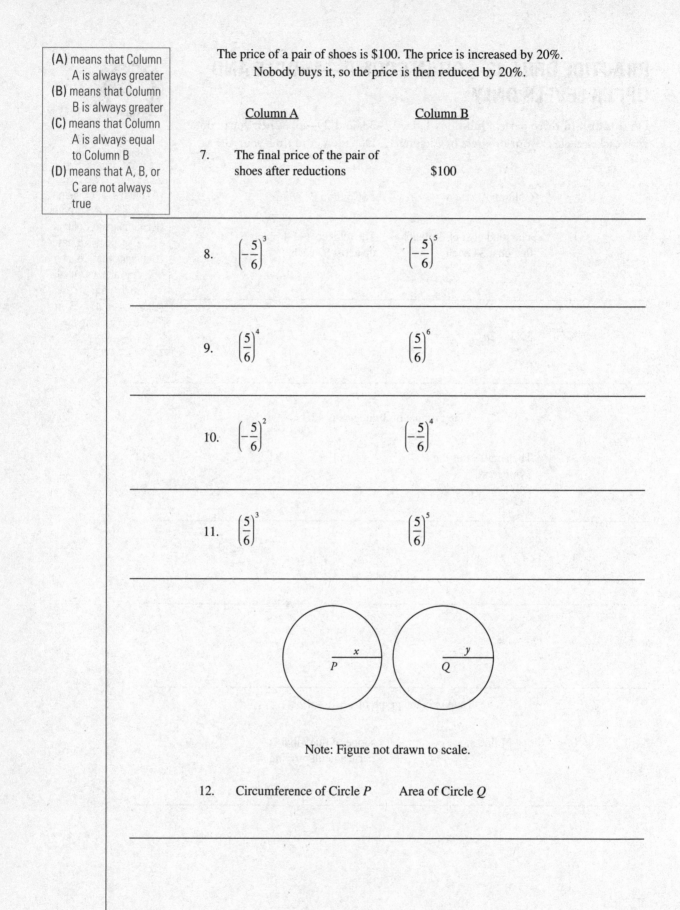

Note: Figure not drawn to scale.

12.   Circumference of Circle P Area of Circle Q

	Column A	Column B

A 6-sided number die, numbered 1 to 6, is rolled.

13. Probability that the number rolled is prime. | $\dfrac{3}{6}$

---

a and b are integers.

$$a + b = 5$$

14. a | b

---

15. $\sqrt{25 - 9}$ | $\sqrt{25} - \sqrt{9}$

Set A: {all prime numbers}

Set B: {all positive multiples of 5 less than 50}

Set C: intersection of Sets A and B

16. Number of elements in Set C | 1

---

17. $\dfrac{3}{4} \times \dfrac{3}{4}$ | $\dfrac{3}{4} + \dfrac{3}{4}$

$$a > 0$$

$$b < 0$$

18. $-(ab)$ | $-ab$

	Column A	Column B

Set A: {1, 3, 8, 11, 15}

Set B: {2, 4, 8, 9, 10, 20}

19. Median of Set A Median of Set B

20. Sum of all consecutive integers between 1 and 10, inclusive   5(11)

21. $2^3 + 2^3 + 2^3$ 2^9

22. $7(x - 3)$ $21 - 7x$

23. The smallest positive factor of 25 multiplied by biggest positive factor of 16   40

24. Probability of a fair penny having heads face up on two consecutive flips   Probability of a fair penny having heads face up on three consecutive flips

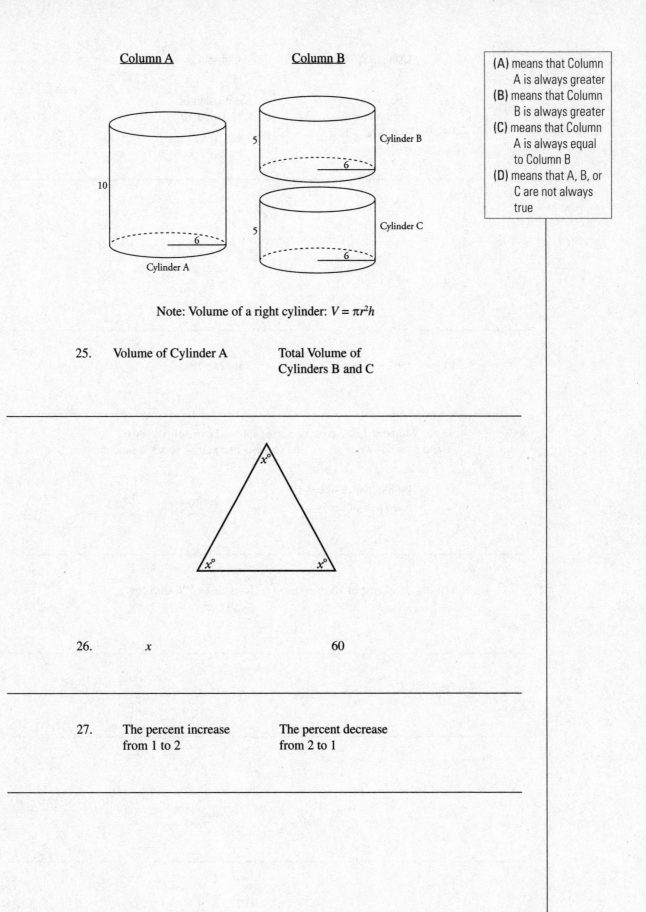

(A) means that Column A is always greater

(B) means that Column B is always greater

(C) means that Column A is always equal to Column B

(D) means that A, B, or C are not always true

Cylinder B

Cylinder C

Cylinder A

Note: Volume of a right cylinder: $V = \pi r^2 h$

25.   Volume of Cylinder A   Total Volume of Cylinders B and C

26. x 60

27.   The percent increase from 1 to 2   The percent decrease from 2 to 1

	Column A	Column B
28.	The average (arithmetic mean) of 4, 6, 8, and 10	The median of 4, 6, 8, and 10

$$x > 0$$
$$y > 0$$

	Column A	Column B
29.	$\dfrac{xy}{2}$	$\sqrt{xy}$

	Column A	Column B
30.	(567.83) (0.40)	(40) (5.6783)

Meredith has 7 pairs of purple shoes, 2 pairs of red shoes, and 1 pair of white shoes. She chooses one pair of shoes at random.

	Column A	Column B
31.	Probability of <u>not</u> picking a red pair of shoes	$\dfrac{8}{10}$

	Column A	Column B
32.	Total cost of 10 shirts at $8 each	Total cost of 20 shirts at $4.50 each

	Column A	Column B
33.	$\dfrac{x^2 x^5}{x^4}$	x^3

$$x^2 = 36$$

	Column A	Column B
34.	x	-6

	Column A	Column B

(A) means that Column A is always greater
(B) means that Column B is always greater
(C) means that Column A is always equal to Column B
(D) means that A, B, or C are not always true

35.   Largest positive factor of 16   Smallest positive multiple of 16

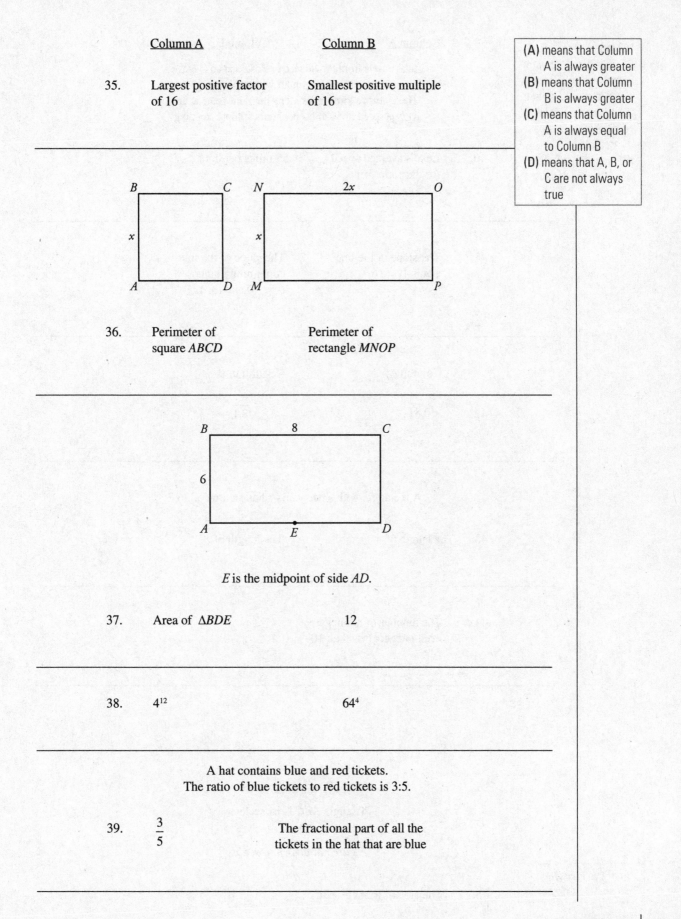

36.   Perimeter of square $ABCD$ Perimeter of rectangle $MNOP$

E is the midpoint of side AD.

37.   Area of $\triangle BDE$ 12

38. 4^{12} 64^4

A hat contains blue and red tickets.
The ratio of blue tickets to red tickets is 3:5.

39. $\dfrac{3}{5}$ The fractional part of all the tickets in the hat that are blue

Column A   Column B

Luke travels from Providence to Boston at an average speed of 50 miles per hour without stopping.
He returns to Providence along the same route at an average speed of 60 miles per hours without stopping.

40.   Luke's average speed   55 miles per hour
for the entire trip

---

41.   The slope of the line   The slope of the line
$12x - 4y = 16$ containing points
$(-3,\ 6)$ and $(3, 12)$

Column A   Column B

42. $\sqrt{0.81}$ $\sqrt{8.1}$

A rectangle with sides y and z has an area of 36.

43.   The length of y The length of z

---

44.   The number of nonnegative
even integers less than 10   4

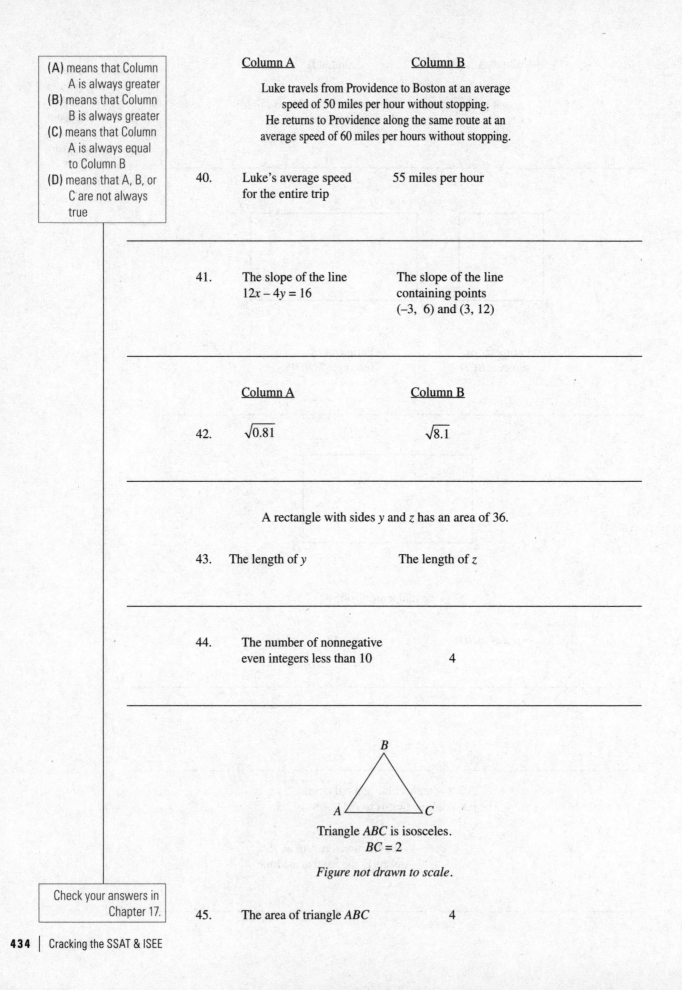

Triangle *ABC* is isosceles.
$BC = 2$

Figure not drawn to scale.

45.   The area of triangle *ABC*   4

MATH REVIEW

Make sure you can confidently answer all of the following questions before you take the ISEE.

1. Is zero an integer? _____

2. Is zero positive or negative? _____

3. What operation do you perform to find a sum? _____

4. What operation do you perform to find a product? _____

5. What is the result called when you divide? _____

6. Is 312 divisible by 3 ? _____

    Is 312 divisible by 9 ? _____

    (Actually dividing isn't fair. Use your divisibility rules!)

7. What does the "E" in PEMDAS stand for? _____

8. Is 3 a factor of 12 ? _____

    Is 12 a factor of 3 ? _____

9. Is 3 a multiple of 12 ? _____

    Is 12 a multiple of 3 ? _____

10. What is the tens digit in the number 304.275 ? _____

11. What is the tenths digit in the number 304.275 ? _____

12. 2^3 = _____

13. In "math language," the word *percent* means: _____.

14. In "math language," the word *of* means: _____.

15. In a Ratio Box, the last column on the right is always the

    _____.

16. Whenever you see a problem involving averages, draw the

    _____.

17. When a problem contains variables in the question and in the

answers, I will _____.

18. To find the perimeter of a square, I _____ the

length(s) of _____ side(s).

19. To find the area of a square, I _____

the length(s) of _____ sides.

20. There are _____ degrees in a straight line.

21. A triangle has _____ angles, which total

_____ degrees.

22. A four-sided figure contains _____ degrees.

23. An isosceles triangle has _____ equal sides; a(n)

_____ triangle has three equal sides.

24. The longest side of a right triangle is called the _____

and is located opposite the _____.

25. To find the area of a triangle, I use the formula: _____.

Check your answers in Chapter 17.

Chapter 15
ISEE Verbal

INTRODUCTION

Take a look at the Verbal section of a practice ISEE in this book. The Verbal section on the ISEE consists of 40 questions (34 for the Lower Level), usually broken into:

- 20 synonym questions (questions 1 to 20)
- 20 sentence completion questions (questions 21 to 40)

That's 40 questions—but you have only 20 minutes! Should you try to spend 30 seconds on each question to get them all done? **No!**

You Mean I Don't Have to Answer All the Questions?

Nope. You'll actually improve your score by working on fewer questions, as long as you're still using all of the allotted time. Even though you shouldn't work on all of the questions, you should still answer them all with your favorite letter because there is no penalty for a wrong answer!

"Allotted Time"?
If you can't define *allotted*, make a flash card for it! Look in Chapter 1 for ideas on how to use flash cards to learn new words.

Remember, this test is designed for students in two to four different grade levels. There will be vocabulary on some of these questions that is aimed at students older than you, and almost no one in your grade will get those questions right. The ISEE score you receive will compare you only with students in your own grade. The younger you are in your test level, the fewer questions you are expected to complete. Sixth graders are expected to complete the fewest questions on the Middle Level test. Eighth graders are expected to do the fewest questions on the Upper Level test.

So, why rush through the questions you can get right to get to the really tough ones that almost nobody gets? That approach only ensures that you will make hasty, careless errors. Work slowly on the questions that have vocabulary that you know to make sure you get them right. Then try the ones that have some unfamiliar words in them.

If you pace yourself, you'll have much more time for each question than students who think they have to get them all done.

Guess?
Yes. Fill in an answer even for the questions you don't read. Why? Because there is no penalty for a wrong answer on the ISEE, so you've got nothing to lose (and plenty to gain when you happen to be right!)..

Which Questions Should I Work on?

Everybody's different. You know some words that your friends don't, and vice versa. Some verbal questions are harder for certain people than they are for others.

So, here's the plan: go through the first section, and work on all the synonyms that are easy for you first. Those are the questions for which you know the definitions of the words involved. Then, go back through and answer the questions with words that sound familiar, even if you are not sure of their dictionary definition—these are words you sort of know. Then, move on to sentence completions, leaving yourself more than half the time in the section. Remember to skip a number on the answer sheet when you skip a question—but do fill it in at some point!

Knowing your own vocabulary is the key to deciding if you can answer a question easily.

Know Yourself

Categorize the words you see in ISEE questions into:

- words you know
- words you sort of know
- words you really don't know

Be honest with yourself when it comes to deciding if you know a word or not, so you apply the techniques that are best for the questions on which you are working. Keep your idea of the word's meaning flexible, because the test writers sometimes use the words in ways that you and I do not! (They claim to use dictionary definitions.)

Of course, the easiest way to get a verbal question right is by making sure all the words in it fall into the first category—words you know. The best way to do this is by learning new vocabulary words *every day*. Check out the Vocabulary chapter (Chapter 1) for the best ways to do this.

You can raise your verbal score moderately just by using the techniques we teach in this chapter. But if you want to see a substantial rise in your score, you need to build up your vocabulary, too.

Eliminate Choices

With math questions, there's always one *correct* answer. The other answers are simply wrong. In a verbal question, however, things are not that simple. Words are much more slippery than numbers. So verbal questions have *best* answers, not *correct* answers. The other answers aren't necessarily wrong, but the people who score the ISEE think they're not as good as the *best* one. This means that—even more so than on the Quantitative sections—in the Verbal and Reading sections you should always try to eliminate choices. Get used to looking for *worse* answers. There are many more of them than there are *best* answers, so *worse* answers are easier to find!

When you find them, cross them out in the question booklet to make sure you don't spend any more time looking at them. No matter which other techniques you use to answer a question, first eliminate wrong answers, instead of trying to magically pick out the best answer right away.

One thing to remember for the Verbal section: you should not eliminate choices that contain words you don't know. It doesn't matter that *you* don't know what a word means—it could still be the answer.

Cross Out the Bad Ones
Even when none of the answers looks particularly right, you can usually eliminate at least one.

Shop Around
Try every choice in a verbal question to be sure you're picking the *best* answer there.

Don't Rule It Out
Don't eliminate answers with words you don't know.

What If I Can't Narrow It Down to One Answer?

Should you guess? Yes. Even if you can't eliminate any choices, you should still guess. We mentioned before that you should leave a minute or two at the end of the section to fill in an answer for any questions you did not get to. Why? *Because there's no guessing penalty on the ISEE.* Nothing is subtracted from your score for a wrong answer, and because there are four choices, you'll get approximately 25 percent of the questions on which you guess randomly correct.

That means that you should *never* leave a question blank. Pick a letter (A, B, C, or D) to fill in for your random guesses. It doesn't matter which letter you use, but stick with one letter-of-the-day so you don't have to think about it.

Of course, the number of questions you get right will increase if you can eliminate some choices before you guess, so we'll teach you techniques to do this.

Bubble Practice
Whenever you do a practice test, use the sample answer sheet so you get used to skipping around and making sure you're always on the same number on the test booklet and answer sheet.

Where Do I Start?

Do synonyms first in the Verbal section, right where you find them. Get them done in less than 10 minutes so you have a little more than half the time in the section for sentence completions. Sentence completions take longer to read and work through, but they have more context to help you get the question right, even if you don't know all the words involved. If you get stuck on a sentence completion, simply fill in the letter-of-the-day and move on. Don't save it for a second pass. Similarly, if you realize you simply don't know the stem word or a synonym, just fill in your guess and keep going.

You'll be answering the questions in the following order:

- synonyms with words you know
- synonyms with words you sort of know
- sentence completions

REVIEW—THE VERBAL PLAN

Pacing and Verbal Strategy

What's the order in which I answer questions in the Verbal section?

1. _____

2. _____

3. _____

How long should I spend on synonyms? _____

What's the technique I'll be using all the time, regardless of whatever

else I'm using to answer a question? _____

How many choices must I have eliminated to guess

productively? _____

Can I eliminate choices that contain words I don't know?

_____

Check your answers in Chapter 17.

If you had trouble with any of these questions, just review this part of the chapter before moving on.

Knowing My Vocabulary

Look at each of the following words and decide if it's a word that you know, sort of know, or really don't know. If you know it, write down its definition.

insecticide (noun) _____

trifle (verb) _____

repugnant (adjective) _____

mollify (verb) _____

camouflage (verb) _____

historic (adjective) _____

Check the ones you thought you knew or sort of knew. Look them up in the dictionary and make flash cards for them.

Be Honest
Do you really know the definition of the word? The ISEE uses dictionary definitions, and these may differ from your own sometimes. If you're not positive, you may want to use the techniques for when you sort of know the word.

SYNONYMS

What Is a Synonym?

On the ISEE, a synonym question asks you to choose the choice that comes closest in meaning to the stem word (the word in capital letters). Often, the best answer won't mean the exact same thing as the stem word, but it will be closer than any of the other choices.

You need to decide which vocabulary category the synonym stem word falls into for you, so you know which technique to use. First, find all the synonyms for which you know the stem word, and then go back and find the ones with stem words you sort of know.

When You Know the Stem Word

Don't Waste Time
Make sure you cross out answers you've eliminated, so you don't look at them again.

Write Down Your Own Definition

Come up with a simple definition—a word or a phrase. Write it next to the stem word. Then look at the answers, eliminate the ones that are furthest from your definition, and choose the closest one.

It's very simple. Don't let the test writers put words into your mouth. Make sure you're armed with your own definition before you look at their choices. They often like to put in a word that is a close second to the best answer; if you've got your own synonym ready, you'll be able to make the distinction.

If you need to, cover the answers with your hand so you can think of your definition before looking. Eventually, you may not have to write down your definitions, but you should start out that way so that you are not influenced by the choices they give you.

As you compare the choices with your definition, cross out the wrong ones with your pencil. Crossing out choices is something you should *always* do—it saves you time because you don't go back to choices you've already decided were not the best.

As always, don't eliminate words you don't know. Try this one. Write your definition of WITHER before you look at the choices.

WITHER: _____
- (A) play
- (B) spoil
- (C) greatly improve
- (D) wilt

The stem word means "shrivel" or "dry up." Which answer is closest? (D). You may have been considering (B), but (D) is closer.

PRACTICE DRILL 1—WRITE YOUR OWN DEFINITION

Write your definition—just a word or two—for each of these stem words.

1. BIZARRE: _____

2. PREFACE: _____

3. GENEROUS: _____

4. MORAL: _____

5. ALTER: _____

6. REVOLVE: _____

7. HOPEFUL: _____

8. LINGER: _____

9. ASSIST: _____

10. CONSTRUCT: _____

11. STOOP: _____

12. CANDID: _____

13. TAUNT: _____

14. COARSE: _____

15. VAIN: _____

16. SERENE: _____

17. UTILIZE: _____

18. VIGOROUS: _____

19. PROLONG: _____

20. BENEFIT: _____

Write Another Definition

Why would you ever need to change your definition? Let's see.

> MANEUVER:
>
> (A) avoidance
> (B) deviation
> (C) find
> (D) contrivance

Your definition may be something like *move* or *control* if you know the word from hearing it applied to cars. But that definition isn't in the choices. The problem is that you're thinking about *maneuver* as a verb. However, *maneuver* can also be a noun. It means "a plan, scheme, or trick." Now go back and eliminate. The answer is (D).

The ISEE sometimes uses secondary definitions, which can be the same part of speech or a different part of speech from the primary definition. Just stay flexible in your definitions, and you'll be fine.

PRACTICE DRILL 2—WRITE ANOTHER DEFINITION

Write down as many definitions as you can think of for the following words. Your definitions may be the same part of speech or different. If you have a hard time thinking of different meanings, look up the word.

1. POINT: _____ _____

2. INDUSTRY: _____ _____

3. FLAG: _____ _____

4. FLUID: _____ _____

5. CHAMPION: _____ _____

6. TABLE: _____ _____

7. SERVICE: _____ _____

PRACTICE DRILL 3—BASIC SYNONYM TECHNIQUES

Try these synonyms.

- Use the definition for the stem word that you wrote down before.
- Look at the choices, and eliminate the ones that are furthest from your definition.
- If there are stem words that you don't know well enough to define, just skip and mark them and come back after you've learned techniques for stem words you sort of know.

1. BIZARRE:

   (A) lonely
   (B) unable
   (C) odd
   (D) found

2. PREFACE:

   (A) introduce
   (B) state
   (C) propose
   (D) jumble

3. GENEROUS:

   (A) skimpy
   (B) faulty
   (C) ample
   (D) unusual

4. MORAL:

   (A) imitation
   (B) full
   (C) real
   (D) upright

5. ALTER:

   (A) sew
   (B) make up
   (C) react
   (D) change

6. REVOLVE:

   (A) push against
   (B) go forward
   (C) leave behind
   (D) turn around

7. HOPEFUL:

   (A) discouraging
   (B) promising
   (C) fulfilling
   (D) deceiving

8. LINGER:

   (A) hurry
   (B) abate
   (C) dawdle
   (D) attempt

9. ASSIST:

   (A) work
   (B) discourage
   (C) hinder
   (D) help

10. CONSTRUCT:

    (A) build
    (B) type
    (C) live in
    (D) engage

11. STOOP:

    (A) raise
    (B) elevate
    (C) condescend
    (D) realize

12. CANDID:

    (A) picture
    (B) honest
    (C) prepared
    (D) unfocused

13. TAUNT:

    (A) delay
    (B) stand
    (C) show
    (D) tease

14. COARSE:

    (A) smooth
    (B) crude
    (C) polite
    (D) furious

15. VAIN:

    (A) conceited

    (B) beautiful

    (C) talented

    (D) helpless

16. SERENE:

    (A) helpful

    (B) normal

    (C) calm

    (D) disastrous

17. UTILIZE:

    (A) pass on

    (B) resort to

    (C) rely on

    (D) make use of

18. VIGOROUS:

    (A) slothful

    (B) aimless

    (C) energetic

    (D) glorious

19. PROLONG:

    (A) affirmative

    (B) lengthen

    (C) exceed

    (D) assert

20. BENEFIT:

    (A) cooperate

    (B) struggle

    (C) assist

    (D) appeal

Check your answers in Chapter 17.

When You Sort of Know the Stem Word

Why should you answer synonym questions quickly? Why can they seem harder than sentence completions, even though you should do them faster?

Synonyms can be harder to beat than sentence completions because the ISEE gives you no context with which to figure out words that you sort of know. But that doesn't mean you're done after the easy synonyms. You can get the medium ones, too. You just need to create your own context to figure out words you don't know very well.

Also, keep in mind that your goal is to eliminate the worst answers and make educated guesses. You'll be able to do this for every synonym that you sort of know. Even if you eliminate just one choice, you've increased your chances of guessing correctly. You'll gain points overall.

Make Your Own Context

You can create your own context for the word by figuring out how you've heard it used before. Think of the other words you've heard used with the stem word. Is there a certain phrase that comes to mind? What does that phrase mean?

If you still can't come up with a definition for the stem word, just use the context in which you've heard the word to eliminate answers that wouldn't fit at all in that same context.

How about this stem word?

ABOMINABLE:

Where have you heard *abominable*? The Abominable Snowman, of course. Think about it—you know it's a monster-like creature. Which choices can you eliminate?

ABOMINABLE:

(A) enormous   the enormous snowman? maybe
(B) terrible   the terrible snowman? sure
(Ø) rude   the rude snowman? probably not
(Ø) talkative   the talkative snowman? only Frosty!

You can throw out everything except (A) and (B). Now you can guess, with a much better shot at getting the answer right than guessing from four choices. Or you can think about where else you've heard the stem word. Have you ever heard something called an *abomination*? Was it something terrible or was it something enormous? Choice (B) is the answer.

Try this one. Where have you heard this stem word? Try the answers in that context.

SURROGATE:

- (A) requested
- (B) paranoid
- (C) numerous
- (D) substitute

Have you heard the stem word in *surrogate mother*? If you have, you can definitely eliminate (A), (B), and (C). A surrogate mother is a substitute mother.

Try one more.

ENDANGER:

- (A) rescue
- (B) frighten
- (C) confuse
- (D) threaten

Everyone's associations are different, but you've probably heard of *endangered species* or *endangered lives*. Use either of those phrases to eliminate choices that can't fit into it. Rescued species? Frightened species? Confused species? Threatened species? (D) works best.

PRACTICE DRILL 4—MAKING YOUR OWN CONTEXT

Write down the phrase in which you've heard each word.

1. COMMON: _____

2. COMPETENT: _____

3. ABRIDGE: _____

4. UNTIMELY: _____

5. HOMOGENIZE: _____

6. DELINQUENT: _____

7. INALIENABLE: _____

8. PALTRY: _____

9. AUSPICIOUS: _____

10. PRODIGAL: _____

PRACTICE DRILL 5—USING YOUR OWN CONTEXT

1. COMMON:
   - (A) beautiful
   - (B) novel
   - (C) typical
   - (D) constant

2. COMPETENT:
   - (A) angry
   - (B) peaceful
   - (C) well-written
   - (D) capable

3. ABRIDGE:
   - (A) complete
   - (B) span
   - (C) reach
   - (D) shorten

4. UNTIMELY:
   - (A) late
   - (B) punctual
   - (C) inappropriate
   - (D) continuous

5. HOMOGENIZE:
   - (A) make the same
   - (B) send away
   - (C) isolate
   - (D) enfold

6. DELINQUENT:
   - (A) underage
   - (B) negligent
   - (C) superior
   - (D) advanced

7. INALIENABLE:
   - (A) misplaced
   - (B) universal
   - (C) assured
   - (D) democratic

8. PALTRY:

   (A) meager
   (B) colored
   (C) thick
   (D) abundant

9. AUSPICIOUS:

   (A) supple
   (B) minor
   (C) favorable
   (D) ominous

10. PRODIGAL:

   (A) wasteful
   (B) amusing
   (C) disadvantaged
   (D) lazy

Check your answers in Chapter 17.

Use Word Parts to Piece Together a Definition

Prefixes, roots, and suffixes can help you figure out what a word means. You should use this technique in addition to word association, because not all word parts retain their original meanings.

You may never have seen this stem word before, but if you've been working on your Vocabulary chapter, you know that the root *pac* or *peac* means peace. You can see the same root in *Pacific*, *pacifier*, and the word *peace* itself. So which answer matches this synonym?

PACIFIST:

(A) innocent person
(B) person opposed to war
(C) warmonger
(D) wanderer of lands

It's (B). In the following stem word, we see *cred*, a word part that means "belief" or "faith." You can see this word part in *incredible*, *credit*, and *credibility*. The answer is now simple.

CREDIBLE:

(A) obsolete
(B) believable
(C) fabulous
(D) mundane

(B) again. What are the word parts in the following stem word?

MONOTONOUS:

(A) lively
(B) educational
(C) nutritious
(D) repetitious

Mono means "one." *Tone* has to do with sound. If something keeps striking one sound, how would you describe it? (D) is the answer.

The only way you'll be able to use word parts is if you know them. Get cracking on the Vocabulary chapter!

Words You Really Don't Know

Don't spend time on a synonym with a stem word you've never seen if you don't know any of its word parts. Simply make sure you fill in your letter-of-the-day for that question.

PRACTICE DRILL 6—ALL SYNONYMS TECHNIQUES

1. PRINCIPLE:

   (A) leader
   (B) established
   (C) theory
   (D) chief

2. CAPTURE:

   (A) secure
   (B) lose
   (C) bargain
   (D) halt

3. BEFRIEND:

   (A) sever ties
   (B) close down
   (C) connect with
   (D) enjoy

4. AUTOMATIC:

   (A) involuntary
   (B) enjoyable
   (C) forceful
   (D) hapless

5. APTITUDE:

   (A) difficulty
   (B) reason
   (C) mistake
   (D) ability

6. CAPITAL:

   (A) primary
   (B) regressive
   (C) capable
   (D) central

7. REPRESS:

   (A) defy
   (B) faithful
   (C) ruling
   (D) prevent

8. ENDURE:

   (A) take in
   (B) stick with
   (C) add to
   (D) run from

9. TRANSMIT:

(A) eliminate
(B) watch
(C) send
(D) annoy

10. DIALOGUE:

(A) speak
(B) conversation
(C) monologue
(D) sermon

11. EULOGY:

(A) attack
(B) tribute
(C) complement
(D) encouragement

12. BAN:

(A) remove
(B) impose
(C) forbid
(D) specify

13. APATHY:

(A) involvement
(B) compassion
(C) contempt
(D) indifference

14. OMNISCIENT:

(A) agile
(B) logical
(C) knowledgeable
(D) invulnerable

15. TRANSGRESS:

(A) transport
(B) eradicate
(C) include
(D) violate

16. VIVACIOUS:

(A) nimble
(B) lively
(C) easily amused
(D) direct

17. HYPERBOLE:

 (A) isolation
 (B) identification
 (C) exaggeration
 (D) sharp curve

18. CONGENITAL:

 (A) innocent
 (B) inborn
 (C) graceful
 (D) acquired

19. SUCCINCT:

 (A) subterranean
 (B) confusing
 (C) blatant
 (D) direct

20. CRAFTY:

 (A) apt
 (B) sly
 (C) agile
 (D) wicked

21. FLUENT:

 (A) spoken
 (B) quiet
 (C) flowing
 (D) fast

22. IDENTICAL:

 (A) broken
 (B) duplicate
 (C) foolish
 (D) related

23. POPULAR:

 (A) rude
 (B) accepted
 (C) understood
 (D) respected

24. WHARF:

 (A) beach
 (B) raft
 (C) flat ship
 (D) dock

25. FAITHFUL:

    (A) hopeful
    (B) unrealistic
    (C) truthful
    (D) devoted

26. OBSTACLE:

    (A) path
    (B) great distance
    (C) ditch
    (D) impediment

27. CONVOLUTED:

    (A) interesting
    (B) expensive
    (C) twisted
    (D) forged

28. ALIGN:

    (A) repair
    (B) command
    (C) straighten
    (D) replace

29. VETO:

    (A) reject
    (B) discuss
    (C) define
    (D) submit

30. MANGLE:

    (A) shine
    (B) wear
    (C) torture
    (D) mutilate

31. FEEBLE:

    (A) fair
    (B) ineffective
    (C) tough
    (D) hardened

32. SLUGGISH:

    (A) aggressive
    (B) slow
    (C) inconsiderate
    (D) wicked

33. REDUNDANT:

   (A) poor
   (B) superfluous
   (C) abundant
   (D) fancy

34. LAMPOON:

   (A) article
   (B) biography
   (C) journey
   (D) satire

35. TREPIDATION:

   (A) boldness
   (B) irony
   (C) rashness
   (D) fear

36. ASSESS:

   (A) deny
   (B) accept
   (C) size up
   (D) dismiss

37. GHASTLY:

   (A) responsible
   (B) erroneous
   (C) horrible
   (D) favorable

38. CENSURE:

   (A) editing
   (B) understanding
   (C) approval
   (D) disapproval

39. DISMANTLE:

   (A) discourse with
   (B) break down
   (C) yield to
   (D) drive away

40. CACOPHONY:

   (A) melody
   (B) harmony
   (C) music
   (D) dissonance

Check your answers in Chapter 17.

SENTENCE COMPLETIONS

What Is a Sentence Completion?

On an ISEE sentence completion, you need to pick the answer that best fills the blank in the sentence they've given you. Just like with synonym problems, you have to choose the best word from the choices, and sometimes it's not a perfect fit. On the Upper Level test, some questions will have two blanks.

Often, however, you'll actually find more than one choice that could fit in the blank. How do you decide which is best to choose?

Just like on the synonym questions, you need to make sure the ISEE test writers don't get to put words into your mouth. That's how they confuse you, especially on the medium and hard questions. You need to have your own answer ready before you look at theirs.

Come Up with Your Own Word

The easiest way to make sure you don't get caught up in the ISEE's tricky answers is to cover them with your hand until you've thought of your own word for the blank. Why waste your time plugging all their answers into the sentence, anyway? Let's look at one.

> **Just Use the Sentence**
> Don't try to use outside knowledge to fill in the blank. Use only what the sentence tells you.

Quite ------- conditions continue to exist in many mountain towns in America where houses do not have running water or electricity.

What word would you put in the blank? Something like *basic* or *old-fashioned* or *harsh*? Write down any words that occur to you. Which part of the sentence lets you know which words could fit? "Where houses do not have running water or electricity" gives you the clue.

When you've come up with one or two words you would put in the blank, write them down. (You may not always have to write them, but during practice you should, so you can compare your answers with the answers in this book.) Then, uncover the answers.

(A) common
(B) primitive
(C) orderly
(D) lively

Which looks most like your words? Choice (B). Any of the other words could appear in this sentence in real life, right? However, because the only context you have is the sentence itself, you have to use what the sentence gives you to get the *best* answer for the ISEE.

Use the Clue

Try this one.

> Museums are good places for students of ------.

What word did you come up with? Art? History? Science? Those words are all different! Don't worry, you will not get a sentence completion like this because there's not enough information to go on—any choice could be defended! There will always be a clue to tell you what can go in the blank.

> Museums that house paintings and sculptures are good places for students of -------.

What's your word? Something like "art." What told you it was art, and not history or science? Underline the part of the sentence that gave you the clue. The clue is the most important part of the sentence—the part that tells you what to put in the blank.

Try another one. Underline the clue and fill in the blank.

> The businessman was ------- because sales were down and costs were up, and his demeanor showed his unhappiness.

Don't be afraid to just reuse the clue in the blank—the clue is *unhappiness* and the word *unhappy* would go well in the blank! When it fits, use the clue itself. Now eliminate answers.

> (A) despondent
> (B) persuasive
> (C) indifferent
> (D) unresponsive

Even if you're not sure what *despondent* means, do the other words mean *unhappy*? No. Choice (A) must be the answer.

Cover the answers, underline the clue, and fill in the blank before looking at the choices.

> To join the soccer team, a student absolutely had to be able to practice two hours a day; however, buying the uniform was -------.
>
> (A) obligatory
> (B) universal
> (C) natural
> (D) optional

Recycle
Often you can use the very same word(s) you see in the clue— or something close!

Your word was probably something like "not required" or "unnecessary." (Don't worry if you're using a short phrase instead of a word—anything that expresses the meaning of what should go in the blank is fine.) But the clue was "absolutely had to," and your words are the opposite of that. What's going on?

Up until now, all the sentences we've seen have had a clue that was pretty much the same as the word in the blank. But sometimes the word in the blank is actually different from the clue—in fact, an opposite. How can you tell when this is true? Well, which word in the sentence told you? *However.* *However* lets you know that the word in the blank would be the opposite of the clue (the clue was "absolutely had to").

There are many little words that can tell you if the blank is the same as the clue or different.

Use Direction Words
Direction words tell you if the blank continues in the same direction as the clue or if it changes direction.

Which of these responses do you want to hear when you've just asked someone to the prom?

I really like you, *but* _____.

I really like you, *and* _____.

Why is the first one so awful to hear? *But* lets you know that the sentence is going to suddenly change direction and not be about liking you anymore. Why is the second one so much better? *And* lets you know that the sentence is going to continue in the same direction and continue to be all about liking you. Some other direction words are below. If you can think of any others, add them here.

Different Direction	Same Direction
but	and
however	thus
although	therefore
rather	so
instead	because
despite	in addition
yet	consequently

Now, cover the answers, underline the clue, circle the direction words, and fill in your own word.

> When people first began investigating the human brain they were unscientific in their methods, but eventually they began to develop methods that were -------.
>
> (A) objective
> (B) inconclusive
> (C) lucrative
> (D) widespread

Going Thataway
Be careful when you see a direction word— make sure you know which way you need to go. Try plugging in opposites as a test.

Which choice is closest to yours? If you underlined *unscientific* and circled *but*, then you could have written *scientific* in the blank. Choice (A) is closest.

PRACTICE DRILL 7—COMING UP WITH YOUR OWN WORD

Underline the clues, circle the direction words, and come up with one or two words for each of these sentences.

1. The leading man's rehearsals were so _____ that the director and producer were already imagining what a hit the movie would be.

2. Once very _____, computers are now found in almost every home.

3. After playing more than a dozen different concert halls, the orchestra was praised by critics for its _____ rendition of Beethoven's famous *Fifth Symphony*.

4. Although Miles had been unable to sleep the night before, he seemed remarkably _____ when he gave his presentation.

5. Julie was _____ to have been in the right place at the right time; the drama coach gave her the lead in our class play.

6. Mr. Jones is an intelligent and _____ teacher; his knowledge is matched only by his concern for his students.

7. To the casual observer, all fingerprints may appear to be _____; but in fact each individual's prints are unique.

8. Hardly one to _____, Josh tackled every project as soon as he got it.

9. In Charles Dickens's *A Christmas Carol*, Scrooge is a particularly _____ character, refusing to give his assistant, Bob Cratchit, a raise, despite his enormous wealth.

10. Alfred Wegener's theory that the continents are slowly drifting apart has recently been confirmed by instruments that measure very small _____ in land masses.

11. Despite their seemingly _____ architecture, the pyramids of Giza are actually intricate marvels of ancient engineering.

12. Unlike animals, which must seek sustenance in their surrounding environments, plants are able to _____ their own food.

13. Great variations in successive layers of polar ice make it possible for scientists to determine how the climate has _____ over the past millennium.

14. Because of the rigors of mountain climbing, the team needs equipment that is both _____ enough to support the members and completely reliable.

15. For a student to qualify for the foreign study program, good language skills are absolutely necessary; however, prior travel to the host country is _____.

16. The task was very _____ because certain parts needed to be carried out over and over again.

17. Because the ground there was steep and dangerous, the mountain guide told us that it was _____ to approach the edge.

18. Most members of the drama club, though reserved in real life, are quite _____ once they get on stage.

19. Physicians offer recommendations about food groups and eating habits to help their patients follow a more _____ diet.

20. Fundraising is only effective when _____ individuals are available, showing their concern by their readiness to give.

21. Not one to be easily intimidated, the corporal remained _____ while the opposing army pressed toward his troop's position.

22. Unlike her confident companion, she tended to be _____ when she found herself among strangers.

23. Although the rest of the class laughed at her antics, the teacher was _____ by Shelly's constant interruptions.

24. To avoid being penalized for tardiness, you should be _____ with your assignments.

25. Carpentry and cabinet-making are such difficult trades that they require great _____ with woodworking tools.

26. One of the most ecologically diverse places on Earth, the tropical rain forests of Brazil are home to an incredible _____ of insect species.

27. Higher math is a _____ discipline; it requires just as much imagination and insight as do any of the arts.

28. Many tribes in New Guinea are known for their _____ societies; all property belongs to all members of the tribe.

29. Because their roots are external and their leaf bases clasp, palm trees are rigid and upright, yet _____ enough to bend in strong winds.

30. Though some assert that all behavior is learned, there are others who hold that some behaviors are _____, existing before any learning occurs.

31. A very outgoing and _____ individual, the mayor loved to talk to her fellow citizens.

32. Staring wide eyed, the crowd was _____ by the magician's amazing feats of illusion.

Check your answers in Chapter 17.

PRACTICE DRILL 8—ELIMINATING ANSWERS BASED ON YOUR WORD

Using what you wrote in the sentences above, eliminate answers that cannot fit.

1. The leading man's rehearsals were so ------- that the director and producer were already imagining what a hit the movie would be.

   (A) indignant
   (B) overacted
   (C) trite
   (D) imaginative

2. Once very -------, computers are now found in almost every home.

   (A) common
   (B) unusual
   (C) obtainable
   (D) simple

3. After playing more than a dozen different concert halls, the orchestra was praised by critics for its ------- rendition of Beethoven's famous *Fifth Symphony*.

   (A) unimaginative
   (B) typical
   (C) moving
   (D) loud

4. Although Miles had been unable to sleep the night before, he seemed remarkably ------- when he gave his presentation.

   (A) worn
   (B) tired
   (C) presentable
   (D) alert

5. Julie was ------- to have been in the right place at the right time; the drama coach gave her the lead in our class play.

   (A) fortunate
   (B) inspired
   (C) dramatic
   (D) impressive

6. Mr. Jones is an intelligent and ------- teacher; his knowledge is matched only by his concern for his students.

   (A) caring
   (B) experienced
   (C) unusual
   (D) original

7. To the casual observer, all fingerprints may appear to be -------, but in fact, each individual's prints are unique.

   (A) different
   (B) complicated
   (C) personal
   (D) similar

8. Hardly one to -------, Josh tackled every project as soon as he got it.

   (A) strive
   (B) volunteer
   (C) procrastinate
   (D) disagree

9. In Charles Dickens's *A Christmas Carol*, Scrooge is a particularly ------- character, refusing to give his assistant, Bob Cratchit, a raise, despite his enormous wealth.

   (A) circumspect
   (B) miserly
   (C) generous
   (D) demure

10. Alfred Wegener's theory that the continents are slowly drifting apart has recently been confirmed by instruments that measure very small ------- in land masses.

   (A) locomotion
   (B) adhesion
   (C) punishment
   (D) erosion

11. Despite their seemingly ------- architecture, the pyramids of Giza are actually intricate marvels of ancient engineering.

(A) revolutionary
(B) complex
(C) archaic
(D) simplistic

12. Unlike animals, which must seek sustenance in their surrounding environment, plants are able to ------- their own food.

(A) find
(B) digest
(C) gather
(D) manufacture

13. Great variations in successive layers of polar ice make it possible for scientists to determine how the climate has ------- over the past millennium.

(A) migrated
(B) altered
(C) tended
(D) petrified

14. Because of the rigors of mountain climbing, the team needs equipment that is both ------- enough to support two members and completely reliable.

(A) weighty
(B) consistent
(C) sturdy
(D) innovative

15. For a student to qualify for the foreign study program, good language skills are absolutely necessary; however, prior travel to the host country is -------.

(A) inevitable
(B) mandatory
(C) plausible
(D) optional

16. The task was very ------- because certain parts needed to be carried out over and over again.

(A) standard
(B) enjoyable
(C) tiresome
(D) common

17. Because the ground there was steep and dangerous, the mountain guide told us that it was ------- to approach the edge.

    (A) encouraged
    (B) forbidden
    (C) important
    (D) possible

18. Most members of the drama club, though reserved in real life, are quite ------- once they get on stage.

    (A) dynamic
    (B) quarrelsome
    (C) threatening
    (D) behaved

19. Physicians offer recommendations about food groups and eating habits in order to help their patients follow a more ------- diet.

    (A) total
    (B) hearty
    (C) balanced
    (D) fulfilling

20. Fund-raising is effective only when ------- individuals are available, showing their concern by their readiness to give.

    (A) popular
    (B) famous
    (C) selfless
    (D) meaningful

21. Not one to be easily intimidated, the corporal remained ------- while the opposing army pressed toward his troop's position.

    (A) commanding
    (B) composed
    (C) aggressive
    (D) communicative

22. Unlike her confident companion, she tended to be ------- when she found herself among strangers.

    (A) lively
    (B) friendly
    (C) crowded
    (D) bashful

23. Although the rest of the class laughed at her antics, the teacher was ------- by Shelly's constant interruptions.

    (A) irked
    (B) amused
    (C) consoled
    (D) confused

24. To avoid being penalized for tardiness, you should be ------- with your assignments.

    (A) original
    (B) punctual
    (C) precise
    (D) thorough

25. Carpentry and cabinet-making are such difficult trades that they require great ------- with woodworking tools.

    (A) adeptness
    (B) alertness
    (C) awareness
    (D) assertiveness

26. One of the most ecologically diverse places on Earth, the tropical rain forests of Brazil are home to an incredible ------- of insect species.

    (A) size
    (B) collection
    (C) range
    (D) group

27. Higher math is a very ------- discipline; it requires just as much imagination and insight as do any of the arts.

    (A) logical
    (B) creative
    (C) new
    (D) surprising

28. Many tribes in New Guinea are known for their ------- societies; all property belongs to all members of the tribe.

    (A) primitive
    (B) communal
    (C) ancient
    (D) savage

29. Because their roots are external and their leaf bases clasp, palm trees are rigid and upright, yet ------- enough to bend in strong winds.

   (A) tropical
   (B) vibrant
   (C) elastic
   (D) flamboyant

30. Though some assert that all behavior is learned, there are others who hold that some behaviors are -------, existing before any learning occurs.

   (A) ostentatious
   (B) innate
   (C) durable
   (D) cultural

31. A very outgoing and ------- individual, the mayor loved to talk to her fellow citizens.

   (A) garrulous
   (B) majestic
   (C) classy
   (D) rambunctious

32. Staring wide eyed, the crowd was ------- by the magician's amazing feats of illusion.

   (A) rewarded
   (B) conjoined
   (C) stupefied
   (D) pleased

Check your answers in Chapter 17.

Use "Positive/Negative"

Sometimes you'll have trouble coming up with a word of your own. Don't sweat it; you can still eliminate answers.

> Gregor was a gifted violinist who was ------- about
> practicing, showing a dedication to his art that even
> surpassed his talent.

If you can't come up with an exact word, decide if it's good or bad. In the sentence above, is Gregor good about practicing or is he bad about practicing? Underline the clue that tells you, and put a little "+" sign if the word is good, and a "−" sign if the word is bad. (You can put an "n" if it's neither.) Gregor is good about practicing, so which of the following choices can you eliminate? We've marked whether they're positive or negative, so cross out the ones you know are wrong.

(A)	diligent	+
(B)	ornery	−
(C)	practical	+
(D)	ambivalent	n

Choices (B) and (D) cannot fit because they don't match what we know about the word in the blank (it's positive). So between (A) and (C), which best expresses the same thing as the clue? Choice (A). If you're not sure what *diligent* means, make a flash card for it. (And if you're not sure what to do with the flash card, get cracking on the Vocabulary chapter!)

PRACTICE DRILL 9—USING POSITIVE/NEGATIVE

Decide if the blank is positive, negative, or neutral. Try to come up with a word of your own, if you can.

1. Our manager was normally so _____ that it surprised everyone when he failed so badly on the test.

2. Frozen vegetables, though perhaps not as nutritious as fresh ones, can be a _____ way to get vitamins into a dietary plan.

3. The five-person team of adventurers almost _____ after ten grueling days in stormy weather.

4. David enjoyed the Matisse exhibit at the museum; Matisse is one of his _____ artists.

5. Petra was so _____ while giving her speech in front of the class that her stomach began to ache.

6. The Neanderthals of Krapina were _____ hunters, possessing great strength and prowess.

7. Mr. Lambert _____ the class for not studying enough for the science exam.

8. The two knights engaged in a _____ fight; it would not end until one of them lay dead on the ground.

9. If Wanda had a better sense of her accomplishments, she would stop making such _____ remarks about herself.

10. As their diet became enriched by energy-laden fat, the populations of early hunters _____ and spread throughout the plains.

PRACTICE DRILL 10—ELIMINATING BASED ON POSITIVE/NEGATIVE

Use your judgment on the sentences below to eliminate answers that cannot fit.

1. Our manager was normally so ------- that it surprised everyone when he failed so badly on the test.

   (A) successful
   (B) conceited
   (C) hateful
   (D) spiteful

2. Frozen vegetables, though perhaps not as nutritious as fresh ones, can be a ------- way to get vitamins into a dietary plan.

   (A) poor
   (B) inadequate
   (C) convenient
   (D) lenient

3. The five-person team of adventurers almost ------- after ten grueling days in stormy weather.

   (A) struggled
   (B) perished
   (C) paused
   (D) lapsed

4. David enjoyed the Matisse exhibit at the museum; Matisse is one of his ------- artists.

   (A) unusual
   (B) respected
   (C) unknown
   (D) cherished

5. Petra was so ------- while giving her speech in front of the class that her stomach began to ache.

   (A) loud
   (B) calm
   (C) anxious
   (D) relaxed

6. The Neanderthals of Krapina were
   ------- hunters, possessing great strength and prowess.

   (A) formidable
   (B) unsuitable
   (C) unstable
   (D) researched

7. Mr. Lambert ------- the class for not studying enough
   for the science exam.

   (A) congratulated
   (B) warned
   (C) chastised
   (D) corrected

8. The two knights engaged in a ------- fight; it would
   not end until one of them lay dead on the ground.

   (A) divided
   (B) humiliating
   (C) tenuous
   (D) perilous

9. If Wanda had a better sense of her accomplishments,
   she would stop making such ------- remarks about
   herself.

   (A) deprecating
   (B) indelicate
   (C) rebellious
   (D) fertile

10. As their diet became enriched by energy-laden fat,
    the populations of early hunters ------- and spread
    throughout the plains.

    (A) divided
    (B) congregated
    (C) thrived
    (D) restored

Check your answers in
Chapter 17.

Two-Blank Sentences—Upper Level Only

Two-blank sentences are usually longer than one-blanks. Does that mean they're harder? Nope. Actually, if you take two-blank sentences slowly, one blank at a time, they can be easier to get right! Check it out.

> Since Europe has been polluting its rivers, the ------- of many species of fish has been severely -------.

Take It Easy

As long as you approach two-blank sentence completions the way we've shown you, they'll be easier because you won't need to know all the vocabulary.

Cover your answers, and look for the clues and direction words. Which blank do you try first? Whichever is easier for you or whichever you have more information for, in the form of clues and direction words. For this example, let's go with the second blank, because we know something bad has been happening to the fish. How do we know? The clues are *polluting its rivers* and *severely*, and the direction word is *Since*, which keeps everything moving in the same direction. We can at least put a "−" sign next to the second blank. Now, when you uncover the answers to check them, only uncover the words for the blank you're working on. Don't even look at the words for the first blank here! You're only going to eliminate answers based on what cannot fit in the second blank.

(A) XXXX ... augmented
(B) XXXX ... observed
(C) XXXX ... approached
(D) XXXX .... threatened

You can eliminate (B) and (C), because they're not negative enough. Cross them out so you don't look at them again. Do you know what (A) means? If not, you can't eliminate it. Never eliminate words you don't know.

Now look back at the sentence and fill in a word or two for the first blank. What is it that can be negatively affected by pollution? Once you've got a word or two, look at the choices that are left for the first blank.

(A) acceptance ... augmented
(B) audacity ... observed
(C) equanimity ... approached
(D) habitat ... threatened

Which sounds better? You may have had a word like *environment* or *survival* filled in. Choice (D) definitely fits better than (A). Notice that if you didn't know what *augmented*, *audacity*, or *equanimity* meant, you could still get this question right. That's because on two-blank sentence completions, as soon as you eliminate a choice based on one of its words, the whole thing is gone—you never have to look at it again, and it doesn't matter what the other word in it is. (However, if *augmented*, *audacity*, or *equanimity* comes up in a one-blank sentence, you do need to know it to eliminate it—so make some flash cards for those words.)

Think of all the time you'd waste if you tried plugging the words for each choice into the sentence. You'd be reading the sentence four or five times! Plus, you'd find more than one choice that sounded okay, and you'd have nothing with which to compare them.

Two-blank sentence completions are your friends on the ISEE. Treat your friends right—do them one blank at a time, coming up with your own words.

PRACTICE DRILL 11—TWO-BLANK SENTENCE COMPLETIONS (UPPER LEVEL ONLY)

Cover the answers, underline the clues, circle the direction words, and come up with a word for one of the blanks. Eliminate answers based on that blank alone, and then go back up to the sentence to work on the other blank. Then, eliminate again.

1. Psychologists have long ------- the connection between violence on television and actual crime; the wealth of different ------- makes it very hard to reach a consensus.

   (A) found . . . facts
   (B) debated . . . opinions
   (C) agreed . . . articles
   (D) argued . . . criminals

2. Jason felt quite ------- about his ability to score well; he had studied ------- the night before.

   (A) frightened . . . thoroughly
   (B) happy . . . poorly
   (C) confident . . . diligently
   (D) resistant . . . lately

3. Although the pilot checked all his instruments before takeoff, the ------- of one of them almost caused the plane to -------.

   (A) malfunction . . . crash
   (B) misuse . . . land
   (C) safety . . . abort
   (D) refusal . . . fly

4. Her treatment of the subject was so ------- that the class was convinced she had only ------- the material the night before.

   (A) spotty . . . skimmed
   (B) thorough . . . misunderstood
   (C) partial . . . memorized
   (D) confused . . . learned

5. Communities need to work not ------, but
------; as a group, they can solve problems more
easily.

   (A)   in groups . . . communally
   (B)   at home . . . detached
   (C)   always . . . constantly
   (D)   in isolation . . . together

6. Despite the best efforts of his coach, Josh remained
------ in his ------ streak.

   (A)   mired . . . losing
   (B)   upbeat . . . winning
   (C)   free . . . consistent
   (D)   taken . . . sportsman

7. Due to the author's ------ handwriting, the typist had
a difficult time ------ the manuscript.

   (A)   perfect . . . transcribing
   (B)   careful . . . reading
   (C)   illegible . . . deciphering
   (D)   readable . . . translating

8. The maid, while appropriately ------ to the guests of
the hotel, was ------ with her employers.

   (A)   indifferent . . . curt
   (B)   submissive . . . pleasant
   (C)   obsequious . . . obstinate
   (D)   reliable . . . obedient

9. The owner is difficult to work for, less for her critical
and ------ nature than for her ------.

   (A)   exacting . . . procrastination
   (B)   perfect . . . assistance
   (C)   meticulous . . . encouragement
   (D)   carefree . . . complaints

10. Smithers hoped that the committee would not
------ a course of action that would ------ an already
bad situation in the workplace.

   (A)   relate . . . assist
   (B)   formulate . . . amend
   (C)   recommend . . . exacerbate
   (D)   present . . . mediate

Check your answers in
Chapter 17.

Text Complete Sentences—Lower Level Only

For text completions, you need to finish a sentence. This might seem hard, but it's not if you use common sense. The correct answer will follow the correct direction (same/opposite) and make sense in context. Let's try one:

> Even though Peter's mom said he wouldn't have
> dessert if he didn't clean his room, _____.
>
> (A)   he was unable to fall asleep that night
> (B)   she decided it was time to go on a diet
> (C)   he continued playing with his toys until dinner time
> (D)   she prepared a delicious and healthy salad

Which answer makes sense? Choice (C) does. The "even though" tells us that Peter didn't do what he was supposed to do. While (B) and (D) relate to food, they have nothing to do with dessert or Peter's room. Choice (A) is just weird.

Guess Aggressively When You've Worked on a Sentence

When you've narrowed a sentence completion down to two or three answers, it's probably because you don't know the vocabulary in some of those answers. Just take a guess and move on—you're not going to be able to divine the meanings of the words (and trust us, the proctor will not let you pull out a dictionary). You've increased your chances of getting the question right by eliminating one or two choices, and there's no guessing penalty, so fill in a bubble and move on.

When to Take a Guess

What if you come across a sentence that is so confusing that you can't even decide if the blank(s) should be positive or negative, much less come up with a word of your own? Don't waste your time on it. Just make sure you fill in your letter-of-the-day and move on.

If you have only a minute left, and you're not yet done, make sure you fill in your letter-of-the-day on all remaining questions.

> **Which Letter Should I Use?**
> No matter what you may have heard, it doesn't matter which letter you use to fill in answers for questions you don't work on. ERB tries to use letters in equal amounts.

Review—The Sentence Completions Plan

One-Blank Sentence Completions

For each and every sentence completion, the first thing I do is _____ the answers.

I look for the _____, and I mark it by _____ it.

I look for any _____ words, and I _____ them.

Then I _____.

If I have trouble coming up with a word for the blank, I decide if the blank is _____ or _____ (or neither).

Then I _____ choices and _____.

Two-Blank Sentence Completions—Upper Level Only

For each and every sentence completion, the first thing I do is _____ the answers.

I look for the _____, and I mark it by _____ it.

I look for any _____ words, and I _____ them.

If the sentence completion has two blanks, I do them _____.

Which blank do I try first? _____

I come up with a word for one of the blanks, and when I uncover the choices, I uncover only _____ and I eliminate based on those.

Then I go back to the sentence and _____ for the other blank, uncover the choices that are left, and eliminate.

Eliminating Choices and Guessing

Can I eliminate choices just because they contain words I do not know?

_____

What do I do if I can eliminate only one or two choices? _____

_____

What do I do if the sentence or the vocabulary looks so difficult that I can't come up with a word or decide if the blank is positive or negative? _____

_____

What do I spend my last minute on? _____

_____

Why should I never leave a question unanswered, even if I did not work on that question at all?
_____

If you have trouble answering any of these questions, go back and review the appropriate section of this chapter before going on.

PRACTICE DRILL 12—ALL SENTENCE COMPLETION TECHNIQUES

Upper level test takers should complete the entire drill. Others should stop after question 13.

1. One of the simple guidelines of public speaking is
    that good presentations require ------- preparation.

    (A) thorough
    (B) fretful
    (C) partial
    (D) solitary

2. Franklin D. Roosevelt was an effective -------, taking
    time out each week to speak to the people of the
    United States by radio in casual "fireside chats."

    (A) writer
    (B) warrior
    (C) communicator
    (D) legislator

3. Compared with Asia, the huge continent to its east,
    Europe is actually quite ------- in size, though not in
    its impressive and numerous cultural contributions.

    (A) mammoth
    (B) modest
    (C) irregular
    (D) predictable

4. Even though she was known to be quite outgoing, Janet could be ------- if she didn't know everyone in the room.

   (A) timid
   (B) extroverted
   (C) diverse
   (D) separate

5. Unlike the convex lens, which brings light rays together, the concave lens actually ------- light rays.

   (A) merges
   (B) dissolves
   (C) assists
   (D) spreads out

6. Usually cool and collected, the coach grew ------- when he saw his best player needlessly injured in the illegal play.

   (A) indifferent
   (B) furious
   (C) realistic
   (D) impatient

7. The ruler of the kingdom was known to be quite a -------; he was domineering and cruel to all his subjects.

   (A) leader
   (B) tyrant
   (C) democrat
   (D) highbrow

8. Most house fires can be avoided through such simple ------- as proper education and a well-placed fire extinguisher.

   (A) previews
   (B) presentations
   (C) precautions
   (D) preventions

9. The dishonest employee ------- his company, absconding with more than two thousand dollars' worth of supplies.

   (A) relieved
   (B) reported
   (C) swindled
   (D) demoted

10. Almost worse than the cast that covered it, the scar on Jennifer's leg was quite -------.

    (A) pleasant
    (B) ghastly
    (C) beneficial
    (D) ingenious

11. Theories of the origin of the universe are far from -------; after all, no one was around to witness the event.

    (A) hypothetical
    (B) plausible
    (C) credible
    (D) definitive

12. The situation called for ------- measures; the solution would not be simple and straightforward.

    (A) complex
    (B) unique
    (C) elementary
    (D) firsthand

13. The day was hardly a ------- one; everything that could possibly go wrong did.

    (A) reluctant
    (B) blithe
    (C) resistant
    (D) frenetic

14. Known for their ------- skills at goldsmithing, the Incas produced some of the most beautiful and ------- gold figurines of all time.

    (A) primitive . . expensive
    (B) early . . religious
    (C) expert . . intricate
    (D) novice . . strong

15. It is hard to imagine that so much modern machinery, from huge oil tankers, cars, and jet engines all the way down to ------- nuts, bolts, and screws, is made from ------- material: steel.

    (A) minuscule . . the same
    (B) tremendous . . the common
    (C) countless . . the perfect
    (D) flimsy . . the unique

16. Once a common and important means of -------,
    sailing has become more of a sport and a ------- than
    a primary way of getting around.

    (A) conveyance . . profession
    (B) transportation . . hobby
    (C) relaxation . . business
    (D) socialization . . vocation

17. Because he was the best at spelling, Michael was
    ------- to be our ------- at the county spelling bee.

    (A) assigned . . principal
    (B) picked . . treasurer
    (C) chosen . . representative
    (D) elected . . washout

18. Martha could no longer keep -------; with unusual
    -------, she spoke out passionately against the
    injustices at her school.

    (A) pace . . speed
    (B) quiet . . timidity
    (C) up . . facility
    (D) silent . . vigor

19. With a multitude of nationalities present, this campus
    is one of the most ------- and ------- in the whole
    country.

    (A) diverse . . fascinating
    (B) uniform . . tremendous
    (C) multifaceted . . bland
    (D) homogeneous . . ethnic

20. Standing on their feet and applauding, the audience
    was ------- the actor's ------- performance of Abe
    Lincoln in Illinois.

    (A) rebellious at . . fanatic
    (B) thrilled by . . weak
    (C) impressed with . . uninspired
    (D) electrified by . . marvelous

Check your answers in
Chapter 17.

Chapter 16
ISEE Reading

AN OPEN BOOK TEST

Keep in mind when you approach the Reading Section of the ISEE that *it is an open book test*. But you can't read the passages in advance of the test to prepare, and you have a limited amount of time to get through the passages and questions. What does this all mean? You will be much better served to take a *strategic* approach.

Read with a Purpose

When you read for school, you have to read everything—carefully. Not only is there no time for such an approach on the ISEE, but reading carefully at the outset does not even make sense. Each passage has only six questions (five for Lower Level), and all you need to read and process is the information that will provide answers to those questions. As only questions can generate points, your goal is to get to the questions as quickly as possible.

Even so, it does help to have a high-level overview of the passage before you attack the questions. There are two ways to accomplish this goal.

- If you are a fairly fast reader, get through the passage quickly, ignoring the nitty-gritty and focusing on the overall point of each paragraph.
- If you don't read quickly enough to read the entire passage in a way that will provide you with the overall point of the paragraphs, read the first sentence of each paragraph.

Once you have identified the point of each paragraph, those points will flow into the overall purpose of the passage and also provide a map of where to find detailed information. Once you have established the purpose and map, you should go right to the questions.

Answering Questions

Some questions are about particular parts of a passage, while others are about the passage as a whole. Depending on how well you understood the purpose of the passage, you may be able to answer big picture questions quite easily. Detail questions, on the other hand, will require some work; after all, you didn't get lost in the details when you got through the passage quickly!

> By reading more quickly up front, you have more time to spend on finding the answer to a particular question.

For a particular detail question, you will need to go back to the passage with the question in mind and *find the answer in the passage*. Let's repeat that last part: you should *find the answer in the passage*. If you know what the answer should look like, it is much easier to evaluate the choices. True, some questions cannot be answered in advance, such as "Which one of the following questions is answered in the passage?" But the general rule is *find the answer* before you go to the choices.

In all cases, you should use effective Process of Elimination. Correct answers are fully supported by the text of the passage. There is no reading between the lines, connecting the dots, or getting inside the author's head. If you are down to two answers, determine which one is not supported by the text of the passage. It takes only one word to doom an otherwise good answer.

In short, follow this process for detail questions:

- Read and understand the question.
- Go to the passage and *find the answer* (unless the question is too open-ended).
- Use Process of Elimination, getting rid of any answer that is not consistent with the answer you found and/or is not fully supported by the text of the passage.

We will look at some specific question types shortly, but if you follow the general approach outlined here, you will be able to answer more questions accurately.

Pacing

Let's amend that last statement: you will be able to answer more questions accurately if you have a sound pacing plan. While reading up front more quickly will generate more time for the questions, getting through all the passages and all the questions in the time allotted is difficult for almost all students.

There are six passages on the ISEE (five for Lower Level), some short and some quite long. Some might seem like fairly quick reads and some might seem a bit dense. They cover a broad array of topics, from history to science to fiction. You may relate to some passages but not to others. On top of that, if you are rushing through the section to make sure you answer every single question, you are likely making a lot of mistakes. Slow down to increase your accuracy.

How many passages should you do? That depends on you. You should attack as many passages as you can while still maintaining a high degree of accuracy. If, for example, dropping to five passages allows you to answer all but one or two questions correctly, while rushing through six creates a lot of silly mistakes, do five.

> Doing fewer passages accurately can generate more points than rushing through more passages.

Always pick your passages wisely. You don't get extra credit for answering questions on a more complex passage correctly. If you begin a passage and are thinking "Uh, what?" move on to another passage. You might end up coming back to the passage or you may never look at it again. What is most important is that you nail the easier passages before you hit the more complicated ones.

STEP ONE: READING THE PASSAGE

Let's put the new reading approach into practice.

Label the Paragraphs

After you read each paragraph, ask yourself what you just read. Put it in your own words—just a couple of words—and label the side of the paragraph with your summary. This way you'll have something to guide you back to the relevant part of the passage when you answer a question. The key to labeling the paragraphs is practice—you need to do it quickly, coming up with one or two words that accurately remind you of what's in the paragraph.

If the passage has only one paragraph, come up with a single label.

State the Main Idea

After you have read the entire passage, ask yourself two questions.

- "**What?**" What is the passage about?

- "**So what?**" What's the author's point about this topic?

The answers to these questions will show you the main idea of the passage. Scribble down this main idea in just a few words. The answer to "What?" is the thing that was being talked about: "bees" or "weather forecasting." The answer to "So what?" gives you the rest of the sentence: "Bees do little dances that tell other bees where to go for pollen" or "Weather forecasting is complicated by many problems."

Don't assume you will find the main idea in the first sentence. While often the main idea is in the beginning of the passage, it is not always in the first sentence. The beginning may just be a lead-in to the main point.

PRACTICE DRILL 1—GETTING THROUGH THE PASSAGE

As you quickly read each paragraph, label it. When you finish the passage, answer "What?" and "So what?" to get the main idea.

Line

1   Contrary to popular belief, the first European known to lay
2   eyes on America was not Christopher Columbus or Amerigo
3   Vespucci but a little-known Viking by the name of Bjarni
4   Herjolfsson. In the summer of 986, Bjarni sailed from Norway
5   to Iceland, heading for the Viking settlement where his father,
6   Heriulf, resided.

7   When he arrived in Iceland, Bjarni discovered that his father
8   had already sold his land and estates and set out for the latest
9   Viking settlement on the subarctic island called Greenland.
10   Discovered by a notorious murderer and criminal named
11   Erik the Red, Greenland lay at the limit of the known world.
12   Dismayed, Bjarni set out for this new colony.

13   Because the Vikings traveled without chart or compass, it was
14   not uncommon for them to lose their way in the unpredictable
15   northern seas. Beset by fog, the crew lost their bearings. When
16   the fog finally cleared, they found themselves before a land that
17   was level and covered with woods.

18   They traveled farther up the coast, finding more flat, wooded
19   country. Farther north, the landscape revealed glaciers and rocky
20   mountains. Though Bjarni realized this was an unknown land,
21   he was no intrepid explorer. Rather, he was a practical man
22   who had simply set out to find his father. Refusing his crew's
23   request to go ashore, he promptly turned his bow back out to
24   sea. After four days' sailing, Bjarni landed at Herjolfsnes on
25   the southwestern tip of Greenland, the exact place he had been
26   seeking all along.

"What" is this passage about? _____

"So what?" What's the author's point? _____

What type of passage is this? _____

Check your answers in Chapter 17 to be sure you're on the right track. You can find detailed explanations in your Student Tools.

STEP TWO: ANSWERING THE QUESTIONS

Now, we're getting to the important part of the Reading Comprehension section. This is where you need to spend time to avoid careless errors. After reading a passage, you'll have a group of questions that are in no particular order. The first thing you need to decide is whether the question you're answering is general or specific.

General Questions

General questions are about the passage as a whole. They come in a variety of forms but ideally all can be answered based on your initial read.

Main idea

- Which of the following best expresses the main point?
- The passage is primarily about
- The main idea of the passage is
- The best title for this passage would be

Purpose

- The purpose of the passage is
- The author wrote this passage to

Tone/attitude

- The author's tone is
- The attitude of the author is one of

Organization and Structure

- Which one of the following best describes the organization of the passage as a whole?
- Which one of the following best describes the organization of the second paragraph?

Notice that these questions all require you to know the main idea, but the ones at the beginning of the list don't require anything else, and the ones toward the end require you to use your map.

Answering a General Question

Keep your answers to "What? So what?" in mind. The answer to a general question will concern the main idea. If it helps, you can go back to your paragraph labels. The labels will allow you to look at the passage again without getting bogged down in the details.

- For a straight **main idea** question, just ask yourself, "What was the 'What? So what?' for this passage?"

- For a **general purpose** question, ask yourself, "Why did the author write this?"

- For a **tone/attitude question**, ask yourself, "How did the author feel about the subject?"

- For an **organization and structure question**, use your map for questions about the entire passage, and use Process of Elimination for questions about a paragraph.

Answer the question in your own words before looking at the choices. Eliminate answers that are not consistent with your predicted answer, as well as those that are too broad or too narrow. They should be "just right."

PRACTICE DRILL 2—ANSWERING A GENERAL QUESTION

Use the passage about Vikings that you just read and labeled. Reread your main idea and answer the following questions. Use the questions above to help you paraphrase your own answer before looking at the choices. When you're done, check your answers in Chapter 17. For more detailed explanations, go to your Student Tools.

1. This passage is primarily about

   (A) the Vikings and their civilization
   (B) the waves of Viking immigration
   (C) sailing techniques of Bjarni Herjolfsson
   (D) one Viking's glimpse of the New World

> What was the answer to "What? So what?" for this passage?

2. What was the author's purpose in writing this passage?

   (A) To turn the reader against Italian adventurers
   (B) To show his disdain for Eric the Red
   (C) To demonstrate the Vikings' nautical skills
   (D) To correct a common misconception about the European discovery of America

Specific Questions

Specific questions are about a detail or section of the passage. While the questions can be presented in a number of different ways, they boil down to questions about WHAT the author said, WHY the author said something, and Vocab-in-Context.

What?
- According to the passage/author
- The author states that
- Which of these questions is answered by the passage?
- The author implies in line X
- It can be inferred from paragraph X
- The most likely interpretation of X is

> Which answer is closest to what the author said overall?

Why?
- The author uses X to
- Why does the author say X?

Vocab-in-Context
- What does the passage mean by X?
- X probably represents/means
- Which word best replaces the word X without changing the meaning?
- As it is used in X, _____ most nearly means

> Why did the author write this passage? Think about the main idea.

Specific interpretation
- The author would be most likely to agree with which one of the following?
- Which one of the following questions is answered in the passage?

Once you have read and understood the question, go to the passage to find the answer. You should be able to find the answer quickly:

- Use your **paragraph labels** to go straight to the information you need.
- Use the **line or paragraph reference**, if there is one, but be careful. With a line reference ("In line 10…"), be sure to read the whole surrounding paragraph, not just the line. If the question says, "In line 10…," then you need to read lines 5 through 15 to actually find the answer.
- Use words that stand out in the question and passage. Names, places, and long words will be easy to find back in the passage. We call these **lead words** because they lead you back to the right place in the passage.

Once you're in the right area, answer the question in your own words. Then look at the choices and eliminate any that aren't like your answer or are not supported by the text of the passage.

For Vocab-in-Context questions, be sure to come up with your own word based on the surrounding sentences. It does not matter if you do not know the word being tested, as long as you can figure it out from context. Even if you do know the word, it may be used in an unusual way. So, always ignore the word and come up with your own before using Process of Elimination.

Questions with Special Formats

I, II, III questions   The questions that have three Roman numerals are confusing and time consuming. They look like this.

> According to the passage, which of the following is true?
>
> I.   The sky is blue.
> II. Nothing rhymes with "orange."
> III. Smoking cigarettes increases lung capacity.
>
> (A) I only
> (B) II only
> (C) I and II only
> (D) I, II, and III

On the ISEE, you will need to look up each of the three statements in the passage. This will always be time-consuming, but you can make them less confusing by making sure you look up just one statement at a time.

For instance, look at the question above. You might look back at the passage and see that the passage says I is true. Write a big "T" next to it. What can you eliminate now? (B). Now, you check out II, and you find that sure enough, the passage says that too. II gets a big "T" and you cross off (A). Next, looking in the paragraph that you labeled "smoking is bad," you find that the passage actually says that smoking decreases lung capacity. What can you eliminate? Choice (D).

You may want to skip a I, II, III question because it will be time-consuming, especially if you're on your last passage and there are other questions you can answer instead. If you skip it, remember to fill in your letter-of-the-day.

EXCEPT/LEAST/NOT Questions   This is another confusing type of question. The test writers are reversing what you need to look for, asking you which answer is false.

> All of the following can be inferred from the
> passage EXCEPT

Before you go any further, cross out "EXCEPT." Now, you have a much more positive question to answer. Of course, as always, you will go through all the choices, but for this type of question you will put a "T" or "F" next to the answers as you check them out. Let's say we've checked out these answers.

(A)   Americans are patriotic.   T
(B)   Americans have great ingenuity.   T
(C)   Americans love war.   F
(D)   Americans do what they can to help one another.   T

Which one stands out? The one with the "F." That's your answer. You made a confusing question much simpler than the test writers wanted it to be. If you don't go through all the choices and mark them, you run the risk of accidentally picking one of the choices that you know is true because that's what you usually look for on reading comp questions.

You should skip an EXCEPT/LEAST/NOT question if you're on your last passage and there are other questions you can try instead—just fill in your letter-of-the-day on your answer sheet.

PRACTICE DRILL 3—ANSWERING A SPECIFIC QUESTION

Use the passage about Vikings that you just read and labeled. Use your paragraph labels and the lead words in each question to get to the part of the passage you need, and then put the answer in your own words before going back to the choices.

1. According to the passage, Bjarni Herjolfsson left Norway to

   (A) found a new colony
   (B) open trading lanes
   (C) visit a relative
   (D) map the North Sea

   > What's the lead word here? *Norway. Norway* should also be in one of your labels.

2. Bjarni's reaction upon landing in Iceland can best be described as

   (A) disappointed
   (B) satisfied
   (C) amused
   (D) indifferent

   > What's the lead word here? *Iceland.* Again, this should be in one of your labels. Go back and read this part.

3. "The crew lost their bearings" probably means that

   (A) the ship was damaged beyond repair
   (B) the crew became disoriented
   (C) the crew decided to mutiny
   (D) the crew went insane

   > Go back and read this part. Replace the words they've quoted with your own.

4. It can be inferred from the passage that, prior to Bjarni Herjolfsson's voyage, Greenland

   (A) was covered in grass and shrubs
   (B) was overrun with Vikings
   (C) was rich in fish and game
   (D) was as far west as the Vikings had traveled

   > What's the lead word here? *Greenland.* Is it in one of your labels? What does that part of the passage say about Greenland? Paraphrase before looking at the answers!

5. With which of the following statements about Viking explorers would the author most probably agree?

   (A) Greenland and Iceland were the Vikings' final discoveries.
   (B) Viking explorers were cruel and savage.
   (C) The Vikings' most startling discovery was an accidental one.
   (D) Bjarni Herjolfsson was the first settler of America.

   > Check your answers in Chapter 17. For more detailed explanations, go to your Student Tools.

STEP THREE: PROCESS OF ELIMINATION

Before you ever look at an choice, you've come up with your own answer, in your own words. What do you do next?

Well, you're looking for the closest answer to yours, but it's much easier to eliminate answers than to try to magically zoom in on the best one. Work through the answers using Process of Elimination. As soon as you eliminate an answer, cross off the letter in your test booklet so that you no longer think of that choice as a possibility.

How Do I Eliminate Choices?

On a General Question

Eliminate an answer that is:

- Too small. The passage may mention it, but it's only a detail—not a main idea.
- Not mentioned in the passage.
- In contradiction to the passage—it says the opposite of what you read.
- Too big. The answer tries to say that more was discussed than really was.
- Too extreme. An extreme answer is one that is too negative or too positive, or uses absolute words like *all*, *every*, *never*, or *always*. Eliminating extreme answers makes tone/attitude questions especially quick.
- Going against common sense. The passage is not likely to back up answers that just don't make sense at all.

On a Specific Question

Eliminate any choice that is:

- Too extreme
- In contradiction to passage details
- Not mentioned in the passage
- Against common sense

If you look back at the questions you did for the Viking passage, you'll see that many of the wrong choices fit into the categories above.

On a Tone Question
Eliminate any choice that is:

- Too extreme
- Opposite meaning
- Against common sense. These are answers that make the author seem confused or uninterested—an ISEE author won't be either.

What Kinds of Answers Do I Keep?
Best answers are likely to be:

- Paraphrases of the words in the passage
- Traditional and conservative in their outlook
- Moderate, using words like *may*, *can*, and *often*

When You've Got It Down to Two
If you've eliminated all but two answers, don't get stuck and waste time. Keep the main idea in the back of your mind and step back.

- Reread the question.

- Look at what makes the two answers different.

- Go back to the passage.

- Which answer is worse? Eliminate it.

REVIEW—THE READING PLAN

The Passages

After I read each paragraph, I _____ it.

After I read an entire passage, I ask myself _____? and _____?

The Questions

The five main types of general questions, and the questions I can ask myself to answer them, are:

_____   _____

_____   _____

_____   _____

_____   _____

_____   _____

To find the answer to a specific question, I can use three clues.

_____

_____

_____

If the question says "in line 22," where do I begin reading for the answer?

_____

The Answers

On a general question, I eliminate answers that are:

_____

_____

_____

_____

_____

On a specific question, I eliminate answers that are:

_____

_____

_____

_____

When I've got it down to two possible answers, I should:

_____

_____

_____

If you had any trouble with these questions, reread this section of the chapter before going further.

Check your answers in Chapter 17. For more detailed explanations, go to your Student Tools.

PRACTICE DRILL 4—ALL READING TECHNIQUES—LOWER LEVEL

Line

1　　The term "tides" has come to represent the cyclical rising
2　　and falling of ocean waters, most notably evident along the
3　　shoreline as the border between land and sea moves in and out
4　　with the passing of the day. The primary reason for this constant
5　　redefinition of the boundaries of the sea is the gravitational
6　　force of the moon.
7　　　　This force of lunar gravity is not as strong as Earth's own
8　　gravitational pull, which keeps our bodies and our homes from
9　　being pulled off the ground, through the sky, and into space
10　　toward the moon. It is a strong enough force, however, to exert
11　　a certain gravitational pull as the moon passes over Earth's
12　　surface. This pull causes the water level to rise (as the water is
13　　literally pulled, ever so slightly, toward the moon) in those parts
14　　of the ocean that are exposed to the moon and its gravitational
15　　forces. When the water level in one part of the ocean rises, it
16　　must naturally fall in another, and this is what causes water
17　　level to change, dramatically at times, along any given piece of
18　　coastline.

1.　Which one of the following is the most obvious
　　effect of the tides?

　　(A) A part of the beach that was once dry is now
　　　　under water.
　　(B) Floods cause great damage during heavy
　　　　rainstorms.
　　(C) The moon is not visible.
　　(D) Water falls.

2.　The word "lunar" most nearly means

　　(A) weak
　　(B) strong
　　(C) destructive
　　(D) related to the moon

3. It can be inferred from the passage that if one were to travel to the moon

    (A) that water would be found on its surface
    (B) that an object, if dropped, would float away from the surface of the moon
    (C) that tides are more dramatic during the day than during the night
    (D) that an object, if dropped, would fall to the moon's surface

4. The author's primary purpose in writing this passage is to

    (A) prove the existence of water on the moon
    (B) refute claims that tides are caused by the moon
    (C) explain the main cause of the ocean's tides
    (D) argue that humans should not interfere with the processes of nature

Check your answers in Chapter 17. For more detailed explanations, go to your Student Tools.

PRACTICE DRILL 5—ALL READING TECHNIQUES— LOWER LEVEL

Line

1   The Brooklyn Bridge in New York has been featured in
2   movies, photographs, and media for over a hundred years, but
3   the bridge is much more than just a pretty sight. It opened on
4   May 24, 1883, and, at 3,460 feet, it was the longest suspension
5   bridge in the world, measuring 50% longer than any previously
6   built. The Brooklyn Bridge was a symbol of American strength
7   and vitality, but its completion followed years of toil and
8   sacrifice.
9   John Augustus Roebling, a German immigrant, envisioned
10   the bridge that would link Manhattan to Brooklyn over the
11   East River. While in preparations for building, however, John
12   Roebling was injured when a ferry pinned his foot to a pylon,
13   and he died weeks later of tetanus. This first setback to the
14   building of the bridge was indicative of the problems that would
15   plague its construction as well as the harrowing tenacity that led
16   to its completion.
17   Washington Roebling took over the project upon his father's
18   death. Washington persevered through many hurdles in the
19   building of the bridge including fires, accidents, industrial
20   corruption, and loss of public support. He continued, however,
21   in his push to complete the bridge. In fact, it is said that he
22   worked harder and longer than any worker he employed in
23   even the most dangerous circumstances. While working in
24   the caissons, underwater chambers that supported the bridge,
25   he was stricken by the decompression sickness that led to his
26   paralysis. Nothing could stop him, though, and he continued
27   construction by sending messages to the site through his wife,
28   Emily.
29   Fourteen years after construction began, the Brooklyn
30   Bridge celebrated its grand opening. The total cost to build the
31   bridge was fifteen million dollars, and 27 people died in its
32   construction, but it stood as a tribute to American invention and
33   industry.

1.   The primary purpose of the passage is to

(A)   convince the reader that the Brooklyn Bridge
      is the longest suspension bridge in the world

(B)   describe Washington Roebling's rise to
      success

(C)   show that Americans have an inborn talent
      for inventiveness

(D)   describe how the Brooklyn Bridge was a
      great success despite the hardships faced in
      building it

2. It can be inferred from the third paragraph that Washington Roebling

   (A) was injured by a ferry
   (B) was determined to build the bridge despite many setbacks
   (C) suffered from depression after his injury
   (D) had a son who completed the building of the bridge

3. Which one of the following is given as a difficulty faced in building the Brooklyn Bridge?

   (A) An excessive number of pylons in the East River
   (B) An outbreak of tetanus among the workers
   (C) The death of the man who envisioned the bridge
   (D) A lack of funds to keep building

4. Washington Roebling can best be described as

   (A) persistent
   (B) weak
   (C) clumsy
   (D) dangerous

5. Which of the following is NOT stated about the Brooklyn Bridge?

   (A) It was a sign of American power.
   (B) It cost millions of dollars to build.
   (C) It was not worth the money lost in building it.
   (D) It has been seen in the movies.

Check your answers in Chapter 17. For more detailed explanations, go to your Student Tools.

PRACTICE DRILL 6—ALL READING TECHNIQUES—ALL LEVELS

Line

1   Immediately following the dramatic end of World War II
2   came a realization that the United States now had to turn its
3   attention inward. Years of fighting battles around the globe had
4   drained the country of important resources. Many industries
5   (such as housing) suffered, as both materials and workers
6   were used elsewhere in the war effort. Once the soldiers began
7   returning, it became clear that new jobs and new homes were
8   among their biggest needs. The homes needed to be affordable,
9   since few people had the time or ability to save much during the
10   war.
11   It was in this situation that many house developers saw a
12   business opportunity. Amid such a pressing demand for new
13   homes, developer William Levitt realized the need for a new
14   method of building. He sought a way to build homes cheaper
15   and faster than ever before.
16   He wasn't the only developer to realize this, but he was one
17   of the best in making it happen. He applied the same ideas to
18   homes that Henry Ford had used 50 years earlier in making
19   cars. Levitt did not build a factory with an assembly line of
20   fully formed homes rolling out of some giant machine. Instead,
21   he adapted the assembly line formula into a system in which
22   the workers, rather than the product, moved for a streamlined,
23   efficient building process.
24   Previously, a developer who completed four homes a year
25   had been moving at a good pace. Levitt planned to do that
26   many each week, and succeeded. He created specialized teams
27   that focused on only one job each and moved up and down the
28   streets of new homes. Teams of foundation-builders, carpenters,
29   roofers, and painters worked faster by sticking to just one task
30   as they moved, factory-style, from house to house. The time
31   and money saved allowed Levitt to build cheap homes of good
32   value.
33   With this new approach, Levitt oversaw the building of some
34   of the first towns that would eventually be called suburbs—
35   planned communities outside the city. Some critics blame
36   developers like Levitt for turning farmland into monotonous,
37   characterless towns. However, most agree that his contribution
38   to the country following a bitter war was mostly positive. He
39   did vary the style of home from street to street, and his work
40   on simpler home features was influenced by the work of
41   architecture great Frank Lloyd Wright.

Line

42   In the end, Levitt's success speaks for itself. After his first

43   success—building thousands of homes in Long Island, New

44   York—he went on to found several more "Levittowns" in

45   Pennsylvania, New Jersey, and elsewhere. Levitt gave home

46   buyers what they wanted: nice pieces of land with nice homes

47   on top. In a way, by creating houses that so many families could

48   afford, William Levitt made the American dream a more

49   affordable reality.

1.   The primary purpose of the passage is to

(A) discuss the final days of World War II

(B) suggest that suburban housing is unaffordable

(C) describe one person's contribution to an industry

(D) prove that the economy changed after World War II

2.   Which of the following statements about William Levitt is best supported by the passage?

(A) He invented the word "suburb."

(B) He was unconcerned with the appearance of the homes he built.

(C) His homes were built in Ford-style factories.

(D) His efficient methods helped make homes more affordable.

3.   Which of the following best describes Levitt?

(A) Courageous patriot

(B) Strict businessman

(C) Ground-breaking entrepreneur

(D) Financial mastermind

4.   It can be inferred from the passage that

(A) Levitt was the only developer working in New York following World War II

(B) Levitt and Henry Ford created homes the same way

(C) other developers did not know how to use the concept of assembly line construction

(D) Levitt built homes much faster than was customary before World War II

5. The passage mentions all of the following
    as reasons for the postwar housing demand
    EXCEPT the

    (A) destruction of American homes during
        the war
    (B) difficulty of saving money during the war
    (C) search for new jobs and new homes by
        returning soldiers
    (D) use of home-building materials elsewhere
        during the war

6. The passage suggests that a potential drawback to
    "assembly-line style" houses is that they can be

    (A) hard to sell
    (B) not very sturdy
    (C) similar-looking
    (D) horrible for the environment

Check your answers in Chapter 17. For more detailed explanations, go to your Student Tools.

PRACTICE DRILL 7—ALL READING TECHNIQUES— ALL LEVELS

Line

1   Etymology, the study of words and word roots, may sound

2   like the kind of thing done by boring librarians in small, dusty

3   rooms. Yet etymologists actually have a uniquely interesting

4   job. They are, in many ways, just like archeologists digging up

5   the physical history of people and events. The special aspect

6   of etymology is that it digs up history, so to speak, through the

7   words and phrases that are left behind.

8   The English language, in particular, is a great arena in which

9   to explore history through words. As a language, English has an

10   extraordinary number of words. This is in part due to its ability

11   to adapt foreign words so readily. For example, "English" words

12   such as *kindergarten* (from German), *croissant* (from French),

13   and *cheetah* (from Hindi) have become part of the language

14   with little or no change from their original sounds and spellings.

15   So English language etymologists have a vast world of words

16   to explore.

17   Another enjoyable element of etymology for most word

18   experts is solving word mysteries. No, etymologists do not

19   go around solving murders, cloaked in intrigue like the great

20   fictional detective Sherlock Holmes. What these word experts

21   solve are mysteries surrounding the origin of some of our most

22   common words.

23   One of the biggest questions English language experts have

24   pursued is how English came to have the phrase *OK*. Though it

25   is one of the most commonly used slang expressions, its exact

26   beginning is a puzzle even to this day. Even its spelling is not

27   entirely consistent—unless you spell it *okay*, it's hard even to

28   call it a word.

29   Etymologists have been able to narrow *OK*'s origin down to

30   a likely, although not certain, source. It became widely used

31   around the time of Martin Van Buren's run for president in

32   1840. His nickname was Old Kinderhook. What troubles word

33   experts about this explanation is that the phrase appeared in

34   some newspapers before Van Buren became well known. As a

35   result, it's unlikely that Van Buren could be called its primary

36   source. Like bloodhounds following a faint scent, etymologists

37   will doubtless keep searching for the initial source. However, it

38   is clear that *OK*'s popularity and fame have exceeded those of

39   the American president to whom it has been most clearly linked.

1. It can be inferred from the second paragraph that English vocabulary

    (A) is easy to learn for speakers of other languages
    (B) can claim many sources
    (C) has a longer history than that of many other languages
    (D) affects American politics

2. The author mentions the words "kindergarten," "croissant," and "cheetah" most likely because

    (A) they are words with unknown origins
    (B) etymologists dispute words like these
    (C) they represent words that are similarly spelled and spoken in two languages
    (D) English speakers find them difficult to pronounce

3. According to the passage, etymologists are

    (A) investigators of word history
    (B) lovers of vocabulary words
    (C) scientists of the five senses
    (D) archeologists of extinct languages

4. Which of the following best states the purpose of the fourth and fifth paragraphs?

    (A) To illustrate another non-English word
    (B) To define the phrase "OK"
    (C) To show an interesting aspect of etymology
    (D) To compare American phrases

5. The primary purpose of the passage is to

    (A) provide information about the English language
    (B) discuss enjoyable aspects of the study of words
    (C) show that language plays an important role in politics
    (D) describe the origin of the phrase "OK"

Check your answers in Chapter 17. For more detailed explanations, go to your Student Tools.

PRACTICE DRILL 8—ALL READING TECHNIQUES—UPPER LEVEL

Line

1   Bob Dylan was born on May 24, 1941 in Duluth, Minnesota,
2   but his name wasn't Dylan. He was born Robert Allen
3   Zimmerman, one of two sons born to Abraham and Betty
4   Zimmerman. Nineteen years later, he moved to New York
5   City with his new name and a passion to pursue his dream of
6   becoming a music legend.
7   Bob Dylan's career began like those of many musicians.
8   He began to play in New York City at various clubs around
9   Greenwich Village. He began to gain public recognition as a
10   singer/songwriter and was even reviewed by the *New York Times*
11   his first year in New York. He signed his first record deal with
12   Columbia Records a mere ten months after moving to New
13   York. From that point on, his career skyrocketed.
14   What is unique about Bob Dylan, given his huge success, is
15   his vocal quality. Dylan's singing voice was untrained and had
16   an unusual edge to it. Because of this, many of his most famous
17   early songs first reached the public through versions by other
18   performers who were more immediately palatable. Joan Baez
19   was one of these musicians who performed many of Dylan's
20   early songs. She furthered Dylan's already rising performance
21   career by inviting him onstage during her concerts, and many
22   credit her with bringing Dylan to his vast level of national and
23   international prominence.
24   In his career, which spans more than four decades, Dylan
25   has produced 500 songs and more than 40 albums. This king
26   of songs has thirteen songs on *Rolling Stone* magazine's Top
27   500 Songs of All Time, including his most famous song, "Like
28   a Rolling Stone," which tops the list. In 2004, Bob Dylan was
29   ranked second in *Rolling Stone* magazine's 100 Greatest Artists
30   of All Time, surpassed only by the Beatles.
31   In a recent television interview, Bob Dylan was asked why
32   he became a musician. He replied that from a very early age, he
33   knew it was his destiny to become a music legend. Certainly,
34   that destiny has been realized!

1. Which of the following best states the main idea of the passage?

   (A) The beginning of Bob Dylan's music career is similar to the beginnings of the careers of most other musicians.
   (B) It is extremely important to follow your dreams.
   (C) Bob Dylan never really knew what he wanted to be in life.
   (D) Bob Dylan had great success despite his unusual style of singing.

2. The word "prominence" at the end of the third paragraph most nearly means

   (A) perception
   (B) status
   (C) obviousness
   (D) protrusion

3. The passage most strongly supports which of the following statements about Joan Baez?

   (A) She was jealous of Bob Dylan's superior vocal training.
   (B) She grew up in Minnesota.
   (C) She has performed more of Bob Dylan's songs than of her own.
   (D) She helped Bob Dylan to become a music legend.

4. The phrase "king of songs" near the beginning of the fourth paragraph refers to

   (A) Bob Dylan's prolific nature as a singer/songwriter
   (B) Bob Dylan's ownership of *Rolling Stone* magazine
   (C) how most musicians regarded Bob Dylan as a king
   (D) Bob Dylan's perception of himself

5. Which of the following is best supported by the passage?

   (A) Bob Dylan has two brothers.
   (B) Bob Dylan was reviewed by Columbia Records his first year in New York.
   (C) "Like a Rolling Stone" is considered by some to be the best song of all time.
   (D) Without Joan Baez, Bob Dylan would never have succeeded.

Check your answers in Chapter 17. For more detailed explanations, go to your Student Tools.

PRACTICE DRILL 9—ALL READING TECHNIQUES— MIDDLE AND UPPER LEVELS

Line

1   It is easy to lose patience with science today. The questions
2   are pressing: How dangerous is dioxin? What about low-
3   level radiation? When will that monstrous earthquake strike
4   California? And why can't we predict weather better? But the
5   evidence is often described as "inconclusive," forcing scientists
6   to base their points of view almost as much on intuition as on
7   science.
8   When historians and philosophers of science listen to these
9   questions, some conclude that science may be incapable of
10   solving all these problems any time soon. Many questions seem
11   to defy the scientific method, an approach that works best when
12   it examines straightforward relationships: If something is done
13   to variable A, what happens to variable B? Such procedures
14   can, of course, be very difficult in their own ways, but for
15   experiments, they are effective.
16   With the aid of Newton's laws of gravitational attraction, for
17   instance, ground controllers can predict the path of a planetary
18   probe—or satellite—with incredible accuracy. They do this
19   by calculating the gravitational tugs from each of the passing
20   planets until the probe speeds beyond the edge of the solar
21   system. A much more difficult task is to calculate what happens
22   when two or three such tugs pull on the probe at the same time.
23   The unknowns can grow into riddles that are impossible to
24   solve. Because of the turbulent and changing state of the earth's
25   atmosphere, for instance, scientists have struggled for centuries
26   to predict the weather with precision.
27   This spectrum of questions—from simple problems to those
28   impossibly complex—has resulted in nicknames for various
29   fields of study. "Hard" sciences, such as astronomy and
30   chemistry, are said to yield precise answers, whereas "soft"
31   sciences, such as sociology and economics, admit a great degree
32   of uncertainty.

1. Which of the following best tells what this passage is about?

    (A)   How the large variety of factors some scientists deal with makes absolute scientific accuracy impossible

    (B)   How Newton solved the problem of accuracy and science

    (C)   How "hard" science is more important than "soft" science

    (D)   Why science now uses less and less conclusive evidence

2. According to the passage, it can be inferred that the scientific method would work best in which of the following situations?

    (A)   Predicting public reactions to a set of policy decisions

    (B)   Identifying the factors that will predict a California earthquake

    (C)   Predicting the amount of corn that an acre will yield when a particular type of fertilizer is used

    (D)   Calculating how much a cubic centimeter of water will weigh when cooled under controlled conditions

3. The author suggests that accurately predicting the path of a planetary probe is more difficult than

    (A)   forecasting the weather

    (B)   determining when an earthquake will occur

    (C)   predicting economic behavior

    (D)   determining the gravitational influence of one planet

4. According to the passage, "hard" science can be distinguished from "soft" science by which of the following characteristics?

    (A)   Finding precise answers to its questions

    (B)   Identifying important questions that need answers

    (C)   Making significant contributions to human welfare

    (D)   Creating debates about unresolved issues

5. The author implies that when confronted with complex questions, scientists base their opinions

    (A)   on theoretical foundations

    (B)   more on intuition than on science

    (C)   on science and intuition, in varying degrees

    (D)   on experimental procedures

Check your answers in Chapter 17. For more detailed explanations, go to your Student Tools.

Chapter 17
Answers and
Explanations for
ISEE Practice Drills

ISEE MATH

Practice Drill 1—Lower Level

1. **D** List the factors of 24: 1 and 24, 2 and 12, 3 and 8, and 4 and 6. This totals 8 different factors of 24. The correct answer is (D).

2. **D** Since 12 is a factor of a certain number, Plug In for that certain number. For instance, Plug In 36 since 12 is a factor, and use POE. 2 and 6 are factors of 36, but they are not the only factors of 36 listed in the choices. Eliminate (A). Similarly, 3 and 4 are not the only factors of 36 listed, so eliminate (B). 12 is a factor, but it is not the only factor listed, so eliminate (C). Choice (D) contains all the other factors listed in previous choices. The correct answer is (D).

3. **B** A multiple of 3 will be 3 times a number. 2 is not a multiple of 3, so eliminate (A). 3 × 2 = 6, so keep (B). 10 and 14 are not divisible by 3, and therefore cannot be multiples of 3. The correct answer is (B).

4. **C** The question asks which number is NOT a multiple of 6. 6 × 2 = 12 and 6 × 3 = 18, so (A) and (B) are multiples. 6 does not divide evenly into 23, so keep (C). 6 × 4 = 24 and 6 × 7 = 42 so (D) can be eliminated. The correct answer is (C).

5. **D** The question is essentially asking for a number that is divisible by both 3 and 5. 10, 20, and 25 are all divisible by 5, but not by 3. Eliminate (A), (B), and (C). 45 ÷ 3 = 15 and 45 ÷ 5 = 9, so 45 is divisible by both 3 and 5. The correct answer is (D). Remember, you can also use the divisibility rules for 3 and 5 to help with this question! All the numbers end in either 5 or 0, so they are all divisible by 5. However, only (D) has digits that add up to a number divisible by 3.

6. **B** Use long division to find the remainder of 1,024 divided by 9. The remainder is 7, so add 2 to the total to make the number be divisible by 9. The correct answer is (B). Alternatively, you can use the divisibility rule for 9—the sum of the digits is divisible by 9. 1 + 0 + 2 + 4 = 7, so if 2 is added to that, the sum is 9, which is divisible by 9. Remember, the question asks for the *smallest* number that can be added to 1,024.

7. **D** Use PITA to solve this question. Since the question asks for *the square of the largest of the five consecutive integers*, label the choices as such. Then, start with (C) to get rid of choices more effectively. If 49 were the square of the largest integer, the integer would be 7, and other consecutive integers would be 6, 5, 4, and 3. The sum of these numbers 3 + 4 + 5 + 6 + 7 = 25, which is less than 30. Therefore, eliminate (A), (B), and (C), since these are too small. Try (D): the square root of 64 is 8, and the other integers would therefore be 7, 6, 5, and 4. 4 + 5 + 6 + 7 + 8 = 30, so the correct answer is (D).

8. **C** Since the question is asking for a specific amount and has real numbers in the choices, one way to solve this problem is to use PITA to test the answers, starting with (C). 75,000 × 6 = 450,000, which works. The correct answer is (C). Alternatively, you can translate the words. *How many times as great as* means divide the two numbers, so $\dfrac{\text{profit in 1992}}{\text{profit in 1972}} = \dfrac{450,000}{75,000} = 6$.

9. **B** Use PITA since the question is asking for a specific value and there are real numbers in the choices. The question asks for Joanne's portion of the furniture, which is one-third of the total. Start with (C): 6 × 3 = 18, which is too large. Eliminate (C) and (D). Try (B): 4 × 3 = 12, which works. The correct answer is (B).

10. C   Since the question asks for a specific value, use PITA to answer the question, starting with (C). The choices represent the amount of oil in the tank now, which is one-third of the total amount. Choice (C) is 30: is 30 one-third of the total amount (90 gallons) the tank holds? $30 = \frac{1}{3}(90)$ is true, so the correct answer is (C).

11. D   Ginger sleeps $\frac{3}{4}$ of each day. To find how many days she sleeps over the course of four days, multiply: $\frac{3}{4} \times 4$. Simplify to solve: $\frac{3 \times 4}{4} = \frac{12}{4} = 3$. The correct answer is (D).

12. A   To find the greatest value, use the choices and ballpark wherever possible to help. Choice (A) is close to 1, so use this as a comparison point. Choice (B) is smaller, since it is less than $\frac{1}{2}$. Pay attention to the division sign in (C): $\frac{1}{12} \div \frac{1}{3} = \frac{1}{12} \times \frac{3}{1} = \frac{3}{12}$, which is also less than $\frac{1}{2}$. In (D), multiply the fractions: $\frac{3}{4} \times \frac{1}{3} = \frac{3 \times 1}{4 \times 3} = \frac{3}{12}$, which is equal to (C) and therefore less than $\frac{1}{2}$. The greatest value is (A).

13. C   Rearrange these values by grouping together fractions with like denominators: $\frac{1}{2} + \frac{1}{2} = 1, \frac{2}{3} + \frac{1}{3} = \frac{3}{3} = 1$, and $\frac{3}{4} + \frac{1}{4} = \frac{4}{4} = 1$. Then add the whole numbers: $1 + 1 + 1 = 3$. The correct answer is (C).

14. D   When multiplying by a factor of 10, simply move the decimal point to the right for each zero. In this case, you are multiplying by 1,000, so move the decimal point to the right 3 places for the three zeros in 1,000. The decimal 0.34 becomes 340, which is closest to 350. The correct answer is (D).

15. C   The question is testing knowledge of decimal places. The answer should not have multiplication in it, so eliminate (A). Eliminate (D) as well since it does not have 2 included. In the number 2.398, 0.3 is equivalent to $\frac{3}{10}$, 0.09 to $\frac{9}{100}$, and 0.008 to $\frac{8}{1,000}$. This correlates to (C), which is the correct answer.

Practice Drill 2—Middle and Upper Levels

1. A   Since 4 is not a prime number and no multiple of 4 will be prime either, there will not be any numbers in common. Therefore, the correct answer is (A).

2. B   First, list all the factors of 24: 1 and 24, 2 and 12, 3 and 8, 4 and 6. Next, list all the factors of 81: 1 and 81, 3 and 27, 9 and 9. The only factors that 24 and 81 have in common are 1 and 3, so there are two factors in common. The correct answer is (B).

3. D   Use PITA here to find the correct answer. Usually, you would start with (B) or (C), but notice that finding $\frac{1}{4}$ (i.e., 25%) of either of these numbers will create a fraction. Try (D): Find $\frac{1}{4}$ of $40: $\frac{1}{4}(40) = \frac{40}{4} = 10$. If the tip was $10 and the price of the dinner was $40, then the total was $50. Since this matches the total in the problem, stop here. The correct answer is (D).

4. **B** First, since there are fewer multiples of 7, list the multiples of 7 from 1–99. The multiples are 7, 14, 21, 28, 35, 42, 49, 56, 63, 70, 77, 84, 91, and 98. The multiples that would also be multiples of 2 would be the even numbers: 14, 28, 42, 56, 70, 84, and 98. This is a total of 7 numbers. The correct answer is (B).

5. **B** Remember, with exponents, you can write it out! $2^3 = 2 \times 2 \times 2$ and $2^2 = 2 \times 2$, so you have $(2 \times 2 \times 2) \times (2 \times 2 \times 2) \times (2 \times 2)$. Count up the number of 2s that you have, which is 8, and make that number the new exponent: 2^8. The correct choice is (B). Alternatively, you can use MADSPM: when multiplying the same base, add the exponents. Simply add $3 + 3 + 2 = 8$. The answer will be 2^8.

6. **B** Use PITA to plug in the choices for m, starting with (C). Plug 3 in for m: $2(3) + 4 = 10$ and $3^3 = 27$, which are not equal. Since 3 is too large, eliminate (C) and (D). Next try (B): $2(2) + 4 = 8$ and $2^3 = 8$. Since this works, stop here. The correct answer is (B).

7. **D** First, solve for x and then find what the question is asking: $x + 10$. Start with $6x - 4 = 38$. Add 4 to each side, and $6x = 42$. Divide by 6 on each side to find that $x = 7$. Now plug 7 into $x + 10$ to find that $7 + 10 = 17$. The correct answer is (D).

8. **D** Let the choices help here. Since the number must be greater than 50, eliminate (A) and (B). 51 is not a multiple of 7, so eliminate (C). 56 is a multiple of 7 and is the only remaining choice. Therefore, the correct answer is (D).

9. **D** For word problem questions, translate the words to their math equivalents: if 4 (the students who chose recycling) is equal to one-fifth of the students in the class, then $4 = \dfrac{1}{5} \times n$, where n is the number of students in the class. To solve, multiply both sides by 5, and $n = 20$. There are 20 students in the class. The correct choice is (D).

10. **A** To find a percentage, find the portion the question asks for out of the total. First, find the total of all the grains: 60 bushels of corn + 20 bushels of wheat + 40 bushels of soybeans = 120 total bushels. The question asks for the percent of corn, so $\dfrac{\text{corn}}{\text{total}} = \dfrac{60}{120} = \dfrac{1}{2}$, which is equal to $\dfrac{50}{100}$, or 50%. The correct answer is (A).

11. **C** To find percent change, use this formula: % change $= \dfrac{\text{difference}}{\text{original}} \times 100$. The difference here is $45 - $30 = $15, and the item was originally $45, so $\dfrac{15}{45} \times 100$. This reduces to $\dfrac{1}{3} \times 100$. To solve, $\dfrac{1 \times 100}{3} = \dfrac{100}{3} = 33\dfrac{1}{3}$%. The correct answer is (C).

12. **C** Use Ballparking! 19.95 is roughly 20, and 35% is close to $\dfrac{1}{3}$, so $\dfrac{1}{3}$ of 20 is between 6 and 7. Eliminate (D) since it is too big. Choices (A) and (B) are too small, so that leaves (C) as the closest. The correct answer is (C).

13. **A** To find percent change, use this formula: % change $= \dfrac{\text{difference}}{\text{original}} \times 100$. The original value is $50 and the final value is $20, so the difference is $30. $\dfrac{30}{50} \times 100$ reduces to $\dfrac{3}{5} \times 100 = \dfrac{3 \times 100}{5} = \dfrac{300}{5} = 60$. The correct answer is (A).

14. **B**   Take this question in bite-sized pieces. If four friends each pay $5 for a pizza, the pizza costs $4 \times 5 = \$20$. Therefore, if a fifth friend joins, then $5 \times p = \$20$. Divide both sides by 5, and each friend pays $4. The correct answer is (B).

15. **C**   The perimeter is all the sides added together. The sides of a square are all equal, so divide 56 by 4 to find that each side has a length of 14. The correct answer is (C).

16. **A**   An equilateral triangle has equal sides. Therefore, if one side has a length of 4, all sides have a length of 4. Add all the sides to find the perimeter: $4 + 4 + 4 = 12$. The correct answer is (A).

More Practice: Upper Level Only

17. **A**   If $b° = 45°$, the other angle must also be $45°$ since $180° - 90° - 45° = 45°$, which makes this an isosceles right triangle. Therefore, the other leg of the triangle is also 4. From here, use the Pythagorean Theorem to find v^2: $4^2 + 4^2 = v^2$. Simplify the left side of the equation to get $16 + 16 = 32$. The correct answer is (A). Be careful here. Notice that the question is asking for v^2, not just v.

18. **B**   Translate this question into math: *one-half of* something means to multiply by $\frac{1}{2}$, *difference between* means to subtract, *degrees in a square* is $360°$, and *degrees in a triangle* is $180°$. Thus, the equation will be $\frac{1}{2}(360 - 180)$. Simplify to get $\frac{1}{2}(180) = 90$. The correct answer is (B).

19. **C**   Since the question asks for a specific value, use PITA to answer this question, starting with (C). If the side length of a square is 4, its perimeter is 16 because $4 + 4 + 4 + 4 = 16$ and its area is also 16 because $4^2 = 16$. Since those are equal, stop here. The correct answer is (C).

20. **D**   First find the area of the rectangle with a width of 4 and length of 3: $A = l \times w = 3 \times 4 = 12$. The area of the triangle is also equal to 12, so $A = \frac{1}{2}bh = 12$. Plug in the given value for the base: $\frac{1}{2}(6)h = 12$. Simplify to find that $3h = 12$, and then divide both sides by 3. The height must be 4, so the correct answer is (D).

21. **B**   First, find the volume of the box that has all dimensions known. $V = lwh$, so $V = 3 \times 4 \times 10 = 120$. Since the other box has the same volume, $120 = 6 \times 4 \times h$. $120 = 24h$, so $h = 5$. The correct answer is (B).

22. **D**   Use the formula for the area of a square: $A = s^2$. If $A = 64p^2$, then to find the side length of the square, take the square root: $\sqrt{64} = 8$. Eliminate (A) and (C) since both choices have 64. For the square root of p^2, you can plug in for p. Pick an easy number like 2. If $p = 2$, then $p^2 = 4$. So $\sqrt{p^2} = \sqrt{4} = 2$, which means your answer should equal 2 when you plug in for p. Choice (B) has p^2, which would be 4, so eliminate (B). Choice (D) has p, which is 2. This matches, so the correct answer is (D).

23. **D**   The length of AB is the same as all the different heights added together on the right-hand side of the figure. Therefore, the perimeter will contain two lengths of 10. Similarly, the length of AC is the same as all the different lengths added together that are across the figure (in this case, above AC), so there will be two lengths of 15. To find the perimeter, add all the sides: $P = 10 + 10 + 15 + 15 = 50$. The correct answer is (D).

24. **C**   Notice the three triangles that have been created within the rectangle. Look at the two right triangles that surround the larger (possibly) equilateral triangle in the middle. Since each triangle has a right angle, the other two angles must equal 90° since 180° − 90° = 90°. Thus, in the triangle on the left side that includes side AB, $w + x = 90°$, and in the triangle on the right side that includes side CD, $y + z = 90°$. Add all these together to find that 90° + 90° = 180°. The correct answer is (C).

25. **D**   Notice that the part that juts out on the left side of the shape would fit into the indented part on the right side of the shape. Filling in the hole would make a rectangle with a length of 8 and a width of 4 + 3 + 4 = 11. To find the area of a rectangle, use the formula: $A = l \times w$. Therefore, $A = 8 \times 11 = 88$. The correct answer is (D).

26. **B**   The length of police tape wrapping around a rectangle is the same as the perimeter. Draw a rectangle and label the length as 28 and the width as 6. Remember, in a rectangle, opposite sides are equal to each other. Calculate the perimeter by adding all the sides: 6 + 6 + 28 + 28 = 68. The correct answer is (B).

27. **D**   To find the distance between two points, draw a right triangle and use the Pythagorean Theorem. Draw a line straight down from point B and directly right from point A. That point will be (7,1), which you can label C. The distance from A to C is 6, and the distance from C to B is 8. Use the Pythagorean Theorem to find the missing side: $6^2 + 8^2 = c^2$. Simplify the left side to get 36 + 64 = 100. Take the square root of both sides to get $c = 10$. The correct answer is (D).

28. **B**   Even though the length of the radius is unknown, it is still possible to find the angle measurements. There is a 90° angle in the center of the circle, and both OQ and OP are radii of the circle, which means they are the same length. Therefore, this is an isosceles right triangle, meaning the two smaller angles are congruent. All triangles have 180°, so 180° − 90° = 90°. The two smaller angles add up to 90°, so $\dfrac{90°}{2} = 45°$. The correct answer is (B).

29. **D**   Notice that the four intersecting lines form a quadrilateral. All quadrilaterals contain 360°, so keep a tally of the vertices and find the missing angle. 80° is already provided, so 360° − 80° = 280°. All straight lines add up to 180°, so use the exterior angles to find the interior angles. If one of the exterior angles is 75°, the supplementary angle must be 105°. Subtract this from 280° to find that 280° − 105° = 175°. The other exterior angle, 108°, is opposite the interior vertex. Since opposite angles are equal, the interior vertex must also be 108°. Subtract this from the current total to find that 175° − 108° = 67°. The missing angle is 67°. The correct answer is (D).

30. **C**   The question states that triangle ABC is equilateral, so all 3 sides are equal to 4. Label AC as 4 and BC as 4. The question asks for perimeter, not area. So, there are two sides of the triangle that are part of the perimeter, so add them together: $AB + BC = 4 + 4 = 8$. Eliminate (A) and (B) since the choice must have an 8 in it. Now, find the rounded portion. The rounded portion is half of the circumference (i.e., a semicircle). Since you labeled BC as 4, you should see that the diameter of the circle must also be 4. If $C = \pi d$, then half of the circumference is $\dfrac{1}{2}\pi d$. Plug in the value for the diameter and simplify: $\dfrac{1}{2}\pi(4) = 2\pi$. The full expression for the perimeter will then read $8 + 2\pi$. The correct answer is (C).

31. **D** Break the trapezoid into two triangles and a rectangle. Next, figure out the missing segment lengths. If $MN = 8$, then $QP = 8$. That means that $20 - 8 = 12$, which is what LQ and PO must total. If each segment were the same, then $LQ = 6$ and $PO = 6$ since $\frac{12}{2} = 6$. Next, find out QM and PN. You may notice that these are 6-8-10 right triangles. Otherwise, use the Pythagorean Theorem to find the height of the triangles: $6^2 + b^2 = 10^2$. Solve for b: $36 + b^2 = 100$; subtract 36 from both sides to get $b^2 = 64$. Then take the square root of both sides, and $b = 8$. To find the area of the triangles, plug in the base and height into the formula for the area of a triangle: $A = \frac{1}{2}bh = \frac{1}{2}(6)(8) = 24$. There are two triangles, so $24 + 24 = 48$. Eliminate (A) since you haven't finished finding the area of the whole trapezoid yet. The rectangle $QMNP$ is actually a square since all sides equal 8. To find the area of a square, use the formula: $A = s^2 = 8^2 = 64$. Finally, add the areas: (2 triangles) + (1 square) = $48 + 64 = 112$. The correct answer is (D).

Practice Drill 3—Ratios

1. **C** When the question asks about ratios, make a Ratio Box. The ratio of single rooms to doubles to triples is 3:4:5, so label the boxes and place this ratio in the top row. Add $3 + 4 + 5$ to find the total for the room types is 12. Put 12 in the total column for the ratio row. The question states that there are 36 total rooms in the hotel, so this number goes in the total column for the actual number row. 12 times what equals 36? Since $12 \times 3 = 36$, the multiplier is 3. Find the number of doubles by multiplying: $4 \times 3 = 12$. The correct answer is (C).

	SINGLES	DOUBLES	TRIPLES	TOTAL
Ratio	3	4	5	12
Multiplier	× 3	× 3	× 3	× 3
Actual	9	12	15	36

2. **C** This question gives information about the total number of players first, so place this information in the bottom row and add 8 and 4 to find the total for the actual number row. Be careful to order the ratio in the way the question asks. There are more right-handed players, so the first number should be the bigger of the two numbers. Eliminate (A) and (B)! Next, divide out the largest possible common denominator, in this case 4, to find the most reduced form of the ratio. That means the ratio of right-handed players to left-handed players is 2:1. The correct answer is (C). Note: if you chose (A), you set up the ratio box backwards, showing left-handed players to right-handed players. Read carefully!

	RIGHT-HANDED	LEFT-HANDED	TOTAL
Ratio	2	1	3
Multiplier	× 4	× 4	× 4
Actual	8	4	12

3.   C   The ratio of goat food to grass is 2:1, so place this in the ratio row of the box. The question also states that the goat eats 15 total pounds per day, so place this number in total column of the actual number row. To find the multiplier, find the total of the ratio, 2 + 1 = 3, and find what times 3 equals 15. 3 × 5 = 15, so the multiplier is 5. The question asks for the total amount of grass the goat eats, so 1 × 5 = 5. The correct answer is (C).

	GOAT FOOD	GRASS	TOTAL
Ratio	2	1	3
Multiplier	× 5	× 5	× 5
Actual	10	5	15

Practice Drill 4—Averages

1.   A   Use an Average Pie to solve this question: . Place 3 in the *# of items* and 18 in for the *average*. Multiply these numbers to find the total, which is 54. The question asks for twice the sum, which is the same as twice the total, so 2 × 54 = 108. The correct answer is (A).

2.   B   Use two Average Pies to organize the information in this question—every time you see the word *average* draw an Average Pie . The first pie represents the information about the boys: 4 boys average 2 projects each, so place 4 in the *# of items* place and 2 in the *average* place. To find the total number of projects the boys complete, multiply 4 and 2 to find a total of 8 projects. Repeat this same process with the girls in the second pie. The 5 girls average 3 projects each, so place these numbers in their respective places in the Average Pie, and multiply to find a total of 15 projects. The question asks for the total number of projects in the class, so 8 + 15 = 23. The correct answer is (B).

3.   A   First, add the three scores to find Catherine's current point total. 84 + 85 + 88 = 257. Next, make an Average Pie with 4 in the *# of items* place since there will be a fourth test, and 89 as the desired *average*. Multiply 4 × 89 to find a total of 356. Subtract the totals to find that 356 − 257 = 99. This means that she must score a 99 on the fourth test to raise her average to an 89. The correct answer is (A).

4.   A   Use two Average Pies to organize the information in this question—every time you see the word *average* draw an Average Pie . There are 6 students with an average test score of 72. Place 6 in the *# of items* place and 72 in the *average* place. Find the total number of points by multiplying 6 × 72 = 432. Make a separate Average Pie for the next portion of the question. If a seventh student joins the class, the *# of items* place now contains 7, and the desired *average* is 76. Multiply these together to find that 7 × 76 = 532. The difference between 532 and 432 is 100, so the seventh student must score 100 to change the average to 76. The correct answer is (A).

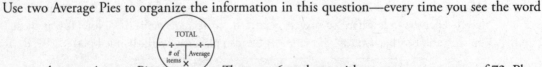

More Practice: Lower Level

5.   **A**   Use an Average Pie to solve this question: . List the number of donuts Anna ate each day: Monday = 2, Tuesday = 4, Wednesday = 2, Thursday = 4, Friday = 2, Saturday = 0, and Sunday = 0. The question asks for the average number of donuts she ate over the course of all 7 days, so add all the donuts she ate: 2 + 4 + 2 + 4 + 2 + 0 + 0 = 14. Put 14 in the *total* spot in your Average Pie. The *# of items* is 7 since the question asks about the whole week. Finally, divide these two numbers to get the average: $\frac{14}{7}$ = 2. The correct answer is (A).

6.   **B**   When you see the word *average*, draw an Average Pie . To find the average for the whole trip, find the total number of miles: 240 mi + 350 mi = 590 mi. Put 590 in the *total* part of the Average Pie. Then find the total number of hours Merry drove: 4 hrs + 7 hrs = 11 hrs. 11 will go in the *# of items* spot. Next, divide to find the average: $\frac{590}{11}$. To save yourself some time, remember to ballpark! Notice that the result will not be a whole number, so the correct answer must be (B).

7.   **D**   To find the profit, find the total amount of ticket sales and then subtract the expenses the school had for stage production and advertising. Since the show sold out, all 300 seats were purchased. If each seat cost $6, then the sales total was 300 × 6 = 1,800. Subtract the expenses from the total sales to find the net profit: 1,800 – (550 + 250) = 1,800 – 800 = 1,000. The correct answer is (D).

More Practice: Middle and Upper Levels

8.   **C**   Use two Average Pies to organize the information in this question—every time you see the word *average* draw an Average Pie .The question states that *Michael scored an average of 24 points over his first 5 basketball games*. Therefore, place 24 in the *average* place of the pie, and 5 in the *# of items* place. Multiply these numbers together to find that Michael scored a total of 120 points over the five games. To find how many points he must score on his sixth game to bring his average up to 25, use the second Average Pie to plug in the given information. Write 6 in the *# of items* place of to account for all six games, and 25 in the *average* place since that's the desired average. Multiply these numbers to find he must score a total of 150 points over the entire 6 games. The difference between 150 and 120 is 30, so Michael must score 30 points in the sixth game to raise his average to 25. The correct answer is (C).

9. **B** Even though this problem doesn't use the word *average*, you can still use Average Pies to help solve this question. The problem gives information about the weekly amount of rain, but the question asks about the *daily amount* instead. The daily amount will be the average (i.e., the amount of rain per day). Place 245 in the *total* spot of the first Average Pie and 7 in the *# of items* place. That gives you an average of $\frac{245}{7} = 35$, which is the average daily amount for the current year. Do the same for the previous year in a second Average Pie. This time, 196 goes in the *total* spot and 7 goes in the *# of items* place. That equals an average of $\frac{196}{7} = 28$. The question asks for *how many more inches*, so you will need to subtract the two daily amounts of rain: $35 - 28 = 7$. The correct answer is (B).

10. **C** Since the question mentions the mean, create an Average Pie. Joe wants to have an average of 230 or more, so place 230 in the *average* spot of the pie. In the *# of items* place, write in 5 because he has already read 4 books that were 200, 200, 220, and 260 pages long, and he is going to read one more. Multiply to find the total number of pages he must read: $5 \times 230 = 1{,}150$. He has already read $200 + 200 + 220 + 260 = 880$ pages, so find the difference between these two totals to see how many pages long the fifth book must at least be: $1{,}150 - 880 = 270$. The correct answer is (C).

Practice Drill 5—Percent Change

1. **D** The question is testing percent change since it asks *by what percent did the temperature drop*? To find percent change, use this formula: $\%\text{ change} = \frac{\text{difference}}{\text{original}} \times 100$. The change in temperature was 20°: $10° - (-10°) = 20°$. Since the question asks for the percent the temperature *dropped*, the *larger* number will be the original number. Thus, the equation should read $\frac{20}{10} \times 100$, which reduces to $2 \times 100 = 200$. The correct answer is (D).

2. **C** The question is testing percent change since it asks *by what percent did the patty increase*? To find percent change, use this formula: $\%\text{ change} = \frac{\text{difference}}{\text{original}} \times 100$. The change in patty size is 4, which is given in the question. The new patty size is 16 oz, so the original patty size must have been 12 oz since $16 - 4 = 12$. The equation will read $\frac{4}{12} \times 100$, which reduces to $\frac{1}{3} \times 100 = \frac{100}{3} = 33\frac{1}{3}$. The correct answer is (C).

Practice Drill 6—Plugging In

1. **B**   This is a Plugging In question because there are variables in the choices and the question stem contains the phrase *in terms of*. Plug In a value, work through the problem to find a target answer, and then check each of the choices to see which yields the target answer. For instance, Plug In $x =$ $3. The question asks for the total amount of money donated, so $3 \times 200 = 600$. $600 is the target answer. Now, plug 3 into the choices for x to see which choice matches your target answer (600). Eliminate (A) because $\frac{3}{200}$ is way too small. Choice (B) works because $200(3) = 600$. Eliminate (C) because $\frac{200}{3}$ is too small. Eliminate (D) because $200 + 3$ or $203 \neq 600$. The correct answer is (B).

2. **D**   This is a Plugging In question because there are variables in the choices. Plug In a value, work through the problem to find a target answer, and then check each of the choices to see which yields the target answer. For instance, Plug In 6 for d dollars. If 10 magazines cost $6, then $3 would buy 5 magazines—you spend half as much money, so you can get only half as many magazines. So 5 is the target answer. Now, plug 6 into the choices to see which answer yields 5, the target answer. Eliminate (A) because $\frac{3 \times 6}{10} = \frac{18}{10} = 1.8$ does not equal 5. Eliminate (B) because $30(6)$ is way too large. Choice (C) is a fraction, $\frac{6}{30} = \frac{1}{5}$, so it will not equal 5. Choice (D) works, as $\frac{30}{6} = 5$, so keep this choice. The correct answer is (D).

3. **C**   This is a Plugging In question because there are variables in the choices and the question stem contains the phrase *in terms of*. Plug In a value, work through the problem to find a target answer, and then check each of the choices to see which yields the target answer. *The zoo has four times as many monkeys as lions*, so, for instance, Plug In 40 for the monkeys, which translates to $4 \times$ lions $= 40$, so there are 10 lions. *There are four more lions than zebras*, which means that $10 - 4 = 6$ zebras, so $z = 6$. The question asks *how many monkeys are there in the zoo*, so the target answer is 40. Now, plug 6 into the choices for z to see which choice matches your target answer (40). Eliminate (A) because $4 \times 6 = 24$ is not equal to 40. Eliminate (B) because $6 + 8 = 14$ is still too small. Since $4(6) + 16 = 40$, keep (C). Remember to try all four choices when Plugging In, so check (D) as well. $4(6) + 4 = 28$, which is too small, so eliminate (D). The correct answer is (C).

More Practice: Lower Level

4. **B** This is a Plugging In question because there are variables in the choices and the question stem contains the phrase *in terms of.* Plug In a value, work through the problem to find a target answer, and then check each of the choices to see which yields the target answer. For instance, say that $y = 10$ pairs of earrings. The total amount of money for 6 pairs of earrings would be $6 \times 10 = 60$, which is the target answer. Now, plug 10 into the choices for y to see which choice matches your target answer (60). Eliminate (A) because $6 + 10 = 16$, which does not equal 60. Keep (B) because $6(10) = 60$. Remember to check the remaining choices when Plugging In. 6^{10} is a very large number, much greater than 60, so eliminate (C). Eliminate (D) as well because $6 + 6(10) = 66$, which does not equal 60. The correct answer is (B).

5. **B** This is a Plugging In question because there are variables in the choices. Plug In a value, work through the problem to find a target answer, and then check each of the choices to see which yields the target answer. For instance, say that p pieces of candy is equal to 5 pieces, and c cents is 10 cents. Therefore, 10 pieces of candy will cost 20 cents—you have twice as many pieces, so it will cost twice as much money. So, the target answer is 20. Now, Plug In your values for p and c into the choices to find the choice that equals your target answer (20). Eliminate (A) because $\dfrac{5 \times 10}{10} = \dfrac{50}{10} = 5$, which is too small. $\dfrac{10 \times 10}{5} = \dfrac{100}{5} = 20$, so keep (B). Remember to check the remaining choices when Plugging In. $\dfrac{10 \times 5}{10} = \dfrac{50}{10} = 5$, so eliminate (C) as well. Cross off (D) because $10(5)(10) = 500$, which is way too large. The correct answer is (B).

More Practice: Middle Level

6. **C** In this question, J is an odd integer, so Plug In an odd integer for J. Since this is a *must be* question, see if there is a number that would make the answer untrue. Plug In 1 for J to make (A) untrue, since $\dfrac{1}{3}$ is not greater than 1. This number for J will also eliminate (B) since $1 - 2 = -1$, which is not a positive integer. Choice (C) is true since $2 \times 1 = 2$, which is an even integer. Eliminate (D) since J could be negative. For example, if $J = -3$, -3 is not greater than 0. Check that value for (C) to be sure it always works. Again, if $J = -3$, then $2 \times -3 = -6$, which is still an even integer. Since it always works, the correct answer is (C).

7. **C** When there are percents or fractions without a starting or ending value in the question stem, feel free to Plug In. What number would make the math easy? 8 is a common denominator for $\dfrac{1}{4}$ and

$\frac{1}{2}$, so draw a picture of a fruit tart and divide it into 8 equal parts. Shade in the number of pieces she has eaten. On Monday, she ate $\frac{1}{2}$ of the pie, so $\frac{1}{2}$ of 8 is $\frac{4}{8}$ or 4 slices, leaving 4 slices for later. The next day, she ate $\frac{1}{4}$ of what was left. $\frac{1}{4}$ of 4 slices is 1, so she ate 1 slice. There are now 3 out of 8 slices left. Beware of choosing (A), however! The question asks how much she ate, so add up the slices she consumed. There should be 5 slices shaded (4 + 1 = 5), so the correct answer is (C).

More Practice: Middle and Upper Levels

8. C   When there are percents or fractions without a starting or ending value in the question stem, feel free to Plug In. For instance, Plug In $100 for the starting price of the suit. It is *reduced by 20%*, so 20% of $100 is equal to $\frac{1}{5}(100) = \frac{100}{5} = 20$. That is the amount the suit is reduced. Subtract that from $100 to find the resulting price: $100 – $20 = $80. The suit is then *reduced by 10%*, so 10% of $80 is $\frac{10}{100}(80) = \frac{1}{10}(80) = \frac{80}{10} = 8$. Subtract this from $80 to find the final price of the suit: $80 – $8 = $72. The final price is $72. The *final price is what percent off of the original* is another way of asking the *final price is what percent less than the original*. So, use the percent change formula: % change $= \frac{\text{difference}}{\text{original}} \times 100$. The difference is $100 – $72 = 28. The original price was $100. Therefore, $\frac{28}{100}(100) = 28$. The correct answer is (C).

9. C   Try Plugging In values that satisfy the question stem, and eliminate choices. It may be necessary to Plug In twice on *must be true* or *always true* questions. If m is an even number, let $m = 2$, and let $n = 3$ since it must be an odd integer. If p is the product of m and n, then $p = (2)(3) = 6$. Now check the choices. Eliminate (A) because p is not a fraction. Eliminate (B) as well since p is not an odd integer. Keep (C) because 6 is divisible by 2. Finally, keep (D) because 6 is greater than zero. Plug In again to compare the remaining choices. Perhaps keep one number the same, so $n = 3$, but make $m = -2$ instead of 2. Now $p = (-2)(3) = -6$. Choice (C) still works since –6 is divisible by 2, but (D) no longer works since p is less than zero. Since it is always true, the correct answer is (C).

More Practice: Upper Level

10. B   Since there are variables in the choices, Plug In a value for p, paying attention to the restrictions in the question. If p is an odd integer, make sure to Plug In an odd integer, for instance $p = 3$. Now, test the choices to see which one can be eliminated. Cross off (A) because $(3)^2 + 3 = 9 + 3 = 12$, which is not odd. Choice (B) works since 2(3) + 1 = 6 + 1 = 7, which is odd. Choice (C) works since $\frac{3}{3} = 1$. Choice (D) does not work since 3 – 3 = 0. Remember 0 is even, not odd. Plug In a second time for the

remaining choices. Try $p = 5$. Choice (B) still works because $2(5) + 1 = 10 + 1 = 11$, but eliminate (C) because $\dfrac{5}{3}$ is no longer an integer. The correct answer is (B).

11. **B** The wording on this problem is tricky: it asks for which CANNOT be true, so try to find examples that COULD be true to eliminate choices. Pay attention to the restrictions in the problem, and Plug In two positive even integers: say 4 and 6. Thus, $4 + 6 = 10 = m$. Next, eliminate choices that WORK. Choice (A) does not work since 10 is greater than 5. Keep it. Choice (B) does not work because $3(10) = 30$, which is even, not odd. Keep it. Eliminate (C) because $m = 10$, which is even, so it works. Eliminate (D) as well because 10^3 ends in a zero, which is also even, so this statement works. Now, Plug In a second time for the remaining choices. Try new numbers, and remember that the numbers do not have to be distinct from one another. Try Plugging In 2 for both positive even integers. Thus, $2 + 2 = 4 = m$. Check the remaining answers and eliminate the choices that WORK. For (A), 4 is less than 5. That works, so eliminate (A). For (B), $3(4) = 12$, which does not work since it's even, so keep it. The only choice left is (B), which is the correct answer.

12. **D** This is a Plugging In question because there are variables in the choices and the question stem contains the phrase *in terms of*. Plug In a value, work through the problem to find a target answer, and then check each of the choices to see which yields the target answer. For instance, Plug In 20 for Anthony. Since Anthony has *twice as many baseball cards as Keith*, Keith has $\dfrac{1}{2}$ the number of cards that Anthony has. Therefore, Keith must have 10 cards, and $k = 10$. Keith has *one-third as many baseball cards as Ian*, so Ian has 3 times as many as Keith has: $10 \times 3 = 30$, or 30 cards. Together, Anthony and Ian have $20 + 30 = 50$. So, 50 is the target answer. Now, Plug In 10 for k to find which choice yields 50, your target answer. Eliminate (A) because $\dfrac{3 \times 10}{2} = \dfrac{30}{2} = 15$, not 50. Eliminate (B) because $\dfrac{6 \times 10}{2} = \dfrac{60}{2} = 30$ is still too small. Choice (C) is still too small, as $\dfrac{8 \times 10}{2} = \dfrac{80}{2} = 40$. Choice (D) works because $\dfrac{10 \times 10}{2} = \dfrac{100}{2} = 50$. The correct answer is (D).

13. **D** This is a Plugging In question because there are variables in the choices. Plug In a value, work through the problem to find a target answer, and then check each of the choices to see which yields the target answer. Let $b = 4$ and $a = 3$. Finding the *product* means multiply, so $\dfrac{1}{2}(4) \times 3^2 = 2 \times 9 = 18$. The target answer is 18. Now, Plug In your values for b and a into the choices to find the choice that equals your target answer (18). Eliminate (A) since $(3 \times 4)^2 = (12)^2 = 144$, which is too big. Eliminate (B) since $\dfrac{3^2}{4} = \dfrac{9}{4}$ and is not equal to 18. Also eliminate (C) since $2(3) \times \dfrac{1}{2}(4) = 6 \times 2 = 12$, which does not equal 18. Choice (D) works: $\dfrac{3^2 \times 4}{2} = \dfrac{9 \times 4}{2} = \dfrac{36}{2} = 18$. Keep it. The correct answer is (D).

14. **D** Use MADSPM to simplify the exponents in the equations first. When raising a power to a power, multiply the exponents together. For the first equation, $\left(x^3\right)^3 = x^{3\times3} = x^9$, so $a = 9$. When dividing by the same base, subtract the exponents. For the second equation, $\dfrac{y^{10}}{y^2} = y^{10-2} = y^8$, so $b = 8$. The question asks to find $a \times b$, so $9 \times 8 = 72$. The correct answer is (D).

15. **B** Since the question involves averages, use the Average Pie. However, save yourself some time by reading carefully! Notice that the classes have an equal number of students donating money. Because of this, simply Plug In values for the averages since it doesn't matter how many actual students are donating money from each class. You only need values for the average of each class, so start there. Those two averages will become the numbers for your total in the next part of the problem. For instance, Plug In $3 as the average, y, for Mr. Greenwood's class, and $5 for z, the average for Ms. Norris's class. Add these two numbers to find the total amount of money donated $(3 + 5 = 8)$, and put 8 in the *total* spot. There are 2 classes donating money, so the *# of items* is 2. Find the average by dividing: $\dfrac{8}{2} = 4$. The target answer is 4. Now, Plug In 3 for y and 5 for z to find which choice yields 4, the target answer. Eliminate (A) because $\dfrac{5}{3} \neq 4$. Choice (B) works because $\dfrac{3+5}{2} = \dfrac{8}{2} = 4$. Eliminate (C) because $3 + 5 \neq 4$. Finally, eliminate (D) because $2(3 + 5) = 2(8) = 16$, which is way too large. The correct answer is (B).

16. **C** First, simplify the first expression: $(3xy)^3 = 3^3x^3y^3 = 27x^3y^3$. While comparing it to the other expression, $3x^2y^5$, you can work in bite-sized pieces. Start with the coefficients: the greatest common factor of 3 and 27 is 3. Eliminate (A) and (D) since those don't contain 3. Both of the remaining answers contain x^2, so compare y in the two expressions. One has $y^3 = y \times y \times y$ and the other has $y^5 = y \times y \times y \times y \times y$. The greatest common factor is y^3 since both expressions have at least 3 y's. Eliminate (B). The correct answer is (C).

Practice Drill 7—Plugging In The Answers

1. **B** The question is asking for a specific value and there are real numbers in the choices, so use PITA to solve. Ted can read 60 pages per hour, which is 60 pages in 60 minutes, and Naomi can read 45 pages in 60 minutes. Combined, they can read 105 pages $(60 + 45)$ in 60 minutes. Now, start with one of the middle choices to see which answer will yield a total of 210 pages. Try (B) since if they read for 120 minutes, they will read double the amount they did in 60 minutes. That will make the math easy. In 60 minutes they read 105 pages, so $105 \times 2 = 210$. This satisfies the question, so (B) is correct.

2. **B** The question is asking for a specific value and there are real numbers in the choices, so use PITA to solve, starting with (C). The choices represent how much Sara pays. If Sara pays $30 and she pays twice as much as John, then John would have paid $15 since $\frac{1}{2} \times 30 = 15$. Paul paid three times as much as Sara, so he would have paid $3 \times 30 = 90$. This added together is more than $90, so eliminate (C) and (D), as these will amount to a total that is too much. Try (B): if Sara paid $20, John would have paid $10 since $\frac{1}{2} \times 20 = 10$. Paul paid $3 \times 20 = 60$. Add these amounts together to find that $20 + $10 + $60 = $90, which satisfies the question. The correct answer is (B).

3. **D** First, translate the English into math and then use PITA to test the choices. *Four less than a certain number* translates to $n - 4$, and two-thirds of a number translates to $\frac{2}{3} \times n$. So the equation is $n - 4 = \frac{2}{3} \times n$. Now, Plug In the Answers to find the one that satisfies the equation, starting with (C). If $n = 8$, then the equation will read $8 - 4 = \frac{2}{3}(8)$. Since $4 \neq \frac{16}{3}$, eliminate (C) and try another choice. Try (D): if $n = 12$, then $12 - 4 = \frac{2}{3}(12)$, which is $8 = \frac{24}{3}$ or $8 = 8$. Since 12 works, stop here. The correct answer is (D).

More Practice: Lower Level

4. **D** The question is asking for a specific value and there are real numbers in the choices, so use PITA to solve. The question asks for how many girls are in the class, so label the choices "girls" and create another label next to it marked "boys." Test the choices, starting with (C). If there are 20 girls in the classroom, then subtract 12 to find the number of boys: $20 - 12 = 8$ boys. $20 + 8 = 28$, which means that (C) is too small. Eliminate (A), (B), and (C). Choice (D) must be the correct answer, so be aggressive if you're worried about the time. If you have time to check, you will see that it works because if there are 21 girls, then $21 - 12 = 9$, so there are 9 boys. $21 + 9 = 30$, which matches the total given in the problem. The correct answer is (D).

5. **B** The question is asking for a specific value and there are real numbers in the choices, so use PITA to solve. The question asks for how much Jonathan paid, so label the choices as such and create 2 additional columns next to it, one labeled as Victor and the other as Russell. Now, test the choices and follow instructions from the question stem, starting with (C). Choice (C) means that Jonathan paid $100. The question states that *Victor paid twice as much as Jonathan*, so Victor paid $100 \times 2 = 200$. The question then states that *Victor paid half as much as Russell*, so Russell paid twice as much as Victor: $200 \times 2 = 400$. Find the total: $100 + $200 + $400 = $700, which is too much, so eliminate (C) and (D). Try (B): if Jonathan paid $80, then Victor paid $80 \times 2 = 160$, and Russell paid $160 \times 2 = 320$. Find the total: $80 + $160 + $320 = $560, which is the amount stated in the question. The correct answer is (B).

More Practice: Middle and Upper Levels

6. **D** The question is asking for a specific value and there are real numbers in the choices, so use PITA to solve. The question asks for Bob's age, so label the choices "Bob" and create 2 additional columns next to it, one labeled as Adam and the other as Cindy. Now, follow the steps of the question and test the choices, starting with (C). If Bob is 18, then Adam must be 9 because *Adam is half as old as Bob*. It is also stated that *[Adam] is three times as old as Cindy* (remember, Adam is the subject of the sentence), so Cindy must be 3 since $\frac{9}{3} = 3$. Find the total of their ages: $18 + 9 + 3 = 30$, which is too small. Eliminate (A), (B), and (C). Choice (D) is the only answer left, so it must be correct. Stop work and move on! If you have time later to check, you'll see that if Bob is 24, then Adam must be 12 and Cindy is 4, which makes the total $24 + 12 + 4 = 40$. The correct answer is (D).

7. **D** The question is asking for a specific value and there are real numbers in the choices, so use PITA to solve. The question asks for a possible value of x. So, Plug In for x and see if there is an integer that would work to make the rest of the equation balance. Start with one of the middle choices. Try (C): if $x = 55$, then $70(55) = 3,850$. Solve the rest of the equation: $3,850 + 33y = 4,233$ to see if y is an integer. Subtract 3,850 from both sides to find that $33y = 383$. You can try dividing, but you could also ballpark. $33 \times 11 = 363$ and $33 \times 12 = 396$, so 383 is not divisible by 33. Therefore, eliminate (C) and try another choice. Try (D): $70(60) + 33y = 4,233$ simplifies to $4,200 + 33y = 4,233$. Subtract 4,200 from both sides to find that $33y = 33$. Divide each side by 33 to find that $y = 1$. 1 is an integer, so this satisfies the question. The correct answer is (D).

8. **A** This question gives a fair amount of information in the question, that the smallest of the three integers is 2, the sum of $2 + x + y = 9$, and the product of $2xy = 24$. Simplify these equations first and then use PITA to solve. Subtract 2 from either side of the sum to find that $x + y = 7$, and divide by 2 in the second equation to find that $xy = 12$. Now Plug In, starting with the largest number to find the largest number as efficiently as possible. Eliminate (C) and (D) right away since 8 or 9 added to another positive integer cannot equal 7. Try (B): Plug In 6 to get $6 + y = 7$, so y would have to equal 1. This cannot be true, however, since the smallest integer has to be 2. Eliminate (B). Choice (A) is the only answer left, so it must be correct. Stop work and move on! If you have time later to check, you'll see that if you Plug In 4 that $4 + y = 7$ means that $y = 3$. These are both larger than 2, the smallest number. Do these numbers work in the second equation? Yes! $3 \times 4 = 12$. The correct answer is (A).

9. **C** Be sure to label the choices very carefully to stay visually organized. The question asks for Lori's age now, so label the choices "L," and create another column to the right and label it "C" for Carol's age. Next, create two more columns and label them as "L + 10" and "C + 10" for their respective ages in 10 years. Now, Plug In starting with (C): if Lori is 20 years now, Carol must be 5 because *Lori is 15 years older than Carol*. This means that in 10 years, Lori will be 30 ($20 + 10 = 30$), and Carol will be 15 ($5 + 10 = 15$). The question states that *in 10 years, Lori will be twice as old as Carol*. $30 = 2 \times 15$, so this satisfies the statement. The correct answer is (C).

10. **A** Let the choices help here. The choices represent how many people are currently in the group. Eliminate (D) immediately since 30 cannot be divided 12 ways (hopefully there aren't partial people in the car!).

Try (B), which is the middle answer of the remaining choices: if there are 6 people renting the car now, the cost would be $5 each since $\frac{30}{6} = 5$. If a seventh person joined, the cost per person would be $\frac{30}{7}$, which is not an integer. Since the problem stated that adding 1 person to the group would result in each person owing $1 less, this does not satisfy the question, so eliminate (B) and try another choice. Try (A): if there are 5 people renting the car, they will each pay $6 since $\frac{30}{5} = 6$. If a sixth person joins, they will each pay $5 because $\frac{30}{6} = 5$. $5 is exactly one dollar less than $6, so this satisfies the question stem. Choice (A) is correct.

Extra Practice

1. **B**   Ballparking is one way to work through this problem. The shaded region looks to be about half the square, and half of 144 is 72, (B). To be more precise, the side of the square must be 12 since $A = s^2$ and $12^2 = 144$, so the height of each shaded triangle is 12. The base for one triangle ends at P and the base for the other triangle ends at Q, and $PQ = 12$ since it's a side of the square. So make the base for each triangle 6 since the two bases must add up to 12. Plug those values into the formula: $A = \frac{1}{2}bh = \frac{1}{2}(6)(12) = 36$. Since both areas equal 36, the total area of the shaded region is $36 + 36 = 72$. The correct answer is (B).

2. **B**   Take this question in bite-sized pieces. The question asks for the shaded region, so you want the part inside the square but outside the circle. In other words, if you find the area of the square and the area of the circle, you can find the shaded region by removing what you do not need (the area of the circle). First, find the area of the square. The side of the square is equal to 4, so $A = s^2 = 4^2 = 16$. Eliminate (A), (C), and (D), since these do not contain 16. For added security, find the area of the circle. The radius is 2, so $A = \pi r^2 = \pi(2)^2 = 4\pi$. Remember to subtract that from the area of the square, so the full answer is $16 - 4\pi$. The correct answer is (B).

Practice Drill 8—Functions

1. **B**   Don't be scared off by these types of questions! Simply follow the directions and plug numbers into the equation where specified. In this case, replace n with the given number (7). Thus, the equation should read $7 = 10(7) - 10$. Simplify the equation to $7 = 70 - 10 = 60$. The correct answer is (B).

2. **C**   The question asks which of the choices will yield a result of 120. Therefore, use PITA to solve, starting with (C). If $n = 13$, then replace 13 for n in the given equation: $13 = 10(13) - 10$. Simplify to find that $13 = 130 - 10 = 120$. This works, so the correct answer is (C).

3. **D**   In this function, simply plug in the number to the left of the weird symbol for d and the number to the right of the weird symbol for y exactly as the example directs. The function should read $d ¿ y = 10 ¿ 2 = (10 \times 2) - (10 + 2)$, which simplifies to $(20) - (12) = 8$. The correct answer is (D).

4. **D**   This question asks to first find the result of the function, and then to find the unknown K. Take this question in bite-sized pieces. Start with the parentheses first. Solve for $4 ¿ 3$: $(4 \times 3) - (4 + 3) = (12) - (7) = 5$. Next, plug 5 into the equation to find K: $K(5) = 30$. Divide by 5 on both sides to find that K equals 6. The correct answer is (D).

5.　**A**　You will need to set the equation up based on the function defined above, and then use PEMDAS to simplify and solve for the end result. Take this question in bite-sized pieces. Start with the first set of parentheses: (2 ¿ 4) = (2 × 4) – (2 + 4) = (8) – (6) = 2. Next, work with the second set of parentheses: (3 ¿ 6) = (3 × 6) – (3 + 6) = (18) – (9) = 9. Put these values back in the original equation: (2 ¿ 4) × (3 ¿ 6) = (2) × (9) = 18. Now, test the choices to see which expression yields 18 as well. Try (A): (9 × 3) – (9 + 3) + 3 = (27) – (12) + 3 = 18. Since this matches, stop here. The correct answer is (A). Remember, if you find a question too time consuming, skip it and move on! You can come back to it later if you have time.

Practice Drill 9—Charts and Graphs

1.　**D**　First, find what District A spent in 1990: $400,000 (pay attention to the note below the table: the numbers are in thousands of dollars). Look for double this amount. $800,000 is listed in the table for the value in 1991 for District E. The correct answer is (D).

2.　**D**　Add across to find which district spent the most, keeping in mind that these are all in the thousands (though this doesn't really matter to find the largest sum). District E has the largest sum: $600,000 + $800,000 = $1,400,000. The correct answer is (D).

3.　**D**　Remember that these numbers are in the thousands. Add down to find the sum of the values in 1990: $1,800,000. Do the same with the values in 1991 to find a sum of $2,600,000. Find the difference of these values: $2,600,000 – $1,800,000 = $800,000. The correct answer is (D).

4.　**D**　Check the graph. Carl owns 5 CDs, so the other two people together must own a total of 5 CDs. Eliminate (A) because Abe has 2 and Ben has 4, totaling 6. Eliminate (B) as well because Ben has 4 and Dave has 3, which is 7. Choice (C) is incorrect since Abe and Ed both have 2, so this amounts only to 4. Choice (D) works because Abe has 2 and Dave has 3, amounting to 5. The correct answer is (D).

5.　**B**　To find which student owns one-fourth of all the CDs, first add all the CDs to find a total. Your work from the previous question will help! Abe = 2, Ben = 4, Carl = 5, Dave = 3, and Ed = 2, which yields a total of 16 CDs. $\frac{1}{4}$ of 16 is $\frac{1}{4} \times 16 = \frac{16}{4} = 4$, so Ben is the student who has 4 CDs. The correct answer is (B).

6.　**D**　To find Matt's earnings for the week, first add up all his hours and then multiply by his hourly salary ($6/hour). He works 3.5 + 4 + 3.5 + 3 = 14 hours over the week, so 14 × 6 = 84. The correct answer is (D).

7.　**B**　Remember, if you see the word *average*, you can use an Average Pie . The previous question helped you find the total number of hours Matt worked: 14. Put that number in the *total* place. He worked 4 days—note the question says *on the days he worked* not the number of days in a week. Put 4 in the *# of items* place. Divide these two numbers to find the average: $\frac{14}{4} = 3.5$. If you're pressed for time, instead of doing the long division, let the answer choices help! Since 14 is not divisible by 4, eliminate all the integers. The correct answer is (B).

8. **C** One way to solve this problem is to translate the words into math: *The hours he worked on Monday is 3.5, accounted for is equals, what percent is* $\frac{x}{100}$, and the *total hours he worked* is 14. The equation is $3.5 = \frac{x}{100} \times 14$. Simplify the right side: $\frac{x}{100} \times 14 = \frac{x(14)}{100} = \frac{14x}{100}$. Multiply both sides by 100 to get $350 = 14x$. Divide both sides by 14, and $x = 25$. The correct answer is (C). You can also find a percent by dividing the desired amount by the total amount: Matt worked 3.5 hours on Monday and a total of 14 hours, so $\frac{3.5}{14} = \frac{35}{140} = \frac{1}{4}$, or 25%.

Practice Drill 10—Quantitative Comparison—Middle and Upper Levels

1. **C** Look at Column B first. $17 \times 2 + 17$ is the same as $17 + 17 + 17$, or 17×3. Thus, the two columns are equal. The correct answer is (C).

2. **A** Draw a picture. For instance, draw a pie and divide it into eight parts since eight is a common denominator for $\frac{1}{2}$ and $\frac{3}{8}$. Since $\frac{1}{2} = \frac{4}{8}$, four of the eight parts of the pie would be colored in. Only three out of eight would be filled in for $\frac{3}{8}$. Therefore, Column A is greatest, and the correct answer is (A).

3. **B** There are variables in the columns, so Plug In twice. For instance, try $b = 10$. $10 + 80 = 90$, and $10 + 82 = 92$. In this case, Column B is greater, so eliminate (A) and (C). Try another number, perhaps a negative number: -10. Perform the necessary calculations: $-10 + 80 = 70$ and $-10 + 82 = 72$. Column B is still greater, so the correct answer is (B).

4. **B** Plug In a value here. Say that Matt is 60 inches tall, making Rob 58 inches tall since *Rob is two inches shorter than Matt*. The question stem also states that *Joel is four inches taller than Matt*, so Joel must be 64 inches tall. This makes Joel taller than Rob, so Column B is greater. The correct answer is (B).

5. **C** When dealing with exponents, write it out! Column A can be rewritten as $16 \times 16 \times 16$. Column B can be rewritten as $4 \times 4 \times 4 \times 4 \times 4 \times 4$. Notice that 16 is the same as 4×4. Therefore, Column A can also be written as $(4 \times 4) \times (4 \times 4) \times (4 \times 4)$. Since each column contains 6 fours, the two columns are equal. The correct answer is (C).

6. **D** The information given does not indicate the direction or orientation of either girl's house. However, the information does state that *Kimberly lives two miles from school*, so Column A is 2. However, Jennifer could live another two miles past Kimberly's house, four miles in the other direction from the school (making the two houses 6 miles apart), or she could even live 4 miles north or south of the school (making the distance between their houses yet another value). Since there is no way to determine the distance between their houses without more information, the solution cannot be determined. The correct answer is (D).

Practice Drill 11—Quant Comp

1. **B** Since there are variables in the columns, Plug In a number. Pay attention to the restriction given: Plug In a number greater than 1 for x. Let $x = 4$. Column A is equal to 4, and column B is equal to 4^2, or 16. Since column B is greater, eliminate choices (A) and (C). Try a different number to see if Column A could be greater or if the quantities could be equal. Since $x > 1$, x cannot be negative, zero, or one. Try a very large number. $1,000^2$ is much larger than 1,000, so Column B is still greater.

You could also try a decimal, like 2.5. In this case, Column B is still greater since $2.5^2 = 6.25$, which is greater than 2.5. Therefore, since Column B is always greater, the correct answer is (B).

2. **C**   Read the question carefully: *b is an integer and −1 < b < 1*. There is only one integer between −1 and 1. Therefore, *b* must be 0. Plug 0 in for *b* into each of the columns. Column A is $\frac{0}{2} = 0$. Column B is $\frac{0}{8} = 0$. The quantities are equal, so (C) is the correct answer.

3. **D**   Since there are variables in the columns, Plug In values for *p* and *m*. For instance, let *p* = 16 and *m* = 3. Since it takes 4 quarts to make one gallon, Column B is less than 1 gallon while Column A is 16 gallons. This makes Column A greater. However, the question does not state anything about requirements for these numbers, and the values could easily be reversed, that *p* = 3 and *m* = 16. The 16 quarts in Column B is equal to 4 gallons, which is greater than the 3 gallons in Column A. Since this could be true as well, it cannot be determined which quantity is larger. The correct answer is (D).

4. **A**   Since there are variables in the columns, Plug In a number. Pay attention to the restriction given: if *x* must be a positive integer, Plug In a positive integer for *x*. For example, let *x* = 3. Column A is $\frac{3}{4}$ while Column B is $\frac{3}{5}$. If you're not sure which value is greater, draw a picture. You can also use Bowtie to compare fractions. Column A becomes $\frac{15}{20}$, and Column B becomes $\frac{12}{20}$. Thus, Column A is greater. Eliminate (B) and (C). Try Plugging In another value for *x* to see if another outcome is possible. Remember the restriction given, so *x* cannot be negative or zero, so try a large integer. Make *x* = 100. Column A is $\frac{100}{4} = 25$, and Column B is $\frac{100}{5} = 20$. Column A is still greater. You could also try *x* = 1, but you will get the same result. Column A will be greater since $\frac{1}{4} = 0.25$ is greater than $\frac{1}{5} = 0.20$. The correct answer is (A).

5. **D**   Since there are variables in the columns, Plug In values for *p* and *w*, according to the information given: *w is an integer less than 4*, so let *w* = 3. You are also given that *p is an integer greater than 10*, so let *p* = 11. Therefore, Column A is (3)(11) = 33 while Column B is equal to 3. In this case, Column A is greater. Eliminate (B) and (C). Now, try Plugging In different numbers to see if another outcome is possible. Let *w* = 0 and *p* = 12. In Column A, (12)(0) = 0. This is equal to Column B since *w* = 0. Since Column A isn't always greater nor are the two columns always equal, the correct answer is (D).

6. **D**   Since there are variables in the columns, Plug In a value for *c*. Let *c* = 2. In Column A, 4(2) + 6 = 8 + 6 = 14. Do the same for Column B: 3(2) + 12 = 6 + 12 = 18. In this case, Column B is greater, so eliminate (A) and (C). Now, try a different number, perhaps a negative number. Let *c* = −10. Now, Column A will read 4(−10) + 6 = −40 + 6 = −34. Do the same to Column B: 3(−10) + 12 = −30 + 12 = −18. In this case, −18 > −34, so Column A is now greater. Since neither column is always greater, the correct answer is (D).

Practice Drill 12—Quantitative Comparison—Middle and Upper Levels

1. **C** Find the total cost in each of the columns. Column A contains the statement *The total cost of 3 plants that cost $4 each*, so 3($4) = $12. Column B contains the statement *The total cost of 4 plants that cost $3 each*, so 4($3) = $12. The columns are equal, so the correct answer is (C).

2. **D** First, simplify the expression in Column A. Distribute the 30 in the expression $30(1 - 2n)$ to get $30 - 60n$. Now, Plug In a value for n to solve each column. Let $n = 2$. In Column A, $30 - 60(2) = -90$. In Column B, $30 - 2(2) = 26$. Column B is greater, so eliminate (A) and (C). Now, Plug In a second time, trying a different number (remember, try 1, 0, fractions/decimals, negatives, or large or small numbers to find different outcomes). Try a negative number here. Let $n = -3$. Column A will now read $30 - 60(-3) = 210$, and Column B will read $30 - 2(-3) = 36$. Column A is greater in this case. Since neither column is always greater, the correct answer is (D).

3. **D** You are given the statement The *product of 3 integers is 48*. There are many ways to reach a product of 48. For instance, $2 \times 3 \times 8 = 48$. Of the three integers, the smallest is 2, so Column A is 2. Compared to Column B, Column A is greater. Eliminate (B) and (C). However, this is not the only way to multiply integers to get a product of 48. For example, $1 \times 2 \times 24 = 48$. In this case, the smallest of the three integers is 1, which means the two columns are equal. Since Column A is not always greater nor are the two columns always equal, the correct answer is (D).

4. **C** First, simplify Column A: $(x + y)(x - y)$ can be FOILed out to be $x^2 + xy - xy - y^2$. The two middle values cancel each other out, so the expression reads $x^2 - y^2$, which is the same expression in Column B. Since the two columns are equal, the correct answer is (C). Note that you can also Plug In values for x and y and solve the problem this way. You should try more than one set of numbers to check for other possible outcomes.

5. **A** Use correct PEMDAS to evaluate the expression in Column A. First, work within the parentheses: $(7 - 4) \times 3 - 3 = (3) \times 3 - 3$. There are no exponents, so the next step is to do the multiplication and division from left to right: $(3) \times 3 - 3 = 9 - 3$. Finally, add and subtract from left to right: $9 - 3 = 6$. Since 6 is greater than 0, Column A is greater. The correct answer is (A).

6. **A** Since line m is equal to $y = x + 4$, the slope of line m is equal to 1. Remember, the slope is the coefficient of x in linear equations. Therefore, Column A is 1. Perpendicular lines will have slopes that are negative reciprocals of one another. Therefore, line l, which is perpendicular to line m, will have a slope of -1 since the negative reciprocal of $\frac{1}{1}$ is $-\frac{1}{1}$. Thus, Column B is -1. Since 1 is greater than -1, Column A is greater. The correct answer is (A).

7. **B** Work through the information provided to find the value of Column A. If the shoes are $100 and *the price is increased by 20%*, find 20% of $100 and add that result to the total. $\frac{20}{100}(100)$ reduces to $\frac{1}{5}(100) = \frac{100}{5} = 20$. The price increased $20, so $100 + $20 = $120. The shoes are now $120. However, *the price was reduced by 20%*. Find 20% of 120 and subtract that result from the total. $\frac{20}{100}(120)$ reduces to $\frac{1}{5}(120) = \frac{120}{5} = 24$. The price decreased $24, so $120 - $24 = $96. The final price of the shoes is $96, so Column A is $96. Since Column B is $100, it is greater. The correct answer is (B).

8. **B** Remember, a negative sign will stay negative with an odd exponent. Both columns contain negative numbers and odd exponents, so both columns will remain negative. With negative numbers, the value that is *closest to* zero will be the greater value (e.g., –1 > –4). When working with fractions, remember that as the denominator gets larger, the fraction will get smaller (e.g., $\frac{1}{2} > \frac{1}{4}$). However, with negative fractions, the one that is "less negative" will be greater (e.g., $-\frac{1}{4} > -\frac{1}{2}$). In Column B, the exponent is greater, so the denominator in Column B will be larger and thus the value of the fraction will be smaller. Since the fraction in Column B will be less negative than the fraction in Column A, the value in Column B is greater. The correct answer is (B).

9. **A** Both fractions are positive and both are being raised to a positive, even power. However, be careful when working with fractions less than 1. When those numbers are raised to a positive power, they become smaller since the denominator increases. Remember, as the denominator gets larger, the fraction will get smaller (e.g., $\frac{1}{2} > \frac{1}{4}$). Thus, the denominator in Column A (6^4) will be smaller than the denominator in Column B (6^6), which means the value in Column A will be greater. The correct answer is (A).

10. **A** The negative sign in both columns will become positive since both columns are being raised to an even power. With fractions less than 1, the larger the denominator, the smaller the fraction. Since the denominator in Column A (6^2) will be smaller than the denominator in Column B (6^4), the value in Column A will be greater. The correct answer is (A).

11. **A** With fractions less than 1, the larger the denominator, the smaller the fraction. Since the denominator in Column A (6^3) will be smaller than the denominator in Column B (6^5), the value in Column A will be greater. The correct answer is (A).

12. **D** There are no instructions as to the values of x and y, so Plug In. For instance, x and y could be equal. Let both x and y equal 4. Column A would be $C = 2(4)\pi$, or 8π, and Column B would be $A = \pi(4)^2 = 16\pi$. In this case, Column B is greater, so eliminate (A) and (C). Since x and y do not have to be equal, plug in a second time to see if a different outcome is possible. Say that $x = 2$ and $y = 1$. Then Column A will be $C = 2(2)\pi = 4\pi$, and Column B will be $A = \pi(1)^2 = \pi$. Now, Column A is greater. Since neither column is always greater, the correct answer is (D).

13. **C** List the prime numbers on the 6-sided die: 2, 3, and 5 (Note! 1 is not a prime number). Since there are 6 sides on the die, the probability of rolling a prime number is $\frac{3}{6}$, so Column A is $\frac{3}{6}$. This is the same value listed in Column B. Since the columns are equal, the correct answer is (C).

14. **D** Since there are variables in the columns, Plug In values for a and b. If a and b are integers and $a + b = 5$, choose numbers to make both statements true. Let $a = 3$ and $b = 2$. In this case, Column A is greater, so eliminate (B) and (C). However, these numbers could easily be reversed because there are no restrictions listed. If $a = 2$ and $b = 3$, then Column B would be greater. Since neither column is always greater, the correct answer is (D).

15.   **A**   Evaluate the expressions, using order of operations. Column A is $\sqrt{25-9} = \sqrt{16} = 4$, and Column B is $\sqrt{25} - \sqrt{9} = 5 - 3 = 2$. Therefore, Column A is greater. The correct answer is (A).

16.   **C**   Start with Set B, since it is a finite set. Set B consists of 5, 10, 15, 20, 25, 30, 35, 40, and 45. Set A contains all prime numbers. The only prime number contained in Set B is 5, so the intersection of these two sets (i.e., Set C) will contain only the number 5. There is only one number in Set C, so the columns are equal. The correct answer is (C).

17.   **B**   When multiplying fractions, multiply the numerators across and the denominators across. Therefore, the value of Column A is $\frac{3}{4} \times \frac{3}{4} = \frac{3 \times 3}{4 \times 4} = \frac{9}{16}$. When adding fractions with a common denominator, add the numerators. Thus, the value of Column B is $\frac{3}{4} + \frac{3}{4} = \frac{3+3}{4} = \frac{6}{4} = 1\frac{1}{2}$. Column B is greater. The correct answer is (B).

18.   **C**   Since there are variables in the columns, Plug In values for a and b, paying attention to restrictions given. Since $a > 0$, let $a = 2$. Since $b < 0$, let $b = -3$. Now, plug in these numbers to the expressions. Column A is $-(2 \times -3) = -(-6) = 6$. Column B is $-2 \times -3 = 6$ as well. The two columns are equal. You can try testing different values for a and b, but the columns will always be equal because the negative signs will always cancel out and the same numbers are being multiplied in each column, so the result will not vary. The correct answer is (C).

19.   **B**   This question is testing math vocabulary. The median of a set is the middle number when the numbers are listed in order from least to greatest. In Set A, the numbers are already in order, so find the middle number: 8. Thus, Column A is 8. In Set B, the numbers are also already in order. However, there is an even number of items in this set, so the median will be found by taking the average of the two middle numbers. The two middle numbers are 8 and 9, so the median is $\frac{8+9}{2} = \frac{17}{2} = 8.5$.

The value in Column B is 8.5. Since Column B is greater, the correct answer is (B).

20.   **C**   *Inclusive* means to include the outer limits—in this case, 1 and 10. In Column A, add up all the integers, including 1 and 10: $1 + 2 + 3 + 4 + 5 + 6 + 7 + 8 + 9 + 10 = 55$. Simplify Column B to get $5 \times 11 = 55$. Since the columns are equal, the correct answer is (C).

21.   **B**   Remember, with exponents, write it out! Thus, Column A can be rewritten as $(2 \times 2 \times 2) + (2 \times 2 \times 2) + (2 \times 2 \times 2) = 8 + 8 + 8 = 24$. Note that in Column A, the quantities are being added, not multiplied. Column B can be rewritten as $2 \times 2 \times 2 \times 2 \times 2 \times 2 \times 2 \times 2 \times 2$, which will equal a value larger than 24. Therefore, Column B is greater. Another way to solve this problem is to use exponent rules. When exponents with the same base and same exponent are being added, simply treat them like any variable. For example, $x + x + x = 3x$. Thus, $2^3 + 2^3 + 2^3 = 3(2^3) = 3(8) = 24$. This is not the same as 2^9, which is a much larger number. Since Column B is greater, the correct answer is (B).

22.   **D**   Since there are variables in the columns, Plug In. First, simplify Column A: $7(x - 3) = 7x - 21$. Now, Plug In a value for x. For instance, let $x = 3$. Plug In 3 to Column A to find that $7(3) - 21 = 21 - 21 = 0$. Now, do the same for Column B: $21 - 7(3) = 21 - 21 = 0$. The columns are equal, so eliminate (A) and (B). Remember, Plug In a second time to see if a different outcome is possible. This time let $x = 2$. In Column A, the expression will read $7(2) - 21$, which simplifies to $14 - 21 = -7$. In Column B, the expression will read $21 - 7(2)$, which simplifies to $21 - 14 = 7$. Now Column B is greater. Since the columns are not always equal nor is Column B always greater, the correct answer is (D).

23. **B** First, take the instructions in Column A into bite-sized pieces. The smallest positive factor of 25 is 1, and the biggest positive factor of 16 is 16. Thus, 1 × 16 = 16. Column A is 16. Since Column B is greater, the correct answer is (B).

24. **A** The probability of getting heads on any single flip is $\frac{1}{2}$, since there are two sides of a coin and only one of those is heads. Column A is the probability of getting heads on 2 consecutive flips, so you need to multiply the probability of the first flip by the probability of the second flip (i.e., Event 1 × Event 2): $\frac{1}{2} \times \frac{1}{2} = \frac{1 \times 1}{2 \times 2} = \frac{1}{4}$. To find Column B, include the probability of a getting heads on third flip (i.e., Event 1 × Event 2 × Event 3): $\frac{1}{2} \times \frac{1}{2} \times \frac{1}{2} = \frac{1 \times 1 \times 1}{2 \times 2 \times 2} = \frac{1}{8}$. Since Column A is greater, the correct answer is (A). Note: If you know that the probability of getting the same result (in this case, heads) on consecutive flips of a coin diminishes with each subsequent flip, you can find the correct answer quickly!

25. **C** Use the formula given to find the areas of each figure. In Column A, the height of Cylinder *A* is 10 cm and the radius is 6 cm. Plug these values into the volume formula to find that $V = \pi(6)^2(10) = \pi(36)(10) = 360\pi$. Column A is 360π. For Column B, you can find the volumes of Cylinder B and Cylinder C separately and then add the results together. Alternatively, since the two figures have the same dimensions, you can multiply the volume formula by 2 to find the total volume. Thus, Column B is $V = 2\pi(6)^2(5) = 2\pi(36)(5) = 2\pi(180) = 360\pi$. Since the columns are equal, the correct answer is (C).

26. **C** Since all the angles are labeled as *x*, they are all equal. The angles in a triangle must add up to 180°; therefore, each angle is equal to 60° since $\frac{180}{3} = 60$. Thus, the value of Column A is 60, which makes the columns equal. The correct answer is (C).

27. **A** To find percent change, use this formula: % change $= \dfrac{\text{difference}}{\text{total}} \times 100$. In Column A, the difference from 1 to 2 is 1. Since you are looking for percent *increase*, the *smaller* number will be the original number. Thus, the original number is 1. Column A is $\frac{2-1}{1} \times 100$, which simplifies to $\frac{1}{1} \times 100 = 100$. For Column B, the difference from 2 to 1 is still 1. However, since you are looking for percent *decrease*, the *larger* number will be the original number. Thus, the original value is now 2. Column B is $\frac{2-1}{2} \times 100$, which simplifies to $\frac{1}{2} \times 100 = 50$. The value in Column A is greater, so the correct answer is (A).

28. **C** Remember, if you see the word *average*, you can use an Average Pie. First, find the sum: 4 + 6 + 8 + 10 = 28. That number goes in the *total* place. There are 4 numbers, so put 4 in the *# of items* spot. Divide to get $\frac{28}{4} = 7$. Column A is 7. Remember that the median of a set is the middle number when the numbers are listed in order from least to greatest. Since there is an even number

of items in this set, the median will be found by taking the average of the two middle numbers, 6 and 8. The average of 6 and 8 is $\frac{6+8}{2} = \frac{14}{2} = 7$, so the value in Column B is 7. Since the two columns are equal, the correct answer is (C).

29. **D** Since there are variables in the columns, Plug In values for the variables and evaluate the expressions. For instance, let $x = 3$ and $y = 5$ since x and y must be positive numbers. Column A is $\frac{3 \times 5}{2} = \frac{15}{2} = 7.5$ whereas Column B is $\sqrt{3 \times 5} = \sqrt{15}$, which is a little bit less than 4 since $\sqrt{16} = 4$. Since Column A is greater, eliminate (B) and (C). Now, Plug In a second time to see if a different outcome is possible. Let $x = 1$ and $y = 1$. Column A is $\frac{1 \times 1}{2} = \frac{1}{2}$, and Column B is $\sqrt{1 \times 1} = \sqrt{1} = 1$. This time, Column B is greater. Since neither column is always greater, the correct answer is (D).

30. **C** This is a common trick on the ISEE. Notice that all the numbers are exactly the same and in the exact same order. All that is different is the placement of the decimals. 567.83 and 5.6783 are off by two decimals, or a factor of 100. Similarly, 0.40 and 40.0 are related by a factor of 100, or two decimal places as well. This cancels itself out, and the product will be the same for both columns. Check if you want to see for yourself, but if you know this trick it will save you some time on the test! The correct answer is (C).

31. **C** First, find the probability of *not* picking red shoes, which is the same as picking purple or white shoes, and then compare the result to Column B's value. There are 10 total pairs to pick from, and there are 8 pairs of shoes that are purple or white (i.e., not red), so the probability is $\frac{\text{not red}}{\text{total}} = \frac{8}{10}$. Column A is $\frac{8}{10}$ which is the value of Column B. Since the columns are equal, the correct answer is (C).

32. **B** Find the total of each column. Column A is $10 \times 8 = 80$, and Column B is $20 \times 4.5 = 90$. Column B is greater, so the correct answer is (B). Remember, you can estimate Column B's value if you're running short on time. $20 \times 4 = 80$; however, since 20 is really being multiplied by 4.5, not 4, you know the product has to be more than 80.

33. **C** Remember, if you see exponents, you can always write it out! You could also Plug In since there are variables in the columns. However, another way to find the values of the two columns is to use the exponent rules (MADSPM). For Column A, $\frac{x^2 x^5}{x^4} = \frac{x^{2+5}}{x^4} = \frac{x^7}{x^4} = x^{7-4} = x^3$. Column B is also x^3. Since the two columns are equal, the correct answer is (C).

34. **D** The information given is $x^2 = 36$. Remember that 6 is not the only solution to this equation. 6^2 is equal to 36, but $(-6)^2$ is also equal to 36 since two negatives multiplied together will equal a positive number. Since Column A can be greater than Column B but could also be equal to Column B, the correct answer is (D).

35. **C** Remember that factors are numbers you can multiply together to equal another number. The largest positive factor of 16 is 16, since $1 \times 16 = 16$. Thus, Column A is 16. Multiples are the result of multiplying two numbers together. The smallest positive multiple of 16 is also 16, since $16 \times 1 = 16$. Therefore, Column B is also 16. Since the columns are equal, the correct answer is (C).

36. **B** Since there are variables in the figure, Plug In a value for x. For instance, let $x = 2$. The perimeter of square $ABCD$ is equal to $2 + 2 + 2 + 2 = 8$. The perimeter of $MNOP$ is equal to $2 + 2(2) + 2 + 2(2)$, or $2 + 4 + 2 + 4 = 12$. In this case, Column B is greater, so eliminate (A) and (C). Try Plugging In a second time to see if a different outcome is possible. Try $x = \frac{1}{2}$. The perimeter of square $ABCD$ is equal to $\frac{1}{2} + \frac{1}{2} + \frac{1}{2} + \frac{1}{2}$, or $1 + 1 = 2$. The perimeter of $MNOP$ is equal to $\frac{1}{2} + 2\left(\frac{1}{2}\right) + \frac{1}{2} + 2\left(\frac{1}{2}\right)$, or $1 + 1 + 1 = 3$. Column B is still greater. Since there are figures, it is not possible to Plug In a negative number or zero; the only possible numbers will be positive. All positive numbers will yield the same outcome since the rectangle has two sides that are double the side length of the square, meaning that the rectangle will always have a perimeter a little bit (or a lot) bigger than the square's. Therefore, Column B will always be greater, and the correct answer is (B).

37. **C** Draw the triangle on the figure provided and write down the formula for the area of a triangle: $A = \frac{1}{2}bh$. Next find the values for the base and height. To find the base, find the value of DE. AD and BC are congruent since the shape is a rectangle. From there, the base must be 4, since E is the midpoint of AD, which splits 8 into two equal parts. The height of the triangle must meet the base at a right angle, so the height of the triangle is the same as the measure of side AB, which has a length of 6. Plug In these values to the formula to find that $A = \frac{1}{2}(4)(6) = (2)(6) = 12$. Column A is 12, which is equivalent to the value in Column B. Since the columns are equal, the correct answer is (C).

38. **C** Remember, with exponents, you can always write it out. However, this is a common trick on the ISEE. Another way to evaluate these expressions is to rewrite them with the same base. In Column B, 64 is the same as 4^3, so the whole expression can be rewritten as $(4^3)^4$. Using the exponent rules (MADSPM), you can further simplify: $\left(4^3\right)^4 = 4^{3 \times 4} = 4^{12}$. Since the value in Column B is the same as the value of Column A, the correct answer is (C).

39.   **A**   When the question asks about ratios, use a Ratio Box. The ratio of blue to red tickets is 3:5, so fill in that information into the top row of the Ratio Box. Remember to add the two numbers together to get the total for the ratio row: $3 + 5 = 8$. No other information is provided. To make things simple, let's say that there are a total of 8 actual tickets. That makes the multiplier 1. Column B asks for *the fractional part of all the tickets that are blue.* Use the numbers from the Ratio Box. There are 3 blue tickets and 8 total tickets: $\dfrac{\text{blue}}{\text{total}} = \dfrac{3}{8}$. Thus, Column B is $\dfrac{3}{8}$. Remember that when the numerators are the same, the fraction with the *bigger* denominator is actually the *smaller* number. Therefore, Column A is greater, and the correct answer is (A).

	BLUE	RED	TOTAL
Ratio	3	5	8
Multiplier	× 1	× 1	× 1
Actual	3	5	8

40.   **C**   Remember, if you see the word average, you can use an Average Pie . Luke made two trips, so the *# of items* is 2. Column A represents the average speed for the entire trip, so to find the total speed, add the speeds from both parts of the trip: $50 + 60 = 110$. Put that value in the *total* spot. Finally, divide to find the average: $\dfrac{50 + 60}{2} = \dfrac{110}{2} = 55$. Thus, Column A is 55, which is the same as Column B. Since the two columns are equal, the correct answer is (C).

41.   **A**   First, rearrange the equation in Column A to $y = mx + b$ form. Subtract $12x$ from both sides to get $-4y = -12x + 16$. Divide by -4 on both sides to get $y = 3x - 4$. The slope is the coefficient of x, so the slope is 3. Column A is 3. Now, find the slope from the two points given in Column B using the formula $m = \dfrac{y_2 - y_1}{x_2 - x_1}$. Thus, $\dfrac{y_2 - y_1}{x_2 - x_1} = \dfrac{12 - 6}{3 - (-3)} = \dfrac{6}{6} = 1$, and Column B is 1. The value of Column A is greater, so the correct answer is (A).

42.   **B**   Don't be intimidated by the decimals under the square root! You probably know that $9^2 = 81$, right? To go from 81 to 0.81, you need to move the decimal to the left two places, so move the decimal one place to the left for each 9 and multiply: $0.9 \times 0.9 = 0.81$. Thus, $\sqrt{0.81} = 0.9$. Column A is 0.9. For Column B, the decimal needs to be moved only one place. That means the two numbers that will be multiplied together will have to be bigger than 0.9. Therefore, Column B will be greater. The correct answer is (B). Note, you can also ballpark. $\sqrt{4} = 2$ and $\sqrt{9} = 3$, so the $\sqrt{8.1}$ will be less than 3 but greater than 2, which is still larger than 0.9.

43. **D** There are infinitely different ways in which the length and width could multiply together to equal 36. For instance, the length of *y* could be 4 and the width of *z* could be 9, or vice versa. The values of *y* and *z* could also each be 6, which would make the two columns equal. Since it is impossible to know if *y* or *z* is the greater value, or if they are equal, without more information, the correct answer must be (D).

44. **A** First, list the nonnegative even integers less than 10. Don't forget about zero! The list should contain 0, 2, 4, 6, and 8. Therefore, Column A is 5. Since this is greater than the value of Column B, the correct answer is (A).

45. **D** Don't make assumptions! As for all geometry questions, use the rules of the shape you are given to help you solve and ignore anything unstated about the illustration. Isosceles triangles have 2 equal sides. There are therefore three possibilities for the two equal sides: 1) both *AB* and *BC* equal 2, 2) both *BC* and *AC* equal 2, or 3) *BC* equals 2 and both *AB* and *AC* equal some other number. Because the shape is not drawn to scale, it's possible that *AB* and *AC* could be equal to, say, 100, which would make the area of the triangle much greater than 4. In other words, there are so many possibilities, many of which have an area greater than 4, that the correct answer must be (D).

Math Review

1. Yes
2. It is neither positive nor negative.
3. Addition
4. Multiplication
5. The quotient
6. Yes   3 + 1 + 2 = 6, which is divisible by 3;
   No   3 + 1 + 2 = 6, which is not divisible by 9.
7. Exponents
8. Yes   3 goes into 12 evenly 4 times;
   No   12 cannot go into 3.
9. No   No integer times 12 is equal to 3;
   Yes $3 \times 4 = 12$
10. 0   The tens digit is two places to the left of the decimal.
11. 2   The tenths digit is one place to the right of the decimal.
12. 8   Write it out! $2 \times 2 \times 2 = 8$
13. Over 100 or $\dfrac{x}{100}$
14. Multiplication
15. Total column
16. Average pie
17. Plug In a number
18. Add; all four
19. Multiply; two (or square one side, since the sides of a square are the same)
20. 180
21. 3; 180
22. 360
23. 2; equilateral
24. Hypotenuse; right angle
25. $A = \dfrac{1}{2}(base)(height)$

REVIEW—THE VERBAL PLAN

Pacing and Verbal Strategy

I will do the verbal questions in this order.

1. Synonyms with words I know
2. Synonyms with words I sort of know
3. Sentence completions

I should spend less than ten minutes on synonyms.

I will always eliminate wrong (or "worse") answers.

If possible, I will eliminate choices before I guess, but even if I can't eliminate any, I will still guess productively.

No, I cannot eliminate choices that contain words I do not know.

SYNONYMS

Practice Drill 1—Write Your Own Definition

Possible Definitions

1.	weird	11.	bend down
2.	introduction	12.	honest
3.	giving	13.	tease
4.	doing the right thing	14.	rough
5.	change	15.	self-centered
6.	circle around	16.	calm
7.	optimistic	17.	use
8.	stick around	18.	full of life
9.	help	19.	stretch out
10.	build	20.	help

Practice Drill 2—Write Another Definition

Look up these seven words in a dictionary to see how many different meanings they can have.

Practice Drill 3—Basic Synonym Techniques

1.	C	5.	D	9.	D	13.	D	17.	D
2.	A	6.	D	10.	A	14.	B	18.	C
3.	C	7.	B	11.	C	15.	A	19.	B
4.	D	8.	C	12.	B	16.	C	20.	C

Practice Drill 4—Making Your Own Context

Possible Contexts (Answers Will Vary)

1. Common cold; common man
2. Competent to stand trial
3. Abridged dictionary
4. Untimely demise; untimely remark
5. Homogenized milk
6. Juvenile delinquent; delinquent payments
7. Inalienable rights
8. Paltry sum
9. Auspicious beginning; auspicious occasion
10. Prodigal son

Practice Drill 5—Using Your Own Context

1. C
2. D
3. D
4. C
5. A
6. B
7. C
8. A
9. C
10. A

Practice Drill 6—All Synonyms Techniques

1.	C	11.	B	21.	C	31.	B
2.	A	12.	C	22.	B	32.	B
3.	C	13.	D	23.	B	33.	B
4.	A	14.	C	24.	D	34.	D
5.	D	15.	D	25.	D	35.	D
6.	A	16.	B	26.	D	36.	C
7.	D	17.	C	27.	C	37.	C
8.	B	18.	B	28.	C	38.	D
9.	C	19.	D	29.	A	39.	B
10.	B	20.	B	30.	D	40.	D

SENTENCE COMPLETIONS

Practice Drill 7—Coming Up with Your Own Word

These words are just to give you an idea of what you could use. Any words that accurately fill the blank, based on the clue and the direction word, will do.

1.	good	12.	produce	23.	annoyed
2.	rare	13.	changed	24.	on time
3.	remarkable	14.	strong	25.	skill
4.	awake	15.	not necessary	26.	variety
5.	lucky	16.	repetitive	27.	creative
6.	thoughtful	17.	risky	28.	sharing
7.	alike	18.	outgoing	29.	flexible
8.	waste time	19.	balanced	30.	inborn
9.	frugal	20.	generous	31.	affable;
10.	movement	21.	steadfast		talkative
11.	simple	22.	intimidated; shy	32.	awestruck

Practice Drill 8—Eliminating Answers Based on Your Word

Below are the correct answers to the problems. You should have eliminated the other choices.

1.	D	9.	B	17.	B	25.	A
2.	B	10.	A	18.	A	26.	C
3.	C	11.	D	19.	C	27.	B
4.	D	12.	D	20.	C	28.	B
5.	A	13.	B	21.	B	29.	C
6.	A	14.	C	22.	D	30.	B
7.	D	15.	D	23.	A	31.	A
8.	C	16.	C	24.	B	32.	C

Practice Drill 9—Using Positive/Negative

1.	+	6.	+
2.	+	7.	–
3.	–	8.	–
4.	+	9.	–
5.	–	10.	+

Practice Drill 10—Eliminating Based on Positive/Negative

1.	A	6.	A
2.	C	7.	C
3.	B	8.	D
4.	D	9.	A
5.	C	10.	C

Practice Drill 11—Two-Blank Sentence Completions

1.	B	6.	A
2.	C	7.	C
3.	A	8.	C
4.	A	9.	A
5.	D	10.	C

Review—The Sentence Completions Plan

For each and every sentence completion, the first thing I do is cover the answers.

I look for the clue, and I mark it by underlining it.

I look for any direction words, and I circle them.

Then I come up with my own word for the blank. If I have trouble coming up with a word for the blank, I decide if the blank is positive or negative (or neither).

Then I eliminate choices, and I guess from the remaining choices.

For each and every sentence completion, the first thing I do is cover the answers.

I look for the clue, and I mark it by underlining it.

I look for any direction words, and I circle them.

If the sentence completion has two blanks, I do them one at a time.

I do the blank that is easier first—the one that has the better clue.

I come up with a word for one of the blanks, and when I uncover the choices, I uncover only the words for the blank that I am working on, and I eliminate based on those.

Then, I go back to the sentence and come up with a word for the other blank, uncover the choices that are left, and eliminate.

No, I cannot eliminate choices that contain words I do not know.

If I can eliminate only one or two choices, then I guess from the remaining choices.

If the sentence or vocabulary looks so difficult that I can't come up with a word or decide if the blank is positive or negative, then I fill in my "letter-of-the-day."

I spend my last minute filling in the "letter-of-the-day" for any questions I have not gotten around to answering.

I should never leave a question unanswered because there is no penalty for guessing.

Practice Drill 12—All Sentence Completion Techniques

1.	A	5.	D	9.	C	13.	B	17.	C
2.	C	6.	B	10.	B	14.	C	18.	D
3.	B	7.	B	11.	D	15.	A	19.	A
4.	A	8.	C	12.	A	16.	B	20.	D

READING COMPREHENSION

For detailed explanations, go to your Student Tools.

Practice Drill 1—Getting Through the Passage

You should have brief labels like the following:

1st Label:	Norway → Iceland
2nd Label:	Iceland → Greenland
3rd Label:	Lost
4th Label:	Saw America; landed Greenland
What?	A Viking
So What?	Found America early
Passage type?	History of an event—social studies

Practice Drill 2—Answering a General Question

1. D
2. D

Practice Drill 3—Answering a Specific Question

1. C
2. A
3. B
4. D
5. C

Review—The Reading Plan

After I read each paragraph, I label it.

After I read an entire passage, I ask myself: What? and So what?

The five main types of general questions, and the questions I can ask myself to answer them, are:

- Main idea: What was the "What? So what?" for this passage?
- Tone/attitude: How did the author feel about the subject?
- General interpretation: Which answer stays closest to what the author said and how he said it?
- General purpose: Why did the author write this?
- Prediction: How was the passage arranged? What will come next?

To find the answer to a specific question, I can use three clues.

- Paragraph labels
- Line or paragraph reference
- Lead words

If the question says "In line 22," then I begin reading at approximately line 17. On a general question, I eliminate answers that are:

- Too small
- Not mentioned in the passage
- In contradiction to the passage
- Too big
- Too extreme
- Against common sense

On a specific question, I eliminate answers that are:

- Too extreme
- Contradicting passage details
- Not mentioned in the passage
- Against common sense

When I've got it down to two possible answers, I:

- Reread the question
- Look at what makes the two answers different
- Go back to the passage
- Eliminate the answer that is worse

Practice Drill 4—All Reading Techniques—Lower Level

What? Tides

So what? Are caused by the moon

1. A
2. D
3. D
4. C

Practice Drill 5—All Reading Techniques—Lower Level

What? Brooklyn Bridge

So what? There were problems building it.

1. D
2. B
3. C
4. A
5. C

Practice Drill 6—All Reading Techniques—All Levels

What? William Levitt

So what? Built homes efficiently

1. C
2. D
3. C
4. D
5. A
6. C

Practice Drill 7—All Reading Techniques—All Levels

What? Etymology

So what? Has many words to explore

1. B
2. C
3. A
4. C
5. B

Practice Drill 8—All Reading Techniques—Upper Level

What? Bob Dylan

So what? Was destined to be a musician

1. D
2. B
3. D
4. A
5. C

Practice Drill 9—All Reading Techniques—Middle and Upper Levels

What? Science

So what? Doesn't have all the answers

1. A
2. D
3. D
4. A
5. C

Part V
ISEE Practice Tests

HOW TO TAKE A PRACTICE TEST

Here are some reminders for taking your practice test.

- Find a quiet place to take the test where you won't be interrupted or distracted, and make sure you have enough time to take the entire test.

- Time yourself strictly. Use a timer, watch, or stopwatch that will ring, and do not allow yourself to go over time for any section.

- Take a practice test in one sitting, allowing yourself breaks of no more than two minutes between sections.

- Use the attached answer sheets to bubble in your choices.

- Each bubble you choose should be filled in thoroughly, and no other marks should be made in the answer area.

- Make sure to double-check that your bubbles are filled in correctly!

Chapter 18
Upper Level ISEE
Practice Test

Upper Level Practice Test

Be sure each mark *completely* fills the answer space.

SECTION 1

1 Ⓐ Ⓑ Ⓒ Ⓓ	9 Ⓐ Ⓑ Ⓒ Ⓓ	17 Ⓐ Ⓑ Ⓒ Ⓓ	25 Ⓐ Ⓑ Ⓒ Ⓓ	33 Ⓐ Ⓑ Ⓒ Ⓓ
2 Ⓐ Ⓑ Ⓒ Ⓓ	10 Ⓐ Ⓑ Ⓒ Ⓓ	18 Ⓐ Ⓑ Ⓒ Ⓓ	26 Ⓐ Ⓑ Ⓒ Ⓓ	34 Ⓐ Ⓑ Ⓒ Ⓓ
3 Ⓐ Ⓑ Ⓒ Ⓓ	11 Ⓐ Ⓑ Ⓒ Ⓓ	19 Ⓐ Ⓑ Ⓒ Ⓓ	27 Ⓐ Ⓑ Ⓒ Ⓓ	35 Ⓐ Ⓑ Ⓒ Ⓓ
4 Ⓐ Ⓑ Ⓒ Ⓓ	12 Ⓐ Ⓑ Ⓒ Ⓓ	20 Ⓐ Ⓑ Ⓒ Ⓓ	28 Ⓐ Ⓑ Ⓒ Ⓓ	36 Ⓐ Ⓑ Ⓒ Ⓓ
5 Ⓐ Ⓑ Ⓒ Ⓓ	13 Ⓐ Ⓑ Ⓒ Ⓓ	21 Ⓐ Ⓑ Ⓒ Ⓓ	29 Ⓐ Ⓑ Ⓒ Ⓓ	37 Ⓐ Ⓑ Ⓒ Ⓓ
6 Ⓐ Ⓑ Ⓒ Ⓓ	14 Ⓐ Ⓑ Ⓒ Ⓓ	22 Ⓐ Ⓑ Ⓒ Ⓓ	30 Ⓐ Ⓑ Ⓒ Ⓓ	38 Ⓐ Ⓑ Ⓒ Ⓓ
7 Ⓐ Ⓑ Ⓒ Ⓓ	15 Ⓐ Ⓑ Ⓒ Ⓓ	23 Ⓐ Ⓑ Ⓒ Ⓓ	31 Ⓐ Ⓑ Ⓒ Ⓓ	39 Ⓐ Ⓑ Ⓒ Ⓓ
8 Ⓐ Ⓑ Ⓒ Ⓓ	16 Ⓐ Ⓑ Ⓒ Ⓓ	24 Ⓐ Ⓑ Ⓒ Ⓓ	32 Ⓐ Ⓑ Ⓒ Ⓓ	40 Ⓐ Ⓑ Ⓒ Ⓓ

SECTION 2

1 Ⓐ Ⓑ Ⓒ Ⓓ	9 Ⓐ Ⓑ Ⓒ Ⓓ	17 Ⓐ Ⓑ Ⓒ Ⓓ	25 Ⓐ Ⓑ Ⓒ Ⓓ	33 Ⓐ Ⓑ Ⓒ Ⓓ
2 Ⓐ Ⓑ Ⓒ Ⓓ	10 Ⓐ Ⓑ Ⓒ Ⓓ	18 Ⓐ Ⓑ Ⓒ Ⓓ	26 Ⓐ Ⓑ Ⓒ Ⓓ	34 Ⓐ Ⓑ Ⓒ Ⓓ
3 Ⓐ Ⓑ Ⓒ Ⓓ	11 Ⓐ Ⓑ Ⓒ Ⓓ	19 Ⓐ Ⓑ Ⓒ Ⓓ	27 Ⓐ Ⓑ Ⓒ Ⓓ	35 Ⓐ Ⓑ Ⓒ Ⓓ
4 Ⓐ Ⓑ Ⓒ Ⓓ	12 Ⓐ Ⓑ Ⓒ Ⓓ	20 Ⓐ Ⓑ Ⓒ Ⓓ	28 Ⓐ Ⓑ Ⓒ Ⓓ	36 Ⓐ Ⓑ Ⓒ Ⓓ
5 Ⓐ Ⓑ Ⓒ Ⓓ	13 Ⓐ Ⓑ Ⓒ Ⓓ	21 Ⓐ Ⓑ Ⓒ Ⓓ	29 Ⓐ Ⓑ Ⓒ Ⓓ	37 Ⓐ Ⓑ Ⓒ Ⓓ
6 Ⓐ Ⓑ Ⓒ Ⓓ	14 Ⓐ Ⓑ Ⓒ Ⓓ	22 Ⓐ Ⓑ Ⓒ Ⓓ	30 Ⓐ Ⓑ Ⓒ Ⓓ	
7 Ⓐ Ⓑ Ⓒ Ⓓ	15 Ⓐ Ⓑ Ⓒ Ⓓ	23 Ⓐ Ⓑ Ⓒ Ⓓ	31 Ⓐ Ⓑ Ⓒ Ⓓ	
8 Ⓐ Ⓑ Ⓒ Ⓓ	16 Ⓐ Ⓑ Ⓒ Ⓓ	24 Ⓐ Ⓑ Ⓒ Ⓓ	32 Ⓐ Ⓑ Ⓒ Ⓓ	

SECTION 3

1 Ⓐ Ⓑ Ⓒ Ⓓ	9 Ⓐ Ⓑ Ⓒ Ⓓ	17 Ⓐ Ⓑ Ⓒ Ⓓ	25 Ⓐ Ⓑ Ⓒ Ⓓ	33 Ⓐ Ⓑ Ⓒ Ⓓ
2 Ⓐ Ⓑ Ⓒ Ⓓ	10 Ⓐ Ⓑ Ⓒ Ⓓ	18 Ⓐ Ⓑ Ⓒ Ⓓ	26 Ⓐ Ⓑ Ⓒ Ⓓ	34 Ⓐ Ⓑ Ⓒ Ⓓ
3 Ⓐ Ⓑ Ⓒ Ⓓ	11 Ⓐ Ⓑ Ⓒ Ⓓ	19 Ⓐ Ⓑ Ⓒ Ⓓ	27 Ⓐ Ⓑ Ⓒ Ⓓ	35 Ⓐ Ⓑ Ⓒ Ⓓ
4 Ⓐ Ⓑ Ⓒ Ⓓ	12 Ⓐ Ⓑ Ⓒ Ⓓ	20 Ⓐ Ⓑ Ⓒ Ⓓ	28 Ⓐ Ⓑ Ⓒ Ⓓ	36 Ⓐ Ⓑ Ⓒ Ⓓ
5 Ⓐ Ⓑ Ⓒ Ⓓ	13 Ⓐ Ⓑ Ⓒ Ⓓ	21 Ⓐ Ⓑ Ⓒ Ⓓ	29 Ⓐ Ⓑ Ⓒ Ⓓ	
6 Ⓐ Ⓑ Ⓒ Ⓓ	14 Ⓐ Ⓑ Ⓒ Ⓓ	22 Ⓐ Ⓑ Ⓒ Ⓓ	30 Ⓐ Ⓑ Ⓒ Ⓓ	
7 Ⓐ Ⓑ Ⓒ Ⓓ	15 Ⓐ Ⓑ Ⓒ Ⓓ	23 Ⓐ Ⓑ Ⓒ Ⓓ	31 Ⓐ Ⓑ Ⓒ Ⓓ	
8 Ⓐ Ⓑ Ⓒ Ⓓ	16 Ⓐ Ⓑ Ⓒ Ⓓ	24 Ⓐ Ⓑ Ⓒ Ⓓ	32 Ⓐ Ⓑ Ⓒ Ⓓ	

SECTION 4

1 Ⓐ Ⓑ Ⓒ Ⓓ	11 Ⓐ Ⓑ Ⓒ Ⓓ	21 Ⓐ Ⓑ Ⓒ Ⓓ	31 Ⓐ Ⓑ Ⓒ Ⓓ	41 Ⓐ Ⓑ Ⓒ Ⓓ
2 Ⓐ Ⓑ Ⓒ Ⓓ	12 Ⓐ Ⓑ Ⓒ Ⓓ	22 Ⓐ Ⓑ Ⓒ Ⓓ	32 Ⓐ Ⓑ Ⓒ Ⓓ	42 Ⓐ Ⓑ Ⓒ Ⓓ
3 Ⓐ Ⓑ Ⓒ Ⓓ	13 Ⓐ Ⓑ Ⓒ Ⓓ	23 Ⓐ Ⓑ Ⓒ Ⓓ	33 Ⓐ Ⓑ Ⓒ Ⓓ	43 Ⓐ Ⓑ Ⓒ Ⓓ
4 Ⓐ Ⓑ Ⓒ Ⓓ	14 Ⓐ Ⓑ Ⓒ Ⓓ	24 Ⓐ Ⓑ Ⓒ Ⓓ	34 Ⓐ Ⓑ Ⓒ Ⓓ	44 Ⓐ Ⓑ Ⓒ Ⓓ
5 Ⓐ Ⓑ Ⓒ Ⓓ	15 Ⓐ Ⓑ Ⓒ Ⓓ	25 Ⓐ Ⓑ Ⓒ Ⓓ	35 Ⓐ Ⓑ Ⓒ Ⓓ	45 Ⓐ Ⓑ Ⓒ Ⓓ
6 Ⓐ Ⓑ Ⓒ Ⓓ	16 Ⓐ Ⓑ Ⓒ Ⓓ	26 Ⓐ Ⓑ Ⓒ Ⓓ	36 Ⓐ Ⓑ Ⓒ Ⓓ	46 Ⓐ Ⓑ Ⓒ Ⓓ
7 Ⓐ Ⓑ Ⓒ Ⓓ	17 Ⓐ Ⓑ Ⓒ Ⓓ	27 Ⓐ Ⓑ Ⓒ Ⓓ	37 Ⓐ Ⓑ Ⓒ Ⓓ	47 Ⓐ Ⓑ Ⓒ Ⓓ
8 Ⓐ Ⓑ Ⓒ Ⓓ	18 Ⓐ Ⓑ Ⓒ Ⓓ	28 Ⓐ Ⓑ Ⓒ Ⓓ	38 Ⓐ Ⓑ Ⓒ Ⓓ	
9 Ⓐ Ⓑ Ⓒ Ⓓ	19 Ⓐ Ⓑ Ⓒ Ⓓ	29 Ⓐ Ⓑ Ⓒ Ⓓ	39 Ⓐ Ⓑ Ⓒ Ⓓ	
10 Ⓐ Ⓑ Ⓒ Ⓓ	20 Ⓐ Ⓑ Ⓒ Ⓓ	30 Ⓐ Ⓑ Ⓒ Ⓓ	40 Ⓐ Ⓑ Ⓒ Ⓓ	

Section 1
Verbal Reasoning

| 40 Questions | Time: 20 Minutes |

This section is divided into two parts that contain two different types of questions. As soon as you have completed Part One, answer the questions in Part Two. You may write in your test booklet. For each answer you select, fill in the corresponding circle on your answer document.

Part One – Synonyms

Each question in Part One consists of a word in capital letters followed by four answer choices. Select the one word that is most nearly the same in meaning as the word in capital letters.

SAMPLE QUESTION: <u>Sample Answer</u>

GENERIC:

(A) effortless

(B) general

(C) strong

(D) thoughtful

Go on to the next page. ➝

VR

Part Two – Sentence Completion

Each question in Part Two is made up of a sentence with one or two blanks. One blank indicates that a word is missing. Two blanks indicate that two words are missing. Each sentence is followed by four answer choices. Select the one word or pair of words that best completes the meaning of the sentence as a whole.

SAMPLE QUESTIONS:

Always ------, Edgar's late arrival surprised his friends.

(A)   entertaining
(B)   lazy
(C)   punctual
(D)   sincere

Sample Answer

Ⓐ Ⓑ ● Ⓓ

After training for months, the runner felt ------ that she would win the race, quite different from her ------ attitude initially.

(A)   confident . . . excited
(B)   indifferent . . . concern
(C)   secure . . . apprehensive
(D)   worried . . . excited

Sample Answer

Ⓐ Ⓑ ● Ⓓ

STOP. Do not go on until told to do so.

Part One – Synonyms

Directions: Select the word that is most nearly the same in meaning as the word in capital letters.

1. GRAVE:

   (A) deadly
   (B) final
   (C) open
   (D) solemn

2. FOMENT:

   (A) articulate
   (B) dissemble
   (C) instigate
   (D) praise

3. INARTICULATE:

   (A) creative
   (B) friendly
   (C) overly sensitive
   (D) tongue-tied

4. AMELIORATE:

   (A) enjoy
   (B) hinder
   (C) improve
   (D) restrain

5. THESIS:

   (A) belief
   (B) paper
   (C) report
   (D) study

6. DEBUNK:

   (A) build
   (B) discredit
   (C) impress
   (D) justify

7. DISDAIN:

   (A) annoy
   (B) contempt
   (C) find
   (D) hope

8. RETICENT:

   (A) anxious
   (B) aware
   (C) informed
   (D) reserved

9. PREVALENT:

   (A) fascinating
   (B) minority
   (C) old-fashioned
   (D) predominant

10. SATIATE:

   (A) deny
   (B) fill
   (C) serve
   (D) starve

Go on to the next page. ⟶

VR

11. CANDID:

    (A) defiant
    (B) dejected
    (C) frank
    (D) stingy

12. EMULATE:

    (A) brush off
    (B) imitate
    (C) perplex
    (D) permit

13. TAINT:

    (A) annoy
    (B) handle
    (C) infect
    (D) master

14. ENIGMA:

    (A) effort
    (B) mystery
    (C) struggle
    (D) tantrum

15. DETRIMENTAL:

    (A) considerate
    (B) desolate
    (C) emphatic
    (D) injurious

16. METICULOUS:

    (A) favorable
    (B) finicky
    (C) gigantic
    (D) maddening

17. JUXTAPOSE:

    (A) keep away
    (B) place side by side
    (C) put behind
    (D) question

18. CONGENIAL:

    (A) friendly
    (B) impressive
    (C) inborn
    (D) magical

19. MITIGATE:

    (A) bend
    (B) ease
    (C) harden
    (D) untangle

20. ELUSIVE:

    (A) real
    (B) slippery
    (C) treacherous
    (D) unhappy

Go on to the next page. ➡

Part Two – Sentence Completion

Directions: Select the word or word pair that best completes the sentence.

21. Jane felt ------- about whether to go to the party or not; on one hand it seemed like fun, but on the other, she was very tired.

    (A) ambivalent
    (B) apathetic
    (C) happy
    (D) irritated

22. Like the more famous Susan B. Anthony, M. Carey Thomas ------- feminism and women's rights.

    (A) championed
    (B) defaced
    (C) found
    (D) gained

23. Morality is not -------; cultures around the world have different ideas about how people should be treated.

    (A) debatable
    (B) helpful
    (C) realistic
    (D) universal

24. Although Ms. Sanchez ------ the student that he needed a good grade on the final exam, he did not study at all.

    (A) admonished
    (B) congratulated
    (C) criticized
    (D) ridiculed

25. Thomas Jefferson was a man of ------- talents: he was known for his skills as a writer, a musician, an architect, and an inventor as well as a politician.

    (A) abundant
    (B) frugal
    (C) mundane
    (D) overblown

26. Monica could remain ------- no longer; the injustices she witnessed moved her to speak up.

    (A) active
    (B) furious
    (C) helpful
    (D) reticent

27. Louisa May Alcott's *Little Women* is really quite -------; much of the story is based on her experiences as a young woman growing up in Concord, Massachusetts.

    (A) autobiographical
    (B) fictional
    (C) moving
    (D) visual

Go on to the next page. ➞

28. Though his lectures could be monotonous, Mr. Cutler was actually quite ------- when he spoke to students in small, informal groups.

    (A) amiable
    (B) pious
    (C) prosaic
    (D) vapid

29. Craig had ------- that the day would not go well, and just as he'd thought, he had two pop quizzes.

    (A) an antidote
    (B) an interest
    (C) a premonition
    (D) a report

30. Far from shedding light on the mystery, Jason's ------- response left people unsure.

    (A) impartial
    (B) opaque
    (C) risky
    (D) systematic

31. Although Marie was a talented and ------- performer, her gifts were often ------- because she didn't know how to promote herself.

    (A) faithful . . . supported
    (B) insulting . . . overlooked
    (C) promising . . . satisfied
    (D) versatile . . . ignored

32. Although she was the daughter of a wealthy slaveholder, Angelina Grimke ------- slavery and ------- her whole life for the cause of abolition.

    (A) desired . . . picketed
    (B) detested . . . dedicated
    (C) hated . . . wasted
    (D) represented . . . fought

33. Rhubarb is actually quite -------, requiring a large amount of sugar to make it -------.

    (A) bitter . . . palatable
    (B) flavorful . . . fattening
    (C) nutritious . . . sickening
    (D) unpopular . . . sticky

34. Because Martha was naturally -------, she would see the bright side of any situation, but Jack had a ------- personality and always waited for something bad to happen.

    (A) cheerful . . . upbeat
    (B) frightened . . . mawkish
    (C) optimistic . . . dreary
    (D) realistic . . . unreasonable

35. Although Edgar was not telling the truth, his ------ succeeded: it ------- the crowd to demand that Edgar's competitor be rejected.

    (A) antipathy . . . questioned
    (B) condone . . . encouraged
    (C) fallacy . . . incited
    (D) lie . . . permitted

Go on to the next page. ➜

36. Even though the critics praised the author's ------- use of words, they found the text ------- at a mere 100 pages.

    (A) hackneyed . . . threadbare
    (B) improper . . . laconic
    (C) precise . . . short
    (D) sure . . . banal

37. Erica's mother could not ------- why Erica would study a subject as ------- as the culture of 13th century French winemakers.

    (A) fathom . . . esoteric
    (B) intend . . . bizarre
    (C) respond . . . gruesome
    (D) understand . . . interesting

38. The threat of the storm did not ------- Ernie's excitement for the race; he had no ------- running in even the most unpleasant of weather.

    (A) diminish . . . reservations about
    (B) improve . . . concerns about
    (C) lessen . . . inclination to go
    (D) understate . . . abilities for

39. Always -------, Mr. Sanford refused to spend any money on anything unnecessary; to him, even a meal at a restaurant was a ------- excess.

    (A) parsimonious . . . gratuitous
    (B) penurious . . . useful
    (C) spendthrift . . . respectable
    (D) stingy . . . selective

40. To her -------, Margie was given the unfair label of -------, even though her love of the arts was far from superficial.

    (A) chagrin . . . dilettante
    (B) frustration . . . adversary
    (C) irritation . . . performer
    (D) surprise . . . mentor

STOP. If there is time, you may check your work in this section only.

 STOP

QR

Section 2
Quantitative Reasoning

| 37 Questions | Time: 35 Minutes |

This section is divided into two parts that contain two different types of questions. As soon as you have completed Part One, answer the questions in Part Two. You may write in your test booklet. For each answer you select, remember to fill in the corresponding circle on your answer document.

Any figures that accompany the questions in this section may be assumed to be drawn as accurately as possible EXCEPT when it is stated that a particular figure is not drawn to scale. Letters such as *x, y,* and *n* stand for real numbers.

Part One – Word Problems

Each question in Part One consists of a word problem followed by four answer choices. You may write in your test booklet; however, you may be able to solve many of these problems in your head. Next, look at the four answer choices given and select the best answer.

EXAMPLE 1:

    What is the value of the expression

    $5 + 3 \times (10 - 2) \div 4$?

    (A)   5
    (B)   9
    (C)   11
    (D)   16

Sample Answer
ⒶⒷ●Ⓓ

The correct answer is 11, so circle C is darkened.

Go on to the next page. ➡

Part Two – Quantitative Comparisons

All questions in Part Two are quantitative comparisons between the quantities shown in Column A and Column B. Using the information given in each question, compare the quantity in Column A to the quantity in Column B, and chose one of these four answer choices:

(A)   The quantity in Column A is greater.
(B)   The quantity in Column B is greater.
(C)   The two quantities are equal.
(D)   The relationship cannot be determined from the information given.

EXAMPLE 2:	<u>Column A</u> 50% of 40	<u>Column B</u> 20% of 100	<u>Sample Answer</u> Ⓐ Ⓑ ● Ⓓ

The quantity in <u>Column A</u> (20) is the same as the quantity in <u>Column B</u> (20), so circle C is darkened.

EXAMPLE 3:	*y* is any real non-zero number		<u>Sample Answer</u> Ⓐ Ⓑ Ⓒ ●
	<u>Column A</u> *y*	<u>Column B</u> $\frac{1}{y}$	

Since *y* can be any real number (including an integer or a fraction), there is not enough information given to determine the relationship, so circle D is darkened.

STOP. Do not go on
until told to do so.

NO TEST MATERIAL ON THIS PAGE

Part One – Word Problems

Directions: Choose the best answer from the four choices given.

___

1. Which of the following is greatest?

   (A) 0.0100
   (B) 0.0099
   (C) 0.1900
   (D) 0.0199

2. Which of the following is NOT the product of two prime numbers?

   (A) 33
   (B) 35
   (C) 45
   (D) 91

3. If x, y, and z are consecutive even integers, then what is the difference between x and z ?

   (A) 0
   (B) 1
   (C) 2
   (D) 4

Questions 4-5 refer to the following chart.

Clothing Close-out

Dresses	Originally $120	Now $90
Coats	Originally $250	Now $180
Shoes	Originally $60	Now $40
Hats	Originally $40	Now $20

4. Which of the items for sale has the greatest percent discount?

   (A) Dresses
   (B) Coats
   (C) Shoes
   (D) Hats

5. Purchasing which item will save the buyer the most dollars?

   (A) Dresses
   (B) Coats
   (C) Shoes
   (D) Hats

Go on to the next page. ➡

6. Amy is three years older than Beth and five years younger than Jo. If Beth is b years old, how old is Jo, in terms of b ?

(A) $2b + 3$
(B) $2b - 3$
(C) $b + 4$
(D) $b + 8$

7. If x is divided by 5, the remainder is 4. If y is divided by 5, the remainder is 1. What is the remainder when $(x + y)$ is divided by 5 ?

(A) 0
(B) 1
(C) 2
(D) 3

8. If x is a factor of p and y is a factor of q, then which of the following is true?

(A) pq is a factor of xy.
(B) pq is a multiple of x.
(C) p is a factor of xy.
(D) p is a multiple of xy.

9. Find the maximum value of y when $y = 3x^2 + 2$ and $-3 \le x \le 2$.

(A) 2
(B) 14
(C) 29
(D) 50

10. If b is a positive integer and $(x + 5)^2 = x^2 + bx + 25$, then b is equal to what value?

(A) 5
(B) 10
(C) 20
(D) 25

11. J is a whole number divisible by 4. J is also divisible by 3. Which of the following is NOT a possible value for J ?

(A) 12
(B) 24
(C) 30
(D) 36

12. The product of 0.48 and 100 is approximately

(A) 0.5
(B) 4.8
(C) 5
(D) 50

Go on to the next page. ➡

13. If the length of a rectangle is increased by 20% and the width of the rectangle is decreased by 10%, what is the percent increase of the area of the rectangle?

(A) 8%
(B) 9%
(C) 10%
(D) 12%

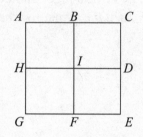

14. Square *ACEG* shown above is composed of 4 squares with sides of 1 meter each. Traveling only on the lines of the squares, how many different routes from *A* to *D* that are exactly 3 meters long are possible?

(A) 2
(B) 3
(C) 4
(D) 5

15. If, in triangle *ABC*, the measure of angle *B* is greater than 90°, and *AB = BC,* what is a possible measure for angle *C* in degrees?

(A) 35
(B) 45
(C) 60
(D) It cannot be determined from the information given.

16. Chumway Motors discounts the cost of a car by 10% and then runs another special one-day deal offering an additional 20% off the discounted price. What discount does this represent from the original price of the car?

(A) 28%
(B) 30%
(C) 40%
(D) 72%

17. David scored 82, 84, and 95 on his first three math tests. What score does he need on his fourth test to bring his average up to a 90 ?

(A) 90
(B) 92
(C) 96
(D) 99

Go on to the next page. ➞

18. Howard has a coin jar filled with only quarters and nickels. If he has a total of 23 coins that equal $2.15, which of the following could be the number of nickels Howard has in the jar?

    (A) 5
    (B) 10
    (C) 18
    (D) 20

19. If $p^2 + q^2 = 25$ and $2pq = 10$, what is the value of $(p - q)^2$?

    (A) 250
    (B) 100
    (C) 50
    (D) 15

20. The ratio of yellow paint to red paint to white paint needed to make a perfect mixture of orange paint is 3 to 2 to 1. If 36 gallons of orange paint are needed to paint a cottage, how many gallons of red paint will be needed?

    (A) 2
    (B) 6
    (C) 12
    (D) 15

Go on to the next page. ⟶

Part Two – Quantitative Comparisons

Directions: Using all information given in each question, compare the quantity in Column A to the quantity in Column B. All questions in Part Two have these answer choices:

(A) The quantity in Column A is greater.
(B) The quantity in Column B is greater.
(C) The two quantities are equal.
(D) The relationship cannot be determined from the information given.

	Column A	Column B
21.	25% of 50	50% of 25

A piggy bank is filled with nickels and pennies, totaling $2.10, and the number of pennies is double the number of nickels. (Note: 1 nickel = $0.05 and 1 penny = $0.01.)

	Column A	Column B
22.	The total value of the nickels	$1.75

360 is the product of 4 consecutive integers.

	Column A	Column B
23.	The greatest of the 4 consecutive integers	6

	Column A	Column B
24.	x^2	x^3

	Column A	Column B
25.	$8 - 20 \div 2 \times 5 + 3$	20

Go on to the next page. ➝

QR

Answer choices for all questions on this page.

(A) The quantity in Column A is greater.
(B) The quantity in Column B is greater.
(C) The two quantities are equal.
(D) The relationship cannot be determined from the information given.

$$(x + 2)(x - 2) = 0$$

	Column A	Column B
26.	x	2

	Column A	Column B
27.	$\sqrt{36} + \sqrt{16}$	$\sqrt{52}$

	Column A	Column B
28.	3^{12}	9^6

The volume of a solid cube is 27.

	Column A	Column B
29.	The height of the cube	3

$$\frac{x + 2}{y + 2} = \frac{x}{y}$$

	Column A	Column B
30.	x	$y + 2$

	Column A	Column B
31.	The sum of the integers from 1 to 100, inclusive	The sum of the even integers from 1 to 200, inclusive

$$\frac{x}{4} = 1.5$$

	Column A	Column B
32.	x	5

Go on to the next page. →

Answer choices for all questions on this page.

(A) The quantity in Column A is greater.
(B) The quantity in Column B is greater.
(C) The two quantities are equal.
(D) The relationship cannot be determined from the information given.

Column A	Column B
33. $\left(\dfrac{1}{5}\right)^{-\frac{1}{2}}$	$\left(\dfrac{1}{5}\right)^{4}$

A card is drawn from a standard deck and a 6-sided number cube, numbered 1 to 6, is rolled.

Column A	Column B
34. If a king is drawn from the deck, the probability of rolling an even number.	If a spade is drawn from the deck, the probability of rolling a number less than 4

When they are in season, a farmer sells turnips for $1.80 per bunch. At the beginning of the off-season, this farmer increases the price per bunch by 10%; however, at the end of the off-season, the farmer decreases by 10% the price of turnips per bunch.

Column A	Column B
35. The price of turnips per bunch at the end of the off-season	$1.80

A box contains 4 cookies, 5 brownies, and 6 doughnuts. Two items are removed from the bag.

Column A	Column B
36. The probability that both items are brownies	The probability that one item is a cookie and the other is a doughnut

A triangle has two sides measuring 4 and 6, respectively.

Column A	Column B
37. The greatest possible area of the triangle	12

STOP. If there is time, you may check your work in this section only.

RC

Section 3
Reading Comprehension

| 36 Questions | | Time: 35 Minutes |

This section contains six short reading passages. Each passage is followed by six questions based on its content. Answer the questions following each passage on the basis of what is <u>stated</u> or <u>implied</u> in that passage. You may write in the test booklet.

STOP. Do not go on until told to do so.

Questions 1–6

Line

1   New Orleans was the site of the last
2 major battle during the War of 1812,
3 a lengthy conflict between British and
4 American troops. The Battle of New
5 Orleans in January 1815 was one of the
6 greatest victories in American military
7 history. However, the great success of this
8 battle did not actually bring about the end of
9 the war. Surprisingly, the Treaty of Ghent,
10 which declared the end of the war, had
11 already been signed by both sides a month
12 earlier.
13   How was that possible? There were two
14 major reasons. The first is that New Orleans
15 was relatively isolated and communication
16 in the growing United States was not as
17 simple as it is today. Thus, it is possible that
18 the British commanders and the American
19 general, Andrew Jackson, did not realize a
20 treaty had been signed before they started
21 their battle. A second reason is that there is
22 a difference between a signed treaty and a
23 ratified treaty. Even if all soldiers fighting in
24 and around New Orleans had known of the
25 treaty, it had not yet been ratified by the U.S.
26 Senate. Thus, though the Treaty of Ghent
27 took place in December prior to the Battle of
28 New Orleans, the war did not officially end
29 until February 1815, when the Senate ratified
30 the treaty.

31   Had the combatants in New Orleans
32 known of the treaty, they might have
33 avoided a tough battle, especially the
34 British. In the battle, a force of about 4,000
35 American troops decisively defeated an
36 enemy of nearly twice its size. At stake for
37 the soldiers was control of the waterways of
38 the Mississippi, and the fighting was fierce.
39 A combination of tactical mistakes and bad
40 weather doomed the British attack, costing
41 them nearly 2,000 soldiers injured or killed.
42 The Americans lost fewer than 200. But
43 was the terrible battle all for nothing? Some
44 historians suggest that victory that day was
45 crucial for the American military in order
46 to enforce and help quickly ratify the peace
47 treaty. Potentially, with an American loss in
48 New Orleans, the British could have found
49 hope to continue the conflict.

Go on to the next page. ➞

1. The primary purpose of the passage is to

   (A) blame the British for fighting an unnecessary war
   (B) celebrate the tactical military maneuvers of Andrew Jackson
   (C) convince readers that peace treaties are often worthless
   (D) provide greater details about the end of a historical conflict

2. The passage suggests that all of the following occurred near the end of the War of 1812 EXCEPT

   (A) Andrew Jackson ignored the orders of President Madison
   (B) Communication with the battle line commanders was slow
   (C) The Treaty of Ghent was signed
   (D) Weather conditions hurt the efforts of the British soldiers

3. Which of the following is implied by the passage?

   (A) Andrew Jackson did not know the difference between a signed treaty and a ratified treaty.
   (B) President Madison did not realize the Battle of New Orleans was possible.
   (C) The British may have had a chance for victory with better conditions and preparation.
   (D) The British troops knew of the treaty but attacked anyway.

4. According to the passage, New Orleans was a strategic battle site because

   (A) it was the only location where American forces were better supplied than the British forces
   (B) the American forces would be trapped in the swamplands if they lost
   (C) the British were attempting to defeat a more numerous force
   (D) the Mississippi River was nearby and control of it was important

5. After which of the following was the War of 1812 officially at an end?

   (A) Both armies signing the Treaty of Ghent
   (B) British retreat from the Mississippi
   (C) The Battle of New Orleans
   (D) The Senate's ratification of the Treaty of Ghent

6. According to the passage, a treaty

   (A) cannot be signed by the president without the consent of the Senate
   (B) has sometimes been ignored by those in battle
   (C) is always used to end a war
   (D) is not effective until it is ratified by the Senate

Go on to the next page. ➜

Questions 7–12

Line

1   According to game maker Hasbro,
2 approximately 750 million people have
3 played the well-known game *Monopoly*
4 since it was invented in the 1930s. Charles
5 Darrow is typically credited as the inventor
6 of the world's most famous board game.
7 However, he likely derived his version of
8 *Monopoly* from one of several other games
9 similarly involving realty buying and selling
10 that were already in existence prior to the
11 1930s when he got his patent for the game.
12   A probable reason that Darrow's
13 *Monopoly* became the hugely successful
14 game that still exists today is that he took
15 a diligent approach to producing it. Other
16 similar games existed, but some of them
17 had no board or regulation pieces. With
18 help from his wife and son who adorned the
19 sets with detail, Darrow personally created
20 the pieces and boards that became the first
21 *Monopoly* game sets. His extra work in
22 creating the entire environment that players
23 needed gave his game something extra that
24 other variations did not have.

25   Darrow had marginal success selling
26 his games in various parts of the country.
27 Several Philadelphia area stores were
28 the first to carry his game and sell it in
29 large quantities. Despite this, Darrow had
30 difficulty selling his game to the major
31 game manufacturer of the time, Parker
32 Brothers. He was told that his game was
33 too complex and had fundamental errors
34 in its design that would limit its appeal.
35 Ultimately, the continued sales he managed
36 on his own forced Parker Brothers to
37 reassess the worth of his game. Eventually,
38 the company agreed to produce the game
39 and shortly thereafter it became the
40 bestselling game in the country.
41   That success turned Charles Darrow
42 into a millionaire, which is the ultimate
43 irony. Darrow initially began work on
44 *Monopoly* to help support himself and his
45 family following the financial troubles tied
46 to the stock market crash of 1929.
47   Thus, Charles Darrow became a
48 millionaire by producing a game that allows
49 "regular" people to feel like they are buying
50 and selling homes and real estate like
51 millionaires.

Go on to the next page. ⟶

7. The best title for this passage would be

    (A) "A Comparison of Several Early Real Estate Board Games"
    (B) "How Hasbro Introduced *Monopoly* to the World"
    (C) "The Early History of Charles Darrow's *Monopoly*"
    (D) "Two Views of Charles Darrow's Life"

8. It is suggested by the passage that

    (A) Darrow decided to make his game less complex after initially meeting with Parker Brothers
    (B) Darrow had no other skills to use after the stock market crash of 1929
    (C) Parker Brothers probably doubted that a complex game could sell well
    (D) Philadelphia was the only major city where he could sell his game

9. As used in line 49, "regular" refers to people who

    (A) rent rather than own property
    (B) are in the top 1% of wealthiest people
    (C) love to play board games
    (D) are in a lower economic class than millionaires

10. With which of the following would the author be LEAST likely to agree?

    (A) Charles Darrow chose to continue to sell his game despite criticisms.
    (B) Charles Darrow is not the first person to conceive of a board-based real estate game.
    (C) Charles Darrow preferred to achieve his goals without the help of others.
    (D) Some of the things Darrow chose to do helped make his game sell better than other games.

11. Which of the following was NOT mentioned by the author as contributing to the ultimate success of *Monopoly*?

    (A) Darrow's efforts to initially sell the game on his own
    (B) The addition of specific pieces and a playing board in each set
    (C) The adjustments Parker Brothers made to the game
    (D) The enjoyment people get in pretending to be millionaires

12. The author suggests in the third paragraph that

    (A) certain errors in *Monopoly* served to limit its appeal
    (B) Charles Darrow sold his game in Philadelphia because he knew it would be popular there
    (C) *Monopoly* was initially too complex to be popular
    (D) some people doubted that *Monopoly* would be popular

Go on to the next page. ➡

Questions 13–18

Line

1   Every year, hundreds of hopeful
2 students arrive in Washington, D.C., in
3 order to compete in the National Spelling
4 Bee. This competition has been held
5 annually since 1925 and is sponsored by
6 E.W. Scripps Company. The sponsors
7 provide both a trophy and a monetary award
8 to the champion speller. In the competition,
9 students under 16 years of age take turns
10 attempting to properly spell words as
11 provided by the moderator. The champion
12 is the sole remaining student who does not
13 make a mistake.
14   Most American students are familiar
15 with the concept of a spelling bee because
16 it is practiced in many schools throughout
17 the country. The National Spelling Bee,
18 however, is a much bigger setting and
19 showcases only the best spellers from all
20 parts of the nation. Students who appear
21 at the National Spelling Bee have already
22 won competitions at local and state levels.
23 Winning the competition nowadays requires
24 the ability to perform under intense pressure
25 against very talented students in front
26 of a large audience. A student who wins
27 the event in the twenty-first century will
28 experience a much different challenge than
29 the first winner, Frank Neuhauser, did in
30 1925 when he defeated only nine other
31 competitors.

32   Clearly, the 90 years of the National
33 Spelling Bee's existence attests to the
34 importance of spelling in the English
35 language. However, struggles with spelling
36 English words goes back much more than
37 80 years. The captivating thing about
38 spelling correctly in English is that it is in
39 many ways without rules. English language
40 has a powerful capacity to absorb new
41 words from other languages and in doing so
42 make them "English" words. As a result of
43 this ability to borrow from other languages,
44 the sheer number of words in English is
45 much higher than any other language. Thus,
46 spelling in many other languages involves
47 fewer words, fewer rules, and fewer odd
48 exceptions to those rules. It turns out that a
49 spelling bee in most other languages would
50 be a waste of time. Why is that? Well,
51 without the myriad exceptions to common
52 vocabulary, there would be very few words
53 that everyone didn't already know.

Go on to the next page. ➡

13. The author mentions "other languages" in line 41 in order to point out that

    (A) English-language spelling bees are unnecessarily complex
    (B) one challenge in English-language spelling bees is the number of words that can be tested
    (C) spelling bees are at least 90 years old
    (D) words are harder to spell in English than in any other language

14. According to the passage, what is a major difference between the first National Spelling Bee and today's competition?

    (A) Spellers in the past did not expect the competition to grow so large.
    (B) The competition no longer focuses on only English words.
    (C) There are more competitors.
    (D) The words used today are significantly harder.

15. In line 51, the word "myriad" most nearly means

    (A) confusing
    (B) dangerous
    (C) linguistic
    (D) numerous

16. Which of the following can be inferred from the passage?

    (A) A competitor at the National Spelling Bee has already won at least one smaller spelling bee.
    (B) E.W. Scripps Company desires to eliminate poor spelling in America.
    (C) Frank Neuhauser would not do well in today's competition.
    (D) The competition has grown too large.

17. The author of the passage intends to

    (A) compare the presentation of the current National Spelling Bee with the structure in the past
    (B) contrast the English language with other languages
    (C) investigate the role that vocabulary plays in our lives
    (D) review the history and current form of the National Spelling Bee

18. The author's attitude toward winners of the National Spelling Bee is

    (A) admiring
    (B) critical
    (C) indifferent
    (D) questioning

Go on to the next page. ⟶

Questions 19–24

Line

1   The idea of black holes was developed
2 by Karl Schwarzschild in 1916. Since then,
3 many different scientists have added to the
4 theory of black holes in space. A black hole
5 is usually defined as a very dense celestial
6 body from which nothing, not even light,
7 can escape. But from what do black holes
8 originate?
9   A black hole begins as a star. A star
10 burns hydrogen, and this process, called
11 fusion, releases energy. The energy released
12 outward works against the star's own
13 gravity pulling inward and prevents the star
14 from collapsing. After millions of years
15 of burning hydrogen, the star eventually
16 runs out of fuel. At this point, the star's
17 own gravity and weight cause it to start
18 contracting.
19   If the star is small and not very heavy,
20 it will shrink just a little and become a white
21 dwarf when it runs out of fuel. White dwarf
22 stars do not emit much energy, so they are
23 usually not visible without a telescope.

24   If the star is bigger and heavier, it will
25 collapse very quickly in an implosion. If the
26 matter that remains is not much heavier than
27 our sun, it will eventually become a very
28 dense neutron star. However, if the matter
29 that remains is more than 1.7 times the mass
30 of our sun, there will not be enough outward
31 pressure to resist the force of gravity, and
32 the collapse will continue. The result is a
33 black hole.
34   The black hole will have a boundary
35 around it called the horizon. Light and
36 matter can pass over this boundary to enter,
37 but they cannot pass back out again—this is
38 why the hole appears black. The gravity and
39 density of the black hole prevent anything
40 from escaping.
41   Scientists are still adding to the black
42 hole theory. They think they may have
43 found black holes in several different
44 galaxies, and as they learn more about them,
45 scientists will be able to understand more
46 about how black holes are formed and what
47 happens as the holes change.

Go on to the next page. ➡

19. The purpose of the question in the first paragraph is to

(A) illustrate how little we know about black holes
(B) indicate the source of the facts quoted in the passage
(C) interest the reader in the topic of the passage
(D) set a goal for independent research

20. According to the passage, which of the following causes a collapsing star to become a neutron star?

(A) Mass greater than 1.7 times that of our sun
(B) Mass less than 1.7 times that of our sun
(C) Remaining fuel that can be used in fusion
(D) Slow, brief shrinkage process

21. The passage suggests that if we were to send a satellite to the horizon of a black hole, it would probably

(A) begin spinning uncontrollably and fly apart
(B) be immediately repelled from the black hole
(C) be pulled into the black hole and not come back out
(D) enter, and then immediately exit, the black hole

22. According to the passage, which of the following is an effect of the process of fusion?

(A) The star does not immediately collapse.
(B) The star generates hydrogen.
(C) The star survives millions of years longer than average.
(D) The white dwarf fails to produce light.

23. Black holes appear black because

(A) only a little energy escapes them
(B) only one galaxy contains them
(C) they are extraordinarily large
(D) they do not eject light they have absorbed

24. Which of the following best describes the organization of the passage?

(A) It discusses the biggest, heaviest celestial bodies before moving on to the smaller, lighter ones.
(B) It introduces the topic and then narrates chronologically the process by which stars become black holes.
(C) It uses a personal story to introduce the topic, and then compares and contrasts black holes.
(D) It uses the example of one specific black hole in order to generalize.

Go on to the next page. ➡

Questions 25–30

Line

1   The midterm elections of 2014 had
2 the lowest voter turnout of any American
3 election cycle since World War II, with only
4 36.4 percent of the eligible voting public
5 casting a ballot. What is most disturbing
6 about this number is that it was less than
7 100 years ago that 200 women marched on
8 the White House, incurring public scorn,
9 arrest, and even torture, to secure the vote
10 for half the American public.
11   Women's Suffrage, the movement
12 dedicated to securing women's right to
13 vote in the United States, began in earnest
14 in the 1840s. Several Women's Rights
15 Conventions were held throughout the 19th
16 century, beginning with the Seneca Falls
17 Convention of 1848, during which attendees
18 officially passed a resolution in favor of
19 Women's Suffrage. Over the next 70 years,
20 many brave women fought for the cause of
21 basic gender equality.
22   This fight came to a head in 1917,
23 when members of the National Women's
24 Party, led by Alice Paul, picketed outside
25 the White House in order to influence
26 President Wilson and Congress to pass
27 an amendment to the United States
28 Constitution that would enfranchise women
29 and guarantee their voting rights. This
30 was the first time in the history of the
31 United States that the White House was

32 picketed, and it was done so in an orderly
33 and peaceful fashion. After months of
34 nonviolent protest, police arrested over 200
35 women for blocking a public sidewalk in
36 July 1917.
37   Paul and many of her followers
38 underwent a hunger strike during their
39 incarceration to protest the deplorable
40 conditions of the prison, which resulted
41 in many women being force-fed and Paul
42 herself being moved to the psychiatric
43 ward of the hospital. The rest were sent
44 to the Occoquan Workhouse. It was at
45 this workhouse that the most terrible and
46 significant event of the Women's Suffrage
47 movement would occur. Dubbed the "Night
48 of Terror," 44 guards armed with clubs
49 attacked 33 women protesters as they
50 returned to the house. They were brutally
51 beaten, choked, and one was stabbed to
52 death. These events infuriated the nation
53 when they were exposed, and within two
54 weeks a judge had ordered the prisoners
55 released and cleared of all charges.
56   Due to the widespread gain of support
57 these women earned through their peaceful
58 protest and physical endurance, as well as
59 the work of countless men and women of
60 the previous 70 years, the 19th Amendment
61 was added to the Constitution three years
62 later, on August 20, 1920.

Go on to the next page. ➡

25. The main purpose of the passage is to

    (A) portray Alice Paul as an integral figure of the Women's Suffrage movement
    (B) attribute the adoption of the 19th Amendment solely to the Night of Terror
    (C) describe the actions taken by part of the American public to secure equal voting rights
    (D) demonstrate the terrible actions of guards against women's rights protestors

26. The word "exposed" as used in line 53 most closely means

    (A) unprotected
    (B) bare
    (C) revealed
    (D) buried

27. Which of the following best expresses the author's attitude toward the percentage of voter turnout mentioned in the first paragraph?

    (A) Shock
    (B) Reassurance
    (C) Pessimism
    (D) Terror

28. According to the author, the most probable legacy of the Night of Terror is

    (A) President Wilson's pardon of the protestors
    (B) the imprisonment of the 44 guards who attacked the protesters
    (C) the desired delay of the 19th amendment for several years
    (D) the right to vote for women

29. Which of the following does the passage imply was a reason for the protestor's hunger strike?

    (A) They were attempting to improve the environment of their captivity.
    (B) They were resisting being force-fed at the prison.
    (C) They wanted to be able to use the sidewalk for peaceful protest.
    (D) They were unable to eat after being choked during the Night of Terror.

30. The author believes that the National Women's Party's tactics are best described as

    (A) calm but pointless
    (B) disorderly but successful
    (C) violent and immediate
    (D) nonviolent and effective

Go on to the next page. ⟶

Questions 31–36

Line

1   He is one of the greatest living
2 scientists of this age. In fact, he is perhaps
3 one of the greatest scientists of any age.
4 Yet he owes much of his success not to
5 mathematics or physics or any other science
6 but to a disease. He is Stephen Hawking.
7   Born in 1942, three hundred years after
8 the death of Galileo, Stephen Hawking
9 had an unimpressive start to his scholarly
10 pursuits. At his revered English primary
11 school, St. Albans, he was considered by
12 his teachers a good, but not exceptional,
13 student. It was not evident at the time that
14 he would become internationally acclaimed
15 as a leader in several scientific fields.
16 He continued this moderately successful
17 academic trend at University College in
18 Oxford. Again, his professors thought him
19 to be intelligent, but not extraordinary in
20 his efforts. Both his cleverness and lack
21 of diligence were noticed by some of his
22 instructors.
23   After graduating from Oxford, he
24 continued to Cambridge, another excellent
25 school. Clearly, Hawking was moving
26 forward into a good science career.
27 However, it was at this time that he
28 encountered a life-changing challenge. He
29 was diagnosed with a disease that affects
30 and damages the nervous system. That

31 meant that he was eventually going to lose
32 control of his muscles and spend his life in
33 a wheelchair. Surprisingly though, Hawking
34 credits this event with making his outlook
35 on life strong again. He claims that until
36 then, he was often bored by life. For a man
37 with such a powerful mind, that makes
38 sense. He was talented, but he saw little use
39 for his talent and felt no pressure to work
40 hard. His diagnosis and impending physical
41 problems forced him to start living life to
42 the fullest.
43   Most of Stephen Hawking's
44 contributions to science have come after
45 learning of his disease. His work in the
46 field of physics has influenced the greatest
47 scientists alive. If the technology ever
48 becomes possible, he plans a trip into
49 space with the help of influential friends.
50 Though he now moves only with a special
51 wheelchair and speaks only with the help
52 of a computerized speech enhancer, he still
53 has the ability to contribute to the world. He
54 credits his disease with forcing him to face
55 the limited time available in one lifetime.
56 Stephen Hawking has made a crippling
57 disease the source of one of the greatest
58 scientific careers the world has known.
59 Through his misfortune, he learned to reach
60 his greatest potential.

Go on to the next page. ⟶

31. The author's tone is best described as

    (A) nostalgic
    (B) admiring
    (C) pitying
    (D) scornful

32. The purpose of the last line of the first paragraph ("He is Stephen Hawking") is to

    (A) reveal an answer to a riddle
    (B) specify a subject who has already been introduced
    (C) answer a question the author asked earlier
    (D) name the greatest living scientist

33. Which of the following describes Stephen Hawking's attitude toward his disease?

    (A) Actively nonchalant
    (B) Bitterly irate
    (C) Ironically appreciative
    (D) Unreservedly giddy

34. According to the second paragraph, Stephen Hawking was seen by some as

    (A) often disrespectful
    (B) particularly brilliant
    (C) somewhat lazy
    (D) uniquely energetic

35. The passage does all of the following EXCEPT

    (A) demonstrate a connection between Stephen Hawking's disease and his success as a physicist
    (B) describe a goal Hawking hopes to achieve
    (C) note particular theories developed by Hawking
    (D) set forth educational institutions attended by Hawking

36. The passage can best be described as focusing primarily on

    (A) biographical details
    (B) medical diagnoses
    (C) scientific discoveries
    (D) technological advancements

STOP. If there is time, you may check your work in this section only.

Section 4
Mathematics Achievement

47 Questions	Time: 40 Minutes

Each question is followed by four suggested answers. Read each question and then decide which one of the four suggested answers is best.

Find the row of spaces on your answer document that has the same number as the question. In this row, mark the space having the same letter as the answer you have chosen. You may write in your test booklet.

SAMPLE QUESTION:

Sample Answer

Ⓐ ● Ⓒ Ⓓ

What is the perimeter of an isosceles triangle with two sides of 4 cm and one side of 6 cm?

(A)   10 cm
(B)   14 cm
(C)   16 cm
(D)   24 cm

The correct answer is 14 cm, so circle B is darkened.

STOP. Do not go on
until told to do so.

NO TEST MATERIAL ON THIS PAGE

1. Which of the following pairs of numbers are the two different prime factors of 36 ?

   (A) 2 and 3
   (B) 3 and 4
   (C) 3 and 12
   (D) 4 and 9

2. For what nonzero value of x will the expression $\dfrac{x-3}{4x}$ be equal to 0 ?

   (A) −3
   (B) −2
   (C) 1
   (D) 3

3. Two positive whole numbers are in a ratio of 3 to 4. If the smaller of the two numbers is 9, what is the average of the two numbers?

   (A) 4
   (B) 10
   (C) 10.5
   (D) 12

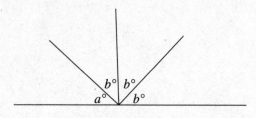

4. The four angles in the figure above share a common vertex on a straight line. What is the value of b when a equals 42° ?

   (A) 38°
   (B) 40°
   (C) 42°
   (D) 46°

5. What is 85% of 50 ?

   (A) 150.75
   (B) 135
   (C) 42.5
   (D) 39

6. A set of three positive integers has a sum of 11 and a product of 36. If the smallest of the three numbers is 2, what is the largest?

   (A) 2
   (B) 4
   (C) 6
   (D) 9

Go on to the next page. ➡

7. What is two-thirds of one-half?

   (A) $\dfrac{1}{3}$

   (B) $\dfrac{7}{6}$

   (C) $\dfrac{1}{2}$

   (D) $\dfrac{2}{3}$

8. If the distance around an oval-shaped track is 400 meters, how many laps does a runner have to run to cover a distance of 4 kilometers?
   (1 kilometer = 1,000 meters)

   (A)   4
   (B)   10
   (C)   15
   (D) 1,000

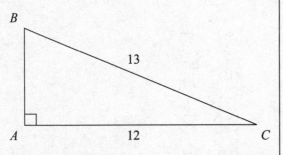

9. In triangle *ABC* shown above, the length of side *AB* is

   (A)   5
   (B)   7
   (C) 11
   (D) 14

10. Find the value of $\dfrac{2.7 \times 10^7}{3.0 \times 10^{-3}}$.

    (A) 9.0×10^{10}
    (B) 9.0×10^9
    (C) 9.0×10^4
    (D) 9.0×10^3

11. MegaMusic decides to decrease the price of a digital song from \$1.60 to \$1.20. The percent decrease for this digital song is

    (A) 20%
    (B) 25%

    (C) $33\dfrac{1}{3}\%$

    (D) 40%

12. There are *x* students in Mrs. Sproul's class, 4 fewer than twice as many as are in Mrs. Puccio's class. If there are *y* students in Mrs. Puccio's class, then what is the value of *y* in terms of *x* ?

    (A) $\dfrac{x}{2} + 2$

    (B) $2x + 4$

    (C) $2x - 4$

    (D) $\dfrac{x}{2} - 4$

Go on to the next page. ➡

Questions 13–14 refer to the following definition.

For all real numbers x,

$\#x = x^2$ if x is negative;
$\#x = 2x$ if x is positive.

13. $\#(-6) - \#(6) =$

    (A)   −24
    (B)   16
    (C)   24
    (D)   30

14. What is the value of $\#[\#x - \#y]$ when $x = 3$ and $y = -4$?

    (A)   −10
    (B)   12
    (C)   32
    (D)   100

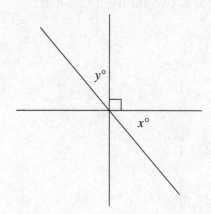

15. In the figure above, what is the value of x in terms of y ?

    (A) y
    (B) $90 - y$
    (C) $90 + y$
    (D) $180 - y$

16. $\dfrac{4a^4 b^6 c^3}{2a^3 b^5 c^2} =$

    (A) $\dfrac{2ac}{b}$

    (B) $\dfrac{ac}{b}$

    (C) $\dfrac{2b}{c}$

    (D) $2abc$

Go on to the next page. ➡

17. In Mr. Johanessen's class, $\frac{1}{4}$ of the students failed the final exam. Of the remaining students in the class, $\frac{1}{3}$ scored an A. What fraction of the whole class passed the test but scored below an A?

(A) $\frac{1}{4}$

(B) $\frac{5}{12}$

(C) $\frac{1}{2}$

(D) $\frac{7}{12}$

18. When buying new clothes for school, Rena spends $20 more than Karen and $50 more than Lynn does. If Rena spends r dollars, then what is the cost of all three of their purchases in terms of r?

(A) $r + 70$

(B) $\frac{r + 70}{3}$

(C) $3r - 70$

(D) $r + 210$

19. In a group of 100 children, there are 34 more girls than there are boys. How many boys are in the group?

(A) 33
(B) 37
(C) 67
(D) 68

20. Samantha made a chart of her students' favorite types of books.

FAVORITE TYPE OF BOOK

Type of Book	Number of Students
Mystery	8
Fantasy	20
Sci-Fi	10
Other	2

A circle graph is made using the data. What is the central angle of the portion of the graph representing Sci-Fi?

(A) 10°
(B) 25°
(C) 45°
(D) 90°

Go on to the next page. ⟶

21. At Nicholas's Computer World, computers usually sold for $1,500 are now being sold for $1,200. What fraction of the original price is the new price?

    (A) $\frac{1}{10}$

    (B) $\frac{1}{5}$

    (C) $\frac{3}{4}$

    (D) $\frac{4}{5}$

22. If $\frac{3}{x} = \frac{y}{4}$, then

    (A) $xy = 12$

    (B) $3y = 4x$

    (C) $\frac{x}{y} = \frac{4}{3}$

    (D) $3x = 4y$

23. The ratio of boys to girls at Delaware Township School is 3 to 2. If there is a total of 600 students at the school, how many are girls?

    (A) 120
    (B) 240
    (C) 360
    (D) 400

24. 150% of 40 is

    (A) 30
    (B) 40
    (C) 50
    (D) 60

25. Jane studied for her math exam for 4 hours last night. If she studied $\frac{3}{4}$ as long for her English exam, how many hours did she study all together?

    (A) 3

    (B) $4\frac{3}{4}$

    (C) 6

    (D) 7

26. $\frac{0.966}{0.42} =$

    (A) 0.23
    (B) 2.3
    (C) 23
    (D) 230

Go on to the next page. ➡

27. Nicole was able to type 35 words per minute. If she increased her speed to 42 words per minute, what was the percent increase in her typing speed?

    (A) $16\frac{2}{3}\%$

    (B) 20%

    (C) 70%

    (D) 71%

28. The first term in a series of numbers is 50. Each subsequent term is one-half the term before it if the term is even, or one-half rounded up to the next whole number if the term is odd. What is the third term in this sequence?

    (A) 13
    (B) 24
    (C) 30
    (D) 40

29. Sophia recorded the number of siblings each student in her class has in the table below.

    SIBLINGS OF EACH STUDENT

Number of Siblings	Number of Students with that Number of Siblings
0	6
1	10
2	8
3	6
4	1
5	1

    What is the mode of the data?

    (A) 1
    (B) 2
    (C) 6
    (D) 10

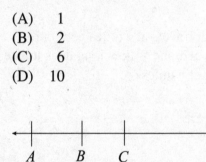

30. On the number line shown above, if segment *BD* has a length of 18, segment *AB* has a length of 5, and segment *CD* has a length of 12, then segment *AC* has a length of

    (A) 6
    (B) 11
    (C) 17
    (D) 23

Go on to the next page. ➡

31. The decimal representation of $2 + 40 + \frac{1}{100}$ is

    (A) 24.1
    (B) 24.01
    (C) 42.1
    (D) 42.01

32. What is the least possible integer divisible by 2, 3, 4, and 5 ?

    (A) 30
    (B) 40
    (C) 60
    (D) 90

33. If a car travels at x miles per hour, in terms of x and y, how long does it take it to travel y miles?

    (A) $\frac{2x}{y}$

    (B) xy

    (C) $\frac{y}{x}$

    (D) $\frac{x}{y}$

34. Triangles ABC and PQR are similar. The length of $\overline{BC}$ is 4 and the length of $\overline{QR}$ is 12. If the area of ABC is 6, what is the area of PQR ?

    (A) 54
    (B) 24
    (C) 18
    (D) 15

35. James buys one halibut steak and two salmon steaks for $30.00. Dave buys two halibut steaks and four salmon steaks for $60.00. If halibut steaks cost x dollars each and salmon steaks cost y dollars each, what is the value of x ?

    (A) $5.00
    (B) $8.00
    (C) $10.00
    (D) It cannot be determined from the information given.

Question 36 refers to the following definition.

For all positive integer values of x,

$(x) = \frac{1}{2}x$ if x is even;

$(x) = 2x$ if x is odd.

36. $(1 + 5) =$

    (A) 2
    (B) 3
    (C) 4
    (D) 6

37. Which of the following equals $2(4z + 1)$?

    (A) $2z + \frac{1}{2}$

    (B) $2z + 1$

    (C) $4z + 2$

    (D) $8z + 2$

Go on to the next page. ➡

38. The stem-and-leaf plot shown represents the length, in minutes, of movies that Janet watched over the summer.

Stem	Leaf
10	8 9
11	1 2 2 5 5 6 7
12	0 3 4 8
13	2 4 6 6 7 7 9
14	2 3 3 8 9 9
15	7

What is the median length, in minutes, of the movies Janet watched?

(A) 130
(B) 132
(C) 133
(D) 136

39. Zoo A has 3 monkeys. Zoo B has 8 monkeys. Zoo C has 16 monkeys. What is the average number of monkeys at the three zoos?

(A) 3
(B) 7
(C) 9
(D) 27

40. A steak costs $4 more than a hamburger, and a hamburger costs $4 more than a grilled cheese sandwich. If six grilled cheese sandwiches cost $2x$ dollars, how much will 4 steaks and 2 hamburgers cost?

(A) $2x + 40$
(B) $2x + 48$
(C) $6x + 34$
(D) $12x + 40$

41. What is the solution set to the inequality $|3 - 2x| > 9$?

(A) $-3 < x < 6$
(B) $-6 < x < 3$
(C) $x < -3$ or $x > 6$
(D) $x < -6$ or $x > 3$

42. $100xy$ is what percent of xy ?

(A) 10
(B) 100
(C) 1,000
(D) 10,000

43. If Matt's home is four miles from school and Laura's home is eight miles from school, then the distance from Matt's home to Laura's home is

(A) 4 miles
(B) 8 miles
(C) 12 miles
(D) It cannot be determined from the information given.

44. Two partners divide a profit of $2,000 so that the difference between the two amounts is half of their average. What is the ratio of the larger to the smaller amount?

(A) 6:1
(B) 5:3
(C) 4:1
(D) 2:1

Go on to the next page. ➞

45. What is the total value, in cents, of j coins worth 10 cents each and $j + 5$ coins worth 25 cents each?

(A) $35j + 125$
(B) $35j + 5$
(C) $10j + 130$
(D) $2j + 5$

46. A box of coins has 6 pennies, 3 nickels, 4 dimes, and 5 quarters. If two coins are selected at random, what is the probability that the first coin is a penny and the second coin is a quarter?

(A) $\dfrac{11}{18}$

(B) $\dfrac{17}{18}$

(C) $\dfrac{6}{18} \times \dfrac{5}{18}$

(D) $\dfrac{6}{18} \times \dfrac{5}{17}$

47. The formula for the volume of a cone is $\frac{1}{3}\pi r^2 h$, where r is the radius of the circular base and h is the height of the cone.

What is the radius of a cone with a volume of 12π and a height of 4 ?

(A) 3
(B) 4
(C) 8
(D) 9

STOP. If there is time, you may check your work in this section only.

Essay

You will have 30 minutes to plan and write an essay on the topic printed on the other side of this page. **Do not write on another topic. An essay on another topic is not acceptable.**

The essay is designed to give you an opportunity to show how well you can write. You should try to express your thoughts clearly. How well you write is much more important than how much you write, but you need to say enough for a reader to understand what you mean.

You will probably want to write more than a short paragraph. You should also be aware that a copy of your essay will be sent to each school that will be receiving your test results. You are to write only in the appropriate section of the answer sheet. Please write or print so that your writing may be read by someone who is not familiar with your handwriting.

You may make notes and plan your essay on the reverse side of the page. Allow enough time to copy the final form on to your answer sheet. You must copy the essay topic onto your answer sheet, on page 3, in the box provided.

Please remember to write only the final draft of the essay on pages 3 and 4 of your answer sheet and to write it in blue or black pen. Again, you may use cursive writing or you may print. Only pages 3 and 4 will be sent to the schools.

Directions continue on next page.

Essay Topic

If you could change one thing about your country, what would you change and why?

- Only write on this essay question
- Only pages 3 and 4 will be sent to the schools
- Only write in blue or black pen

NOTES

_____

_____

_____

_____

_____

_____

_____

_____

_____

_____

_____

_____

_____

Chapter 19
Middle Level
ISEE Practice Test

Middle Level Practice Test

Be sure each mark *completely* fills the answer space.

SECTION 1

1 Ⓐ Ⓑ Ⓒ Ⓓ	9 Ⓐ Ⓑ Ⓒ Ⓓ	17 Ⓐ Ⓑ Ⓒ Ⓓ	25 Ⓐ Ⓑ Ⓒ Ⓓ	33 Ⓐ Ⓑ Ⓒ Ⓓ
2 Ⓐ Ⓑ Ⓒ Ⓓ	10 Ⓐ Ⓑ Ⓒ Ⓓ	18 Ⓐ Ⓑ Ⓒ Ⓓ	26 Ⓐ Ⓑ Ⓒ Ⓓ	34 Ⓐ Ⓑ Ⓒ Ⓓ
3 Ⓐ Ⓑ Ⓒ Ⓓ	11 Ⓐ Ⓑ Ⓒ Ⓓ	19 Ⓐ Ⓑ Ⓒ Ⓓ	27 Ⓐ Ⓑ Ⓒ Ⓓ	35 Ⓐ Ⓑ Ⓒ Ⓓ
4 Ⓐ Ⓑ Ⓒ Ⓓ	12 Ⓐ Ⓑ Ⓒ Ⓓ	20 Ⓐ Ⓑ Ⓒ Ⓓ	28 Ⓐ Ⓑ Ⓒ Ⓓ	36 Ⓐ Ⓑ Ⓒ Ⓓ
5 Ⓐ Ⓑ Ⓒ Ⓓ	13 Ⓐ Ⓑ Ⓒ Ⓓ	21 Ⓐ Ⓑ Ⓒ Ⓓ	29 Ⓐ Ⓑ Ⓒ Ⓓ	37 Ⓐ Ⓑ Ⓒ Ⓓ
6 Ⓐ Ⓑ Ⓒ Ⓓ	14 Ⓐ Ⓑ Ⓒ Ⓓ	22 Ⓐ Ⓑ Ⓒ Ⓓ	30 Ⓐ Ⓑ Ⓒ Ⓓ	38 Ⓐ Ⓑ Ⓒ Ⓓ
7 Ⓐ Ⓑ Ⓒ Ⓓ	15 Ⓐ Ⓑ Ⓒ Ⓓ	23 Ⓐ Ⓑ Ⓒ Ⓓ	31 Ⓐ Ⓑ Ⓒ Ⓓ	39 Ⓐ Ⓑ Ⓒ Ⓓ
8 Ⓐ Ⓑ Ⓒ Ⓓ	16 Ⓐ Ⓑ Ⓒ Ⓓ	24 Ⓐ Ⓑ Ⓒ Ⓓ	32 Ⓐ Ⓑ Ⓒ Ⓓ	40 Ⓐ Ⓑ Ⓒ Ⓓ

SECTION 2

1 Ⓐ Ⓑ Ⓒ Ⓓ	9 Ⓐ Ⓑ Ⓒ Ⓓ	17 Ⓐ Ⓑ Ⓒ Ⓓ	25 Ⓐ Ⓑ Ⓒ Ⓓ	33 Ⓐ Ⓑ Ⓒ Ⓓ
2 Ⓐ Ⓑ Ⓒ Ⓓ	10 Ⓐ Ⓑ Ⓒ Ⓓ	18 Ⓐ Ⓑ Ⓒ Ⓓ	26 Ⓐ Ⓑ Ⓒ Ⓓ	34 Ⓐ Ⓑ Ⓒ Ⓓ
3 Ⓐ Ⓑ Ⓒ Ⓓ	11 Ⓐ Ⓑ Ⓒ Ⓓ	19 Ⓐ Ⓑ Ⓒ Ⓓ	27 Ⓐ Ⓑ Ⓒ Ⓓ	35 Ⓐ Ⓑ Ⓒ Ⓓ
4 Ⓐ Ⓑ Ⓒ Ⓓ	12 Ⓐ Ⓑ Ⓒ Ⓓ	20 Ⓐ Ⓑ Ⓒ Ⓓ	28 Ⓐ Ⓑ Ⓒ Ⓓ	36 Ⓐ Ⓑ Ⓒ Ⓓ
5 Ⓐ Ⓑ Ⓒ Ⓓ	13 Ⓐ Ⓑ Ⓒ Ⓓ	21 Ⓐ Ⓑ Ⓒ Ⓓ	29 Ⓐ Ⓑ Ⓒ Ⓓ	37 Ⓐ Ⓑ Ⓒ Ⓓ
6 Ⓐ Ⓑ Ⓒ Ⓓ	14 Ⓐ Ⓑ Ⓒ Ⓓ	22 Ⓐ Ⓑ Ⓒ Ⓓ	30 Ⓐ Ⓑ Ⓒ Ⓓ	
7 Ⓐ Ⓑ Ⓒ Ⓓ	15 Ⓐ Ⓑ Ⓒ Ⓓ	23 Ⓐ Ⓑ Ⓒ Ⓓ	31 Ⓐ Ⓑ Ⓒ Ⓓ	
8 Ⓐ Ⓑ Ⓒ Ⓓ	16 Ⓐ Ⓑ Ⓒ Ⓓ	24 Ⓐ Ⓑ Ⓒ Ⓓ	32 Ⓐ Ⓑ Ⓒ Ⓓ	

SECTION 3

1 Ⓐ Ⓑ Ⓒ Ⓓ	9 Ⓐ Ⓑ Ⓒ Ⓓ	17 Ⓐ Ⓑ Ⓒ Ⓓ	25 Ⓐ Ⓑ Ⓒ Ⓓ	33 Ⓐ Ⓑ Ⓒ Ⓓ
2 Ⓐ Ⓑ Ⓒ Ⓓ	10 Ⓐ Ⓑ Ⓒ Ⓓ	18 Ⓐ Ⓑ Ⓒ Ⓓ	26 Ⓐ Ⓑ Ⓒ Ⓓ	34 Ⓐ Ⓑ Ⓒ Ⓓ
3 Ⓐ Ⓑ Ⓒ Ⓓ	11 Ⓐ Ⓑ Ⓒ Ⓓ	19 Ⓐ Ⓑ Ⓒ Ⓓ	27 Ⓐ Ⓑ Ⓒ Ⓓ	35 Ⓐ Ⓑ Ⓒ Ⓓ
4 Ⓐ Ⓑ Ⓒ Ⓓ	12 Ⓐ Ⓑ Ⓒ Ⓓ	20 Ⓐ Ⓑ Ⓒ Ⓓ	28 Ⓐ Ⓑ Ⓒ Ⓓ	36 Ⓐ Ⓑ Ⓒ Ⓓ
5 Ⓐ Ⓑ Ⓒ Ⓓ	13 Ⓐ Ⓑ Ⓒ Ⓓ	21 Ⓐ Ⓑ Ⓒ Ⓓ	29 Ⓐ Ⓑ Ⓒ Ⓓ	
6 Ⓐ Ⓑ Ⓒ Ⓓ	14 Ⓐ Ⓑ Ⓒ Ⓓ	22 Ⓐ Ⓑ Ⓒ Ⓓ	30 Ⓐ Ⓑ Ⓒ Ⓓ	
7 Ⓐ Ⓑ Ⓒ Ⓓ	15 Ⓐ Ⓑ Ⓒ Ⓓ	23 Ⓐ Ⓑ Ⓒ Ⓓ	31 Ⓐ Ⓑ Ⓒ Ⓓ	
8 Ⓐ Ⓑ Ⓒ Ⓓ	16 Ⓐ Ⓑ Ⓒ Ⓓ	24 Ⓐ Ⓑ Ⓒ Ⓓ	32 Ⓐ Ⓑ Ⓒ Ⓓ	

SECTION 4

1 Ⓐ Ⓑ Ⓒ Ⓓ	11 Ⓐ Ⓑ Ⓒ Ⓓ	21 Ⓐ Ⓑ Ⓒ Ⓓ	31 Ⓐ Ⓑ Ⓒ Ⓓ	41 Ⓐ Ⓑ Ⓒ Ⓓ
2 Ⓐ Ⓑ Ⓒ Ⓓ	12 Ⓐ Ⓑ Ⓒ Ⓓ	22 Ⓐ Ⓑ Ⓒ Ⓓ	32 Ⓐ Ⓑ Ⓒ Ⓓ	42 Ⓐ Ⓑ Ⓒ Ⓓ
3 Ⓐ Ⓑ Ⓒ Ⓓ	13 Ⓐ Ⓑ Ⓒ Ⓓ	23 Ⓐ Ⓑ Ⓒ Ⓓ	33 Ⓐ Ⓑ Ⓒ Ⓓ	43 Ⓐ Ⓑ Ⓒ Ⓓ
4 Ⓐ Ⓑ Ⓒ Ⓓ	14 Ⓐ Ⓑ Ⓒ Ⓓ	24 Ⓐ Ⓑ Ⓒ Ⓓ	34 Ⓐ Ⓑ Ⓒ Ⓓ	44 Ⓐ Ⓑ Ⓒ Ⓓ
5 Ⓐ Ⓑ Ⓒ Ⓓ	15 Ⓐ Ⓑ Ⓒ Ⓓ	25 Ⓐ Ⓑ Ⓒ Ⓓ	35 Ⓐ Ⓑ Ⓒ Ⓓ	45 Ⓐ Ⓑ Ⓒ Ⓓ
6 Ⓐ Ⓑ Ⓒ Ⓓ	16 Ⓐ Ⓑ Ⓒ Ⓓ	26 Ⓐ Ⓑ Ⓒ Ⓓ	36 Ⓐ Ⓑ Ⓒ Ⓓ	46 Ⓐ Ⓑ Ⓒ Ⓓ
7 Ⓐ Ⓑ Ⓒ Ⓓ	17 Ⓐ Ⓑ Ⓒ Ⓓ	27 Ⓐ Ⓑ Ⓒ Ⓓ	37 Ⓐ Ⓑ Ⓒ Ⓓ	47 Ⓐ Ⓑ Ⓒ Ⓓ
8 Ⓐ Ⓑ Ⓒ Ⓓ	18 Ⓐ Ⓑ Ⓒ Ⓓ	28 Ⓐ Ⓑ Ⓒ Ⓓ	38 Ⓐ Ⓑ Ⓒ Ⓓ	
9 Ⓐ Ⓑ Ⓒ Ⓓ	19 Ⓐ Ⓑ Ⓒ Ⓓ	29 Ⓐ Ⓑ Ⓒ Ⓓ	39 Ⓐ Ⓑ Ⓒ Ⓓ	
10 Ⓐ Ⓑ Ⓒ Ⓓ	20 Ⓐ Ⓑ Ⓒ Ⓓ	30 Ⓐ Ⓑ Ⓒ Ⓓ	40 Ⓐ Ⓑ Ⓒ Ⓓ	

Section 1
Verbal Reasoning

This section is divided into two parts that contain two different types of questions. As soon as you have completed Part One, answer the questions in Part Two. You may write in your test booklet. For each answer you select, fill in the corresponding circle on your answer document.

Part One – Synonyms

Each question in Part One consists of a word in capital letters followed by four answer choices. Select the one word that is most nearly the same in meaning as the word in capital letters.

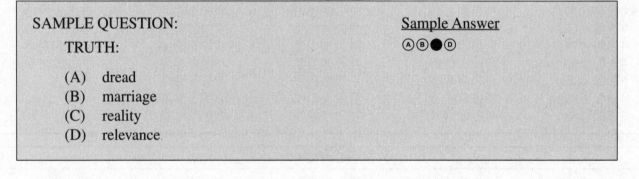

SAMPLE QUESTION:

TRUTH:

Sample Answer

Ⓐ Ⓑ ● Ⓓ

(A)   dread
(B)   marriage
(C)   reality
(D)   relevance

Go on to the next page. ➡

VR

Part Two – Sentence Completion

Each question in Part Two is made up of a sentence with one blank. Each blank indicates that a word is missing. The sentence is followed by four answer choices. Select the word that best completes the meaning of the sentence as a whole.

SAMPLE QUESTIONS:

The question was so ------- that the best student in class got it wrong.

(A) coarse
(B) difficult
(C) funny
(D) long

Sample Answer

Ⓐ ● Ⓒ Ⓓ

Part One – Synonyms

Directions: Select the word that is most nearly the same in meaning as the word in capital letters.

1. UNUSUAL:

   (A) friendly
   (B) happy
   (C) new
   (D) peculiar

2. ASSISTANCE:

   (A) call
   (B) disability
   (C) service
   (D) teaching

3. REALITY:

   (A) dream
   (B) fact
   (C) rarity
   (D) security

4. DIMINUTION:

   (A) assessment
   (B) leniency
   (C) reduction
   (D) restitution

5. CONTENTED:

   (A) diplomatic
   (B) disgusted
   (C) mammoth
   (D) satisfied

6. BOUND:

   (A) badgered
   (B) confused
   (C) obliged
   (D) relieved

7. FALTER:

   (A) drop
   (B) hesitate
   (C) question
   (D) replenish

8. CONTAINED:

   (A) eliminated
   (B) held
   (C) raging
   (D) wooden

9. REVERE:

   (A) disdain
   (B) esteem
   (C) faith
   (D) reliance

10. DILIGENT:

   (A) defensive
   (B) hardworking
   (C) lazy
   (D) obsessive

Go on to the next page. ➡

VR

11. DETRIMENTAL:

(A) harmful
(B) knowledgeable
(C) tentative
(D) worrisome

12. VOW:

(A) argue
(B) claim
(C) please
(D) pledge

13. ASPIRATION:

(A) focus
(B) hope
(C) injury
(D) trend

14. BASHFUL:

(A) argumentative
(B) serious
(C) shy
(D) tolerant

15. SINISTER:

(A) elderly
(B) erratic
(C) uncomfortable
(D) wicked

16. DISCLOSE:

(A) hide
(B) remove
(C) reveal
(D) undress

17. CONGEAL:

(A) coagulate
(B) help
(C) recede
(D) weaken

18. INUNDATE:

(A) enter
(B) flood
(C) migrate
(D) strive

19. STEADFAST:

(A) constant
(B) optional
(C) quick
(D) restful

20. RUTHLESS:

(A) counterfeit
(B) unofficial
(C) unsparing
(D) victorious

Go on to the next page. ➞

Part Two – Sentence Completion

Directions: Select the word that best completes the sentence.

21. Myron was able to remain completely ------- ; he never took sides in any of the disagreements around the house.

    (A) biased
    (B) interested
    (C) neutral
    (D) thoughtful

22. Since the great drought left the soil completely useless, the people of that country were forced to ------- food from other countries.

    (A) export
    (B) import
    (C) report on
    (D) sell

23. Because he was annoyed by even the smallest grammatical error, Mr. Jones reviewed all the students' papers ------- before grading them.

    (A) crudely
    (B) helplessly
    (C) inefficiently
    (D) meticulously

24. Eric doesn't merely dislike racism; he ------- it.

    (A) abhors
    (B) moderates
    (C) questions
    (D) studies

25. Sharon's anger was too great: David simply could not ------- her with his charm.

    (A) irritate
    (B) manipulate
    (C) pacify
    (D) terrify

26. Even though the accident led to serious damage to our property, our ------- lawyer didn't present a convincing argument and we received no compensation.

    (A) discerning
    (B) fatalistic
    (C) incompetent
    (D) professional

27. After months of petty disputes, the two countries finally decided to sit down at a table and have a ------- discussion.

    (A) friendly
    (B) hostile
    (C) lengthy
    (D) pressing

28. Although the thief claimed that he accidentally picked up the stolen watch, the jury judged his action -------.

    (A) deliberate
    (B) frantic
    (C) impractical
    (D) misguided

Go on to the next page. ➡

29. In order to be a good doctor, you don't need to be ------- yourself, just as a good architect does not have to live in a fancy house.

    (A) educated
    (B) handsome
    (C) healthy
    (D) thoughtful

30. Pete ------- his coach when he followed up his winning season with an even better performance this year.

    (A) disappointed
    (B) gratified
    (C) relieved
    (D) upset

31. While many species, such as wolves, travel in groups, the cheetah is a ------- animal.

    (A) dangerous
    (B) pack
    (C) solitary
    (D) territorial

32. During his years in the Senate, Jones felt ------- about speaking up at all, while most of the other senators were aggressive and argumentative.

    (A) blithe
    (B) contented
    (C) favorable
    (D) timid

33. The politician's speech was so ------- that nearly everyone in the room decided not to vote for him.

    (A) feeble
    (B) monotonous
    (C) persuasive
    (D) unique

34. The corporation did not have a ------- system for promotions; each department was free to use its own discretion in advancing employees.

    (A) dignified
    (B) favorable
    (C) forgiving
    (D) uniform

35. Only from years of training can a gymnast hope to become ------- enough to master Olympic-level techniques.

    (A) agile
    (B) mature
    (C) passive
    (D) strict

36. Though Mr. Fenster was known to be ------- toward his neighbors, he always welcomed their children as trick-or-treaters at Halloween.

    (A) belligerent
    (B) cheerful
    (C) courteous
    (D) direct

Go on to the next page. ➡

37. The ------- young man talked back to his parents and teachers alike.

(A) dreary
(B) insolent
(C) nervous
(D) respectful

38. While the painting's brushstrokes seem -------, they are actually carefully planned out.

(A) flagrant
(B) haphazard
(C) intricate
(D) paltry

39. The Declaration of Independence is premised upon ------- principles, such as protecting life, liberty, and the pursuit of happiness.

(A) united
(B) lofty
(C) predictable
(D) variable

40. Our teacher advised us not to get too caught up in the ------- of information in the textbook, or we could lose the "big picture" of its theory.

(A) minutiae
(B) principles
(C) scope
(D) thought

STOP. If there is time, you may check your work in this section only.

QR

Section 2
Quantitative Reasoning

This section is divided into two parts that contain two different types of questions. As soon as you have completed Part One, answer the questions in Part Two. You may write in your test booklet. For each answer you select, remember to fill in the corresponding circle on your answer document.

Any figures that accompany the questions in this section may be assumed to be drawn as accurately as possible EXCEPT when it is stated that a particular figure is not drawn to scale. Letters such as x, y, and n stand for real numbers.

Part One – Word Problems

Each question in Part One consists of a word problem followed by four answer choices. You may write in your test booklet; however, you may be able to solve many of these problems in your head. Next, look at the four answer choices given and select the best answer.

EXAMPLE 1:

What is the value of the expression

$1 + 3 \times (4 \div 2) - 5$?

(A) 2
(B) 3
(C) 4
(D) 8

Sample Answer
● Ⓑ Ⓒ Ⓓ

The correct answer is 2, so circle A is darkened.

Go on to the next page. ➜

Part Two – Quantitative Comparisons

All questions in Part Two are quantitative comparisons between the quantities shown in Column A and Column B. Using the information given in each question, compare the quantity in Column A to the quantity in Column B, and chose one of these four answer choices:

(A)   The quantity in Column A is greater.
(B)   The quantity in Column B is greater.
(C)   The two quantities are equal.
(D)   The relationship cannot be determined from the information given.

EXAMPLE 2:	Column A	Column B	Sample Answer
	$\frac{2}{3}$ of 9	$\frac{1}{3}$ of 18	Ⓐ Ⓑ ● Ⓓ

The quantity in <u>Column A</u> (6) is the same as the quantity in <u>Column B</u> (6), so circle C is darkened.

EXAMPLE 3:   Sample Answer

Ⓐ Ⓑ Ⓒ ●

When integer x is multiplied by 2, the result is greater than 10 but less than 16.

Column A	Column B
x	7

Since $10 < 2x < 16$, $5 < x < 8$. Thus, as x can equal 6 or 7, there is not enough information given to determine the relationship. Circle D is darkened.

STOP. Do not go on
until told to do so.

NO TEST MATERIAL ON THIS PAGE

Part One – Word Problems

Directions: Choose the best answer from the four choices given.

1. $54 \times 3 =$

   (A) 123
   (B) 150
   (C) 162
   (D) 172

2. What is the area of a square with a side of length 2 ?

   (A) 2
   (B) 4
   (C) 6
   (D) 8

3. $3 \times 2 \times 1 - (4 \times 3 \times 2) =$

   (A) 18
   (B) 6
   (C) –6
   (D) –18

4. Vicky scored 80, 90, and 94 on her three tests. What was her average score?

   (A) 81
   (B) 88
   (C) 90
   (D) 93

Questions 5–6 refer to the following graph.

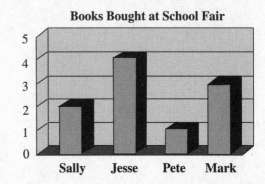

5. Who bought the most books at the school fair?

   (A) Sally
   (B) Jesse
   (C) Pete
   (D) Mark

6. Sally and Mark together bought how many more books than Jesse?

   (A) 1
   (B) 2
   (C) 3
   (D) 5

Go on to the next page. ➞

7. $\frac{1}{2} + \frac{3}{4} =$

   (A) $\frac{3}{8}$

   (B) $\frac{5}{4}$

   (C) $\frac{3}{2}$

   (D) $\frac{5}{2}$

8. What is the value of the digit 7 in the number 4,678.02 ?

   (A)   7
   (B)   70
   (C)   700
   (D)   7,000

9. Jason has several books in his room, 20% of which are fiction. The other books are nonfiction. If he has 5 fiction books, how many nonfiction books does he have?

   (A)   5
   (B)   10
   (C)   20
   (D)   25

10. $\frac{7}{0.35} =$

   (A)   0.2
   (B)   2
   (C)   20
   (D) 200

11. Which of the following is closest in value to 5 ?

   (A)   4.5
   (B)   5.009
   (C)   5.01
   (D)   5.101

12. Janice went to the butcher and bought six pounds of hamburger. If the bill was $18.50, which of the following is closest to the cost per pound of the hamburger?

   (A) $2.00
   (B) $3.00
   (C) $5.00
   (D) $6.00

13. Which of the following numbers is closest to the square root of 175 ?

   (A)   9
   (B)   13
   (C)   22
   (D)   30

14. Laurie was reading a book that had an illustration on every odd-numbered page. If there are 32 numbered pages in the book, how many illustrations are there?

   (A)   15
   (B)   16
   (C)   17
   (D)   31

Go on to the next page. ➔

15. If $6y + 8 = 20$, what is the value of $3y + 4$?

    (A) 2
    (B) 8
    (C) 10
    (D) 12

16. A lecture hall's maximum capacity of 56 has increased by 75%. What is the new seating capacity after the increase?

    (A) 42
    (B) 70
    (C) 98
    (D) 112

17. When a number is divided by 8, the quotient is 11 and the remainder is 2. What is the number?

    (A) 11
    (B) 22
    (C) 72
    (D) 90

The following graph shows the amount of rainfall in Miller County for the years 1942–1946.

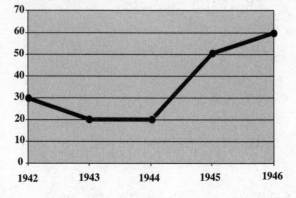

Average Inches of Rainfall in Miller County, 1942–1946

18. When did the greatest increase in rainfall occur in Miller County?

    (A) Between 1942 and 1943
    (B) Between 1943 and 1944
    (C) Between 1944 and 1945
    (D) Between 1945 and 1946

19. The temperature at 6 A.M. was 32°. If the temperature increased at a constant rate of 3° per hour all day, what was the temperature at 1 P.M.?

    (A) 35°
    (B) 43°
    (C) 47°
    (D) 53°

20. What is the volume of a box with length 4 cm, width 3 cm, and height 2 cm?

    (A) 6 cubic centimeters
    (B) 9 cubic centimeters
    (C) 12 cubic centimeters
    (D) 24 cubic centimeters

Go on to the next page. ➡

QR

Part Two – Quantitative Comparisons

Directions: Using all information given in each question, compare the quantity in Column A to the quantity in Column B. All questions in Part Two have these answer choices:

(A) The quantity in Column A is greater.
(B) The quantity in Column B is greater.
(C) The two quantities are equal.
(D) The relationship cannot be determined from the information given.

	Column A	Column B
23.	$\sqrt{9} + \sqrt{25}$	$\sqrt{9 + 25}$

125° / x

	Column A	Column B
21.	x	55

A rectangle with sides x and y has an area of 12.

	Column A	Column B
22.	The length of x	The length of y

A — B

3

D — C

The quadrilateral *ABCD* has an area of 12.

	Column A	Column B
24.	The perimeter of *ABCD*	15

Go on to the next page. ➡

> **Answer choices for all questions on this page.**
>
> (A) The quantity in Column A is greater.
> (B) The quantity in Column B is greater.
> (C) The two quantities are equal.
> (D) The relationship cannot be determined from the information given.

Martha had $20. She gave half of her money to her sister, Linda. Linda now has $30.

Column A	Column B
25. The amount of money Martha now has	The amount of money Linda had originally

$$4x + 7 = 63$$

$$\frac{y}{3} + 6 = 15$$

Column A	Column B
26. x	y

Column A	Column B
27. The area of a rectangle with length 3 and width 4	The area of a square with a side of 3

Number of Cookies Eaten Each Day

Wednesday	3
Thursday	2
Friday	1
Saturday	3

Column A	Column B
28. The average number of cookies eaten each day	The number of cookies eaten on Thursday

Column A	Column B
29. $\sqrt{0.64}$	$\sqrt{6.4}$

Go on to the next page. ⟶

QR

Answer choices for all questions on this page.

(A) The quantity in Column A is greater.
(B) The quantity in Column B is greater.
(C) The two quantities are equal.
(D) The relationship cannot be determined from the information given.

Amy bought 5 oranges and 6 peaches. The total price of the fruit was $1.10.

Column A	Column B
30. The cost of one orange	The cost of one peach

Column A	Column B
31. $-(5)^6$	$(-5)^6$

a represents an odd integer greater than 9 and less than 15.

b represents an even integer greater than 9 and less than 15.

Column A	Column B
32. $a \times 3$	$b \times 4$

A 12-sided die with faces numbered 1 through 12 is rolled.

Column A	Column B
33. The probability that the result is even	The probability that the result is prime

Go on to the next page. →

Answer choices for all questions on this page.

(A) The quantity in Column A is greater.
(B) The quantity in Column B is greater.
(C) The two quantities are equal.
(D) The relationship cannot be determined from the information given.

	Column A	Column B
34.	The fractional part of the figure that is shaded	$\dfrac{3}{20}$

Melvin brought home a large pizza with 12 slices.

	Column A	Column B
35.	The number of slices left if Melvin eats 50% of the pizza	The number of slices left if Melvin eats one-third of the pizza

The original price of a shirt now on sale was $50.

	Column A	Column B
36.	The price of the shirt after two 20% discounts	The price of the shirt after a single 40% discount

	Column A	Column B
37.	The slope of the line with points (3, 8) and (5, 2)	The slope of the line $6x - 2y = -8$

STOP. If there is time, you may check your work in this section only.

Section 3
Reading Comprehension

This section contains six short reading passages. Each passage is followed by six questions based on its content. Answer the questions following each passage on the basis of what is <u>stated</u> or <u>implied</u> in that passage. You may write in the test booklet.

STOP. Do not go on until told to do so.

Questions 1–6

Line

1　　When most people think of the history
2　of transportation, they think of the invention
3　of the wheel as the starting point. The
4　wheel was invented around 3500 B.C.E.,
5　more than 5,000 years ago. Before then,
6　transportation was a difficult process,
7　especially for those who had anything to
8　carry. During prehistoric times, the only
9　way to get around was to walk. Children
10　and possessions were strapped to someone's
11　back if they needed to be carried. If the
12　load was too heavy for one person, it could
13　be strapped to a pole and carried by two.
14　The sledge was developed as a way to
15　drag a heavy load. Sledges were originally

16　just logs or pieces of animal skin upon
17　which a load was strapped and dragged.
18　In time, runners were put on the sledge,
19　and it evolved to what is now called a sled.
20　Around 5000 B.C.E., the first animals were
21　domesticated, or tamed. Then, donkeys and
22　oxen were used to carry heavy loads and
23　pull sledges. It wasn't until almost 1,500
24　years later that wheeled vehicles appeared.
25　It is believed that the wheel was invented
26　in Mesopotamia, in the Middle East. About
27　300 years later, the Egyptians invented the
28　sailboat. These two inventions changed
29　transportation forever.

Go on to the next page. ⟶

RC

1. The primary purpose of the passage is to

   (A) describe some of the things people used for transportation long ago
   (B) describe the reasons that led to transportation discoveries
   (C) explain the evolution of the sled
   (D) give a detailed history of transportation

2. The passage suggests that prehistoric man used all of the following for carrying things EXCEPT

   (A) animals
   (B) children
   (C) poles
   (D) primitive sleds

3. The passage implies that early man

   (A) was incapable of inventing the wheel any earlier than 3500 B.C.E.
   (B) was interested in farming
   (C) was interested in finding ways to help carry things
   (D) was outgoing and friendly

4. It can be inferred from the passage that the reason animals were domesticated was

   (A) to help carry large loads
   (B) to move people and possessions around quickly
   (C) to provide family pets
   (D) to ward off danger

5. Which of the following describes the author's attitude toward the invention of the wheel?

   (A) Admiration
   (B) Disdain
   (C) Indifference
   (D) Regret

6. The passage suggests that the sledge was

   (A) a precursor to the sled
   (B) invented in conjunction with the wheel
   (C) made exclusively of animal skin
   (D) the only tool used for transportation at the time

Go on to the next page. ⟶

Questions 7–12

Line

1   Bison and buffalo are not the same
2 animal. For years, American bison were
3 mistakenly referred to as buffalo. Due to
4 this confusion, there are many references
5 to buffalo in the United States. There is the
6 city of Buffalo in northwestern New York
7 state. In addition, the buffalo appeared
8 on the U.S. nickel for many years at the
9 beginning of the twentieth century. This is
10 often referred to as the "Buffalo Nickel" to
11 distinguish it from the current nickel with
12 Thomas Jefferson on the front. Buffalo are
13 actually found in Asia, Africa, and South

14 America. Bison roamed the North American
15 western plains by the millions just a couple
16 of centuries ago. Because the bison were so
17 widely hunted, however, their numbers fell
18 greatly. In fact, as of a century ago, there
19 were only about 500 left. They were deemed
20 near extinction, but due to conservation
21 efforts, their numbers have increased. There
22 are approximately 50,000 bison living today
23 in protected parks. Though they may never
24 be as abundant as they once were, they are
25 not in danger of extinction as long as they
26 remain protected.

Go on to the next page. ➜

7. The primary purpose of the passage is to

    (A) applaud conservation efforts
    (B) explain the genetic difference between the bison and the buffalo
    (C) explain why people confuse the buffalo and the bison
    (D) give some background on the American bison

8. The passage implies that the primary difference between the buffalo and the bison is

    (A) their geographic location
    (B) their number
    (C) their size
    (D) when they existed

9. As used in line 19, the word "deemed" most closely means

    (A) found
    (B) hunted
    (C) ruled
    (D) eaten

10. According to the passage, what can be hoped for as long as the American bison is protected?

    (A) They will be as plentiful as they once were.
    (B) They will disturb the delicate ecological balance in the plains.
    (C) They will face even greater dangers.
    (D) They will probably not die out.

11. According to the passage, the primary reason that the American bison is no longer near extinction is

    (A) conservation efforts
    (B) lack of interest in hunting them
    (C) loss of value of their fur
    (D) the migration of the animals

12. In line 6, the author mentions the city of Buffalo in order to

    (A) criticize a hunting practice
    (B) establish the reason for a particular currency
    (C) illustrate a common misunderstanding
    (D) pinpoint the first sighting of buffalo in New York

Go on to the next page. →

<u>Questions 13–18</u>

Line

1   The Greek philosopher Aristotle
2 had many students, but perhaps none so
3 famous as Alexander the Great. As a child,
4 Alexander was known for his intelligence
5 and bravery. The lessons he learned from
6 Aristotle left him with a lifelong love of
7 books and learning. But it was not his love
8 of books that made him famous. Alexander,
9 in 336 B.C., became the king of a small
10 Greek kingdom called Macedonia. He was
11 only twenty at the time. He went on to
12 invade country after country: Persia (now
13 known as Iran), Egypt, and all the way
14 to parts of India and Pakistan. Alexander
15 conquered most of what was then the
16 "civilized world." He brought with him the
17 Greek way of thinking and doing things. He
18 is considered one of the great generals and
19 kings of history and is responsible for the
20 spread of Greek culture throughout much of
21 the world.

Go on to the next page. ⟶

13. Which of the following would be the best title for the passage?

    (A) "Alexander the Great: King and Conqueror"
    (B) "Aristotle: Teacher of the Kings"
    (C) "Greek Culture"
    (D) "The History of Macedonia"

14. As used in line 16, the word "civilized" most closely means

    (A) barbaric
    (B) educated
    (C) friendly
    (D) well-mannered

15. The tone of the passage is most like that found in

    (A) a diary entry from an historian
    (B) a letter from an archeologist
    (C) a philosophy journal
    (D) a reference book

16. According to the passage, one of the things that was so impressive about Alexander was

    (A) his ability to teach
    (B) his great integrity
    (C) his handsome features
    (D) his intelligence and culture

17. The passage suggests that Aristotle

    (A) encouraged Alexander to spread culture
    (B) helped foster Alexander's love of books
    (C) supported Alexander's military career
    (D) taught Alexander military strategy

18. According to the passage, when Alexander invaded a country, he

    (A) enslaved citizens
    (B) freed oppressed people
    (C) spread Greek ideas
    (D) toppled monuments

Go on to the next page. ⟶

Questions 19–24

Line

1   Everyone has had attacks of the
2   hiccups, or hiccoughs, at one point in his or
3   her life. Few people, however, think about
4   what is happening to them and how hiccups
5   begin and end.
6   The diaphragm is a large muscle,
7   shaped like a dome, that sits at the base
8   of the chest cavity. As one breathes, the
9   diaphragm gently contracts and relaxes
10 to help the process. Occasionally, an
11 irritation near the diaphragm or a disease
12 may cause the muscle to spasm, or contract
13 suddenly. The spasm will suck air into the
14 lungs past the vocal cords. A small flap
15 called the epiglottis tops the vocal cords so
16 that food will not accidentally enter into
17 the windpipe. The sudden spasm of the
18 diaphragm causes the epiglottis to close
19 quickly. Imagine the pull of air into the
20 vocal cords from the spastic diaphragm
21 hitting the closed epiglottis. This moves
22 the vocal cords, causing the "hic" sound
23 of the hiccup. Although most people don't
24 really worry about the hiccups, attacks may
25 last for days. The exhaustion of hiccupping
26 for days on end has been fatal in certain
27 rare cases. Home remedies abound—from
28 breathing into paper bags to squeezing on
29 pressure points that supposedly relax the
30 diaphragm.

Go on to the next page. ➡

19. The primary purpose of the passage is to

    (A) describe a common occurrence
    (B) prescribe a treatment
    (C) settle a dispute
    (D) warn about a danger

20. According to the passage, one possible cause of hiccups is

    (A) a sudden rush of air
    (B) an irritant near the diaphragm
    (C) breathing in and out of a paper bag
    (D) the closing of the epiglottis

21. As used in line 24, "attacks" most closely means

    (A) advances
    (B) assaults
    (C) bouts
    (D) threats

22. The passage suggests that which of the following makes the "hic" sound of the hiccup?

    (A) The diaphragm
    (B) The lungs
    (C) The stomach
    (D) The vocal cords

23. According to the passage, the hiccups can be fatal due to

    (A) fatigue from days of hiccupping
    (B) home remedies that are toxic
    (C) the humiliation of hiccupping for days on end
    (D) the irritant to the diaphragm

24. The author mentions "hiccoughs" in line 2 in order to

    (A) correct an improper usage
    (B) define a technical term
    (C) indicate an alternate spelling
    (D) weaken a misguided argument

Go on to the next page. ➞

Questions 25–30

Line

1   During the winter months in many
2 regions, food can be extremely scarce. For
3 the wildlife of these areas, this can be a
4 great problem unless animals have some
5 mechanism that allows them to adapt. Some
6 animals migrate to warmer climates. Others
7 hibernate to conserve energy and decrease
8 the need for food. Prior to hibernation, an
9 animal will generally eat a lot to build up a
10 store of fat. The animal's system will "feed"
11 off the fat stores throughout the long cold
12 winter months. When the animal hibernates,
13 its body temperature decreases and its body
14 functions slow down considerably. The
15 dormouse's heartbeat, for example, slows
16 down to just a beat every few minutes. Its

17 breathing also becomes slow and its body
18 temperature drops to just a few degrees
19 above the temperature of the ground around
20 it. All these changes decrease the need for
21 fuel and allow the animal to survive long
22 periods without any food. It is a mistake
23 to think that all hibernating animals sleep
24 for the whole winter. In fact, many animals
25 hibernate for short spurts during the winter.
26 They may wake for an interval of mild
27 weather. Scientists have now discovered
28 the chemical that triggers hibernation. If
29 this chemical is injected in an animal in the
30 summer months, it can cause the animal to
31 go into summer hibernation.

Go on to the next page. ➞

25. The primary purpose of the passage is to

    (A) compare the hibernating dormouse to other hibernating animals
    (B) debunk some common myths about hibernation
    (C) discuss the discovery of the chemical that causes hibernation
    (D) explore some basic information about hibernation

26. As used in line 7, the word "conserve" most closely means

    (A) expend
    (B) help
    (C) reserve
    (D) waste

27. According to the author, each of the following happens to a hibernating animal EXCEPT

    (A) it goes into a dream state
    (B) its body temperature drops
    (C) its breathing slows
    (D) its heartbeat slows

28. Which of the following can be inferred as a reason a hibernating animal may interrupt its hibernation?

    (A) A day or two of stormy weather
    (B) An overabundance of food
    (C) A week in which there was no snow
    (D) A week in which the temperature was well above freezing

29. According to the author, if the chemical that triggers hibernation is injected into an animal when it would not normally hibernate, the chemical may

    (A) allow the animal to shed extra fat stores
    (B) cause an out-of-season hibernation
    (C) cause body functions to slow to a halt
    (D) decrease an animal's need for food

30. The tone of the passage is best described as

    (A) amazed
    (B) concerned
    (C) indifferent
    (D) informative

Go on to the next page. ⟶

Questions 31–36

Line

1   The theater is one of the richest art
2 forms. The excitement of opening night
3 can be felt by the people waiting to watch
4 a performance and by the performers and
5 workers backstage waiting for the curtain
6 to go up. Live theater is thrilling because
7 no one really knows how well the play
8 will go until it is performed. Many people
9 collaborate to bring a play to life. There
10 are playwrights, directors, set designers,
11 costumers, lighting technicians, and,
12 of course, actors. If the performance is
13 a musical, the skills of a songwriter, a
14 choreographer (the person who composes
15 the dances), and musicians are also
16 required. The word *theater* comes from the
17 Greek *theatron*, which means "a place for
18 seeing." One concept from Greek theater
19 that is still seen in some plays today is the
20 "Greek Chorus." This consists of several
21 actors/characters watching the action of the

22 play (almost like the audience) and then
23 commenting on what they just saw with
24 either reactions or dialogue. Although most
25 people think of the theater in terms of a play
26 performed on the stage, theater has taken
27 on a much broader meaning in the modern
28 world. You may find yourself walking into
29 a theater with no seats in the rows. Instead,
30 you are seated among the set pieces, which
31 makes you part of the setting. Sometimes
32 theater may come to life on a street corner,
33 or in a classroom. The excitement of theater
34 is in its very nature—it is an art form that
35 changes as it is interpreted in different
36 ways by different people. That is probably
37 why the works of the greatest playwright
38 of all time, William Shakespeare, are still
39 performed and enjoyed today, both in
40 classic and new interpretations.

Go on to the next page. ⟶

31. The best title for the passage might be

    (A) "A Brief History of Theatrical Productions"
    (B) "Modern Theater: Adventures in Acting"
    (C) "Shakespeare: Our Greatest Playwright"
    (D) "The Excitement of Theater"

32. According to the passage, the primary reason that theater is so exciting is that

    (A) it derives from a Greek custom
    (B) it is performed live
    (C) plays are often well written
    (D) there are so many people working on it

33. The passage suggests which of the following about modern theater?

    (A) It always draws great attention from the audience.
    (B) It has been interpreted in a more varied fashion.
    (C) It is less exciting than classic theater.
    (D) There are mostly Shakespearean plays performed.

34. The author's attitude toward theater can best be described as

    (A) admiring
    (B) ambivalent
    (C) apathetic
    (D) neutral

35. In line 1, the word "richest" is best understood to mean most

    (A) diverse
    (B) entertaining
    (C) terrifying
    (D) wealthy

36. The passage suggests that the plays of Shakespeare

    (A) are more often given new interpretations today than at any other time
    (B) are more popular today than during Shakespeare's time
    (C) have been performed in a variety of ways
    (D) will always be considered the world's greatest

STOP. If there is time, you may check your work in this section only.

Section 4
Mathematics Achievement

Each question is followed by four suggested answers. Read each question and then decide which one of the four suggested answers is best.

Find the row of spaces on your answer document that has the same number as the question. In this row, mark the space having the same letter as the answer you have chosen. You may write in your test booklet.

SAMPLE QUESTION:

Sample Answer

Ⓐ ● Ⓒ Ⓓ

What is the perimeter of an equilateral triangle with a side length of 4 in?

(A)   8 in
(B)   12 in
(C)   16 in
(D)   24 in

The correct answer is 12 in, so circle B is darkened.

STOP. Do not go on
until told to do so.

NO TEST MATERIAL ON THIS PAGE

1. In the decimal 0.0987, the digit 9 is equivalent to which of the following?

   (A) $\frac{9}{10}$

   (B) $\frac{9}{100}$

   (C) $\frac{9}{1,000}$

   (D) $\frac{9}{10,000}$

2. What is the least common multiple of 6, 9, and 12 ?

   (A) 3
   (B) 36
   (C) 72
   (D) 324

3. Which of the following equals 5 ?

   (A) $30 - 12 \div 2 \times (3 + 7)$
   (B) $30 - 12 \div (2 \times 3 + 7)$
   (C) $(30 - 12) \div 2 \times 3 + 7$
   (D) $30 - 12 \div 2 \times 3 - 7$

4. $\frac{5}{7} + \frac{2}{11} =$

   (A) $\frac{10}{17}$

   (B) $\frac{10}{77}$

   (C) $\frac{7}{18}$

   (D) $\frac{69}{77}$

5. $7\frac{1}{2}$ hours is how many minutes more than $6\frac{1}{4}$ hours?

   (A) 45
   (B) 60
   (C) 75
   (D) 90

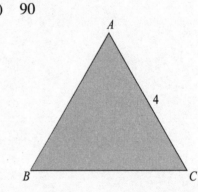

6. What is the perimeter of equilateral triangle *ABC* shown above?

   (A) 12
   (B) 15
   (C) 18
   (D) It cannot be determined from the information given.

Go on to the next page. ➜

7. Which of the following is 20% of 200 ?

    (A)   20
    (B)   30
    (C)   40
    (D)   100

Questions 8–10 refer to the following chart.

Day	Temperature (in degrees Celsius)	Snowfall (in centimeters)
Monday	2	3
Tuesday	6	3
Wednesday	3	4
Thursday	13	1

8. What was the total amount of snowfall for the four-day period shown?

    (A)   44 cm
    (B)   40 cm
    (C)   11 cm
    (D)   10 cm

9. On which day was the snowfall the greatest?

    (A)   Thursday
    (B)   Wednesday
    (C)   Tuesday
    (D)   Monday

10. What was the average temperature for each day in the four-day period?

    (A)   24°
    (B)   20°
    (C)   11°
    (D)   6°

11. $\dfrac{100}{0.25} =$

    (A)   4
    (B)   40
    (C)   400
    (D)   4000

12. $5 \times 31 = 100 + \underline{}$

    (A)   55
    (B)   51
    (C)   50
    (D)   36

13. Gwen planted six tomato plants. Half of them died. She then planted one more. How many tomato plants does Gwen have now?

    (A)   3
    (B)   4
    (C)   5
    (D)   6

Go on to the next page. ➔

14. The public library charges one dollar to rent a video game overnight, with a fifty-cent charge for each day the video game is late. If Tracey returns a video game three days late, how much does she owe all together?

(A) $1.50
(B) $2.00
(C) $2.50
(D) $3.50

15. $0.45 \times 100 =$

(A) 4,500
(B) 450
(C) 45
(D) 4.5

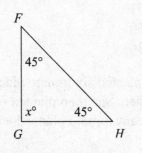

16. In triangle *FGH* shown above, the value of angle *x*, in degrees, is

(A) 30
(B) 45
(C) 50
(D) 90

17. If a dozen eggs cost $1.20, then 3 eggs cost

(A) 30¢
(B) 36¢
(C) 40¢
(D) $3.60

18. Boris and his friend Bruce collect baseball cards. If Bruce has 12 baseball cards and Boris has three times as many baseball cards as Bruce, what is the average number of cards in the boys' collections?

(A) 7.5
(B) 18
(C) 24
(D) 48

19. What is the perimeter of a rectangle with length 3 and width 2 ?

(A) 6
(B) 8
(C) 10
(D) 12

20. $\dfrac{3}{5} \times \dfrac{2}{7} =$

(A) $\dfrac{3}{8}$

(B) $\dfrac{6}{35}$

(C) $\dfrac{31}{35}$

(D) $\dfrac{21}{35}$

Go on to the next page. ➞

21. If Kenny can run three miles in 45 minutes, how long will it take him to run five miles?

(A) 1 hour
(B) 1 hour 15 minutes
(C) 1 hour 30 minutes
(D) 2 hours

22. Which fraction is greater than $\frac{5}{11}$?

(A) $\frac{3}{8}$

(B) $\frac{2}{7}$

(C) $\frac{4}{9}$

(D) $\frac{4}{7}$

23. If the perimeter of a square is 36, what is its area?

(A) 16
(B) 36
(C) 64
(D) 81

24. Maureen studied for two hours before school. After school, she studied for twice as long as she had before school. What was the total number of hours she studied in the day?

(A) 4
(B) 6
(C) 8
(D) 12

25. $\dfrac{40(37+63)}{8} =$

(A) 450
(B) 500
(C) 1,250
(D) 4,000

26. $0.347 =$

(A) $\dfrac{7}{10} + \dfrac{4}{100} + \dfrac{3}{1,000}$

(B) $\dfrac{3}{100} + \dfrac{4}{10} + \dfrac{7}{100}$

(C) $\dfrac{4}{100} + \dfrac{3}{10} + \dfrac{7}{1,000}$

(D) $\dfrac{3}{10} + \dfrac{4}{1,000} + \dfrac{7}{100}$

27. Which is the prime factorization of 36 ?

(A) $3 \times 3 \times 3 \times 2$
(B) $3 \times 3 \times 2 \times 2$
(C) $3 \times 2 \times 2 \times 2$
(D) $6 \times 3 \times 2$

Go on to the next page. →

Questions 28–30 refer to the following chart.

Train Fares from Monroeville to Perkins' Corner

Fares	Weekday Peak	Weekday Off-Peak	Weekend & Holiday
One Way	$6.00	$5.00	$4.50
Round-Trip	$12.00	$10.00	$9.00
10-Trip Ticket	$54.00	$45.00	$40.00
Children Under 11	$1.00	$0.50	Free with Paying Adult

28. How much would it cost two adults and one child under the age of 11 to travel one way from Monroeville to Perkins' Corner on a weekend?

    (A) $25.00
    (B) $20.50
    (C) $18.00
    (D) $9.00

29. The price of a weekday peak fare ten-trip ticket is what percent less than the cost of purchasing ten one-way weekday peak fare tickets?

    (A) 10%
    (B) 20%
    (C) 50%
    (D) 100%

30. How much more does it cost for one adult to travel one way during the weekday peak fare period than for one adult to make the trip on the weekend?

    (A) $0.50
    (B) $0.75
    (C) $1.00
    (D) $1.50

31. Mr. Schroder swims laps at the community pool. It takes him 5 minutes to swim one lap. If he swims for 60 minutes without stopping, how many laps will he swim?

    (A) 8
    (B) 10
    (C) 12
    (D) 14

32. $10^3 =$

    (A) 10×3

    (B) $10 + 10 + 10$

    (C) $10 \times 10 \times 10$

    (D) $\dfrac{10}{3}$

Go on to the next page. ➡

MA

33. A DVD player initially cost $100. During a sale, the store reduced the price by 10%. Two days later, the store reduced the new price by 20%. What was the final price?

    (A) $68
    (B) $70
    (C) $72
    (D) $80

34. Mr. Hoffman has a rectangular box that is 10 centimeters wide, 30 centimeters long, and 4 centimeters high. What is the volume of the box?

    (A)   44 cm^3
    (B)   120 cm^3
    (C)   300 cm^3
    (D) 1,200 cm^3

35. Dr. Heldman sees an average of nine patients an hour for eight hours on Monday and for six hours on Tuesday. What is the average number of patients she sees on each day?

    (A)   54
    (B)   63
    (C)   72
    (D) 126

36. If $q + 9 = 7 - p$, what is the value of $q + p$?

    (A) −16
    (B)   −2
    (C)   2
    (D)   16

37. Which of the following is the product of two consecutive even integers?

    (A)   0
    (B) 15
    (C) 22
    (D) 30

38. Two triangles, *ABC* and *XYZ*, are similar. Triangle *ABC* has lengths of 3, 4, and 5. Which of the following could be the corresponding lengths of triangle *XYZ* ?

    (A) 3, 3, and 3
    (B) 4, 5, and 6
    (C) 6, 8, and 10
    (D) 13, 14, and 15

39. The perimeter of a square whose area is 169 centimeters is

    (A) 52
    (B) 48
    (C) 44
    (D) 42

40. If three-fourths of the 240 employees at Tigger's Toys are at a party, how many of the employees are NOT at the party?

    (A)   60
    (B)   80
    (C) 120
    (D) 180

Go on to the next page. ⟶

41. Jose and Greg are going on a 20-mile walk for charity. If they walk $\frac{1}{4}$ of the distance in the first two hours, and $\frac{1}{5}$ of the entire distance in the next hour and a half, how many miles do they have left to walk?

(A)   9
(B)   10
(C)   11
(D)   12

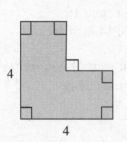

42. What is the perimeter of the shaded area in the figure above?

(A)   15
(B)   16
(C)   24
(D)   It cannot be determined from the information given.

43. A field hockey player scored an average of 3 goals per game for 12 games. How many points did she score in all 12 games?

(A)   4
(B)   20
(C)   24
(D)   36

44. What is the volume of a box with length 8, width 4, and height $\frac{1}{4}$?

(A)   8

(B) $12\frac{1}{4}$

(C)   32

(D)   128

45. The price of a $30 hat is decreased by 20%. What is the new price of the hat?

(A) $10.00
(B) $12.00
(C) $20.00
(D) $24.00

Go on to the next page. ➡

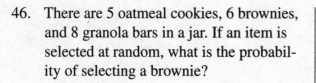

46. There are 5 oatmeal cookies, 6 brownies, and 8 granola bars in a jar. If an item is selected at random, what is the probability of selecting a brownie?

(A) $\dfrac{1}{6}$

(B) $\dfrac{6}{19}$

(C) $\dfrac{8}{19}$

(D) $\dfrac{6}{13}$

47. Which of the following is equivalent to $\dfrac{2}{3}x = 6 - y$?

(A) $2x = 6 - 3y$

(B) $3y - x = 6$

(C) $2x + 3y = 18$

(D) $2(x + 3y) = 18$

STOP. If there is time, you may check your work in this section only.

Essay

You will have 30 minutes to plan and write an essay on the topic printed on the other side of this page. **Do not write on another topic. An essay on another topic is not acceptable.**

The essay is designed to give you an opportunity to show how well you can write. You should try to express your thoughts clearly. How well you write is much more important than how much you write, but you need to say enough for a reader to understand what you mean.

You will probably want to write more than a short paragraph. You should also be aware that a copy of your essay will be sent to each school that will be receiving your test results. You are to write only in the appropriate section of the answer sheet. Please write or print so that your writing may be read by someone who is not familiar with your handwriting.

You may make notes and plan your essay on the reverse side of the page. Allow enough time to copy the final form on to your answer sheet. You must copy the essay topic onto your answer sheet, on page 3, in the box provided.

Please remember to write only the final draft of the essay on pages 3 and 4 of your answer sheet and to write it in blue or black pen. Again, you may use cursive writing or you may print. Only pages 3 and 4 will be sent to the schools.

Directions continue on next page.

REMINDER: Please write this essay topic on the first few lines of page 3 of your answer sheet.

Essay Topic

If you could change one thing about your school, what would you change and why?

- Only write on this essay question
- Only pages 3 and 4 will be sent to the schools
- Only write in blue or black pen

NOTES

_____

_____

_____

_____

_____

_____

_____

_____

_____

_____

_____

_____

_____

Chapter 20
Lower Level
ISEE Practice Test

Lower Level Practice Test

Be sure each mark *completely* fills the answer space.

SECTION 1

1 Ⓐ Ⓑ Ⓒ Ⓓ	9 Ⓐ Ⓑ Ⓒ Ⓓ	17 Ⓐ Ⓑ Ⓒ Ⓓ	25 Ⓐ Ⓑ Ⓒ Ⓓ	33 Ⓐ Ⓑ Ⓒ Ⓓ
2 Ⓐ Ⓑ Ⓒ Ⓓ	10 Ⓐ Ⓑ Ⓒ Ⓓ	18 Ⓐ Ⓑ Ⓒ Ⓓ	26 Ⓐ Ⓑ Ⓒ Ⓓ	34 Ⓐ Ⓑ Ⓒ Ⓓ
3 Ⓐ Ⓑ Ⓒ Ⓓ	11 Ⓐ Ⓑ Ⓒ Ⓓ	19 Ⓐ Ⓑ Ⓒ Ⓓ	27 Ⓐ Ⓑ Ⓒ Ⓓ	
4 Ⓐ Ⓑ Ⓒ Ⓓ	12 Ⓐ Ⓑ Ⓒ Ⓓ	20 Ⓐ Ⓑ Ⓒ Ⓓ	28 Ⓐ Ⓑ Ⓒ Ⓓ	
5 Ⓐ Ⓑ Ⓒ Ⓓ	13 Ⓐ Ⓑ Ⓒ Ⓓ	21 Ⓐ Ⓑ Ⓒ Ⓓ	29 Ⓐ Ⓑ Ⓒ Ⓓ	
6 Ⓐ Ⓑ Ⓒ Ⓓ	14 Ⓐ Ⓑ Ⓒ Ⓓ	22 Ⓐ Ⓑ Ⓒ Ⓓ	30 Ⓐ Ⓑ Ⓒ Ⓓ	
7 Ⓐ Ⓑ Ⓒ Ⓓ	15 Ⓐ Ⓑ Ⓒ Ⓓ	23 Ⓐ Ⓑ Ⓒ Ⓓ	31 Ⓐ Ⓑ Ⓒ Ⓓ	
8 Ⓐ Ⓑ Ⓒ Ⓓ	16 Ⓐ Ⓑ Ⓒ Ⓓ	24 Ⓐ Ⓑ Ⓒ Ⓓ	32 Ⓐ Ⓑ Ⓒ Ⓓ	

SECTION 2

1 Ⓐ Ⓑ Ⓒ Ⓓ	9 Ⓐ Ⓑ Ⓒ Ⓓ	17 Ⓐ Ⓑ Ⓒ Ⓓ	25 Ⓐ Ⓑ Ⓒ Ⓓ	33 Ⓐ Ⓑ Ⓒ Ⓓ
2 Ⓐ Ⓑ Ⓒ Ⓓ	10 Ⓐ Ⓑ Ⓒ Ⓓ	18 Ⓐ Ⓑ Ⓒ Ⓓ	26 Ⓐ Ⓑ Ⓒ Ⓓ	34 Ⓐ Ⓑ Ⓒ Ⓓ
3 Ⓐ Ⓑ Ⓒ Ⓓ	11 Ⓐ Ⓑ Ⓒ Ⓓ	19 Ⓐ Ⓑ Ⓒ Ⓓ	27 Ⓐ Ⓑ Ⓒ Ⓓ	35 Ⓐ Ⓑ Ⓒ Ⓓ
4 Ⓐ Ⓑ Ⓒ Ⓓ	12 Ⓐ Ⓑ Ⓒ Ⓓ	20 Ⓐ Ⓑ Ⓒ Ⓓ	28 Ⓐ Ⓑ Ⓒ Ⓓ	36 Ⓐ Ⓑ Ⓒ Ⓓ
5 Ⓐ Ⓑ Ⓒ Ⓓ	13 Ⓐ Ⓑ Ⓒ Ⓓ	21 Ⓐ Ⓑ Ⓒ Ⓓ	29 Ⓐ Ⓑ Ⓒ Ⓓ	37 Ⓐ Ⓑ Ⓒ Ⓓ
6 Ⓐ Ⓑ Ⓒ Ⓓ	14 Ⓐ Ⓑ Ⓒ Ⓓ	22 Ⓐ Ⓑ Ⓒ Ⓓ	30 Ⓐ Ⓑ Ⓒ Ⓓ	38 Ⓐ Ⓑ Ⓒ Ⓓ
7 Ⓐ Ⓑ Ⓒ Ⓓ	15 Ⓐ Ⓑ Ⓒ Ⓓ	23 Ⓐ Ⓑ Ⓒ Ⓓ	31 Ⓐ Ⓑ Ⓒ Ⓓ	
8 Ⓐ Ⓑ Ⓒ Ⓓ	16 Ⓐ Ⓑ Ⓒ Ⓓ	24 Ⓐ Ⓑ Ⓒ Ⓓ	32 Ⓐ Ⓑ Ⓒ Ⓓ	

SECTION 3

1 Ⓐ Ⓑ Ⓒ Ⓓ	9 Ⓐ Ⓑ Ⓒ Ⓓ	17 Ⓐ Ⓑ Ⓒ Ⓓ	25 Ⓐ Ⓑ Ⓒ Ⓓ
2 Ⓐ Ⓑ Ⓒ Ⓓ	10 Ⓐ Ⓑ Ⓒ Ⓓ	18 Ⓐ Ⓑ Ⓒ Ⓓ	
3 Ⓐ Ⓑ Ⓒ Ⓓ	11 Ⓐ Ⓑ Ⓒ Ⓓ	19 Ⓐ Ⓑ Ⓒ Ⓓ	
4 Ⓐ Ⓑ Ⓒ Ⓓ	12 Ⓐ Ⓑ Ⓒ Ⓓ	20 Ⓐ Ⓑ Ⓒ Ⓓ	
5 Ⓐ Ⓑ Ⓒ Ⓓ	13 Ⓐ Ⓑ Ⓒ Ⓓ	21 Ⓐ Ⓑ Ⓒ Ⓓ	
6 Ⓐ Ⓑ Ⓒ Ⓓ	14 Ⓐ Ⓑ Ⓒ Ⓓ	22 Ⓐ Ⓑ Ⓒ Ⓓ	
7 Ⓐ Ⓑ Ⓒ Ⓓ	15 Ⓐ Ⓑ Ⓒ Ⓓ	23 Ⓐ Ⓑ Ⓒ Ⓓ	
8 Ⓐ Ⓑ Ⓒ Ⓓ	16 Ⓐ Ⓑ Ⓒ Ⓓ	24 Ⓐ Ⓑ Ⓒ Ⓓ	

SECTION 4

1 Ⓐ Ⓑ Ⓒ Ⓓ	9 Ⓐ Ⓑ Ⓒ Ⓓ	17 Ⓐ Ⓑ Ⓒ Ⓓ	25 Ⓐ Ⓑ Ⓒ Ⓓ
2 Ⓐ Ⓑ Ⓒ Ⓓ	10 Ⓐ Ⓑ Ⓒ Ⓓ	18 Ⓐ Ⓑ Ⓒ Ⓓ	26 Ⓐ Ⓑ Ⓒ Ⓓ
3 Ⓐ Ⓑ Ⓒ Ⓓ	11 Ⓐ Ⓑ Ⓒ Ⓓ	19 Ⓐ Ⓑ Ⓒ Ⓓ	27 Ⓐ Ⓑ Ⓒ Ⓓ
4 Ⓐ Ⓑ Ⓒ Ⓓ	12 Ⓐ Ⓑ Ⓒ Ⓓ	20 Ⓐ Ⓑ Ⓒ Ⓓ	28 Ⓐ Ⓑ Ⓒ Ⓓ
5 Ⓐ Ⓑ Ⓒ Ⓓ	13 Ⓐ Ⓑ Ⓒ Ⓓ	21 Ⓐ Ⓑ Ⓒ Ⓓ	29 Ⓐ Ⓑ Ⓒ Ⓓ
6 Ⓐ Ⓑ Ⓒ Ⓓ	14 Ⓐ Ⓑ Ⓒ Ⓓ	22 Ⓐ Ⓑ Ⓒ Ⓓ	30 Ⓐ Ⓑ Ⓒ Ⓓ
7 Ⓐ Ⓑ Ⓒ Ⓓ	15 Ⓐ Ⓑ Ⓒ Ⓓ	23 Ⓐ Ⓑ Ⓒ Ⓓ	
8 Ⓐ Ⓑ Ⓒ Ⓓ	16 Ⓐ Ⓑ Ⓒ Ⓓ	24 Ⓐ Ⓑ Ⓒ Ⓓ	

Section 1
Verbal Reasoning

| **34 Questions** | **Time: 20 Minutes** |

This section is divided into two parts that contain two different types of questions. As soon as you have completed Part One, answer the questions in Part Two. You may write in your test booklet. For each answer you select, fill in the corresponding circle on your answer document.

Part One – Synonyms

Each question in Part One consists of a word in capital letters followed by four answer choices. Select the one word that is most nearly the same in meaning as the word in capital letters.

SAMPLE QUESTION:

    AGGRAVATE:

    (A) apply
    (B) enjoy
    (C) irritate
    (D) present

<u>Sample Answer</u>

Ⓐ Ⓑ ● Ⓓ

Go on to the next page. ➝

VR

Part Two – Sentence Completion

Each question in Part Two is made up of a sentence with one blank. Each blank indicates that a word or phrase is missing. The sentence is followed by four answer choices. Select the one word or phrase that best completes the meaning of the sentence as a whole.

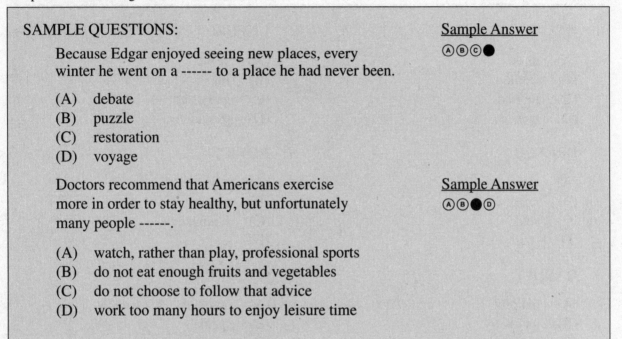

SAMPLE QUESTIONS:

Because Edgar enjoyed seeing new places, every winter he went on a ------ to a place he had never been.

Sample Answer
Ⓐ Ⓑ Ⓒ ●

(A) debate
(B) puzzle
(C) restoration
(D) voyage

Doctors recommend that Americans exercise more in order to stay healthy, but unfortunately many people ------.

Sample Answer
Ⓐ Ⓑ ● Ⓓ

(A) watch, rather than play, professional sports
(B) do not eat enough fruits and vegetables
(C) do not choose to follow that advice
(D) work too many hours to enjoy leisure time

STOP. Do not go on until told to do so.

Part One – Synonyms

Directions: Select the word that is most nearly the same in meaning as the word in capital letters.

1. BASIN:

    (A) desk
    (B) frame
    (C) mound
    (D) sink

2. DRENCH:

    (A) clean
    (B) rain
    (C) soak
    (D) twist

3. HASTILY:

    (A) happily
    (B) passively
    (C) quickly
    (D) quietly

4. HEAP:

    (A) grain
    (B) imprint
    (C) pile
    (D) volume

5. ADORN:

    (A) average
    (B) decorate
    (C) sew
    (D) visit

6. UNFURL:

    (A) close
    (B) flap
    (C) gather up
    (D) spread out

7. NOVICE:

    (A) beginner
    (B) player
    (C) sickness
    (D) story

8. COMPREHEND:

    (A) compare
    (B) speak
    (C) understand
    (D) wonder

9. MALICE:

    (A) fear
    (B) hatred
    (C) joy
    (D) opinion

10. UNKEMPT:

    (A) free
    (B) frequent
    (C) messy
    (D) obvious

Go on to the next page. ➡

11. RUSE:

   (A) laugh
   (B) partner
   (C) sale
   (D) trick

12. OBSOLETE:

   (A) historical
   (B) old-fashioned
   (C) popular
   (D) uncommon

13. WILY:

   (A) careful
   (B) crafty
   (C) loud
   (D) thin

14. BRITTLE:

   (A) breakable
   (B) lumpy
   (C) sharp
   (D) small

15. ORATOR:

   (A) curator
   (B) listener
   (C) orchestra
   (D) speaker

16. POLL:

   (A) argument
   (B) discussion
   (C) election
   (D) survey

17. PLEA:

   (A) appeal
   (B) explanation
   (C) remark
   (D) response

Go on to the next page. →

Part Two – Sentence Completion

Directions: Select the word that best completes the sentence.

18. Sasha's friends think she is outgoing and talkative, but when she meets people for the first time she is often -------.

    (A) friendly
    (B) privileged
    (C) shy
    (D) sociable

19. Ms. Lin reviewed all the essays so that she could ------- each student's writing.

    (A) deny
    (B) emphasize
    (C) evaluate
    (D) ignore

20. A snapping turtle's neck can ------- to catch fish far away from its body.

    (A) blend
    (B) extend
    (C) retract
    (D) wander

21. The young man dressed carefully for his job interview because he wanted to ------- the interviewer.

    (A) annoy
    (B) discourage
    (C) employ
    (D) impress

22. Scientists spend a lot of time studying ants, bees, and other ------- insects that live and work together in large groups.

    (A) aquatic
    (B) social
    (C) uninteresting
    (D) wingless

23. Because the domestic cat cleans its fur thoroughly with its rough tongue, it rarely becomes -------.

    (A) distracted
    (B) soiled
    (C) tidy
    (D) washed

24. Everyone said Jaquinta was an ------- person because she always asked a lot of questions.

    (A) inquisitive
    (B) intense
    (C) organized
    (D) unpredictable

25. Although Wanda has taken violin lessons for three years, her ------- is actually to play sports.

    (A) possibility
    (B) preference
    (C) question
    (D) routine

Go on to the next page. ➡

26. People who obey the law and try not to hurt anyone are not likely to become -------.

    (A) happy
    (B) infamous
    (C) quiet
    (D) serene

27. At one time, Western movies were released -------, but now they are hardly ever made.

    (A) frequently
    (B) informally
    (C) quickly
    (D) seldom

28. Mr. Thomas placed celery in colored water in order to ------- the way plants can absorb liquids.

    (A) compress
    (B) cover
    (C) demonstrate
    (D) ignore

29. Most goods were produced in people's homes before industrialization, but as the factory system became common, ------- production of goods decreased.

    (A) domestic
    (B) energetic
    (C) foreign
    (D) high-speed

30. Frederick Church built a large Moorish home that was ------- as a visitor came up the long driveway, but came into view suddenly at the end.

    (A) beautiful
    (B) concealed
    (C) uninteresting
    (D) visible

31. To keep Cassidy's baby sister safe once she begins to crawl, her family will -------.

    (A) take lots of pictures
    (B) stay close to the ground
    (C) buy new baby shoes
    (D) baby-proof the house

32. Even though most of the students looked confused, the teacher -------.

    (A) wondered what she would have for lunch
    (B) explained the solution to the problem a second time
    (C) sent a student to the principal's office for misbehaving
    (D) moved on to a new topic without asking whether anyone had questions

Go on to the next page. ➞

33. Although the weather forecast predicted freezing temperatures and wet snow, Jason -------.

(A) decided to learn how to ski
(B) did not wear a coat when he went outside
(C) worked twice as hard as he usually does
(D) put on his favorite wool sweater

34. Because Ronnie was terrified of the ocean and never learned to swim, -------.

(A) she did not accept an invitation to her friend's beach house
(B) her parents never took her on their vacations to Kansas
(C) she became an A student and was the president of two clubs
(D) her brother decided to try out for the Olympic swimming team

STOP. If there is time, you may check your work in this section only.

Section 2
Quantitative Reasoning

| 38 Questions | Time: 35 Minutes |

Each question consists of a word problem followed by four answer choices. Read each question and then decide which one of the four suggested answers is best.

Find the row of spaces on your answer document that has the same number as the question. In this row, mark the space having the same letter as the answer you have chosen. You may write in your test booklet.

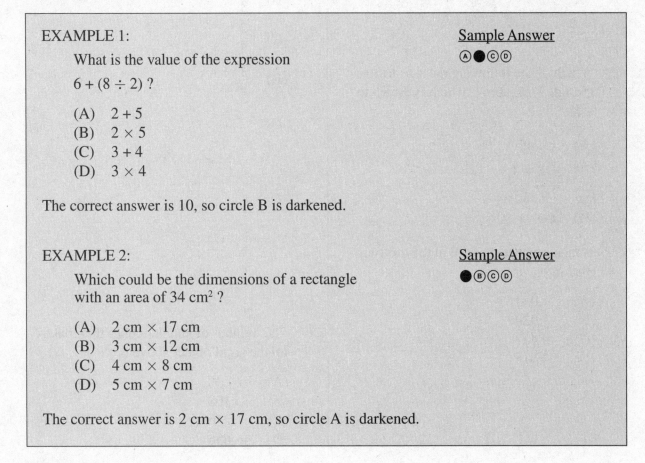

EXAMPLE 1:

What is the value of the expression

$6 + (8 \div 2)$?

(A) $2 + 5$
(B) 2×5
(C) $3 + 4$
(D) 3×4

Sample Answer

Ⓐ ● Ⓒ Ⓓ

The correct answer is 10, so circle B is darkened.

EXAMPLE 2:

Which could be the dimensions of a rectangle with an area of 34 cm² ?

(A) 2 cm × 17 cm
(B) 3 cm × 12 cm
(C) 4 cm × 8 cm
(D) 5 cm × 7 cm

Sample Answer

● Ⓑ Ⓒ Ⓓ

The correct answer is 2 cm × 17 cm, so circle A is darkened.

STOP. Do not go on until told to do so.

1. Which is seven hundred ninety thousand twelve?

    (A)   7,912
    (B)   79,012
    (C)   709,012
    (D)   790,012

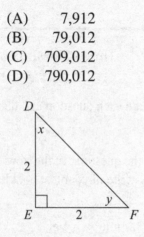

2. Which of the following must be true of triangle *DEF* above, which is drawn to scale?

    (A) $x = 45$
    (B) $\overline{DF} = 2$
    (C) $\overline{DF} = 4$
    (D) $x + y > 90$

3. Which number shows 9 in the thousands place?

    (A)   1,039
    (B)   7,920
    (C)   9,437
    (D)   94,016

4. Which of the following is the product of two distinct prime numbers?

    (A)   1
    (B)   4
    (C)   8
    (D)   14

5. Which is the smallest fraction?

    (A) $\dfrac{2}{5}$

    (B) $\dfrac{3}{8}$

    (C) $\dfrac{3}{4}$

    (D) $\dfrac{4}{9}$

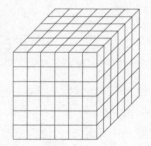

6. The number of smaller cubes that make up the solid object above is

    (A)   36
    (B)   108
    (C)   216
    (D)   46,656

Go on to the next page. ➡

7. It takes Ms. Weiss ten minutes to drive 4 miles. If she continues to drive at the same speed for 25 more minutes, how many more miles will she have driven?

   (A)   4
   (B)   10
   (C)   14
   (D)   25

8. A painter uses 3 gallons of paint to cover 2 square yards on the inside of a house. How many gallons will it take for him to cover a wall that is 12 feet tall and 60 feet long? <u>Note</u>: 3 feet = 1 yard.

   (A)   40
   (B)   120
   (C)   180
   (D)   240

9. Which of the following is equal to $\frac{1}{6}$?

   (A) $\frac{3}{6}$

   (B) $\frac{3}{9}$

   (C) $\frac{3}{18}$

   (D) $\frac{3}{24}$

10. When a number is divided by 8, the remainder is 3. Which could be the number?

   (A)   11
   (B)   14
   (C)   17
   (D)   21

11. Which of the following equals 90 ?

   (A) 5×18
   (B) 5×16
   (C) 4×15
   (D) 9^{10}

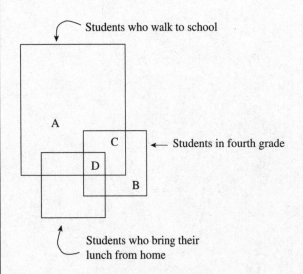

Students who walk to school

Students in fourth grade

Students who bring their lunch from home

12. In which region of the figure above would you find Stephanie, a fourth-grade student who walks to school and buys her lunch in the cafeteria?

   (A)   A
   (B)   B
   (C)   C
   (D)   D

Go on to the next page. ➡

13. Which of the following shows a line of symmetry?

(A)

(B)

(C)

(D)

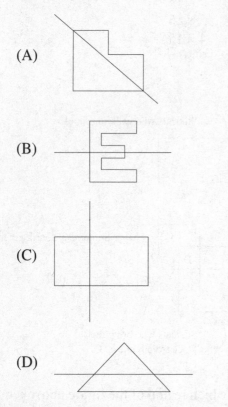

14. What is the area of the shaded region in the figure above?

(A) 12
(B) 13
(C) 14
(D) 24

$$\begin{array}{r} 16 \\ \times\ M \\ \hline A\,0 \end{array}$$

15. In the multiplication problem shown above, if A and M represent distinct positive integers, which of the following is the value of A ?

(A) 0
(B) 4
(C) 8
(D) 9

Go on to the next page. ➡

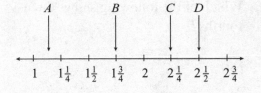
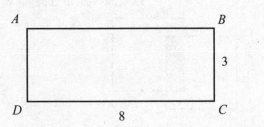

16. What is the perimeter of rectangle *ABCD* above?

(A) 5
(B) 11
(C) 22
(D) 24

17. Which shows 7 in the hundreds and thousandths places?

(A) 2,793.4701
(B) 5,704.2371
(C) 7,421.9783
(D) 8,072.7634

18. Which is seventy two thousand fourteen?

(A) 7,214
(B) 72,014
(C) 72,140
(D) 720,014

19. Which point on the number line above indicates the correct placement of $\frac{10}{4}$?

(A) *A*
(B) *B*
(C) *C*
(D) *D*

20. Which of the following is closest in value to 7 ?

(A) 6.8
(B) 7.009
(C) 7.01
(D) 7.1

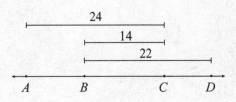

21. The length of *AD* in the figure shown above is

(A) 30
(B) 32
(C) 38
(D) 46

Go on to the next page. →

22. Which of the following shows three-fourths?

(A)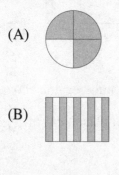

(B) ▮▮▮▮▮

(C) ▭

(D) ▲

23. Which of the following is NOT equal to 16 ?

(A) $2^2 \times 4$
(B) 2^3
(C) 2^4
(D) 4^2

24. Which is the largest fraction?

(A) $\dfrac{3}{5}$

(B) $\dfrac{2}{3}$

(C) $\dfrac{1}{6}$

(D) $\dfrac{1}{2}$

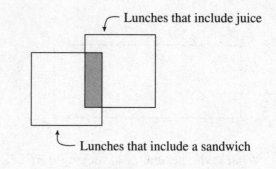

Lunches that include juice

Lunches that include a sandwich

25. Which lunch menu can be found in the shaded part of the figure above?

(A) Yogurt and soda
(B) Ham sandwich and apple juice
(C) Pizza and milk
(D) Cheese sandwich and water

Go on to the next page. ➡

26. Which of the following shows a reflection?

(A)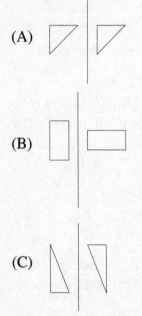

(B)

(C)

(D)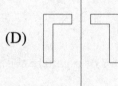

27. Which of the following produces a remainder of 3 ?

(A) $72 \div 9$
(B) $57 \div 6$
(C) $49 \div 9$
(D) $39 \div 7$

28. Sam's Pizza uses 24 slices of pepperoni on 8 pieces of pizza. How many slices of pepperoni would be used on 6 pieces of pizza?

(A)   3
(B)   12
(C)   18
(D)   48

29. Evan is making a quilt out of 6-inch squares of material. How many squares will he need to make a quilt that is 6 feet long and 5 feet wide?
Note: 1 foot = 12 inches.

(A)   15
(B)   30
(C)   60
(D)   120

Go on to the next page. ➡

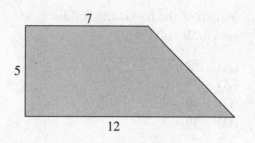

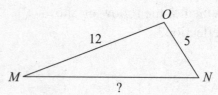
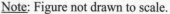

Note: Figure not drawn to scale.

30. What is the area of the figure shown above?

(A) 24
(B) 35
(C) 47.5
(D) 60

31. Which of the following shows 48 as a product of primes?

(A) 3×8
(B) $2^4 \times 3$
(C) $2^3 \times 6$
(D) 2×3

32. Which of the following CANNOT be the length of side *MN* in triangle *MNO*, shown above?

(A) 8
(B) 11
(C) 16
(D) 19

33. When a number is divided by 8, the remainder is 2. What is the number?

(A) 11
(B) 22
(C) 72
(D) 90

34. What is the perimeter of a square with a side of length 2 ?

(A) 8
(B) 6
(C) 4
(D) 2

Go on to the next page. ⟶

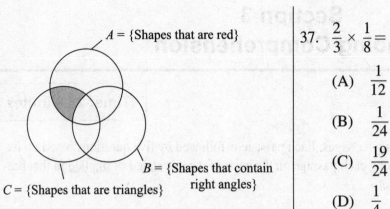

A = {Shapes that are red}

C = {Shapes that are triangles}

B = {Shapes that contain right angles}

35. Which of these shapes would fall into the shaded region of the figure shown above?

    (A) A red right triangle
    (B) A red equilateral triangle
    (C) A green rectangle
    (D) A blue circle

36. Melissa had 20 words on her spelling test. If she spelled $\frac{1}{4}$ of the words incorrectly, how many words did she spell correctly?

    (A) 4
    (B) 5
    (C) 15
    (D) 16

37. $\frac{2}{3} \times \frac{1}{8} =$

    (A) $\frac{1}{12}$
    (B) $\frac{1}{24}$
    (C) $\frac{19}{24}$
    (D) $\frac{1}{4}$

38. The distance from Amy's home to Los Angeles is 2,281 miles. The distance from Dave's house to Los Angeles is 1,912 miles. How much closer is Dave's house to Los Angeles than Amy's house?

    (A) 379
    (B) 369
    (C) 359
    (D) 269

STOP. If there is time, you may check your work in this section only.

Section 3
Reading Comprehension

| 25 Questions | Time: 25 Minutes |

This section contains five short reading passages. Each passage is followed by five questions based on its content. Answer the questions following each passage on the basis of what is <u>stated</u> or <u>implied</u> in that passage. You may write in the test booklet.

STOP. Do not go on until told to do so.

NO TEST MATERIAL ON THIS PAGE

<u>Questions 1–5</u>

Line

1   "What's that noise?" my brother asked.
2   I listened carefully. Just when I thought
3 I heard a small noise, the thunder crashed
4 again. The rain was hitting the roof hard,
5 too, making it difficult to hear anything. "I
6 don't hear it," I said.
7   "What do you mean you don't hear
8 it? It's so loud!" my brother whispered.
9 Then I heard it. It was a *click-click-click*,
10 and it sounded like it was coming from the
11 bathroom.
12   "Maybe it's a monster. We should go
13 get Mom," my brother said. I didn't want
14 to be a scaredy-cat, and I knew Mom was
15 probably asleep. Besides, I'd have to walk
16 past the bathroom to get to her.
17   *Click-click-click.* I told my brother to
18 go to sleep, but he said, "I can't. We have to
19 see what it is."

20   "Okay," I said. I pretended I was
21 very brave, and got up and marched to the
22 bathroom. When I saw what was making the
23 noise, I laughed out loud. My brother came
24 running down the hall, asking, "What is it?"
25   Then, he poked his head in the door and
26 looked in the bathtub. There was our dog,
27 Mack. He was so scared of the thunder that
28 he was hiding in the tub! He sat there with
29 his head down, shivering. His toenails went
30 *click-click-click* against the ceramic tub as
31 he turned to look at us.
32   "Poor Mack! He's more scared than
33 we were," I said. We brought Mack into our
34 bedroom and petted him until he stopped
35 shaking. Then, we all went to sleep.

Go on to the next page. ⟶

1. At the beginning of the story, the narrator's brother thinks the noise is made by

   (A) a monster
   (B) his mother
   (C) the dog
   (D) the narrator

2. When the narrator says, "Besides, I'd have to walk past the bathroom," (lines 15–16), you know that he

   (A) is afraid of getting in trouble
   (B) is not familiar with the house
   (C) is scared to go near the noise
   (D) would rather go to the kitchen

3. In line 21, "marched" most nearly means

   (A) hopped loudly
   (B) ran sneakily
   (C) sang a military song
   (D) walked with a purpose

4. Why does the narrator laugh out loud (line 23) when he gets to the bathroom?

   (A) He is amused because he sees that it is just the dog making a noise.
   (B) He is happy that there is nothing making a noise in the bathroom.
   (C) He is nervous about opening the door.
   (D) His brother has just told him a good joke.

5. According to the passage, the dog was in the bathtub because

   (A) he needed a bath
   (B) he was hungry
   (C) he was trying to hide from the brothers
   (D) he was trying to hide from the thunder

Go on to the next page. ➡

Questions 6–10

This story is adapted from an African folktale that explains why the sun and moon are in the sky.

Line

1   Long ago, the sun and the moon and the
2 water all lived on Earth. The sun and moon
3 were married and they were friends with
4 the water. The sun and moon often went to
5 visit the water where he lived, but the water
6 never returned their visits.
7   One day, the moon said to the water,
8 "Why do you never come to visit us?"
9   The water replied, "My people and I
10 take up a lot of room. I do not think you have
11 enough room in your house for all my people
12 and me. I would like to visit you, but I do not
13 want to crowd your home."
14   The moon said, "Well, then we shall
15 build a bigger house so that you can visit."
16   "I would like that," said the water, "but
17 it must be a very big place."
18   So the moon and the sun built a huge
19 palace. It took many months, but finally it
20 was finished. They sent word to the water to
21 come and visit.
22   The next day, the water came. It stayed
23 outside the gates and called inside. "I have
24 arrived, my friends. Shall I come in?"

25   The sun and moon said together, "Yes,
26 of course. Come in." So the water came
27 through the gates. So, too, came the fishes
28 and the crabs and the other water-dwelling
29 creatures.
30   The water filled the palace so much that
31 the sun and moon were forced to move up
32 to the top floor. "Are you sure you want me
33 to continue?" the water asked.
34   "Of course, come in," said the sun and
35 moon. So the water continued.
36   Soon the water had filled the house
37 completely, and the sun and moon were
38 perched on the roof. "Are you sure?" asked
39 the water.
40   "Yes, yes. You are welcome here," said
41 the moon and sun. And so the water flowed
42 more, until the moon and sun had to jump
43 into the sky. They have stayed there ever
44 since.

Go on to the next page. ➞

6. The primary purpose of this passage is to

   (A) describe how to build a large and expensive palace
   (B) describe how water flows in a flood
   (C) explain how the sun and moon got into the sky
   (D) provide information about sea creatures

7. The sun and moon can best be described as

   (A) assertive
   (B) friendly
   (C) grumpy
   (D) selfish

8. In the beginning of the story, why does the water never come to visit the sun and moon?

   (A) The sun and moon have never invited the water to their home.
   (B) The water does not really like the sun and moon.
   (C) The water lives too far away from the sun and moon to make the trip.
   (D) The water thinks there is not enough space where the sun and moon live.

9. When the water says "my people" in line 9, he is referring to

   (A) the creatures that live in the trees
   (B) the creatures that live in the water
   (C) the sun and the moon
   (D) the workers who build the palace

10. In line 38, "perched" most nearly means

    (A) got very thirsty
    (B) laughed heartily
    (C) looked like a fish
    (D) sat on the edge

Go on to the next page. ➞

<u>Questions 11–15</u>

Line

1   Not all bees live in colonies. Some
2 bees live all alone in a nest built for one.
3 Most of us, however, when we think of bees
4 and wasps, think of huge groups of insects,
5 working together in a cohesive social
6 unit. The hive is, in many ways, a perfect
7 example of a social system. Inside the hive,
8 bees raise their young and store honey. The
9 queen honeybee, for example, may lay up to
10 1,500 eggs a day in the summer. The drone
11 bees mate with the queen and die. The
12 worker bees gather food, care for the hive
13 and the young, and protect the hive. The
14 stored pollen and honey will feed the colony
15 throughout the cold winter months. Inside
16 a hive there is one queen, a few hundred
17 drones, and as many as 40,000 workers.
18 The expression "busy as a bee" is certainly
19 appropriate when you consider the work
20 that bees perform.

Go on to the next page. ➞

11. According to the passage, the purpose of the drones is to

    (A) care for the hive
    (B) gather food
    (C) mate with the queen
    (D) supervise the workers

12. According to the passage, the purpose of the honey and pollen is to

    (A) attract a queen to the hive
    (B) fertilize flowers
    (C) provide a place for the queen to lay her eggs
    (D) provide food for the hive

13. According to the passage, the hive is an example of a social system because

    (A) different members of the hive perform different jobs, yet they work together
    (B) the queen rules over all the bees
    (C) there are workers to do all the work
    (D) there is no conflict in the hive

14. The word "cohesive" in line 5 most nearly means

    (A) connected
    (B) hardworking
    (C) sacred
    (D) sticky

15. The tone of the passage is most like that found in a

    (A) diary entry of a modern naturalist
    (B) general science textbook
    (C) laboratory report
    (D) letter to a friend

Go on to the next page. ⟶

Questions 16–20

Line

1   A wealthy contributor to the arts,
2 Isabella Stewart Gardner was born in New
3 York in 1840. She married John Lowell
4 Gardner, a wealthy heir, and settled in
5 Boston, Massachusetts. When her only son
6 died as a young child, she devoted her life
7 to the arts. Assisted by Bernard Berenson,
8 a young art critic, she began collecting
9 important works of art. After her husband
10 died in 1898, she purchased land for the
11 construction of a museum and worked for
12 years overseeing its creation. She actually
13 lived in the museum until her death in 1924.
14 Her museum became a gathering place for
15 artists, writers, and celebrities. She was
16 considered quite eccentric, often shunning
17 Boston "society" in favor of more colorful
18 characters. She gave her wonderful museum
19 to the city of Boston, to be preserved as a
20 public museum. Today, if you visit Boston,
21 you can admire the work of Isabella Stewart
22 Gardner.

Go on to the next page. ➞

16. Which title would be most appropriate for the passage?

    (A) "An Eccentric Woman"
    (B) "Isabella Stewart Gardner— Museum Maker"
    (C) "The Beginnings of a Museum"
    (D) "Two Deaths in a Family"

17. In line 17, the word "colorful" most nearly means

    (A) beautiful
    (B) brilliant
    (C) unusual
    (D) vivid

18. The passage suggests that Isabella Stewart Gardner began collecting art

    (A) after the death of her husband
    (B) after the death of her son
    (C) to impress art critics
    (D) to spend her husband's money

19. According to the passage, the museum built by Isabella Stewart Gardner was used for all of the following EXCEPT

    (A) a place for artists to congregate
    (B) a place for art to be viewed
    (C) a school for aspiring artists
    (D) her home

20. The author's attitude toward Isabella Stewart Gardner can best be described as

    (A) admiring
    (B) critical
    (C) jealous
    (D) skeptical

Go on to the next page. ➡

Questions 21–25

Line

1   Charlotte Perkins Gilman lived from
2   1860 to 1935. She lived during a time when
3   most women in America and Europe had
4   few educational opportunities. For most of
5   Gilman's life, women could not even vote.
6   Gilman had many ideas for how to improve
7   women's lives.
8   Because she grew up in a family that
9   was not wealthy, Gilman read a lot in order
10 to educate herself. When she was eighteen,
11 however, she attended the Rhode Island
12 School of Design. She worked her way
13 through school by tutoring and teaching.

14   Gilman eventually began publishing
15 books, articles, poems, and even a monthly
16 magazine of her own. She also lectured
17 to large groups. Much of her writing and
18 speaking focused on allowing women to
19 use their natural talents and intelligence by
20 giving them access to education and jobs
21 that paid well. By offering lots of different
22 ideas and ways to change society, Gilman
23 helped women gain the right to live full,
24 productive lives.

Go on to the next page. ➞

21. The primary purpose of the passage is to

    (A) convince the reader that women are able to work and study outside the home
    (B) describe how one woman focused on helping to improve others' lives
    (C) prove that people who are not wealthy can still gain access to education
    (D) show that everyone needs to find a way to help others

22. According to the passage, during Gilman's life women did not have

    (A) any ideas about how to change things
    (B) any way to publish their writing
    (C) a way to travel between America and Europe
    (D) many options for school and work

23. It can be inferred from lines 8–10 that Gilman

    (A) did not like to read by herself
    (B) planned to become a writer and speaker when she was young
    (C) preferred to spend time alone
    (D) was not able to attend school very often as a child

24. The main point of the third paragraph (lines 14–24) is that

    (A) Gilman enjoyed writing and speaking to large groups
    (B) Gilman worked to spread ideas about how women could live fuller lives
    (C) it was very easy to publish your own magazine at the turn of the century
    (D) most women did not have access to education and well-paying jobs

25. Based on the information in the passage, you could most likely expect one of Gilman's books to be titled

    (A) *Europe: A History*
    (B) *Growing Up Rich*
    (C) *Why Women Don't Need to Vote*
    (D) *Women and Economics*

STOP. If there is time, you may check your work in this section only.

Section 4
Mathematics Achievement

30 Questions		Time: 30 Minutes

Each question is followed by four suggested answers. Read each question and then decide which one of the four suggested answers is best.

Find the row of spaces on your answer document that has the same number as the question. In this row, mark the space having the same letter as the answer you have chosen. You may write in your test booklet.

SAMPLE QUESTION:

Sample Answer

Ⓐ ● Ⓒ Ⓓ

Which number is divisible by 7 without a remainder?

(A) 26
(B) 35
(C) 18
(D) 60

The correct answer is 35, so circle B is darkened.

STOP. Do not go on
until told to do so.

NO TEST MATERIAL ON THIS PAGE

1. $6\frac{1}{2}$ hours is how many minutes more than 5 hours?

   (A) $1\frac{1}{2}$

   (B)   30

   (C)   60

   (D)   90

2. Which numeral represents twenty-four thousand, six hundred and three?

   (A)   2,463

   (B)   20,463

   (C)   24,603

   (D)   24,630

3. $\frac{2}{3} + \frac{8}{9} =$

   (A) $\frac{14}{9}$

   (B) $\frac{28}{27}$

   (C) $\frac{10}{9}$

   (D) $\frac{9}{14}$

Questions 4–6 refer to the pictograph shown below.

Letters Delivered on Mrs. Adler's Mail Route

Monday

Tuesday

Wednesday

Note: Each 🖂 represents 2 letters.

4. How many letters did Mrs. Adler deliver on Tuesday?

   (A)   None

   (B)   2

   (C)   3

   (D)   6

5. How many more letters did Mrs. Adler deliver on Monday than on Wednesday?

   (A)   1

   (B)   2

   (C)   3

   (D)   4

6. How many letters did Mrs. Adler deliver on Monday and Tuesday?

   (A)   24

   (B)   18

   (C)   16

   (D)   8

Go on to the next page. ⟶

MA

7. In the decimal 0.42537, the digit 2 is equivalent to which of the following?

   (A) $\dfrac{2}{10}$

   (B) $\dfrac{2}{100}$

   (C) $\dfrac{2}{1,000}$

   (D) $\dfrac{2}{10,000}$

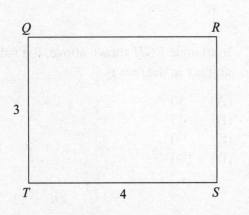

8. What is the perimeter of rectangle *QRST* shown above?

   (A) 7
   (B) 10
   (C) 12
   (D) 14

9. $\dfrac{1,000}{25} =$

   (A) 400

   (B) 40

   (C) 4

   (D) $\dfrac{1}{4}$

10. $3 \times 64 =$

    (A) 128
    (B) 182
    (C) 192
    (D) 256

11. $3 \times 2 + 4 =$

    (A) 7
    (B) 10
    (C) 14
    (D) 16

12. Wu had 18 marbles. He lost half of them, and then his friend gave him 3 more marbles. How many marbles does Wu have now?

    (A) 6
    (B) 9
    (C) 12
    (D) 21

Go on to the next page. ➡

School Supplies	
Pad of Paper	$1.25
Notebook	$1.50
Box of Pencils	$2.00
Pens	$1.00

13. Ian visits the store and buys 2 pads of paper, 1 notebook, and 3 boxes of pencils. How much money does he spend?

    (A) $10.00
    (B) $8.00
    (C) $5.75
    (D) $4.75

14. $\frac{1}{5} \times 400 =$

    (A) 20
    (B) 40
    (C) 80
    (D) 120

15. Evan has 26 comic books. Mark has twice as many comic books as Evan has. How many comic books does Mark have?

    (A) 13
    (B) 26
    (C) 42
    (D) 52

16. If 12 eggs cost $1.80, then how much will 36 eggs cost?

    (A) $0.60
    (B) $1.80
    (C) $3.60
    (D) $5.40

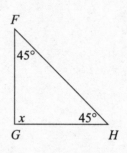

17. In triangle *FGH* shown above, the value of angle *x* in degrees is

    (A) 30
    (B) 45
    (C) 90
    (D) 180

Go on to the next page. ➞

Questions 18–19 refer to the following graph.

Amount of Time Alicia Spent Doing Homework

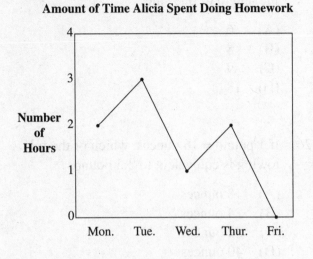

18. On which day did Alicia spend the same amount of time doing homework as she spent on Monday?

(A) Tuesday
(B) Wednesday
(C) Thursday
(D) Friday

19. How many more hours did Alicia spend doing her homework on Tuesday than on Wednesday?

(A) 1
(B) 2
(C) 3
(D) 4

20. $6 \times 20 = 150 - $ _____

(A) 130
(B) 90
(C) 30
(D) 10

21. Which fraction is less than $\frac{3}{4}$?

(A) $\frac{2}{3}$

(B) $\frac{5}{6}$

(C) $\frac{7}{8}$

(D) $\frac{9}{10}$

22. All of the following are multiples of 3 EXCEPT

(A) 120
(B) 210
(C) 462
(D) 512

Go on to the next page. ➡

Questions 23–24 refer to the graph shown below.

Favorite Ice Cream Flavors of Helen's Class

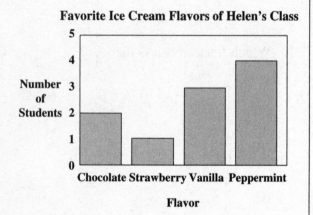

23. How many students chose vanilla ice cream as their favorite?

(A) 1
(B) 2
(C) 3
(D) 4

24. Which flavor was the favorite of the greatest number of students?

(A) Peppermint
(B) Vanilla
(C) Chocolate
(D) Strawberry

25. If the perimeter of a square is 36, what is the length of one side?

(A) 6
(B) 8
(C) 9
(D) 18

26. If 1 pound = 16 ounces, which of the following is equivalent to 2.5 pounds?

(A) 18 ounces
(B) 24 ounces
(C) 32 ounces
(D) 40 ounces

27. Jessica worked $5\frac{1}{2}$ hours on Tuesday and $3\frac{3}{4}$ hours on Wednesday. How many hours did she work on Tuesday and Wednesday?

(A) $1\frac{3}{4}$

(B) $2\frac{1}{2}$

(C) $8\frac{1}{4}$

(D) $9\frac{1}{4}$

Go on to the next page. ➡

Questions 28–30 refer to the price list shown below.

Fast Ferry Price List

	ADULTS	CHILDREN
Weekday Mornings	$15.00	$9.00
Weekday Afternoons	$12.00	$6.00
Weekends	$10.00	FREE

28. How much will it cost for 2 adults and 1 child to ride the Fast Ferry on a weekday afternoon?

(A) $30.00
(B) $27.00
(C) $24.00
(D) $18.00

29. How much less will it cost 1 adult and 2 children to ride the Fast Ferry on a weekday afternoon than it would cost them to ride on a weekday morning?

(A) $6.00
(B) $8.00
(C) $9.00
(D) $18.00

30. The price for 2 adults and 1 child to ride the Fast Ferry on a weekend is what fractional part of the price for 2 adults and 1 child to ride the Fast Ferry on a weekday afternoon?

(A) $\dfrac{1}{2}$

(B) $\dfrac{1}{3}$

(C) $\dfrac{2}{3}$

(D) $\dfrac{3}{4}$

STOP. If there is time, you may check your work in this section only.

Essay

You will have 30 minutes to plan and write an essay on the topic printed on the other side of this page. **Do not write on another topic. An essay on another topic is not acceptable.**

The essay is designed to give you an opportunity to show how well you can write. You should try to express your thoughts clearly. How well you write is much more important than how much you write, but you need to say enough for a reader to understand what you mean.

You will probably want to write more than a short paragraph. You should also be aware that a copy of your essay will be sent to each school that will be receiving your test results. You are to write only in the appropriate section of the answer sheet. Please write or print so that your writing may be read by someone who is not familiar with your handwriting.

You may make notes and plan your essay on the reverse side of the page. Allow enough time to copy the final form onto your answer sheet. You must copy the essay topic onto your answer sheet, on page 3, in the box provided.

Please remember to write only the final draft of the essay on pages 3 and 4 of your answer sheet and to write it in blue or black pen. Again, you may use cursive writing or you may print. Only pages 3 and 4 will be sent to the schools.

Directions continue on next page.

> **REMINDER:** Please write this essay topic on the first few lines of page 3 of your answer sheet.

Essay Topic

If you could plan your perfect vacation, what would you do?

- Only write on this essay question
- Only pages 3 and 4 will be sent to the schools
- Only write in blue or black pen

NOTES

_____

_____

_____

_____

_____

_____

_____

_____

_____

_____

_____

_____

_____

Chapter 21
Answer Key to
ISEE Practice Tests

ANSWER KEY

Detailed explanations can be found online in your Student Tools.

ISEE UL Verbal 1

1. D	5. A	9. D	13. C	17. B	21. A	25. A	29. C	33. A	37. A
2. C	6. B	10. B	14. B	18. A	22. A	26. D	30. B	34. C	38. A
3. D	7. B	11. C	15. D	19. B	23. D	27. A	31. D	35. C	39. A
4. C	8. D	12. B	16. B	20. B	24. A	28. A	32. B	36. C	40. A

ISEE UL Quantitative 2

1. C	5. B	9. C	13. A	17. D	21. C	25. B	29. C	33. A	37. C
2. C	6. D	10. B	14. B	18. C	22. B	26. D	30. B	34. C	
3. D	7. A	11. C	15. A	19. D	23. C	27. A	31. B	35. B	
4. D	8. B	12. D	16. A	20. C	24. D	28. C	32. A	36. B	

ISEE UL Reading 3

1. D	5. D	9. D	13. B	17. D	21. C	25. C	29. A	33. C
2. A	6. D	10. C	14. C	18. A	22. A	26. C	30. D	34. C
3. C	7. C	11. C	15. D	19. C	23. D	27. C	31. B	35. C
4. D	8. C	12. D	16. A	20. B	24. B	28. D	32. B	36. A

ISEE UL Math 4

1. A	6. C	11. B	16. D	21. D	26. B	31. D	36. B	41. C	46. D
2. D	7. A	12. A	17. C	22. A	27. B	32. C	37. D	42. D	47. A
3. C	8. B	13. C	18. C	23. B	28. A	33. C	38. B	43. D	
4. D	9. A	14. D	19. A	24. D	29. A	34. A	39. C	44. B	
5. C	10. B	15. B	20. D	25. D	30. B	35. D	40. A	45. A	

ANSWER KEY

Detailed explanations can be found online in your Student Tools.

ISEE ML Verbal 1

1. D	5. D	9. B	13. B	17. A	21. C	25. C	29. C	33. A	37. B
2. C	6. C	10. B	14. C	18. B	22. B	26. C	30. B	34. D	38. B
3. B	7. B	11. A	15. D	19. A	23. D	27. A	31. C	35. A	39. B
4. C	8. B	12. D	16. C	20. C	24. A	28. A	32. D	36. A	40. A

ISEE ML Quantitative 2

1. C	5. B	9. C	13. B	17. D	21. C	25. B	29. B	33. A	37. B
2. B	6. A	10. C	14. B	18. C	22. D	26. B	30. D	34. C	
3. D	7. B	11. B	15. C	19. D	23. A	27. A	31. B	35. B	
4. B	8. B	12. B	16. C	20. D	24. B	28. A	32. B	36. A	

ISEE ML Reading 3

1. A	5. A	9. C	13. A	17. B	21. C	25. D	29. B	33. B
2. B	6. A	10. D	14. B	18. C	22. D	26. C	30. D	34. A
3. C	7. D	11. A	15. D	19. A	23. A	27. A	31. D	35. B
4. A	8. A	12. C	16. D	20. B	24. C	28. D	32. B	36. C

ISEE ML Math 4

1. B	6. A	11. C	16. D	21. B	26. C	31. C	36. B	41. C	46. B
2. B	7. C	12. A	17. A	22. D	27. B	32. C	37. A	42. B	47. C
3. D	8. C	13. B	18. C	23. D	28. D	33. C	38. C	43. D	
4. D	9. B	14. C	19. C	24. B	29. A	34. D	39. A	44. A	
5. C	10. D	15. C	20. B	25. B	30. D	35. B	40. A	45. D	

ANSWER KEY

Detailed explanations can be found online in your Student Tools.

ISEE LL Verbal 1

1. D	5. B	9. B	13. B	17. A	21. D	25. B	29. A	33. B
2. C	6. D	10. C	14. A	18. C	22. B	26. B	30. B	34. A
3. C	7. A	11. D	15. D	19. C	23. B	27. A	31. D	
4. C	8. C	12. B	16. D	20. B	24. A	28. C	32. D	

ISEE LL Quantitative 2

1. D	5. B	9. C	13. B	17. B	21. B	25. B	29. D	33. D	37. A
2. A	6. C	10. A	14. C	18. B	22. A	26. D	30. C	34. A	38. B
3. C	7. B	11. A	15. C	19. D	23. B	27. B	31. B	35. B	
4. D	8. B	12. C	16. C	20. B	24. B	28. C	32. D	36. C	

ISEE LL Reading 3

1. A	5. D	9. B	13. A	17. C	21. B	25. D
2. C	6. C	10. D	14. A	18. B	22. D	
3. D	7. B	11. C	15. B	19. C	23. D	
4. A	8. D	12. D	16. B	20. A	24. B	

ISEE LL Math 4

1. D	5. B	9. B	13. A	17. C	21. A	25. C	29. C
2. C	6. C	10. C	14. C	18. C	22. D	26. D	30. C
3. A	7. B	11. B	15. D	19. B	23. C	27. D	
4. D	8. D	12. C	16. D	20. C	24. A	28. A	

NOTES